Hilltop Farm

Hilltop Farm

Journals and correspondence
from a rural Vermont experiment
in subsistence living during
World War II;
how it began,
and why it ultimately failed.

Compiled by
Piers Anthony Jacob &
Teresa Jacob Engeman

The Write Place
Kennett Square, Pennsylvania

Copyright © 2021 by Piers Anthony Jacob and Teresa Jacob Engeman

All rights reserved. No part of this book may be reproduced in any form or by any electronic or mechanical means including information storage and retrieval systems without permission in writing from the publisher, except by a reviewer who may quote brief passages in a review. Inquiries should be addressed to the Vermont Historical Society, 60 Washington St., Barre, VT 05641.

Library of Congress Cataloging-in-Publication Data is available upon request.

Printed in the United States of America
23 22 21   1 2 3

ISBN: 978-0-578-31146-3

First Printing, December 2021

Designed by James F. Brisson

Contents

Acknowledgments vii

Editor's Note xi

Introduction 1

1941 7
1942 66
1943 142
1944 297
1945 356

Epilogue 433

Appendix 1: Jan Long, "My Experience in Civilian Public Service Camps" 435

Appendix 2: Norma Jacob, "Community Examined. . . . Community—But Not Utopia" 439

Index of Happenings, 1941–45 443

Acknowledgments

The support of local Vermont author and historian Greg Joly has been invaluable in the preparation of this material. From the beginning he encouraged its completion and provided suggestions and contacts that widened its scope as a meaningful memoir. He and Jim Dauchy, present owner of the Hilltop property who lives nearby, accompanied Teresa and her daughter in 2018 on a visit to the old farmstead, finding it much changed, yet familiar, its story needing to be told.

We are also grateful for the patient assistance of our editor, Alan Berolzheimer, whose suggestions clarified the sometimes unpolished narrative based on our parents' own words.

We thank them, Greg, Alan, and Jim, for their willingness to help bring this story to light.

Abandoned Farm

Through the deep woods, dim with the end of day,
The road winds upward, tortuous and slow.
Walls of rough stone are tumbled in decay
From where their builders ranged them long ago.
A ruin covered by the spring's new green
Makes absolute the triumph of the wood—
Stone for a hearth, a hollow dimly seen,
And fallen timbers where a barn once stood.
Here is a spring, still pool beside a stone;
A rose-bush there, that once some woman tended;
And there a crumbling chimney stands alone.
Life had a pattern here, but that is ended.
All that was man is gone; the delicate deer
Leave cloven prints to mark their passage here.

—Norma Jacob, 1944

Editors' Note

THIS NARRATIVE IS BASED on a 75-year-old collection of daily journals, correspondence, and long-afterward recollections. The documents, contained in a crumbling cardboard carton and somehow surviving countless moves throughout the decades, were tattered and faded and quite often lacked a specific date, so that the chronology had to be inferred from the context.

Piers and Teresa, who were young children at the time, appear in the background of a few of the old photos.

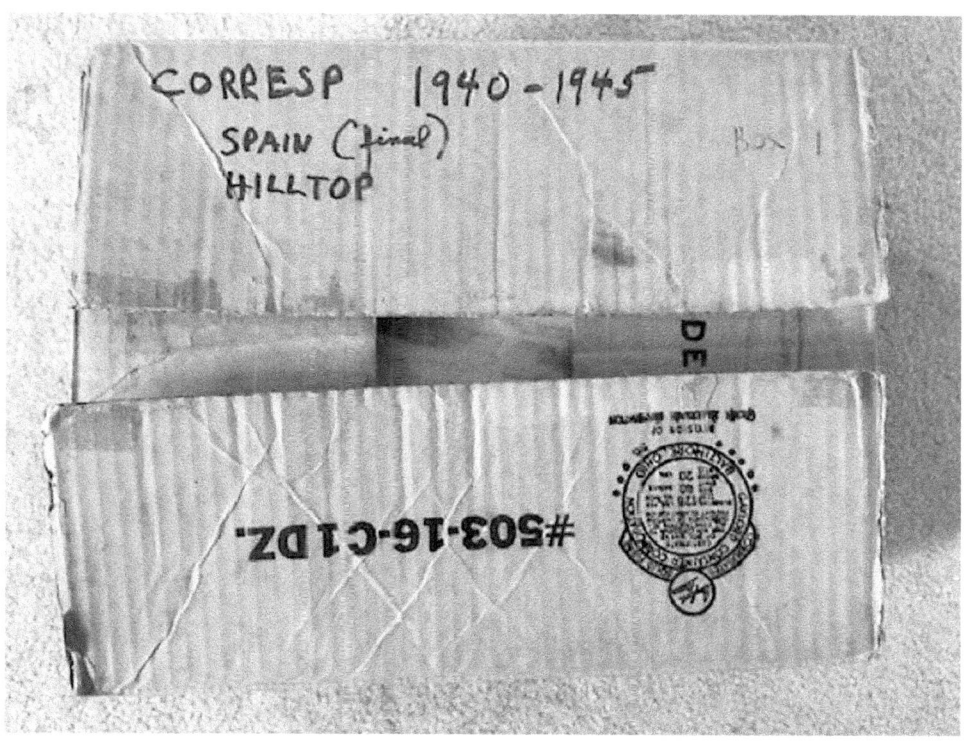

IMAGE 1: *Cardboard box of correspondence.*

IMAGE 2: *The cottage in 2019.*

Introduction

We believed we could demonstrate by our actions how armed conflict was unnecessary, by living together in a new community, cooperatively and in harmony.

THE VISION THAT BECAME HILLTOP FARM may have started in Spain. The Spanish Civil War raged from 1936 to 1939; Generalissimo Francisco Franco eventually won and was settling in. Adolf Hitler was in the process of starting World War II, having used Spain to test new weapons and techniques. Pablo Picasso's huge iconic painting of the bombed-out village of Guernica emphasized the devastation resulting from warfare.

To ensure their safety, children were evacuated from the cities, arriving in the countryside exhausted and hungry. Relief organizations began to plan how best to help them.

Alfred Jacob, a 26-year-old American-born Oxford University graduate who spoke fluent Spanish but had no leadership experience, was asked by the Friends (Quakers) Service Council in London to head up its mission in Spain. For four years he and his British wife, Norma, aided by a small staff, supervised the distribution of food to the refugees from their office in a former mansion in Barcelona.[1] Both were fluent in three languages, though inexperienced in handling large-scale challenges.

Ironies abounded. Alfred was from a well-to-do family in West Chester, Pennsylvania, Norma was from England. Both were from privileged backgrounds, with servants to handle routine tasks such as housekeeping, cooking, and childcare. Alfred did not have to make his own bed. Norma never learned to cook, sew, or clean and was educated by a private tutor. Alfred's father, one of 13 children who had emigrated from Ireland in 1880, had made his fortune growing and selling edible mushrooms, becoming known as the Mushroom King. Norma's father was a doctor, the head of a psychiatric hospital that housed patients with mental afflictions, some of whom worked in their home. Her later career in the mental health field probably had its genesis in this environment. The two young people, more intellectual than practical, had done well at Oxford University where they met, Norma at Somerville College, Alfred

---

1. This harrowing endeavor is related in detail by Farah Mendlesohn in *Quaker Relief Work in the Spanish Civil War* (The Edwin Mellen Press, 2002).

at Exeter. They married only a few months after meeting, and set up housekeeping in a rented, somewhat primitive (no indoor toilet) thatched cottage in Charlbury, outside of Oxford proper. Two children arrived in a little over two years. They had not been part of the initial plan, and were causing some familial tension. The call to Spain provided a way for Alfred and Norma to bring aid and comfort to hundreds of needy children rather than (they maintained) selfishly focusing on their own. It was therefore with a measure of relief that Piers and Teresa, ages 2 and 1, were left with Norma's parents and a nanny in the grandparents' comfortable home in England.

Norma returned from Spain from time to time (often to regain her somewhat fragile health, as food rations were limited and the work exhausting) but was careful not to spend too much time with the children, so they would not miss her when she had to leave again. It was not clear to them that she was their mother, this role having been undertaken by the nanny for several years. When it came time for her to depart, distracting the child and then slipping away unnoticed was believed to be kind—she assumed the toddlers would quickly forget. Piers and Teresa learned not to bond with anyone too closely, as they might unexpectedly disappear.

After four years working in Barcelona, Alfred traveled to Madrid in mid-1940 with money to buy food for the refugees when their train would stop there. It never arrived. The authorities arrested him, took the money, and put him in jail on a trumped-up charge of possessing an illegal vehicle. Another prisoner in the crowded group holding cell agreed to let him hide a postcard inside a thermos brought by a visitor, when the empty bottle was taken away. Outside, the friend mailed the smuggled card, and in due course it reached Norma, who had been frantic with worry about the unexplained disappearance of her husband.

She went to the authorities, who denied they had arrested him. She then produced the card, evidence they could not refute. The government, its bluff having been called, did not want to forfeit the money being provided by aid agencies to assist the refugees, and reluctantly revealed where he was being held. She went to see him in the cold, stone-floored cell, bringing extra food for the other prisoners.

To avoid headlines about how they had arrested an international relief worker without cause, with possible resulting sanctions against Spain, Alfred was released, on condition that he leave the country immediately. Piers and Teresa, by then 5 and 4 years old, had recently joined their parents in Barcelona, leaving behind their beloved nanny, Bunty. In Barcelona they were cared for by a motherly cook, Señora Borás, and her 14-year-old son, Jorge.

Forced by the government to abandon their humanitarian efforts after Alfred's arrest, the family traveled to Lisbon, Portugal, and boarded the HMS *Excalibur*, the last ship out of Europe, barely escaping the erupting

INTRODUCTION

World War II. Teresa had just had her tonsils removed—without anesthesia, which, unbeknownst to her mother, was not available during the war. It was a horrifying experience that Piers, who witnessed it, has never forgotten. Teresa's own recollection is mercifully blank.

British royalty, Edward VIII and Wallis Simpson, the Duke and Duchess of Windsor, were also aboard the *Excalibur*, having been permanently exiled from the ex-king's homeland after his shocking abdication in 1935. He was on his way to assume the governorship of the Bahamas, a ploy to keep him occupied and safely distant from Britain, where his presence might create dissension. The disgraced royals and their sumptuous motorcar were offloaded in Hamilton, Bermuda, watched by less important passengers who lined the rail to gawk. The Spanish artist Salvador Dalí was also aboard.

Soon after, the Jacob family arrived in America, where they were met on the dock by his father, Edward (whom Alfred had not seen for several years, though they had corresponded), and new stepmother Caroline Nicholson, who had worked with relief organizations in Germany following World War I. She had taught German at Westtown, a prestigious Quaker boarding school outside Philadelphia, for 23 years, and was assistant to the headmaster, James Walker. Edward had lost two wives to cancer and met Caroline at Westtown when his youngest son, Philip, was enrolled.

At Pendle Hill, a Quaker study center 15 miles from Philadelphia where they spent several months, and with recollections of the devastation and horror of wartime fresh in their minds, Alfred and Norma joined with a group of idealistic young people who believed they could demonstrate by their actions how conflict, particularly armed conflict, was unnecessary. They would live together cooperatively and in harmony, making decisions jointly with the good of the community always paramount. Simple! The seekers and atmosphere at Pendle Hill fitted well with the young idealists' views.

"Quaker" is the popular designation of the Religious Society of Friends, whose underlying precepts include integrity, pacifism, financial responsibility, and the belief that an individual needs no intermediary between their self and God, who, Quakers believe, dwells within all of us. Quakers do not condone war, and many were conscientious objectors to the military conscription of the time. Some were imprisoned for their refusal to serve in the military forces, and others were assigned to Civilian Public Service (CPS) camps around the country, where they would perform "work of national importance." The conscientious objectors' refusal to fight was not viewed kindly by the majority of the population, who believed they were simply shirking warfare out of cowardice.

Alfred, from a staunchly Quaker family—his Irish grandfather Joshua was an itinerant Quaker preacher—was comfortable with these principles. "I have lived in a warring country and been subjected to perhaps five hundred bombardments from sea and air. I am convinced that war is the craziest, most nonessential, most unproductive way of attempting to achieve anything that can be imagined, and I am determined to have absolutely nothing to do with it in any country, for any purpose."

But his experience in Spain made him wary of the postwar period, which he believed might be as bad. "I think some of us should prepare for the breakdown of the structure of society... for me this means experimentation with a small, closely knit community of friends close to the soil."

There, in a few words, was the rationale for Hilltop Farm, with which Norma agreed. She suggested that they try forming such a community. "There are about half a dozen of us here, possibly more, who are being driven to the position that the present state of society is so intolerable that we must contract out as far as we are able and make a new beginning on more rational lines. We are seriously thinking of renting a farm with maybe 100 acres next Spring and trying to run it on a kind of Christian Socialism."

Neither Alfred nor Norma had any farming experience whatsoever, knew nothing of crop management or animal husbandry, indeed were unfamiliar with even ordinary daily routines, including childcare, never having had to organize a household themselves. Nevertheless, they were confident that this lack of experience would not be an impediment. They were intelligent, motivated, and could quickly learn! The goal was admirable, the group was dedicated, and details would work themselves out in a spirit of harmony and shared purpose. It was an exciting prospect.

They checked real estate ads. On the advice of a friend, Alfred bought a green 1934 Dodge telephone truck with a covered bed and tool drawers along the sides for $60, and set out to visit a number of properties. The plan began to take shape.

Norma wrote in November 1940 that, "At present we are vacillating on the edge of acquiring, for the ridiculous price of $700, a thousand acres of forest in Vermont. The agent also says the timber on the property is worth the purchase price. Alfred's father will put up the money." Although the actual price turned out to be quite a bit more than that, it remained an excellent value.

In December 1940 they made their decision. In January 1941 they purchased, sight unseen, 800 acres for $3,650 in cash. The tract was comprised of several contiguous properties in the Green Mountains of Vermont, near the village of Jamaica (pop. 567). It included an uninsulated, century-old one-and-a-half-story house with no heat, running water, or electricity, and a barn in imminent danger of collapse, reached by a three-mile-long, rutted dirt road up the mountain. Home to legions of mice and spiders and gnawed by porcupines, it had been used as a hunters' camp for 20 years. It

INTRODUCTION

was abandoned completely following the stealth hurricane of 1938 that laid waste to much of New England.[2]

It was perfect.

Alfred: The house was just what we aspired to: a house that was pretty well tumbling down—the wind blew right through the walls. In the years leading up to 1938 it was known as the King Farm, though the Kings had left in the early 1920s.

Thus did the social experiment that became Hilltop Farm have its genesis. There would be problems, but with cooperation and a shared vision, any difficulties could soon be ironed out. Three intrepid couples would be the pioneers: Alfred and Norma, Leslie and Valerie Johnston, and a third couple that is not named, and in the end did not participate. Many other young idealists expressed support and their intention to help establish the new community.

---

2. The Hurricane of '38, which occurred in September, was one of the U.S.'s worst-ever natural disasters, ripping across Long Island and up through New England with 130 mph winds, leaving 700 dead and millions of sugar maples destroyed. There had been no warning to the populace, although the weather service had been tracking the storm for some time. It is doubtful that many residents would have been listening to their radios, and in any event the word "hurricane" was virtually unknown in New England, and few homes had telephones with which to spread the warning.

IMAGE 3: *Norma was aghast when she arrived with two small children and saw what their future home was like*

1941

Other than the house, there is no place which can even be used without repair, unless it be the horse stable. The house is not at all inviting. The magnitude of the task is indeed impressive; it will take a good deal of work.

ALFRED AND BILL BRINTON, son of Pendle Hill directors Howard and Anna Brinton, had journeyed up the mountain in the early spring of 1941 when four feet of snow still lay deep along the road, to view the new property. (Sixty years later, Alfred mused that, "We were there in midwinter, never realizing what kind of winters were going to take place up there. When I asked the postman whether he had ever considered moving south, he laughed. I had no way to know what to expect."[3]) Alfred rarely asked for information, preferring to maintain that he "had no way to know" something and was therefore a victim of circumstance. Any villager could have warned him what the winters would be like.

May 1941

Primitive though the premises clearly were, Alfred was undaunted. He returned on May 13, three days before his 32nd birthday, with the Dodge truck loaded with household goods. Reaching Jamaica at three in the afternoon, it took another two hours to navigate the remaining four miles to the farm, three of them little more than a dirt track through the woods. The road was both muddy and steep in places, and he had to fill the ruts with sticks and leaves. What luck that the Dodge truck had an extra low-low gear, as the last bit of hill would have defeated an ordinary truck. He would not encourage anyone to attempt to drive up on a rainy day without chains! (Later, the labored whine of a vehicle engine as it toiled up the final slope would signal the arrival of a visitor long before anyone actually appeared. "Car coming! Car coming!" the children would shriek excitedly.)

The house, built on a rocky outcropping that fell away steeply on three sides, was much the same as when he had left it at the end of March. The

---

3. Toward the end of Alfred's life (he died in 2002 at age 93) Teresa spent many hours reviewing each journal entry with him and recording his responses. His comments are included in the narrative retrospectively.

ramshackle barn was sagging, but had stalls for possible future livestock, and a hay mow. In the lowest level, underneath, were piles of old wooden sap buckets, which later were repurposed as kindling. Outside was a pile of well-rotted manure, which would be used to fertilize the planned garden, and a small pond that, when filled, was home to frogs and—briefly, before the foxes discovered them—to ducks. The water table was high, and much of the surrounding area was swampy. He looked around, seeing the property for the first time without snow, filled with awe both at the possibilities inherent in it, and the magnitude of the challenge. The well at the southwest corner of the house was smelly and full of insects, so he poured old engine oil and Cresylic disinfectant on it, a quick fix that he later realized was environmentally undesirable. The lowland to the east and northeast needed to be drained.

But the apple trees were in bloom. He found it somewhat breathtaking to see Spring in possession of the woods. There was also a ubiquitous animal with a black face, black and white bristly fur, stubby tail, and waddling legs, that he learned later was a porcupine. It was slow of movement, stationary when surprised, and it gnawed on wood both outside and inside the house, including the joist between the cellar stair and pantry, and even truck tires. The porcupine became Alfred's bête noire, to be dealt with swiftly and ruthlessly. He had not anticipated that brutal killing would be a component of the farming experience. Out in the field, he spied a couple of animals that "looked like dogs, but had tails that were white underneath which bobbed up and down as they ran." He surmised, correctly, that these might be deer. Mice and spiders were everywhere. He had taken an intensive four-day course in horticulture at Fellowship Farm[4] under Richard Johnson, and confidently expected that this would suffice for tackling the real thing. There would be challenges, but he felt prepared to meet them.

He made himself at home in the house as best he could. There were three rooms downstairs; two had a fireplace and the third had a wood stove and a rudimentary sink. Upstairs were two relatively spacious rooms and, under the eaves, several spaces that could be utilized for sleeping. There was a claustrophobic attic, reached by a narrow, almost perpendicular staircase, containing piles of ancient *National Geographic* magazines. (Later, the children would giggle over photos of bare-breasted native women.) It was reasonably adequate for a family, and for guests if they were prepared to rough it for a time.

---

4. A cooperative enterprise promoting social justice, environmental awareness, and individual initiative. "The Mission of Fellowship Farm is to nurture in each person the vision and skills to foster the ways of peace."

1941

Wanting to provide what he anticipated would be a useful guide for followers, Alfred commenced his very detailed, though brief, daily journal entries, which have here been combined for the most part into a single narrative.

The next morning the temperature was 32°F at 5:30. The porcupine, having gnawed at the cellar stairway all night, was far out on a branch of a nearby tree. Others were busy in the barn. He cleaned out the spring about 200 yards away, and dug drainage ditches around it, then explored the woods to the west and southwest and cleaned out the other spring.

It was a start.

Thursday morning a local farmer, Mr. Stark, and his son came at 9 with a team of horses, plow, and harrow. (*Note*: This entry is almost certainly misplaced, as Alfred, a complete stranger, would surely not have been able to hire someone as he passed through the village on his way up the mountain, before he had even seen or evaluated the property! A year later Mr. Stark did bring the team, and plowed out a garden area. Nevertheless, the entry exists.) They plowed the field to the southeast, the future vegetable garden, for $7.25. The man's good humor was exemplary as he overrode the boulders to plow a piece 120 by 140 feet, then harrowed it. Alfred worked alongside, heaving stones out as fast as they came to light. Stark said he was born in a house of which there was now no trace, near the schoolhouse, which had some traces, just off this property. "An acre of this land is worth four in the valley," he asserted.

Alfred recalled that, "At that time I hadn't read *Plowman's Folly*,[5] which explains why it's a mistake ever to disturb the surface of the ground. Ideally you would apply a thick mulch, which would crowd out anything beneath it and break down into fertility. The conventional view at that time was that the first thing you do is to plow it. It turned out to be the wrong thing, but that developed later."

The garden site prepared, Alfred finished unloading the truck. He painted the kitchen sink with enamel undercoating. It was another day of slow but significant accomplishment. It was not rich living, as he had to make meals from what he had brought in the truck: bread, oranges, cocoa, oat flakes, raisins. Supper was soup, kidney beans with molasses, bread, and tea. Hardly gourmet dining, but cheap, reasonably nutritious, and easy to store and prepare.

---

5. The author, Edward H. Faulkner, believed that crop yield could be greatly increased by simply disking plenty of green manure into the surface. Crops would be protected against the vagaries of the weather, not seriously affected by either drought or a wet season, and be virtually immune to insect ravages. The book was published in 1944.

IMAGE 4: *Mr. Stark and his son plow the long-abandoned turf to establish the garden.*

("I don't know why I wrote everything down," Alfred remarked decades later. "I wanted to keep an accurate record. It's something I've always done."[6])

---

6. In retrospect, Alfred is believed to have had some form of Asperger's Syndrome, on the autism spectrum, which can include an almost obsessive attention to detail. He also exhibited other characteristics such as singleness of purpose, difficulty with social relationships, lack of empathy, and discomfort with change. When frustrated, because they have limited coping skills and don't know how to work with others to resolve an issue, individuals may become enraged and even physically abusive.

1941

Friday morning was Alfred's 32nd birthday. He left at 9 a.m. for Brattleboro, 30 miles away, where he picked up a Sears Roebuck order and bought seeds, lime, and fertilizer. He also loaded 300 pounds of seed potatoes from the Brattleboro Grain Company, and bought sundry hardware, stationery supplies, and food. There was no time for lunch.

On the way back, he saw the Brownings (representatives of the Youth Hostel system) in Bondville (a village in the town of Winhall), and picked up a long-handled pump with which to draw water from the spring. Back home he enjoyed chocolate cake, provided by a Pendle Hill friend. It was his birthday, after all!

The next day he did a general cleanup of odds and ends and put a third undercoat on the sink—he was always meticulous about preparing a surface prior to painting it. He swept and arranged the kitchen and "living room," and set traps and poison for the vermin.

Then came the hard work: He created a makeshift harrow by hammering four-inch nails through an old gate and dragging it across the plowed soil so that the nails would scrape it level. It was ingenious, but hardly functional. "It looked right, but it didn't penetrate the earth, it just rode over the top of the furrows." Two and a half hours of backbreaking labor did not produce a very satisfactory result. "I thought I could go over it with this contraption I had invented, and it would all be harrowed." If, contrary to reason, the Starks *had* in fact plowed an area, they had their own harrow, and Alfred would not have had to invent one. Where did he find the materials, so soon after arriving? The record continues to be confusing at this point.

He transplanted tomatoes into pots, which took another two hours, and warmed up some leftovers for supper.

Alfred: I must have built a fire in the living room stove, but it was all coming apart. Eventually we took that stove out and dumped it in the woods, when we had bought another one at an auction. We got a stove that had an oven with a door on each side, so you could get into the oven from the left or from the right.

Sunday was nominally a day of rest, which meant finishing up odd jobs. Wishing to be together at least in spirit with Pendle Hill's Sunday morning worship group, he read *Divine Human Society* by Howard Brinton, one of Pendle Hill's directors. This was perhaps ironic during his self-imposed isolation, in which society was being intentionally avoided. He tried baking in the oven of the wood-burning stove, but didn't get it hot enough.

On Monday morning he walked to the post office in Jamaica, four miles downhill, in one hour, and walked back—briskly—in another hour. It was windy and cold, so the four-mile-an-hour pace down and then uphill wasn't unduly hot. On this day the gardening consisted of leveling off places around the plow-site boulders that could not be wrenched from the soil, spreading old manure on part of the section nearest the house, and adding 50 pounds of hydrated lime on the next section. He made a planting chart after studying the available literature, which largely consisted of government agricultural pamphlets. In view of the lack of space, it seemed advisable to try the "two-story" system utilized by Native Americans, in which low-growing plants such as beans are placed below tall ones like corn. (This plan was, in fact, put into practice the following summer. It is surely out of sequence here.)

May 20 marked Alfred's first full week working on Hilltop Farm, concentrating on outdoor work, leaving the cobwebs to the spiders and the barn timbers to the porcupines. He transplanted cabbages, planted cucumbers in boxes, set carrot seeds to germinate, and planted rows and patches of corn, peas, onions, lettuce, beans, tomatoes, parsnips, radishes, beets, chard, potatoes, and spinach. He manured one quarter of the garden, limed one quarter, and left the remainder for experiments with fertilizers.

The care of seedlings required a good deal of time, as they had to be carried out in the morning and back inside the house in the evening. If they were left out overnight, Brother Porcupine ate the paraffin off the pots and trampled the plants. "The porcupine was a mystery to me; it would gnaw all night as if trying to get through the door. I just had never had any contact with them. We didn't have them in England."

And he finally enameled the sink with the first coat.

Day after day he planted the garden, enameled the sink with a total of six coats, cleared out a stoppage in the sink drain that simply emptied out onto the ground outside, and went to Jamaica for parcels and to West Townshend for the state inspection of the truck. The old mechanic there said his wife had taught school on that hill fifty years before, down at Lumbercamp Corner.

He also explored the neighborhood, trudging along the old dirt logging roads, "up past the Clark place and several more abandoned farms. Came out on Stratton Road. Came up the Bondville road. Got lost on the heights."

He planted beans and peas, hauled manure, and did some laundry, carrying water from the spring. The manure was spread over one quarter of the field, where he planted nine rows of potatoes, removing sod from directly above the chunk that would produce the new plant.

A one-page circular letter was sent to interested friends, using carbon paper to create multiple copies. He had to type it twice to get enough copies, as the carbons, on coarse yellow paper, not thin onionskin, faded to illegibility after the first two or three layers.

1941

"When I look around on the cobwebs, the fallen plaster, and the cracks in the floor; on the cavities in the roof of the barn, the chilled rubbish in the damp obscurity of the basement, the weeds, brush & abandoned objects everywhere, I am driven for encouragement to remember the first beginnings of the relief work in Spain—in their way just as inauspicious, yet because the principle of growth was in them, they expanded astronomically. Hilltop Farm does not need to expand in that sense. Its success will depend entirely on the way in which it is carried on; not that the way leads to 'success,' but the right way is its own success." This ingenuous assumption was to prove flawed soon enough.

He thanked others for their contributions. "What a blessing those gifts have been which poured in from all sides!" Louisa, his father's sister, provided almost complete culinary supplies for a one-man household. "Uncle Bert's fork did the first digging, and the Fieldston [the name of his father's house at the end of Walnut Street in West Chester, built in 1929] assortment of saucepans have graced the stove from the beginning. It is nice to be surrounded by the evidence of friendship."

In a letter to Leslie Johnston—he and his wife Valerie were to be the other founding couple of the experiment—the next day, he got into some of the tension between philosophy and reality, as well as an extended description of the challenge being addressed.

"From any point a dozen tasks-to-be-done stand out. It is difficult to be temperate in action, but I have tried to persuade myself that I am here first to plant something, second to remove rubbish from the house. This means that matters such as water supply, sanitation, setting up the saw, buying lumber to season & all the visits off the property will remain static. But something at least can be achieved by planning in advance, and following the plan during the summer; else, if others are like me, a thousand sundry tasks will be begun & left off to begin a prior one preliminary to it."

Alfred was confident that the other pioneers would agree with his evaluation and the best way to approach the goal. Hadn't they discussed it at length at Pendle Hill?

"Other than the house, there is no place which can even be used without repair, unless it be the horse stable. The sugar house[7] in the woods some distance away is made of vertical board siding and roof with cracks between, set up on stones with space between the sleepers & the earth. It is a framework, but not usable in its present state, except for sugar, for which it is good.

---

7. Sugaring, the conversion of watery maple tree sap into syrup, was an important cottage industry in Vermont. Most farms had some equipment for this use, whether for themselves or to sell on the open market. Forty gallons of sap had to be boiled down to make one gallon of syrup, requiring a considerable commitment of time and space.

"The barn flooring has fallen in, in several places, and the upper level, where cots might have been put, seems too insecure. It is only a matter of work to fix it up, and boards. There is nothing hopeless about it, but it will take a good deal of work. The chicken houses look essentially sound, but will have to be gone over, re-covered with roofing & siding paper, & protected against animals. So everyone will have to sleep in the house, & the house is not at all inviting; nor ought we to make it so during the summer, since that is winter work."

The priorities were clear, at least to him.

"I don't know what scale of 'roughing it' Americans are used to,[8] but I don't want prospective workers here to be romantic about it. It will be a case for many adjustments, and willingness to let a bad thing go on being bad, in order to do work of long-term importance. It is a nuisance to have most of the doors half-hinged, for instance. But I am leaving them, because I take it our policy would be gradually to carve wooden hinges. Also, the window casings are in a terrible state; but from the long view, that is a refinement.

"Even the matter of sanitation seems to be secondary, in a sense, since it inevitably solves itself somehow. I mean, I would not take much time for building a temporary privy, if that time was to delay the completion of the permanent one. There are always the woods—much pleasanter than any outhouse.

"On the other hand, I do see need of creating a water supply. The spring is stone lined, about three feet deep, but impossible to dip water out of without stirring up a fine silt. I dipped the thing empty in a few minutes, to clean it out. There is not enough reserve supply. Moreover, other water issues from the field slightly higher up. My view would be to dig out the swampiest portions, make a stone facing along the back & a concrete reservoir for front and sides, cover it over, and run a pipe down towards the spot nearest the house, and there construct a main reservoir, pump room, wash house, bathroom, refrigerator, etc. It would be just across the road, facing the kitchen windows, where there is already a dry watering trough. Something of the sort has been done twice before: once, an aqueduct, now buried; and once a pipe, now burst. I am working on the pipe to see if it will work again. But the clay subsoil means there is inevitably a suspension of clay and water, like a white cloud which settles to the bottom in about two days; and this must be left undisturbed by drawing water off other than by dipping.

---

8. Alfred had become a British subject during his years there, affecting British spelling and terminology and tending to look down on so-called pampered Americans. Born into privilege and lacking practical experience, he nevertheless worked tirelessly to bring order into the Hilltop chaos and believed others would do the same.

"As to a lower level, [I envision] sanitary privies accessible to the North door, now unused [there were two doors in the back vestibule, one of which led directly to the old privy, and the other was an entrance] and a dormitory above. This needs to be carefully planned, to conserve the characteristic architecture, preserve the view, cut off the wind, and serve all future purposes. Such a thing might not be finished during the summer, but it could at least be well begun."

Not one of these ambitious plans ever came to fruition, although a woodshed was eventually built on the west side. Holding back decay was in itself a full-time project.

He continued to itemize the envisioned tasks: "The barn is slightly akimbo, and some timbers have collapsed. The foundations have to be gone over, the environs drained, the doors rebuilt, half the roof redone, & the structure made porcupine-proof. The house itself, in the first instance, should have only outside repairs, to leave as much as possible for winter inside work. This means a roof, inspection of foundations, and storm windows. Even the outside paintwork could wait, except the windows and frames.

"There are other tasks, however, not so obvious. There is about a mile of road between the house and the edge of the property, on which the trees

IMAGE 5: *The back door, with the old privy at the side. The front door was rarely used.*

have so encroached that it never dries out and is always slippery. Those trees should be cut back to the wall. [Dry-laid stone walls utilizing the abundant local boulders bordered every road and pasture.] They will make good fence posts and bean poles.

"There is swampy land on two sides, once drained and farmed [one wonders how he knew this], but now useless. This should be re-drained, if we are to keep the mosquito population down."

Alfred's confidence that even a few of these tasks could be accomplished in one summer by total greenhorns speaks to the level of naivete and inexperience that quickly undermined the success of the project.

He continued with a numbered itemization of the necessary projects, which he estimated could be handled by seven teams of people. His opinion about the relative importance of the many tasks that lay before them would often turn out to be at odds with the goals of others, a circumstance that would, across time, not lend itself to the kind of harmonious resolution of difficulties that had been so confidently anticipated.

He described a simple but, in his view, adequate diet and a daily routine from 5 a.m. to 9 p.m.: a 16-hour day. He saw no reason why others would not be ready to follow this sensible plan.

One day was spent on the water system. He thought there might be enough of a drop from a higher spring to operate a hydraulic ram, a mechanism whereby the slow flow of water is caused to pump a portion of itself to a higher level with no other power required, invaluable for a farm without electricity. Water would have to be stored up in a reservoir, and the ram operated intermittently. Another project for the future. The spring discovered beyond the barn in the woods was a thousand feet away, and one in the meadow, 600 feet. Neither was a practical source of water.

On the 30th he dug 16 post holes and set 11 posts. "The corn is visible, the onions well started and the beans visible." The next day he wrote letters and took them to the village. "Tugged up two poles found along the roadside. Got into difficulties on steep bit and had to saw and load them. Also, self-starter died. [This would mean the truck had to be started with a hand crank: "Don't put your thumb around it, it could snap back and break your finger!" Teresa remembers being warned.] Hauled in remaining poles of earlier batch."

In a letter of May 31, Alfred wrote to Norma about the practical details of getting Hilltop shaped up for family occupation, and made this comment:

"The temptation to beautify is awfully strong. I have such nice clippers, & the brush is growing all along the walls, & I want the place to be tidy so you won't have too bad an impression of it. Likewise the sink corner, somewhat painted now, is so cheering that I long to finish it. Likewise I ought to prepare some vestige of sanitation for those not accustomed to the great open spaces: and also the house has yet to be cleaned. So life is full of temptations, but the main struggle is between the garden & the fence."

Bringing small children into such surroundings did not trouble him. Their needs were not important, and they would learn to adjust. They should not be treated any differently from the adults, and were expected to have adult patience, judgment, and logic.

Fencing the garden was a long-term project, with holes to be dug, posts set, and fence wire strung. It could not wait indefinitely, because the plants were coming up and would soon be eaten down by the creatures of the forest if not protected. In his ignorance, Alfred believed that a few strands of barbed wire would discourage the intrusion of hungry deer, and later, goats. "I hadn't learned that deer can negotiate fences."

Bugs were a problem, as gnats made working outside at times almost intolerable.

One Sunday he made a batch of chocolate drop cookies with ground flour, passing it through the finest sieve. This left considerable bran, which he toasted in a large shallow pan and would test for making home style "coffee," or as breakfast food.

June 1941

In June, Alfred had some visitors: Leslie Johnston's friend Vernon Squires; Mr. Hanford, "a kindly old man, a retired florist"; and Charles Jackson. Vernon opined that there was no future in the project, in which "we were doing everything wrong." Charles, who with his much younger wife later purchased a vacant house a couple of miles down the road, became a regular visitor as time went on, and was very helpful in fencing the garden and other heavy work.

Although he believed residents could just go out in the woods to answer nature's call, Alfred was willing to make some concessions for those with particular sensibilities. The old red one-hole privy, which had been blown about 50 yards away by the hurricane of 1938, was returned to its original location outside the back door. He fitted a hinged flap to the back for removal of the waste receptacle—the procedure was to drop a scoop of earth on top of your deposit, to discourage flies and hasten decomposition—put a cover on the seat, leveled the floor, patched up holes, and fitted fasteners to the door. Users would now be able to take care of business in privacy.

Sometime after June 9, Alfred returned to Pendle Hill, where he had a term paper to read, "Reclaiming an Abandoned Farm."

The Dodge truck was packed at Pendle Hill, and the next day, wishing to get an early start, Alfred, Leslie Johnston, and Walter Bethel left after midnight to drive north. Fatigue caught up with them, and at 6 a.m. one of the truck's slightly wider rear tires hit a tree near Far Hills, New Jersey.

Norma, Valerie Johnston, and the children—Teresa, age 5, and Piers, 6—left Pendle Hill the next morning in the Oldsmobile, Alfred's father's almost-new car that he had loaned them, unaware of the stresses it would be subjected to when climbing the mountain. They passed through Far Hills, saw the damaged truck, left money to pay for its repair, and drove on, after pausing for lunch with Alfred and a friend, Jim Corsa, who had been picked up at Fetzer's Farm about 4 a.m.

Near Bear Mountain Bridge the Oldsmobile overtook Leslie and Walter, hitchhiking. There was no room in the car to pick them up, so they continued on their own, reaching Hartford, Connecticut, about 9:30 p.m. and spending the night with friends. The women and children reached Fellowship Farm in West Acton, Massachusetts, soon after midnight.

The truck reached Hilltop Farm at 8 a.m. on Sunday, June 15. Leslie and Walter arrived about 6 p.m. Norma, Valerie, and the children arrived about 6:30, having walked most of the last half mile when the Oldsmobile got stuck in the mud. The nascent community was taking shape!

The new arrivals were soon to discover what life on a remote farm was like: With no electricity or running water, light at night was provided by a kerosene lamp, and water was carried up from the spring in a bucket, pending the installation of a hand pump in the kitchen sink. To get from one place to another, even miles away, you walked. None of this was considered a hardship. It was what everyone did.

The next day Jim Corsa left to drive the Oldsmobile back to Philadelphia. Alfred and Leslie rode down with him to collect mail. The remainder of the party explored the old sugar house in the woods beyond the upper field, the barn, the two chicken houses, and the general layout, and looked for a place to create a swimming pool (!). It rained at intervals all day.

They found rhubarb growing in a plot near the barn, and cooked it for supper. Later, asparagus was discovered growing wild in one of the pastures. The cabbages in the vegetable patch had been eaten by some animal, and the beans were attacked by fungus. Farming was not going to be easy.

They held a business meeting to decide whether Alfred should go at once to Brattleboro, about 30 miles away, to buy chemical sprays, and decided in the negative. They also considered purchasing animals, which Norma felt were essential for a proper farm. Alfred objected, believing that their care would inevitably siphon away the time needed for more urgent survival tasks. The question of how to provide food suitable for young children—milk, eggs—was not foremost in his mind. Children would have to eat whatever they were given, and were not entitled to special treatment.

Next morning Leslie sawed firewood and Alfred planted potatoes, while Norma, Valerie, and Walter weeded vegetable rows. Then came more rain. They decided that one of the chicken coops needed only minor repairs in order to house half a dozen Rhode Island Red hens, immediately.

They read the first two chapters of Brinton's *Divine Human Society* and planned to make this reading a part of the daily routine. The enterprise was getting off to a good start.

The next day had a fine morning, followed by rain most of the afternoon. They worked inside, scraping wallpaper off red wooden walls in the kitchen and back hallway. When the rain finally ceased, they went out to plant potatoes again, as Alfred thought they were an easy, carefree crop to grow and would provide nourishment during the winter. They would not be going hungry!

John Barstow arrived about 5:00 p.m. with his father and brother. John was a boy whom Leslie had volunteered to take care of for the summer, although he "wasn't quite balanced, you didn't know what he would do next." Alfred recalled that, "He was put to sleep up in the attic, which got very hot by day. I don't know what he did for a bed. Leslie noticed as time went on that there was no evidence of his having washed his arms; the rest of us took turns washing in the kitchen." Since there was no private bathroom or running water, only sponge baths could be undertaken.

Norma rode down to Jamaica with the Barstows to fetch the mail and then walked up again, an eight-mile round trip she was to make two or three times a week over the years, reading a book as she trudged. A letter was received from Ernst Sollwitz, possibly a German medical student, asking to join them. It seemed that word of the project was getting around!

The last hundred pounds of potatoes were planted, and in the afternoon they cleared the space beside the back door where an annex would eventually be built. (It never was.) The area on the west side of the house was littered with trash discarded by previous occupants, but cleaning it up was not a priority. A couple of years later, a teenaged visitor undertook this task on her own initiative. They cleaned out the chicken coop, weeded the garden, and fixed a shower beside the outdoor pump that Alfred's brother John, a builder, had donated. They discovered that brief hot showers were possible when the sun had been shining on the pipe. While Alfred saw nothing wrong with bathing naked outdoors, others did not share that view. Bathing was difficult to arrange and did not happen very often.

Alfred made most of a screen door. Valerie cut Walter's hair. The children, left to their own devices as usual, developed a game where one squatted

IMAGE 6: *The men put together a crude outdoor shower and Piers tested it out.*

down and the other jumped over from the stone wall. Piers misjudged the distance and landed on Teresa's head, giving her a nasty cut.

It had been a busy day.

1941

The next day they planted peas, beets, and corn, and repaired the chicken house. In the afternoon they prepared a flower garden and planted seeds given by friends. It was very hot, peaking at 88° in the shade.

A business meeting was held in the evening. Regular business meetings were an essential part of what Alfred conceived to be the long-range plan.

On Saturday Alfred, Norma, and Leslie left in the truck at 6 a.m. to go to Brattleboro to do the marketing. After lunch Valerie walked down to a sale at Rawsonville, where she met Albert and Helen Baily, who helped her to pick up several bargains. Later the Bailys came up to Hilltop and gave much good advice. Helen Baily was always called "Ma'am," which was a problem for Alfred, as he had recently lived in a country where the only person addressed in that manner was the Queen. Ordinary women were "Madam," as is still the practice today.

On its return journey from Brattleboro the truck had a number of adventures, including being overtaken by Vernon Squires and his girlfriend Abbie, and later overtaking Alfred's brother Ed, with his wife Dorothy and son "Teddy," on their way up to Hilltop. A record number of 13 sat down to supper. The diary does not reveal where they all spent the night, or what they ate. Ed had brought his house trailer but had to leave it at Hanford's, more than two miles down the road, so perhaps that family walked back to it for the night. They lived on an 18-acre estate outside West Chester and were not accustomed to roughing it.

The three children, Piers, Teresa and cousin Teddy, ages 5 and 6, hid in a shack and played doctor: "I'll show you mine if you'll show me yours." As long as they didn't get in the way or require attention, children were pretty much free to do as they pleased. Little thought had been given to their needs, as children were not relevant to the larger, globally significant purpose of saving humanity.

On Sunday, Leslie, Valerie, Vernon, and Abbie attended church in Jamaica. The whole party had a picnic lunch on the hill, with a delectable salad prepared by Alfred's sister-in-law, Dorothy. After lunch the visitors left.

Toward supper time there came heavy rain with lightning and thunder, continuing most of the night and all the next day, so they did odd jobs around the house. Valerie made some "really good" bread. Alfred and Leslie walked down to Jamaica to find a lawyer to arrange the deed of partnership. It was believed that an immigrant (Leslie was British) who could demonstrate that he owned property would not be considered a "public charge," and would not be deported.

Walter and Valerie worked on the second chicken house, now known as the Shack, to make it ready for human habitation. Leslie and the boy, John, cut down trees that were blocking the view on the horizon. John would chop a tree down, but fail to call out the customary warning—*Timberrrrrr!*—for others to get out of the way as it fell. This was a hazard, and for that and other reasons Leslie soon arranged for John's father to come and pick him up. "His father was always hunting for places where he could live and be watched over."

One day at lunchtime Ernst Sollwitz arrived. He had inquired by letter a week before, and of course was welcomed.

Alfred: I remember him, because the truck needed some kind of repair job, which was my responsibility, but other work needed to be done first. Ernst had this German accuracy; in order to achieve some goal, it was suggested to take the truck down to the village. I said no, the truck was not fit to run now. It was a repair I suppose I could have done, but I was involved in other things that were coming up. Ernst said, 'Why has not something been done about it?' Well, because I can't do that and do the other things too. One of my jobs was baking bread. I had to take care of that, because if I didn't someone would say, 'Why is there no bread?' If I was doing one thing, I couldn't do another." Alfred felt controlled by others' expectations. His "tunnel vision" made it difficult for him to change a plan he was focused on or to consider the value of someone else's suggestion. And in working at another's direction he could not be blamed for unexpected outcomes.

After lunch the entire party went to the abandoned lumber camp down the road and demolished one of the buildings. The road from the village made a fairly even ascent up to that point, then made a left turn to scramble up the steep slope (still known as the King Road on maps) for the final half mile to the top. The location, known as Lumbercamp Corner, was part of the Hilltop property and available for salvage.

Just as they were gathering for supper, Edwin Keller arrived in a car driven by a dashing girl in pink slacks, a noteworthy sight for these isolated premises.

The next day most of the party worked at stripping the top covering from the roof. John and Valerie worked in the garden. Leslie set up a camp bed. The Shack was finally disinfected and two wood-and-canvas "army cots" were moved in. Leslie cut the grass with a scythe. Alfred visited the outer world and brought back the mail. Everyone was busy.

Walter, Ed, and Ernst worked on the roof the next very hot day, crouching precariously on the black tarpaper.

After lunch, Leslie and Valerie left for Canada to attend to some business matters there, expecting to return in a couple of weeks. John and

Norma walked down to the village for mail and groceries, and decided that the eight-mile hike was not worth the effort.

Norma wrote to Mrs. Donald Hadley, a goat keeper, to inquire whether she would have a suitable goat to sell: not an award winner, just an ordinary milker for family use.

The blueberries were ripening, and Ernst made two blueberry pies. Beyond the house to the east were what were called Strawberry Hill and Blueberry Hill. It was all one hill, partitioned by one of the ubiquitous stone walls. On the near slope, beyond the new vegetable garden, strawberries grew, tiny and very sweet compared to the commercial variety. On the far side the hill leveled off and was covered by wild blueberry patches. When they came in season later in the summer the blueberries ripened on a daily basis, and quarts were picked, canned, and eaten. It was slow, pleasant work that everyone participated in, each person picking a patch to settle by and harvest.

One day Teresa, who like Piers routinely went barefoot all summer, stepped on a rusty nail and had to be taken to the doctor in Townshend for a tetanus shot. The danger of infection was taken seriously, with scary tales of possible lockjaw that lurked on old farmsteads.

July 1941

Tuesday, July 1: A sad day. Walter Bethel and Ernst Sollwitz left the community before breakfast, following a disagreement with Alfred. Norma wrote to Leslie and Valerie that there had been an argument between Alfred and the trio of Walter, Ernst, and Ed Keller; they didn't wish to attend the regular morning worship meeting, preferring to go down to the lumber camp after breakfast to get some more planks for the roof, as the prior supply of planks was exhausted. Alfred took exception, feeling that they should attend the meeting, as the original plan, formulated with the now-departed Johnstons, anticipated that all participants would gather in this way each morning.

The dissidents did attend, but under protest, forming an opposition clique of three. They resolved to leave, Walter and Ed immediately, and Ernst as soon as Leslie and Valerie had returned from Canada. It was the beginning of the disintegration of the project, barely two weeks after it began, because of personality conflicts.

"I shall write a book on *Why Communities Fail*, my contribution to posterity," Norma reflected sadly. (See Appendix II.)

A note in Alfred's private personal journal dated July 4 makes only a passing reference to the situation: "History repeats itself. Ernst Sollwitz objected to meetings for worship. Evident differences of opinion, requiring discussion and negotiation." Later he would write to Leslie at considerable length, explaining his views. Alfred was not good at negotiation, unable to see past his own carefully thought-out plans, and having little patience with what motivated others, particularly if they had not been part of the original organizing group.

The remaining member of the trio, Ernst, built a scaffolding for the roof while the others worked at some late planting in the vegetable garden. Work on the roof continued for the next three days. Early harvest started, with a few onions, a little lettuce, and more radishes. Norma cleaned out and disinfected a stall for the expected new goat.

On Saturday Piers got stung on the lip by a wasp. The next day Ernst left after breakfast to return to Bryn Mawr, having spent ten days participating in the Hilltop experience and finding it not to be as idyllic as perhaps he had anticipated. Four people (including John, the unstable boy) had now abandoned the experiment within the first three weeks, and two others, the Johnstons, were temporarily absent.

IMAGE 7: *Working on the roof.*

A really significant change was just ahead: the arrival of the first of the goats. Alfred passed the driving test in Brattleboro, and a goat named Junie from Mrs. Truesdell of Townshend joined the family. The weather was thundery, with still more rain in the evening. The local minister, Mr. Watts, visited in the afternoon.

The children immediately got to know Junie. Since the family surname began with a J, it seemed fitting that Junie was a J name. She was a Toggenberg, brown with two white stripes on her nose, her horns cropped short in the manner of most farm goats, and she seemed gentle and companionable. They led her to the barn where she would live, and of course, they assumed, she would have the whole landscape in which to forage. The wire-strung garden fence, the neophytes were confident, would keep goats out, as well as deer. The children developed a permanent affection for goats.

(One night later on, Alfred slept out in the garden in the hope of discovering whether it was deer eating the young vegetables, and if so, how they got in and out, as the high fence was by then complete. What he detected was a woodchuck, eating the garden plants. The deer were innocent, so far.)

Vernon Squires and Abbie visited after lunch and drove the family to Jamaica for marketing and mail retrieval before driving back to Brattleboro. There was heavy rain during the night, but the repaired section of the roof proved to be watertight. Alfred recalled that, "Vernon didn't believe in our project. He got the county agent to come and tell us that it was impossible. He thought that protection from forest fires could be achieved by cutting a 20-ft wide strip around the outer limits of the property, so the fire would die out."

Dorrit Weil, a friend of Karl Schultz, came to lunch, bringing two others, a father and daughter named Bernard. Vernon returned about bedtime.

On July 14 the Hilltop Ghost first revealed itself: Mysterious footsteps were heard in the attic at 3 a.m. No material cause was discovered for this phenomenon. Teresa recalls that manifestations such as smoke issuing from a chimney when no one was home would jokingly be attributed to Ann Boleyn, one of Henry VIII's doomed wives, who "Walked the Bloody Tower/ With her head tucked underneath her arm/ At the midnight hour."

Alfred and Vernon opened a window into the cellar, a dank, earth-floored cave suitable only for storage of canned goods, root vegetables buried in sawdust, and the propagation of earthworms in a dirt-filled box. About teatime Vernon drove down to Brattleboro to bring back his girlfriend Abbie, Pat Beatts, his wife Sheila, and their baby, Barbara. Abbie stayed for supper.

Alfred wrote a long, long letter to Leslie Johnston, reviewing the problem of July 1 when Walter and Ed had unexpectedly departed.

"Walter's departure seems to have revealed a series of differences of thinking which have worried me during the past week and made me wonder whether, after all, I may be the one who is out of touch with the real aims planned for this place. I was keen to have regular discussions at Pendle Hill so that we could get over the preliminary knowledge of each other and our differing emphases in advance, and not have to contend with them amidst the problems of material adjustment on the farm [which could hardly have been anticipated before anyone had even seen the place, nor had they any experience of farm life, or of local weather conditions].

"I think it was a pity the discussions did not continue. In fact, if we are to pursue the course I had thought was our common mind [here in a nutshell is the basis of nearly all future difficulties, the divergence between what Alfred believed was the proper course of action and what others proposed] it seems to me that much time for joint reflection must be allowed as part of the program. Surely the planning is a legitimate part of the execution, and emphasis on execution to the exclusion of mutual reflection cannot benefit the project.

"Vernon and Abbie came yesterday, and he will return today permanently. Pat & his family come tomorrow. We are thus on the verge of the same problem which we faced when Walter, Ed, John and Ernst were here—a majority of newcomers, unacquainted with our past deliberations or the needs out of which our present actions have evolved, each with ideas of his own as to what should be done and how, and each bringing a proportion of the standard ideas of the civilized world which, if we were to follow, would make us identical with the world and remove our raison d'être [reason for being].

"It is clear to me that there is not existing a unified community to receive them into. By attempting to continue [with] about the same arrangements as we had when you were here, I got into trouble all around. Can it be that the real group is any group that may casually be here at one time? Or is the real group composed of those who are committed to a permanent project? I incline to the latter view, but it must be obnoxious to newcomers (and I think it offended Walter and Ernst) to give considerable influence to absent members.

"I am thrown into [an expression he often uses, implying helplessness] opposition on countless points, either because I want to continue the outward arrangements we agreed on, like meeting [for worship], department responsibility, collective planning of daily work: or because I want progressively to apply the principles I believed we had united on, such as simple living, conservation of resources, acceptance of manual tasks, experimentation in subsistence, and so on.

"My position has come to be unenviable, yet I cannot readily change the ideas which made me interested in this type of project from the beginning, and to have them and to wish to apply them seem to me to be of one parcel.

"I see only two alternatives:

"One: to live here quietly as a double household with friends, spending the income that the group enjoys, devoting ourselves to reading, sundry outward activities, and some productive labor as a hobby: feeling free to come and go, take part time employment, write and indulge our interests. This would be an attractive life, and has its possibilities, particularly since it would free us from the more burdensome tasks, all of which could be covered by the cash income. It is something of this sort that I imagine our guests and short-term workers think we wish to achieve.

"Two: a serious experimental project involving self- and group-discipline, united effort, careful planning, close cooperation; a way of life at once satisfying for us and capable of universalization, keeping an open mind to religious values, and adhering to certain religious practices, planning step by step the characteristics of our life without following existing models uncritically, so arranging our material life as to rely less and less on unearned income, which could then be applied to supporting similar projects or other useful works.

"I am open to both alternatives, but in myself I feel the need to explore the more difficult way. Having seen Europe recently, having friends who are in great distress, I feel the call to take life seriously rather than frivolously, working out a way of life I should not be ashamed of even if I lived next door to European friends, and getting a practical preparation in case there is need of future service here or elsewhere.

"For myself, I should like to find a way of life with the maximum simplicity of feeding and living arrangements and the consciousness that God is there, and we are just frittering away our time unless we are trying to find out and to do His will. [This Christocentric view is not shared by all Quakers.]

"I do not like abstractions, unless they have an immediate material reference; that is, a meaning in conduct.[9]

"I had imagined that the first year of our project, the year in which we had arranged that it would be unnecessary to do any productive or remunerative work unless we wished, would be dedicated to the necessary adjustments to rural life, and the adjustments in our habits and needs, leading towards an ability to live decently with the least cash outlay. I visualized such nominal 'sacrifices' as the use of wood for coal and oil, use of foot power for internal combustion engines [bicycle? Shank's mare?]; margarine for butter, dried milk for liquid milk, home ground flour, handmade hinges, home-cooked foods, and so on.

---

9. Individuals with autism are very literal-minded and do not understand fantasy or abstractions. Such children, for example, do not play make-believe or pretend that a doll or an animal is "talking," because obviously they cannot actually talk.

"I call them nominal, because there is no material sacrifice. The result is identical. Milk is milk, whether dried or liquid; there is only the adjustment to the different form and flavor; one fat and another are much of a muchness in the diet; and so on. There are only matters of adjustment. Nothing is 'done without' except familiar forms and flavors.

"I would hope that we would not be afraid of genuine sacrifices as well: if we were not ready to produce eggs, we could discover the function of eggs in the diet and meet the need by other means; or at a time when one foodstuff might be running low, devise ways of making the remaining foods more attractive until such time as a journey to the village might be justified; to adjust ourselves to a lesser area of warmed air during the winter; and to substitutions for oranges, tobacco, bananas, and things incapable of production in this climate.

"If I had to choose between chopping wood for 8 hours in order to warm the whole house, or chopping for 4 in order to warm half of it, I should prefer to adjust myself to less space and have more free time, rather than insist on more warmed space and have less free time.

"The same thing is true of the tailor-made cigarette you mentioned in a letter. It is only easier to buy [rather than make] things for people who happen to have money automatically. If we sold wheat at 60¢ a bushel, we should stop before trading the plowing, harrowing, planting, reaping, seasoning, threshing, storing, sacking and transportation of a quarter bushel for a pack of cigarettes. It would be infinitely easier to roll them by hand. [*Teresa*: Out of curiosity I learned to roll cigarettes at Hilltop, using tobacco intended as feed for the goats. We were allowed to try smoking it and quickly became ill, thereafter losing all interest in pursuing this unhealthful habit.]

"This explains part of what I feel about butter. The difference between butter at 42¢ and margarine at 15¢ a pound, means that either you have struggled to economize on something else, in order to enjoy butter; or you have dug, planted, weeded, sprayed, harvested and transported so many peas or cabbages to get the extra 27¢, valuing your time at about 1¢ an hour, and receiving little actual value nutritionally from the time and money so spent. To me it seems logical to make the adjustment to the difference in color and flavor, rather than spend all those hours weeding, or lumbering, or dish-washing. [*Teresa*: Margarine came in white blocks that were colored by working an orange powder through with a fork, or in a plastic bag with a capsule of orange coloring that was pinched open and worked in with the hands. Pre-colored margarine would, it was thought, unfairly compete with real butter in the marketplace.]

"In the case of installations of a permanent nature, I would not think so much of economies. There is no possible adjustment to a roof the wind has torn off because it was improperly fastened. You cannot use a [wood] plane that won't shave, or a saw that won't bite. I see no point in living on a hill top in order to enjoy the same fried oysters and caviar as at a seaside resort. I should prefer to see how far our own ingenuity will go towards taking a handful of basic foods and providing a diet sufficiently varied and nutritious to maintain us in efficiency.

"The object is conservation of resources. The absence of oranges, cream cheese, ham and tinned peaches will be compensated [for] by leakless roofs, storm-tight windows, and a dry wood pile. We cannot expect to have both. I would prefer a more studied economy of living to a more comfortable one, if only for the reason that we could then keep an open door to newcomers, even if they added no property to the common pool.

"Of course, there is the conventional alternative, that of making money. To set up a large-enough poultry or dairy business here to make money would mean the abandonment of our original plan. Something can be made of forestry, but not enough to maintain us like lords, and during the time we have an unearned income [Alfred's father was underwriting the initial maintenance costs and had provided the funds with which to purchase the farm] I should think it is right to discover what must be our standard of living. I am wary of all obvious means and solutions. Even the goat will cost more to maintain than the milk would cost us to buy. I would have taken the other way, of using other foodstuffs more freely during the time it is not possible for us to maintain livestock economically.

"It seems more likely that you, Valerie, and Norma will agree in general than that any of you will agree with me. As you have observed, my mind works in a way of its own. But even so, there is plenty of common ground to stand on, which can be discovered by patient search, and I should think it worthwhile to make the search and hold together, rather than refuse to do so and fall apart.

"I do not think I could feel committed to a project which did not give full weight to the very serious state of the world and did not represent an honest effort to live rightly in a wrong world. I feel uneasy at any attempt to consider larger responsibilities. I have seen enough irresponsibility in people who did not know the disasters they were helping to cause; and though I think we should have fun and enjoy life, I also think we should use our intelligence to the full and diligently search for divine guidance where our wits are not enough, in order to live in the sort of way that men have ultimately got to live in the world.

"You and I had discussed and decided that our Godward relation was to be regarded as important. I tried to explain this to Ernst, and he and Walter came to Meeting under a sense of compulsion, and soon left altogether. Meeting since then has been only formal. So even this must be taken up once again, as part of a general discussion of What is important? If we go to the extreme of crowding out the Godward reference and organizing life on a money-making basis, I do not see that we differ from any other business.

"If only there were a way to proceed, deciding unitedly and carrying out our decisions cooperatively. It is what I thought we wanted, and what I want, yet if I try to apply it, I am thrown into a position of obstructionism and am regarded as slowing up the works. Was it true that I obstructed the purchase of a goat and hens? If you think so, it can only mean that we did not have a full enough discussion. Are we going on to do more things without a full enough discussion? What becomes of our project then? We either have to slow up the goat and chickens, or slow up the spirit of the community, and I would rather the former.

"Come down for the day, if you can, and let's hash over some of these matters."

Alfred viewed a God-concept as a motivating and sustaining force, making Hilltop skew toward being a religious rather than a secular community. That may have been the reason the three men departed: If it was to be a religious enterprise, a sort of monastery, there was more profession of faith than they were comfortable with. It might have been better to leave God out of it, and let each person interpret the situation as he or she chose.

But this is conjecture; the records do not ever quite support it. Again and again, Alfred's only partially self-aware comments make clear the difficulty he had in conforming to societal norms and understanding the vagaries of human behavior, as could be typical of someone exhibiting an autistic mindset.

And so, only six weeks after Alfred's initial arrival in mid-May, and less than three weeks after the arrival of the first settlers, Hilltop Farm had suffered its first serious upheaval, resulting in the "resignation" of three members, the exile of two others, and the banishment of a sixth, and occasioning much thought about purpose and means. But the project limped along, and perhaps, they hoped, it would be possible to avoid future altercations of this nature. Communities, like individuals, could learn from experience, however painful that might be.

Meanwhile, Pat Beatts mowed grass with the scythe, while the others worked at gardening and cleaning out the larder [pantry], covering mouseholes with bent tin can lids. In the afternoon the men went out to survey the property and the women and children picked blueberries for canning. There was some excitement when it was discovered that Junie had unfastened her chain and disappeared. After a search she was found…in the barn. Village people showed up and asked permission to pick blueberries, apparently a local tradition.

1941

IMAGE 8: *Pikes Falls, a pleasant but icy-cold recreational option.*

One day Alfred's older brother Edward, his new stepmother Caroline, his aunt Louisa, and sister Elinor arrived in time for lunch. Pat did not turn up for lunch, causing some anxiety. It turned out that he had made a grand tour, returning via Jamaica village. Other visitors for the afternoon and evening were Vernon's girlfriend Abbie, Mr. Buchanan, the county agent from Brattleboro, and the forester, Mr. Turner, who stayed to supper and gave much valuable advice. All hands turned out to pick blueberries, picking enough for several quarts of blueberry preserves.

Norma wrote a letter to "Dick and Cynthia":

"It is utterly disgraceful to have let more than a month go by before writing to thank you for your hospitality, which was so wonderfully welcome on our way north. What *would* my mother say! But maybe you can imagine the kind of pressure under which we have been living these past four weeks, with absolutely everything to get started at the same time. Also, we had a disagreement with Walter, which set us back a good deal in our adjustment to the new life: it was a saddening thing to have happen but I hope we shall learn from it some of the mistakes to avoid making with new people in the future."

She went on to mention some of the details: the potatoes were full of weeds, blueberries needed to be picked for preserves, haymaking, and patching up the barn so they could put a horse in it when they got a horse.

"All last week when Alfred and I were alone, we just floundered. I could barely keep up with the cooking, cleaning and laundry [and child-minding, tasks she had never before had to handle herself, always having lived where there were servants to deal with such things], and Alfred with looking after garden and goat. It is wonderful to have more manpower again."

She resolutely concluded, "Still, life is pretty good, the weather and the scenery are perfect, the local people very friendly, and we have discovered a wonderful swimming-hole four or five miles away." This would be either Pikes Falls (at left), a frigid torrent coursing over huge boulders into a rocky pool, or more likely the Salmon Hole, a wide, shallow portion of the West River that passed near Jamaica village.[10]

Vernon and the children began to excavate the cellar, trying to find rock bottom in the sloping floor of dirt. Others scrubbed the future kitchen walls and floor. Pat made a Dutch door for the front bedroom. The stove, reclaimed from the lumber camp, was brought in and put in position in the temporary tool room that was shortly to become the kitchen.

Many hours were devoted to haymaking, weeding, making jam, sandpapering the lumber-camp stove, and other odd jobs. A two-gallon jar was filled with marmalade made from orange peels. This surely would have required a lot of white sugar, despite Alfred's aversion to it and his contention that "since we weren't producing sugar, we shouldn't be using it." Once the war began, sugar was strictly rationed.

---

10. In 2010 an archaeological dig revealed that there had been Native American (Abenaki) encampments along the West River for thousands of years. "Evidence suggests that present-day Jamaica had been a center for hunting, fishing, plant gathering and tool making for a period of more than 8,000 years." The area is now cordoned off from souvenir seekers as it awaits further funding. From the Vermont State Parks trails guide.

A letter was received from Leslie and Valerie announcing their return, planned for the end of the coming week, joyous news indeed! Alfred made a wheelbarrow and Norma painted the stove black.

The Jacob family and the Squires drove to Arlington the next day to spend the afternoon with their friends the Baumgardts, and met Dorothy Canfield Fisher, an author of some repute. This was the first purely frivolous excursion undertaken since the colonists had settled in. Abbie drove the party and stayed to supper.

Alfred's private record remarked that they were having many discussions about purpose, with increasing verbal discontent. There was consideration of the economics of raising goats for sale.

They worked on the garden and made canvas cots. Pat built a playpen for Barbara. In the afternoon there were visits from Mr. Gottlieb of the State Forestry Service and Mr. Root, the county agent, driven up by Abbie. At Vernon's suggestion an evaluation meeting was held in the evening, discussing progress and future possibilities.

July 22 was Alfred and Norma's eighth wedding anniversary. To celebrate, they removed the old kitchen stove from what was to be the living room and unbricked the original fireplace behind it. (This room was never furnished, as most social interaction took place in the kitchen.) The stovepipe had made a bend to feed into the fireplace chimney, and there turned out to be large brick-lined chambers—beehive ovens—that would be heated by the fire in the fireplace, for slow baking. The century-old house was revealing some of its secrets.

Some people from nearby Pikes Falls valley came to pick blueberries. Mrs. Smith, whose sons Oscar and Elmer would later attend the one-room schoolhouse to which Piers and Teresa walked, brought a large quantity of lettuce, Swiss chard, and beets. Sheila, Pat, and Barbara walked to the village for mail. Vernon built a stand for a power saw, though no such equipment existed as yet. Pat and Alfred finished fixing the garden fence. Vernon finished the saw table. The grinder was fixed to the rear wheel of the truck, and some wheat was ground, from which Vernon made bread.

Although it appeared that daily life was progressing satisfactorily, Alfred's journal somewhat ominously noted that, "My temper is violent, and I express it with the goats." The man of peace, who confidently expected to demonstrate to the rest of the world how to avoid war, was finding it difficult to align his personal goals with those of others, and resentment flowered. Unfortunately, it was not only the goats but his own family on which he focused his frustration.

The truck ground some more wheat and corn and powered the saw to make firewood. Norma left to attend the Green Mountain Festival in

HILLTOP FARM

IMAGE 9: *Teresa looks on as Alfred works to enable the revolving wheel to power an appliance.*

Middlebury. Abbie brought Ellen Gould, of Brattleboro, for supper. Vernon went back to Brattleboro with them. The children occupied themselves as best they could without adult guidance.

On Saturday Herbert Leader, of Tunbridge, Vermont, came to spend the day, and a general holiday was observed. Herbert was a powerful man; Alfred liked to say that he was as strong as two men. He was a free spirit who arrived and departed without notice as the mood suited him, drifting in and out of the Hilltop experiment for several years.

Alfred wrote again to Leslie and Valerie, saying in part:

"Those of us who are here are in no way unified in our approach to problems. Vernon asked to know more about the origins of Hilltop as soon as he arrived, but what with the irregularity of work, meals, rising and retiring, the children and the dishes, it has only been possible to explain a fraction of the preliminaries.

"Norma [who suffered from stomach ulcers exacerbated by the coarse food and constant stress, with which Alfred, with his Christian Science just-ignore-it background, was not sympathetic; his mother believed in the principles of Christian Science and he no doubt absorbed some of those convictions] appears to have been laid up when each important decision was made, so I am the only one who is acquainted with the general lines which were proposed when this thing was started and am often in conflict with the general tendencies of the rest of the group.

Since we have regularly had butter, vacuum sealed coffee, tins of milk, joints of meat [British term for a roast], and 'bought' bread, did we need to come to Vermont to buy and consume the things advertised in the *Ladies Home Journal*?

"What is important is something that must be lacking as long as you [the Johnstons] are away: a unity of approach, and a determination to find grounds for agreement in every situation, realizing that there are differences but that they need not be obstacles to action or to fellowship. At present I feel as if I were regarded as the obstacle to such action and fellowship because of the stands which I cannot help making: if I am responsible for the garden, I must oppose any effort to harvest vegetables which I don't think ready for harvest, and I continue to oppose popping down into the village in the truck to see if there is any mail and bring up a sack of beans.

"I can quite easily see how anyone accustomed to Americanized life and not familiar with the philosophy which guided us here would be very critical of my opposition; and arguments on this sort of subject tend to leave me very confused. I don't see that anything worthwhile [it was becoming clear that Alfred's definition of worthwhile differed significantly from that of others] will be achieved unless it is reasonably consistent; I don't think this ought to be a frivolous affair in which we make bread if we happen to feel like it, and buy it if we happen to feel like it. Unless it is a conscious effort to follow out some ordered plan, facing the difficulties which the application of the plan engenders, I shall not understand it very well.

"Fundamentally, I think what I am searching for is honesty. Is this a labor holiday, or a religious experiment, or a business? I have some business instincts, and a group business project has its constructive side. But I do earnestly object to pretending that we are moving toward community when there is not even a unified desire for such element of discipline and planning as might lead towards community."

But he also remarked, "Life is not all problems. The goat milk production has gone up; the circular saw is mounted and has had a tryout; the kitchen is moved; evening fireside chats take place; Pat has got some hay in for the goat; the garden is growing and the fence is enough repaired so the woodchuck's ravages are not in evidence; Herbert Leader has visited and proved interesting—much farther advanced into subsistence farming than we are (if we are to be), and we look forward to Philip J's visit sometime next month." (It became clear after some time that Herbert's professed knowledge and expertise were largely a product of his own imagination. Nevertheless, he was a hard worker and good company.)

Morning rain on July 27 prevented work outside. Alfred plastered above the revealed mantelpiece in the living room, and Norma returned from Middlebury.

The kitchen was finished and soon became the center of the community, because the constantly burning stove heated it in winter, making it the only reliably comfortable room in the house. Once, although it was freezing outside, in the kitchen it was 100º!

Norma walked to the village for mail, as she was to do regularly in any weather. One might think an eight-mile round trip for letters was excessive, but everyone was used to walking, and the mail was the main means of contact with friends in the outside world. (It was, frankly, also an opportunity to get away from the frequent discord in the house.)

Unsettled as the situation already was, intimations of disaster surfaced when Abbie brought a Special Delivery letter from the Johnstons, asking the others to meet them on the Canadian border to talk over future plans, as their supposedly routine application for a visa now seemed likely to be refused.

Vernon, Abbie, Alfred, and Norma drove up to Derby Line on the Canadian border, and Vernon and Abbie drove on to Montreal and spent the night in Johnston friend Kay's flat there. They returned with Leslie and Valerie, and a conference was held on the lawn behind the Immigration Office. "We had to straddle the boundary line and do our talking, each in his own country," Norma noted.

All too soon, Kay came to take the Johnstons back to Montreal. The others drove home in stunned silence, arriving at midnight after experiencing three blowouts on the way. It was a grim occasion, for the Johnstons had been integral to the plans for the Hilltop community. This was particularly devastating for Norma, who had counted on Valerie's support during the difficult first weeks and months of the project, and now found herself the lone woman, with no one to talk to who fully understood the challenge, or could assist with household tasks.

A letter from John's mother Dorothy Barstow, perhaps somewhat in denial about her son's mental issues, said in part: "I want to thank you and the others there, who so kindly took in my son John on your brave experiment of simple living and hard work. I was very sorry that he left you so suddenly. The two main reasons for his withdrawal [he had been asked to leave, but perhaps she did not know this] were that he didn't like the food, and he found it very lonely. He had just come from two years' life on a farm where they had lots of fresh milk and eggs and fruits and vegetables, and where there were many young people of his age, and I am afraid the contrast was too much for him."

August 1941

On August 1, the Jacob and Beatts families went to Brattleboro in the truck. Preliminary inquiries were made about renting a house in Jamaica village for the winter months, because it was becoming clear that the community, such as it was, was not yet prepared for the rigors of an isolated winter. Alfred recalled that they needed "a place where we could live so Teresa and Piers could go to school. Norma tried teaching them, and found it hopeless. She didn't have the patience." This makes it sound as though Alfred would have been fine with spending the winter in the frigid, drafty, mouse-ridden old house if it weren't for the children's scholastic requirements. At ages 5 and 6, school was not yet a priority, but provided a convenient excuse to escape the anticipated winter trials.

The truck went down to Jamaica to fetch lumber to make a bathroom partition and the entrance vestibule floor. Further inquiries were made about a house, but so far none seemed to be available for rent. The Jacksons arrived to spend the night. Mrs. Jackson and her daughter Lucy left for a camp in northern Vermont the next day. Charles Jackson and his son Tommy stayed to help. There was a picnic on the top of Blueberry Hill, and nine and a half pounds of blueberries—five quarts—were picked and bottled.

A space behind the stairs was turned out, and holes in the walls were plastered, preparatory to making it into a mouse-proof larder, as what was later to become the pantry was being used as an office for writing the many letters needed to remain in communication with other subsistence communities.

Mr. and Mrs. Porter arrived to visit the Beatts and took them away to spend the night in Newfane, about ten miles south of Jamaica. The Beatts then left for Rose Valley (not far from Pendle Hill) with Mr. Porter. An afternoon's work was done at the lumber camp, collecting a truckload of timber and other materials.

Norma answered Dorothy Barstow's letter of July 31:

"We quite understand why John left, in fact it seemed to us from the first that we hadn't made it clear enough how difficult life up here was bound to be in the early days of our experiment. If it turns out as we plan, it should be just what John hoped to find here, but that will be a matter of years of work and considerable sacrifices all around. At the present time we are in some difficulty because our friends the Johnstons have been practically refused permission to re-enter the country from Canada. We don't know just what we are going to do, but meanwhile we are carrying on and hoping something can be arranged to get them back. There is practically nothing we can do in their absence except just the day-to-day jobs of gardening, mending the roof and so on."

August 6 was Piers' 7th birthday, his first in America, which was appropriately celebrated. His 6th birthday had occurred on the refugee ship, the *Excalibur*, where the staff created a mock cake for him out of sawdust, as sugar, eggs, and flour were not available because of the war in Europe.

Janet Jackson arrived back from leaving Lucy at her camp. In the afternoon a party drove over to see Scott Nearing, a neighbor on the Bondville side, whose birthday coincidentally was the same as Piers', albeit 51 years earlier. (Scott, a robust 58 at that time, was to live to age 100, at which point he brought his life to an end by declining to eat or drink anymore.) Someone at Pendle Hill had exclaimed, upon learning of the move to Jamaica, "Oh, you'll be near Scott Nearing!" Alfred was amused at the repetition: Near… Nearing.

Later on, Helen, Scott's partner in life, came to visit and Norma introduced her as Mrs. Scott Nearing. "Oh no," she exclaimed, "I'm Helen Knothe!" (kuh-no-thee). The fact that she and Scott weren't married caused some raised eyebrows among traditionalists. (They did marry some years later, after Scott's first wife, Nellie Seeds, had died.)

Roof repairs were finally completed. The next day Alfred, Vernon, and Charles Jackson excavated a hole to make a door into the cellar on the east side, so they could more readily access it from outside.

Norma wrote a Dear Friends letter to the Johnstons, saying in part:

"Vernon, Alfred, and Charles Jackson have been busy all day on the east side, where a large section of the house is just floating on thin air. Vernon announced regretfully that the aperture would not be sufficient for the truck to be driven in. 'Tis not so deep as a well, nor so wide as a church door, but 'twill serve.'[11] The ostensible purpose is so that we can get our tons of firewood, potatoes and the like into the cellar without having to carry them piecemeal down the cellar stairs."

What, out of ignorance, they hadn't reckoned on was that the new aperture took away the insulation provided by the ground, so that the cellar froze in winter while they were away, and the entire crop of potatoes was reduced to a slimy, smelly mess.

Norma went on, "I find recent experiences, both good and bad, have left me convinced of several things.

"1) The Community idea is the right idea and must be tried.

"2) Vermont is an excellent place for such an experiment, because of the peculiarly vigorous character of democracy here. Most of what we thought

---

11. From Shakespeare's *Romeo and Juliet*: Romeo's friend Mercutio explains why he is sure the battle wound he has just received will ultimately be fatal. Norma's correspondence is peppered with quotations from the Bible, Shakespeare, the classics, poetry, philosophy and literature in general. Books were her joy and her escape.

we should have to keep alive among ourselves for posterity is existing here among the small local communities. In fact, in many ways the New England Town Meeting set-up resembles that of the City State, with the great advantage of not being based on slave labor, but on hard work by every single person concerned.

"3) We need a new kind of education and it is up to us to create it. Our first step in that direction I think will be extra buildings, to be undertaken next summer if funds permit and labor is available.

"4) Our first task right now is to get you two back into the country. With that in mind we are writing to any people we can think of who might be able to help. Even if you had to go and teach in a college somewhere, that would mean contact could be maintained, and the future would be open to us. I find I have brought with me from Europe [because of the civil war in Spain] the habit of not being able to look even a month ahead, but clearly we must discipline ourselves and learn to think in years again, even if most of what we plan may in fact be wrecked by the by-products of world disintegration. [This doomsday scenario is alluded to again and again.]

"5) You are the people with whom we can work best; it would warm the cockles of your hearts to know how much we want you back. Vernon and Charles Jackson are our kind of people too, but both have matrimonial entanglements which pretty well disqualify them as raw material for the Community."

That same day she wrote to Dorothy Canfield Fisher:

"Just now, though, we are in serious difficulties because our friends and fellow-experimenters, the Johnstons, on whom the whole thing depends, are finding it practically impossible to get back into this country from Canada as permanent residents. They were here on student visas, which expired at the beginning of July, and though they went off provided with all sorts of papers, including an affidavit of support from some friends, the Consul in Montreal doesn't feel able to give them immigration visas and has referred their application to Washington. He tells them this means a delay of several months and probably a final refusal, as a mere affidavit of support from a person not a relative isn't considered sufficient nowadays.

"There is the further complication that Leslie Johnston registered as a conscientious objector. The only practicable alternative seems to be for him to get a teaching post in a college somewhere. He has good teaching qualifications, and an M.A. degree from Haverford [College], but still we don't know whether anything can be arranged so late in the summer.

"Altogether we feel fairly depressed about the future, for even when we have tried everything there will still be a long time-lag before we can know anything definite. In the circumstances we think we shall have to move ourselves from this very remote outpost into Jamaica village for the winter months, and send the children to the school there."

A letter to Mr. Henry C. Taylor, of the Farm Foundation in Chicago, stated:

"This farm was originally bought last January by a group consisting of three young married couples, who hoped to live on it and work towards subsistence production, with the idea of becoming, insofar as possible, self-supporting before the economic crisis which we seem to see ahead. The idea is not as selfish as it sounds, because we believe that the discoveries which we make about the best way for people like ourselves, with limited capital and not born and bred on a farm, to achieve a fair degree of economic independence will be valuable to the thousands who will, in the next few years, be thrown back on the land as their only source of livelihood."

The U.S. would not enter the war for another four months, which could not have been anticipated at that time, so this ominous prediction no doubt applies to the already war-torn countries abroad, for which they believed they could provide guidance and instruction.

She continued: "We also have an interest in discovering the mechanics of social life: what for instance are the personal difficulties and strains which make people less happy and efficient than need be in the management of their individual lives for the greater good of the community, and beyond that, what are the elements in human conduct which, on a large scale, produce war and all its attendant horrors unless they are checked at the start?

"This is very ambitious, but we feel that it is at this moment the chief task before humanity as a whole, and we don't know where the discovery of a better way of living together is to begin unless it is among individual small groups dedicated to this very purpose. One of our hopes for the future is the building up of a small community here which would have its own school run on progressive lines, but a great deal of merely material work will have to be done before that becomes possible."

Six hens were purchased from Mr. Browning in Bondville. Fresh eggs were coming to the farm! The next day the Jacksons left for Boston. Miss Hanford, whose house was halfway between Hilltop and the village, came to pick blueberries. Seven quarts of green beans from the garden were canned.

Alfred wrote, somewhat grumpily, to Leslie and Valerie. "The problems outstanding when we met are being solved, I think, by abandoning all thought of self-sufficiency & conservation of resource[s] except insofar as both are convenient. Consequently, I have ordered a small concrete mixer to help with foundations, water cistern & wall plastering (I have tried out plaster made with sawdust instead of sand & it seems satisfactory, but should be very well mixed) & I shall allow myself somewhat more than the most essential tools & materials. If a group life evolves in the future, we can decide by common consent whether to explore self-maintenance at that time."

1941

It had taken only a few weeks for Alfred to discover that his rock-bottom subsistence plan was not going to work, and that some previously scorned mechanical aids were in fact desirable.

"This past week's work, with Vernon & Charles Jackson, has been the most satisfying of the summer, largely, I think, because we all understand one another. We brought the garden up to date, finished the roof, and excavated an entrance to the cellar on the East side large enough to back the truck in, or tie up the goat there. The other jobs I have in prospect are some sort of shelter outside the west door [it never happened], and some arrangement to get water inside the house.

"We are fairly well decided to buy Mrs. Hope's house for $800. She says the taxes are only $10, & that would give us a pied a terre [temporary lodging] in the village, & room for more visitors, & (again abandoning subsistence production) since there is electric current there, small electric tools could be used, ironing done, etc. [Ironing was accomplished with a heavy iron heated on the stove to a temperature that would achieve results without burning the fabric. It was a tricky balance to maintain, and scorch marks were common.] There is a large gravel pit which should help with my cement work & also from time to time might be sold at 5¢ a cubic yard. Vernon has been over the house & thinks it is a good buy with its two acres, small barn & two chicken houses (all derelict) even though there are 5 large timbers in the basement that are totally rotted away. We can pay for the house theoretically out of this year's income (if you do not need any of it) & subsequently the only cost would be taxation. Norma wants to fix it up with a view to renting in the summer.

"We have encouraged the Jacksons to feel free to club together with us if they feel led, just as we have encouraged the Johnstons. I feel it would be all to the good if all four families were concerned in this place. CJ is certainly a good worker, & Janet is very congenial, from what we have seen this week.

"The goat is nearly up to 3 quarts now, and yesterday Norma bought 6 hens from the Brownings, hens he proposed to execute this autumn, & we could do so after we can get some pullets or ducks." (There were ducks, briefly, that paddled on the small swampy pond near the barn. Their purpose was never clear, unless as an additional source of eggs. They were quickly devoured by foxes. The pond was home to frogs, whose jelly-like egg masses and subsequent tadpoles fascinated the children.)

Alfred continued: "Also I think Norma wants one of CJ's puppies. They are cute, but have to eat meat, which involves cash. Again, if we are not to be self-sufficient, this doesn't matter.

"We are shifting the larder to the office today, leaving room to develop a new office in the [old] larder & a bathroom at the north end of it, accessible from the staircase. I have ordered pipe-cutting & threading equipment & a blowtorch & should have no difficulty in setting up a bathroom. [The facility consisted of a never-used claw-footed tub and a washstand with jug and basin. There was no door, only a curtain over the aperture. No one ever actually bathed there.] It is all very interesting work for me, facilitated much by the possibility of buying small things [a curious comment from someone who had eschewed reliance on commercial aids of any kind]; & it is very constructive in our own family life for Norma & me to work on something of common interest, even an office or bathroom. The one drawback about taking Mrs. Hope's house is that it will slow up the work on this house; but it justifies the purchase of tools."

Alfred also reported on the garden: "The corn is showing tassels now, the lettuce has at last recovered from the nocturnal consumers, the beets are showing red & the squash are blooming. Tomatoes hang heavy on most of the vines, but are not red. The little ones are not 12 inches high yet: in fact, all the tomatoes are more like bushes than vines. [Tomatoes naturally sprawl, they are not climbers. Alfred may not have known this.] We have had some nice larger radishes, anyway. I haven't got after the compost heap, except the one made of night soil [human waste]. It's a pity to lose the summer, since not much decomposition can take place in the winter. I suppose it means I must buy fertilizer for next year, since the difference between fertilized & non-fertilized rows is marked, & the biodynamic system[12] cannot be worked without farm animals." Alfred was learning through experience what generations of farmers had long since discovered.

Vernon, Abbie, and Vernon's mother came to fetch Vernon's things and say goodbye. "Abbie wasn't going to tolerate having Vernon spend much time [with us]. She thought the enterprise was hopeless."

A letter from Anna Brinton (who, with her husband Howard, was a codirector at Pendle Hill) dated August 11, 1941, says in part: "A long letter from Leslie and Valerie Johnston makes us realize that you have all agreed to let the farm wait for some further developments. It does take time and such an infinite amount of adjustment to build up a new undertaking. I realize this from our own experience at Pendle Hill [founded in 1935], where it has taken some years to come to being the kind of place we hoped it would become."

Wednesday had a very cold wind and showers. Alfred's younger brother, Philip, and his wife Elizabeth Linton, known as Teddy, arrived for a visit of a few days. Phil was perhaps the member of the Jacob family most firmly committed to the concept of God as an all-knowing, all-controlling spirit. A person could ask Phil a question about the price of beans in Bohemia,

---

12. Biodynamic agriculture is an organic and some would say mystical system of farming developed by Rudolph Steiner in the 1920s; it is still popular today.

and he would say, "I don't know the answer, but I know Someone who does." Then the subject became exclusively God.

Alfred and Phil repaired barn timbers while Norma and Teddy painted doors and windows. It rained from lunchtime onward. Phil and Teddy left the next day.

Teresa: I always thought that Teddy was "the perfect mother," though I knew I was supposed to believe that my own mother was perfect. *Alfred*: I remember how they always consulted together, which I wasn't in a position to do. Norma always knew what was the thing to do, and what had to be done. The idea of working it out, consulting together, was alien to her. *Teresa*: Since Alfred refused ever to take the initiative, Norma had to go forward on her own, making it inevitable that she would be blamed for difficulties.

Alfred wrote again to Leslie and Valerie:

"I confess that your last epistle depressed me very much indeed. So probably I had better not say much, because I recognize that my state of mind is largely due to extreme physical fatigue. I was just beginning to feel the cumulative effects of nine weeks of unremitting hard work accompanied by several disappointments, when your letter arrived to administer the coup de grâce [a merciful blow that puts a wounded animal out of its misery]. From what you say there doesn't really seem to be any loophole at all through which we can squeeze to continue hoping for the fulfillment of our plans."

A letter dated August 22 from Norma to Dick and Cynthia lamented, "We have just heard from Leslie that apparently insuperable difficulties have now arisen on the Canadian side, and barring a miracle, it seems we must say goodbye to Community for the present, at least as far as they are concerned."

Two days later came a visit from some people from Grafton, Vermont, including one of the King children whose family homestead Hilltop used to be. (*Alfred*: There were a dozen children, so it would have been interesting to find out just where they put them all in the house! It wasn't really a very large house.) Unfortunately, the record does not include any reminiscences by the King "child," which would have fascinated the present occupants.

Alfred cleaned out the goat shed, but found Junie preferred to sleep on quicklime. Alfred and Piers made an expedition to The Pinnacle[13] and found the marks showing the farm's boundary.

---

13. The Pinnacle was a nearby mountain top; local lore maintained that a group of Seventh Day Adventists had once donned white garments and ascended the peak to await The Rapture, in which they would somehow be transported up to Heaven. When nothing happened, they returned to their farms to await the next spiritual imperative.

Norma wrote to her family in England:

"We are in doubt at present as to what is to happen next, as it now seems almost certain that the Johnstons will not be able to rejoin us for several months—perhaps never. We never anticipated there would be any real difficulty about their coming back, but unfortunately a lot of new regulations went into effect at the beginning of July both on this and on the Canadian side.

"If only they had left a week earlier!

"We are making arrangements to spend the winter down in the village, where we shall have electric light, neighbors, a school for the children and other amenities which are lacking here. Alfred expects to come up quite frequently and do the various jobs which have to be done up here during the winter, mostly inside the house. We are making great progress with making it more comfortable, but there is an enormous amount still to be done."

Norma was determined that her family should not know her true circumstances, and made the house seem much more spacious and comfortable than it actually was.

"I'm afraid I haven't made at all clear what are our objects in taking up this kind of life. We regard what we are doing now as a necessary part of the preparation for the reconstruction work that will have to be done when the belligerents have worn themselves out. The A.F.S.C. [American Friends Service Committee, a Quaker relief organization] now is training people in languages for relief work later on. We have this kind of preparation [both Alfred and Norma were fluent in three languages], and also the first-hand experience of relief work, and what we are acquiring is knowledge of agricultural work, building and so on, which is obviously going to be essential, as it was after the last war.

"Living on a farm is hard work, make no mistake about that, especially for those who, like ourselves, were brought up to a different kind of life. You don't need feel we are shirking our responsibilities to society at large and having a soft life at someone else's expense, though I suppose there is really nothing I can say that will persuade you otherwise. Perhaps you would do better to look back over the past and decide whether I have ever shown a predilection for soft and easy jobs and comfortable living."

Also: "We were greatly amused the other day to read [a petition] from 127 citizens of Jamaica (and about a dozen other places in the state of Vermont). What do you suppose our fellow-townsmen were petitioning Congress about? The hours of barbers in the District of Columbia, i.e. the City of Washington! I should very much like to know who signed the petition, and why Jamaica stood first on a list of towns and cities, including among others Montpelier, the state capital. We must have someone very public-spirited in our midst."

1941

Also: "I have just been down to the garden to pick the ingredients for a green salad for lunch. In spite of various handicaps, such as our inexperience, late planting, and deer getting into the garden, we are now getting all the fruit, green vegetables and salad ingredients that we need. It always surprises me that things like tomatoes and cucumbers, which can hardly be grown out of doors in England where the climate is so much milder, do so well here. But though our summer is short, it is of high quality. We have now picked fine, ripe tomatoes weighing half a pound apiece. When I look at the tomato plants and think of the canning ahead, my heart fails me a little, but we shall be glad of it all in the winter, no doubt.

"You have to make such elaborate preparations for a winter here. Storm windows (otherwise the combination of 60 degrees inside and minus twenty outside would break the glass), felt boots, ski trousers, earmuffs. Sleds for the children. Rock wool insulation for the roof. And above all, stoves. My trip to Brattleboro was to try and pick up a wood-burning stove, second hand. The prices of these are shooting upward even faster than the prices of everything else, and they are so ugly, too. The first one we saw (which I realized later was a remarkable bargain) I rejected outright because in addition to the steel lace-work pagoda which they all have on top, and which can usually be removed, it had polished steel frills all around its middle and bottom, for all the world like a Victorian petticoat. [This embellishment probably served to dissipate the heat.] Now, we can't find one at a price we are willing to pay. We are going to an auction next Thursday and hope to pick one up there.

IMAGE 10: *A country auction.*

"Country auctions are really wonderful affairs, especially for people like ourselves, who are furnishing on a minimum of money. At the last one I bought a handsome green-painted bedstead for fifty cents—no one else bid for it at all. Generally, the things that fetch the highest prices are things I wouldn't have as a gift—they are bought by summer people on the lookout for souvenirs of Vermont. One can get tools of all kinds, china (miscellaneous) and kitchen oddments for practically nothing."

The truck went down to the village in a heavy rain and picked up orders from Sears Roebuck and Montgomery Ward. (Alfred later mused that, "I'm glad the truck was still operating. For most of the war years it was parked. We knew nothing about the war, we were protected from it at Hilltop. I only found out much later what really was going on.") Teresa remembers that, rather than spend a few cents to purchase a newspaper, whoever went to the village would simply read the headlines and report the news, back on the mountaintop.

The pioneers went to a sale at South Vernon, Massachusetts. Norma bought a Singer treadle sewing machine in a cabinet for five dollars, on which, years later, 12-year-old Teresa learned to sew, using torn-up bed sheets for fabric. (Decades later, Alfred grumbled that he "was glad it was useful, after sinking all that money.")

There was a fine display of Northern Lights after dark.

At the end of August, Kay Laubach and Verna Dotter, friends of Leslie and Valerie Johnston, were driven up by a friend and took over the Shack as sleeping quarters. The next day Charles, Janet, and Tommy Jackson arrived. (Alfred sighed that, "Different people turned up from time to time and were useful, and then they disappeared again.")

(The following paragraph is out of sequence, as the Dartmouth College sojourn had not yet happened at this time.)

Reg and Rica Brown were friends Norma had made during the semester at Dartmouth. Alfred had not wanted to continue teaching there, explaining that, "I never wanted to teach. My hopes were all attached to Hilltop, our effort to find how the world could live without war. Dartmouth would be just conventional living. It was a project I wanted to make headway with; I wasn't thinking in terms of people." Reg taught at Dartmouth for another year and then returned to England and trained to become an army officer, where the recruits were put up in the best hotels and given the best equipment: training to be gentlemen.

Alfred: At that time there were enough people around trying to find an alternative to war. In our time, how could people tolerate war? Everybody was going into it, but it didn't achieve anything, it wasn't any use, a lot of wasted equipment, hundreds of thousands of war tanks, all being built just for destruction. How could people lend themselves to that? There was such a terrible amount of destruction, corpses all over the place, and bodies being loaded into deep pits. And then there were the Nuremberg Trials, where the officers who commanded all of this disaster, sat, properly dressed, around a table. Those officers were tolerating the war, the whole idea of war. How could they carve out for themselves such a different life from the people that were massacred by the guns and the tanks? [Alfred is looking back on the war many decades after it had ended: The Holocaust had not been general knowledge during the Hilltop years.]

Verna and Kay turned out and rearranged the library. At an evening session around the fire, the relative merits of English and American education were discussed.

Routine chores continued: logging for the men, cleaning up for the women, who also picked apples and made apple butter and apple jelly, and canned beans and carrots. The month finished out with very heavy rain.

September 1941

A cloudburst in the middle of the night revealed unsuspected holes in the patched-up roof. "Water got in and poured down over and into everything."

Kay and Verna left early in the Jackson's car to catch the bus to Brattleboro. Mr. Mills came to fetch John Barstow's bed and belongings.

Janet Jackson spent a day hunting for houses in Jamaica, and one day Norma and Janet drove to Jamaica and Pikes Falls in search of young Mr. Crowninshield, owner of a closed-up red house near the Hanford house, about a mile from Hilltop. Alfred and Charles Jackson went to see it. In due course the Jacksons bought that house and stored their furniture in it. An expedition was also made to the village to clean up Hope House and put in some furniture.

When the Jacksons departed, they left a puppy, Juliet, who became part of the J family along with Junie. Although a dog would have been company for him in the absence of other people, Alfred felt negative. "It would have been one more mouth to feed," he explained. "A dog wouldn't have contributed to my notion of a warless world." He did not know how to relate to animals, did not talk to them, and resented their demands on his time, which was to him a precious commodity.

Upon returning from a sale in South Londonderry, visitors from Pendle Hill were found: Anna Brinton with her teenage children Ed and Joanie,

Teresina Rowell, and Venice Baker. They stayed for about an hour. Anna Brinton, the doyen of Pendle Hill, was a kind, motherly woman who, a few years later, was very helpful to Norma in arranging a place for the Jacobs to live after they came down off the mountain.

Scott Nearing visited. Alfred took Norma's broken typewriter apart, then could not get all the pieces back together. He laid the pieces out on a table; they somehow fell off and he had to crawl around on the floor trying to find them all.

The children had their first day's home-school lessons. Five-year-old Teresa could read well beyond her grade level, but Piers, later believed to have some form of dyslexia, struggled.

Although Friday brought the first frost in the village, the days at Hilltop remained hot. Since cold air sinks, it would always be colder at the base of the mountain. A load of gravel was fetched from the Hanford's gravel pit, to be used in fixing the road. The next day Mr. Boynton, the village postmaster, drove up after breakfast to bring a letter for Charles Jackson, announcing the arrival of his furniture. Personal mail service! Charles spent the night.

The furniture was placed in the Jackson's newly acquired house, but as no precautions were taken to protect it from porcupines, over time the pieces became badly gnawed. The Jacobs returned home, walking through the woods up the hill to the Blanding's farm, a 200-acre adjacent property that could have been part of the Hilltop parcel if it hadn't been considered an unnecessary expense.

Having worked on it for several days, Alfred finished the repairs to the barn roof. He found a large barrel and attempted to create silage out of the corn stalks. "I knew you should put chopped corn into it, but that's all I knew. It didn't work, and all was lost."

Norma wrote to Valerie, using Hope House as the return address.

"I made five loaves of bread (good bread, too, though I says it) ['Though I says it as shouldn't' is a wry British expression], gave the children some lessons, swept out the chicken house, corrected about 20 pages of the manuscript of Baumgardt's forthcoming book on Bentham, canned seven pints of sweet corn and started to make four double-bed sheets.... Did I tell you about the sewing machine I got for $5? It works perfectly and there are all sorts of things lining up to be done when I finish with the canning. Just at the moment we are working against time trying to get the tomatoes and corn safely canned as quickly as they ripen, and before the frost. Jamaica had its first frost last night, but we hope to be spared another week or so. It's too bad you aren't going to be able to taste the Hilltop sweet corn, it is simply delectable when eaten out of the garden." They probably did not know that tomatoes can be picked green, wrapped in paper, and will slowly continue to ripen.

Alfred wrote to Bill [Brinton?]: "I'm not sure just what became of the community idea. We can't claim to be anything now but a family with an open door. Leslie has given up hope of returning from Canada and has got a job teaching. No one else has cared to stay, though we have had an infinity of visitors. [It] may have been the vicissitudes of the summer, so we are learning fast. We keep on hoping that something useful will result from all this, though we don't claim to know now what it will be. We are working out a scheme whereby a group of young men could work at forest improvement on this place & maintain themselves on the small payment the government gives for it. The trouble, as always, is to find the right people. We feel that there are infinite opportunities here for any who want to use them."

Alfred wrote to Domingo Ricart (a colleague with whom they had worked in Spain): "My life is devoted to gardening, roofing, and general repairs necessary before the winter. Just now we are bottling corn and tomatoes as rapidly as possible, expecting the frost to cut off our crop almost any night. Later there will be about two tons of potatoes to dig up and store, as well as turnips, carrots, beets and onions. Also, I must try to protect our water supply from freezing, for the temperature may go down to 20 below zero during the winter; and the house has to be made wind-tight and cold-proof, and an abundance of firewood sawed up and stacked, and so on, ad. inf [*ad infinitum*; endlessly].

"We have decided to live in the village for this first winter and not risk being 4 miles from the nearest neighbor. This will also give the children a chance to go to school, and enable us to get to know some of the local people better. But it means two houses and properties to take care of instead of one, so neither one will benefit so much from my manual activities.

"We have one goat and 6 chickens. I look after the goat and Norma makes the chickens comfortable. We have just acquired a little dog, too, and the Baumgardts have promised a cat. The children will play all day with the goat and dog and amuse themselves making little houses out of pieces of lumber, stones, and bricks, and secret hiding places in the nearby bushes."

(Juliet the dog sometime later jumped out of the back of the truck while it was parked at a rest stop, and ran off. "She wasn't tied, but we thought it would be all right," Alfred shrugged. Although a brief search was undertaken, he was intent on continuing the journey and soon drove on, unmoved by the children's tears. He had not wanted a dog, and was unable to comprehend the bond that existed between her and the children, as he had never experienced such feelings himself.)

He went on: "I have applied for a temporary job at Dartmouth College in the Spanish department, but I doubt if anything will come of it. It is the same college I attended for a year before going to Woodbrooke, and is not far from here. I do very little reading and no studying, except to find solutions to immediate agricultural problems. On the other hand, I think this experience of farming will equip me much better for the future than anything else. It gives a wide practical knowledge which is valid in any country; and so much information is available in America that this is a good place to get this sort of training. At some future time, when you and I are able to work together again, it will be interesting to see how we can turn to account the knowledge we have each gained in the meanwhile."

One day, softening his usual policy of "You lost it, you lose it," Alfred went with Piers to look for Piers' sweater in the woods, and found a gravel pit and a camp site beside a spring.

He wrote to his father Edward and stepmother Caroline:

"Norma has been busy canning and I have been mending roofs and trying to conserve the buildings for the future. It takes a long time for me alone to get anything done, but it is a satisfaction when it is done. My next jobs are: dig potatoes, cover two more roofs, get in firewood for the winter, protect spring and pipeline from freezing, make door for cellar entrance, concrete the foundations, and if possible, build a woodshed. Also, windproof the house and do essential outside painting. When the weather gets so bad that these jobs are impossible, I can turn attention to interior decoration on snowy days, and forest improvement on clear ones. The government Soil Conservation Service makes it worth the farmer's while to cooperate in conserving both forest and soil resources by paying him $3 an acre for forest improvement, and this may be a source of cash income for us during the winter. It is work I should much enjoy because it seems really constructive, and in learning to do it properly I should get knowledge which would be valuable in other countries too.

"I am trying to get hold of a plow and hitch it on behind the truck to turn over some of our land and plant potatoes and corn outside the fence next year. If we could raise some corn and some hay, then next year we could consider having a horse, or oxen, or pigs, or whatever animals we thought we could feed. Corn seems a good thing to go for because it can be harvested by hand and need not be threshed, and the green stuff is good for silage. I am experimenting with a little silage in a large maple-sap hogshead. Probably it is too little to work out well, but that is the largest container I had. We have so little hay and so poor, that I need something else to feed the goat on.

"We have only had one frost. The thick foliage all over the garden has protected it and I think things are still growing, except the cucumbers. I want to try to find time today to put all available material onto compost heaps so it can be rotting until next spring. I have bought some commercial fertilizer in advance (anticipating a price rise) but it seems better to use natural compost and manure if possible. It looks as if I would have to drive 70 miles and back to get a ton of lime, too. I wish I could combine that journey with a visit to Dartmouth College. But no doubt I shall shortly hear whether they require my services there, and I had better wait & not make two journeys."

The letter was concluded by Norma: "I am sending off various letters today to see whether a trip South about the 6th of October would be convenient for various other people whose plans I have to fit in with; for instance, there is a possibility Charles Jackson might be free to come and stay with Alfred and Piers, as I don't altogether like the idea of leaving just the two of them all alone up here for any length of time. [She must have realized that Alfred was not a reliable child minder, fully engrossed as he was in his own projects.] My original idea was to go to Philadelphia towards the end of the month and see them settled down in the village first, but that means shortening the period during which useful work can be done up here, and besides I think when Piers first goes to a strange school (which will be very different, I'm afraid, from the Friends school at Media) I ought to be on hand to make the various adjustments easier. As soon as I know more definitely when it will be possible for me to go, I will write."

Toward the end of September, a large quantity of corn was picked, blanched, and put in the solar dryer that Alfred had fashioned. Unfortunately, the sun was less hot than on previous days, though there was no rain. A makeshift silo was filled with corn. About a dozen soybeans were harvested: the entire crop. Alfred maintained that though they were "tiny," they were "very nutritious! A dozen soybeans would last a long while." He must have spoken in jest.

The Johnston's belongings were packed up, ready to ship back to them, surely a sorrowful task. Norma wrote to them that "Alfred is digging a long and deep ditch to lay the pipes in from the spring. His plan (worked out scientifically in conjunction with Vernon) is to have a gravity flow of water into a large underground cistern between the house and the road, then a short length of exposed pipe which can be drained to avoid freezing, and a pump by the kitchen sink. I plan to leave for Philadelphia in about a week, to take Teresa for what I hope to goodness is the final visit to Dr. [Joseph] Stokes [of Children's Hospital in Philadelphia]." Because of her recent bout with tuberculosis in Spain, Teresa had for many years to have regular X-ray checkups.

"We are still waiting for definite news about our refugees [probably referring to the anticipated visit of Herr Faller at the end of October]. The last news we had was that the ship was due to dock on the 25th, but whether it actually did, we haven't heard. Any day we expect a telegram saying one or all of the family is on the way up here. Tomorrow we plan to spend the day in Jamaica, working on Hope House and ready to dash off to Brattleboro if the telegram does arrive. We have been in this painful state of suspense more than two weeks, and I wish something would happen one way or the other."

Norma then wrote to Bill [Brinton?]:

"Things are very quiet around here just now, though the countryside is looking beautiful. The flood of summer visitors has ceased, and we are having a peaceful period collecting ourselves together again. We have done heaps of canning (much to my surprise) and most of the outdoor repair work. Alfred is now busy on a major engineering job, which is piping the water into the house; he has to dig a long trench from the spring to just this side of the road, then dig a large reservoir and arrange to pump the water up the last short stretch into the house. It sounds like quite a good scheme.

"Before long we expect to be moving down to the village for the winter, so that the children can go to school. This will mean all sorts of compromises with the existing system, such as joining the local ladies in Bundles for Britain, and the children saluting the flag, and so on. I hope my independent tongue won't get me into serious trouble! Work up at Hilltop will go on however, whenever the weather permits, which we anticipate will be most of the time. We want to try some tree planting and some forest improvement (both jobs for which the government pays) as well as selling the wood that is cleared away to allow better trees to grow straight. And I suppose we shall try our hand at [maple] sugaring in March. Come up, anyway, any time you are at a loose end."

Despite the difficulties, Norma was still on board with the overall plan.

October 1941

Excerpts from the Acting Treasurer's Report of October 1, 1941:

"This seems a good time to close Hilltop's financial year, as the summer's activities are definitely over, and most of the harvest is in or at least can be roughly estimated.... Expenditures on food have averaged just under $10 a week, which is not bad considering that from the middle of June to the end of August the average family numbered 7, and during this period we were only producing a small part of what we needed.

"The expensive tastes of some of our guests have also to be reckoned with; for instance, there were some who wouldn't eat anything but store bread and would go out and buy their own if it wasn't provided! We shall have to decide on a definite policy before next year's crop of visitors. In any case we should from now on be producing at least 75 percent of what we need to eat. Or perhaps a safer figure would be 50 percent this winter, 75 next summer and thereafter.

"Clothing will be an expense for some time yet, as the children get through things so fast and we are not even within sight of producing any of the needed raw materials.

"Transport seems likely to cost more, rather than less, in future."

Summary of Hilltop Expenditures
January 2—September 30, 1941

Purchase of Hilltop Farm	3,850.00
Building, Repairs, Tools	541.78
Housekeeping	342.18
Office	33.87
Truck and Transport	273.20
Livestock	42.83
Garden	28.10
Library	37.06
Miscellaneous	113.00
The grand total is	$5,362.02

This concluded Hilltop's first financial year.

Mr. Butler, the soil conservation agent, came to visit and promised to deliver five tons of lime. "We spread it on the fields [although] we weren't going to grow anything there. I thought it would be a benefit to the soil to have the lime on it. The government gave free lime according to the number of livestock you had."

At a sale in Jamaica they bought a plow for 50 cents. For the first time they lighted a fire during the day. Alfred dug out a large hole near the house on the north side for the water reservoir, and fitted a loose frame inside it for pouring the concrete. He and the children spent all day mixing and pouring concrete. Miss Robinson from Jamaica, and her uncle, visited.

Norma wrote a family letter describing their activities, and quoted a famous verse written by Sarah Cleghorn, an advocate for child labor laws, whom she would later meet:

The golf links lie so near the mill
That almost every day
The laboring children can look out
And see the men at play.

After Alfred had poured concrete into the cistern framework and Norma had packed their things, the family, including goat and dog, went down to the village to attend a town meeting, and spent their first night at Hope House. "Even a fire in the new porcelain enamel heater didn't remove the bareness and emptiness of the place." Teresa remembers sharing a bed with Piers, with a roll of tarpaper between them to enforce personal boundaries.

The next day Norma and Teresa took the bus for West Chester, after shipping off Leslie and Valerie's goods on the express truck that would take them to the Brattleboro train. Alfred and Piers cleaned up a bit, collected the animals, and drove to the Hanford's to get a load of gravel. Mr. Worden was there, loading hay that he had bought from Wallace Crowninshield to feed the two horses he had bought at the Brooks sale.

Alfred then directed Piers, barely 7 years old, to walk on alone with the goat and dog. Alfred saw no reason for concern. "He couldn't get lost if he stayed on the road." The possibility that the goat or dog might run off, or that such a young child might become frightened, did not occur to him. Following behind, he drove up by stages, loading abandoned bridge timbers and logs. The two parties rejoined at Lumbercamp Corner, where they picked apples.

When they arrived at Hilltop, they found Herbert Leader there, on his way to Stratton, Vermont, after working at a variety of jobs in Connecticut. They tested the new fifty-cent plow, dragging it behind the truck, and it worked, but the beam pulled apart in the middle. Herbert said that a stronger plow should work better, a fairly obvious conclusion.

It blew up windy and Herbert prophesized that snow was coming, so they got in wood and water, put the animals to bed and made themselves a sumptuous supper. "Norma kept saying that the children wouldn't like this or that, so I made up a name for whatever it was, and the children ate it, and all was well." Teresa recalls the made-up names applied to such things as rancid lard and rotten eggs. "Fizzly Pudding," made with sour milk, was one such invention. Food, no matter how unappetizing, was not to be wasted. An exception was made one day when Teresa found several cooked cabbage worms on her plate. Since that day she has avoided eating cabbage in any form.

Herbert stayed the night. He was interested in buying a farm in northern Vermont and doing subsistence farming, which was one of Alfred's stated goals. The next morning, he set off for Stratton by the Pikes Falls road. Alfred worked in the planned kitchen, somewhat hampered by hanging tomato vines and sacks of beans. He cleaned the dirt-floored cellar and sprayed the potato bin with cresylic disinfectant and put hay in it to keep the potatoes from touching the rotten wood. Several wheelbarrow loads of rubbish, including old bottles, tins, and sacks, were removed.

Alfred put together "a supper that Herbert and I would eat, and there wasn't anybody else. Oh yes, Piers. I don't know what his tastes were." Children's preferences were not sought.

Decades later, Alfred referred to the Hilltop project as "a romantic adventure." Teresa responded, "It's hard to see how you could have looked at a house that had holes in the roof, no way to heat it, no plumbing, and how you could not have realized how difficult it would be just to exist! Wouldn't you have thought, this place is just going to require too much work—we need a place that's already snug and heated and has water and is close to a school, and *then* we can figure out how to save the world?"

Alfred responded, "We thought we'd fit in with the march of time. We had to buy a house that was in ruins and then count on ourselves to fix it up to make it livable. At least there was some kind of house, and there was an unlimited supply of firewood, so we'd never need fear being cold in the winter, and water. It was an opportunity that just couldn't be passed up. For three years I was convinced that, as we were surrounded by trees, there should be no shortage of firewood. I didn't know firewood had to be seasoned. I thought you just cut it and burned it. It wasn't until Scott Nearing drove up to visit and left some chunks of seasoned wood that he'd been using as ballast in his truck, and we found it burned so differently and made such a welcome fire, that we realized that wood should be seasoned."

Alfred poured the floor of the reservoir using Hanford gravel and cement. Water soon leaked in and covered it (concrete will harden under water, via a chemical process). He lighted a fire in the fireplace for the first time, and Piers fell asleep by it, stretched on the floor with his head on a log. He seemed to like fitting into tight spaces, and liked to lie on the wooden ventilation tunnel that ran behind the kitchen stove, or even to curl up inside the wood box, perhaps seeking the comfort of feeling enclosed. Alfred, focused on whatever task was at hand, seemed not to realize that the little boy's tendency to fall asleep in odd and uncomfortable places, even outside in a field, indicated that he was overtired and needed parental guidance to establish regular naps and bedtimes. One day Piers added too much hot pepper to his mashed potato, and began breathing in gasps. Alfred suggested that the dog, Juliet, could finish his plate. More than 75 years later, Piers noted, "I remember. I loved hot pepper, but this was a lesson I did not forget. It was possible for there to be too much of a good thing!"

Recurring tensions notwithstanding, it was plainly lonely without Norma and Teresa. Housework was piling up and decisions had to be made whether to focus on inside or outside chores. Anticipating the arrival of freezing weather, the trench from cistern to cellar was excavated, and a pipe run through the foundation wall, with a platform for a pump in the cellar.

Hilltop would have running water! Imperfections in the cistern tank were patched up.

Junie got into the garden, leaping over the barbed wire fence and injuring her rather large udder. She enjoyed eating the cabbages, which partially solved the problem of how to store them over the winter. Piers got a nail in his foot while "racing around with the dog," but Alfred did not think it necessary to take him to the doctor for a tetanus shot, which would have consumed valuable time needed for other things. In Alfred's Christian Scientist view, Nature was a more reliable healer than the medical establishment, whose motives were always suspect.

One day Piers was given the task of scrubbing potatoes for supper while Alfred milked the goat, and dutifully did so with a scrub brush and Ivory soap. Alfred probably had not thought it necessary to show him how to do it. Helen Hanford and a friend walked up for a neighborly visit. Soon they would close their house for the winter.

Anticipating Norma's return, a number of small jobs were undertaken, though Alfred lamented that "before you do any job you have to do a prior job, which can't be done until there's an earlier job done. You spend all your time getting ready, and the main job never gets done." Alfred was meticulous about preparations for any task; this was why the Hilltop project moved ahead so incrementally. He and Piers set out early and got the truck inspected at West Townshend, then drove down to Brattleboro to meet Norma and Teresa as they arrived by train.

October 22 was Teresa's sixth birthday; no mention is made of any special notice having been taken. Alfred installed the pump in the cellar and arranged for water to run into the reservoir. The channel that crossed the road was "filled in with boards and sawdust, topped with earth." He did not know about digging deep enough to be below the frost line, but "thought it would be all right," to use a familiar Hilltop phrase.

Norma wrote a letter to Marian [no last name], saying in part:

"During the summer we had a constant stream of visitors, but none of them permanent. Thanks to them, however, we got a lot of work done and the house is now in good shape, though we don't plan to spend this first winter up here all alone. It is too remote, too much risk of being snowed in for weeks at a time, and of course the children ought to go to school now that Leslie is not here to teach them. So we are moving to Jamaica village pretty soon, to stay down there until the spring.

"We agree with you about the virtues of decentralization, in fact during my recent trip to Philadelphia I was more than ever convinced of the unhealthiness, both physical and moral, of life in a city under the best conditions. I wish I could think that these huge cities could be broken up into smaller, more or less self-supporting units. War might hasten the breaking-up process, but how much better if people would realize the need for it without that! Vermont is a very fascinating study in the essentials of democracy, and I am planning to spend a good part of this winter seriously studying the New England Town Meeting as a guide to more intelligent living.

"We also feel more and more the need for a back-to-the-land movement, and we think our discovery that it actually is possible for city people like ourselves to support themselves off the land is potentially of social value. Land here doesn't cost much, anybody with some savings could buy a few acres, a goat, hens, and a pig, and become very nearly self-supporting on a modest scale in a very short time. We have made heaps of mistakes but still we believe we may manage to grow the greater part of all the food we need by this time next year.

"More important still are the possibilities of what might be done by three or four families joining together. The all-in Community idea presents a good many difficulties and probably it shouldn't be undertaken by people who aren't fully ready for it, but co-operative farming is another matter. Several families could club together to buy a team of horses and some farm machinery, and they could all work together on a piece of land and divide out the product between them. We should like very much to find two or three young couples who would make this experiment with us, either buying or renting a piece of our land which they could turn back to the community any time they wanted to come in on a full partnership basis.

"Half a dozen of us could solve problems which are too much for just one family alone. For instance, we can't afford a horse this year and shall have to pay some farmer to do our fall plowing. On the other hand, with one more goat and some more hens we could provide eggs and milk for twice as many people, and grow more vegetables with the extra labor. Leslie and Valerie's absence has of course made havoc of many of our schemes; perhaps we should have foreseen it, but none of us had any idea they would find real difficulty in coming back."

October 24 was Norma's 32nd birthday. Alfred spent most of the morning making toll house cookies for a birthday cake. There was a solemn inauguration of the new indoor pumping system: no more carrying water in buckets! Now it could be pumped directly into the kitchen sink. It was much colder, and for the first time the stove burned all day. During a trip to the village for mail a big fox was seen in the road below Hanford's.

A "boundary commission" consisting of Alfred and Teresa in the morning and Alfred, Piers, and Junie goat in the afternoon explored the eastern boundaries of the Mason and Parker land, finding some marked trees and marking others. Norma worked at printing a circular letter with the hectograph, a copying device made of gel in a flat pan that picked up the dark print typed onto a master page, then transferred it to a sheet of blank paper pressed against it. Several copies could be made before it faded. This was a marvel of modern technology prior to the invention of the mimeograph.

Still more potatoes were harvested. They were expected to be a staple of the winter diet, "since we weren't producing anything else much to eat."

A saw table was set up for the power-operated saw to cut the logs collected during the summer, to be stored in the cellar, as there was no outside shelter for them, although the cramped, dirt-floored cellar would hardly hold more than a cord of wood, and was being filled with potatoes.

Norma wrote a long letter to their Spanish friend, Jorge Guillen.

"Perhaps I'd better tell the story from the beginning, apologizing for the bits you may have heard before. They threw us out of Spain after we'd struggled to keep a footing (and our patience) under Franco for thirteen months. Things got worse and worse and finally at the beginning of July 1940 they put Alfred in jail, apparently on suspicion of being an agent of the British government! He was there a week and they let him out finally, on condition he left the country at once, so we bustled about and by great good fortune (which we didn't appreciate at the time) within a month we had got our American visas and passage on a boat and sailed from Lisbon on August 1.

"We arrived here and had a wonderful welcome from Alfred's family (I still think they are grand people, even after more than a year!) The first thing that happened was that Teresa was taken ill; it seemed absolutely trivial, though mysterious, till a doctor diagnosed it as rheumatic fever, which is about the most serious of the childhood complaints. He warned us she might have to stay in bed perfectly quiet for anything up to a year and might be a semi-invalid for life. We tried to adjust ourselves to this idea. Finally, she saw another doctor at the Children's Hospital in Philadelphia, who threw the previous diagnosis out the window, and after a period of observation and many tests finally discovered it was tuberculosis. Everybody congratulated us, because tuberculosis is not considered dangerous in children of her age. She had to spend six months in bed [Teresa remembers being on the screened porch on the second floor of Pendle Hill's main house, where she could see people coming and going on the terrace below, but was mostly left to her own devices], and several more months after that taking life very quietly, and even now she isn't completely well, but she is coming along splendidly and able to lead a normal life."

Alfred once remarked that he believed Norma had shopped Teresa around to a number of doctors until she found one who agreed that the child was sick.

"In the midst of all this I began to suffer from a return of the indigestion I'd had in Spain, and by means of X-rays (what this family has spent on X-rays in the past year!) it was discovered to be due to a duodenal ulcer. You remember this was what my father had, the time he was so ill. I was pretty frightened, but I went on a diet of milk and raw eggs for two months, then worked up through porridge and mashed potatoes and steamed fish, and now I am practically back to normal again [though] there are still some things I can't eat.... [This palliative diet was not available at Hilltop until Norma arranged to get the goat and a few hens, which Alfred grumbled about as requiring time needed for more important tasks. The belief was that such bland and smooth foods would not irritate the ulcer. It wasn't known at that time that milk triggers the production of stomach acids. Ulcers today are routinely cured with antibiotics.]

"So perhaps it will sound queer if I say that this past year has been the happiest and most significant of my whole life up till now. We spent October to mid-June at Pendle Hill, a Quaker graduate school near Philadelphia, often referred to as 'The American Woodbrooke.'[14] The people who go to Pendle Hill are exceptional and I never before spent so long amongst so many people who were worth knowing in so many different ways.

"Between the lot of us we evolved the plan which we are still hoping someday to put into practice here—it's a plan for cooperative farming, on an all-in basis (pooling of incomes and responsibilities) in the belief that somebody, somewhere, has got to set about trying to find a more rational way of living in society. You notice the top-heaviness of the social order when you've seen it topple over, as we did in Spain, and then come here and contrast what we saw there with the still-flourishing capitalism here: a few people at the top with a fantastically high standard of living, a great mass of people in the middle with no idea but to get to the top, i.e., to have a more widely advertised type of refrigerator, a larger and shinier and faster car, and send their children to a more snobbish college, and finally the enormous mass at the bottom, industrial workers, Negro sharecroppers and the like, who have never had enough to eat or any of the ordinary decencies of life.

"The whole thing is utterly crazy from the top to the bottom. We feel certain that part of the solution is decentralization and a huge movement back to the land, away from the cities. American cities are really horrifying, take Philadelphia for instance, where municipal corruption is the rule and

---

14. Woodbrooke, former home of George Cadbury, the well-known chocolatier, was a residential Quaker study center in Birmingham, England. Alfred had studied in its—he felt—idyllic setting for a time. Today it is a highly rated bed-and-breakfast accommodation.

conditions of life in the Negro quarters are as bad as anything in Europe ever was in this century. It just can't go on.

"Here in Vermont and in lots of other states there is land lying idle because it can't be cultivated at a sufficient profit to pay for 'the American way of life,' i.e., the way a few Americans can afford to live, and all the others would like to. Farming seems one obvious outlet for the energies of people who want to do something about it. This farm was bought with money borrowed from Alfred's father, and we are trying to run it on an absolute minimum, doing all our own repairs with our own materials and growing more and more of our own food.

"Many others are interested and come to help, though they don't feel like coming in on a full-time basis. They still think something can be done either by tinkering with the existing order or by setting up as an entirely new one on the ruins of the old, after the Russian model.

"You'd laugh if you saw me baking bread, making marmalade and pickles, canning spinach and sweet corn from the garden, feeding the hens and so on. It's all useful experience and may come in handy if we ever get back into the relief field, as I expect we probably shall someday. We'd like to make this a kind of training school where people who want to help with reconstruction after the war could learn a few really useful things. I think there are possibilities in that direction.

"It's a hard life in a way, but enjoyable, especially when some of our more congenial friends are with us. You remember [Alfred's brother] Phil? He married a girl from Vassar, the American Somerville [Norma's alma mater in Oxford], the daughter of shockingly wealthy Quaker parents, and they live in a fishing village in Maine very much as we do, only they do concede a little more to progress, for instance they have electric light! But basically it's the same kind of experiment. There seems to be something which drives the Jacobs to do these odd things.

"Up here (nearly 2,000 feet) snow lies on the ground from November to March. I wish you could see how totally different it looked in summer with everything green. I never lived in such a beautiful spot, except possibly at Puigcerdà [puh-cher-da],[15] which was similar in many ways.

"Well, it's time for me to get lunch. After lunch I'm going to walk down to the Post Office, four miles of exceptionally bad road, and of course four miles back, and all of it uphill. We go down to Jamaica on Saturdays in the truck and get groceries and letters and parcels and if I want a letter or a

---

15. A mountain resort village about one mile from the French border. Norma and the children had stayed there at one time. Most of its 12th-century buildings were bombed to rubble during the Spanish civil war

newspaper or a pound of butter in between I just have to make up my mind to the eight-mile walk. Actually, it's rather enjoyable, through the woods, which are full of deer, foxes, pheasants and (reputedly) bears. We never saw a bear yet, but Alfred has seen their tracks in the snow. They are said to be quite harmless and live on berries." (During Teresa's visit to the area in September 2018, near Scott Nearing's former homestead in Pikes Falls, three small black bear cubs were sighted crossing the entrance lane, following their mother, who was not seen.)

As the month ended there was a visit from Herbert Leader with his two sisters and Herr Faller, a refugee who wanted to talk about the position of the Jews in Germany. Alfred stated that he had not known, and did not care, that Herbert was Jewish, as "I'm not a good observer."

November 1941

On November 1 it was pouring rain all day: The truck had to have chains put on to make the trip to the village, where they collected 1,000 young trees. Half were two-year-old tamarack, and 500 were four-year-old arbor vitae. Alfred and Teresa started planting the trees in the overgrown field on the north side of the house, and continued for the next two days. Alfred told Teresa that she could think of the trees as her birthday present, and she was thrilled. *Her* trees! She still refers to them that way to this day.

As to why a thousand trees were planted in an area already surrounded by forest, Alfred later explained that "These were open fields, and they would grow into underbrush unless trees were planted. The fields would have been wasted if they hadn't been planted with something useful. I had to find some kind of tree that could be planted that couldn't possibly have any war use. The tamarack, the only use it had was for making the masts of sailing vessels, so I thought that was clear of contamination. The other variety was arbor vitae, the tree of life, that was symbolically good." Despite his original concern, Alfred never went back in the following years to check on the progress of the little saplings that were just across the road.

One day Myron Stark and a lady friend came to visit. Mr. Stark was born in this house 55 years before, and left it around 1900; his grandmother sold it to Mr. King. He recalled what crops had been grown in the different fields and related a number of anecdotes about his childhood here. Difficult to envision, at that time it was a two-family house, with his grandparents living downstairs and his parents upstairs, with an outside staircase coming down from the door in the wall of the spare bedroom. This door is visible in the painting on the kitchen wall (see the image on the cover of the book).

He confirmed the local reports that it had been a good farm, only allowed to go out of production because Mr. King became too old to carry on, after his many children left home. Norma rode down to the village with them when they left, to get mail and groceries, and walked the four miles back up in complete darkness and heavy rain.

The next day the remaining potatoes and turnips were harvested. The new stove, purchased at an auction in South Vernon, Vermont, proved to be very effective. The children built a complete model farm with the toys Mr. Stark had brought on Sunday. Since the needs of children had not been considered relevant when planning the experiment, Piers and Teresa had few playthings and relied on their own creativity for entertainment. Teresa remembers a wooden horse on a little wheeled platform that could be pulled about, and a plastic doll named Alice for which she crocheted a pink outfit. There were also a handmade Raggedy Ann and Andy, that Teresa still had as a boarder at Westtown School. There were no children's books as such. A picture book contained a photo of a gorgeously caparisoned black Arabian horse that Teresa loved to pore over.

The first light fall of snow came in mid-November. Mr. Bennett of Jamaica came to visit and suggested expanding their production next year, "in the interests of national defense," which raised some awkward questions. Nevertheless, it was believed that production could be increased as suggested. It was not known that the U.S. would officially enter the war in another month.

One day Teresa had a temperature of 101°. They decided to move down to the village, at least for one night, after piling sawdust around three sides of the house for insulation. The fourth side, above the dug-out lower entrance, could not be reached. At Hope House Teresa was put to bed, and the doctor summoned. He pronounced it simply a digestive upset. Sure enough, the next day she was much better. Alfred installed a new cook stove, which worked beautifully, and improved the chimney arrangement for the other stove.

They returned to Hilltop, where Alfred killed and dressed one of the chickens. As he was a vegetarian "from the moment I had set foot on European soil," this would have been a particularly distasteful task. Teresa remembers the grisly process, with the chopping block, the axe, and the desperately flapping, squawking bird, which lurched around even after losing its head. The next day the remaining five hens were dispatched, and Norma dressed and canned them.

Herbert Leader turned up again and helped with chores. "He was very helpful, and we depended on him, never realizing how little he [actually] knew," Alfred mused decades later. On the next trip to the village Herbert got a letter asking him to come to Rutland, Vermont, at once to get his friend Henry Little out of jail. He left immediately.

1941

Back home, the remaining household goods were loaded onto the truck on top of the wood, and the house was swept out and closed up for the winter. Junie walked down the hill to the crossroads behind the truck, and then rode on the running board the rest of the way, with Norma's arm out the window firmly holding on to her. Barely had they settled in before the family, with two adults and two children crowded together in the front seat, and the goat in the back, left to drive to Alfred's brother Phil's home in Sebasco, Maine, stopping at Townshend to have the vehicle greased and the windshield wiper repaired. After returning library books in Brattleboro, they proceeded to Royalston CPS (Civilian Public Service)[16] camp to see Francis Hall, arriving at Fellowship Farm about 7 p.m.

The expedition continued the next morning around 10, broke down in Salisbury at 12:30, left again at 3:30 p.m. after changing tires, got lost in Portland, and finally arrived in Sebasco about 9:30 p.m. on the 23rd. A one-sentence summation of what must have been a nightmarish trip!

The family stayed with Phil and Teddy for nearly three weeks. This was a practical community experiment, with the daily jobs divided among the four adults so that neither Phil nor Teddy had extra work on account of the visit. When Phil was ill for a couple of days, Alfred and Norma were able to take over the barn work and relieve their hosts of all responsibility for the animals or the distribution of the milk. Alfred remembers that he was occupied gluing felt strips around the truck doors for insulation against the intrusion of frigid air when a newsboy came by, shouting that war had been declared!

The villagers came and went freely in their home and held theological "disquisitions" based on the beliefs of the local Nazarene Church, with which Alfred disagreed. Phil had been invited to preach in their church, but soon found that they relished sermons about hellfire and brimstone. Having been raised in a Quaker family where waiting silence was the customary form of worship, his addresses were not satisfactory in that regard. However, he was attracted to the basic principles of the sect, and slowly grew more and more radicalized by it. (As his convictions grew over the years, he required his four children to repudiate their mother, Teddy, altogether. In despair, she eventually committed suicide. It was a tragic end to what had been a warm, loving family at the time when Alfred and Norma were separately relying on them for moral and emotional support.)

When they returned to Hilltop Junie was left behind for treatment by the local vet, as she had failed to come in heat and they wanted to start out their planned herd with kids from Phil's buck, who had a notable pedigree. They bought two more goats, Harriet and Deborah, both due to freshen in

---

16. For a first-hand account of life in a Civilian Public Service camp, see Appendix 1.

February, which they anticipated would provide a continuous milk supply as soon as Junie returned. It was arranged for her to be taken down to Fellowship Farm and shipped to Hilltop from there in a crate, a routine method of transporting farm animals.

After stocking up on a winter's worth of supplies—a 60-pound tin of honey, crates of raisins and apricots, non-instant dried milk, and other staples—they headed west, taking Freemont Johnson, one of the draft resisters from Fellowship Farm, who wanted to visit relatives in Jamaica. No doubt he had to ride in the open, freezing cold back of the vehicle, as there would have been no room in the front. At least he did not have to share space with the goat!

Stopping at the CPS camp, they talked to a small group about Spain and Hilltop. The listeners asked intelligent questions but disagreed with the thesis that man must wean himself from dependence on machines. Here they learned of a Mrs. Spruyt [pronounced Sprite] who raised goats, with the intention of shipping them overseas after the war. They stopped to see her and admire her model goat barn and herd of Toggenbergs. The truck ran perfectly the whole way, averaging 12-13 miles per gallon. The only problem was a flat tire. The spare tire was also flat, costing unfortunate time.

They returned to Hope House in mid-December, to find the kitchen frozen up and the floor covered with ice from the barrel under the tap. Providentially, the dozens of glass jars of canned fruit and vegetables had not broken, as this would have destroyed an entire summer's work. Stalls were built for the three goats. One day they met Helen Knothe at the post office, and she said she and Scott Nearing planned to visit soon.

Alfred found it reassuring to discover how many people were committed to the same kind of life, and how much they all had in common, though they seldom had opportunity to visit one another and exchange ideas. Phil and Teddy turned out to be compatible. It was cheering to discover that pacifists everywhere were taking the actual outbreak of war very calmly and were quite aware of what was involved. But there was also some depression, because those who might be ready to join Hilltop were likely to wind up in CPS camp, or jail, before very long. They agreed it would be helpful to have a newsletter to help unify the movement.

Unexpectedly (though he'd applied for the job in August or September, as referenced by letters in those months), thanks to his brother Edward's influence, Alfred was offered a temporary position teaching Spanish at Dartmouth College, not far to the east in Hanover, New Hampshire. The family moved there for the remainder of the winter, where the children went to school. Teresa, age 6, remembers setting out to walk to school by herself one day. When getting dressed she had neglected to put on any panties, which had to be hastily purchased on the way to school after she was apprehended.

Deborah Goat gave birth to two buck kids. In March they lent Deborah to a local resident who had no goats. Norma complained about giving Deborah away so soon, because now there was a shortage of milk, as the other goat, Polly, had not yet freshened. "That made me angry and ironical," noted Alfred's journal entry of March 30. It is not clear exactly what it was that made him angry, but he tended to disagree with Norma's views in general.

There are no further journal entries or correspondence until the return to Hilltop on May 2, 1942.

IMAGE 11: *Mischievous and lively young goats are hard to corral!*

1942

Our experience seems to confirm that neither we nor others will make any fundamental change in our way of living on purely moral grounds, but will only consider it reluctantly when forced by circumstances to do so.

May 1942

On May 2, 1942, the family returned to Hilltop from Hanover, bringing along a student, Roger Robison. Alfred recalled that, "At Dartmouth there was a group of boys who identified themselves as the Peace Service Fellowship, and every week they would go out to offer manual help to widows and handicapped people who needed help gathering firewood or mending the roof or something else that a group of boys could help with. That impressed me, and I went with them during the time I was there. Roger Robison was one of them, and Bob Blood, the son of the governor of New Hampshire."

The road was still very muddy. Roger's and Norma's cars sank in up to the axles just before the lumber camp turn; luckily the truck coming up behind was able to pull them out onto the side. However, it seemed best to leave the two cars where they were, overnight.

The trees were leafing out and many wildflowers could be seen in the woods. Double daffodils bloomed near the wood pile opposite the house. The new arrivals picked rhubarb growing in what became known as the Pepper Garden, near the barn. An exploratory tour of the farm and woods revealed a number of flowers, including wild white and blue violets.

Alfred and Roger went back down the hill, brought one car up, and transshipped the load of the other car to the Dodge truck. The next day both cars went back down the hill. On the way they met Charles and Janet Jackson exploring the boundaries of their new property. They rode to the village with the Jacksons and then brought the entire Jackson family back up to Hilltop. The Jacksons left after supper to spend the night at Hope House, as the spare beds were all down there. (*Alfred*: "They bought the land and the house to store their furniture from Boston, including a piano. I wasn't in any way involved, but I discovered that porcupines were getting in and gnawing away at everything. They never said a word.")

1942

Roger began digging up the southeast corner of the garden, while Alfred reconnected the water pump. Work focused on the garden. Roger drove to the village for mail and brought back the walking plow and a tricycle the Jacksons had left for the children. (Teresa recalls how excited the children were to have this new toy to ride around and around the big north room, even though they were really too big to ride it properly. Riding outside was not possible, as there was no level terrain.)

Roger left to go back to Hanover for graduation. Norma put bread dough in the sun to rise, only to come back later to find the pan empty and Junie the goat "sitting by it with a satisfied air."

They made a trip to Brattleboro to fetch part of the order for fertilizer and vegetable seeds, and from there they went down to Greenfield, Massachusetts, to bring back five yearling does they had agreed to pasture for Mrs. Spruyt for the summer: Hannie, Judy, Bluette, Ginger, and Columbine. The goat herd was growing rapidly.

Herbert Leader showed up, and he and Alfred took the truck down to the village to fetch furniture and try to hire a team of horses so that Herbert could do the plowing, and brought back six hens and six tomato plants. The large table for breakfast was unpacked, and in the process a porcupine was discovered gnawing the furniture in the truck.

In the afternoon the road-mending gang came up with a large truck and graded the last section of road. Alfred and Roger's friend Howie tried out the walking plow, a gift from Richard Gregg[17] via Fellowship Farm. It was a small plow designed for one man to drag behind him. It didn't penetrate very deeply, merely turning the soil over—on which weeds quickly sprang up. (*Alfred*: At the beginning of the war supplies were short, and this was an alternative way to plow if you didn't have a horse or an ox. It was pretty tough going, pulling it with just a single manpower!) They quickly discovered that in Vermont there is only a fairly thin layer of soil covering bedrock and clay, very difficult to work. They dug up a large part of the south end of the garden, and sowed beans, corn, onions, carrots, and parsley, and planted the six tomatoes. After that they cleaned out the hen house and turned the new poultry loose. The six new hens laid six eggs!

In the evening Mrs. Spruyt arrived with six more goats, Trap Rock, Shonyo, Elizabeth, Trudy, Farthing, and Cilla. The Spruyts had a youth hostel on their farm in Northfield, Massachusetts, but they had too many goats, so a good number of them came to live at Hilltop on a temporary

---

17. Richard Gregg was a pioneer in the pacifist community, author of *The Power of Nonviolence* (1934). Eventually Scott Nearing gave him a piece of land and he built a stone house on it. He was a respected authority on nonviolence at that time.

basis. Alfred remarked that, "It was more involved than we realized." Having no experience with goats, or for that matter any kind of animal, he assumed that the herd, now totaling 15, would just wander around the open fields and take care of themselves. The fallacy of this expectation quickly became apparent, to his chagrin.

Work continued. Two porcupines were dispatched, one near the barn and one at the front doorstep. As they did not scuttle away when surprised, it was easy to accomplish their demise by simply bashing them with a shovel. The black flies were very troublesome. In the kitchen, before a meal or when the room was needed, occupants lined up along the back wall and flapped dishtowels in unison to herd the flies out the door. This worked temporarily, at least until the door was opened again. Porcupine casualties continued to mount: Two more were terminated in the barn before breakfast. (Teresa remembers that something called Paris Green was painted on surfaces the porkies liked to gnaw, like truck tires or wood. This either discouraged or poisoned them; at least that was the theory.)

Paul Rosenthal, another friend of Herbert Leader, arrived. The bedrooms were reorganized, putting the children in a larger room formerly occupied by Alfred and Norma, who moved into Piers' little room. There were only two rooms upstairs, one above the kitchen that was somewhat warmer in the winter, and the other at the head of the stairs. "Mattress space" could be utilized under the eaves at one side and the back. Between the east and west sides of the house was the central chimney, with attic stairs going up beside it, so steep and narrow that one climbed them on hands and knees, and an eaves space both behind and across from it.

On Saturday, Herbert Stark came up with two horses and a plow and harrow. He and Paul plowed up about half an acre in the big west field and harrowed part of the vegetable garden. (The earlier reference to Mr. Stark coming with his son in May 1941 remains unexplained.)

Norma walked to the village for mail and groceries and was picked up by Robert and Thelma La Morder on their way to visit Hilltop. Robert had lost his job in Brattleboro for refusing to "help buy a bomber." They were invited to come to live at Hilltop while deciding what to do next.

May 16 was Alfred's 33rd birthday. (He later mused that, "The great work of my life [organizing the feeding program for refugee children in Spain] I completed before I was 30." Hilltop was probably anticipated to be his greatest life's work, but instead became a bitter disappointment, as indicated in the many letters he wrote to the Johnstons and to his brother Phil.)

Mr. Connolly of Jamaica, with three friends and a baby, came to see about renting, or buying, Hope House. After they left, the entire party set out to walk to Scott Nearing's farm, blazing a trail through the forest. This was over three miles as the crow flies, not far by the standards of the time, but they turned back about halfway as the journey seemed too long for the children, who were then 6 and 7. Later the children would make almost this same trek through the woods every day, winter and summer, to reach the one-room schoolhouse in the valley.

On Monday, Paul and Alfred wormed 17 goats before breakfast—this required pushing a large capsule down their throats—and began building a fence to keep goats to the region of the barn. Paul continued to work on the goat pen and had his first recorder (a wooden flute)[18] lesson. They quickly discovered that a post-and-rail fence was not going to deter these curious and determined animals. Paul and Alfred walked to the village and brought back ten small fruit trees, and Jim Stewart, another of the Dartmouth Peace Service Fellowship boys, arrived. Jim planted the new fruit trees, with Piers' help, while the other men dug in the garden and sowed soybeans. Alfred clipped three goats, and trimmed their hooves.

IMAGE 12: *Alfred takes a break to practice the accordion, trailed by Piers, who later inherited it.*

---

18. Norma was a proficient recorder player and Alfred also played at times. He played the accordion, and liked to stroll through the fields while picking out tunes. In another life Norma had also played the piano and violin, and Alfred the bassoon, which he had sold to a musician in the London Symphony Orchestra when they lived in England. The composer Samuel Barber had been a schoolmate of his in West Chester, Pennsylvania.

IMAGE 13: *Seated on the overturned iron bathtub, Jim canes one of the antique walnut kitchen chairs.*

Friday was a third consecutive day of heavy rain. In the afternoon the group sat by the fire and read, as outdoor work was impossible. Paul and the children got haircuts, and Jim began recaning a chair, a task requiring considerable expertise. Long afterward, these walnut kitchen chairs were found to be valuable antiques; in 2021 Teresa still had two of them.

That Sunday the party set out again to walk to Scott Nearing's through the woods, and this time they were successful. They admired Scott's new stone house, built against a rock wall, and with a "flush" toilet into which one dumped a bucket of graywater to cleanse the bowl. After a generous meal of pancakes and maple syrup they were driven part of the way home. Paul and Jim had a swim in the stream by the stone bridge (perhaps the bridge by the former Seventh Day Adventist church, now converted to a private dwelling), while Alfred and Teresa took a shortcut through the woods and arrived home first.

Paul and Jim spent the next morning sawing firewood while Alfred cleaned out the barn and arranged pens for the bucks and kids. Just before lunch Leona gave birth to one doe kid, which they named Leonora. Paul, wanting to be useful, had built a goat shelter out of rough-sawn lumber they found on the property. It was at some distance from the house, out of sight, and the goats never used it, preferring to be closer to the action. Teresa remembers noticing smoke coming from a pile of hay that was stored there, and alerting someone in time to avoid a spontaneous conflagration. For this she received a rare expression of approbation from her father.

Later in the week Paul and Piers finished the goat shelter, while the rest took the truck down to Brattleboro and brought back a load of fertilizer, roofing, wallboard, plywood, and groceries. They visited Mrs. Starkberger of East Jamaica, who had a number of goats, and took the truck to Townshend for state inspection.

Paul and Herbert spent a day hunting for horses (perhaps to pull a plow?) but returned empty handed. Scott Nearing and Helen Knothe visited after supper and brought asparagus, onion plants, dry wood, and a mailbox. Mr. Welch of East Jamaica came, to offer a team.

The journal notes on May 28: "Everybody very tired and disinclined to work. Hot. Herbert Leader arrived after supper." The next day there was a trip to Townshend to see about buying a team of horses, in spite of the fact that Alfred was adamantly opposed to the acquisition of draft animals—indeed, any animals—surmising, correctly, that they would consume valuable time and resources.

There was heavy rain all night and into the early morning. Ralph Noyes of Bondville came over, wanting to sell his horse. Will Connolly came to make final arrangements for buying Hope House. It had been purchased for $800, but was really never occupied, as the family unexpectedly went to Hanover that winter. In the interests of fairness Alfred intended to sell it for the same amount, despite having made some improvements. Mrs. Starkberger of East Jamaica arrived, with her mother-in-law and children.

June 1942

Work began on the new ceilings and partitions at the head of the stairs, chiefly demolition and building the partition framework. This became Piers' room. Alfred mended three pairs of shoes. The next day the men hewed flooring timbers for the barn and started putting them in place. Mr. Roberts' team of horses from Bondville plowed up the remaining part of the garden and about half an acre in the hay field behind the barn. Horse teams would have had to plod several miles on the rutted woods road, with their equipment, in order to reach the farm.

Herbert Leader appeared and chopped up all the wood Scott Nearing had brought. Alfred spent Wednesday trying to make the accounts for the past year balance. The next day he plastered most of the sloping ceiling in the small room at the head of the stairs, using hair clipped from Lulu the goat. Junie Goat gave birth Saturday to one very large buck kid, who was named Jonathan and destined to be a pet for a friend of Jim's. Teresa remembers a long-ago photo of herself, age 6, feeding Jonathan with a bottle. Herbert went with the family to Jamaica to load up on lime, furniture, and lumber, and made preparations for the Moore family to occupy Hope House.

Sunday was gloomy, because Ginger Goat, who belonged to Mrs. Spruyt, accidentally choked to death on a misplaced worming capsule. They were quite large and had to be placed on the back of the animal's tongue to be sure they were swallowed. Teresa was present when this happened, and clearly remembers looking on in horror as poor Ginger struggled desperately to breathe, and then died. Alfred and Jim spent the day cutting her up to ascertain the exact cause of death, once again a distasteful task for a vegetarian who had no experience butchering an animal.

There was no time to mourn: Soybeans, corn, and potatoes had to be planted. The gnats were very bad. Jim stretched Ginger's hide on a frame in the attic and then began building a new henhouse. All the potatoes harvested the previous summer and stored in the cellar had unfortunately frozen into a slimy, smelly mess during the winter when the house was unoccupied. Nevertheless, potatoes were still viewed as the basis of off-season nutrition.

Two days later nine more hens were brought back from Mrs. Waite and put in the new enclosure. Ken and Roberta Kramer stopped by on their way to the youth hostel in Bondville "and brought news of the pacifist world in and around Philadelphia." Word of mouth was the only way to learn of the outside world. During a trip to the village for mail, Norma learned that Dr. Ebeling, about three miles down the road, was giving away the materials from his old barn. The truck made a hasty trip to the Ebeling's for a load of old lumber, and fetched a second load on another day.

One morning Paul and Herbert got up at 4 a.m. to work in the darkness in hopes of outwitting the gnats, but found the small black flies to be even more annoying. There were two kinds of "no-see-ems": the ones that itched as they bit, and the ones that were not felt but left small wounds that bled. Only bug repellent could keep them away. Herbert tried to drive them off with the fumes from his corncob pipe, without noticeable success. Alfred recalled that, "Later on we sprayed each other with something that provided protection. We didn't like coating our bare skins with commercial animal spray, but we found from Agway one type of spray that was nontoxic, so we used that. It was a test of patience to be attacked all the time by the gnats."

Herbert went exploring in the woods and brought back about a pint of wild strawberries, the first of the season. The afternoon temperature was

92°. Paul and Herbert chopped down a number of spruce trees to use in shoring up the barn. The truck took them down to the local sawmill to be made into boards, and brought back two stoves, the mower, and other miscellany from Hope House. Paul took the cream separator to pieces and decided that it would work. (Teresa recalls that this contraption, purchased for 25¢ at an auction, had a flywheel that one could vigorously crank, which would then continue to spin while making a droning noise. Since at that time there was no cow, it was just a plaything.) The flies and gnats were still very bad.

"Herbert was overcome by the fumes from his corncob pipe and missed [lost?] his lunch." Jean Aldrich, a nurse, arrived on the evening bus from Brattleboro. A letter was received from Fran and Judy Bacon saying they had decided not to come. They had been awaiting the birth of their first baby, Bert (who would grow up to marry Alfred's as-yet-unborn niece, Dotsy, daughter of his brother Edward), before making a decision. Fran had been at Hilltop some time earlier and had repaired the garden fence with barbed wire, which damaged Junie's large udder when she tried to get through the fence.

To celebrate the one-year anniversary of the family's arrival at Hilltop, an expedition was made to Weston, where they visited the Vermont Crafts Guild with its grist mill, looms, and other equipment. In Cuttingsville they visited Mrs. Edna Hower of the Stoddard CPS camp and dropped off Jim Stewart, who hoped to get a ride to Rutland and thence back to Hanover. Paul stayed at the farm.

The next day was spent in weeding for most, while Paul and Herbert cut more than a cord of pulpwood. The truck fetched the rest of the furniture from Hope House. The women and children picked strawberries. Herbert and Paul sowed buckwheat in the field behind the barn, which "completed the immediate planting program." One wonders whose program that was, since Alfred's initial preference was that nothing at all should be planted for two or more years, until the ground had been adequately "prepared" with compost, rotted manure, and cover crops. He said later that even if nothing had been planted, he believed the family could subsist on potatoes, cabbage, and animal-feed wheat berries during the winter months. His understanding of basic nutritional requirements was still in a formative stage.

Lowell Naeve arrived from Danbury prison (in Connecticut) to spend some time at Hilltop. He was just out of draft-resister jail, and one evening came dashing through the house, stark naked, to cavort in the open fields, perhaps hoping to rid himself of the trailing miasma of imprisonment. He set to work to construct a sod hut in an outlying field and even bought a goat for companionship and milk, so that he could be independent of the group. Mrs. Starkberger drove up soon after to tell him she had made a mistake about the price of the goat. (Too much? Too little?) She and her son stayed and talked for some time. The journal records that, "Their Scotty killed one of our chickens, which was fried for supper."

Alfred and Herbert spent a long time fixing the mower that had been brought from brother Philip's place in Sebasco. It was hitched behind the truck and successfully mowed a strip down the middle of the hayfield behind the barn.

It having become evident that the farm would, contrary to Alfred's wishes, include livestock, an excursion was made to Manchester, Dorset, and Rupert, on the New York border, in search of sheep and rabbits. They returned with three sheep as the foundation of a flock. The purebred ram lamb of the Blackface Heath breed had been recommended by the owner of the country store in Weston, Vrest Orton. He was named Ramsay MacDonald (a British statesman and Labor Party prime minister) to honor his Scottish ancestry, and of course as a pun on his name.

Paul and Herbert worked on bracing the floor of the barn. Some went to Manchester and others to an auction in Townshend, where they bought "a flax wheel, a sap storage tank, and several parts of a wagon," a dressing table with mirror, and a buffalo robe for Paul—a hide with the hair left on.

Dr. Ebeling's corncrib, a small, ventilated outbuilding with in-sloping slat walls, used for storage of unhusked corn ears, was disassembled. The Hilltop version was somewhat larger, with a loft and closed vertical walls, and was used for a tool workroom, study office, and temporary guest quarters. From Mr. Worden they bought a wagon, loaded the corncrib parts on it, and towed them up the hill, to be reassembled at the top of the rocky slope overlooking the house. (It burned down many years later when a mentally unbalanced guest placed hot wood ashes next to the foundation. Only the stone entrance step remains.)

A partition was built to divide the front bedroom into two smaller rooms. The door in the outside wall that opens in mid-air remained a mystery. (Perhaps Mr. Stark's explanation of the two-family arrangement was not known to the diarist.)

Good haying weather enabled Herbert to cut a section in the east field with the scythe. More mowing was done the next day with the mower towed behind the truck. The day after that everyone worked in the hayfield; the cut hay was raked and gathered in and another section was cut. Norma went to the village and got caught in a rainstorm on the way home.

She wrote to a Pendle Hill friend, Larry Hall, a medical student, congratulating him on his employment with Dr. Stokes, Teresa's physician who arranged her regular X-rays. "Is it really *the* Dr. Stokes? I didn't know that was one of his lines, but anyway my appreciation for him is unqualified and I think he must be a grand person to work with. The farm is really getting to feel like a farm at last. Just now haying is in progress. We have been trembling on the verge of buying a horse.... [We] hunted all over for horses at the price we'd decided to pay and could find none [so] we changed our minds and decided a horse wasn't an economic proposition. Since then, horses for even less than we'd calculated are positively falling into our laps. I suspect we shall stage a comeback one of these days, by which time probably all the desirable horses will have been commissioned for the cavalry.

"Yesterday a woman in the village wanted me to subscribe to the U.S.O [United Service Organization]. Taken completely aback, I could think of nothing to say but 'What *is* the U.S.O.?' She rightly treated that with the contempt it deserved and said they were always explaining it on the radio. My feeble protest that we hadn't a radio she obviously didn't believe. So I fell back on Eve's method (at least I think it must have been Eve) and said I must consult my husband. All the men are against contributing to the U.S.O. but I am the one that will have to tell the village gossips that I'm not interested in the comfort and wellbeing of their brave boys. The woman always pays. Just how long it will be before we are pariahs I don't know, in fact I expected it before this, and have even invited it by getting into a scrap with the storekeeper because he said he'd like to kill Hitler inch by inch. The money [for the U.S.O.] wouldn't actually go to support the war, but I'm sure Alfred will not see it that way.

"We have three men here just now, all possible permanent residents. One [Lowell Naeve] is just out from Danbury [prison] after a year and a day, most of it in almost solitary confinement. He seems to have acquired a taste for it and we scarcely see him even at meals; he is building himself a house in the most beautiful spot in the whole nine hundred [*sic*] acres and lives up there idyllically on pork and beans and the milk from his own pet goat.

"The other two do lots of work around the place. We are turning over in our minds a kind of Hilltop Association, a kind of excuse for examining our aims and the technical means of reaching them, and the first step towards a genuine planned economy, which has not been possible up to now with so many uncertainties about personnel. I could have wished that whatever [organization] was to grow here could have been more spontaneous and less a matter of agreeing on rules and setting them down in black and white, but perhaps we are just spoiled by Pendle Hill, maybe it doesn't happen in other places.

"On the first of August we hope the N.E. Pacifist Farmers' conference will meet here. We recently bought an old sheep (because we wanted the lamb, which was not yet weaned) and are turning over in our minds the possibility of roasting her on a spit to feed some 30 possible conferees. Rather a medieval spectacle for a pacifist gathering! I know the end of it will be we shall keep her till she dies a natural death, from sheer inability to make up our minds. We now have five buck [goat]s where one would have been sufficient." (As male animals are of little use on a farm, newborn males should be killed immediately, but this disagreeable task is not always undertaken.)

Toward the end of the month a trip was made to Londonderry to get hen feed and other things. Paul and Herbert loaded the remaining pieces of Dr. Ebeling's corncrib on the wagon. The following day was ideal haying weather and all hands worked all day in the east field and then in the small field beyond the barn. Before supper time it had all been gathered in.

From the record: "The Moore family arrived, and room was found for them in the new large bedroom upstairs." (*Alfred*: That would be Arthur Moore and his wife. She was an opera singer. They didn't stay, because [he assumes] Mrs. Moore couldn't bring herself to use the outhouse. They moved to the other side of Brattleboro and rented an old house and spent the rest of the time down there.) Paul and Lowell tried to sleep in Lowell's half-built sod hut, but were driven in again by mosquitoes.

After supper a general meeting was held, "at which we discussed our basic purposes and some of the ideas by which we are guided." They decided:

1) to invite three young men from Ohio who recently wrote asking to come and work;
2) to make further inquiries about joining the Farm Bureau;
3) to encourage the Bacons—Fran, Judy and the baby—to bring their hive of bees with them if they came, but not the goat;
4) to buy two young Angora rabbits and two Angora goat kids; and
5) to inquire from the county agent about the possibility of buying flax seed for cultivation.

Paul cleared out the Shack, one of the two former henhouses, and moved in there to live. It was very small, maybe 10x12 feet.

In the evening there was another meeting. A statement of aims was agreed to and a number of problems discussed, such as that of individual vs. cooperative exploration. Individual initiative resulted in Lowell's field being plowed by a hired team and planted with corn and soybeans. (The field wasn't fenced, and after Paul and Lowell left, the deer made short work of the new shoots. As it was their project, Alfred had felt no obligation to take any protective measures.)

On Sunday, the agreed-upon day of rest, they had a picnic lunch and then walked five miles down to the Salmon Hole in the West River outside Jamaica to swim. Some years later, Piers and Teresa walked there to get swimming lessons, and were mentioned in the Brattleboro newspaper: "Piers Jacob and his sister, the children who walked five miles." Teresa was annoyed that *her* name wasn't mentioned.

Herbert left to visit a friend at West Dover, Vermont, and the Moores left before lunch on Monday to find more acceptable lodgings elsewhere. Paul "caught a crab" [a term rowers use to describe dipping an oar too deeply into the water] with the mower knife, bit his tongue, and knocked off his hat. Jean, the nurse, was stung five times by a hornet. At teatime Herbert returned, and Fran Hall, a draft refuser, arrived. He discovered an abandoned shack in the woods and planned to stay there until the FBI came to get him, which he anticipated would be soon.

After supper the ends and means discussion continued.

On the last day of June, Fran walked to the village to get the mail. He came back empty-handed, because he had not gotten the Hilltop box number and the postman didn't know him. Paul got up early to spray the potatoes but couldn't do it because there had been no overnight dew. Alfred finished fixing the truck and drove it a short distance before it balked again. More hay was gathered from the west field. The first spinach was harvested from the garden.

It was discovered that some of the beech wood they had cut was on an adjacent property, which meant they had to pay Mr. Rawson $7.00 per thousand board feet plus $5.00 for the tops.

Yet another long "discussion about our ends" took place in the evening between Paul, Herbert, Jean Aldrich, Lowell, Norma, and Alfred. (*Alfred*: I doubt if anybody agreed to anything, but it would be a lively discussion. Norma's idea was everybody eagerly expressing opinions and cluttering up . . . she thought that was the ideal discussion.)

July 1942

Herbert restacked the spruce lumber near the house and barricaded the barn door against goats. Paul hoed potatoes. Fran set out to climb the Pinnacle, and Alfred worked in the garden. Jean walked to the village. The first blueberries of the season were made into a pie.

Mr. Tucker of Ferrisburg, Vermont, to whom Herbert had written about the lumber cabins on the place next to Hilltop down the Bondville road, drove up with his family to discuss selling one of the cabins. The Bondville road had formerly been used for logging, but after the hurricane of 1938 that washed out the bridge and blew trees down across the road, that enterprise was abandoned. It still served as a walking trail.

Still more discussion took place in the evening.

NEW ENGLAND PACIFIST FARM COMMUNITIES CONFERENCE NEWSLETTER

No. 2, July 4, 1942, reproduced by hectograph.

This paper is intended primarily for the farm projects, to permit exchange of ideas, goods, and services. However, we shall publish information for the benefit of those who may desire to visit or work with these communities.

Listed are CHRISTIAN HILL FARM in Barre, Mass., with one cow, 100 chickens, a full acre garden from which they expect to put up 400 to 500 quarts, haying for themselves and to sell.

GOULD FARM in Great Barrington, Mass. "While sympathetic with and interested in the pacifist movement, Gould Farm is not allied with it."

FELLOWSHIP FARM, West Acton, Mass.

HILLTOP FARM, Jamaica Vermont. "We have acquired 3 sheep, including a ram of a special long-haired breed, which we hope will help us to produce good-quality wool for our own and others' needs." Their Angora rabbits are increasing, as rabbits do.

CLARENCE CARR, Southfield, Mass. Negotiating for purchase of property to set up a community in the form of a school and farm ashram.

SEBASCO, Phippsburg, Maine. Occupied with the goat milk business, gardens, and the fishing community.

Paul and Herbert cleaned out the potatoes that had frozen and rotted in the cellar during the winter while the family was at Dartmouth, and were almost overcome by the stench.

Letter to Leslie and Valerie Johnston, July 7, probably written by Norma:

"The latest from the Bacons is that they have changed their minds again. We shall not quite believe in them till we see them, but still it's more hopeful. And on Sunday the men went swimming in the Salmon Hole and picked up, or were picked up by, a woman whom they describe as possible Hilltop material. She was married to a Russian Jew who jumped off a bridge somewhere in New York City. She came over to speak to them after overhearing snatches of the kind of conversation one doesn't hear too often in Jamaica or Townshend. They invited her to come up and see us, and now we await developments.

"The livestock are all flourishing except little Ramsay MacDonald, who seems to be going into a decline. He won't eat of his own accord and now we have to pump milk down him four times a day with the enema syringe, as even a feeding bottle doesn't seem to meet the need. It will be too bad if we can't raise him—ten dollars [Norma's British typewriter did not have a $ key] gone west—but I can't say I feel much affection for him, pathetic as he is. He just isn't likeable, like the kids. The 27 goats aren't really as bad as they sound. Eleven are boarders, only here for the summer grazing, then there are several extra bucks who will have to be got rid of one way or another when the time for stall-feeding arrives, and the only ones that require food and attention now are the milkers and doe kids. Jamaica is becoming very goat-conscious, chiefly because of Lowell Naeve, who walks the eight miles to the post office and back with his pet, Beauty, following at his heels like a dog.

"Valerie, what about next summer? Think how [their expected baby] would enjoy playing with Albert Lloyd Bacon! The place is really becoming fairly comfortable. I wish we could persuade Jean Aldrich to move in permanently, she makes the greatest difference to everybody's comfort and happiness, as we've found this weekend, which she has spent visiting friends in the Rutland direction.

"We are all a little ragged just now after spending ten days in vehement discussions about Hilltop's ends and means. Everyone is short of sleep, and we still don't know how far we agree. Once late at night Paul produced a formula which was satisfactory to all parties, but he, and we, had forgotten it by next morning. He is really in earnest about the community business, I think, and I feel the similarity in our fundamental ideas is more significant than differences in externals. He has many of the thought and speech mannerisms of both Walter [Bethel] and Larry [Hall] in their less serious moments, but I am no longer much put off by the typical New Yorker idiom in things of this kind.

"Herbert I don't know about, he certainly has great possibilities, but there is a fundamental instability about him which may or may not be an obstacle to his permanence here. The two of them the past week have been cutting beech lumber to sell to the local sawmill; the job is worth fifty dollars and theoretically could have been completed in 3 days, but things kept going wrong. It's an interesting experiment, though, to discover the actual cash potentiality of the forest. Alfred has drawn up a budget for 8 people on a basis of one hundred dollars cash spending a month, and we should be able to raise this in a week or ten days, but it probably won't work out that way. However, it does look for the very first time as though there is a real possibility of our becoming self-supporting financially if we have the men willing to work in the forest. Then we could put our unearned income into a special revolving fund to help others get a start. Anyway, it may not be impossible for us to send Valerie some money this winter if she finds she needs it, though we dare not at the moment stake anything on the future. I am hopeful, but have learned from experience not to hope too much."

Norma wrote to "My dear Mercedes," their former secretary in Spain (the carbon is almost too faint to read, noted here by empty parentheses):

"We got your Air Mail card of June 6th yesterday and I am writing at once to tell you that we have sent three or four letters during the past few months—I do hope that you will have received at least one of them by the time you read this. I meant to send my last letter by Air Mail but I was posting several at once and didn't remember until I had dropped them all into the box. I will try the Air Mail this time, though Alfred thinks it is not any quicker. [Air mail to Spain would surely be faster than boat mail!]

"Up here on the farm we are very busy, with 27 goats of all ages—the smallest one has to be fed with a bottle like a baby—3 sheep and ( ) hens and small chicks. The men are working in the forest, cutting down trees to sell to a man in the village who makes chairs; there are so many trees that the forest is not damaged if they are carefully chosen, and for us it is a means of getting money for our needs by our own work.

"You will understand that we are not happy about living on money that is given us by someone else, even though we hope we are making better use of it than others might make. If we could earn enough by our own work to pay for the few things that [it] is necessary to have, we could make a special fund with the extra money out of which to help others in whom we are interested, both here and beyond the sea, who are not able to get along by themselves, but so far it is hard enough to manage even with what there is.

"To feed four men who work all day in the open air is almost like running a canteen! We still buy beans and such things in hundred-pound ( ) sacks, though a sack of ( ) flakes lasts a little longer now than it used [to]. But our larder here looks a great deal like our larder in ( ) ( ) ( ). I wish we could be really Spanish and use oil for our cooking, but it is far too expensive. We eat a great many salads; the lady I spoke of before (she is a trained nurse) knows a great deal about what kinds of weeds are good to eat, and she goes out into the fields and gathers all kinds of things which the men eat with interest, even if they are not quite sure whether they like it or not.

"We haven't sent you any pictures for a long time and I will try and choose one or two from a very good collection taken by a friend who was here last month. They will show you the kind of country we live in, very much like Puigcerdà I often think, except that at Puigcerdà the surrounding country went upwards in all directions, and here it goes downwards in all directions—and yet, strangely, Puigcerdà was twice as high above sea level to start with. But the greenness, the hills, all would make a person from Cerdaña [the countryside] feel at home here.

"The children are very well and happy. Teresa has to go and see the doctor in Philadelphia again during the next few weeks, but I hope he will say that she is quite cured. She is getting fat and brown in the sun. They both enjoyed going to school last winter and did very well.

"At the beginning of August some friends are going to meet here to discuss with us all the problems of learning to be a farmer. We hope Alfred's brother Philip will come, and several other people whom we have met recently, some of them quite well known. Our neighbor here [Scott Nearing] is a man who is quite famous as an author and lecturer, but who prefers to be a farmer. He has the piece of land next to ours, but there is a mountain between us, and if we go to visit him, the distance by road is eleven miles!

"In a letter which he wrote to you not long ago, Alfred asked whether you could send him any Spanish text books on goat-keeping—'capriculture.' It would be interesting to know what are the usual breeds found in Spain, how they are managed, and so on. In this country there is a breed called 'Murciana,' but there are not very many of them. The only goats I remember seeing in Spain are the small black ones, which are quite different from ours.

"Now you will have had some of our news and will know we are still thinking of you all—though I hope you never doubted that anyway! Please give our best greetings to Francisco and all your family. Alfred was very glad to have Francisco's letter not long ago, and he answered it at once.

"Your affectionate friend, Norma"

Janet (Larry's fiancée) wrote on July 12. Some excerpts:

"Your letter seemed to indicate a pleasant state of affairs at Hilltop.

"Teresa running around in her little shorts sounds as though she had the right idea.

"Rather exciting news is that Howard Johnson's [a restaurant in Media] has asked Pendle Hill please not to bring its Negroes along with them, as time before last five other customers are alleged to have walked out. Anna Brinton was there the last time, so got an eyewitness account of just what went on."

Paul and Norma drove over Tyler Hill, stopped for lunch with Scott Nearing and Helen, and called on Harold and Natalie Field from Downingtown, Pennsylvania, outside Philadelphia, who had just moved into the farm below the Nearings on the other side. Later in the day the Fields drove up to visit Hilltop (a 25-mile round trip by car).

(There is a short gap in the journal at this point.)

July 18, Norma replied to Janet:

"At present I'm thinking in terms of taking Teresa to see Dr. Stokes as soon as the conference here is out of the way, that is, as soon as possible after

August 4th. I could do with a rest and change from the bustle and stress of community life in the country. There's hardly been a day of quiet home living for at least two weeks. People rush up the hill with supreme disregard of gas or other rationing[19] (perhaps they all work in defense industries, like the young Quaker who visited us a couple of days ago). Right now there are eight of us more or less permanent, three more expected at any moment—and no place to put them—and I have letters from three or four more whom ordinarily we would have been glad to welcome, but there simply isn't the accommodation. That doesn't mean you, by the way. If any of the Old Gang turn up here, we'll put them in if we have to raise the roof another story to do it.

"I am a little wistful this afternoon because I have suddenly realized that if this *does* become a real community it will not be with the people I most want to live with, who are mostly in Canada or Pennsylvania, and I shall have to submit myself to the discipline of not being able to buy so much as a postage stamp to write to an absent friend except by the grace of the Community. [Norma sighed years later that the last straw had been when a community meeting was called to decide whether she should be authorized to spend 10¢ to buy baking powder.] Well, I suppose it's all discipline and good for the soul. The silly part is, I was sold on this Community idea because it originally was to consist of people I really liked, and now I have no hand in choosing them at all. The idea is still just as good, of course, and the people are good people too, it just happens I don't know them as well as I do those who belonged to the original group.

"Anyway, it's touch and go, we may definitely jell during the next 2 weeks or we may come completely unstuck. Some days we all feel everything is fine, other days (like today) it doesn't look so good. What is most definitely lacking here is just what the predominantly Quaker group had—a common field of reference, and a method tested by time of reconciling conflicting opinions and desires and making a new whole better than anybody's piecemeal idea.

"We have been picking berries all this week—*The Grapes of Wrath*[20] has nothing on us. First it was raspberries, for which we had to walk two miles, delightful miles through the forest but very time-consuming when you

---

19. Gas rationing had been instituted on May 15, 1942. Drivers were issued coupons and a windshield sticker marked with a letter to indicate how much gas they could purchase (at 19¢/gallon). Most drivers were in the A category and could get two gallons a week; thus, the Hilltop truck could travel about 24 miles in a week. Off-road or farm vehicles were R, clergy and physicians were C, etc. The black market became very profitable, and gas siphoning and ration book forgery were common. A "Victory speed limit" of 35 mph was instituted.
20. John Steinbeck's novel, published in 1939. The title comes from the hymn, "John Brown's Body": "Mine eyes have seen the glory of the coming of the Lord/ He is trampling out the vintage where the grapes of wrath are stored."

think what a lot of raspberries it takes to fill a one-quart jar. Then yesterday blueberries, and today blueberries again, only I have contracted out because Saturday is the day the mail goes out. With organizing this conference, I am up to the eyes.

"Looks like the mail man is going now, so I must hastily conclude. Never mind, I hope to be with you soon (the community business didn't get organized in time to thwart that, anyway! Oh, how un-communal I am today.)"

Alfred wrote a letter to their Spanish colleague, Domingo Ricart, in which his frustration is evident.

"Our experiment here is evolving somewhat. We were supposed to be aiming towards maintaining ourselves off the land. [This] being the second harvest year, we are in sight of the possibility; but we encounter that there is an unwillingness to make the change voluntarily from the type of living to which we are accustomed, to the type which the farm can maintain. Our own experience seems to confirm that neither we nor others will make any fundamental change in their way of living on purely moral grounds, but will only accept them reluctantly when forced by circumstances or superior power to do so.

"This seems to be the death of civilization [!], for unless we can live morally because we wish to, we cannot claim to be living morally at all, nor to be headed towards a moral goal. If we cannot bring ourselves to do the right thing even when we see it to be right, we are really living on the level of criminals and maniacs. [Alfred's doom-and-gloom perspective may not have been the best way to further the original aims of the project.] The right thing, in our case, is conceived to be living a life which, if universalized, would make war impossible. We have reached the point where we can see what would be involved in such a life, but have not reached the point of acting on it.

"In this month's *New England Goat News*, Norma has an article on the desirability of raising milk goats now to have in reserve for shipping to Europe after the war as a practical means of rehabilitation while dairy herds are being rebuilt. I wonder if you have heard of this idea, or whether you see it as practicable. The assumption is that farmers who have lost all their stock would feel like farmers once more if they had even one goat, and even that small amount of milk would do good. Something of the sort was done in Austria after the last war, with cows."

On the back of that letter Norma had an addendum: "I am adding a short note because I don't think Alfred has expressed quite fairly what the position is in this matter of making our standard of living match what we believe to be right. We have given up the possibility of living comfortable, bourgeois lives on Alfred's salary as a college professor, because we no longer believe that kind of life is right; we cannot put that kind of gulf between ourselves and our good friends who are going hungry now in Spain, because if we ever went back, we should have grown into the kind of people who rely on middle-class comforts and can't do good work without them, and that would make it quite impossible for us to understand them anymore.

"Also, we don't believe in that kind of life because it is not capable of universalization—it isn't possible, or even desirable, for everybody to have the kind of life that is thought necessary by the American middle class. But it *is* possible and desirable for everyone to have a life in which there are enough of the things that make the good life possible, among which we must certainly count sufficient and good food, and surroundings that are pleasant even if not luxuriant.

"If I am not agreeing to lower my standard permanently below this, it is not because I see that it is right to do so now but am not willing to give it a trial—it is because I do not think it is right. In my opinion we are living now at the lowest standard which will provide a decent life for the human race in general. I certainly think one can and should live at a lower standard during short periods for a definite purpose. We did, in fact, live on a good deal less food in Spain during and after the [civil] war. But when we came here, we were all in such poor health we spent very large sums of Alfred's father's money on doctors, hospitals, special foods and vitamin preparations, and even now you could not say that we are a healthy family, [as] both Teresa and I still feel the effects of the time we spent on an inadequate diet in Spain. I cannot accept the theory that it is right to live on such a standard as a permanent thing, however right and necessary it may be in special circumstances such as we faced in Spain."

The hair shirt as a means to salvation was clearly unlikely to appeal to the masses.

On the last day of July the whole party spent the day preparing for the forthcoming Farmers Conference. Paul built a table under the butternut tree; Fran Bacon (apparently they had decided to come after all) fixed up a men's toilet behind the barn; Jean cleaned up and scrubbed the whole of the lower floor of the house; Judy and Norma arranged beds.

About 10 p.m. they were sitting around the fire, listening to the rain, when Alfred's brother Phil arrived, having walked up from the village. (Alfred commented, "I was glad he came. He was the fountain of all our farming experience. He knew the experts in the biodynamic field and the principals.")

Ramsay MacDonald, the special Blackface Heath lamb, having, it was surmised, been taken from his mother too soon, died and was skinned, only a month after he was acquired. So much for the dream of pedigreed sheep production. One of the original three sheep is pictured in the kitchen wall mural that was painted October 4, 1943, by Clif Bennett.

August 1942

Saturday, August 1, was the first day of the conference. Several parties arrived during the morning and afternoon; three people from Stoddard CPS and eight from Fellowship Farm arrived in time for supper. The afternoon session was devoted to news of Hilltop and other people's projects, and the evening to philosophical questions. The Bacons—Fran, Judy, and baby Bert—drove down to the village during the morning hoping to borrow a baby crib, but returned without one. About 22 participants were present on Saturday afternoon. It continued on Sunday in the morning and afternoon, starting with philosophical subjects and concluding with a discussion on economics led by Scott Nearing.

Some of the projects of those present included (these remarks are taken directly from the report in the journal):

Webb. Worked four years on the beginnings of a cooperative farm community, now a boys' camp. Now trying to get the farm on a paying basis. Two families in residence. Four hundred acres near Plymouth Pond. Hope to have a printing press, crafts, school. The boy and girl campers help in the farm work.

Winchester. Businessman who wants to persuade his family of the value of farm life.

Jacob. Started with group exempted from war service, thinking about obligation to society. Need to abandon conventional way of doing things. Question of subsistence. Hope to create expanding nucleus of way of life based on cooperation rather than competition. Difficulty of learning these things while learning farming. Hope of establishing school.

Homer. 140 acres. Hopes to have cooperative Catholic group, about five families with 15 children.

Phil Jacob. Has lived in Maine about four years. Trying to fit into existing community and make it more cooperative. Subsistence insofar as not conflicting with other aims. Goats, milk, eggs, and vegetables.

Miles. Teaberryport—tea importing business of N. and N. Leeman. To become cooperative the first of next year. Gladys and Irwin Parker arriving first of September. $50 per person for membership. Office of R.C.C.C. [Rural Cooperative Communities Committee] founded to coordinate information. Not necessarily pacifist. Ultimately to be craft business—starting with toys.

Root. Volunteer Land Corps founded by those who remained in Camp William James (Tunbridge) after outbreak ODF [?] war. Non-pacifists. Post-war land service. Recruited boys and girls, also older people—about 600 working in Vermont now. What to do in Fall uncertain. Long range aim—to direct shift from competitive city life to cooperative rural life.

Lindhein. Palestine cooperatives. Necessity of training for living together. Cooperative group—each family has separate 25 acres, all the rest of life in common. Collective—common ownership. Collective medicine, marketing, buying. Training farm in New Jersey for transfer to Palestine. New commandment—not to exploit anybody.

On Saturday evening, about 24 were present.

Fellowship Farm. Started out to build a strong pacifist action group. Believe value for pacifist movement in owning land. Hope to let underprivileged group use the farm. Thinking of taking Japanese family. Cooperative house in Cambridge slum, friendly contacts with other people in street.

Barretts.[21] Bought farm as place to grow and start future. Wish to be affiliated with farm group. 35 acres of blueberries. May develop into community farm, but neighbors hostile to idea of pacifism. Could use more helpers—board and lodging.

R.C.C.C. Outgrowth of conference in New York in February. Trying to compile file of cooperative communities. Hope to get out periodic news sheet; some suggestions asked for. They ask appointment of delegate from New England.

Consideration of Ends and Means. Necessity of cohesive forces. Is learning to live together our primary purpose? Special problems—at Fellowship Farm, rapid turnover of personnel at farm and inadequate contact with community. Wish for sponsors to share living standards of farmers and be more clearly identified. No personal problems between those actually on the farm. Should farm-city relation be avoided? Problem of subsidization. Can we start from scratch without either money or skill? Necessity of religious basis to attempt to live together. How shall we get a burning desire to achieve a certain aim, to combat the excessive mobility of pacifists? "Self-improvement" versus help for others.

Sunday morning, August 2, about 33 present.

X. Read extracts from *Community Broadsheet*. Some topics:

    Techniques for bringing our life more closely in accord with our principles. Does Board's method help?

    Importance and difficulty of changing habits.

    How to achieve burning desire for new way of life—place of meditation in this process.

    Methods used by Catholics at Stoddard.

---

21. Alfred recalled that, "That wasn't their real name. They bought a place on Wimpole Hill and decided to identify themselves as the Barretts of Wimpole Hill." The reference is to the 1930 play, *The Barretts of Wimpole Street*, about the romance between Elizabeth Barrett Browning and Robert Browning.

Does community provide basis to change material life leading to possibility of change in spiritual life?
How much are we hampered by too high a standard of comfort?
Question of leadership. Is it dangerous to have one person do the planning?
Experience with co-ops on the West coast (Upton Sinclair[22]) showing success of spreading leadership over the whole group.
Value of a higher authority than that of the individual community.
Does a Quaker Yearly Meeting exercise influence over policy of individual meetings?
Should there be some overriding principle of fellowship such as unites the Masons, etc?

XX. Relationship to R.C.C.C.
Let us try to keep ourselves without organization.
Should we turn in surplus of conference fees to R.C.C.C.?
Newsletter—Bill Kriebel?
Date—October 30 and 31 for next meeting. Place—Northfield or Gould Farm? Fellowship Farm? Lake Buell? Write Gould Farm re date, cooperative eating, etc. Arrangements to be entrusted to Albert Scott or Clarence Carr.

Should we have a monthly round robin [a letter in which each recipient adds a paragraph or two, then sends the letter on to the next person on the list, dropping the final entry] to keep us in touch with one another?

Sunday afternoon. About 31 present.

Economics of subsistence farming. Scott Nearing defines this as "maintaining a solvent economic unit with land as a basis" (e.g., exporting more than we import). Special problems of communities seeking to live off the land. 2 stages—period of development, financed by subsidy or adequate working capital, or by good cash crop, and period of genuine subsistence once economy is established.

Problems of early period—need for some austerity of living. Community must choose between solvency and American standard of living. Must also raise some cash to meet legitimate demands of larger community (e.g.,

---

22. Upton Sinclair was famous for his muckraking novel *The Jungle*, which exposed unsavory conditions in the U.S. meatpacking industry, causing a public uproar that contributed in part to the passage in 1906 of the Pure Food and Drug Act and the Meat Inspection Act (Wikipedia). He lived for a time in the intentional community of Arden, Delaware, where he was known as 'Uppy."

taxes). You can build up a community if you can regulate your standard of living, build up a money crop, and adjust yourself to the demands of nature (e.g., sufficient food, fuel and shelter—if you don't have fuel, you simply cannot survive).

Speed of becoming self-supporting depends on nature of cash crop. Lumber not adequate as basis of farm economy. Allow at least 2 years for change-over.

Place of machinery in economic system. A minimum of simple machinery increases efficiency.

Cooperatives in New England. Scott Nearing says mostly Government subsidized.

What is a moral cash crop? Can we dissociate ourselves entirely from current immoral economy? Necessity for some degree of compromise in order to continue association with fellow humans. Insurance—is it moral? Or money in the bank?

Should we ask people to pay for privilege of working with us?

After the conference Alfred and Norma, with Lowell Naeve, drove brother Phil down to Brattleboro in the hope of arriving in time for the Boston bus at 6:55 a.m., but did not get there until 7:30. They decided to drive on to Greenfield and catch a train. At Greenfield they visited Mrs. Spruyt and picked up another goat, Ann, probably for sale to the Fields. On the way home they visited the Moores in their new, less rigorous, home at Westminster West.

Norma wrote to Dear Friends:

"I feel deflated, debunked, de-enthused and altogether ready to sing 'Immunity from Community' with evangelical fervor. The conference came and went, and as far as I could determine through a mist of activities it was a success—Bob Brainerd thought even better than last time. There certainly were more people, just under fifty at one time or another, and how we fitted them all in I leave you to guess. Well, we had sixteen sleeping in the house (and could have slept two more, had they been of the right sex) and ten men in the hay-mow, not to speak of the two in the chicken house. Everything went well, even the Bacon baby came up to scratch and attended two of the sessions.

"Two or three of the goats insisted on attending too, and on Sunday afternoon I shut one of them up five times—each time she came back and mingled with the people sitting on the grass, some of them very dignified, and it really was very funny to see them jump when she began to nibble their ears. But by the time the tumult and the shouting[23] had died and the last car bumped away I was ready to lie down and die of sheer exhaustion, and I'm not so sure I'll live even yet.

"Luckily we had great efficiency in the kitchen department. I wasn't able to do much, on account of having to look after the introductions, gathering of names, collecting fees, etc. but Jean Aldrich and Judy Bacon did wonders. We fed them beans and then again beans—dried and green—and squash from the garden and hot dogs. It was extremely simple fare, but they didn't object very audibly. Paul managed most of the sessions very successfully and got into an argument with Scott Nearing which produced some wonderful verbal fireworks. Bob Brainerd said some useful things and I also was much amused to see him solemnly wringing out the baby's washing for Judy on Sunday morning!

"Phil came first and left last, which was as it should be, and gave us much helpful sympathy on the very difficult question of a standard of living. I hope and believe we are going to arrive at a modus vivendi [manner of living] soon on this point. Paul has gone away for a change of air, and much as I like and admire him, I think we may get on faster now in his absence, chiefly because we now have a group which accepts the discipline of the Quaker method. I hope we are going to be able to arrange things so that what seems important to him is looked after all right. His clear-headedness, his cheerfulness and his capacity for hard work are assets it would be a pity to lose.

"We have a black kitten named Daphne, the smallest thing you ever saw away from its mother, coal black with a white spot under the chin, she has been here ten days and hasn't got any bigger and her ways are just those of a grown-up cat—I believe she is a miniature or something, maybe we ought to send her to a museum. We still hope for a dog someday.

"Then there were Arthur Root, who organized the Volunteer Land Corps (an outgrowth of Camp William James), and a Mrs. Lindheim, a member of his committee, who lives in a Jewish settlement in Palestine and has torn herself away from a completely satisfying life to come to America and spread the good news. They were very worthwhile people, perhaps the most worthwhile, even though they are all out to beat Hitler, and drove up in a magnificent car given by a Rockefeller. Which shows how little externals really matter.

---

23. From "Recessional," a poem by Rudyard Kipling composed for Queen Victoria's Diamond Jubilee in 1867. "Lord God of Hosts, be with us yet/ Lest we forget—lest we forget! / The tumult and the shouting dies." The refrain, "Lest we forget," is often used at war commemorative events, though this poem had nothing to do with war (Wikipedia).

[On this page the carbon is so faint it is almost illegible.]

"And there was Shirley Miles from Stephen Leaman's place down at Kew City. She brought with her Margaret Edelman, another of those lost souls looking for a home who thought she might find it here. Well, she may, but I hardly think we ourselves are that stable as yet. We didn't really realize, when we encouraged her to come, that she was a person with so many inner conflicts of her own. However, she has been with us a week and done lots of hard work, though we haven't gotten to know her very well. She is a [per] diem, by the way.

"After supper we got into a philosophical argument that went absolutely nowhere because people kept falling asleep, then waking up and joining the discussion again at the point where they'd left off. Herbert Leader looked in again too, but I think the bond between him and us is definitely broken, and personally I am relieved. Maybe someday he'll decide to build a cabin in a distant corner of the property and become a modern Thoreau. Meanwhile we have his wonderful library, which makes the term library applied to our end room really mean something.

"Scott Nearing and Helen came over with the Fields (who have bought a farm just near the Nearings and whose team we hope to borrow, a beginning of real cooperative farming here).

"We had 35 to lunch Sunday and it was quite a scramble, but everybody seemed to get something to eat. We are off to spend the day with Arthur Moore, an old friend of Alfred's, who with his wife and children has taken a house over at Westminster West, near Putney. They took one look at Hilltop and ran! I think Arthur would have liked it if he'd been on his own.

"In haste and fraternal affection."

Thursday, August 6, was Piers' 8th birthday: Judy baked him a beautiful cake. Jean picked and washed several kettles full of turnip greens and Norma canned forty pints. Alfred clipped all the unclipped goats and trimmed their hooves, and Fran cut firewood. Fran and Alfred dipped all the goats in disinfectant.

Different people had different priorities, and as there was no master plan, each did what they thought would be most helpful. (*Alfred*: We had a lot of discussion from time to time. Each person thought that what *he* wanted was the only way to proceed. There was no control over that.) The lack of a clearly understood plan, and acceptance of the leadership necessary to carry it out, continued to sabotage the Hilltop goals.

Saturday the whole party, except for Margaret and Lowell, drove over to spend the day with the Moores and discuss some of the implications of pacifist living, spending an hour in the morning and two more hours in the afternoon. They enjoyed the day but failed to solve any of the problems of practical pacifism. The next day was occupied with further discussion of the points brought up during the previous day's deliberations.

Four cockerels (male chickens) were killed and canned, and Fran cut poles to mend the goat fence. Alfred worked in the garden.

Fran Bacon spent the day answering a draft questionnaire, and walked down to the post office with it, riding back with Mr. and Mrs. Pineo of South Ryegate, Vermont, "who paid us quite a long visit." Judy and Norma painted the library walls and canned seven quarts of peas and nine of beans. Yet another discussion after dinner focused on "Where are we heading?"

Paul walked down to Lumbercamp Corner to look at a possible site on which to build himself a home. The next day he didn't turn up for morning meeting, "no doubt a part of his excursion into individualism." He was interested in Lowell's experiments with a diet of soybeans and sprouted wheat, which Lowell claimed made him feel "100 per cent better."

Ed Levin, a friend of Gloria Edwards, arrived. A house meeting was held in the kitchen while Norma canned blackberries. Paul and Lowell left in the middle to play recorder and guitar duets in the library. From the daily record, a disgruntled comment, perhaps by Alfred: "No very connected discussion took place. In our house meetings there is not yet a searching for truth nor a sense of caring for and responsibility for each other."

On Saturday, Norma, Jean, Teresa, Paul, Lowell, and Alfred set off for Manchester. Paul and Lowell went about their business and Alfred monopolized David Baumgardt during the morning on the subject of ethics, searching for the validity of training in ethics, and in the afternoon on possible convergences between MacMurry and Baumgardt, which led to difficulties. When Alfred touched on objectivity, D. B. mentioned Master Morality, and they seemed to move in different spheres. They had hoped to study the nature of a life designed to be wholly moral, but hardly got that far before Paul and Lowell walked in, tea was served, and preparations made for return. A bottle of New York Chablis brought by Ed Levin was sampled. Norma offered to type Sarah Cleghorn's manuscript, for which she was very grateful and contributed a box of Whitman's chocolates.

Milking was done after dark in total confusion. The Bacons made an excursion to visit Scott Nearing, and Ed Levin and Paul sat up talking until midnight. Ed then slept until midday on Sunday. That weekend Broody Hen[24] hatched her first egg. The milk report showed about 12 quarts a day, with a consumption of 75 pounds of grain. Thus, the feed costs alone for

---

24. Sometimes hens "go broody" and want only to sit on eggs. Broody Hen, a Rhode Island Red, was useful as a surrogate mother for fertilized White Leghorn eggs purchased separately. One of the chicks hatched in this way was part red and part white. Half Chick became a sort of pet for a long time. Eventually she made the ultimate sacrifice and ended up in the school lunch stewpot. When there were no real eggs, Broody Hen was given a darning egg—a wooden egg shape inserted into a sock to facilitate darning—to incubate as a substitute.

milk production ran at about three cents a quart. A financial discussion was scheduled. However, Fran walked down to the village with Ed Levin, the Bolsters came up to see about buying another goat and "took [some of] us through the woods and along an old road to the Spencer place"; then Paul went down with them to see about a job, so the session after supper was a purely Bacon-Jacob one.

Norma offered a plan that could provide greater clarity; it consisted in a voluntary pooling of such resources as participants wanted to pool, an agreement as to what maintenance expenses would be chargeable to the pool, and a division of the remainder among individuals to use as they wished for their personal needs. She suggested that visitors might be required to engage in a certain amount of work, or provide an equivalent amount of cash, or some combination of the two. This plan was very similar in all respects to one that Paul had proposed. Unfortunately, he felt that *his* suggestions had fallen on uninterested ears, so he lost hope and turned individualist from then on. Norma's plan suffered much the same disability, in that those concerned had other interests that prevented them from giving it a just consideration. In the evening, when Norma's plan was on the verge of discussion, Gordon Goley (or perhaps Goldey) arrived, and conversation went into other interesting fields.

Monday, Alfred and the Bacons continued the Sunday evening discussion, and it became clear that they needed to know each other's views and needs, the bedrock of Quaker conflict resolution, quite apart from judging as to the rightness or wrongness of them. Boiled down to essentials, it appeared that what Judy wanted was a home suitable for children; Fran wanted a normal working farm; Alfred wanted a consistent plan of action that could be followed through.

Later in the week Margaret walked to the village for mail and Lowell and Piers walked down in the evening to fetch Lowell's guitar. Fran continued to work on the cellar wall. The library painting was finished, and so was the little washroom at the foot of the stairs. Although there was a cast iron bathtub, no one used it to bathe, as water had to be heated on the stove and carried in pot by pot, and would quickly have cooled. Sponge baths were the only option. The children sometimes shared a galvanized washtub of warm water in the kitchen, behind a makeshift screen of towels draped over the back of chairs.

Charles Jackson turned up on a bicycle to work for a week on his house, about one and a half miles down the mountain road. The women went down with him to help him decide what to do, taking the herd of goats for a walk. When Norma returned, the goats were not yet ready to come back, so she left them for Charles. When he was ready, they had already gone, but on his arrival at Hilltop, no goats were there. Alfred set off to bring them up, but found no trace at the Jackson's or Hanford's. Charles, who left three minutes after Alfred, found no trace of either goats or Alfred. After supper they, and Paul and Fran, set off in the car to search the surrounding roads and give the alarm in the village and at houses along the road.

The next morning all hands joined in the search, and Paul and Charles found 17 goats, with bursting udders, in the woods between the east field and the road. Junie was not among them. They proceeded to search for her through the brush-filled fields, three abreast, shouting, blowing whistles, and ringing bells. They marveled that so many goats could have left so few traces of their passage. The next day the hunt continued, exploring the thickets in case Junie was injured and couldn't respond. They gave up at midday when there had been no sighting, confident she would not starve in the woods.

By afternoon Fran Hall, who had just arrived, with Lowell and Gordon, had decided to establish a contemplative order in Lowell's sod house rather than in the shack down the road toward Bondville that Fran had expressed interest in, and they slept there.

Charles and Alfred continued the Junie hunt, enlivened by very searching discussion of the place of the principled individual in an unprincipled world, and whether a decent, upright life was enough. There was no doubt that no one in the group was complacent; everyone was in varying stages of search, dissatisfaction, or unrest, but no manner of common thinking had been worked out, so it resembled those ancient comedies in which two men chase each other around a haystack and neither can catch the other even though they are going over and over the same ground. They did not find Junie.

During various discussions it was decided, despite there being no clear group leading, that Alfred should attend the Friends World Committee conference in Wilmington, Ohio, and Norma should try to return from Philadelphia (where she planned to take Teresa for her appointment with Dr. Stokes) by August 30 to take over his responsibilities. Paul planned to leave with Norma for New York the next day. Alfred looked up trains to Wilmington.

Two FBI men in business suits and wingtip shoes drove up, looking wildly out of place among the hirsute colonists, and, as he had anticipated, took Fran Hall to Rutland for questioning. After supper there was singing and folk dancing. The next day Charles and Alfred, ostensibly knocking off from strawberry picking to hunt for Junie, came back laden with berries. Fran Bacon tried dehorning Beauty, Lowell's goat, renamed Esperanza, with rubber bands fastened tightly around the horns' base, but she didn't like it; her horns seemed to be her chief dignity.

The subject of an agricultural plan was brought up. Fran thought they should lose no time in getting the fields into production and should sow winter wheat to harvest next year, either as hay or grain. Alfred still felt strongly that the fields should be built up with compost and rotten manure for a year or two before attempting to take crops from them, and while legume hay would be valuable if they could grow it, wheat would probably cost just about as much to produce as to buy and would consume valuable time (always his focus), this fall and next spring. The discussion was full of asides and excursions and was more a matter of throwing out readymade opinions than of searching for the right thing. (Journal entries were not always completely objective, though an effort was made to keep them so.)

Saturday's plan was for Fran Bacon and Alfred to work with Charles Jackson at his place. Fran and Charles went down, and Alfred would follow when he had fueled the truck and pumped up its tire. The truck was uncooperative, but by midday Alfred had persuaded it to run downhill, and he set off, taking Hannie to show the Eastmans.

Poor Junie, surely in great discomfort from her over-filled udder, was still lost. During a trip for the mail the postmaster said that Mrs. Twing had phoned him to say she had seen Junie the night before. The goat hunt was resumed. The Bergmans had seen her two days ago—*and* that morning! Two men in a car had seen her two hours before, around Charlie White's place! Piers and Alfred ranged the woods, field, and river, but there was no sign of her. At nightfall they returned; the truck engine balked at Hanford's. Adjustments were made, and the vehicle labored up the hill with its load of gravel. They met Judy, who had driven down for Charles, who had run a nail through his foot. When they got back, Fran was in the barn, milking by lanternlight.

Norma, Paul, and Teresa set off for New York in the Ford. The five remaining men carried the roofs up to the corncrib, and the house meeting was rather late. Jean picked a gallon of berries. The season's first sweet corn was served for supper. Alfred, Gordon, and Lowell talked until midnight. Ruth had put the garden in order during the day and Jean and Judy carried the household.

Although Sunday was customarily a day of inactivity, Ruth continued working in the garden, unable to rest while there was so much to be done. She walked to the village in the afternoon. Charles brought back news of Junie, that she was safe with the Charlie Whites! Alfred and Piers went down in the truck to fetch her and bring back more gravel. The Fields came with a load of hay and took the goats Ann and Button, and the cement mixer. Gordon and Lowell brought some soy-wheat-corn-miscellany bread that all enjoyed. The next day Charles set off on his bicycle to catch a train at Greenfield, "after penetrating final discussions with Jean and others on his immediate and perennial problems." (*Alfred*: Charles had married a much younger woman, almost the same age as his own daughters, and they just couldn't agree about anything.) The Bacons and Lowell went to Brattleboro, Ruth to Hanover. Alfred got a telegram from Norma asking him to leave the next day and take advantage of a free ride from Philadelphia to Ohio Yearly Meeting for the FWCC conference. A telegram would probably have been sent to the Jamaica post office, and from there driven up the mountain to be delivered, as there was no other means of communication.

The truck continued to have problems and a local trucker suggested that the water pump might be out of order. (*Alfred*: The water pump required a special kind of grease, but I didn't know that. I was greasing it with [?] grease, which was no good.)

The Bacons and Lowell came back from Brattleboro about 7 p.m. with a trailer load of goods. The next day Alfred left for the Ohio conference, Fran worked on the fence around the garden, and the women canned peas. Fran walked over to consult with the Fields and Nearings about possible winter lodgings.

Gordon Goley and Fran jacked up the front of the house to make it level, while the women canned green beans and corn. Fran began to rebuild the foundation of the house. He and Lowell drove to Jamaica to meet Norma and Teresa returning from Philadelphia on the afternoon bus. Lowell Naeve's brother Ennis unexpectedly arrived on the same bus, and all enjoyed one of Lowell's cooking experiments, prepared from whole soybeans, corn, wheat, and sundry other things.

On August 30, Sunday, they awoke to find that Joe, a friend of Gordon's and Lowell's, had arrived during the night. Joe and Ennis left in the afternoon. The Bacons began to scrape rusty spots on their blue Ford in order to save what was left of the finish. The meditative group began to read *The Code of Christ* by Gerald Heard.

Norma wrote to Edith Pye, saying in part:

"We can't help believing that the mess Europe is going to have to clear up will be so colossal that anyone at all able to join in the work will have to do so, and whether or not we may ever be needed we are trying our best to fit ourselves for some kind of useful service. Even if our knowledge of goats isn't destined to be any use, we are learning a good deal about agriculture— peasant farming, horses, hens and pigs, rather than large-scale farming with tractors as practiced in the Middle West—and we hope we are fitting ourselves to help ultimately with some program of rural reconstruction. We are also learning something about simply building and repairs, something about forestry, and lots about human nature.

"And we are trying to achieve in ourselves the kind of balance and adaptability which in Spain we felt was our greatest lack, and which we feel must proceed from a much better integration of the individual on the religious plane. Does that sound terribly American? I don't want to find myself beginning to think in abstractions with capital letters! We just would like you to know we are still here and still caring about the same things and still hoping to have some very small part in the making of the post-war world."

The next day she wrote to Dear Friends:

"Well, we [she and Teresa had been to Philadelphia] finally got back after a nightmare journey. I slept fitfully between Philadelphia and New York. At Grand Central a soldier took us in charge and carried the suitcase to the train and much to everyone's embarrassment a box burst open and spilled intimate garments all over the platform! Perhaps it was this that upset him, but anyway he put us on the wrong train, and we didn't find out till we were well away; I would have made sure for myself if I hadn't been so sleepy. By the mercy of Providence, the other train drew up beside ours at New Haven and with a wild rush we transferred ourselves—leaving our tickets in the first train and once again scattering undergarments far and wide. On the last stretch of the journey I fell asleep once more and was rudely awakened by a fat, red-faced, intoxicated stranger tickling me under the chin. I was so startled that my customary meekness fled, and I told him off good and proper. After that we reached home without further untoward events.

"It wasn't altogether a cheerful homecoming. Somehow when one is coming back to a place one hopes to make home and people one hopes to make friends, there is something chilling about courteous indifference. I keep asking myself, what have we done wrong? Why can't we make friends with the people here when I, at any rate, have never found any difficulty in making friends before? I don't think it can be all our fault.

"Feeble as it seems, I can't help seeing the hand of ill-luck in the thing too. We know there are people we can work happily with, in fact many of them have been here and the experience of co-operation has been satisfying, but always they were people who could only come for a short while. The people who are here now are much younger and just married and very sure of themselves—but that would apply just the same to you two, and I don't find it hard to be on friendly terms with you! What I seem to lack is an outgoing something, an interest in the other party for his own sake—and this lack, you'll understand, fatally reinforces the similar tendency in Alfred. It's all very difficult."

Norma's clear-eyed, though painful, assessment of the challenges they faced and her part in them was not matched by any others, who tended to look for a scapegoat rather than accept responsibility for (not) forming a harmonious community.

September 1942

Norma walked to the village and returned with numerous postcards from Alfred and a long letter from Herbert Leader, who was in San Diego, California. An abbreviated version of his rambling letter described his adventures:

"Leaving all my belongings except a blanket at the 'Y' in Los Angeles, I set out to enjoy California, afoot. A fellow stopped to talk with me. He invited me to ride with him to Tijuana, across the line in Mexico. We set out. At the line, I was stopped. The customs people quizzed me a long while. I was finally allowed to enter. The inspector gave me a quarter, 'So I'd be sure of one meal anyway.'

"On Sunday I attended a pleasant little Catholic church. My beard and overalls caused no one distraction. A book dealer by the church told me of a Russian colony seventy miles farther down in Baja California. No one knew whether they were Doukhobors.[25] I decided to visit the colony.

"The farms were individually owned, everywhere in the deep, beautiful valley, unconnected with the houses in the village. They were bi-lingual, and Spanish was the language of the schoolbooks. The older people wore Russian dress, home-made, but the young were Mexican, save for their blond hair. They seem to have lost their old industry, and are not particularly prosperous. I was fed wonderful vegetable soup (borscht) and a chunk of white and rye bread. Also some fruit.

"When I took stock, I decided I had made a mistake in coming to Mexico so early in the fall, so I am back in the Estados Unidos, bound for Montana. In the spring I shall go by bus to South Dakota to visit a Hutterite settlement on the James River there."

Gordon and Lowell left Hilltop after breakfast for Brattleboro and parts unknown. Gordon was convinced the Department of Justice wished to see him soon ... if they could find him. Lowell was to see his dentist and was expecting further communication from his draft board.

Norma wrote to Mildred Young on September 2:

"I've just come back from a trip to Pennsylvania, designed partly as recuperation after a rather wearing summer. The visit to Pendle Hill was re-creative in the best sense, though not perhaps exactly restful, but it left lots of our problems much where they were. Constantly this summer I've found myself referring to your writings to help elucidate obscure points,

---

25. An independent religious sect originating in Russia, believing in the supreme authority of the inner voice, and in the transmigration of souls, rejecting the divinity of Christ and the establishment of churches, refusing to pay taxes or do military service.

and now I feel moved to write and ask whether, out of your much wider experience, you can't throw a little light into the dark places. I had naively supposed that among people who accepted, at least in theory, the vocation of 'poverty' according to your definitions of it, there wouldn't be much room for disagreement on the subject of a standard of living. But among those of us who think we are emancipated from the 'American Standard' there are as many gradations as in an army.

"All this summer I've been struggling—almost entirely alone—to build a middle course between those who think our standard here is too high, and those who think it's too low. No one will give an inch, and the dissatisfied have apparently no other solution but to throw up the whole thing and go. We had, for instance, a boy who gave us up as a bad job because we wouldn't agree—at once, that same day—to forswear entirely all our unearned income and live exclusively off what the land would provide. I wouldn't agree to that because I don't believe enough has yet been put into this land to make it capable of supporting a group of people at an adequate standard (allowing for food, shelter, clothing, outside contacts and recreation) without any kind of subsidy from outside. I agree with Scott Nearing, our neighbor, who has actually tried just that on land almost the same as ours—maybe just a little better—and says it takes two years to achieve a minimum standard of self-sufficiency.

"And I think we ought to look to the time when we can dispense with a subsidy, and that the time ought to be soon, but it ought to be a time when we really can dispense with it once and for all and not get ourselves into such trouble that we have to fall back on it again in a few months to pay our debts and doctors' bills. On the other hand, to illustrate the opposite extreme, there was the old and trusted friend of Alfred's who came here with his wife and children but left again after three days. His wife subsequently told me they wouldn't stay because they simply couldn't bear the house. Well, I'll admit that the house is in a good deal of a mess still, because we have to provide our necessities first, and we haven't felt that new plaster on the walls was so urgent a necessity as food. But can you imagine a man surrendering the chance to live and work with a dear friend whom he hasn't seen for a long time, just because the friend lives in an ugly house? The friend, incidentally, neither confirmed nor denied this version of their unwillingness to stay with us: perhaps he didn't dare. Still, these people are extremes, they do represent the 'American Standard,' and perhaps it's hardly fair to quote them, except that this incident was a very clear specimen of the kind of pressure to which we are constantly exposed from the side of those who want us to live at a higher standard or else they won't stay.

"I am beginning to think there is going to be nothing for it but for Alfred and myself to decide on a standard and let others conform to it, or go away. There's the rub: Alfred and I can't even agree upon a standard between ourselves. He, for instance, thinks eggs are without food value and a pure waste of [time] and begrudges the time and money spent in raising hens. I find it's impossible [because of her ulcer] for me to digest coarse home-ground cereals, and believe it would be healthier for everyone if we mixed a certain proportion of white flour with our bread to make it lighter. And so on throughout the whole sphere of dietetics.

"What do you do in such a case? The point is that before we can look forward to doing without our unearned income, we must have a very definite plan for a year's production in all spheres; we can't make such a plan until we can agree upon the standard which such a plan is to provide for us; and without a plan there's nothing but uncoordinated and largely wasted effort leading to discouragement, recrimination and desertion.

"It's easy to say, 'Of course all parties must be able to give way a little so as to reach a compromise.' But when I come down to brass tacks, I find that I have already lowered my standard and the children's as far as I feel is consistent with safety and my responsibility to them. And how can I ask others to give way when I'm not prepared to give way myself? Anyway, that wouldn't meet the needs of those who want us to have a higher standard, meat two or three times a week, for instance, and as many eggs as we feel inclined for."

Piers, 75 years later: I believe Norma is on target here. I liked the Hilltop diet well enough, but did have trouble digesting it. I had daily stomach aches and my growth slowed, so that I became the smallest boy of my age. Later, in high school, on the "inferior" standard American diet, I grew another foot and gained a significant amount of weight. The supposed ideally healthy Hilltop diet was *not* ideal for a growing child, and left me with considerable catching up to do.

Norma continued: "Do you think you could give us a few details from your own experience about this matter of feed? For instance, do you eat meat and if so, how often? How many eggs a week do you regard as a reasonable quantity for a family of four? Do you use all whole wheat bread or allow a little white for variety? Do you buy grapefruit juice if you can't produce your Vitamin C needs from your own garden? Do you drink coffee? And how much, roughly, do you spend on food other than what is home-produced? We have a very variable group; a lot of our buying is done in bulk and covers several weeks or months, but still, as far as I can discover our food from outside the farm is costing us something like one dollar per person per week.

"Then there's the question of surroundings. Does it seem reasonable to you to take time off in the middle of the summer to paint a room—even if the room is in a horrible mess? How much are you worried by dirty and eroded plaster or bare lath? Do you feel these things have to be put right before your house can be a center for the Good Life? Does poverty really mean making do with what there is, even [if] it's ugly and mean [shabby]—or can you justify taking time and money from the business of keeping body and soul together to beautify the surroundings even in a modest way? I know people say cleanliness is all that's required, but believe me, in a house that's falling to pieces cleanliness is not only difficult, but it doesn't produce any noticeable beautifying effect! You can't even wash the windows when the glass is likely to fall out if touched.

"Finally, how do you feel about children? Would there be anything to be said for our dividing what income we have into two separate parts and devoting the unearned part entirely to the children, sending them to a progressive school, buying them the necessary clothes, and paying a fixed sum into the household exchequer during their vacations so that they may have the foods that seem necessary to them even if these are not produced on the farm?

"I'm beginning to wonder if this isn't a possible way out. Alfred and I could probably reach an agreed standard if I weren't worrying all the time about my duty to the children; I don't care much for myself and would rather feel I was living off the results of my own labor."

On September 3, Fran killed another porcupine and they ate some of it along with one of the red hens. The next day, "We canned the remaining roosters together with some chicken soup and some porcupine." They made blackberry jam and marmalade with the oranges that Alfred's father regularly shipped up from Florida. The children were intrigued by the tiny kumquats that were sprinkled in with the larger fruits. No one was sure whether they were edible, or merely decorations. (They are, but are quite sour, better for marmalade.)

Jean left to return to her job, and Fran and Judy Bacon drove up to Plymouth (probably Vermont) to see the Webbs about a possible job for the winter months. They had almost decided to rent the Nearing's old house for the winter until they found it was no longer available. Norma found Jean's absence made a big difference, as she now had to look after the chickens and rabbits as well as doing the milking herself.

A few days later Fran packed up and drove to Plymouth to take over the management of the Webbs' farm. As he was driving down the hill, he met Alfred coming up, returning from the conference in Ohio. Fran returned unexpectedly, and the family spent the afternoon packing up. Around noon the next day they were ready to depart. Just then several local people showed up for a visit. (Alfred, whose focus was always on work rather than socialization, grumbled that "People constantly came and went, and the work didn't get done. They just dropped in for a while and went off again.") For several days work continued on the corncrib; Alfred finished the roof while Norma laid the floor.

At an auction in Bondville, a man was approached about exchanging Hilltop pulpwood for a radio. "On the way home we called on Mr. Horsley, who lent us his ram." (Presumably for breeding purposes, as little Ramsay McDonald, whose responsibility this would have been, had not survived the separation from his mother.) The next day Mr. Stark and a friend drove up and took five pullets. A sixth pullet suddenly dropped dead while being captured.

After they left, the southern boundary was explored. A large beech tree was found that contained carving indicating that someone named Hurd had been killed by a hog in November of 1902!

Norma wrote again to Leslie and Valerie Johnston in Canada:

"Alfred and I have been turning over in our minds the question of whether we can't have a different arrangement here which would give more visible reality to the original group idea. The feeling that we are united with you in a common project is very strong to us, but naturally it hasn't any meaning to others, and it is a source of much misunderstanding. Could we not form some loose kind of association which would be bound to what's being done here by some real ties, that is, have a voice in policy and help us to decide on some of the thornier questions that confront us? We ought to have some kind of constitution, and some idea of what kind of people we'd like to associate with, and on what terms.

"It's extremely desirable that the financing should be put on a different basis, as it seems to be a difficulty in many of these projects. I don't mean the actual raising of the money, but the deciding of how far those who raised it were to be responsible for the way it was spent. Something in the way of a centralized financing department seems needed, a kind of glorified credit union, to be administered possibly by the Rural Co-operative Communities Committee. [RCCC] This would mean a big expansion of their work, but perhaps they should get a percentage of all the money they handle on behalf of these different projects.

"Let us have your thoughts on this matter. If from our collective intelligences we could evolve anything that even looked like a scheme, there would be no harm in trying it out on the next conference, scheduled to meet at the end of October. They need something to get their teeth into and this would give them plenty.

"Apart from that, however, maybe we could unite together in some way that would give you people some real voice in the management of affairs here, and us a much stronger sense of belonging to something, a kind of visible Church instead of just having our citizenship in Heaven, so to speak. Larry [Hall], I believe, might like to be connected with something like this. And by the way, in the strictest secrecy, he and Janet are hoping to be married around Christmas and live in what Larry flatteringly refers to as 'the Jacob apartment.' It transpired that the closely-guarded secret was known to almost everybody. But don't go telling the world anyway, because it *was* told to me as a secret after all.

"However, to return to our muttons[26]—this group or association or whatnot ought to include at least one person who is weighty [Quaker-speak for experienced] and fairly widely known, for instance Stephen Leeman of the R.C.C.C. And Paul should be asked if he wanted to join. He has done such a lot of work around here and really has some glimmering of what it's all about, which can't be said for anybody who's been here since you left except Roger Robison perhaps, but he is at Oberlin and not a possible settler, worse luck. Perhaps too, one ought to except Fran Hall, who is certainly one of the most valuable people we know—but what must he do but hie [an archaic British expression meaning to go quickly] in here, in defiance of his parole board, so that they came and fetched him away at once. He's back in Danbury [prison] now, we don't know for how long. Lowell Naeve is rather a problem. He certainly has a stake in the project as the owner of a practically-completed house [actually a sod hut] on the property, but he is so entirely set on going his own way, and there's absolutely no knowing where it may lead him next.

"That about exhausts the possible partners at present. Oh, the Bacons of course, but they, like Lowell, are a problem. They seem to consider themselves identified with us and expect to come back in the spring (though as we've now learned they are apt to change their minds pretty quickly—Anna Brinton warned me of this, too late of course) but while the decision to move out for the winter with the baby was an eminently sensible one, they seem to have chosen the actual place to move to—fifty miles away—without any regard for the exigencies of the common life here. And the Webbs wanted them to come [to manage the farm] at once, which leaves things here very much up in the air. They don't seem to have felt that moving out in the middle of the harvest, instead of looking for some place to stay nearer at hand, was in any way inconsistent with making a life for themselves here. Still, they are good people and I think will do all right here if something doesn't whiz by and entice them to California or Florida.

---

26. Originally a French phrase, "*revenons à nos moutons* [sheep]," meaning, get back to the subject at hand.

1942

"The essential, anyway, of the kind of thing we're considering would be, first, that it would transfer ownership to a group, and second, that we would have a definite status here as caretakers for that group. We may not know much about farming, but still we've hung on so far without major disaster and look like being able to continue. We would much rather feel like your representatives or even employees than our own masters in this particular sphere. Of course, the right to fire us would automatically be vested in you!

"Will you find out whether there are any restrictions (as there are in England) about sending secondhand books into or out of Canada? If not, we'll send up some books from here to beguile Leslie's weary hours. Often of late, browsing along our now well-filled bookshelves (thanks to Herbert Leader) I've thought 'Here is something Leslie ought to read.' I'd like among other things to send you Cecil Day Lewis's [the father of film actor Daniel Day Lewis] poems, which seem to be much more significant than those of Auden. He put, in a verse, what seems like the essence of what we've blunderingly been trying to say to other people since we came here:

> *Burn then with new desires,*
> *For where we used to build and love*
> *Is no man's land, and only ghosts can live*
> *Between two fires.*
>
> —from "The Conflict"

"Well, we've progress to report. All week we've worked hard on the corncrib we got from Dr. Ebeling. The roof is up, the floor is laid, the door and windows set in and the walls nearly finished. It will make good storage in winter and a house for one or two in summer. Then we are hoping to start work at last on the woodshed, and when the kitchen's cleared we shall put in a new double sink with a small pump and lots of cupboards. All that ought to be finished this fall with any luck.

"We are also on the verge of buying a small wind generator, which will give us one very badly needed bright light in the kitchen and a few dimmer ones elsewhere. [In 2018 Teresa observed a wall outlet in the old kitchen, anticipating the possible future availability of solar or wind power.] And if we get a radio, that can be run by the wind. I really think we must have a radio. We need more good music, and above all we need to be more closely in touch with how the other half lives. [A wind-up Victrola in a cabinet and an assortment of 78 rpm records made it possible to listen to music: Glen Miller, Ezio Pinza, classical masterpieces, Burl Ives square dances. Single-use *thorn* needles replaced the steel needles that were not available during the war. Diamond needles had not yet been invented.]

Norma received an answer from Mildred Young, to whom she had written earlier, dated September 20, 1942.

"Your problems certainly have a familiar and urgent ring to my ear. I suspect you are right that there is really nothing for it but for you and Alfred to claim the right to set the standard, since after all it is your home and the others are transients. We never regard the question of what we are having on the table one that the short-time members of the group are eligible to discuss! Occasionally there is some humor about it; I have a good deal of fun to poke at it myself, but for the most part everybody has seemed pretty happy to eat what came to the table. One rule that we have is that whatever is going currently in the garden is eaten, providing it offers the needed values. That means that during May we may have garden peas every single day but no cabbage, and during June we shall have cabbage almost every single day, and probably very few peas.

"In August the garden goes into a decline, and we expect people to be content to eat the humble okra and the 'sweet' pepper because you still need your vitamins A and C and there isn't much else, and we don't want to start opening what was canned in June and July. We have almost no fresh meat. It has been nearly impossible to buy it in Abbeville this summer anyhow, but even when it was there, we didn't go in much and have no refrigeration, so that we could never get more than [just] enough for a meal. Maybe three times this summer we had a big treat—meat balls. We do use salmon and tuna from cans when they are to be had—tuna disappeared here last spring and salmon grows scarce now. Tinned 'bully' [corned] beef we also buy sometimes as being the cheapest all-meat can of beef available as far as we know. Bacon we keep on hand in the piece and slice it as needed. It does not spoil and adds to the palatability of many dishes.

"We disagree heartily with Alfred about the hen. She is such an ingratiating animal to start with, and the eggs are such a help in making meals interesting, quite apart from their value as eggs! Until now we had less than a dozen hens, and as only a few will lay at any one time in hot weather, we had eggs only for cooking as a rule. Five per week is said by the government authorities on the 'minimum safe diet' to be the rule for each member of the family. There have been plenty of times before we kept hens when we hadn't that many, and sometimes we had none for weeks together. This summer we figured at the end of the lowest egg month and found we had *just* averaged five per person per week, by using all we got. In winter we get a surplus, eat all we want, and take the others to town. Apart from minerals and Vitamin A, I believe the egg is rated at 70 calories per egg. I realize there are a few dietetic theories that condemn it—we have a book which says, 'Never use eggs as food.'

"[In] the matter of bread, we always use about half white flour. I make a baking of white bread too, about every third time. We use some cornbread, a purely southern habit—that contains only whole corn, ground rather fine. It is not made as in the north with eggs and shortening. I made bread with all whole wheat flour when we first went south, and it was so solid that, while we liked it at first, very soon we weren't eating enough, because it was so boring.

"You asked some specific questions that I must be specific on. I should have said that I think the various makeshift meats mentioned above would average about three or four times a week on our table when we have young folks, less when we are alone. Bacon in the form of a seasoning to other dishes about as many times again.

"Yes, we buy a few cans of grapefruit juice every winter, mainly for variety as we really have enough tomatoes to do the Vitamin C need, taken with the kale, collards, peppers and other vegetables rich in that, some of which we can have growing in the garden all winter. We even buy a few raw grapefruits when they get down to six for a quarter, as they usually do for a bit in the winter here.

"Our cost for food (all that was not home-produced) ran 5½ cents per person per meal during the year March '41 to March '42. We hope it may be somewhat less this year. This includes the cost of canning, but nothing for fuel.

"Surroundings. I do believe most firmly in the propriety of having them beautiful. I claim they needn't be expensive to be that, but maybe our place wouldn't look as beautiful to others as it does to me! We inherited here a house that was not in very bad shape but was terribly dirty and had bed bugs in it. Wilmer put certain repairs to it, and I spent a large part of the first winter painting inside. We got it clean and attractive, though it's pretty bare.

"Children need at least one place where they can leave what to them is a project and to the others is a mess, but I do not think they can leave these projects just any place they happen to be. In winter a good deal of enduring of each other's projects has to be done by everybody because of the limited spaces that are warm enough.

"About subsidies. I think you are right not to bite off more than you could perhaps chew and maybe also unduly risk your children. When we first left Westtown, we had an allowance of 100 dollars per month. We did not quite make out on it. Wilmer had fixed all his insurance in such a way that it could be used as needed for the children's education. We bit into that some. But the second year we didn't, and the third year at the Delta, we were able to cut our allowance to $50. We have had that amount ever since. In addition, we have an equipment loan of about $600 from the AFSC, secured by our inventory here and with 2% interest. We are not expected ever to repay it as long as we remain in charge of the farm here.

"We are supposed to pay rent for our farm at the same rate as others. So far we have had to have a crop loan also, which is repaid at the end of each crop year when the crop is sold. This is about the same as our neighbors do, except their loan is from Farm Security Adm. So you see I'd be a queer one to advocate trying to start farming all of a sudden with no subsidy. And of course, as I indicated above, we did arrange the savings of past years in such a way that we didn't have to ask too much of our children. They were able to go through Westtown as they had always supposed they would, even with very much the same clothes and spending money, and they have each about two hundred dollars to start them in college.

"Each person's problem is different from others, but we need not expect that people of our background will be able to be comfortable with our children having no better education than, for instance, my neighbor's children are getting, and no better diet, or health care. We have to face ourselves as we are, and fit our children in the program as we can. Our children won't wait to grow up until we have the kind of community we'd like them or any others to grow up in."

Toward the end of September, the weather grew much colder and several rows of beans and tomatoes were brought inside to finish ripening. Mr. Oikle drove up to inquire about borrowing a goat. He left with Harriet and, for company, Barbara. Beatrice got bred by accident.

Norma wrote again to Dear Friends:

"We just barely escaped a frost early this week, and though the peril seems to have passed for the moment I am making plans for harvesting the perishable stuff in the garden as quickly and methodically as possible. Yesterday I spent an intensive day in the kitchen, the result of which was canned tomato juice, apple sauce and two kinds of corn, three loaves of bread and a roast chicken. Beans—green, soy and lima—are next on the canning schedule. Thanks to the frost holding off there'll be a good late crop of green beans. It was touch and go Monday, they just weren't big enough to be worth picking, and we hesitated a long time whether or not to uproot the whole garden. In the end we took a chance and were justified. Tomatoes are piling up too.

"On Saturday we went to an auction and bought rather a good-looking table for the new kitchen. There was a beautiful bit of linoleum and I bitterly regret having lost my nerve and failed to bid high enough on it, as it went for well under what it was worth. Most likely the best and cheapest kitchen floor covering would be two coats of the very best porch enamel. [Teresa's recollection is that half the floor, where the table and chairs were, was painted tarpaper, and the other half was linoleum. As the men liked to tip back in their chairs after a meal, the tarpaper was significantly dented.] The two new sinks look fine, though they are rather small, and it might be a good thing to keep the old one for extra dirty pots and milk utensils.

"Paul writes that he is visiting a Jewish cooperative down in New Jersey and promises a long letter about it soon. Greetings from Jean, no word from Lowell except that he is now (or was until recently) in Newton, Mass. I can't think what he is doing there.

"Another news item is that Fellowship Farm has closed down and Bob Brainerd is in the C.P.S. camp at West Campton, N.H. Arle Brooks[27] is starting out on a round of visits and we are writing to urge him to take us in. Outside our own original group there's never been anybody who understood so perfectly what we thought we were about. We hoped for him as a fellow worker at one time, but he had to go South because his health is not strong enough for northern winters, also he's a Texan and feels the South's special problems have first call on him.

"Phil and Teddy wrote suggesting we spend the winter with them. This has very obvious attractions but equally obvious difficulties, principally the livestock. In any case I still want to hang on here as long as humanly possible. We worked hard on the corn crib last week and it's almost finished and looks beautiful. Barring unexpected difficulties, we hope to begin work on the woodshed next week. Dimensions and design are agreed upon and most of the materials [are] to hand."

A day or two later the Rev. Lloyd B. Schear of Hughesville, Pennsylvania, dropped in unexpectedly. He was looking for Lowell, whom he had met in prison. He stayed overnight and had a long talk with Alfred. In the morning he helped saw some wood and then left after lunch to catch the bus to Brattleboro. The family harvested potatoes and had soybeans from the garden for supper. (Soybeans were the chief source of protein and appeared in some form at nearly every meal.)

(Journal entries for September 25 to October 3 are missing.)

A handwritten letter from Arle Brooks is dated September 28:

"Dear Alfred & Norma: Thank you for your letter, your invitation and the information about milk goats. I do want to come, but I must be back here

---

27. During World War II, Arle Brooks would have been exempted from combat because he was a minister. However, he had the courage to stand up for a principle and refused to register for the draft. He served one year for refusing to register and another two for not having a draft card. After his release he spent much of his time visiting men in "places of detention" such as prison, jails, and army disciplinary barracks. Arle died of cancer in 1953 at age 44.

Nov. 2. Not that I am so important to our farm, but I have an appointment with my great uncle, and I must not break my appointment. Uncle Sam called on me again. All of his little helpers have been so very nice to me. I was picked up, investigated, etc. but not arrested. The Dist. Att. said he didn't want to arrest and saw no need for it if I [am] here when ( ) Nov. 2 so they could come after me whenever they wanted me. I promised that I would be here, so I really must be here. My plans for travel are already far beyond what they should be for the kind of visiting and the ( ) in which I wanted to visit. I'm afraid I shall find myself '( )king along' but I trust not.

"I do feel the need for visitation among us. There are so many things we must consider, skills we must learn. We should discuss so many of the angles of communal living. I'm glad you are pushing ahead on trying to get the different farm community people of that area together. Should my Uncle [Sam] (and incidentally I think related to many others) decide to postpone or drop the case I shall try to head your way. I would love to visit with you, to see your place, to learn about milk goats. We want to get a few next year, also some hens & a few sheep. I'm convinced we can raise potatoes, soybeans & peanuts. These crops have been good, but corn has not been too good. We do have a good place for a community development and hope I can stay on. James Ball, who is with me, will be picked up for investigation when he returns. We're both in the same boat—no registration card. We are trying to make plans for the continuation of ( ) in hands of like minds in case we go away for a while. I'm convinced that we are on a right track. We have much to learn & far to go. Will you stay at the farm through the winter? Have you been able to do the farming & repairing you had hoped? Have you found & kept time for meditation? Farming is good for the soul, isn't it, at least it is for mine.

"If at all possible, I shall come up. It does seem a long way, but maybe we should cover it occasionally regardless. We must not just blunder along but we must make our lives & communities intentional. I could stand a lot of help—in the work & on the thinking.

"Have you heard from Leslie? Still in Canada and how faring? If I don't get there this time keep the place going & growing and someday I shall be a guest of your community.

"In Fellowship, Arle."

October 1942

Norma wrote to Leslie, apparently in response to one of his that asked some searching questions:

"'What are we here for?' I am absolutely clear about it in my own mind, though I don't find it easy to express. 'Are we doing it?' On that also I am perfectly clear, and the answer is ... No.

"But one of the reasons for this is the vagueness and indefiniteness of our organization on the purely material side. Since circumstances have separated us from all of the group who originally conceived this project, those who come here now have no means of knowing how we designed this place to be run, unless we have something definite to tell them and to show them in action.

"Do we believe in communal ownership? We have consistently evaded, behind a screen of fine words about our ideals, the challenge to take any definite action, however small, in the direction of sharing. And in what, exactly, are we asking them to share? We can't even state that clearly to ourselves, let alone to them. That, very briefly and baldly, is why I feel an urgent need to transfer real ownership to a group, preferably in some way the original group, which will be able to define and offer something definite for others to accept or reject. I feel we are like the man in the parable with his talent which he buried in the earth.[28] "Fundamentals are important—the most important thing of all, far transcending, as Gerald Heard[29] points out, the day-to-day considerations of means. But I am not the only one who, this past summer, has been first amused, then wearied, finally nauseated by listening to hour after hour of talk about the magnificence of our ideals, without any action at all to show that we are in earnest, or have any conception of what is needed to give our ideals a chance to become realities.

"It is a necessary soul discipline for us to stop talking until we have done everything to show it isn't merely hot air. The need to become a different kind of person is basic, but even that requires action rather than talk. I think Alfred will agree that I have been trying very hard lately to persuade him that we do need to become different people. Frankly, I no longer have time for simply sitting around for a vague period each morning doing absolutely nothing. It is a form of mumbo-jumbo for which I don't think there is time in anybody's life. That our morning meeting has from the start been completely without life, a mere vacuum in the middle of the day,

---

28. A reference to the Biblical parable (Matthew 25:18) involving a man who, having been given but one talent (a gold or silver coin) where others had received more, "went away and digged in the earth and hid his lord's money," thus failing to make use of even that modest amount in any way that might benefit him.
29. Henry FitzGerald Heard (1889–1971), commonly called Gerald Heard, was a British-born American historian, science writer, public lecturer, educator, and philosopher. He wrote many articles and over 35 books (Wikipedia).

and that those who talk about its necessity are apparently unaware that it is dead—I believe that's the center of death and demoralization from which all our troubles sooner or later grow.

"I think we could afford, if our own life were rightly grounded, to ally ourselves with people who think community is sensible, economically or philosophically. I am thinking particularly of Paul Rosenthal: he doesn't speak our 'language,' but of all the people who have been here he is the only one to whom the community idea does have real meaning. Probably most of the people in the Jewish collective farms don't talk about the Kingdom of God, but would you doubt that they are in fact helping to bring it about?

"Paul is a keen and discriminating reader of 'Community Broadsheet,' the significance of which has been totally wasted on all our other visitors. He and we want the same thing, and are we going to stick to our Christian terminology and lose the reality of the thing we both want? Mightn't you have advocated community on largely materialistic grounds when you were twenty-one? And didn't you learn more about it very soon? Paul had a genuinely open mind and stayed with us three months before he finally decided we were hopelessly given over to talk rather than action.

"Then you ask, 'Can we afford to bring people into the group who are concerned with safe jobs, insurance policies, standard of living, and so on?' No, perhaps not, but the trouble is we know hardly any people who are not concerned with these things. I can think only of a handful—the Littles, Arle Brookes, Fran Hall, Lowell Naeve. But the first two already have farms of their own, Fran Hall is in Danbury, and Lowell is so completely divorced from material ties that you can't rely on him for anything at all. He comes and goes like birds of the air and neither he nor we have any idea whether he plans to spend the winter here. Paul, I think, genuinely despises material safety. But he likes things clear; he wants to throw our stake on the table and let it lie there, not keep on picking it up again and wondering whether perhaps a smaller coin would do as well.

"Yes, I think we honestly do agree about our ends. There are differences of emphasis; I think two people who think the same things important are likely to disagree at times about their relative importance. The physical strain of life here is a complicating factor, since so often we are below our best. And the time consumed in learning new skills and managing with makeshifts is rather appalling. But we can do a lot better [in] this sphere and I hope we shall."

On October 5, 6, and 7, Lowell returned, and work continued on the woodshed and canning. Four red hens were killed and canned. Mrs. Spruyt drove up and collected her goats. She brought grapes for jelly, buttermilk, and other delicacies. After she left it was discovered that Honey had been left behind. On the way down the hill, she met Harold Field coming up on his motorcycle. He had just missed Lowell, who was walking through the woods to his house.

Another visit from clergy occurred when the Rev. Clifford Simpson of Springfield, Vermont, came by with a friend on his way to Brattleboro. Norma, who suffered from debilitating migraine headaches, took to her bed. Alfred and the children drove down to Hanford's to get a load of lumber, and Piers stayed there while Alfred and Teresa walked to the village. The kitchen pump arrived. One afternoon Monroe Smith of the AYH (American Youth Hostels) came with a truck to fetch goats Shonyo, Judy, and Hannie. Alfred drove down to Hanford's again to get the hay that Mr. Crowninshield was selling for $15 a ton, as the hay in the barn was unsuitable and not much had been cut with the scythe. (Efficiency improved greatly after a neighbor suggested sharpening the blade!)

A letter came from Eleanor Garst inquiring whether she and a friend might find a place to live up at Hilltop. Mr. Bullis, the superintendent of schools, came to advise about books for the children this winter. Alfred again appeared clueless about—or indifferent to—the particular needs of children. He fixed a leak in the kerosene storage tank. Kerosene was used for the evening table lamps and for the lanterns that illuminated the barn after dark. Teresa thinks she remembers carrying a lantern on their way to school before daybreak in darkest winter, although this would seem to have been prohibitively dangerous and may be apocryphal.

Norma did a lot of baking, cooking, and canning while Alfred unloaded the hay purchased from Mr. Crowninshield. The next day she took the bus to Brattleboro and then the train to Northfield. (The record does not reveal why she went, but Northfield was where Mrs. Spruyt lived.) The others helped with the hay and then had a picnic lunch.

Alfred collected $40 from Mr. Petrie for 4,000 feet of beech lumber, of which he paid $34 to Mr. Rawson. (*Alfred*: Logs were what we had, though I don't recall cutting any at that time. What I recall is not relevant because I'm not recalling much. Norma recalled much more, but it wasn't accurate.) Alfred began work on the air intake to feed the living room fireplace so that the draft wouldn't suck cold air from the corners of the room. There were many bends in the duct, which went down to the cellar and then through an opening in the foundation.

Mr. Oikle brought Harriet back to be bred, and also brought Barbara, as Harriet had been bullying her unmercifully. Harriet's temper seemed very bad, so he took Polly with him instead. Norma came home after supper.

On October 14 Norma wrote to Eleanor Garst in response to her query about coming to Hilltop with a friend to live.

"I sent you a hasty postcard as soon as I got your letter; we are so far from the Post Office that we only collect mail twice a week and for urgent outgoing letters we have to depend on chance visitors, so we try to have them ready and hope for the best.

"Lowell probably told you as much as I could about the physical characteristics of this place. The reason we acquired such a lot of land that is considered valueless from the commercial farmer's standpoint was that we argued, as you do, that subsistence farming would soon become almost the only honorable means of life for people of our views, and we wanted to have plenty of space in which we and as many others as possible could practice it.

"What we most need is all-in collaborators, people who will share all the risks, responsibilities and rewards on an equal footing with us, but it takes time to find such people, and we'd be more than glad to sell you a few acres at the local price of five dollars an acre. You might have to pay even if you only rented the place, because in some towns they assess your personal belongings at a hundred dollars and make you pay that. State taxes tend to be high (Vermont is a poll tax state, believe it or not) but they mostly tax items which don't figure much in the budgets of people like ourselves."

(The poll, or head, tax had been used for decades as a prerequisite to eligibility for voting, which disenfranchised primarily Black and poor citizens. The poll tax in federal elections was terminated by the 24th Amendment to the U.S. Constitution in 1964, though it did not apply to state elections.)

Alfred began excavating for the cement foundation for the new "sanitary privy" that would be situated near the rear entry door, following the instructions provided in a government pamphlet. An expedition was made to investigate a field where Eleanor Garst and her friend might live. (*Alfred*: Eleanor Garst was writing a book on cooperatives and she kept coming with a man, I forget his name. He and I chopped a tree together. It took all day to cut the tree, and then he asked me how much I thought the tree would be worth when we sold it. I said I thought about a dollar and a quarter, and I think he was dismayed.)

The old sugar house up in the woods was examined as a possible dwelling. (*Alfred*: When the forester came to visit, he asked why there was a sugar house in an area where there were no sugar trees. It never occurred to me to look for sugar trees around the sugar house. None could be found.) There were, in fact, sugar trees in that location, as was determined later. Alfred may not have known how to identify them.

Teresa's 7th birthday was October 22, unremarked in the journal. Norma walked four miles to visit the Fields, Scott Nearing and Helen, down in the valley. Alfred finished the privy excavation. The next day he built the lower part of the foundation, and Norma canned tomatoes and pears (?—probably should be beans). Only nine more jars were needed to reach a total of 300.

1942

The page that would have mentioned Norma's 33rd birthday on October 24, two days after Teresa's, is missing.

Norma's Dear Family letter to England of October 29 said in part:

"The children have recently had their periodical medical examination and got excellent reports. [Piers'] bed-wetting is still a nuisance—this is likely to be tied up in some way with his general nerviness, which is still rather noticeable, though as his general health is excellent there seems nothing to be done about it. I have wondered once or twice lately whether a house like this with people constantly coming and going is a very satisfactory environment, and whether he might not actually get a more stable atmosphere at a good school. I saw a really excellent school on my recent trip way from home. I have an idea I mentioned it in a recent letter—it's down at Pawling, near Poughkeepsie, on the Hudson River perhaps 50 miles north of New York. A friend of ours teaches there and so does an English girl, Nancy Montague, an Oxford girl and wife of a brother or some near relative of C. E. Montague. She is there with her three small children. In fact, all the staff seemed to have children in the school and they all said how happy the children were, and they certainly looked it.

"It's a farm school, in buildings only slightly less dilapidated than our own, and run on thoroughly unconventional lines, though apparently with great regard for what I should feel were the essentials. Their scholastic standards are good according to all reports, there is abundant evidence that the children are happy, and they have a resident doctor who looks each child over three times a day as it comes in to meals, which seems as good an insurance policy as one could want against infectious diseases or ill-treatment of smaller children by bigger ones.

"If it were financially possible I should much like to send both children there, to solve at one blow the problem of education, companionship and health supervision; but it would take practically the whole of our income, and so far we don't see our way to making a living off this place. So probably nothing will come of it at least for this year.

"They have a Jewish refugee doctor and among the children are representatives of all the races. It's the only boarding school I know of that takes Negroes. They only have one Negro child at present, but they say he is far and away the most intelligent child in the school—has an I.Q. of 180, whatever that may mean. So often the outstanding Negro child simply cannot get adequate education—and though the better colleges such as Harvard and Dartmouth do take Negroes, their graduates nine times out of ten can't get any better job than as waiters or lift [elevator] attendants. It's a tragic and potentially terrifying state of things—a most dangerous state of mind is working up, especially in many parts of the South.

"About the winter we are still undecided. If it got too severe, we could always rent rooms in the village for a few weeks, but there is so much work to do up here. The Superintendent of Schools paid a friendly visit and sent a big parcel of books which arrived today; characteristically, Teresa fell at once on the advanced reader and Piers on the arithmetic books. These are done very attractively in the form of short stories and I hope his love for figures may help to overcome his lack of interest in reading. Teresa's reading is really coming on very well. I got them a good illustrated geography book, and a friend is looking about for a history [book], so I think we'll do all right.

"They are very strict about education in Vermont, so I half expected trouble with the superintendent, but they are pretty used to people living on inaccessible farms. Vermont has a deserved reputation as the healthiest state in the union, free of all the scourges that bedevil American life almost everywhere else—no rattlesnakes, rabies or Rocky Mountain spotted fever—but against these advantages there is the one disadvantage, which is the length and severity of the winter. However, if one has a tight house, plenty of good stoves, and unlimited fuel, one ought to come through all right. [Hilltop had none of these. Norma did not want her family to know how grueling her true circumstances were.] The snowplow will open the road to within half a mile, and for the last bit we'll rely on snowshoes and skis, until such time as we can afford a yoke of oxen and a sleigh!"

At the end of October, Norma left to go to the Communities Conference at Gould Farm. Alfred tried to work out a plan for storing sacks of winter feed that had been brought from South Londonderry, but seven sacks remained on the barn floor. A barrel of goat feed made of oats, wheat, 32% supplement, and corn in the proportion of 2:2:2:3 was prepared. He worked out a winter feeding plan for the animals in which hay was strictly rationed. Each goat would get two pounds of hay a day, each sheep, three pounds. This they consumed in no time.

November 1942

A page in the record contains a chart showing where five kinds of fruit trees were set out on November 4: Montmorency cherry, Windsor sweet cherry, Burbank plum, Fellenberg prune, and Bartlett pear. None ever produced a crop, as they were nibbled by the goats.

Norma wrote to Judy (Bacon):

"I feel guilty not having answered either of your cards asking about the Thanksgiving trip. The fact is I've been through a very unhappy week, trying to weigh everything up and decide whether I can face the winter here—

with no wood cut or anything—or whether the children and I ought to be looking for some place to move to before it snowed. But my correspondence with Eleanor Garst has encouraged me at least to hang on till the end of this month, as she and her friend plan to visit Gene at Danbury at Thanksgiving and come on here after that to survey the land. If they feel like moving in here some time during December, I guess I can stick it out, and with another man we'll be able to keep ourselves in green wood, at any rate. There were a few cords of beech tops which were fairly seasoned, but we are getting through them pretty fast. Last week we had an awful cold spell, and I felt winter was on top of us long before we were ready, and we just wouldn't be able to meet it."

Despite the difficulties, including her own fragile health, Norma was determined to continue with the original plan.

"I won't give up any sooner than I have to, because moving elsewhere, even temporarily, would almost certainly mean leaving the inside plastering and painting for another whole year, since we can't possibly take time off for it during the summer. By the way, we have now got in materials for covering the ceiling of the main living room, which will not only look better but we hope will be a measure of fly control, as we suspect thousands of them live during the cold weather in the cracks of the ceiling. [Teresa remembers this ceiling being covered with sagging, tacked-up lengths of fabric.] Materials for permanent window screens are also on hand and now [that] we're getting the holes blocked in the cellar we ought to have gone a good way towards meeting the menace another year.

"Paul and Herbert—the old firm—are back at present. Paul came back briefly to finish the pulp job, which he hopes will be done tomorrow, and then he expects to collect from Louis Roberts and go to Cornell some time next week. At least that was his original plan, but now I don't know, he talks of getting a job and making some more money first, as he is short on winter clothes. In any event I don't imagine he will be here when you come.

"About Herbert [Leader] one never knows. Tuesday night at dusk Alfred said, 'Someone is walking up the road.' I said, 'What do you bet it's Herbert,' and it was—though the last news from him was that he expected to spend the winter in Montana. I believe the fact is, he is completely at a loose end. If he stayed here this winter to keep Alfred company I could move out with an easier mind (except for the plastering!) but he won't commit himself to anything. I told him I was very likely moving because he doesn't have any better opinion of me than I have of him. In a stable group we could probably get along, we have much in common really, many intellectual interests, but I do feel a chronic drifter is a serious liability when one is in the difficult early stages of building any kind of group, and he feels I am altogether too much wedded to material values, like what the children get to eat. When I came to think back over the summer, I couldn't help realizing what a lot of harm had been done by our egos—Alfred's and mine.

"We have had the most awful weather and the second half of the potato crop still isn't in. Did I tell you Helen's idea of storing root vegetables in dead leaves?"

A long letter from Janet Hall dated November 9 gives news of several mutual acquaintances:

"We have just finished having the C.P.S. assistant camp directors here for a week. Betty Baker's friend, also Betty, and her husband, Francis Duveneck, son of the Great Josephine,[30] were here with their young child. Now they are in Washington for three weeks' intensive training in the Selective Service Act, records and files, forms, etc. then a return to Pendle Hill for three days to top it off."

By mid-November, Norma had reached the end of her rope. She wrote a desperate letter to Alfred's brother Phil and his wife, Teddy, in Maine:

"I'm wondering whether it would be possible for the children and myself to spend a short while with you, maybe a week, maybe two. The fact is that Alfred and I have arrived at a profound divergence of opinion as to what we are trying to do here; this is making us extremely unhappy, and being cooped up together here, hardly seeing another soul, and having no opportunity to get advice or let a fresh wind from outside blow through our difficulties and perhaps blow some of them away, is making it all much harder.

"I think that a short absence from one another would help us to see things straighter. It may be that our difference is actually irreconcilable. In any case I think the odds are that we should not plan to spend the winter together at Hilltop, the circumstances being what they are. I have two or three other possibilities in mind—the most helpful being to spend some months down at the School of Living, learning all the homesteading arts and crafts at which I am so ignorant, while the children could go to school there, and another of our problems would be at least partly solved."

Many years later Norma revealed to Teresa that she had feared for the children's safety, as Alfred was prone to sudden destructive rages, of which they [and she] were sometimes the focus.

"But this will take a little while to arrange—and anyway we have only twenty dollars to our names and the children need some new clothes

---

30. Josephine Whitney Duveneck (1891–?) and her husband were Boston aristocrats who became philanthropists and welcomed disadvantaged visitors of all kinds—Japanese-Americans, World War II refugees, Muslims, Native Americans—to Hidden Villa, their sprawling estate in Los Altos, California.

before they can appear in a snooty place like Suffern, so any arrangement I made wouldn't be able to start much before the first of December when our next money comes in. Besides, I very badly need a short time of rest among friendly people, not to talk over my troubles but just to try and relax somewhat and see them for myself in a more normal light. And I know no one to whom I would rather go in such a state of mind than yourselves. Would you be willing to give us a hole to crawl into for a short while? And if so, could we come some time next week? I don't know what possibilities there are for transportation from Bath to Sebasco. Maybe you don't have any more gasoline—ours is all gone—but if you should be making a trip into Bath any day next week, and if it's convenient for us to come, perhaps you could say which day and we could arrange to arrive by the train that gets to Bath at 1.05 according to our timetable. It's out of date now, but there must be some train still that gets there about the middle of the day, and that's the one we should try to catch.

"It would be a two-day journey anyway and I imagine we'd have to break the journey in Greenfield, which would be cheaper and pleasanter than Boston. Probably our twenty dollars, or maybe it's twenty-five, will cover that all right if there is a bus, or even if one could take a taxi: be sure to let me know about that. Is there a bus as far as Philippsburg [sic], perhaps? I haven't any experience of hitch-hiking and I feel in winter, with two children, is not the time to start!"

Phil responded immediately: "We'll be very glad to have both you and the children pay us a visit for any length of time. Please don't feel that you have to set a time limit—we'd prefer that you just come and stay until it seems right to go again. Our harvest is about completed now, and you need have no fear about depleting our resources. The local children remember Piers and Theresa and will be glad to have them back to play with again. I'm sure that they could go to school while they are here if you wanted them to.

"I plan to be in Bath on this coming Saturday in order to haul out a load of Co-op stuff and lumber, and I'll arrive at the station before or after the 1:03 p.m. train, so just wait there until I turn up. We're sorry about the divergence of your opinion. We know both how hard life can seem under these circumstances and how nice it is when two see eye to eye with each other. Perhaps you are right about getting out to let things settle a bit and get a new perspective. It certainly helps us whenever we have the opportunity to discuss things with you or with others who are working along related lines.

"Please give our regards to Alfred. We'd like to see him too, but we realize that even if it were possible for you both to leave at once it might defeat the purpose of this move if he came too."

This courteous and civilized dialogue in the face of what must have been, for Norma, an agonizing situation, is characteristic of the Quaker acceptance of opposing views and lack of condemnation for either side in a dispute.

The daily log, which had lapsed for a time through a misunderstanding, was resumed. Catching up: Herbert Leader "turned up unexpectedly," as was his habit, and was considering spending the winter at Hilltop. Paul Rosenthal went off to a Zionist[31] farm in New Jersey. The Angora goats that were to have been shipped to Brattleboro did not arrive: the owner said they were too difficult to capture. The truck ran out of gas on the way up the mountain and they had to put in the last two-gallon reserve. The spare tire had blown out on the way down the hill, "so it looks like not running much in the future." It snowed heavily and the temperature went down to zero with a northeast wind. The little black cat, Daphne, froze to death in the barn. Herbert left again to attend a conference in Boston and visit friends.

The temperature rose back up to 40° and the pump pipeline thawed out. The children had fun sledding. Mr. Oikle brought Polly back. After nightfall Herbert returned from Boston and his home in Bennington. The next day steady rain melted most of the remaining snow. Alfred spun a little Angora rabbit and sheep wool and Norma knitted it. Alfred proposed to spin a little every day.

Letter from one "Phil," with no last name, dated November 18, 1942.

"Dear Sydney Alfred Jacob!

"You will probably be surprised to hear from me again, considering your last letter to me was dated July 12, but I've just never had enough leisure and inclination coinciding to do it before. It seemed an especially difficult task, as I found myself in violent disagreement with practically all your present ideas, and knowing my own weakness for getting into downright uncivilized argument, thought it best anyhow to wait a period equivalent to a count of ten before replying. I think four months should have tamed me down sufficiently so that I can say 'Live and let live,' 'Everyone to his own taste,' etc. etc.,—however I still think you're all wrong!

"Of course you will want to know with what I disagree, and why, and it's going to be difficult to tell you simply. However, I've got to register my disapproval somehow, so here goes.

"No one could think the world today was in very good shape—but certainly it is better, even with its faults, than it was a century ago. And that

---

31. The term "Zionism" refers to an international movement originally for the establishment of a Jewish national or religious community in Palestine, and later for the support of modern Israel.

century, in the long run, was an improvement over the century preceding it. The progress of our 'civilization' has brought many evils with it, without a doubt, which we must continue to overcome, but it is my deep-seated conviction that over the years the improvements have far outweighed the evils, and in the last analysis that's what counts. War is horrible, but war has always been with us, which simply means that it is one of the problems still unsolved. It does not mean that our 'civilized' life as we lead it today is responsible for war. One of the greatest, if not the greatest war mongers of all time to wage a complete 'World War' was Genghis Khan[32]—and certainly his age was not 'civilized,' nor did it have any of the problems attendant on our way of life that you could blame for that war.

"I'm damned if I can see how burying one's head in the hills of Vermont and refusing to face and cope with the problems remaining, will ever help accelerate the progress toward the perfect state. Personally, I would feel that I might just as well quit reading the daily papers, studying the opinions of those in touch with the situation, and go back to my kindergarten primers and just forget the whole thing.

"At one time you worked for the Friends Service, and you certainly know the good they are doing in the world to help alleviate the sufferings brought on by this war. They daily work toward eventual world peace. I was very proud of you when you were affiliated with them, and for your work in Spain. Not so, now. The peaceful, domestic, negative life you describe, surrounded by Harriet the goat and Euphoria the ewe, whilst you labor away doing many simple tasks the hard way that our ancestors did them simply because they didn't know any better yet—all this makes me slightly sick at my stomach when I think of all the education and experience you possess that you could be using to help in the fight to make things better. Have you lost your religion too? Jesus certainly lived the 'simple life' if anyone did. But he didn't bury himself in his carpenter shop away from the problems of his day. He got out and did something about it, in the end even dying very uncomfortably on a cross. But he did a tremendous amount of good in the world to relieve the suffering of the poor and the oppressed, first.

"I realize that you probably believe that you are working toward the eventual betterment of the world. You feel that by withdrawing into the hills with this handful of 'pacifists' you can start some sort of a peace movement that will eventually spread and save the world—at least that's how I interpret

---

32. Genghis Khan launched the Mongol invasions that conquered most of Eurasia and included large-scale slaughters of local populations, causing great demographic changes and a drastic decline of population as a result of mass extermination and famine (Wikipedia).

your motive. I feel there are active physical needs to be tended to first and put right before we have the right to minister to its soul. For instance, if there were some man walking down a road and you beside him trying to convince him that you had the answer to the proper way of life, and suddenly three or four thieves jumped out to attack you—would you then run up on a hillside and shout advice to your luckless friend being beaten up below, or would you pitch in, roll up your sleeves and first get rid of the marauders, then bathe and bind his wounds before continuing your preachments?"

To which Alfred responded on November 20:

"Dear Phil, You wrote with admirable clarity and restraint. Norma is going off to my brother's in Maine for a while, and will take this down.

"I thought it was preposterous two years ago when I learned that my brother Philip was taking up farming. I was amused that all his talent should go into the earth. [Another reference to the Biblical man who buried his one talent/coin, a rather clever pun.] But his doing so opened the way for me. I recognize that unless someone opens it, it remains closed, as it is to you at present. I don't want to justify this activity, but I do want to have an exchange of views, so that more or less I can understand and [know] what you think about it, and you can understand what is going on here. I'm not claiming that this is right for all men everywhere, but I think it is right for me.

"Our effort here is to undo, not civilization, but some of the things that have gone wrong in civilization. One of them is the acquisitive instinct, which leads people to live a lifetime of self-centeredness, getting, getting, and getting in order to have more and more. We are interested in exploring a philosophy of giving: sharing and sharing until we all have what we need. [The Marxist slogan, "From each according to his ability, to each according to his need," was posted on the wall at Pendle Hill. Alfred interpreted it quite literally.] We thought that acquisitiveness, raised to a national level, causes international competition and ultimately wars; we cannot stop the wars, but we can stop those impulses in ourselves, which, magnified to a national scale, cause wars.

"This enterprise is really the outgrowth of my period of international service, which taught me how futile is the patching up of the consequences of wrongs. We fed many people in Spain who starved after the relief work ended. I have been wanting to dig down to the very roots of the world problem; and strangely enough I find them in the land. I also find that rural labor and planning is by no means an escape, unless it is an escape from escapism. No city person can know the real problems that confront the producer on whom he depends for the milk on his doorstep. But I am immersed in those problems. It seems to me more fundamental to worry about problems that I can conceivably affect sometime, than to grasp for news about the Russian front which I can in no way influence. Anyway, that front is the result of something wrong in human society, and it is that something wrong which I am groping to understand.

"I am worried about the future of this and all countries. When the present artificial boom is over, a great army of unemployed will have to vegetate in a nation replete with manufactured goods that no one has money to buy or work to earn the money for. The only solution I can see for this is home production of essentials. That is why we have two sheep, two Angora rabbits & are expecting two Angora goats; not for our amusement, but to find which wool is best raised and spun at home, and will therefore be available to people who have no work and therefore no money to pay anyone to spin and weave for them. This looks to you like moving the clock backward, and I understand that. But I have had to work with people [in Spain] who had no hope of buying clothing, and for whom a sheep's fleece would have been a godsend.

"I don't want you to think I am trying to convince anyone of anything. I'm trying to get at the root of the social problem, and the root is probably somewhere near the problem of insecurity. We have such a lot of land here that hundreds of families, if they wished, could settle on it (we would gladly share it) and thenceforth no one could rob them of their home, their garden, their productive labor, or their cloth.

"This will look like dreaming to you. But I want you to see that there is a concrete element in what I am trying to do. It is a self-identification with the great problem of humanity. It may achieve nothing, but it is an effort to achieve something, not for me, but for everyone in need. It is the direct outgrowth of my experience of relief work under the Friends Service Council, and it certainly utilizes all the talents I have been able to assemble, and more.

"I am as critical of the city way of life as you are of [ours]; our neighbor Scott Nearing said the other day that, 'City life provides some of the requisites for decent living; [but not] fresh air, nor pure food, nor freedom of movement, nor contact with the earth, nor leisure, nor a clean environment.' What I deplore in city life is that it is not fundamental. It does not produce, it manipulates. It is not a community, but a fortuitous aggregation. When the time comes that you are sick of [city life], I hope to have worked out a way whereby you can make ends meet in the country and be subservient to no man.

"You want to help in the war, [while] I want to help towards the world-community in which further civil wars will not take place. So long as the instinct to help is given expression, we are by that much saved from the self-centeredness which seems to me to be the ruination of human society."

Alfred was sure that whoever opined that, "The love of money is the root of all evil" (1 Timothy 6:10) had the right idea. He envisioned a world in which money itself is of little necessity.

Life went on. General cleanup day. Strawberries mulched, mower and wagon stowed under the barn, wood stacked, cheesecloth fly screens removed from windows. "By 2:00 the Bacons had not appeared for the Thanksgiving dinner we had prepared, so we ate it." Herbert walked to the village and Alfred dug carrots and cabbages.

Norma left for Sebasco with the children. Alfred wheelbarrowed their three suitcases down through the shortcut.

(Alfred, claiming that he had had no idea of her plans, commented decades later that, "Norma just picked up and left, and I didn't realize, because people were coming and leaving all the time, I didn't realize that she had decided to run away. She took the children and ran away to Philip in Maine. We had visited Philip before, and I imagine Norma thought of him as someone who would be ready to listen to her. I didn't realize [how desperate she felt]. I had poor communication with her, so I didn't realize what was in her mind. I was a world-saver, I wanted to do what was best for the world. I was probably more aware of ideas than of persons.")

Herbert and Alfred dug the last of the rutabagas. Lowell Naeve appeared in an old Chevrolet to collect his things. He had found a job working in a hotel in Northfield that provided room and board, and had the rest of his time free. The next day Herbert and Alfred had a sumptuous meal of mashed pumpkin with molasses, baked potato, hot rolls, chicken, raw cabbage, carrots, and fried pumpkin seeds. Rain changed to sleet in the afternoon and then snow, with the temperature dropping to 18°. They carried on.

Alfred wrote to Norma five days later, catching her up on the ongoing activities. He made no reference to her state of mind or any precipitating events, such as those for which he might have been responsible. "Herbert is chef, since meal preparations coincide with milking, and we are enjoying an abundance of raw carrots (which are very sweet) cabbage leaves, etc., with potatoes, pumpkin & rutabaga for our hot food. We found that pumpkin seeds, well fried & well salted, are the next thing to roasted almonds.

"Yesterday I installed the new sink drain pipe and filled in the foundation, as well as searching for cracks to fill with mortar. The actual sink installation will have to wait until some more outside jobs are done, though it would be quite easy to put them up in a temporary way with the drain working. We also spent another bad day cleaning out the cellar, so that now there is no junk, and only a long shelf full of glass bottles. We threw away the tins, & Herbert removed the pile of earth. We may have to stack turnips where the earth was.

"I have done some spinning daily and am sending you the product to date in the hope you may be able to make a pair of gloves for my father. I have never made him anything, and they certainly won't be well spun, but he might appreciate the gesture. The brown I spun all last evening. That goes very quickly. But the Ramsay-Angora mixture is quicker now than before. . . .

"That seems to be about the news. I won't say anything about us—you and me—because I expect you will say what is needful when you have had your change and rest. We are getting on quite nicely here, and there's no need to worry about us." This could have been meant as reassurance, or, "So don't hurry back."

Norma responded on November 27:

"My dear, I had hoped for a slightly more human letter and for that reason had postponed yet once more the other letters I have to write if I am to be obliged to take on myself the responsibility for what is done this winter. Since you give me no lead of any kind, I suppose I must just go ahead according to such light as I see. But still I am glad to know you are happy and fairly comfortable, and getting the turnips eaten. As I expected, the tangle in my ideas began to straighten out as soon as I got away from Hilltop, and by about midnight things seemed wonderfully clear—and unexpectedly hopeful.

"It was, as you supposed, a pretty awful journey. To begin with, the train at Brattleboro was 45 minutes late so we waited 1 hour on the cold windy platform with no place to sit down. At Greenfield we ate our picnic supper and I telephoned Mrs. Spruyt and had half an hour's talk with her for my nickel, during which I nearly stifled in the telephone box.

"About 15 minutes later she suddenly appeared, having decided that she and an English friend who was staying with her would like to borrow the children while I went on to Bath alone. However, the children were determined they were going to visit Phil and I was too tired and confused to alter all the plans at a moment's notice (the Boston train being practically due) so it seemed better to proceed as planned. I asked if she'd like to have them later, as it seemed clear I'd have to go back to Hilltop some time in December if any preparations were to be made for Eleanor Garst.

"The Boston train finally arrived, very late indeed, and was even later in leaving; troop trains and freight trains were going through all the time and we were pretty tired of Greenfield before we finally got away. We reached Boston at 12.15 instead of 11. The children lay down in the station but didn't get to sleep before the next train left at 2:30 a.m. This was pretty crowded; there were several men occupying four whole seats with various sprawling limbs, and when I'd got the children lying down I no longer had even a place to sit, until I squeezed myself in beside one of the men and managed to doze uncomfortably for a while.

"We got to Portland at 6.30 and had a good breakfast there (we needed it by that time, fortunately the coffee was strong). Then we took the train for Bath and arrived at 8.45. It was raining there and we had no money to speak of except two $5 bills which I didn't want to break into, so we spent four miserable hours in the station till Phil came to pick us up at 1.

"I was glad I hadn't planned to stop overnight, as we should almost certainly have missed a connection, with all the trains so disorganized. Almost the worst part came last; Phil had heaps of marketing to do, loading the truck in one big drafty warehouse after another, and my feet were wet through and frozen (it had turned very cold) and the children of course tired, cross and hungry. I was about all in when we finally did arrive. For a day or two I felt completely exhausted and apathetic and just mooned around depressing everyone, but my normal spirits are beginning to return.

"Here's as far as my thinking has got so far. As far as I am clear about anything, two things seem to stand out: one, that I ought to spend this winter up at Hilltop; two, that the children ought not. So, seeing nothing to be gained by putting it off any longer, I shall write today or tomorrow to Manumit and see if we can agree on terms for them to take the children in January. I shall thank the School of Living people for being willing to take us for $50 a month, but say that as far as I can now foresee, I can't leave home this winter after all. I have already told Eleanor Garst that unless she hears to the contrary, she can count on my being at Hilltop from January on.

"According to present plans I'll start back when Phil makes his next regular trip to Bath on the 12th. I shall ask Mrs. Spruyt if she will take the children at least for a week, and come on alone, possibly arriving back by the late bus that night, since connections are much better going in the other direction. Where we'll spend Christmas I don't yet know, but very likely at Hilltop, since the school in any case won't take the children before some time in January and they can hardly stay with Mrs. Spruyt all that time. If the school won't have them, of course we'll have to start all over again and make new plans.

"If I had the faintest indication that the conditions were beginning to exist within which we could have a normal family life, such as they have here, I would still bring them back to Hilltop and see the winter through, but I must write to the school and prepare for other plans if the first doesn't work out. I have already waited too long, hoping for a miracle. I think that if in these two weeks I can adjust myself to the fact that you don't love me or them, and find some way at least to begin to find another outlet for the need for love which at present makes me so wretched—then we'll do better from this time on. At present it still hurts like hell to see Phil play with his children and pay little attentions to his wife. Already last year they had noticed what your attitude was, but they are kind and don't ask me to say more than I want to, and it's good to be here, apart from the difficulties that always arise when one has children in someone else's house.

"They have much to occupy their minds, too. When I came, they described themselves as 'in a condition of having back-slidden,' that is, they had abandoned the daily quiet time, finding no further need for it. But this last week things have happened which have made Phil feel the need for it again and yesterday, after a long but by no means empty period of silence, Teddy told us she believed she should not register for the conscription of women."

The journal resumes. Hunters came and went, including one from Massachusetts who had kept Toggenbergs. In the evening the [goat] kids and rabbits got a ration of milk. (*Alfred*: The idea was to find a home craft that didn't involve execution [killing]. My dream was that taking care of Angora rabbits would be an ideal responsibility for Norma. And of course, she wasn't going to take it from me. So that didn't work out.)

The following summer Norma did, in fact, care for the rabbits—*and* the cow, the goats, the sheep, the horse, and the hens, not to mention her own and several visiting children, the garden, and the household, with only intermittent assistance from visitors who came and went.

Herbert harvested the cabbages, leaving only turnips and carrots in the ground. "A. has achieved more skill in spinning and, weighing the two blobs of yarn, found they weighed ... one ounce. The goats stayed in all day and the sheep went around with icicles in their fur. Calculations on a basis of weight show that two rabbits will cost $5.80 a year to feed. The cash cost of their wool would therefore be about $3 a pound." (*Alfred*: Norma was knitting all the time, and using knitting wool, but she wasn't there. Things could be made out of home-spun and home-knitted wool, mittens were available, and other such things, though we didn't carry it that far.)

Alfred made two bread loaves into cake by adding fat, sugar, and half a cup of alfalfa leaf meal. Both bread and cake were entirely of coarsely ground wheat. Though heavy, they had risen fully and were full of air spaces. When they had finished eating, it was milking time.

Alfred: Herbert was open to innovative ways of eating. People [did] have trouble making the adjustment, but we were trying to find a simple and effective way of living. Piers and I found [a few years later when they were there together] that if we got hungry [enough], anything tasted good. We were attempting to live on $22 apiece for the summer. One day we'd eat rice and the next day we would eat wheat. And we looked forward to it, once we got hungry. We found it was possible to live that way. We didn't have milk. What we didn't have, we didn't use. It was all experimental.

This minimalist diet would not have supported healthy bodies, as it lacked many essential nutrients, such as protein and calcium.

Journal entries continue: "Still drizzling or snowing alternately. Herbert finished lining the kitchen floor with building paper while A. stuffed rock wool into the cracks in the north wall of the Lulu room [where baby goats were housed at times], stairway ceiling, cupboard & blue room, filling also the partition with rock wool, wood wool & old plaster. Lunch of yesterday's vegetable stew with bread with roasted grains, unsoaked: very tasty, but hard on the teeth." After lunch they installed the west sill of the west wing, with many difficulties. Two hunters were at first mistaken for Eleanor Garst and her friend Herb Willits.

"Barbara came in heat. Our 3 tons of agricultural lime [arrived] so A. rode down to the village with the truck to fetch mail and cider and see the Bolsters about purchasing the Hope property. About lunch time Harold Field came with his gun and stayed till about dusk. Then we carried half a ton of lime up to the west field and spread it beside the plowed part."

Alfred voiced a familiar lament: "Milk is only one of many foods and production of an amount sufficient for a family is supposed to take only a few minutes a day." Sunday was a day off, but by 12.30 he had done nothing but milk, eat breakfast, let the goats out, test them for heat, mend billy goat Patrick's door, chase them out of the garden three times, mend three places in the fence they had broken down, mend the holes he tore in his gloves hooking and unhooking the wire ends of the fence, and cover the feed stored in the large red barrel which the mice have been at. And still the weekly milk records are not done.

Alfred mused that "where milk is a principal part of one's responsible activity, it can rightly take a large slice of one's time; but if we added up the time it takes to build fences, build stalls, let goats in and out, warm water & carry it to them, feed them, dehorn and delouse them, plant, weed, harvest & store roots for them, carry roots & chop them: grow, cut, carry, store, and serve hay for them, chase them out of the garden hundreds of times in the year, replace the fence they tear, stretch, bend or break; replace the vegetables and fruit trees they ruin, besides find the money for feed & the time for routine milking, it would seem like more time than was proportionate to the two or three quarts of milk which are supposed to be necessary in the diet." He relished opportunities to list all the ways a project would not work, and how he had been the victim of others' misguided decisions.

Alfred: That's the picture of rural life, all sorts of little things to be done. I kept careful records of everything [a lifelong habit]. The goat shed was my domain. I may have kept things there for long periods. I valued that, because I was in control, and I greatly resented not being in control of anything else. In a community everyone shares the work—or fails to work. That's why people end with a powerful leader, or a king or someone like that [whom] everyone has to obey.

Teresa: You didn't seem to comprehend the way a situation could develop that would result in there being a war. Hilltop was a microcosm—a few people who couldn't agree on anything.

Alfred: I certainly learned that. And I had to yield, because if I didn't yield, the other people would go ahead and do things according to their own business, like Fran Bacon and the barbed wire. If I wasn't there, he would have put up the barbed wire anyway. It's part of such a situation. There was no harmony between Norma and me, so she felt justified in doing things her own way.

Teresa: It must have been clear that Norma was not accustomed to that kind of living, had no skills, but was doing the best that she could. She had to take care of the children, who were simply considered noisy nuisances who got in the way and made demands on others' time. She had to deal with that. Anybody reading this will marvel that anybody could have lived this way. The other participants didn't plan to spend the winter there, they just wanted to come for the summer and work at things that interested them, and then leave. They couldn't be expected to want to spend time canning food, say, or stuffing cracks in the wall, if they would really prefer to be out picking berries.

Alfred: The governing principle of voluntary societies boils down to one or two systems. Either there must be a patriarch, that is, a man in leadership whom everybody respects, [or] a binding religious commitment. Probably nobody wants just to obey somebody else, somebody else's thinking. I worked things out that made sense to me, but I didn't allow for the fact that they might not make sense to . . . for example [he reflects], the big initial failure was, if you mean to farm the land, you must take some years to prepare the land for plowing. That is, with cover crops, composting and so on. [As the farm had been abandoned for many years, there would have been multiple layers of "green compost" already in place.] The people who were coming to help wanted to plant something right away, as if something were to be achieved by planting instead of preparing the ground for planting. There was no binding, no shared, no communal philosophy.

Teresa: If you hadn't planted anything, what would people—your family—be living on? What would you be eating?

Alfred: It did work out, because our visitors were there with their good will and so on, and they planted things, so we did have cabbages and potatoes and a number of things. I didn't get a chance to implement my ideas. I opened up the whole east end of the basement and took down the foundation, imagining that we would be wheelbarrowing great loads of potatoes in from the garden and storing them [during] the summer. So we would have eaten potatoes, and we depended on bags of wheat [labeled "Not for Human Consumption"] that cost $3 a hundred pounds, so we expected to have plenty of wheat. We had cabbages, that I hung from the ceiling of the cellar. They would have given us some green food, except the goats got in and ate away the cabbages by standing on their hind legs and reaching up for them. I hadn't taken that into account. The potatoes got frozen and thawed and smelled awful. That's how we learn.

We moved down to Hope House before Christmas. [Referring back to the previous year.] The call from Dartmouth was very unexpected. Edward[33] had told them that if they asked me to come, I would be likely to accept, and that's what happened. But I didn't want to teach, I wanted to farm.

Continuing the November 29th entry: "Snow fell in the evening, but fortunately we had spent half an hour getting some wood for the library fire. By bedtime it was rather warmer, around 32°. All the lactations were short and filled with detrimental incidents."

Alfred: I wanted to raise high-quality goats that would give people appreciable amounts of milk. I thought that it takes no more to raise a high-quality goat than a low-quality one, and we could confine ourselves to high-quality goats that gave lots of milk, and we could sell them to people for the going price; people would be getting better goats than they would get if they bought locally. A goat was reputed to provide enough milk for a small family, and that would meet people's needs. Everything was along the line of saving humanity.

November 30: "We decided to do small jobs around the place so as to be free to start the wood-cutting program tomorrow. Though we came in at one, lunch took a long time heating and it was 3 or later before we set out to putty some windows preparatory to setting the storm windows. It was

---

33. As a child Alfred had been mercilessly bullied by his older brother. Although Edward did his best to patch up this relationship when they became adults, Alfred never forgot, and to the end of his life found it difficult to accept Edward's generous overtures or even to express his opposition to them.

1942

very cold work and imperfectly done. A. dealt with the goats in 43 minutes instead of 55, because of doing it by daylight. The evening was devoted to sitting around the fire and reading, as usual. During the day the goats broke down the garden fence in several places. The sheep have learned to clear a patch of snow to get at the grass underneath." (*Alfred*: Goats had a tendency to push down the fence to get at the garden and eat the remaining cabbages and so on. That was another unforeseen . . . I had thought goats were well-behaved and would stay in their own territory.)

December 1942

"Just when we thought no more motor vehicles would come this winter, up came a truck this morning, and it was the snow plow. We set out to chop a cord of wood along the Pikes Falls road, clearing out everything between the walls. About midday it began to snow, and the longer the harder. By 5:30 a cord was stacked, representing 14 man-hours. We were both wet through, so the hot vegetable stew & hot fire were doubly welcome. The goats enjoyed eating the twigs and buds we chopped & we foresee another possible winter feed for them."

Alfred: Herbert had the idea of taking our sleeping bags outside and spending the night in the snow! He was dismayed when I refused.

"It snowed all night at thawing temperature, and this morning there was a deep, sticky snow. Soon it turned colder & continued to snow, until by evening it was quite deep and much drifted, particularly into all corners of the barn. Herbert made a stew & A. made bread, wrote letters & worked on goat registry applications. Too stormy to go to village.

"It was windy the next day, turning colder. The building paper blew off the corncrib S & N walls and was largely destroyed. All the inside, including the tools & seeds, is covered with snow. This involves sufficient loss of time & money to constitute a lesson. It is one more of those things which, for lack of doing it through to the end, involved a good deal of extra work & expense. The goat fencing was another example. We should have put up the outside boards the very afternoon of the morning we put up the paper, but instead filled in the S. foundation. There is little justification for shifting about from job to job like that; less still for leaving a job unfinished in a way which threatens to undo all the work done on it. The rule for the future ought to be: if a thing is worth doing at all, it is worth doing properly."

Alfred: We always "hoped it would be all right," and things happened that meant it wasn't all right.

"From a subsistence point of view, the loss of building paper, working hours, and tools through rust & decay are evidence that we have not yet weighed up in earnest the meaning of a simplified life on a subsistence basis. About 2:30 the snowplow came up. A. told them that since Norma wasn't here, they needn't bother, but she would be glad to hear that they could come up. Herbert went down to the village while A. dehorned Dinah and dehoofed [trimmed] Patrick."

Norma, in Maine, received a letter, undated but it must have been in early December, from Bill Clark, evidently a medical professional of some kind associated with Gould Farm,[34] to whom Norma had evidently written in her despair. From his language he may be British and therefore someone Norma would be drawn to:

"I have no kind of assurance that talking with me would help at all, but that you opened the possibility makes me loath to accept its being closed untried. Since yours is a matter which has extended over some years [perhaps referring to Alfred's abuse], hurry is not as desperately necessary as it may seem. 'Irrevocable' decisions and deeds do not prove to be irrevocable at all, since the recent moves are not the crucial ones, and a solution of the earlier, crucial ones carries the solution of all else along rather readily.

"Whereas apparently things are 'building up,' [and] becoming more and more difficult and intense and insuperable, the fact is that resolution of the initial problem makes later problems sink in significance. Suppose you have moved, that is rather inconsequential compared to the real matter which started the series of events which led on to this.

"The point is this: there is plenty of time still. A few weeks are agony enough, but not cataclysmic, not final. I am anxious to try to be the stimulator to help you think back to the point of insight, and forward to renewal. I frankly think you would do better to go to a good psychiatrist. I cannot bring expert analysis and suggestion; I can only bring a rather intelligent and very warm sympathy, developed out of some rather agonizing personal experience. But you turned to me for some reason, and if a feeling holds, my reaction holds as well: I should like to come, or have you come here. As a passing but not unsuggestive thought, would you like to come to Gould Farm for a bit? I should be very grateful to be asked to come up to see you a

---

34. Gould Farm was "A residential therapeutic community dedicated to helping adults with mental health and related challenges move toward recovery, health and greater independence through community living, meaningful work, and clinical care."

few weeks from now; I should be delighted to see you here. Or if you wish to let it drop, say the word. If you have no definite feelings one way or another, let me come to you. The matter has become of deep concern to me, because I was so taken by you and your family. I cannot believe it insoluble."

Norma replied, writing from Sebasco:

"Dear Bill: I do appreciate your letter, but I can't say much at present except that I am away from home taking the vacation that seemed an absolute necessity, and don't know when I shall be back. I do hope and intend to go back, but I have somehow to get back my strength, and some extra strength too, to face an almost impossible situation, and also I have to make some other arrangements for the children, for this winter at least.

"My hope is to go back to Hilltop around the 15th of the month. If I don't solve the problems I can't go back, because I don't feel it is wise to expose myself again to a strain under which I shall almost certainly crack and greatly increase my own and other people's unhappiness. I would like above everything to visit Gould Farm for a while—when I was there, I longed to stay—but I have things to do before I can consider anything like that.

"It's true that no one action or event in itself is irrevocable. But it's also true that in a long series of events, sooner or later a point will be reached after which there is really no turning back, even though no one event in the series was any more significant than all those that went before. I felt I had to go when I did or they might have taken me out of there finally on a stretcher, or in a straight [sic] jacket! It seemed the best way of preventing the irrevocable. Here I am among friends, the children can go to school, and I am able to feel a release of strain and see things in a more rational light.

"If and when I get back to Hilltop, it would be grand to have you come and visit us, but I hope you won't leave your [newly pregnant] wife if her health is the way you say. So many of my own troubles I can trace back to unexpected troubles during my first pregnancy." Norma may be referring to her health, or to Alfred's failure to be supportive.

Norma wrote to Janet Hall from Sebasco, repeating much of what she had earlier written to Alfred. Some excerpts:

"My dear Janet: Your [letter] of November 9th reached me just as I was making plans for a vacation that was so much needed that I ran around like a chicken without a head (not that I've ever seen a chicken do that, actually. [They do.]) Packing and unpacking suitcases, looking up trains and changing my mind, and altogether exhibiting a fine case of feminine indecision.

"Next time [Walter] makes one of his descents (or ascents) tell him that, a) I know I owe him a letter, and b) that I am ordering some Bach arrangements for 2 recorders, unaccompanied, and look forward to perfect orgies of counterpoint at Hilltop from now on. I am having a severe struggle with the urge to blow a whole twenty-five dollars (which since taking this vacation I definitely can't spare) on a tenor recorder. But our neighbors over the hill have at least one. When you and Larry come up to visit us, we'll have quartets and quintets and sextets to our heart's content. Wouldn't Larry get a thrill out of playing recorder duets with Scott Nearing?

"Part of my mental agony was not being able to decide what to do for the winter. On the one hand I felt utterly incapable of facing what threatened to be an early and long winter with the children in the existing conditions (only one room warm-able, no place to do the laundry, no wood cut for the stoves and so on). [Reading between the lines, one could infer, "and a husband who might fly into an abusive rage without warning." Norma had experienced this at times, even as a newlywed, and it was why she felt the children needed to be somewhere else during the claustrophobic winter months.]

"I am expecting to be back at Hilltop on the 15th. I feel so much better [that] I believe I could cope with almost anything. I hope in my absence Alfred will have fixed the new pump and sink drain in the kitchen and cut piles of wood so we can be warm. We have excellent stoves and there's no reason why the parts of the house we live in shouldn't be warm, though I don't suppose we'll bother heating the bedrooms except in case of illness.

"Come and see us, bringing recorders and skis!"

Continuing the journal: "No further snowfall, but a 15 degree cold, or 10, acc. to the outside thermometer. Once the morning chores were done at 10:30 H. felt it was too gusty to attempt chopping in the morning. A. was feeling under the weather & not keen to go out, so both sat around mending or reading. The days are short anyway, and the space of time between milkings, once meals and washing & cleaning are out of the way, water fetched & wood chopped, isn't long."

Next day: "A nice morning, not too windy, fine for chopping. The dishes (wooden bowls and jelly glasses—jelly used to come in decorated glasses which could then be used at the table) & cleaning were done by about 12 & both went to the North birch-spruce-poplar grove to chop. A. felt weak & uncertain & soon came in & wrapped in a blanket, but H. continued to chop." (*Alfred*: I never realized that I had yielded to nature to that extent. Very strange.) [Alfred's habit was simply to ignore any kind of physical ailment and wait for the body to heal itself.]

"Snow fell again. After milking there was the third process on Ramsay's hide, the German reading, the spinning & then an evening of reading. A. fell asleep reading [Gregory] Vlastos' *Christian Faith & Democracy* [1939] but was able to read *The D.A. Draws A Circle* [Erle Stanley Gardner] until 12:30. H. always settles down in a corner, alternately snoozing & standing up, from about 8 on."

1942

Alfred wrote to Philip on December 5:

"I am very glad Norma has had this time with you, and only wish she had considered staying longer, if the way seemed open from your point of view. I hope you have had a chance to talk fully. It seems clear to me that within a general framework of similarity, she and I want quite different things. I have never learned exactly what it was she wanted to do, and this has made it difficult to come to an understanding. I want to try to tell you what I want to do, partly as a clarification of my own thought. Perhaps you can find out any points on which she and I may be in agreement."

He went on to explain, at considerable length, his vision of a just and peaceful society. Some excerpts:

"Having formulated the theory that a man must be able to live by the work of his hands or else there would be no human race [!], I wanted to put this theory to the test. This means actually doing the work by hand in the first instance, to see what the results are of the labor expended; as a corollary it involves simplifying the work so it can be done by hand. This means bringing our needs, for the purpose of the experiment, within the limits reachable by hand labor.

"I see, therefore, a need to enjoy an abundance of what we can readily produce; but draw in tight and skimp to the utmost on those things which are beyond our sphere of production. This is, I believe, the point where Norma and I are in fundamental disagreement. I am convinced of the need to bring cash expenditure down to the level where it is humanly possible to meet it by extra labor, but she believes we should bring our productive capacity up to the level where it coincides with our cash needs.

"My problem is, should I throw in my lot with Norma in what she appears to want, and if I don't, what alternative have I? Just to stick out like a sore thumb all the rest of my life, thinking in terms of another life I might have been living, which would have seemed to be making a contribution to the world's need, but which was impossible because Norma wouldn't share in it? Do I exist for the world or for Norma? And even if I exist for her, does that mean that her judgment is in every case correct and I should follow it? But if I don't follow it, what alternative have I? It is because I have not always followed it in the past that serious breaches have occurred."

During this time Norma had been making arrangements for the children to go to a small farm school in Pawling, New York, which she had visited and felt would be a safe and educational place for them to be. Unfortunately, the children's sojourn there, especially Piers' because of his social reticence, was for the most part negative, as they were often bullied for looking and sounding (they still had their English accents) different, and lacking the other children's life and family experiences.

The journal continued: "More snowfall, but apparently not so cold. Herbert reports an egg production average of one daily, for eleven hens. A. worked on the goat & money accounts & wrote letters; H. read & chopped." (*Alfred*: According to the records that I tried to keep, it cost us more to produce our own eggs than it would have cost to buy them in the village. The wood was green; the tar dripped down the chimney. It was all stone, so nothing was nearby to ignite. It took us three years to learn that it's a mistake to burn green wood. Fortunately, we never had a chimney fire.)

Alfred typed a note to himself:

"Further reflections after chopping, Monday Dec. 7.

"We have just worked eight hours from 8 till 4, cutting about 250 feet of hardwood logs, worth about $3.50. This represents two men's time for a full day, with frosted feet, nipped fingers, slips on the logs, tumbles in the snow and so on. We found we could only saw about an inch through the big log, then rest; then another inch and rest.

"It is fun, in a way, in itself, and useful if it's for something. In a normal week we might be able to work three days at it and earn $13.50 if the sawyer accepts the logs & the measurements. Since the other days are likely to be snowy, windy, or unsuitable, it means suspending other outdoor jobs to do even that. In the spring the gnats would be formidable, and gardening would have to be brought to a minimum to carry a three-day logging week. By sticking to it, two men might bring in $400 a year if all went well.

"But what's the use? Norma proposes to spend $900 in four months sending the children to school [they had a generous scholarship and Alfred's father paid most of the tuition], plus journeys for the three of them, plus a lot of clothing [most of the necessary clothing was hand-me-downs from Mrs. Spruyt] & incidentals. What is the use of sawing inch by inch through a log, if the product is to be scattered to the winds?"

The emotional needs and education of his children were not on Alfred's mind. Children were viewed only as a drain on limited resources.

"If today's work bought us a sack of soybeans, it would be worthwhile; but if it only buys the children a new pair of shoes because they left their old ones lying around up in the woods, it is not worthwhile. Just as essential as for us to chop wood, is for the children to learn to take care of their things. And so, I find when Norma buys needlessly, I feel if only she knew what sweat, what patience it takes to cut a large tree; if she had to do it herself, she would find it was less work and more satisfactory to not buy those things. [He felt that children should experience the consequences of their unheeding behavior: let them go barefoot, or shiver, or feel hunger! This would be a valuable lesson. It would serve them right, to use a favorite expression.]

"I cannot escape the feeling that if she is going to spend freely, then let's all spend freely—have done with it, and do no work, and buy everything. Would you weigh out your feed ounce by ounce to the animals to have it last the winter if someone came along after you and upset the sacks & scattered it all around? Surely you would think, if I am to weigh the feed & conserve it at feeding time, others must be equally careful to conserve it at other times. We must all work together. That is what I feel. I do not feel in the least like earning money in the woods unless the outcome is just as carefully handled as the income is laborious, but if the household & the workers would cooperate & both work effectively, it would be a going concern.

"Apart from the educational rightness or wrongness, I am afraid sending the children to an expensive school will have an unfavorable psychological result, for if we can afford to spend money on ourselves (or children) that freely, in spite of the poverty & suffering in the world, there is little point in laboring steadily just to increase by a mite the amount to be spent. Why, if the children came home a month early, we would have money enough [saved] to see us through the rest of the year without productive activity.

"Surely if the children go away it is a confession to the world that we think farm life is unsuitable for children; that we think that Vermont is too cold for children; that we could not advise anyone to undertake a community project if he has children. I realize they are being sent away for other reasons: namely because my increasing sense of frustration in what I most wanted vented itself on them or in their presence. And their being sent away of course will increase the basis of my frustration, as our project now is to become patently invalid as a way of family living.

"I have always thought it was not right to maintain a special standard as between parents and children. If the parents feel the laws in one country are unjust & migrate to another [as his own grandfather Joshua had done, leaving Ireland to come to Pennsylvania in 1880 as a protest against mandated vaccination], the children should share in that & go with them. It is difficult for me, then, to see that I ought to feel that one way of life is right (as I thought this was) without feeling it is right for families as well as adults. To remove the children from it is a confession that it is not right. [Perhaps the word "realization" should be substituted for confession. Alfred never understood that children are not miniature adults, with adult judgment, patience, and self-control, and was harsh in his response to perceived failures in these respects.]

"Circumstances here were not ideal for them, but could have been made so. That could be said of many other aspects of this farm. So instead of making a home here, the home is to be broken up. Instead of sharing all together on a level of life accessible to all mankind, the children are to go to a school accessible only to the rich. Unless we pull together [read: do things my way], we shall just go on being pulled asunder. I think it is too much of this sort of thing that has put me on edge & made it seem undesirable for the children to remain with us. Though the remedy is worse than the disease."

December 9: "Chopped at same place to the S. of the road, on a beech tree, & stacked up half a cord above the first one. Knocked off at 2 for A. to go to village. He returned & had milked by 7."

Alfred: That was one reason I objected to Norma's trips to the village. We had lots of work to be done on the farm, and she would simply drop the work and decide to walk to the village, completely oblivious of the work waiting to be done. It was the mail that made life livable for Norma. For the rest of us, if we got the mail once a week, that was perfect. She wanted to keep up with it, her mind was on that, but my mind was on the firewood and so on, which wasn't a reality to her.

December 10: "Cooking day. Somewhat warmer, thawing around midday. No snowfall. Herbert set himself to launder & sharpen saws. A. set himself to bake bread, put up storm windows & clean the goat barn. But the trouble is, so many various small jobs intervene. The sink had to be unfrozen; the green wood wouldn't get the oven up to proper heat, the goats had to be let out, & there are always small jobs to do [in the barn] and water to carry for them. The outhouse had to be emptied & first unfrozen. So nothing moves quickly. One can spend a lot of time trying to make a fire burn.

"Nineteen pounds of bread got baked, partly with soybeans and partly with roasted wheat kernels. One storm window got shaved down, fitted & painted & 6 goat stalls were hurriedly cleaned out. The tanning of Ramsay's hide was finished, with doubtful results on the skin side, though a nice fur on the wool side. Mashed potato & jelly for supper. A. fixed the reservoir so the spring water would play on the pump suction pipe, in the hope of keeping the latter from freezing above water level. Dinah spent the night under the barn.

"Herbert decided to return to Bennington, because he did not feel that life at Hilltop would be self-sustaining from the time Norma returned, and would as soon live off his family in Bennington [Vermont] as the Jacob family in West Chester [who were providing funds to sustain Hilltop]." (*Alfred*: My father had started to distribute his estate and we all benefited. It wasn't much, but a little money went a long way on the farm. Herbert may have had the idea of living off somebody else, and he had his family in Bennington that he could live off.)

"Herbert and A. went down to Jamaica, whence Herbert departed. The gasoline people had authorized a ration, so A. walked up again to fetch [the ration book] then down again, then up again, a total of 16 miles. This amounts to a whole working day spent on the truck. Inspected Jackson house improvements & chatted with Wallace Crowninshield."

Letter from Caroline Nicholson Jacob, Alfred's stepmother, to Norma on December 12:

"From thy letter I presume you are leaving Maine today. It isn't such sunny weather here as Florida [where they customarily spent the winter months] ought to have, but outside our window are green trees and flowers and hanging bunches of grapefruit, which is no doubt very different from the landscape you will be passing through.

"Thy letter and one from Alfred arrived in the same mail this morning, and we will hasten to answer so that we may reach thee at Brattleboro early next week.

"We do approve of your going ahead with the Manumit School idea. Father suggests that he advance an additional 'principal' gift of $330 which will cover the $80 deposit and the first two monthly payments. This would care for additional monthly payments with some left over for your own expenses, and in the meantime you and father together could go ahead more slowly to make some sort of permanent trust arrangement."

December 14: "Thermometer at 6 below. Decided house insulation was the most urgent task. Discovered that extreme cold robs one of vigor & initiative. Decided to leave a log in the evening so it could be sawn first thing in the morning. Internal heat is worth more than external. Nailed on all storm windows without fitting, that is, placing them over the aperture rather than in it. Working was not unpleasant once circulation was aroused. Sitting around is fatal. I was wearing two undershirts, shirt, two sweaters, chore coat with Ramsay sewn in the back, and sheepskin corduroy coat. Indoor temperature didn't get up to 32°. Put lamp under water tank with low flame. Harold Field came over in the afternoon with the mail & a Christmas present of nuts. Invited me to spend the night with them, but I didn't feel easy about breaking away. He appreciated the bread & took 9 lb of soybeans."

December 15: "Library stove smoked during the night. It doesn't do to turn the damper off when there is green wood on the fire. The kettle was boiling when I came down. Apparently it is yellow birch that works wonders with a fire. It occurred to me that wasting and saving time are geometrical progressions, not arithmetical. Not lighting the kitchen stove this morning saved time twice over, by not having to chop for it and not having to tend it. Finished putting Celotex [over the windows] in bathroom, 1 main room, 1 library and half a library window."

Wednesday December 16: "Placed rockwool in the ceiling above the cellar entrance & to the west. At 3:30 walked to the village & was there when Norma arrived at dusk. [No mention of the children.] I had worked several hours to get the truck ready to go & it was lucky I didn't risk it, because the ration [for gas] hadn't come.[35] 800 lb of agricultural phosphate came. We put all the luggage & a basket of oranges on the sled & pulled it up with great difficulty to the lumber camp, where it upset & we left some things. [The implication of "We left some things" is telling.

Imagine their mental and physical state at that point.] On arrival the thermometer read 15° below zero, & at bedtime 18° below.

The next morning it was still at 18° below, but the spring was still running and the goats still alive. The children spent all day in the library with a roaring fire. Alfred chopped wood while Norma unpacked and cooked. The next day she did laundry, wrote letters, and baked bread while Alfred chopped more wood and did chores around the house.

Alfred: So now Norma was making a big adjustment. Philip had persuaded her to come back [not so, he encouraged her to stay longer!]. She tried to do what she believed to be her duty, so she deserves a word of praise for that. I'm sure it was a bleak return.

Norma responded to mother-in-law Caroline on December 18:

"We left Maine on Saturday morning and went to our good friends the Spruyts at Greenfield. Mrs. Spruyt turned out a huge pile of outgrown clothing; she has three children all going to school (two at Putney, one at the University of Minnesota) and they are all growing so fast that their clothes never wear out. There were heaps of wonderful things that either fitted our children or could be easily altered—leather jackets, thick socks, underwear, work shirts and overalls, all just the kind of thing they need. So I spent three days very busily altering, mending and sewing on name tapes, and there's practically nothing now we shall need to buy for the children except shoes, raincoats and more socks—the school list calls for eight pairs each! How glad I am that it's the kind of school where smart clothes are not required. They wear work clothes practically the whole time.

"We came home Wednesday afternoon. It was pretty cold and Piers' cold still wasn't quite better, but the Spruyt children came home from school

---

35. Gas rationing was instituted during World War II (1942), in order to help control gasoline usage. The U.S. Office of Price Administration (OPA) rationed gasoline on May 15, 1942, on the East Coast, and nationwide that December, to assist in the war effort, which had created massive shortages.

and [would have] had to sleep on the floor and anyway I was afraid if we waited longer it would get even colder. As it turned out, we picked the coldest day of the winter so far—when we finally staggered up to the house, our baggage thermometer said fifteen below zero. I would rather not have brought them back, but there seemed nowhere else to go for Christmas without putting someone else to a lot of expense and inconvenience.

"We are slowly getting on with putting the house into some kind of shape—for adults, that is. But the winter started early and has been exceptionally cold even up to now (when lots of people reckon winter hasn't even started) and my being away for nearly four weeks didn't help at all. A good beginning has been made with the kitchen, which of course is what I feel most strongly about as it's where I have to do most of my work.

"I'm much relieved that you approve of [the school plan]. How to provide the children with the things they ought to have, without sacrificing the experiment Alfred feels so strongly about, has been a perfect nightmare to us during the last few months. Much as I regret having the children go so far away for so long, I will draw a deep breath of relief from the constant load of worry when they are safely delivered to a place where they have civilized amenities and proper supervision.

"We are looking for a long-promised visit from the Bacons one of these days. What to do about them next year I don't know. I feel almost certain Judy would never be happy in the kind of conditions that have to be met by anyone that wants to live here. She simply wants to do what Fran wants and that is not a satisfactory basis for pioneering—you have to want it for yourself too. And more than one person has spoken about Fran's reputation for instability, which is another thing there isn't much room for here. On the whole I shall not be very surprised or disappointed if they decide they don't want to come back—though best of all would be if they decided they did want to come back, and meet the conditions as they actually exist.

"Much love and best Christmas wishes to you both."

Saturday morning the temperature was 10° below zero. Norma got letters ready and Alfred did small jobs, going to the village in the afternoon. All the talk in the post office was about the cold weather. When he returned it was 18° below, and got steadily colder. By morning it was 31° below.

December 21: "Wind. Library was 24°, with the fire out. Parlor stove still burning, but the heat loss is too great in that room. A. was expecting to begin work on the kitchen sink as soon as the routine jobs were out of the way. He chopped wood for the various fires, dealt with the goats, who now get a hot feed of beet pulp & calving ration at midday, mixed up 3 weeks supply of a mixture of corn, oats, wheat, 32% supplement, soybean meal, bran, and alfalfa leaf meal, thawed and emptied the outhouse, carried water, got in boards to be thawing for the carpentry jobs, and by that time it was night."

Alfred: For me it all had a purpose [the salvation of mankind], but I think for Norma it didn't, and that made it all the harder for her.

December 22: "Morning temp about 6° above. Wind again. N. baked, did laundry & routine jobs. A. worked all day on the new kitchen sink, and by about midnight it was in place in its essential structure. A. had stomach upset." (*Alfred*: I cut the drainpipe for the sink too long, so the sink was unusually high, and I had to make a little platform for people to stand on while working at the sink.)

December 23: "Norma went down and fetched up Reg and Rica Brown [friends she had made at Dartmouth] in the afternoon. In her absence Harold Field came over to invite us all for Christmas, so we invited him. Further work on sink."

December 24: "A. worked all day to get the sink painted and functioning. The others made the usual Christmas preparations [Teresa remembers a tree with tiny red candles clipped to the branches, an alarming fire hazard!] and tried skiing, but the snow was too soft. Reg dealt with the firewood."

Alfred: They were staying in New York and they didn't realize what conditions we ... nobody would realize what the conditions were [like] up at Hilltop until they experienced it.

December 25, Christmas Day: "A. and Reg decided to chop, but by the time A. had the multifarious chores and jobs done there was no time left. [Alfred returns again and again to this complaint.] Chicken dinner. The Nearings, Fields and Mr. Stark's housekeeper came over in the afternoon, with children."

December 26: "Again planned to chop, & since the goats and chores were out of the way by 12, we did about 2 hours, and skied in the afternoon. N. went to the village. Rica scrubbed, puttied & painted the kitchen. Temperature declined towards zero in the evening."

Monday December 28: "The Browns left. Reg managed to ski down, though there was an ice crust on top of the snow. Rica tried part way. The walk up was tiresome."

Alfred: When I was teaching at Dartmouth it seems to me one day Norma went out and bought a complete set of skis and boots and all the equipment, which she never used [above references notwithstanding]. Just like the horse, which she never used. [The horse, Dickie—see following chapter—was actually used quite a bit. Alfred could never let go of his resentment about the purchase of Dickie.]

On December 29 and 30 there was sleet freezing on the trees, which became so heavily laden that branches were breaking with almost continual gunshot-like sounds in the forest.

Thursday, December 31, the last day of the year, remained icy. Alfred spent the day alternating between the goats and the woodpile. The snow in the woods was too deep to carry logs down, but they came singly on the sled.

There was some conversation in the evening about the future of Hilltop, inconclusive. Alfred felt that economic self-sufficiency must be abandoned as an aim, since they were obviously not heading toward it. He felt that the abandonment of all religious emphasis, and loss of contacts with like-minded others, had placed Hilltop on a simple family basis.

Norma retained hopes of gathering together a group that would then work out its own economic basis. Alfred felt that too much time was being spent on wood chopping, goat herding, water carrying, and other routine jobs that were meaningless in themselves [at least as far as the salvation of civilization was concerned] and wasteful of time, unless the end in view was laudable.

Failing to see any such end in view, or to convince others of its importance, he was inclined to give it over and put the farm on a cash basis for things like food, clothing, travel, and more particularly the children's education—which, in his opinion, would consume more cash in six months than two men could earn in a year in the woods, and therefore render their efforts virtually meaningless.

1943

There is so infinitely more to this business of living together happily than meets the eye, and so much of what is, and must remain, invisible and intangible is at the same time so vitally important that one's inner resistance fails when it is lacking for too long.

January 1943

NORMA WENT DOWN TO THE VILLAGE and reported that many trees had been blown across the road. On Sunday the 3rd, she and the children left for Manumit,[36] the farm school in Pawling, New York, often sliding down on the thick snow crust.

Alfred wrote letters in the morning, and in the afternoon boiled a 20-pound pumpkin, made pumpkin pie, made "crumpets" out of a yeast sponge kept from Norma's last baking, roasted pumpkin seeds, finished making two batches of marmalade from the oranges sent by his father in Florida, and worked on other routine tasks. He didn't cook in Norma's absence, just warmed up porridge boiled the night before. In the evening he ate mashed pumpkin "with bits of bread or potato."

A letter to Norma from Janet Hall on Pendle Hill stationery is dated January 4. Some excerpts:

"We all want to know about Piers and Teresa. Are they with you at Hilltop (supposing you are at Hilltop)? You must have a veritable fiery furnace if you can keep even one room up to 60° with the competition you have from the elements. Mary Evans [head of housekeeping, who later married Walter Bethel, for a short time one of the Hilltop pioneers] says we must keep Pendle Hill down to 65°, which seemed a hardship at first, but the Midwinter Institute old women are here, and we stoke hourly and the place seems stifling. Usually the office is slightly below 60°, and the hands have a tendency to congeal, as you probably know very well.

---

36. Manumit School (the name in Latin means "freedom from slavery") was founded in 1924 as an elementary level, coeducational boarding school on a working farm. Closely associated with a number of New York City labor unions, it was intended to provide a progressive type of "workers education" during a time of increasing socialist optimism in America. Scott Nearing's wife, Nellie Seeds, was the director in 1927/28. It was there that Scott met Helen Knothe, who was the music teacher.

"The Brudercoop[37] is talking of moving out to the country where vegetables can be raised. You know that they have had a negro living with them for some months, apparently without interference from the neighbors. I think the police visits are greatly minimized now, too.

"I suppose your own grapevine has told you that Arle Brooks is back in prison. A boy from P.H. went to the county jail today—a case of someone with clergy status who sent back his papers & went down to the FBI to report.

"Mary and Edith and Larry and Walter all send regards.

"P.S. I neglected to tell you the sad news by cable today that the ship on which Tom Tanner sailed for India about a month ago has been torpedoed and all passengers and crew are missing. One hears of such miraculous savings that perhaps this may be the case here too, but it is a great shock."

Norma returned from Manumit on the 9th, having spent the night with friends in Brattleboro.

On an unknown date she wrote to Ed [no last name given]:

"Dear Ed, You will think we never received your letter—indeed we did, and were very glad to have it. I took it with me when I went for a short visit to Maine, thinking there I would be sure to have time for letter-writing, but my brother-in-law's typewriter proved so erratic that writing with it was rather more of a pain than a pleasure, and since having a machine of my own I have almost lost the use of my hands when it comes to holding a pen! And as letter-writing is one of my chief pleasures, I like it to be unhindered by mechanical defects, so I put off all my correspondence yet once more. I wouldn't be writing letters today probably, if the weather weren't so bad.

"Your letter was particularly welcome because it fell in the middle of a period of deep discouragement due to fatigue and a feeling of having failed in most of what we set out to do this summer. But if people like you like coming to see us, then we (so to speak) have not lived in vain, even if we didn't get the carrots harvested in time. Carrots or company? Me for the company every time. But what a pity it is that even though a man can't live by bread alone, he still has not found out how to live without it. The tug-of-war between the demands of the soul and those of the stomach sometimes threaten to tear us in two. [Truly a prophetic statement.]

"It is funny that you in your semi-militaristic environment are getting, as you say, more hopeful about the possibilities of educating people, while

---

37. A cooperative household on North 24th Street in Philadelphia, modeled on the Bruderhof, "a Christian movement that practices community of goods," something Hilltop aspired to and that Pendle Hill more or less achieved.

we find ourselves moving the other way. Pacifists (beginning with ourselves) do seem rather a hopeless lot. I think our worst trouble is complacency, the feeling we have chosen the right path and are automatically justified thereby. There have been moments when I've felt I could respect myself more if I did an honest day's work in an honest defense factory with honest people who knew what they wanted (even if it were a lesser good) and meant to have it. Don't mistake me, I have no doubt at all as to which is the right course, I just am rather considerably discouraged at the moment about the caliber of the people who have chosen to follow it. Quite possibly they just show up worse because they are attempting much more.

"At present we are alone, though expecting a further accretion any minute—Eleanor Garst (whose husband is doing 5 years in Danbury) and Herb Willits. They are leaving their comfortable jobs in New York because of the new Victory tax[38] and want to become permanent settlers, but they are choosing the very worst time of year to start, and I am somewhat afraid for their morale. A prolonged dose of zero weather, in this very imperfectly-insulated house, with the thick blanket of snow making it impossible for them even to see the promised land—that would demoralize almost anyone. It certainly would me.

"Lowell, when we last had direct news of him, was dishwashing at the big hotel in Northfield, Mass. He seemed very enthusiastic about it. Lately however, we have had communications suggesting he is either with Gordon Goley in Manchester, N.H. (was Gordon here when you came?) or planning to return to his sister's home in Iowa. A letter or card to the Hotel Northfield might reach him, however.

"The Bacons got scared (not unnaturally) at the prospect of wintering up here with the baby, and accepted an offer to spend the winter taking care of a friend's farm in West Bridgewater, Vermont, where it looked as though material conditions would be better, but judging from Judy's letter they have not proved to be so much better after all. Their idea has been to return here in April and help get the house in shape so we can spend next winter more pleasantly. We are expecting a visit from them one of these days, having in fact been expecting it for 2 weeks, during which the weather has been impossible for traveling."

Nanny goat Euphonia was discovered to have no teeth, no doubt explaining why she didn't eat hay.

At the end of the week the road commissioner came up and said the road could not be plowed, but he'd do anything else he could to help. Since

---

38. Congress had passed legislation imposing a Victory Tax of 5% upon net income in excess of $624 for each taxable year, beginning after December 31, 1942.

1943

no gasoline could therefore be obtained, time was spent sawing wood, barrowing manure, and carrying logs. Alfred spent time writing a paper for the *Intentional Subsistence Pacifist*.

On Sunday the 8th Mr. Eastman came up and decided to buy Beatrice Goat.

Norma wrote to Dear Friends [Leslie and Valerie Johnston, in Canada] on January 10:

"I suppose this ban on pleasure driving is going to cut out finally your projected visit down here. Would you like us to see whether we can send the skis? Railway express would be very roundabout and expensive, but the local carrier could take them up as far as Londonderry and maybe you know some way of getting them beyond that point.

"I am just back from depositing the children at school. Two or three letters have come saying they are settling in nicely, so I hope all is for the best, but does one ever know? On the way home I stopped for four days at Gould Farm, which is a good place to be when one is as tired as I was by Monday night. Friday morning, I was to have been driven to the nearest place to get an early bus home, but the ban on pleasure driving stopped that, so I came a long way around and didn't fetch up in Brattleboro till 6 p.m.

"To fill the time before the Jamaica bus left at 10:30 I went into Bob White's church where there was a service going on, and afterwards he and his wife invited me up to the house and persuaded me to stay the night, as it was getting so very cold. What with one thing and another I didn't get back from my jaunt till midday yesterday. Now I have to get the children's things packed into a trunk and take it down the hill tomorrow. The ice storm blocked our road so completely that we had to leave on foot with a few things in suitcases, however the road gang did a nice job and it is open again, plowed out as far as lumber camp corner.

"This morning Alfred and I had a Brains Trust session and had several bright ideas. We both feel (though for slightly different reasons) that the original plan with which we came here is gone with the wind, and a new one must be made right away. The trouble about that is that as we are the only people on the spot at the crucial time, we will have to make the plan. But I believe in any case we should have to decide before this next summer exactly what we want to do.

"First, Alfred feels the garden the last two summers has been too big; no one but himself has cared to work in it, and it has taken all his time and energy and he has not been able to join in much of the other work that was being done. In one or two things we had a bigger crop than we needed or could harvest without help. So, this year he plans to reduce the acreage for vegetables for family consumption by at least half and put the rest of the enclosed area under root vegetables for goats and experimental patches of various cereals, I mean grains. The smaller acreage can be dug by hand, and with intensive cultivation there won't be nearly so much time weeding or thinning the rows, and most likely we can get practically as much as we did from the larger area.

"He thinks we ought to cut down on the canning. It's quite true that took an appalling amount of my time in September and October, but still, when I open the jars of peas or green beans, I feel it has been worthwhile. This probably needs more consideration. I think most likely I shan't embark on such a big canning program this next fall unless I am reasonably sure another woman will be there to work with me, because by the time I had sealed and stacked the 300th quart I was practically dead.

"Second idea: why don't we have a little extra-community cooperative farming? As a nucleus we have ourselves, the Fields and possibly Eleanor Garst and Herb Willits, whom we expect here tomorrow. Why shouldn't we do something like this: the three families (or four if you are in, unless we count Hilltop as one family) join together to pay the cash cost of, say, 50 day-old chicks, a brooder and the necessary feed. One party (say, ourselves) takes entire charge of said chicks till they are pullets. By raising 100 instead of 50 and selling them locally we might even get back the original cash investment (but see below). Then we combine similarly to buy three or four young pigs and get Harold Field, maybe, to raise them and slaughter them when the time comes. We could all help if he would just stick in the knife. Oh, I remember, Fran is an expert on hogs, isn't he?! [*Teresa*: I witnessed a pig-sticking at Mrs. Kuusela's house and have never forgotten the grisly procedure, with the animal suspended from a tree branch by its hind legs. The origin of the expression "bled like a stuck pig" was clear.]

"Then the same plan might be followed with something else like a hive or two of bees. Alfred also suggested the possibility of getting a Jersey heifer and using her milk as a source of extra fat, that is, making all or most of the cream into butter, salting it down to keep the year round, and feeding the skim milk to pigs and poultry. No reason why this shouldn't be on a cooperative basis too. Harold Field is probably going to get a cow too, why shouldn't he get a couple [of them] while he's about it?"

Sensible as they seemed, Norma's ideas did not catch on.

The children's trunk was packed and taken to the village. Brother Edward's raccoon coat, which he was donating, was brought back up. (*Alfred*: When he was at Dartmouth it was the style of being a 'college man.' He tried to sell it to me for $35 but I refused, and eventually he gave it to us. It was a good source of warmth.) The next day, while Alfred was digging turnips in the frozen garden in 14° temperature, Eleanor Garst and Herb

1943

Willits arrived. Eleanor had left her half-written book on philosophy on the bus, and had to start over again.

Alfred and Herb took Beatrice down to deliver to Mr. Eastman, "riding part way on a load of Wallace Crowninshield's logs." Beatrice was lodged "in a cozy house under the chicken house." Alfred and Herb lunched luxuriously on creamed potatoes. Alfred helped Mr. Crowninshield load the two new Angora goats, in their crate. (*Alfred*: My recollection is that they had come all the way from Texas.) The goats—in their crate—were dragged part way on the sled, then encouraged to walk. "After much struggle they more or less learned to walk, but wanted to browse all the time." Norma and Eleanor met them at Lumbercamp Corner.

That evening they worked out a planting plan, aiming for great variety in a small space. "It can probably be done by crop succession and by alternating hills of early and late corn, early and late tomatoes, and spacing certain things like carrots close, and using dwarf varieties to the full, which won't cast much shade."

The Angoras settled in and seemed comfortable. Herb made the fires and Eleanor got breakfast, with some difficulty, in the dark. In the afternoon Herb and Eleanor went to the village and Alfred made a goat harness and attempted to persuade billy goat Patrick to pull the sled, without noticeable success. Herb and Eleanor returned, wondering how long it would take to become used to the trudge up and down the mountain! They had left their luggage, which Mr. Crowninshield was to bring up as far as the Jackson's.

The next day it was much warmer—the temperature went above freezing! Three people went down, through seven or eight inches of drifting snow, to collect the luggage. Mr. C. had not yet brought anything, so they returned, "rather glad there had been nothing to carry." Alfred went to chop a yellow birch on the Pikes Falls road and found the snow sometimes waist deep.

Alfred worked on his paper on subsistence pacifism. The road commissioner brought some of the luggage and offered to pay $20 if the owners collected it themselves, since the road couldn't be plowed. "We arranged to carry it for 40¢ an hour as if we were working on the road." (Perhaps that is a misprint, as it would require *fifty* man-hours of labor to earn the proffered $20 at that rate.) The wood supply had gotten low, but the snow was still deep. Lulu still hadn't produced a kid.

The next day there was sleet most of the day, with wind and drifting. Herb was learning to manage the fires, which kept going out. Alfred's idea of making the breakfast porridge the night before was not taken up, nor was the suggestion of making double the amount of coffee for dinner and saving half of it in a thermos bottle for morning. Although Alfred had intended to chop wood, he first had to finish the following jobs in the barn: "Made a door between the barn floor and the south end, fixed a narrow entrance to the secondary kidding pen so that the sheep couldn't get in and the Angoras could, fixed a feeding rack for sheep and another for Angoras, blocked up two large gaps in the outer siding where snow blows in in quantities, covered two windows with sacks, closed off ¾ of the door near Patrick, which is normally open to let the sheep in and out, cut off a draft from Lulu's kidding pen and from the top of the milking room door, blocked up a large hole on the west side where the wind blows in on the rabbits, rubbed all the goats in lime except Leona and Harriet [? possibly to control parasites], and cleaned out manure from [three stalls]." He found that it took one hour to cut, carry, and buck (cut to stove length) a five-inch yellow birch, and one and a quarter hours to split it and stack it near the stove.

On Tuesday and Wednesday there was great trouble starting the fires because the wood was so green. Very cold. Herb kept going out for more wood and Norma knitted him a pair of mittens in record time. Herb overslept the next morning. Alfred carried up—on his head—a 100-pound sack of feed from Lumbercamp Corner where the town had delivered it. (With luck, the sacks would have been deposited in something like tightly lidded metal cans to frustrate predations by deer and porcupines.)

In the evening they played rummy and Alfred did a little spinning. (*Alfred*: I wanted to learn how to spin, and then I got blamed for not spinning enough. I only needed to learn *how* to do it, I didn't need to spend all my time actually doing it. And I was hoping someone else would take it up. There were other things waiting to be done.)

On Friday there is the following entry; it is not difficult to guess who the frustrated diarist was!

"Friday, Jan. 22. 16° below. The diarist cannot understand why, since water freezes, it can't be left overnight in the warmest room; why, since fires take a long time, the porridge cannot be made the day before and warmed up as the fire is getting going; why it isn't simpler to fetch water than wait for ice to melt; why the coffee can't be put in a thermos flask overnight to be ready anytime in the morning; why, if there is a crust of ice on the water, the crust can't be broken and the water poured out. It is all a great mystery and is interpreted by the diarist as simply evidence of the unreality and non-urgency of this life. We are playing, not working; suiting ourselves, not laboring for principle; not in any way equaling the efforts of CPS-ers, prisoners, soldiers, ambulance workers, nor anyone."

Herb and Eleanor went down to the Jacksons and returned laden with parcels—their own belongings at last! Alfred spent three and a half hours cutting and stacking wood in the kitchen. The yellow birch lasted three days in the kitchen fire, just over one day per hour of effort.

1943

Letter from co-director Mildred Fincke of Manumit School dated January 11:

"Teresa seems to be getting along beautifully in her dormitory of girls. I cannot say as much for Piers, however, who, although his physical health is fine and his appetite good, finds even mild aggressiveness of the other little boys very difficult to handle. He told us that he is not interested in fighting, that he hates the whole idea, and he wishes to be protected from the attacks of other eight-year-olds. It is an old battle, which Piers will have to work out. It makes him say he does not like Manumit, and I believe that he does not at present. He does enjoy a number of the class activities, though.

"If you are getting tearful reports from him, I hope you will be as understanding as you were the day you brought him, and know that the job of getting along with a group of his peers is not easy and he is finding the adjustment at the moment arduous. I have no doubt that he will begin to take hold before very long, however."

Piers: The reason I liked class activities was that there, adults were present and the bullies could not get at me. And, freed of harassment, I was able to get along with other boys. Bit by bit, I learned to fight. After we left, the school burned down; I wondered whether one of the oppressed students had anonymously fought back.

Phil Jacob wrote to Alfred on January 14:

"Teddy and I have certainly done a lot of thinking and a lot of talking about the problem of Hilltop Farm. We were very glad to hear about it from Norma's side when she was here, and it was good to get your letter going into your side of it about the time she left. Both of you seemed to be very fair with the other.

"We have had various ideas at different times about the basic difficulties and solutions of the problem. In fact, shortly after Norma left, I started out to write in detail. However, it is not we who will have to solve the problem, no matter how much we say. No one can solve it for you, for that only you, there, can solve. So, we shall be content to make a few general suggestions.

"Teddy and I both got a decided impression from your letter which we cannot think you really intended to convey. It sounded as if you are now interested in a purely material experiment of finding out to what degree people can become subsistent, starting with nothing. You made no mention of experimenting at the same time with community or with experimenting with living with people. Perhaps you could set us straight on this point. Did you intend us to take it for granted or has your interest really shifted to the material aspects? We do not mean to minimize the importance of such a physical experiment, for it *is* important. But for a pacifist, anxious to rid the world of the seeds of war, is it enough to limit your activities to a purely material experiment?

"And another question, are there really [only] two alternatives, as your letter implied to us: 'Do I exist for the world or for Norma?' Certainly, it can be said for humanity, but it isn't very complimentary to class one's wife as outside of humanity! In fact, isn't the first rung in the ladder of personal relationships one's own family? It all seems to hinge on the first point above. Is your interest now in the material aspects of subsistence, or does the other seem important too? We'd be interested in hearing further about it from you if you feel so inclined."

A letter from Marguerita of Manumit, maybe the dorm mistress:

"Piers' adjustment is wonderful. He has almost completely stopped asking for protection. Yesterday he joined a snowball fight & his whole face & body were simply lit with fun. (I watched him from a window without him knowing it.)...I've been making strong suggestions at night that he try his best to have a dry bed—succeeding so far."

Norma wrote to Roger [perhaps Robison]:

"Verily, as the psalmist ought to have said, you are a spring of water in a thirsty land.[39] Just when I feel at my lowest, a good letter like yours comes to cheer me up from one or other of our friends. We may be rotten farmers and still poorer pacifists, but we do have some wonderful friends! That you should say you still feel 'a part of the Hilltop institution' is as encouraging as anything could be. When one is so much alone, physically, as we are, the consciousness of being in some way united with like-minded people at a distance is particularly valued. My contacts have been poor lately because I have been too busy to write letters, with the children going off to school and all. This week I am trying hard to catch up, and for once start level when the next bunch of mail comes in. We are snowed in at the moment, otherwise it would have been coming in today.

"If I was discouraged when I last wrote, it was probably largely the weather (which has been perfectly devilish) plus physical fatigue. But I want to make it clear that if I am discouraged with the peace movement as a whole, I am even more fed up with ourselves as representatives of it. From now on, anything I say about pacifists (in a derogatory spirit) should be prefaced by: 'Beginning with me.'

"No doubt the failure of a group to develop has been largely due to circumstances we couldn't foresee when it was first planned, but I know we too have [been] much at fault, and what depresses me more than anything is the wonder as to whether we on our side are able to overcome our faults

---

39. Isaiah 44:3, "For I will pour water on the thirsty land, and streams on the dry ground."

while people on (so to speak) the other side are overcoming theirs. In a few months, a year at the outside, there ought to be an unparalleled opportunity for service for us and the place. But are we going to be able to seize that opportunity, or are we going to rob the peace movement of something that by rights belongs to it, and a number of people, of their chance for a fresh start in life? [A possible reference to their belief that after the war the land would be desolate and the population struggling to survive.]

"I feel strongly that the order of the day for us is Hang on! And I know if you do come in June, you will help us do that. What we need supremely here, and have all along, is a small semi-permanent nucleus of people who all want the same thing and want it badly, and who in addition are able to meet on a deeper level than that of mere expediency, or a pacifism which may be largely a surface matter. When Jim was here he was a great asset in that respect, and looking back, I think of his month here last summer as the most fruitful of all the months.

"There is so infinitely more to this business of living together happily than meets the eye, and so much of what is, and must remain, invisible and intangible is at the same time so vitally important that one's inner resistance fails when it is lacking for too long. The pleasures of fellowship have been denied to us here for far too long a period; that's really why we feel demoralized when the weather gets bad, and why we fail to make proper use of even our material resources. [Alfred usually preferred to be, and to work, alone, as his social skills were limited.]

"Your friend Bob Mueller sounds like the sort of person with whom one could get along very nicely indeed. I do hope none of the overhanging uncertainties will interfere with your visit.

"As regards girls, we always need extra help on the feminine side, but on the other hand, most girls find life here rather oppressive. Don't bring any unless they are tough! The jobs, for females anyway, are likely to be weeding the garden and painting the house. Anyone who has a suppressed urge to climb a ladder and splash away with red paint should be able to satisfy it fully here next summer.

"For men, I imagine it will be building (log-cabin construction as likely as not), wood-cutting for next winter's fuel, and odd jobs like insulating the chicken house and building fences. Letting the visiting men dictate agricultural policy proved so disastrous last year that I at any rate have a strong feeling we ought to keep them busy enough this year so they don't feel an urge to go out and cultivate an extra acre of corn!

"Just now we are four—four against the elements, you might almost say. I took the children to school last week, but soon after I came back Eleanor Garst and Herb Willits came to join us. Eleanor's husband is in Danbury [prison] about half-way through a five-year sentence. He may just possibly be paroled without warning, and for this and other reasons she wants to get some sort of small subsistence farm started as soon as possible. The idea at present is that they might buy an acre or so of our land and build a cabin on it next summer; that's where extra manpower would be useful.

"We're learning many interesting things about the insides of Federal prisons. Eleanor's husband is now apparently the senior convict at Danbury, having been there longer than anybody else! I am beginning to wonder what the women's prisons are like inside. Not that I expect to land there, but I expect to have a good many friends there if the registration of women becomes a fact.

"I wish I knew how I'd feel if it were not for the business of being an alien. But I am clear enough on the evils of registration in itself to take a firm stand at just that point, and I feel any stand one takes must be the result of absolutely inescapable convictions. A mere feeling that registration is the first step in a fatal downward movement somehow doesn't seem quite strong enough in itself."

Norma's letter to Lucia, a resident of the Brudercoop, said in part:

"Among other complicating factors, Alfred is now liable for military service under the conscription laws of both England and America. Eleanor and Herb plan to build in the spring and set up one or more separate establishments (no, no scandal here). We are living now almost exclusively on the stuff I canned last fall. It was such a nuisance at the time, but so wonderful on a cold dark evening when one doesn't feel inclined to cook, to pop down to the cellar and bring back a whole meal in glass jars. The hens have not yet begun to lay or the goats to give milk, so the farming end of things shows a heavy deficit at the moment.

"I'm forgetting the big piece of news, which is that the children finally did go away to school. They went off two weeks ago to Manumit, which is just exactly the kind of school we hoped at one time Hilltop might become (and still may, barring every kind of accident). We reached an arrangement with the school about finances and even so [Alfred's] parents have to help out, but I feel it's worth doing. They will get the maximum chances of development there in a specially sympathetic environment. I am hoping that Piers will prove to have some artistic talent, and I have great confidence in the person who has immediate charge of him. Teresa, the little extrovert, is doing fine according to accounts. Well, one never quite knows with Teresa, but I think she ought to be all right. Every letter I get from the school comments on what wonderful appetites the children have—I'm afraid they must be making positive exhibitions of themselves!" (*Teresa*: Our appetites resulted from the abundance of well-prepared, tasteful foods, in contrast to what was offered at Hilltop, where variety and flavor were unimportant and negative comments were not tolerated. As long as food would sustain life, it did not matter how it looked or tasted—nothing was to be wasted.)

On January 18 the morning temperature was 16° and it sleeted most of the day. Herb and Eleanor worked on the plastering until they ran out of sand, and when they thawed some, it was too wet. Odd jobs continued. Friday it was -16° by dawn. Meals were inefficient and delayed because of problems starting the kitchen stove fire for lack of dry wood, and other particular problems that Alfred, frequently frustrated, noted but refrained from remarking on.

Alfred wrote to Leslie on January 19:

"Your analysis of our trouble here was helpful. Still, you must have felt as impotent in analyzing as I do living in the midst of it. I see no way out, except to sacrifice my own convictions, and try to fit in with whatever evolves here, however inadequate it may appear. It seems impossible to get into the more individual and personal side of it. Apparently the difficulties which arise in the domestic sphere are supposed to be hush-hushed. [?]

"Certain things are clear, anyway. Too much liberty allowed to occasional visitors is undesirable. Each new person wants to start a new project, and at the end of summer those of us who are left have to finish off their projects for them instead of harvesting and woodcutting. This year therefore, insofar as I have influence, I want to insist that the farm should be brought to the place where it can be used for production. We embarked too soon trying to produce things before we had the wherewithal; trying to put hay in the barn before it was braced; trying to grow things before there was an adequate fence; trying to plant field crops before the soil was in condition, and so on. Unfortunately, there is no real way to control these things. It always looks like a veto. I'm not good at it. But it will help if Norma is convinced, as I think she is now, of these things.

"In the garden, if I am in charge again, I want to achieve this year variety rather than abundance, to see what the soil will grow, and what plants give the best yield for energy expended; keeping careful record of hours worked and taking care to harvest, not leave things in the ground like this past year. Though this is difficult too. If this past year I had done the normal harvesting and woodcutting, Judy [he conjectured, without basis] would have been offended because of not getting on with the woodshed she so much wants to see go up. You can't do things that are going to offend people. [Alfred seemed always to anticipate being "punished" for nonconformity, perhaps as had been his childhood experience.]

"I plan to use all hand labor, and dig a relatively small area, of perhaps 2500 square feet, and work it as intensively as I know how, with prior- and follow-crops, alternate early and late corn and tomatoes, alternate legume and non-legume, cucurbits [climbing or trailing plants such as squash, cucumber, and melon] all around the edge, and so on; and use all available fertilizer on it. Even if this doesn't produce as much as we want, it seems more intelligent to underproduce rather than overproduce, since the overproduction is just wasted effort; while the time saved in underproduction is fully utilized in the forest, buildings, or other necessary work.

"The two plowed fields I hope to put into a hay mixture and let them be; then cut hay early, again with hand labor. We'll cut as much as we conveniently can; but it doesn't matter if there isn't enough. Nothing is gained by maintaining dozens of goats by hand labor, unless the dozens are necessary to livelihood, which they are not. I do want to see, however, whether one or two goats can be entirely maintained off the farm, without taking too much time from other things. For the rest, we may as well continue buying the grain and hay. Perhaps some of the cost can be covered by sale of stock.

"Norma plans to continue with chickens, in spite of all the statistics I haul out for her to see: that a hen is only 18% as efficient a food producer as a cow; that production of only 1 egg a day would entail digging and working ½ acre of land (the equivalent of our present garden); that many small farm flocks have been given up as uneconomic beside the efficient commercial producers; that it is costing just as much to feed chicks for six months and hens for production, as it would cost to buy the eggs; particularly since in the latter case there would be no overproduction; and that the egg isn't an essential in the diet (a nice thing to have, no doubt, but not essential if you are hard pressed for time and money: we never fed starving populations [in Spain] on eggs); and that during the first years of the farm it is more important to get the productive mechanism in order and make ends meet on a simple level than it is to start out providing everything we always thought we would like to have. But she clings to the idea that anything you produce on a farm costs nothing, even if you buy the hens, buy the feed, and don't take the trouble to give them the conditions in which they can produce. So we shall be supporting a flock of hens for a while to come. I do not, however, propose to try to produce any feed for them. If you're going to use hand labor, you have to stick close to essentials.

"The forest has been left unattended. Herbert Leader and I, in cutting cordwood, tried to cut only the weed trees, though he complained that it slowed up the work. (Here I had to be 'negative' again, to preserve the future timber trees). He thought we might cut some for sale, but we shall be short even on our own immediate needs, let alone preparing for next winter. By now the snow is too deep to avoid wasting the lower part of the trunk.

"The children are off to school and we have less complication in the household. I rather regretted spending such a large amount of money on them when several simpler arrangements [?] would have seemed to me more in keeping with the manner of life we anticipated here. I have never been able to accept the idea that some children deserve to have a lot spent on them even if others go unfed, unclothed and unschooled completely.[40] I should have liked to see that money sent to the Bruderhof, for their children, who really need the things our children had before they went off to school, and have free schools provided for them all over the place anyway. But Norma thought she had sufficient cause to take the step, and she took it. It makes the simple life, hand production, economy, and so on, seem rather unreal in comparison."

That same day he wrote a long letter to Philip: "It was nice to get a letter from you. I wondered what you had been thinking. Norma so often tells me that you could explain what is wrong better than she can; yet I keep thinking, as you say, that perhaps it is a matter between us which no one else is really going to want to intervene in, if he is the sort of person whose intervention would be valuable.

"You were of course right in your assumptions. I have thought of numerous examples to make it clear. I am interested in the economic basis of this farm, but not principally nor to the exclusion of all else. I had thought from the very first that we all accepted a balanced economy on a simple plane and there would be no need to give further attention to that part of life, any more than a [Quaker] Monthly Meeting keeps deliberating on its meeting house—whether it ought to have a gable, a small organ, be a different color, be reconstructed in a slightly different place and so on. They deliberate on what is important, but they do it in a meeting house which is tacitly accepted.

"I had thought our economic basis was accepted, that we would produce rather than buy, and adjust ourselves to a life in which we can't or ought not to try to produce everything we think we would like to have. I do not see that we can escape the responsibility of a material life. I would give it much less importance than Norma does, and get it out of the way more quickly, because I want to do the thing I came here for—live in a way which avoids the causes of wars, and wars are caused ultimately by people.

"On the other question, which was a rude one, I admit: 'Do I exist for the world or for Norma?' your comment is striking, but I think not sound. You imply that I am meeting my obligation to the world in giving up my life and will to her. [?] I cannot get around the belief that we both have an obligation to the world. At present, when half my available time is spent producing milk for her (at about the same cost it would cost to buy) and the other half in fixing

---

40. Piers and Teresa, mere toddlers, had been left in England for three years precisely so that, in Alfred and Norma's view, other more needy children in Spain could benefit from their assistance.

the house to make her comfortable (which after a certain point ought to be a subsidiary, not a main activity), I am reminded of what my situation would have been in Spain if it had been parallel: with thousands of hungry children waiting for food which I was somehow in a key position to get provided, if I had time to spend all my mornings producing milk for her and all my afternoons making her more comfortable, we might have represented the ideal honeymoon couple, but the hungry would have starved. I needed all my time for the work I felt was urgent. [The work, though undeniably stressful, took place in a former mansion and garden in Barcelona with running water, electricity, and staff to attend to the cooking and childcare. Alfred and Norma had no experience with the usual demands of family life, as they focused exclusively on the needs of others in that war-torn country.]

"We are faced with the whole issue of war and peace, and want to deal it a blow at its very roots. We must either (a) not take time to produce our food, clothing and shelter & hire everything done by others to leave us free to the maximum. This I reject, since it contains the seeds of war, according to my reckoning. Or (b) get our material maintenance out of the way as expeditiously as possible, as a good housekeeper gets her tasks done early, to leave time and energy available for our main task in life. If this were done, then time for fellowship, relationship, sharing, mutual aid, inter-visitation, meditation and all worthwhile things would be available. [Over and over again Alfred goes into resentful detail about the demands on his time that prevent the achievement of his long-range goals, which included countless discussions. He had not found a way to get *his* tasks "done early."]

"In the face of this situation, I can't help saying: if we are going to spend that money on ourselves anyway, let us do it in the way which at least frees our time; but infinitely preferable would be to live by our own production and not by outside support. However, whatever we do, let us not cut ourselves off from our main task in the world [the salvation of civilization], either by our use of time or our use of money.

"You know the views I have always held on the stewardship of wealth. Norma must have had her reasons, sufficient for her, for sending the children away to school.[41] I don't think money was given to us to spend on ourselves. I regard it as part of our work in the world. We are to use our time working toward the fellowship of all mankind; and we are to use the money which has been entrusted to us for the same purpose. Some of it, no doubt, may rightly be used to maintain us. In present circumstances, perhaps $200 or

---

41. In an earlier chapter Alfred admits that his own frustration expressed itself around the children in unhealthy ways. He occasionally lost control, and his rage manifested itself in physical outbursts for which Norma was unfortunately the focus. She did not want a 7- and an 8-year-old exposed to such disagreeable and frightening situations.

$300 a year. But the bulk of it seems to me to belong of right to the peace movement; and in withdrawing it from the use of the peace movement in order to send our children to an expensive school and save ourselves a number of readjustments, we are in fact taking a trust, of which we are the stewards, and using it for our own benefit and convenience. My feeling is that this is immoral.

"That is what lay behind my wondering, do I exist for Norma, or do we both exist for the wider purposes to which we both are inclined to give lip service? If the latter, we must honestly spend the money on ourselves to free us for our main work, or we must deliberately so reduce our sense of need for material things that they are cared for with a minimum use of time, leaving most of our time for what is important. This lies behind my condemnation of certain foods, certain activities and practices: if they are not efficient uses of time [something Alfred invariably focused on], if they tie us instead of freeing us for our task, we ought to condemn them. If corn and oats will feed us equally well and corn will grow twice as well on our land, let us use the corn to the full and oats to the minimum, because we feel our time is urgently required for things more important than whether we eat corn or oats.

"I want to make all these considerations true in my manner of living. The thought that it is impossible, and that Norma is somehow involved in its impossibility, is very painful. To me it seems that it is she who gives such importance to relatively unimportant material items, that our whole time is spent on them and there is none left even to balance our income and outgo, let alone do a constructive job in the world.

"I am convinced you will find a way to think the best of me, no matter what. Go on doing that and I expect it will help as much as anything."

On the 19th the morning temperature was 8° below zero, with wind. It was very difficult to start the fires with the green wood. A start was made on fitting ½-inch ceiling board between the joists in the kitchen every 16 inches. In the evening they enjoyed the Eroica Symphony played on the wind-up gramophone.

The next day was still very cold and the fires took a long time to burn, so that breakfast wasn't until 8:30 a.m. Alfred worked on his typewriter and Eleanor instituted a regular schedule of work and writing her book, and fixed up a corner of the library to serve as an office.

The journal notes that, "The morning passed in hovering over the fire, complaining of the cold. A. shifted the hinges to the other side of the library door. The rest of the day went in the usual wood, water and goats, with a little work on the kitchen ceiling. Rummy was played in the evening, while A. spun."

Norma wrote to Family [in England] on January 22, saying in part how dreadful the weather was with temperatures down to 20° below, hardly even up to zero in the day, so that they had to live essentially in one room and wear several layers of clothing. "If this sort of weather lasted, no morale would be likely to survive it, but luckily it is usually limited to three days....

"About English children growing into hardened little brutes, I certainly don't think that, but I had some experience of children who had been subjected to prolonged heavy bombardment in Spain, and my impression is that it does irretrievable damage to them in less obvious ways. [Life at Hilltop might be considered a type of emotional bombardment; it certainly had long-term consequences.]

"I was interested a while back to see in one of the American monthly magazines an article by an English child psychologist, who had studied the subject, saying much the same thing. What has really been done to this generation's children—not only English but all over Europe—we probably shan't find out till the next holocaust in fifteen or twenty years. I notice that Pearl Buck[42] has lately been on record as saying that the major objectives of this war, apart from the purely military, have already been lost and that she sees no possibility of avoiding the next.

"I think regular medical supervision will help to fix up a number of little things which are too slight for treatment in the ordinary way. Piers is really very powerfully built and I think will be like the older Jacob brothers, not tall but thickset and sturdy. Teresa is as tall as he by now, if not actually a little taller, but she has nothing like the same ruggedness that is so striking in him.

"As regards the bed-wetting, I have felt all along that it was a matter of getting the suggestion to penetrate to the deeper layers of his mind, since there was no physical cause that could be discovered and he himself, poor child, was very unhappy about it. I came to the point where I believed that only the experience of group life and the need for being as grown-up as his contemporaries would really provide a solution. [Alfred frequently referred to Piers and Teresa dismissively as "infants," and mocked their childish mispronunciation of certain words, including his name, "Owfud."]

"I am planning to have the children's room completely re-designed before they come back, and start Piers off with a beautiful new mattress as a proof of confidence. It's a matter of breaking the vicious circle—most easily done by a complete change of environment—and then taking pains to see it doesn't re-form. You would be surprised at the number of things I have tried, but all in vain." [*Piers:* She tried everything except eliminating the constant tension in the family that I was responding to. Someone once remarked that in her observation, the tics I exhibited occurred only in

---

42. Some years later Pearl Buck spent time in Pikes Falls with her family, and Teresa became pen pals with her daughter.

Norma's presence. *Teresa*: Perhaps because of her then-undiagnosed bipolar disorder, or simply the unavoidable daily stress, Norma's manner could be like "an overwound mainspring." But, if she were the only cause, why did the problem persist at Manumit? Norma appeared to be, once again, a convenient scapegoat.]

The journal continues on January 23: "Temp 6° below. Mr. Crowninshield brought the Garst things up to Jackson's and Herb spent most of the day fetching them, with help from others. Also, a new crate of oranges. Alfred brought up two more sacks of feed, building a flat-bottomed sled for the second. Number of hours worked on goats this week: 23½."

Alfred: It's hard to resent the goats, but there were other things about the place that were waiting to be done and time had to be consumed on the goats because Norma had decided that how can you call it a farm if there's no livestock?

Teresa: The children needed milk. You could have gotten rid of all the goats but one.

Alfred: Well, I don't know. Communication was always very poor. She was the decider.

The evening temperature was 16°, marking the end of the cold spell, to everyone's relief. Discussion at supper on cooperation and methods of building the new world. (*Alfred*: That's what we wanted to do, that was the basis of the Hilltop philosophy. [At least for him.])

Herb and Eleanor fetched their remaining parcels from the lumber camp. Herb, Eleanor, and Norma went to the Fields while Alfred stayed to watch Lulu, who at 2:15 finally produced an 8.3-lb. buck and 6-lb. doe. The buck caused her considerable labor. It had been very much alive from the first moment, but was dispatched immediately upon its birth, a sad necessity on a farm, as male animals have no value. Lulu, a first-time mother, hovered over her daughter, uttering low sounds, and ate a pan of warm mash and a drink of her own milk.

The travelers returned from the visit to the Fields at 9:00 p.m. exhausted, having taken three and a half hours in each direction to accomplish the four-mile journey. Herb and Eleanor were satisfied that it is not right to settle in the Day home. They admired the newborn kid before retiring.

Norma wrote to Mercedes, their secretary in Spain:

"The summer is so beautiful, and there is so much satisfaction in working with one's hands to produce one's own food, and in learning skills which we may perhaps be given an opportunity of using later on to help others less fortunate. Now I wish I could send you one of my little goats! Our first of this season was born yesterday. I don't know if I have sent you any pictures showing how sweet they are; I don't send pictures now in my letters because I find they are apt to make the letter take even longer on its journey.

"At present I am happy because another woman is with me, and she and I get on very well. There have been several other women here at one time or another but with most of them I have not felt so much at ease as with this one, who is much like me in many ways—especially in having little patience with domestic duties! In one or two ways she reminds me of you, and I often think what fun you and I would have together learning to be farmers. She and another friend are planning to stay here permanently if all the new laws which are passed do not make it necessary for them to go away. In fact, nowadays no one can be certain of being able to continue in any particular place; we do the best we can and try not to waste too much of our precious time in guessing what may be going to happen within the next few months.

"One thing you will be interested to know is that the children are away at school. Teresa has learned [to read] all by herself and now reads quite difficult words. Piers is not interested in books; he likes to do things with his hands, like drawing or building model houses. I am afraid they have forgotten all their Spanish."

Alfred: Norma [tried] to do the teaching. It quickly wore her out; she saw she couldn't do it.

Teresa: When you were deciding to live there, you hadn't thought about what the children's requirements would be?

Alfred: Never gave it a thought.

Teresa: But isn't that a little odd? The children are members of your family, they have needs, it seems strange that their needs were never considered.

Alfred: My mind was on world needs, not on local children.

Teresa: "Local children?" Your *own* children!

Alfred: Maybe I just assumed that Norma would teach them, but she found it didn't work. And that led to Manumit. I thought a child should enjoy home life as long as possible, but my sister pointed out that my children had no home. Home was just the center of chaos.

Teresa: We didn't have any home, or any family in the usual sense, or even a "Mom" and "Dad." [Because we had always called our parents by their first names.]

Alfred: I don't know how you survived it.

Teresa, 75 years later: Alfred's comment was surely more than a little sarcastic, as he felt there should be nothing to "survive" under his plan.

1943

Norma wrote the same day to Johanne [no last name]: "I was very glad to have your letter forwarded from Friends House. When we left Pendle Hill we decided to take up farming—if possible, cooperative farming, with a small group of like-minded people from there. But the only ones who kept up their interest in the plan were Leslie Johnston and his wife Valerie. They were here with us for a while, but then had to go to Canada to get new immigration visas, and were not allowed to come back. Without them it has often been difficult to see our way ahead and keep up our courage, since we have not found any others to really share our hopes and ideas for this place. But we have learned a great many things which we hope may be useful to us in helping, later on, to rebuild a devastated world."

Their assumption apparently was that when the war finally ended there would be nothing left but scorched earth and smoking ruins. No one would have any money and there would be nothing to buy anyway. While this would be true in London and other bombed-out areas, it was hardly the case throughout the globe, and not at all in America, which the war had not touched. Few would be interested in learning to subsist on turnips and oatmeal. They anticipated that, with their Hilltop experience and language expertise, they would be qualified to go back to war-torn areas abroad and demonstrate how life could rise again from the ashes. Norma had written about this dream at some length in August and October of 1941 and July 1944, as had Alfred in November 1942 and April 1943. Or, if that appeared a better solution, Hilltop included enough land that dozens of families could become homesteaders there. These unrealistic presumptions sustained them through difficult times.

Norma continued: "I think one of our most important motives in coming here and cutting ourselves off, as many people think, from the troubles of our fellow-man and any opportunities of doing anything to help them, was what you said in your letter—the idea that 'a sane, happy, balanced life is the best contribution one can make.' I don't feel we ourselves have done much in this line. We seem to have run into too many difficulties of one kind or another, but I do think some of those who have spent short or long periods up here with us in the summer, when everything is so beautiful and peaceful, have been encouraged to go back to their hardworking lives in cities with more strength and calmness of mind than before. One very definite service we may be able to perform is in giving homes and opportunities for starting a new life to some of our friends who are in difficulties because of the [pacifistic] beliefs which we too, share.

"As for me, I have made a big compromise and sent our children away to a small farm school with an excellent reputation. It is terribly lonely and cold up here in winter and I felt I was not giving them the security they ought to have. After much thought and consulting with others I came to feel that they ought to have whatever advantages I could get for them if they were to grow up happy, useful and emotionally well-balanced citizens. I don't think Alfred feels quite as I do about it. Certainly it is a most difficult question, which confronts all parents of our way of thinking and doing."

That day Alfred cleared up the tool room somewhat, then began to tan Lucifer's (Lulu's buck kid) hide, and completed it in the next few days. He also tried carding and spinning some angora wool and found it very cohesive and hard to draw out, with fluffy lumps causing tangles.

Alfred commented, decades later: "We bought a spinning wheel at an auction, but we didn't know how to work it. We had two of them, one was smaller, and one was larger. Someone told us that the larger one was for flax. For a while I had lessons, and I practiced on it one winter. One of the goats had long shaggy hair and I tried to spin it, but it didn't work out very well. We were learning. At least I was learning. I was open to criticism because once I had learned what I was trying to learn, like how to spin, then I didn't spin any more. I just wanted to know how to do it. Some of the others thought that once I knew how to spin, I should spend my time spinning. (From each according to his ability.) But that wasn't what I was there for. I was trying to practice the philosophy of pacifist living, but Norma doubted that anyone would want to do it that way. She didn't think others would agree."

The goats were out nibbling bark, floundering in the snow. Routine chores continued.

Herb worked on plastering their bedroom ceiling, running into difficulty because "the lime is more or less slaked to begin with and the sand is wet." Lulu's baby, Lucy, capered [from a Latin word meaning "little goat"], always entertaining to watch.

The journal, January 28: "For about a week A. has been rising at 6:15, H. shortly after, and the girls get up at various times. E. sleeps in the library. Breakfast and other meals are at various times. H. is chopping for the library & upstairs and A. for the kitchen. The beech will last six days, maybe more. A. added a division to the Angora goat manger to keep them from climbing, put an old window from the green Ford in Patrick's stall and mixed up 200 lbs. of feed. The rate of consumption since last mixing Jan 12 was 7 lbs. daily when fed mornings only. A. is active in mental plans for garden & fields."

The next day Herb and Eleanor went to the village, and six inches of snow fell. Alfred worked on the kitchen ceiling, and chopped down an ironwood tree, which turned out to be very difficult to split and stack, as the wood was hard and internally twisted (hence the name!).

On the 30th Alfred worked until midnight putting his typewriter together with a replacement part that the Royal supplier had sent. All the tiny parts had been spread out but somehow ended up on the floor, and

Alfred had to crawl about on hands and knees trying to find them. (*Alfred*: I know I severely blamed *you* [Teresa] if you lost anything. That didn't mean that *I* shouldn't lose something. [This rueful, self-deprecatory comment was unusual for Alfred.]) Time expended on fixing the typewriter: Nine hours and 20 minutes.

IMAGE 14: *In this corner "office" the letters and journals that form this book were typed by a succession of diarists.*

The women worked in the kitchen producing bread and baked beans. A discussion at supper focused on, "How are we going to live when our syrup and honey run out?" Honey was obtained in large, square metal cans weighing 60 lbs. It was believed to be more healthful than the reviled white, or even brown, sugar. There was also strong-flavored blackstrap molasses, supposedly a good source of iron. ("About 5 tablespoons of blackstrap molasses contains 50 percent of the recommended daily allowance of calcium, 95 percent of iron, and 38 percent of magnesium," see Wikipedia.)

January 30, Norma wrote to a Mr. Rowley as follows:

"I enclose a check for $3.20 in settlement of your account, and am sorry that it was delayed by an oversight.

"There is another matter about which I feel obliged to write to you; this is the question of the shipping of goats in crates to Brattleboro, and of the empty crates back to Jamaica again. I understand that you have a great deal of freight to handle and many difficulties to contend with, but still I feel I must make clear just how much inconvenience is being suffered at this end.

"To take the most recent example—last Thursday I brought a goat down to Jamaica to be shipped, but was unable to ship it because our crate had not come back. In fact, neither crate had come back, since two had been sent out and should have been returned. I spoke to one of your drivers, who told me that a crate was in Brattleboro and would probably be brought back that day. I explained to him that I had this animal to send off and that the delay was very inconvenient and thus it was very important that the crate should be back by Saturday.

"I walked down again on Saturday morning, but found still no crate. Now, I very much hope that I shall manage to get this particular animal off this coming Wednesday; even if I do so, I shall have walked in all 24 miles and wasted about 12 hours of my time.

"What is more important is the possible effect on the animal. These goats are pedigreed stock of considerable value; you probably know that highly-bred animals are delicate and extra nervous, and may become sick and even die if not properly handled. This little one is already in bad condition because of the upset and delay in getting her to her new home. If she gets sick, or even dies, as is perfectly possible, who will compensate me for the loss?

"This, or something like it, happens every time I have a goat to ship off. One wretched animal spent two weeks shut up in a crate, chiefly because your driver didn't take the trouble to send us a verbal message to let us know he hadn't been able to take her. The raising of dairy stock for sale is a perfectly legitimate and patriotic business; I don't intend to stay in the business any longer than I can help, chiefly because of the transportation difficulty, but with things as they are now, I can't even liquidate it without the co-operation of yourself and your drivers. I just can't continue shipping off stock under these conditions.

"Although I appreciate your difficulties, I don't think the problem of taking one not very large or heavy crate to Brattleboro can possibly be so hard as the problems that are confronting me because the crates aren't taken. We are not asking a favor, we are paying for the service and I feel we are entitled to have it, and that livestock has a certain right to priority.

"Would it be any help if I undertake to notify you at least two days in advance each time a goat has to be shipped off? What I should prefer would be to send one regularly each Wednesday morning; I have three waiting to go at present and shall probably have others before three weeks are up. And I can assure you that I am making every possible effort to find other methods of getting the crates to the express office and back, and for my own and the animals' sake will not ask you to carry a single one if I can avoid it."

The next day Junie gave birth to a daughter, 8.6 lbs. Alfred fashioned a spring closing device for the stairway door with a long string interspersed with rubber jar rings. Eleanor produced an excellent lunch of tuna fish, green peas, and raspberry shortcake, "much to the satisfaction of all." (*Alfred*: She must have gotten that on her trip to the village. Visitors usually want samples of the food they're accustomed to.)

Norma wrote to a friend, saying in part:

"Here on the farm, life goes on very quietly indeed, in startling contrast to life outside. The big events are the birth of the season's first kids (two this past week, the funniest little things imaginable) and the occasional bursts of Polar weather. Thirty below zero has been the worst we've experienced so far, and as our house is old and little time or money has been spent on making it weather-tight, we really have experienced a good deal of sheer physical misery during the past six weeks. But signs of Spring are already visible to the farmer, who has to live several months ahead of himself anyway.

"About the time you get this probably we'll be starting sugaring—gathering maple syrup along with our neighbor Scott Nearing, who gets his cash income for the year that way. I understand he formerly had a lurid reputation in some quarters as a Red [Communist] and other dreadful things, but we only know him as a good neighbor always to be relied on for help, advice, and intellectually stimulating conversation! Many interesting people live around in these parts, including some pretty well-known in the peace movement. If only transportation weren't getting so impossible, we could see more of them than we do.

"Our very sincere greeting to all our friends; share the news with them and beg them to write."

Undated letter from Marguerita Rudolph at Manumit, to Mrs. Jacob:

"Piers' habits of personal care are excellent, and he is very reasonable and cooperative. He is very alert and much interested in all activities, and these snowy days enjoys sledding more than anything. If you have a sled at home for them you might send it up. His important problem is what to do with aggressive tendencies of other children. Fighting is a strange thing to Piers, but he will learn enough of it as necessity arises. He will learn, too, other social resources.

"He is very free with me about his needs and sensitivities. He explained to me that he would not wet his bed while the place was still new, but that when he is all used to it, he might have an accident. M.R."

Piers: I did slowly learn to fight, and was stronger than I looked, and eventually was able to take any boy within ten pounds of my weight.

February 1943

Alfred and Herb had planned to chop for an experimental day, but it was windy and snowing, so Alfred plastered above the stairway and along the north part of the cupboard and blue room, putting a few spring closures on doors before retiring. (*Teresa*: Door-slamming was a punishable offense: If you allowed a door to slam you had to go back and open and close it silently ten times.) The next day they did chop from 9 to 1 just beyond the 10-acre field on the road, and felled a yellow birch and a 15-inch maple across the road.

After lunch, Herb mended the kettle and Alfred installed the new little stove in the office, hoping to begin his home holiday the next day. Norma went to the village, setting out on snowshoes, but found she sank in just the same. She was late getting back, so Alfred went to meet her at 7:15 in the darkness and returned with her at 8:30.

Eleanor prepared a delicious soup. No sooner had it been served than there was a booing outside, and Herbert Leader was there, having walked up from Bondville on his snowshoes "with hopes of doing our pruning."

Little Janet, Junie's kid, had to be helped to find the teat, but enlivened during the day. She was large, with a high rump, probably an indication that she would make a big goat. Herbert and Alfred chopped down a large basswood, which did not burn well enough to please the kitchen department. The Herberts (Willits and Leader) also chopped together.

Thursday, Bobsie gave birth to a 9.3-pound daughter, Buttercup, without warning. No preparation had been made as it was not officially her time yet, and the baby was born in her dirty stall. Herbert L. sorted potatoes and then walked over to the Fields.

"A. finds that over the six weeks he has kept a time account, the goats have consumed 3½ hours a day. This is roughly what the cook needs to get all the meals, and seems to mean that the milk is equal in value to all the rest of the food prepared, and of course much more costly—around $4.00 a week plus $275 capital outlay." (*Alfred*: That might have been the purchase price of the goats. If I still had the account book that would be clear.)

On Sunday morning they had French toast for breakfast, indicating that eggs were available. Alfred spent the afternoon spinning, hoping to finish his father's Christmas/birthday mittens, which Norma would knit. (*Alfred*: The policy was that on Sunday we were allowed to do something different. It didn't have to be anything pious; we just could abandon the requisite jobs and do something different.)

Norma wrote to the Family on the 8th:

"The little goats are beginning to arrive; little Lucy trots around after me everywhere. A trick of hers is leaping into the air, executing a half turn and coming down facing the other way. The next one was Green Mountain Janet, born a week later and already bigger than Lucy—she is tall and lanky and not nearly so skittish, with a gentle and timid expression, whereas Lucy looks positively pert. The third kid, Buttercup, is causing some anxiety at present because her mother doesn't like her and is not giving her proper care. I suspect I may have to adopt little Buttercup, as I did all the kids born last year. Her mother is the champion milker, an old goat of the very most aristocratic family, who has borne dozens of kids and probably never been allowed to raise one before. Either she thinks it beneath her or else she still hasn't got over being offended at the manner in which the kid was born. It came a day early and without the slightest warning—I was up in the barn about an hour before it came asking her how she felt, and she said she felt all right, and when Alfred went up to milk there was a strange kid running about the barn, so to speak! Bobsie was furious about the whole business and would not even look at the kid. We had to bring it down to the house to be dried, because she wouldn't lick it clean. You have to be careful with goats, if their feelings once get hurt there is all kinds of trouble.

"The snow drifts are well above the windowsills and it has been snowing for the past three days. However, now that the days are getting longer and the sun stronger, I hope the drifts may begin to diminish. We haven't had any really cold weather for nearly three weeks, either, which is a wonderful relief. For about a week after Eleanor and Herbert arrived it simply wasn't possible to get warm, and we all slept in all our clothes.

"Now we are busy working on the house, blocking up the cracks on the north side through which the wind blows, and plastering where the lath is bare, so the heat won't escape so fast through the roof. The snow which had been on the roof since early December suddenly let go a couple of days ago and a perfect avalanche landed on the south side of the house—I'm glad no one happened to be standing there at the time! I never saw so much snow before, but I gather it is nothing exceptional. And when one gets used to it, it's really not so bad. I got my snowshoes fixed and now I can walk about anywhere on top of the drifts without sinking in.

"If this paragraph seems disjointed, it's because the pressure cooker has blown off steam twice in the course of the last five minutes; I am cooking some beans, the fire is hotter than it should be and the safety device on the cooker is getting plenty of exercise. I ought really to go and sit by it for the next half hour, but I am in a hurry to get this finished, because Herbert Leader has suddenly decided to walk down to the village. It is still snowing and we had not planned to go until tomorrow, but he doesn't mind any kind of weather.

"In a couple of weeks I've been invited to lead a discussion group at the United Pacifist Conference. This is a remarkable and quite unexpected honor. I hope I shall not suffer from stage fright, as all the big people in the movement will be there.

"On the way back I plan to visit the children, as it will only be a little out of my way. But any journey in this enormous country is such an undertaking, especially in present conditions. Just to deviate a few miles from the direct route and spend three or four hours with the children will make me a whole day later getting home. Altogether I'll be away from Friday till the following Tuesday, if all goes well.

"We have no idea what is going on in the world. You can't buy newspapers any more in the village, you have to order them and we never know what day we'll be able to get down the hill, so it is not worthwhile. Whoever goes down for the mail is supposed to read the headlines on someone else's paper but Herb Willits last week forgot to do this, so we are completely out of touch. It's a strange feeling. One of these days we shall have to buy a radio or get someone to give us one—more likely the latter, as money is going to be pretty short with the children at school. However, we don't need to buy any food, as last year's harvest looks as though it will see us through till next year's begins, so money doesn't matter very much. The suggestion has been made that our income should be put into a trust fund for the children. Nothing much has been done about it yet, however.

"I am sorry to send such a brief and disjointed letter—I have to keep jumping up to run in the kitchen and look at the gauge on the pressure cooker [especially when cooking beans, if the pressure got too high the pot could explode], and besides life here is so utterly uneventful, just snow and more snow, [goat] kids getting born and hens laying more or fewer eggs.

"By the way, I never told you about the hot water bottle. You remember the one you sent me to Spain? Well, it went the way of all hot water bottles after a long and honorable life, but I knew it would come in useful, so I saved it. Sure enough, Alfred used it to cut out little rubber disks to keep the water from running out of the two drains in the new double sink. After we'd tried every other way to keep the water in, in vain, he thought of this and it worked like magic. So you see, we don't waste anything!

"We have now made a much better arrangement in the kitchen, opening up the front hall which had been blocked practically ever since we came in. Now we can run to and fro from the new kitchen on one side of the front of the house, to the room we all live in on the other, without going through the back parts which are horribly cold and bare and untidy. One of these days we'll fit on the front door, but there are about six feet of snow at present blocking the place where it ought to be, so we are managing quite all right with the collection of boards nailed together which has served as a front door until now."

That week the office behind the stairs caught fire, possibly because the new chimney of the little stove was tied in place with string. Alfred came in and saw the papers on the shelves burning, called for help, tore down the old blanket that served as a curtain, tried to smother some flames without success, burned his face, and called for water, which the others were meanwhile fetching. He somehow got down to the cistern first and stepped on the ice thinking it was solid frozen, but it gave way and he went in waist deep. He ran back with two buckets: They were half empty, but did some good. Another bucketful carefully placed by small quantities controlled the fire. Most of the woodwork was catching, but thanks to the plaster on the ceiling it didn't get upstairs.

Teresa: I remember the charred shelving and burnt papers. The whole old, wooden house could so easily have gone up in flames, with no way to stop it. Some of the papers used as references for this book have singed edges. When I was away at school years later, there were fire buckets filled with water in the corner of some hallways. Probably such a bucket in the little office would simply have frozen solid and not been of much use.

Alfred: The shelves weren't wide enough for the papers placed on them, which drooped over the edge and quickly caught fire. I tried to put out that fire with the blanket and burned myself in the operation. I did not want to have to answer questions in the village about how that had happened, how we had had open flame in a roomful of loose papers, so I put off going there for a time.

The mittens for Alfred's father were finished and mailed off, still damp from washing.

That weekend Herb Willits cut wood, Herbert Leader laid rockwool above the living room ceiling, and Alfred connected the tap to the new kitchen pump. They still had not cleared up the mess from the fire. Norma was reading *Look to the Mountain*, Herb, *Out of the Night*, and Alfred, *Tess of the d'Urbervilles*. Snow lay up to the window sills. The kitchen was keeping warmer now. Alfred finished *Tess* on Sunday and began *The Return of the Native* as well as continuing with *Creed of Christ*.

Monday morning the temperature was 38° below zero. All regular work was suspended in favor of trying to stay warm. Alfred worked for several hours on the garden plans. That night there was a plan for everyone to sleep in the library to keep warm, but then three people "fortified by hot molasses milk" went upstairs as usual.

The next day, although it was still 34° below zero, Norma went down to the village and arranged for the snowplow to bring groceries up as far as Lumbercamp Corner on its next trip.

Norma wrote another Family letter.

"Since my last letter was so scrappy, I determined to write again soon. I noticed when I got up that it had got colder in the night and when I went out and looked at the thermometer I had to search for a while to find where the mercury had got to! At present it is still daylight and it has fallen to 25° below, so judging by last night's performance, next morning it should say -50°—it can't say any more, because that's as low as our thermometer goes.

"What I find very reassuring, though, is the fact that it isn't nearly as cold in the house as previous cold spells, which weren't anything like as bad. We have been working very hard lately on plastering, insulating the roof and blocking up cracks, and it looks as though we have done a good job. One can hardly expect to be very warm in a room where there are only a few old bits of lath and a board roof covered with thin tarpaper between one's bed and the elements outside.

"In spite of the improvement, I am very glad the children aren't here. Five adults can get along all right and even find it funny—as when the bread was frozen so hard that Alfred had to take his best pulp saw to it at lunch time. The idea is that all five of us will sleep tonight on camp beds in the one warm room. And tomorrow or the day after it will all be over and forgotten, that's the beauty of this climate. We were quite worried about our tiny kids in the barn, but Alfred found they were just as cheerful as usual this morning. He gets the worst of it because he has to go out before dawn and milk, and it takes him nearly an hour in the unheated barn. The hens didn't make any fuss either, they even laid two eggs. All in all, I think Man is pretty inefficient."

Herbert Leader went to visit Scott Nearing, and Eleanor and Herb decided to go to Danbury in case Eleanor's husband Gene was paroled. Norma planned to hitchhike along with them. They spent the day getting ready.

Alfred, alone in the house, planted a variety of vegetables in soil-filled wooden frames that he placed in the library.

"Mr. Albert Jacob" received a letter dated February 26 from Clark's Summit, Pennsylvania.

"Dear Sir: Some weeks ago there appeared in *The Rural New Yorker* one interesting but all too brief paragraph about your community. It was signed by a Mrs. White. She most graciously gave me what information she had about your self-sufficient community, and suggested I get in touch with you.

"I am an ordained minister and a student of religio-communism, which I believe in with all my heart. While my present setup does not permit of joining such a colony, I think they are splendid. There was at one time a colony called The Harmony Society located at Economy which became wealthy and fame [*sic*], but died out after nearly 100 years because they practiced celibacy. There is a book by Charles Nordhoff, published in 1875 [by the Dodo Press, now out of print], called 'Communistic Societies of U.S.'[43] which might be helpful to you. Nearly any large library has it. Also there was an interesting article written in the Bulletin Index, April 25, 1940, on old Economy. This article was an inspiration to me. In the same magazine on April 11, 1940 there was another article. This magazine is published in Pittsburgh, Pa., Investment Bldg.

"Am making a scrap book on the subject and any information you have on what you have accomplished and on what you propose to do will be appreciated. Is the colony a religious group? If so, what denomination, etc. Anything will be most appreciated.

"I am in His service, (signed) Carl Covey."

The routine continued through February. Norma attended the United Pacifist Conference. On the 28th she wrote to parents-in-law Edward and Caroline, saying in part, "The worst we had here was 38 below, which seems to have been a good deal warmer than anyone else we know: two friends

---

43. When this book was first published in 1875, the major utopian communities in America, including the Shakers, the Harmonists, the Wallington and Oneida Perfectionists, the Aurora and Bethel Communities, the Bishop Hill Colony, and others, were still flourishing enterprises.

have written from New Hampshire reporting 50 below, and 60 below was claimed by someone in Londonderry, not far from here. Let's hope it won't happen again as long as we live in Vermont.

"Alfred's face [burned in the office fire] is lots better now and I believe he may not even have a scar—at one time it looked as though he might have several [especially since Alfred's manner of dealing with physical ills was simply to ignore them]. All in all, we were very lucky, as we even found the two or three dollars' worth of seeds that had just come from Burpees for the vegetable garden. Now the only thing I really miss is my one film that I had meant to have the enlargements made from, and perhaps even that will turn up somewhere. The effects of the fire look much worse than they actually are. We did lose several hundred envelopes and will have to re-order them from Sears—I still think it's cheaper to buy them in bulk even if they do burn up once in a while!

"I am just back from the United Pacifist Conference, having taken advantage of the trip to visit a number of other places and people, including the Harlem Ashram. Very interesting people live there. At present they are conducting a campaign about India—picketing the British Embassy and so on, and also trying to give some training in nonviolent action to the Negroes who have decided to use this method to try and get rid of Jim Crow in the south. I think I admire their courage more than their judgment, but certainly it is an awful problem and if one hasn't anything else to suggest I suppose one should back up those who do have a plan of action.

"We have started the summer garden in wooden boxes inside the house and one or two things are coming up already; I am also ordering a few plants for my flower garden. I want a simple old-fashioned English garden, things like lavender and foxgloves and aubrietia [*sic*; produces cascading blankets of purple flowers in April and May] which you don't see so much around here, and consequently it is hard to get the plants—I didn't have any success at all last year trying to raise them from seed. This year I'll have to make a great effort to see the goats don't eat my new plants, but once they are properly established, they ought to go on indefinitely. Then we have our fruit trees, and some nut trees we are ordering from Swarthmore.

"Another excitement is maple syrup. There was some wonderful spring weather last week and we got enough sap to boil down to just a few spoonfuls of syrup. [It requires 40 gallons of sap to produce one gallon of syrup.] I did have an idea of sending our own maple syrup to all the family, but actual experience of how much it takes has discouraged me a good deal.

"Since I came home, I've seemed to spend a good part of my time tidying up. We now have the kitchen well enough organized so that it can be kept fairly tidy, and now that the worst of the cold weather is over (I hope), perhaps for the first time since we moved in, we can begin to live like fairly civilized people. When the weather gets warmer we can take our meals in the kitchen as originally planned; at present it's still so cold that there's only one room warm enough to sit in.

"I had hoped to have the children's room all plastered and redecorated when they came back from school, but hadn't counted on a vacation coming quite so soon. Perhaps I can manage at least to get the paintwork done in their room next week and the beds nice and tidy with new covers. But the plastering is too big a job and I'm afraid anyway it would not be dry in time. By June, when they come home for good, the house ought to look really nice. Progress is very slow, but all the more gratifying for that reason."

Undated script letter from Piers to Norma, probably dictated, as Piers could not write script at that age. "I hope the snow is not too deep for Lucy to go out and play. And I hope everything is all right. Maybe you have some trouble getting up and down the hill. It is very icy at Manumit, and people often fall when they walk.

"We are going to have a movie this afternoon—part of it is Charlie Chaplin. We have had several short movies before in the evenings—but not as long as the one we will have this afternoon. Yesterday was Parents day & we had a big play by the older children. I hope you will come & have Parents Day, just for me! (Aside—'If Teresa read this, she'd be mad!') And I should have lots of things, presents & company. Love Piers." There is an added note by housemother M.R: "I think this is an exceptionally well-composed letter."

March 1943

Norma's Family letter of March 1 indicated that she hitchhiked to Manumit to pick up the children, as well as taking a bus part of the way.

"The first thing that struck me, as you'll be sad but not surprised to learn, was Teresa's really appalling accent. The only consolation is that she'll lose it just as rapidly as she got it. I know the other children had been teasing her for her English accent which she has kept untarnished all this time. Piers seemed very contented, Teresa somewhat less so, but though I made exhaustive inquiries I couldn't discover any reason at all why anyone thought she shouldn't be happy. All agreed that Piers had had a bad time the first week or so, but no one had any ideas about Teresa not getting on well. [*Teresa*: I believe I may have been sexually molested, which could explain my behavior and why no one would talk. I remember being touched intimately by a teacher, but nothing further.] I talked with everyone in any way connected with the children, and had plenty of time to sit on the porch with them and their friends and hear all they had to tell me. Then I took the bus back to Danbury.

"By this time I had a first class sick headache coming on and knew I ought to stop in Danbury for the night and let Eleanor look after me [Eleanor must have already given up on roughing it at Hilltop], but I had sent a telegram to friends in Philadelphia saying I would be down to see them and didn't want to give up unless I absolutely had to. So I took the New York bus, with many misgivings but telling myself I could get out anywhere if I felt too bad and stay the night. Several times I resolved to get out at the very next stop, but the bus always stopped in some completely desolate-appearing spot where there was nothing faintly resembling a hotel, and I just didn't feel equal to hunting for a place to sleep, so the long and the short of it was I finally arrived in New York.

"I got out of the bus prepared to lie down and die pretty well anywhere. Then all of a sudden, I felt better. I went down to the Pennsylvania Station, took the train to Philadelphia, spent a happy evening and night with all my Pendle Hill friends who live in a cooperative house there, and came back to New York next morning in time for the first session of the conference. Naturally by then I was pretty tired and remained so throughout the proceedings, so altogether I think the hitchhiking was a mistake, except for the experience gained and the money saved.

"I put in some time sending out letters to the Press on some aspect of Gandhi's fast. There is enormous excitement about this over here, and in the most unexpected quarters; I'm afraid the prospects for future British-American cooperation have had as bad a blow—from the other side—as I gather they did over the Darlan incident.[44] "Monday morning I got up very early and went to Grand Central to meet Valerie Johnston and [baby] David arriving from Montreal. Because Leslie gets away so seldom from his camp, they decided there wasn't much point in having Valerie struggle for a living with the baby in Montreal, so they accepted Anna Brinton's offer of a job at Pendle Hill. I hope that means she will be able to spend some time with us this summer.

"I had to leave her at breakfast in the station to hurry off to my conference, where I enjoyed meeting several people I previously knew only by correspondence."

---

44. A reference to the assassination of Francoise Darlan, admiral of the French fleet, who was killed in 1942 after a series of military maneuvers, sabotage, and betrayals between the French, Germans, and Allies that culminated in the scuttling of 77 warships and other vessels of the French fleet at Toulon to prevent them being used to aid the Germans.

1943

Alfred wrote to Miss Marjorie Thayer of New York City on March 4.

"I was very glad to hear from you about your active interest in rural life. Our particular farm may not be what you mean by a farm at all; but like yourself we are people of city background who find greater satisfaction in country living than in conventional civilization.

"If there is any prospect of your paying us a visit, I won't go into detail now, because these things can be talked about at length and with apparent clarity; yet a day or two of actual experience may knock the structure to bits. It is a very real changeover from urban to rural ways, and involves much more than anyone can realize who hasn't done it, or tried to.

"We are of course eager for colleagues, and can fit them into our established life and activity without financial embarrassment to them (we are keen to do so, since so many good people seem tied to the city through fear of lack of funds) but it is important that there be agreement on fundamentals. Ours is a pacifist emphasis; in our living we favor simplicity; in our production, hand labor and ingenuity. We are interested in production for consumption, not for sale, and have no cash crop except selling a few dairy goats locally to encourage home production. There are several possible cash crops which we have the beginning of: Angora rabbits, Angora goats, sheep, and timber, and any colleague who wanted to develop any one of them would be welcome to.

"We have been fully occupied up to the present with the indispensable building and maintenance work, gardening, winter-proofing, and so on. A lot of labor has to go into an old farm before it can be productive again, even if it is not intended to produce for sale. We have no horse, tractor, or similar equipment, and do not expect to have until there are a sufficient number of participants to own such things cooperatively. At present we are alone, with a large and constantly reappearing circle of friends and well-wishers.

"Here in New England there are half a dozen groups or cooperatively minded families that need help and friends. You would do better to visit them, and perhaps find a way to fit in to mutual advantage. We ourselves feel that this land, which is several hundred acres, belongs to the pacifist movement (though we hold the deeds) and parts of it can readily be made available to persons seeking a rational way of life. Indeed, there is a girl who was attached to Scribner's (your envelope read Funk & Wagnalls) who moved up soon after Christmas and is sharing our life until she has found the way to build on a part of the land she has chosen. There are an infinite number of ways to do it; and they are best discovered by talking with those who have made some sort of beginning.

"We have been thinking quite recently that for anyone who does not mind producing a commodity which might have a semi-military application, angora rabbits have great promise. We should like to see someone come here and, starting with the trio we have, let them develop into a herd, flock, or whatever it is. The wool sells through a cooperative marketing agency for $6 a pound; but interesting articles can be spun and woven at home for direct sale. There is a lady at Wilmington, Vt, who might be very glad of help with her rabbits. Her husband died, and she depends on an aged farmer, subject to many infirmities. We could put you in touch with several such people, according to your ideas and needs.

"Please allow us to help you in any way we can, either with further information, with hospitality, or even with the initial tools of work. I have thought a great deal about this sort of thing. My thinking is stimulated by my experience of war relief in Spain and I too readily give too much advice. But I do also have access to interesting statistics, and hope I can produce authority for anything I say.

"My wife and I are English and came to this country with two small children in 1940 from Spain, where we had been working [with] Quaker relief. We are both graduates of Oxford University, though we do not pretend to be awfully intellectual. The house is very old and inconvenient, with none of the usual amenities, though we have recently managed to arrange to pump water directly to the kitchen. There is no workable bathroom nor indoor sanitation; little privacy; little warmth in winter. We feel relatively warm now, and the thermometer reads 48°; it was 28° for breakfast. This is just to frighten you off if you are frightenable, because no one is going to stick to the realities of productive life in the country unless his principles are stronger than his tastes. Physical discomfort is really one of the minor evils in the world; and there are ample compensations for that.

"Please let us hear from you further if there is anything more we can add. Don't hesitate to ask questions, if you really think you might make the break. We would love to persuade you to do it, only it's no use unless you are very irretrievably inwardly persuaded."

In early March it was still cold. At milking time Alfred noticed that Prudence, Polly's kid, got up out of the box, scratched herself, and wagged her tail. Two hours later she was dead. They tried to revive her, to no avail. Internally she seemed all right. They concluded that it might have been bloat from overfeeding.

On Saturday, Norma went to Brattleboro to fetch the children, and in the afternoon Alfred went to Jamaica to meet the three of them. It was a long walk up the hill on snowshoes.

The next day Norma wrote to Leslie Johnston, in part:

"The children are home from school for a brief vacation. In many respects I find them greatly improved, Piers especially. But I notice about them a kind of unconscious arrogance, an assumption that the world exists by and for them, as indeed it is bound to do in the environment of a boarding school. This leads me to some reflections, probably not in any way new to you, about the necessity of making the school only one function of a properly integrated community life, so that the children see themselves in their right relation to the whole picture of human life. I would almost urge that if we take children from outside ourselves, we take only such as have no family background of their own—refugees or orphans. It would give me much pleasure to give a completely homeless child a world to live in, and partly for that reason I am keeping in touch with the Children's Aid Society of Vermont in case the day ever comes that we are able to do that.

"Teresa asked me did I buy War Bonds and stamps, and when I said No, she said 'That means you want the Japs to win the war.' And this morning Piers was singing some song, I didn't hear what, and she insisted he ought to stand up to sing it, and if not, it was a sin. What a concatenation of ideas they are getting into their heads!" (*Teresa*: "Off we go, into the wild blue yonder, climbing high…". Evidently I learned this at Manumit. Norma seemed more amused than alarmed at our indoctrination into wartime attitudes.)

Norma went to a home demonstration meeting in the village and returned with a Mr. McCuhn of the FBI, "who made a note of all our activities in this country."

The next day work continued on the garden plan, making an alphabetical list of vegetables, with spaces to indicate which row, what yield, days to maturity, etc. There are to be 98 varieties, mostly in the 50-by-60-foot garden. (*Alfred*: That was probably the year when I had seen a book about three-story gardening and I wanted to practice it. The idea was to plant lettuce and such things in the row, and every four feet plant pepper plants or something like that that didn't cast much shade, and then every eight feet or so plant corn or something that cast a good deal of shade but would be so widely spaced that the shade wouldn't disturb the garden much. I wanted to see how much food I could get out of 50x60 feet. It got to be so dense I could hardly get through it!)

Norma received a letter from Janet Hall at Pendle Hill:

"The time of the singing of birds[45] has come here, and the time for one to ensconce oneself on the fire escape and take in the sunlight … the shoots of the rosebush by Mrs. Sollman's doorway are green clear to the roots, and it was only two days ago that a heavy, wet snow bent the pine branches higher than your head clear to the ground! At the [Philadelphia] art museum last Sunday the parkway leading up to it was full of people,

---

45. Song of Solomon 2:12: "The flowers appear on the earth; the time of the singing of birds is come, and the voice of the turtle is heard in our land."

and the steps too, and even inside. Lots of soldiers and sailors and civilians and quite a few little colored boys who were playing hide-and-seek in the section 'Oriental and Medieval Art'!

"This evening a yet-to-be-inducted WAVE [Women Accepted for Volunteer Emergency Service, the women's branch of the United States Naval Reserve during World War II] is arriving to await the Induction Day. She has been teaching home economics at a small church college upstate. We also have a remarkable young Negro who has been drafted into the Coast Guard, but his station is quarantined for smallpox.

"I saw the letter that Alfred wrote to Glenn Gray which gives a nice factuo-philosophical description of what's been done this winter, but I long to hear the lighter touches from you. I took your calling one of the goats Janet to be a great compliment! Valerie came this week and is wonderful to have around. David is a beautiful child and gurgles upstairs all during Meeting [for worship]. A. B. [Anna Brinton] had a luncheon last Friday to welcome Valerie and the Spring, which was festive and a great success. We want to know how Piers and Teresa are getting along."

Norma wrote to Family on March 19:

"Your letter of Feb 9th arrived yesterday to remind me that my next one was sadly overdue. The children have been home for nearly two weeks, and it has been hard work keeping up with them and with the sugaring too. At this time of year we suddenly get a cut of fine, warm days and frosty nights, which is the ideal sugaring weather, as the sap begins to rise in the maple trees.

"We had hoped to be sugaring co-operatively this year with Scott Nearing and the Fields, as over there they have all the modern equipment and make a thousand gallons or more for the market. But it's four miles away, and Alfred didn't feel he could leave the goats, especially just now with the new kids coming along. So when the sugaring weather came, we just couldn't resist going out and hanging a few buckets. We have about a dozen out now and could hang at least a hundred, as it turns out we have some excellent sugar trees, but we have no proper equipment for boiling down. Even ten or fifteen gallons takes up more space than I can easily spare on the kitchen stove, and one day's run takes all the following day to boil down.

"So far we've made about a gallon. It is delicious with pancakes or corn bread or milk puddings and is a useful substitute for sugar in cooking, though as it sells for about three dollars a gallon, only poor farmers like ourselves, ironically enough, can afford to cook with it. You can boil it down further and make a delightful crystallized candy, which sells for even fancier prices.

1943

"Since I've had the job of carrying those five or ten gallons daily in milk pails for about half a mile over a hillside coated with icy snow,[46] I have had more respect for the stuff and shan't be tempted to use it just to indulge a weakness for sweet things.

"We had quite a business getting the children home. The vacation began on a Saturday, and they wrote to me that I could meet the children at Grand Central Station at 9:20 a.m., or the Travelers' Aid Society could put them on the next train for Brattleboro and I could meet them there. I wrote back asking them if the Traveler's Aid couldn't manage to send them by bus instead, as the bus is much more direct and cheaper—to get to Grand Central they have to go 60 or 70 miles in the wrong direction. But this proved too complicated, and if I had gone down myself and fetched them by bus, I should have had to spend the night somewhere en route which, together with my fare both ways, would have made the whole thing prohibitive.

"It seemed best for them to be put on the train at Grand Central, but the Jamaica bus leaves at 3:00 p.m. and the only train to get to Brattleboro in time left Grand Central ten minutes before the Pawling train arrived. I was in despair. Finally the school authorities used a little imagination and wrote to say that they would make a special effort and send the children [ages 7 and 8, traveling alone] into New York by the 6:11 train so that they could catch the 9:10 to Brattleboro and get home the same night, and so it was.

"They arrived back just full of energy and high spirits. They both are much more self-reliant, able to think of ways to amuse themselves and so on, and Teresa can pick up almost any book and read it—which adds some new terrors to life. All in all, I am pretty well satisfied with what the school is doing for them. It certainly is expensive, though—all these train fares (I'll probably have to take them down to Grand Central again on Monday) and new clothes constantly, and one thing and another."

March 20: Wood, water, goats, saws, and work on the two-wheeled cart.

Alfred: I had built some kind of sled and I wanted to train Patrick to pull a cart, so I bought wheels from Sears, Roebuck and made a cart and then…

Teresa reads from the journal, "Began to train Patrick to pull N. to village in afternoon."

Alfred: Like an ox, just drag it behind. I thought it would be very handy to have a goat cart to go down to the village and bring things up. But he didn't think so.

---

46. The old sugaring facility was on the far side of the upper field. Dozens of old wooden, steel-banded sap buckets remained, and eventually were chopped up for kindling. Today, they would doubtless be pricey tourist souvenirs or decorator items.

The rabbits were losing weight on the reduced diet. At noon Leonora produced one hornless buck and later Dinah had two bucks, one of them hornless. Patrick had sired seven bucks and eight does. The seedling vegetables were beginning to appear in the flats planted during Norma's absence in February.

Norma and the children set off early to return to school, going via a series of buses. (*Teresa*: I don't remember much about the school. I know we were teased and bullied because we talked funny and looked funny, and as our family was atypical, we didn't have the same growing-up experiences that the other children had had. We could not talk about what Mommy or Daddy had said, or what the family had done together, as we never did anything as a family.)

Alfred went with them to the village to pick up the last five gallons of gasoline that their ration entitled them to. He stopped to see Mrs. Bolster but she was away, so he visited Deborah and trimmed her overgrown hoofs. He also saw Mrs. Clayton and did Hyacinth's hoofs. He offered to help with her kidding in return for the kid and Hyacinth's feed. In the village he met Mr. Eastman and went with him to see Beatrice and Bambi. Both were doing fine; Beatrice kept getting her head in the sap buckets and running around like a blind man in an amusing way. Mr. Eastman helped Alfred with the sled and showed him where the old road came out that connected the Hilltop road to the main road near his house.

On the way back up the hill Alfred read *Home Vegetable Gardening* with great interest and later "went onto a milk diet and drank his fill." Norma returned, with Good Luck Seeds and "other interesting items."

Alfred began work on a fence. (He recollected: "I cut down young trees, saplings, and made a fence out of them, quite unaware of how quickly a goat would get through anything I constructed. It meant nothing to the goats, as they preferred to hover around the house.") He sent an order to Eastern States for two tons of feed and fertilizer, to be brought up by McDean.

One day Norma walked four miles to the Fields' at midday. She returned the next afternoon, bringing with her a new little goat, Marietta, whose ears were bent at the tips. She weighed only eight pounds. They taught her to nurse from Harriet. (*Teresa*: I remember we had one goat whose wattles, normally under the chin, were at the base of her ears!)

Herbert Leader turned up at supper time. He "was wandering around, trying to be useful in one place or another." The next day he left again. Louise Strandes arrived, exhausted from climbing the hill. "Norma lay around trying to rest her insides, and Louise buzzed around." (Alfred, as usual dismissive of physical ailments, opined that Norma "had [an ulcer] because her father had one, so it was a familiar situation for her. It never got any worse or better, so whether there was really one there, I have no way to know. Maybe she was ready to interpret something as a symptom, I don't know." Clearly, he believed she was malingering.)

The next day Norma continued to rest while Louise tended to the chores. Two new books came, *Grow Your Own Fruit* and *Vegetable Crops*. Alfred worked all afternoon on the two-wheeled cart for Patrick to pull, and he did in fact pull a sledload of earth the next day.

Letter from Marguerita Rudolph of Manumit School dated March 28, 1943:

"Yes, I think Piers is giving himself wholeheartedly to the adjustment and growth here; he is using all his powers and is very happy. He is enjoying being independent, even to the point of being argumentative and naughty—all of which is indicative of real growth. Asserting himself and rebelling is an important experience to a child, and I don't think Piers has had it. [*Teresa*: Perhaps because his father responded to children's initiatives with sarcasm and mockery rather than encouragement, and demanded conformity to adult standards of behavior without indicating what they should be.]

"I will speak with the doctor about the physical or physiological aspects of Piers' bed-wetting. But so far, I think the cause is psychological. It's somehow tied up with his nervousness and confusion (which he is naturally outgrowing). When he stopped for a couple of weeks in the beginning, he was still quite tense and timid in social adjustment. Since then he's been playing with much more abandon, and much thrilled with the newness of asserting himself; and so he is too excited in doing much now in controlling the old habit. However, he is reasonable about the consequences and not scared and suffering as he seemed at first.

"One afternoon when the other boys scattered all over the place, I could find only Piers for a hike in the forest nearby. We had a lovely time! Piers skipped and leaped and ventured rock climbing and brook crossing unhesitatingly; and made many observations and comments with delicacy and sensitivity. On the way back we made up a story of our adventures, and Piers let his imagination really go (from lion hunting to skipping rope with a bear!)"

Norma wrote to a friend on March 29:

"Some while back we had from your office a request for information about interesting small occupations in our neighborhood. We did nothing about it because there seemed nothing of interest to report from here, but just the other day I came across something that I thought might be of use to you. It concerns one of the run-of-the-mill occupations in Vermont—the production of maple syrup—but is being organized in a new way by Scott Nearing, our neighbor just over the mountain.

"He makes a large part of his yearly cash income from maple products, like many farmers in these parts, and this year he has worked out with the owners of nearby farms an interesting co-operative system. Each farmer contributes what he has in the way of equipment—thus Scott Nearing has the maple trees, the big evaporator, much minor equipment and the acquired skill of several years in the business; our friend contributes his team of horses, a sled, a large gathering tank, and so on, and I suppose others make their contributions too.

"Everyone who works gets paid as a labor unit at the rate of 45¢ an hour (the two horses counting as one labor unit) and in addition, on a basis of these units and of the equipment provided, the product of everyone's work is divided up, so that our friends get 17½% of the total output. This way they are free to sell, as it is far more than they can use at home, and the market is in a very healthy condition. Democratic methods are followed in making plans and dividing up the work, and arrangements are made on a basis of an eight-hour day, six days a week, unless there is something unusual due to weather conditions.

"This is something of an innovation, because I gather the usual maple syrup farmer drops everything else when there's a good run and keeps the evaporator going day and night till the next cold spell, but it can be spread out more evenly with good management and the use of big storage tanks for the sap. The total volume of the business can be roughly judged from the fact that they hope this year to make over a thousand gallons of syrup; the highest grade sells for well over \$5.00 a gallon (three dollars, sorry). There are about four men and two women working full-time (the women look after the evaporator, the most highly-skilled part of the whole business).

"In the same valley, which is famous for its high-quality syrup, there are two other farmers producing syrup for the market, but apart from that, I believe Scott Nearing employs nearly everybody able to work at this time of year. So it is becoming an industry with real community significance. I don't know what you are doing with this information and I forgot to ask him whether he had any objection to its being publicized, so just remember he is still a very dynamic person if displeased!"

In a letter to friends, Norma described her involvement with the sugaring process:

"We are sugaring, and if I ever thought maple syrup was dear [costly] at three dollars a gallon I know better now. At school we used to sing a mournful song called 'Caller [Fresh] Herrin'[47] about what agonies the fishermen went

---

47. One verse of several: "When ye were sleepin' on yer pillows / Dream'd ye ought o' our puir fellows / Darkling as they faced the billows / A' to fill the woven willows [creel]."

through to provide us with the humble breakfast fish, and I am thinking of making an adaptation for the maple syrup farmers. The theory is simple, you just bore a hole in the tree, push in a perforated piece of stick, hang a bucket underneath and wait 12 hours, then you boil the contents of the bucket till 39/40ths have disappeared, and there's your maple syrup.

"However, the 39/40ths business means 10 gallons of sap to 1 quart of syrup, and that means the entire stove occupied all day—no room to cook anything at all except in the oven. We started out on a Sunday with Saturday's product and by 10:30 p.m., when I gave up and went to bed, we'd reduced it by about 50%. I lay in bed gloomily calculating that at this rate we'd finish Saturday's sap by Monday evening, then Tuesday and Wednesday we could boil down Sunday's sap and so on—and sugaring lasts anything up to two months.... [T]he syrup is supposed to be done when it boils at 219 degrees, but according to my thermometer it boils at about 202 [perhaps because of the 2,000-ft. elevation], which the cookbook says only happens in Denver, Colorado. After reading all the textbooks I abandoned modern precision instruments and went back to the traditional Indian method of tasting with a spoon.

"Mountain Lucy still leads all the newcomers in personality, beauty and vivacity. She also has a silkier coat. Strictly between ourselves, there is some doubt about her paternity, and I can't help suspecting that the other buck was responsible, since she is so different from the rest. Luckily, we know her father was a gentleman even if we aren't certain of his name.

"I do hope you decided to make room somehow for the second Japanese-American. Did you read in the *Christian Century* about the meeting in Indiana where all the farmers had agreed to take Japanese workers and then the American Legion got up and led everybody by the nose till the meeting ended by passing a resolution to send them all back to Japan or something of that kind? Every time I go out into the World it gives me the cold shudders.

"The other day I was walking back from the village and was just struggling up the last steep bit when I stopped to rest, happened to look back, and there was a man just behind me. I couldn't have been more surprised if it had been an ostrich. He was all dressed up in city clothes and the snow of course was seeping in over the tops of his rubbers [British for overshoes]. Such a nice-looking young man, I thought he must surely be one of our friends, only I couldn't remember just which. I said, 'Hello!' and we went on walking up together. It soon transpired that he had come on some sort of official business, and sure enough it was the F.B.I. Someone had written them about a conference we held here last August—eight months it had taken them to get around to investigating! He apologetically said, 'We get this kind of stuff all the time.'

"We sat him down by the fire to dry out his feet, gave him our life histories which he solemnly wrote down, produced all our supporting documents, and sent him off well primed with goats' milk and pacifist literature and an invitation to visit us when the weather was nicer, and make a longer stay. I'm surprised we haven't had the F.B.I. here sooner. The fact that they couldn't bring forward anything worse encourages me to think that maybe after all the village doesn't know about Fran Hall's arrest here last summer. I have embarked on a campaign for greater neighborliness and think of inviting the local ladies up to pick blueberries in the summer."

There follows a long digression about the many philosophical and other books she has been reading. "I am planning to send to England for T. S. Eliot's latest long poem . . . the reviewer compares it to Beethoven's posthumous quartets. I am sure I shall find the new Eliot to my taste. A perverted taste, some people think."

April 1943

April came at last, with a feeling of spring. Rain exposed enough ground for the sheep and Angoras to graze, and the hens emerged from their house for the first time and pecked at the new ground. Ducklings arrived. Two had died on the journey and another after it. Alfred fashioned a brooder heated by one of the oil lamps. Mrs. Bolster, who had been "duck sitting" for two days, expressed an interest in the two buck kids and in wool. The hens laid nine eggs.

Alfred: I kept records, and found that it cost as much to produce a dozen eggs as it would to go down to the village and buy them. The hens were supposed to have water, but it froze as soon as we took it up to the henhouse. We just poured it out and hoped it would be all right, which was the way we managed much of the Hilltop business.

Sunday, April 3: Alfred tried to encourage the plants to germinate by sitting the box on the stove until the soil felt warm. As usual, once the chores were done, he found there was only an hour left for his planned reading. Norma returned [no record of where she had been, or why] about 3:00 a.m., having walked up the hill in pitch darkness, snow, and sleet.

(The modern-day "journal interviews" with Alfred end here; only one page, in November, remains.)

1943

Norma wrote to Leslie and Valerie, in part: "It's snowing at the moment, but we are surrounded by spring. The library, our one warm living room, is full of seedlings and ducklings, all growing vigorously. The seedlings have the virtue of being silent but they are much less entertaining. Both smell about equally bad.

"The barn is full of goats. I even got another given me by someone who didn't want it. She was a wild, unloved little creature and has fastened all her frustrated affections on us in a very touching manner. Who would keep a dog or cat if they could keep a baby goat instead? We are so successful with animals [that] I sometimes feel we can't be quite such a flop as human beings as I sometimes think. . . .

"I cannot honestly feel we have more than a fifty-fifty chance of being able to maintain continuity at Hilltop anyway, if Alfred goes to jail, or CPS (and what the chances are of that nobody knows). This is not the sort of place I could manage alone, and no definite collaborators are in sight at the moment.

"Valerie, couldn't you plan a short visit in June? Things look like being good then, so good I am tempted to arrange for the children to be sent from school down to the relations in West Chester to wait a little while till I come down to fetch them back. That might give them a chance to go to the seaside too, which I know they are eager for. Speaking of prepositions, did you ever hear the story about the little boy who said to his mother at bedtime 'What did you bring that book for me to be read to out of for?'"

Norma wrote to Marguerita Rudolph on April 6:

"Your letter about Piers was very helpful and I do feel glad he is in the hands of a person who understands him so well. Certainly his general nervousness and tenseness is very much better since he has been at school, and it's also true, as I have often noticed, that there is a tie-up of some kind between this nervousness and the bed-wetting. I have thought for instance that he shows an increase of nervous mannerisms of one kind or another during a period when he is managing to avoid the bed-wetting.

"I have tried not to worry him about it too much, but it does worry me, for a number of reasons. First, the question of health. In a house like this, with no proper arrangements for laundry, it becomes impossible sometimes if we have a long spell of bad weather to keep him supplied with really dry bedding, and that naturally is a danger to his health. I had thought I might let them go down in June to visit their grandparents and spend time with them by the sea, but how can I send Piers off without me to look after the laundry and so on? A child should be able to go visiting on his own, I think it's a necessary part of his education. I do appreciate hearing from you from time to time about how he is getting on. We still hope you really will manage to come up and visit some time.

"P.S. I don't feel I answered your letter at all adequately—I didn't have it by me when I wrote the above. He has always been unaggressive and very much dependent on grown-ups. I am not conscious of having repressed him, in fact I think from Teresa's behavior you can judge that I am no disciplinarian! And lots of people tell me I show favoritism to Piers. I think it is just born in him to be gentle and rather different from other children. But Teresa's influence has certainly been very bad, and I have long wanted to get Piers into an environment where she was not the most important object. Thank you again for taking such good care of him."

From a Dear Family letter that Norma wrote the same day:

"No letter from you since I last wrote, more than two weeks ago. There certainly must be a number of your letters at the bottom of the Atlantic! Mine seem somewhat more fortunate; I just got word that the precious manuscript about the New England Town Meeting arrived safely at the editorial offices of THE FRIEND. But the letters we send to Spain never seem to arrive; I suspect censorship in this case rather than submarines.

"On the way back to their school, I managed to do something about the children's health certificates. The school requires that every child produce a certificate saying he or she isn't suffering from any contagious disease, though as our own children had spent the whole two weeks in splendid isolation on top of the mountain, it seemed quite impossible for them to have come in contact with any germs. However, they have mumps in the village, so I had kept them away and there had not been any opportunity for them to see the doctor either. Pittsfield [Massachusetts] is full of doctors, and luckily all their offices were in one large building in the center of town, and they were all receiving patients during the hours between two and four. We wandered through the building opening the door on one waiting-room after another, but every one was full, and we only had half an hour.

"Finally we found a doctor with no one in his waiting room, so I led the children in and said, 'Will you please take a look at these children and certify that they aren't infectious?' His jaw dropped a little—it turned out he was a surgeon—but he duly looked down their throats and wrote out the necessary paper. We were lucky he wasn't a chiropodist or a veterinarian—everyone with any kind of degree gets called 'Doctor' in this country.

"When we finally arrived, both children raced off to the dining room, it being supper time, scarcely waiting to say goodbye. That seemed about as cheerful an omen as I could have wished for.

"After that we had a short interlude of relative peace and quiet, except for the daily task of boiling down maple syrup. At the end of the week, I walked over the mountain to visit the Fields and the Nearings, and stayed the night. Although it was a wonderfully warm day, the snow was still almost waist-deep in the forest, and with the warmth the crust was beginning to give way, so I wished many times I had brought my snowshoes.

"Over at the Nearings I admired the way they make maple syrup in a huge evaporator—fifty or sixty gallons of syrup a day, compared with the one quart or less I can produce on the kitchen stove! However, they consoled me by saying that they started out in just the same way several years ago. Four families are cooperating and they hope to make over a thousand gallons altogether, each gallon of the finest quality syrup selling for nearly three and a half dollars. Many small farmers make all their cash for running expenses during the rest of the year during the few weeks of the maple syrup season, which luckily comes before the ground is thawed out enough to plow.

"Opposite the Nearings, working with a slightly smaller evaporator but making, so Helen told me, even finer syrup, are an elderly English couple who have been here a great many years. Mrs. Lightfoot's accent puzzled me for a time. I finally analyzed it as a very heavy dose of 'refined' speech on top of an honest north-country accent—she had been the parlor-maid in some big house before her marriage. They seem very nice people except that Jack Lightfoot is regarded as somewhat brutal in handling his horses. These are the things that make for the respect or otherwise of one's neighbors in these valleys.

"Our peripatetic friend Herbert Leader, who after spending several weeks here disappeared without a word and was not heard from for over a month, suddenly reappeared the day after I got home and announced that he was going to help the Lightfoots with their sugaring, so I suppose that is where he is now.

"Perhaps people are right about the lack of a class system in this country, at least as compared with England. Herbert's people are wealthy and much respected socially in the town of Bennington but no one thinks it in any way beneath his dignity to work at sugaring under the orders of someone's ex-parlor-maid. Of course Herbert is a complete vagabond and would probably defy even the most rigid class system, but still I find it hard to imagine the same situation occurring in the England I used to know, even though I have often defended England against the common accusation of being an excessively class-conscious nation.

"I always score, however, when I mention the color question. Do you know there are no Youth Hostels in this country below the Mason and Dixon Line, because racial equality is one of the planks of the Youth Hostel program, and a Negro who entered a Youth Hostel in the South would stand an excellent chance of being shot or beaten practically to death. It's a long way they have to travel, and I often wonder whether they are ever going to travel it, or whether civil war is going to break out again. All the elements are there."

Norma wrote to Eleanor Garst (who apparently had not, after all, wanted to stay at Hilltop despite her and Herb's extensive preparations) on April 16:

"I write the date with some incredulity, for believe it or not, it is STILL SNOWING and looks as though it might go on forever. [Teresa recalls that, a year or so later, the only day she and Piers could not get to school down in the valley was April 15, because their little bear-paw snowshoes sank into the light, powdery snow.] I am ready to agree with [T. S.] Eliot that 'April is the cruelest month.' According to the papers, more snow has fallen this past week than in the whole month of March. A week or ten days ago nearly everything was clear, though it was pretty cold, no sap running, and thermometer down to zero at least one night.

"But now... it looks like midwinter all over again. You never saw anything so discouraging. Three people are coming to spend Saturday night—two are goat purchasers and they are coming with a truck, but they can't possibly get it up the hill. If only it stops snowing long enough for them at least to walk up in some comfort! Junie, our very first goat, is leaving us, but by all accounts she is going to an excellent home. Still, I hate to part with her, for sentimental reasons. Little Penny, my special pet, is also going. Lately she has been giving more milk than anyone else, even Bobsie.

"Excuse typing, but I am cold—have been all day, since getting thoroughly chilled rising at 6 a.m. to force pills down goats' throats while Alfred held their mouths open. Bobsie just refused to open her mouth and after the third futile attempt we had to give her up. Alfred kept warm struggling with the goats, but all I had to do was stand, clutching the tongs which held the pill, and wait for the opening to become visible down which tongs and pill had to be pushed."

Referencing the recipient's—Eleanor's—father's insistence that all family members experience the consequences of his obstructive decisions, she observed that, "I've always felt children come in the category [of innocent bystanders], since they didn't choose to be pacifists' children and shouldn't be made to suffer for it. Apart from that, judging by my own record in Spain when I lied, evaded, broke the law and would cheerfully have stolen to get my children food, I probably would not be willing to stand up to anything much if it were going to leave them helpless. I don't seek to defend such an attitude on ethical grounds (though it may be quite easily defensible, of course) but my experience of mothers in a tight spot is that it's in their nature to stop at nothing where the children's well-being is concerned."

Routine work continued, with the weather mixed. On April 17 the journal noted that: "Penelope milked a red fluid out of her left side, smelling like yeast or ether, and very little out of the other. We brought her to the house where she spent the day singeing her beard on the stove."

1943

Norma wrote to Family on April 21:

"I look out of the window at an almost unbroken expanse of white. In this devastating month of April it has snowed—heavily—almost every day. At the end of March many of the fields were very clear, and it looked as though spring were really almost here, but every sign of spring has vanished since. Even the maple syrup hasn't been running. People say it's exceptional, of course, like practically all the other weather we've had since we came here. This time last year there was a heat wave and we were having our meals out of doors—but of course that was exceptional too. We are starting our garden and vegetables inside the house, but it's very difficult to give them the warmth and sunshine they need, and pretty soon they ought to be going outdoors.

"I am just back from a dash up to Hanover to see what is probably the last of the Browns [Reg and Rica]. The Dartmouth term ends this week and after that they are waiting to be summoned back to England at any moment. He may get only two days' notice, but if they get a longer time they will very likely be out to see us once more and bring you a last-minute report. [*Alfred commented with apparent satisfaction*: When Norma came back from Hanover she was furious, because she had plans for the library, she was going to make it all pretty, and I had destroyed it by filling it with plants.]

"Reg actually got several months' more freedom through his decision to go back to England, as the American army was ready to take him in January. His case is similar to Alfred's, and this leads us to feel that we may expect action soon. Leslie Johnston is likely to do better than anyone; after about nine months in the forestry camp he has now been given permission to go and work on a farm, where Valerie can join him (she is at present with the baby at Pendle Hill—I hope they'll have time to visit us on their way back to Canada).

"We sent away four goats last weekend. Two purchasers came with a truck on Saturday afternoon, but thanks to the snow they couldn't get within two miles of the house. They stayed the night and on Sunday after lunch we started to walk the goats down the hill. We were already in trouble because one of the goats we had agreed to sell had injured herself and obviously couldn't travel, so we had to ask one buyer to take what from his point of view was an inferior substitute; then this substitute decided she didn't want to leave Hilltop and she had to be dragged, protesting loudly, practically the whole way down the hill. Everybody was worn out and all our feelings lacerated in the process.

"I had meant to ride with them as far as their home in Claremont [New Hampshire] and then take the bus or train to Hanover the same night, but with all these troubles we didn't get to Claremont till 11 p.m., so I spent the night with our friends, the ones who had adopted Junie.

"This woman's husband is an artist named David Fredenthal, who I gather has quite a reputation.[48] They live in a very agreeable farmhouse and though she doesn't know much about animals, her mother is accustomed to cows, so I hope they will get along all right. We also took along little Pepper, a buck kid whom we were sending to some other friends in Northfield. He had to go in a crate and didn't want to leave home either, so we had to carry him and drag the crate. It took us several hours to go the two miles and I [the following line is illegible].

"This coming Sunday (Easter) is Parents' Day at the school again, but I simply can't go. Even if I traveled by bus all night and again all Sunday night it would still cost a preposterous amount. I am afraid the children will have to resign themselves to the fact that I live too far away to come over and see them during term time. Our budget is pretty tight already and going to be tighter soon, as the arrangement of the investments from which we get our income is going to be changed—we are thinking of having a trust fund established for the children, and this apparently will mean much less income, as the speculative element will be removed. I am not quite sure how the school bills are to be met in future without drawing on capital, but he [Alfred's father] seems willing for us to do this, up to a point.

"What seems certain is that every non-essential expense (like long train journeys to spend a couple of hours with the children) will have to be cut out. However, in consideration of the fact that I was saving money by not going myself, I allowed myself to buy each child a really good toy. Such things are fearfully expensive here and until now I have had to harden my heart and say 'No' when they pressed their noses against the windows. There was a particular shop in Hanover just opposite the Post Office, which we never passed without trouble of this kind, so I went back there and chose a delicious black lamb for Piers and a doll in a red dress for Teresa." The doll cost three dollars—about 15/ [shillings] at par—but there was simply nothing cheaper. (*Piers:* I remember that lamb. It was my favorite and I took it everywhere with me. I named it Boss. One day when we were playing in a field, I set it at the base of a tree while we played, then forgot to pick it up when we went home. Remembering it at dusk, I raced back out to the field, but it was gone.)

---

48. David Fredenthal (1914–1958). was "one of America's most respected watercolor artists. He was famous for his bold, intensely vigorous and complex paintings and drawings" (see davidfredenthal.com.) After they split, Miriam and the two young children, Robinson and Ruthann, nicknamed Sparrow, spent time at Hilltop, and after the war they briefly lived with Norma, Piers, and Teresa in the tiny house in Wallingford, Pa. Robin and Ruthann became recognized artists themselves: Robin was a sculptor whose massive modernistic works were displayed in prominent locations in Philadelphia, and Ruth's abstract monochromatic paintings have been exhibited in Italy and the U.S.

1943

Norma continued: "I also got a pattern and some wool [yarn] to make her a pretty little sweater for next winter and was horrified to find that the price of wool had gone up to nearly 2/ [shillings] an ounce. It is actually cheaper to buy garments ready-made, as I found when I started to knit Alfred some socks. However, other things can still be made at home more cheaply and I have just got some exciting flannel in a variety of different stripes to make next winter's pajamas.

"The sister of Mrs. Fredenthal (where I spent the night) is a determined-looking young woman of 15 who, I am told, flies so well that a special dispensation is to be provided to get her into the Army at 15! Rica by the way is going into the A.T.S which I gather is [Norma's 10-years-younger sister] Rowena's branch of the service. It is certainly hard to imagine Rowena as the compleat soldier. As Teresa gets bigger, I find it increasingly difficult to tell them apart in my own mind, in fact I sometimes confuse the names.

"As for the marriage question, when I consider the Browns, who knew each other for years before they decided to marry, and who are now as happy a couple as you could wish to see, I feel the auspices for Rowena are at least as good as for many of these marriages which are the result of people getting swept off their feet, marrying people with whom they have nothing in common, and then regretting it the rest of their lives. A large shared interest is an enormous help.[49] "I wonder if you got any indication of an address for Anthony Baines [a close friend of Alfred and Norma's in England and possibly Piers' namesake]—if we knew more, we might be able to send him some kind of parcel through the Red Cross. It's strange to think of Anthony without some kind of musical instrument, however simple, though when I said this to Rica, she at once remarked 'Of course he has a comb.' [A pocket comb such as men carried at the time could be made musical by folding it in wax paper, and humming through it.] I am sure wherever he is, he's brightening life for the other captives."

Spring returned, and the goats were able to do some grazing, though they preferred bark and twigs. Some patches of grass appeared as the snow melted, though there could still be frosty nights.

A letter from S. Francis Nicholson, Edward Jacob Senior's brother-in-law and financial manager, advised Alfred on the purpose and method of managing the capital fund that enabled Hilltop Farm, concluding, "I suppose you have a will now, in accordance with the Quaker admonition of providing for one's affairs 'while in health.' If not, you ought to do so, particularly in view of your residence in Vermont, your ownership of real estate and the

---

49. Rowena, resolving to add some variety to the gene pool, married a Persian (Iranian) man, with whom she had six children.

presence of your minor children, all of which might cause complications in the event of your death, which might be costly and troublesome to your family." Quakers were not just pacifists, they were good at business. An oft-repeated joke is that, "The Quakers came to the New World to do good, and they did very well."

Norma wrote to Mildred Loomis on April 29, in part:

"We are headed for changes here, as Alfred has received word that he has been classified 4-E.[50] He is now trying to find out how long it is likely to be [before he is called up], so that we know what to do here—whether, for instance, to go ahead with the summer planting as planned, or whether to start right away selling off stock and getting the house into more leave-able condition. It may be that I'll be able to stay on, if I can only find someone to stay with me, but in any case, things will have to be reduced to about the minimum while Alfred has to be away. I feel we have learned much from our two years here and it hasn't been wasted, though perhaps in the nature of things it could never have turned out just as we had planned."

It was risky to plan too far into the future during war, when the military draft was sucking men in. The top classification was 1-A, ready to be called up immediately, and the bottom was 4-F, unqualified for military service. 4-E meant alternate service as a conscientious objector, still disruptive of personal life. The alternative to serving was prison, so this was a serious matter.

Norma also wrote to Eleanor [Garst] on April 29:

"The scandal [?] that seemed about to break over Alfred's head has been averted, at least for the moment. I got some information from an English friend which suggested that the next step would be orders to report for a medical examination prior to re-classification, and so feared the worst. What came, however, was a card saying he had been classified 4-E. He feels now that most likely he'll go when they send for him, because, the cases of Murphy et al. [no reference could be found] notwithstanding, he thinks the authorities are showing slightly more tendency to move in the direction of work of genuine national importance." [Civilian Public Service was organized to use conscientious objectors for performing "work of national importance."]

That same day Alfred wrote to another "Phil," not his brother, probably the same person he corresponded with in November 1942:

---

50. Following the air raid attack on Pearl Harbor and the subsequent declarations of war by the United States against the Empire of Japan and then a few days later against Nazi Germany, the selective service period, originally 12 months, then 18 months, was extended in early 1942 to last for the duration of the war plus a six-month service in the Organized Reserves.

1943

"I'm glad you kept out of the army, even if it wasn't on principle. I have never understood why slight physical defects make one ineligible. Surely the army exists in order to provide [create] those defects, in itself and others, at a maximum of cost.

"My own classification has come. Being an alien [although Alfred was born in the U.S., he became a British subject during his years spent there], a farmer, and a family man will save me no longer. They very kindly put me in their nearest category to where I stand—4-E, for those who think a constructive civilian service is better than a destructive campaign of war. Still, I may be called away, and it raises the problem of what is to happen to the farm and the livestock, and whether to plant anything at all or attempt to cut any hay.

"I wonder what is the other job I could be doing right now? I grant this one isn't world-shaking; but then I live my life in spurts of preparation and spurts of activity. Most people think the urgent thing is for the war to be won. The press campaign has made it inevitable that most people think this. But what is the point in finishing off one way if you go right on living in the sort of way which inevitably gives rise to wars?

"Since I grew up a little (if I have) I have never wanted to take one side in a conflict, but to understand the conflict. This is the attitude of a parent with his children—he does not take sides with one against the other, for both are his. And so the world is ours, and it is in civil war. Let's try to see what can be put right, so that no future civil war will occur. The military instinct to dominate the civil government was just as strong [in Spain] as here, and I saw its results. The whole thing is catastrophic.

"Now, as to the land here. You want to prove that ownership of this land originated in the capitalist system and therefore I should support big business. Not so. Our view is that when we had decided it was right to go all pastoral, we were enabled to acquire a suitable place. Does it matter so much where the money comes from? Ownership of this land was regarded as vested in a group, but legal title has been passed around from one to another of the group, and at present my wife has it. The money was raised by group action and interest. [The initial funding was provided by his father.] As for the postwar jobless millions (it will be no joke then) it was thought that the government would make poor land available when the crisis got severe enough. That is why we chose poor land to work on here.

"You're welcome to your bit of land, but you ought to come up and choose it. You could spend a week or two exploring all the acres and tell us what you find, since there's much of it we've never seen. (Pastoral interlude: I have just tied a hot water bottle underneath a goat whose tummy is swollen.) You could try out our arrangements and learn two things: that life is possible this way, and that you prefer it the other way. Of course, we prefer things the way we have always known them. But is that necessarily the right way or the best way? You have a preference for fancy plumbing—so necessary in the city, so superfluous in the country. We like to give the pump handle a push and feel the water being drawn right from the spring. Where does your water come from? From miles and miles of pipe laid in the sunless cavities under dusty streets. You're welcome to it. You can think it's sweet and clean because you just polished the handle of the faucet. But there may have been a cow standing in the brook it came from. Now, we would see a cow standing in our spring. You see how much more sanitary the simple life is!

"When you have seen one of our baby goats you will want one for a pet. A goat has all nature's devices for keeping clean. And when you milk your own milk, you know what's in it. Do you think the farmer who ships your nice shiny bottles of milk would throw out a 40-quart can because he found a dead mouse floating in it? No, he would just make a mental note to draw the milk for his own house from one of the other cans. Problem solved. The mouse you don't taste won't hurt you. [!]

"Now I must build some fence, in the hope of keeping the goats in the pasture instead of around the house."

The same day he wrote to Leslie, in part:

"Norma thinks I should soft-pedal my view that people make themselves unhappy by developing needs which require them to spend all their time finding the wherewithal to meet such needs. My mind dwells on it. I keep thinking there is something basically simple which we have missed.

"I forwarded your draft board card. I also am 4E. It raises the problem of what to do here—if I am to leave during the summer, I must spend my time on roofs, foundations, and exteriors; if not so soon, I can carry on the agricultural program planned. I don't know what we could do with our stock. We have ordered another ram to replace the one we lost, and more rabbits are coming. There is nothing inherently impossible about Norma's staying here with suitable company, but she ought not to have leaky roofs or a frozen storage cellar to contend with."

May 1943

On May 1 the new Abundance Japanese Plum tree arrived. Alfred began to dig a hole for the tree, then walked over to the Fields', following a blazed trail and felling a tree across a stream to get across. He lunched on pancakes there and got some lessons in saw and file management. Then he went to the Nearings', and while they dug, talked with Scott about the problems of moral investment and of the real number of hours involved [a theme to which he invariably returned] in modern machine labor. Scott thought the war would go on for 150 years like the one between Rome and Carthage, in order eventually to determine the successor to the world domination of the English Channel nations.

A letter arrived from Elizabeth Graham Thorsen, offering to trade her Angora rabbits for rabbits Hilltop might send in the future. "Now I'll be frank—I am much more anxious to find decent care and love and the right feeding and handling for these rabbits than I am to get the money out of them. I can't help this—you would be exactly the same if you had to sell rabbits you had raised and tended. So if this is not a good trade for you—then I'll be more than open-minded to some other sort of trade which will secure your home and your care for these rabbits. I don't want to ask any money for this group now—don't I understand how ready cash is just minus unless one has had time to grow it, or create it, or otherwise produce it! I don't want any cash for this group of animals until their wool, and their sale, has produced it."

Norma answered on May 2:

"Your suggestion about the rabbits would suit us wonderfully, only a major snag has developed. Just last week Alfred had a card saying he had been re-classified in 4-E, which means that, provided he passes the medical examination, he will in course of time be taken off to a C.P.S. camp. We have no idea how long it may be—he has written to the draft board explaining that as a farmer he needs to know whether to go ahead with this year's program or whether to sell the stock and be prepared to go off at once. By next Wednesday I hope we'll have an answer to this. There's quite a chance that they may say 'All right, as you are a farmer, we won't send for you till the end of the present season'.

"However, the whole question of our future here is in doubt. I obviously couldn't manage alone, but there still are a few possibilities in the way of people who can come and help out, and in any case, we'll do our best to see the summer through. If for nothing else, I want the children to have their vacation up here.

"Well, how would this be for an interim solution? You bring us on Saturday as many hutches as you can get in your car, each containing a rabbit. We'll do our very best to fulfill our part of the arrangement, but if we find we do have to leave here we'll let you know as soon as we know ourselves, and work together on finding them another home. There's a chance I might be able to stay somewhere locally and keep a few animals that were easy to look after. All these possibilities we'll have to start exploring when we know more about Alfred's probable future. In any case, it should solve your immediate problem of getting everything out before June 1st."

Letter possibly of May 1943 from Ed [no last name, probably Levin] in Chicago:

"As you can guess merely from the address above, things have happened since I wrote you last. I have found God, quit my job, filed my C.O. form, been classified 1A, filed my appeal, come to Chicago to do some sort of work of social importance—and now I am waiting for the final decision on my case.

"I could write an 'As ever—Ed' on the bottom of this & it would be quite complete—factually. But we know the soul of a letter is not fact, & you two, of all people, deserve a soulful letter. Now I have a real feeling—understanding of the fact that if one lives a good life, a life consistent with the ordering power of the universe, the fruits of his life will inevitably be good. When I was with you last summer, Alfred was quite worried about moral criteria, and I believe, felt a need to justify your 'living apart' from society & its problems. I remember his pointing out—as if to refute an incriminating charge—that society did not question when a young man left it for four years to live isolated in a college. We, like the college man, are trying to find a way of life—a way to cope with certain of its problems.

"Perhaps I have taken us too far afield, for this is what I would like to say: you need no rationale, your work is good and as such will necessarily bear good fruit. What I have found is to some extent your fruit, although neither of us realized it then. And it is as important to society as to oneself, that each find himself.

"Several days later. . . . I'll mail this, before it goes astray, to assuage my conscience & because I so much want to hear from you. And when I can, I'll complete the letter.

"Gloria, who often talks about you and the children, sends her love, as do I.

"PS—I used your name in my C.O. form. Sorry I neglected to get your permission. Hope you don't object. Ed"

Alfred added a postscript to a letter that perhaps Norma wrote, separated from the original letter, maybe circa May 1943:

". . . because it is often in my mind: 'What can be done with means available to absolutely everyone? With poor land, hand tools, no or little livestock, simple shelters, natural fertilizers, home produced seeds, and so on.' Everyone who comes here says to me 'You ought to have a horse. He would save you a lot of work.' The answer is, a horse involves a lump sum of capital, and specialized knowledge, which most people do not have and can't get. I want to see what can be done with means that everyone can have and get. What is it that any man could do on any piece of land?

"This is a long story and I won't go into it. It is generally misunderstood, mostly by those whose unconscious philosophy [Alfred assumes] is: why should you do a piece of work if you can avoid it? As if the whole end and aim of life were to reach the point of no work. I am interested in rightly-ordered work and rightly-ordered consumption. [Whether something is, or isn't, 'rightly ordered' is a common Quaker conundrum.]

"It seems to me tragic that most people should spend most of their time just getting the food, clothing, and shelter with which to spend most of their time getting food, clothing and shelter (not a misprint). If a goat spent all its time keeping itself alive, we should put it in the stew pot. We expect it to produce. A man ought to ask himself too: 'Besides keeping myself and family alive, what am I producing?' But with most, the exercise of keeping alive (at the level of refrigerators, train journeys and steam laundries) exhausts them, and they fall back on the excuse: 'Well, anyway, I am raising some children and maybe they can do some good in the world.'

"This is just one of my notions. Ultimately, I suppose it means that men can only live rightly and creatively when we have reduced our sense of need for material things to the point where we can meet them by expending only part of our time producing them, and use the rest as the goat does, in producing whatever is the equivalent, on the human level, of milk."

Alfred's letter to Edward Senior and Caroline, dated May 1, said in part:

"We thought spring was here but it snowed last night, and the morning temperature of 22° will have done no good to the things in my cold frame [a flat outdoor planter covered with a glass panel that trapped warmth] . . . I have been reclassified 4-E, which removed the immediate danger of going to jail for refusal of the physical examination; but I may still have to go somewhere, and it is difficult to plan the farm work not knowing how long I shall be allowed to be here. I suppose I must just carry on as usual, simplifying where possible; but there are many things that would have to be done soon if I were going away, to keep the mice and porcupines and the weather out. . . .

"If I have to go to a CPS camp, Norma wants me to apply for the Reconstruction unit at Haverford. In that case I might see something more of you, and that would be nice. If I have to leave here, it doesn't matter to me much where I go, so long as it is some constructive activity. The Coast and Geodetic survey would attract me too, or farm work elsewhere; but I don't lean toward the mechanized, speed-up, factory type of farm. I wouldn't want to regard farming as a business, but rather as a way of life. If you can't live in what you're doing and get your enjoyment out of it without needing vacations, something is wrong. I wouldn't want a vacation from farming. It is the vacation already."

Letter from Norma dated May 2, to Piers and Teresa:

"You know this is the day last year that we came back from Hanover with Roger, but it all looks quite different—no leaves on the trees, no daffodils (although there are some that will be flowering soon) and the road is still so wet and muddy that you can't drive up or down it.

"Herbert Leader came over to see us last week, and when he left to go to the Fields', little Marietta followed him all the way. So yesterday Harold Field came over to bring Marietta back, and brought his dog with him. When he left the dog stayed behind, so today we are going over the mountain to take the dog back. I shall take this letter over to leave in the Fields' mail box so you'll get it a little sooner.

"Be sure to tell me when your vacation starts so I can write to Dr. Stokes.[51] We mustn't leave it too late because he is so busy. Teresa, didn't I give you another whole bottle of pills at the end of March? Have you eaten all those, or did you lose the bottle? Look about a little and see if you find it. If you don't, I expect it will not matter going without them for a few weeks now summer is coming.

"I'll be sending off a small parcel this week—nothing very exciting, just Teresa's knitting and some new name tapes which I hope you will like. It was nice to have Teresa's letter, and I hope Piers will write and tell me about the play on Parents' Day.

"We are getting ready to have a nice garden and some plants are coming in a few days. I hope the goats and hens won't eat them, as they did last year."

Norma wrote to the Family on May 6:

"In my last letter I said something to the effect that I suspected we might not be here much longer, and now it looks as though I may have guessed right. Just a few days after I wrote, a card came from Alfred's draft board down in Media saying he had been re-classified 4-E, the special category for conscientious objectors which means 'work of national importance' in a Civilian Public Service camp or elsewhere. That would normally mean that he would have to leave here within from one to four months, according to other friends whom we've consulted.

"However, Alfred wrote to the draft board explaining that it was very important to him as a farmer to know how much time he had left, as he might have to arrange for selling stock, and also if he was to go soon, it wouldn't be worthwhile going ahead with the summer's planting program (some of it of course is already started).

"They wrote back asking for particulars of his farm work; it's unlikely they will re-classify him as a farmer, unless they count the rabbits (we have

---

51. Dr. Joseph Stokes was Teresa's physician at the Children's Hospital of Philadelphia. Because of her illness with TB, she required regular check-up X-rays at the hospital.

just made arrangements for increasing our Angora rabbit family to 24, and wool of all kinds is naturally an important crop just now). But they may perhaps have the good sense to leave him where he is till November; this will mean the production of a whole year's food for one family or more, which isn't to be sniffed at in these times.

"In any case it seems likely we'll have to make other arrangements for next winter, unless I can find someone else to keep me company here, and that gets harder and harder as time goes on, as more and more men get drawn into the machine. The wife of a man in prison or C.P.S. would do well, if I could only find one with enough courage to face the conditions here.

"In many ways we have an easier life than people in cities—better food, less wear and tear on the nerves [a curious statement!], freedom from illness and so on—but it looks very terrifying to one used to the comforts of city life, and certainly loneliness and hard physical work are enough to deter many women.

"Another possibility is that Alfred may be turned down at the physical examination on account of the really shocking condition of his teeth (a legacy of hard work, inadequate food, and incessant mental strain in Spain, but he hasn't actually lost many of them, and anyway they are overlooking such minor defects pretty generally now.)

"All in all, it looks rather as though I should be hunting for a place to spend next winter. I have a number of possibilities in mind. Best of all I'd like to go back to Pendle Hill and spend some months working on the book called 'Quaker Spanish' which they are planning. But that would mean getting rid of all the animals and losing my New England connections, which are becoming quite important—I occupy quite a key position, being such a prolific letter-writer, and am the one who always gets the job of organizing meetings and so on.

"At present I am editing a newsletter to keep people in touch with one another now that visiting is becoming so difficult. So I may try to join up with one of the other farmer's groups, for instance the one at Fellowship Farm near Boston with which we have always had close links. The sheep, the best of the goats, and the rabbits could probably find lodging there. [*Teresa*: I have no recollection whatsoever of rabbits, which is curious since there were apparently two dozen of them in one of the chicken houses.]

"Finance is likely to be a difficulty; it's true that if we move from here we are likely to be near a school where the children could go for nothing, but I am so very anxious to let them have one more full year at Manumit, though it's crazy economics. It will cost more than our entire year's income and will have in any case to be financed from capital, but I feel it's time the children's interests were put first, and I am quite sure Manumit is the right place for them at their present stage of development.

"As a compromise they might go to one of the Quaker boarding schools, where scholarships would be available to them as birthright Friends,[52] but I am much against these schools because of their snobbishness and racial discrimination—two tendencies which seem to me so utterly un-Quakerly as to outweigh any advantages. It will also cost 30 dollars a month to keep Alfred in a C.P.S. camp; so I may have to go out and work to support the family.

"One possibility, however, which seems to me very hopeful, is that Alfred might get into the reconstruction unit at Haverford College, only a few miles from Pendle Hill. The men they take there have been given the 4-E classification but not yet assigned to a camp, and with Alfred's background they might think him something of an acquisition. This would most likely mean a pledge to volunteer for European relief right after the war, but I had been expecting to do that anyway, I even have my branch of service all picked out—the re-settling of peasant refugees in deserted villages in France, already begun by the American Friends. It would also ease the financial situation, because I fancy the members of this unit are paid maintenance (many of them are married men) instead of having to keep themselves.

"On the other hand, life in Haverford would probably be as expensive as anywhere in the country. So far, the rise in the cost of living has scarcely affected us, but I am afraid if we go out into the world again we are due to get some disagreeable shocks. However, we could be together, and I could get work of some kind. Perhaps a co-operative house for the wives of C.O.'s could be tried down there.

"All this is highly speculative as you will see; no doubt by the time I write again we'll know something definite from the draft board. There is always the possibility that Eleanor may come back, but she is still working hard to get her husband out of prison, and I think there is quite a chance she may succeed. She finds that her anti-war activity has been held against her husband, which seems rather unfair.

"The weather continues unspeakable. Here we are well into May, and not a leaf or a flower to be seen. This time last year lilac, apple and daffodils were all blossoming away for dear life. I do see a few tentative buds on the lilac, and there were some big fat buds on the daffodils which either a goat or a sheep has just eaten, to my mortification, and a little rhubarb is timidly beginning to appear, and two or three tulips poking up; but that's absolutely all.

---

52. Children had automatic membership in the Society of Friends if both parents were members at the time of their birth.

"Today the sun is shining for the first time in about a week (though a cold wind still blows from the north) and I have been out most of the day preparing rock gardens here and there and sowing a few packets of seed. When the animals are safely in the barn, I shall put out my three precious aubretia plants. You wouldn't believe the trouble I had to get them, and they cost more than a dollar. The stuff is practically unknown over here. Lavender, carnations and foxgloves are also ordered, and I expect them any day now. My plan is for a series of small gardens here and there on the rocky ledges which surround the house. A formal bed would have to be painstakingly constructed of earth carried from way off, and I think small patches will be both less work and more in keeping with the landscape. I am no gardener, of course, and can only hope for the best."

Teresa: I do not recall that there were flower beds of any kind at Hilltop. Since the goats wandered freely it would have been impossible to protect the plants from them. Norma's attempts to create a homelike environment were constantly being frustrated by the realities of climate in Vermont, the indifference of other residents, and farm life in general. To Alfred, beautification efforts of any kind were a needless waste of time. Even the trash surrounding the entrance door was not cleared up for two years, and then by a visitor.

Norma continued: "Thanks to the weather, the road is still impassable. There is even still snow in some stretches, and it is likely to be a week or ten days before any vehicle can get up the hill. This is a serious situation, as our stocks of food of all kinds are almost exhausted. We ordered in six months' supplies in November, but of course couldn't foresee the abnormally late season.

"The hen food is all gone, and the hens are subsisting mainly on household scraps, of which, with our frugal cooking, there are only a few; naturally this means low production of eggs. And I am at my wits' end what to feed the seven ducklings, with enormous appetites and constant loud clamor for food. Even the humans are running short; we have an abundance of vegetables, but things like flour and breakfast foods are all gone. Yesterday I carried 12 lbs. of miscellaneous groceries up the hill on my back. Everything is ordered, only waiting to be picked up by the truck which is to bring the grain, etc. as soon as the road is open again.

"Alfred is building a fence to try and keep the goats to their half of the property—an almost impossible task, but one that has to be done, whatever else may be left undone. As for me, I have been doing a little landscaping, and have built a dam and thus created a duckpond between here and the barn. It is not a very watertight dam and a good deal seeps through, but still the result is undeniably picturesque, particularly as just on the far side stands a weeping willow which we planted last year to try and screen the barn from view. It hasn't begun to weep yet, but we hope for the best. . . .

"I expect to be sending you a copy of a pamphlet by Vera Brittain;[53] I got so engrossed in reading it that I let all the supper burn and never noticed the evil-smelling smoke spreading through the house! I can't escape agreeing with her statement that 'This (the starving of Europe's children) is one of the most terrible things that has ever happened in the history of the world'. No justification I can possibly think of can be brought forward to support it. There are some things one can't allow oneself to be a party to whatever the provocation, though that fact seems to be pretty generally lost sight of in time of war. Will it really be better for a nation to survive and be hated by the rest of the world for hundreds of years? Might it not be better not even to survive? Vera Brittain's latest book is here waiting to be read; I wonder if you have seen it, I remember you used to enjoy her writing."

Norma's letter of May 6 to Mrs. Spruyt discussed problems of several goats—one had a badly split udder, and a new buck kid got stepped on by a neighbor's horse. Then, "Letters from the children come quite often. I think Teresa is much happier now [that] summer is coming on and there is more to do out of doors, also she seems to be getting on better with the other children in her dormitory. Piers seems to have been perfectly contented after the first few days."

Mrs. Thorsen arrived with the rabbits and hutches, and much of the day went to that encounter.

On May 16, Alfred's 34th birthday, he tried to have a day of idleness, without much success. After milking, he waited around to see where the goats got out, and excavated part of the brook to make the water more accessible for drinking. The goats climbed over the wall to the south field, and Alfred went on to see which way to extend the fence. Then he got to exploring the boundary, and brought back five little balsam trees and set them between the house and barn near the compost.

By then it was breakfast time, then time to go down and wait for Norma. (No mention of where she had been.) The snow was gone and the grass green, and there was plenty of animal activity—including mice in the house and rats in the barn. The birthday was celebrated with a cake and a

---

53. Vera Mary Brittain, a graduate of Somerville College, Norma's alma mater, was an English "Voluntary Aid Detachment" nurse, writer, feminist, and pacifist. Her best-selling 1933 memoir, *Testament of Youth*, recounted her experiences during WWI and the beginning of her journey toward pacifism (Wikipedia).

present: Duke Ellington's 'Sophisticated Lady' for the gramophone. (Alfred played several instruments and had been the leader of a musical group while in high school.)

A dramatic change in Hilltop's circumstances was about to occur.

A letter from former Dartmouth student Roger Robison, now a Methodist minister, to Norma and Alfred, said in part: "The Lord giveth and the Lord taketh away, however. It looks as if He might be giving you, for a month at least, one Norm Williams, who is also writing you. Norm is a college student here, the chairman of our F.O.R. [Fellowship of Reconciliation] group, sort of a missionary in India, a good man. I feel confident he would work in with you perfectly if you can use anybody at all during the summer. He has been classified 1A and is waiting for the results of his appeal, so it is a bit indefinite. I hope you and he can work something out. It will be good for him to discover that there are some Englishmen who are not anti-Gandhi!"

And from Norm Williams, May 18: "I believe that my friend Rog Robison of the seminary here has already mentioned me to you in his last letter. In case he hasn't, I'd better introduce myself.

"I hail originally from the other side of the globe, India to be exact, where my parents are in mission work under the Methodist Board. In 1941 I came over to the United States, after completing high school, and entered Oberlin. Now that my sophomore year is ended and the summer months are ahead of me, I'm casting about for work which will be useful and at the same time do something toward preparing me for life in a C.P.S. camp, which I expect to be entering before many months.

"Of course I am a C.O., although just now the Selective Service does not seem to be in any hurry to recognize the fact, and I want to get with people who are seriously attacking the problem of cooperative living and practical pacifism. The only thing of which I am certain from my thinking on the problems of these types, is that my experience and spiritual equipment is quite pitifully inadequate for meeting them constructively by myself, and that I need help.

"Rog has talked this over with me several times. I told him that a work-camp with the Friends or the F.O.R. seemed to be most valuable for what I had in mind, but that I would like to get in some farm experience before. He suggested you, and told me about his experiences with you. It all sounded very good to me, although I know little or nothing about farms.

"Now I would like to know if you would be willing to take me for a month or more, beginning early in June. I'm pining away for some good, hard, earthy work, so you needn't have any worries that I'm expecting a life of idyllic bliss, or a bed of roses. Rog was kind enough to let me read some of your letters to him, of which he is very proud, and I must say that they make me feel that you must be folks well worth knowing. Rog, of course, makes no bones about that at all, and highly recommends Vermont as well.

"As soon as you can write me, I'll be very glad to hear from you."

Alfred started the truck and hauled most of the remainder of the old (1941) compost to the field, making 17 barrowloads. He spread them and plowed them under with the Gregg one-man plow, which worked pretty well, though it didn't go at all deep. This was satisfactory, however, for Alfred had just read in Ehrenreid Pfeiffer's *Grow a Garden and Be Self-Sufficient* that "A wet, heavy soil which has not been worked in the Fall should not be spaded in the Spring but simply cultivated with a crile [scissor-like forceps, today only for surgical or medical use]. Better results are obtained in such a case from shallow plowing."

The goat Penny's bad side of her udder was hanging from a shred and Alfred cut it off. The flesh was raw underneath, but presumably it would skin over. She spent the day with her head in the darkest corner of the old hay mow, and Norma hand fed her some grass in the evening. The goats passed the house only once, and spent the day grazing at some distance.

Norma went to the village and returned with a new goat book from England sent by Mrs. M., which described poor Penny's symptoms. Another porcupine was dispatched in the barn, about the tenth one.

Alfred wrote to Leslie:

"Since your last letter I have been writing mentally to you much of the time, and today, being rainy, I have finished off early and can write a little.

"Your interpretation of the farm as a meat-producing factory seems proper; the question is, is that what will redeem society? Or, in other words, is that what we ought to be doing here?

"I have always been against the farm as a factory for the production of meat, milk and fiber, for as a factory it must be devoted to labor-saving: i.e. throwing men out of work in order to produce more with less & get higher profits by paying lower wages. Farming seems to me to be desirable as a way of life, not primarily as a means of production. As a means of production it meets some people's purely economic needs: wages, food, profits, etc.; but as a way of life it can meet all needs: creative living, art, invention, poetry, fellowship, security.

"I have found myself opposed to any tendency towards the farm factory, and [am] longing for the farm life. This I hope explains some of my reserves. It seems to begin at the point of saving labor; for a third of the time 'saving labor' really means saving my immediate labor because someone else had labored to produce a machine for me to save my labor with, and will have to labor elsewhere to get the cash to buy the machine with which to save my labor; and a third of the time it means saving labor by (ultimately) throwing someone else out of work. But I grant that saved labor by applied intelligence, improved methods, better organization of time, simplification of procedure, etc., is all to the good, and fully compatible with the family farm.

"The over-mass-productioning of farms seems to me to be intimately connected with war. It achieves war, through displacement of families, seasonal labor, insecurity on the farm, low prices that only highly mechanized mass production can meet, squeezing the family farmer out into the unemployed when war must employ; and on the boomerang, war of course requires further mechanization of the farm in order to produce for mass-waste. [Alfred's plan seems to be for a coalition of individual farms that support only the resident families, not contributing anything to society as a whole.]

"A book I have been looking at, *Cooperation as a Way of Peace*, is very outspoken as to who gains by war. Even without reading it, one has only to open one's eyes and look around one. The fact of war just solves everything for big business right down the line—full use of machinery, immense profits, guaranteed market, fully solvent customer (the gov't), no need to advertise. But what occurs to me is Sherlock Holmes' phrase, cui bono? ['Who is benefitting?'] If we are to look for the causes of war, ought we not to steal a page from him? How is the average man to get out from under this burden? To me it seems clear. A re-thinking of agricultural means is in favor of the small producer instead of in favor of the highly mechanized one (such as McCormack-Deering would like every farmer to be) would reduce the need for heavy equipment and valuable draft animals, and thus reduce the hold of the money-lender on the throat of the farmer who believes all the advertisements; and open up small-scale farming to many for whom the cost of horses, harnesses, stables, cats [?], wagons, mowers, tenders, side-delivery rakes, hay loaders, choppers, blowers, silage cutters and the like would have meant selling their souls to the big dairy companies.

"So, we come back to where we started, where Hilltop started. Farming as a way of life, as a way of education, as a creative activity for everyone, would contain none of the substance of which war is made [Alfred naively overlooks the destructive stresses inherent in group activities, despite personal experience at Hilltop, for which he tended to blame others], and would undercut those whose names are in the list under cui bono?

"I would want children to enjoy an education available to every child—hence one based on very simple talents and materials; for what does the world gain if one or two children have a ten thousand dollar education while 98 or 99 live in Tennessee? Even if the one or two are specially interesting to me. [Alfred's conviction that what he personally is doing will have a global impact seems unshakable.] All this, and more, is what goes on in my head as I plant beans and peas and add rails to the pasture fence. You will want to know, though, what action we have taken in our own case.

"It is not very satisfactory, but I wrote to the investment expert who is to supervise the reinvestment of the funds in my name, and said if I had to concur, I would take exception to 4 types of investment: in businesses in which profit was the primary actuating motive; in security pools; in government bonds; and in enterprises selected because of their security or rate of interest. I have not had an answer.

"I went and had a preliminary physical examination for the draft. Another is to come. I feel uneasy about cooperating even to this extent, but take the view that I had better go ahead, not until I think I ought to do otherwise, but until my whole self cries HALT. I don't know when that will be. I hope I have learned from my Spanish friends that the reason a reed is not broken in the wind is because it bends. Possibly the time comes when it would rather cease to be a reed than to continue to bend before that wind.

"Our earliest peas are above ground; and though planting my 50 x 50 [an earlier reference stated the dimensions as 50 x 60, which is probably correct] three-story garden takes a lot of time, I hope with the pull-plow to sow some legume hay too, even though we may never use it. One can't simply sit down under events and resign one's will, though there is a temptation. We are arranging to disperse the stock; though I should like so to arrange things that I could come back at any time. This is probably vain hoping. Scott Nearing's view is that this war will go on for 150 years, and it is probably true that none of us will live to see the end of it. I can't help feeling that induction into the CPS is just the beginning of a long dark tunnel.

"Our apple blossoms are not yet showing. The poplars are the only trees showing what you might call leaves. But our new nut trees are leafing out."

Alfred clipped three goats, then got out the Gregg one-man plow to work on the west field. The plow needed constant adjustment, but during the day he plowed about 12 feet in width, about a quarter of the whole. A good many potatoes rolled out that had not been dug the previous fall. The best way to store them seemed to be not to harvest them!

Norma wrote to Norm Williams:

"Of course we'll be delighted to have you come and work with us for as long as you may be able. Any friend of Roger's is welcome here any time, and besides, we are in considerable need of help for this summer. As I just wrote to Roger, Alfred will probably find himself in C.P.S. by the end of the summer, which makes it look as though unless something unexpected turns up, this place will have to be closed for the duration, but we still have a summer's food to be grown and harvested, and we feel that is worth doing in any circumstances.

"We also want to leave the home in such a state that it can be reopened for use at any time, either by ourselves or others. There is lots of work to do before it is really in condition to be left, as well as all the gardening, haying etc. If we can't use the food we grow this summer, we may be able to donate it to C.P.S.

"Our farming isn't very extensive, but it would give a miniature cross-section of what goes on in the average farm, except that we don't have draft animals or machinery. We are trying to experiment with subsistence agriculture chiefly on a manual-labor basis, with the idea that we might work out a pattern available to [a] family going back to the land without much capital or experience, but willing to work hard for the chance to live a self-respecting life.

"We feel much as you do about the inadequacy of our equipment for meeting today's problems, and we always welcome a chance to talk over these things with others going the same way and share such experience as we have managed to acquire here. One thing which we can guarantee is that goat-keeping is one of the finest schools of non-violence! We've also learned a lot about the things which keep people from living peacefully and co-operatively together, though not so much as we'd like about how these obstacles can be overcome. We especially welcome anyone with an Indian background, because India has long been one of our interests. My husband met Gandhi in England and is a great admirer of his."

She also wrote to Phil and Teddy, saying in part:

"Did we tell you our best yearling, Penny, was very sick indeed with what we finally identified as the worst kind of mastitis [inflammation of the mammary gland]? We finally got the diagnosis from a little book on goats sent by a friend from England—[none] of the American books listed the symptoms she had. It seems it's a miracle she didn't die during the first few days of the illness. But she seems in good shape and after 5 weeks is still milking from half her udder though the other half dried up and came right away. We can't dry her off, though we are trying hard, because the loss of half the udder left a split in the remaining side through which the milk runs. It will probably have to have stitches [put] in finally, but we hesitate to tackle this ourselves.

"This has been a calamity, [as] we had her sold to David Barrett and he actually came for her all the way from Claremont the day she fell ill. Her suffering, which we could do little to help, has been distressing too." (*Piers:* My memory is that Junie's first kids were Peter and Penny. It is sad that Penny, which was my late daughter's name, suffered so.)

One rainy day Alfred and Norma worked on the children's room. Norma also wrote a Dear Family letter, saying in part:

"Good news continues to come from the children, including a letter from Teresa [several illegible words]. I also got a picture which I'll send, showing Piers with a Negro and a German refugee; evidently he is learning to be catholic in his friendships, as we hoped. Moreover, the Negro boy is supposed to be far and away the most intelligent child in the school, with an I.Q. of 180, whatever that may mean. [Since the customary tests don't go nearly that high, it is not clear how this score could have been calculated. In any case, the boy would have been in a tiny fraction of 1% of the population.] I don't know what Piers' I.Q. would be, probably not much above par, but it seems he is able to hold his own with the intelligent."

Norma wrote to her friend Lucia at the Brudercoop at the end of May:

"Summer is at last almost here, but we are still pretty much beleaguered on the hill top. The road has been closed to traffic since early December and it's already two weeks past the date when the road gang should have been up to fix it. I've been doing some work on it myself and yesterday put in a couple of hours with spade and hoe reopening drainage channels and so on to try and get the water to run off a little quicker. At one point I saw the marks where a truck had tried to get up, become imbedded and finally given up and gone home. I hope this was the truck containing the urgent supplies for the household and animals for which we've been waiting since the beginning of the month, and I hope the driver, who is a busy man, has by this time called up the Road Commissioner and told him what we all think of him in no uncertain terms. There's practically nothing left in the larder except soybeans, and this has been the state of things for the last three weeks. [*Teresa*: We ate soybeans at almost every meal, squeezed for milk, ground for flour, cooked for beans. They provided the protein that was not available in other ways.] The animals are eating the seed corn, buckwheat, etc. You might almost describe it as a famine. Every now and then I haul up ten or twelve pounds of cereals [grains] of various kinds in a knapsack. 'Rugged' is the word that describes me nowadays. I think I would rather enjoy being fragile and feminine again when I'm through here.

"A few days ago a truckload of Angora rabbits came for us, belonging to a friend who has to move out in a hurry and asked us to give them a temporary home. This truck couldn't get up the hill either, though we waited as long as possible, so there was nothing for it but to put them in the barn of the nearest house, two miles away. I don't know what the owner will think if she arrives suddenly for a weekend and finds her barn full of rabbits. Meanwhile I have to walk the four miles down and back each day in order to feed and water them. Perhaps in another three or four weeks the road will have dried out sufficiently for our own truck to go down and fetch them up, but we'll probably all be dead of hunger by then anyway.

"Sorry I sound so gloomy. These, you know, are the times that try men's souls.[54] Never mind, summer must eventually come, or so they always told me."

Routine chores continued through May. The entry for May 31 discussed the economics of having a horse: Alfred calculated that it would eat six pounds daily of oats or 65 bushels a year, or two acres, plus two tons of hay for the winter, and about a hundred hours a year to care for it. He was certain that it wasn't worth it.

June 1943

Letter from Teresa, undated, probably June: "Dear Norma,[55] How are you. I am fine. I finished the bottle of pills. Please send me my shorts."

Another: "Dear Mommy, I am feeling fine. I am having fun. Are you having fun. The gardens are growing fine. I am coming home soon. Love Teresa."

Letter from Elizabeth Thorsen, who took the goat kid, Janet:

"Janet, the little lovely girl, made the nicest trip down with me! She cried as far as Jamaica. Then her cry turned into a little low talk which went on for some time—as if she were talking very confidentially to me. She was all settled, lying down on the seat with her little head in my lap, and my arm around her shoulder, by the time we were five miles south of Jamaica. She changed positions three or four times. But she always came back to lay her head on my lap. And now—of all the comical things—she gets up into my lap every time I go out to the farm. We are such devoted friends—you just don't know! I think she has the nicest little face of any goatling I have seen anywhere."

Alfred wrote a mournful letter to Philip:

"I wonder if you ever question the validity of what you are doing. I know that you have, and I would not question it for a moment. But what about me? There are times when I simply enjoy the work, planning, and small successes, and times when I am conscious that so far as social construction [the salvation of mankind?] goes, I am doing exactly nil [British for nothing].

---

54. This statement was the introduction to a series of morale-boosting pamphlets written by Thomas Paine in 1776 during the Revolutionary War.
55. We called our parents by their given names, so in effect we did not have a Mommy and Daddy, as they did not refer to themselves with those terms. We scarcely knew them during our toddler years in England; we seldom saw Norma and never saw Alfred, for three years. It's not surprising that there was not a close parental bond. The second letter was probably written down by a concerned teacher who presumed the customary form of address.

My hopes for this place have undergone a decline until there seems no more downhill possible. It is difficult to avoid assigning blame, but I am trying to see the facts just as they are. All I can see that is happening here is that we are living peacefully on the product of investments in the economic system we deplore; and that I am learning about crops and small stock.

"Everything else is gone. The religious emphasis, gone. The pacifist emphasis, gone. The community emphasis, gone. The possibility of a way of life open to everyone, gone, for not everyone has a guaranteed income. [And very, very few would want to, or could, live in the stringent manner he advocated.] Self-identification with those in need, gone, for we give ourselves whatever we like to have, rather than give them what they suffer for lack of. An ideal home environment for the children, gone, for they don't live here anymore. [It's hard to believe that Alfred thought Hilltop was an ideal environment for children!] An opportunity for services to the nation, gone. Our time is occupied with our own affairs, and in any extra time we have, we increase our affairs. As a working analysis of the world's economic problem, no good. I feel too much opposition to any clear thinking I attempt to do along this line.

"In short, as an answer to a world at war, this is a fizzle. We are at war here."

Alfred came late to this painful realization, though to others it was glaringly obvious.

He continued: "Does the fact of learning something about crops and stock justify us in continuing here, or on any farm? Neither Norma nor I have the personal companionship we feel we need. She needs people who are alert, intellectually acute; and I need people who, like myself, are able to puzzle things out over a long period of deliberately fair thinking, intending to apply the results at any cost. I have thought that learning how to produce food and clothing in the very simplest way with the minimum of tools would be useful in the reorganization of human society. But so much of it is not in the learning but in the doing; and it is such a stiff pull not only to do the work but do it in the face of opposition and un-understanding [something Alfred clearly felt he was faced with], that I wonder whether the whole world may not be so much wedded to the 'easy' way that no program of production for use would make any appeal to it. For there still is nothing which seems to me to be worthwhile, so ultimately constructive, as what I came here to do: a way of life totally divorced from the seeds of war. If that is impossible (whatever the reason) have I any right to stay here because it is pleasant to be free?

"It has long seemed to me disproportionate that I should spend my whole time simply producing some of our food and some of our dairy produce when there is no objection to buying the whole of it, and the money is there. Could I perhaps be doing something more constructive with my time? Could I take the time consumed in chores, in gardening, in planting, in haying, in fencing, and so on—perhaps 5 or 6 hours a day—and use it in a more constructive way than just in producing things which we are quite ready to buy? It seems rather like a childish game, which can be carried on too long. At first it was worthwhile producing for the children's sake; but now we buy their food anyway [?]. Norma doesn't eat any produce [not true!]. No, I am really just working for myself, and I could do [that] on much simpler things that would take much less time.

"The alternatives that one visualizes are things like work in the AFSC, in the FOR and so on. But I am no organizer of people. It runs against the grain to smooth them and pet them to make them do what I want. [A curious interpretation of how leaders achieve results.] I visualize always a group bound by a common determination, and each member functioning efficiently as part of the total, conscious purpose. Such could have been the case here.

"The very prospect of life in a city, or among people swayed by the war fever, is uninviting. Campaigning for funds and so on seems conventional and fruitless. Perhaps the thing to do would be boldly to close up here and remove to the next best collective farm we can find. If we believe in collectivism, apply it. Instead of waiting for it to come here, go to it. But there is none in this country that seems to be well enough established to absorb us as we are.

"And for me, the matter of the search for truth is all important. Perhaps I should be in some state experiment station. I want to deal with facts and accept them. I want to get at the facts, and find out at what point, and in what circumstances. In Spain I met a man who said, 'I too, am a Quaker.' He agreed with some of the things he had heard that Quakers believe, so he called himself one. Quakerism is a whole way of life from beginning to end. You don't pay a subscription & become a Quaker.[56] One can say to oneself, 'I am aware of being handicapped by what is fundamentally an inability to love, but I also see that others are so handicapped and manage to get along when they learn to understand themselves and one another.'[57] "The conclusion is, among other things, that marriage between two people, one or both of whom are self-frustrating, needn't be a failure if there is an honest attempt to understand, and if one knows what one may be up against and

---

56. Becoming a Quaker requires considerable study and review, followed by application to, and acceptance by, an established Monthly Meeting. If you are not a member of an established Meeting, you are not a bona fide Quaker, though you may share their views.
57. Persons with autism have deficits in social-emotional reciprocity as well as difficulty developing and maintaining relationships. Alfred recognized this lack in himself but was unable to modify his beliefs or behavior.

how to meet it. But the trouble is, most people rush into matrimony without knowing any of this about themselves or one another and then it comes as an awful shock and they go through life futilely blaming one another and never really finding out what is wrong. [Of course, he is speaking about himself: Alfred blamed others for not telling him in advance 'what marriage was really like,' and blamed Norma for what he saw as her determination to wed, representing himself, as was his habit, to have been a helpless pawn unable to withstand an implacable force.]

"There's an awful lot more I'd like to go into, but one must stop somewhere. At the moment we are nine, and five more are expected today. It's a harmonious group. I am sorry for some of the things I said about its prospective enlargement, they were fundamentally uncharitable, and it didn't work out as I feared at all. [An extraordinary admission, as he rarely, if ever, accepted responsibility for a negative outcome.]

"Hilltop has been responsible for two engagements in the past two weeks—at least, we haven't been officially informed about the second, but there are all the signs! It's a good place for the clarification of any human relationship. One sees the other party in an essentially natural state, not elaborately 'presented' by society. If you can't get on with a person, probably it's as well to know it."

Another porcupine was caught under the tool house.

Alfred wrote to "Ed" [Levin?]:

"Your letter is challenging as usual and has given me much to think about the last few days, while scrubbing floors and the like.

"As for the 're-thinking on new lines,' I've only got so far as vague intimations of what some of those new lines ought to be. Here are some of the things I've been wanting to explore and see others explore. The one that comes first to mind is the whole question of the nature and purpose of life. We keep animals, we achieve a relationship with them which can only be described as personal, and yet we are exploiters; we may love a goat dearly but if she is unprofitable she must go into the stewpot.

"What are we to think of the outcry against the Japanese for the perfectly logical and, I maintain, perfectly just act of shooting the men who come to drop bombs on their cities and kill their children? The fact of what the Japanese themselves have done with bombs in China isn't relevant. When they did that, they were playing the game according to the rules; when they shot [our] pilots, they were breaking the rules. [If Alfred shared these views with others it is not surprising that he had difficulty finding any common ground.]

"I say to myself 'What is it [that] makes these people, basically just like me, able to do this? What could make me capable of the same thing?'

1943

As a first step, we'd want to get together and make a thorough study of ourselves. When I know what makes me tick, I will presumably be a good way along the road to knowing what makes Hitler tick, and what to do about it." (*Piers*: Maybe Hitler saw Jews the way Hilltoppers saw porcupines, that is, merely vermin. Alfred shows no sympathy for porcupines, though they are living creatures too. I see a parallel here that he clearly did not. He bashed undesirable creatures to death; they gassed them.)

Alfred continued: "There are real and fundamental and possibly irreconcilable differences between people in their way of thinking, but the lines of demarcation would probably run in very different places from those we expected when we started the exploration. And I don't think any difference is so fundamental as to be a barrier to friendship, if it is frankly faced and not in a spirit of trying to convert the other party, but of seeing how far you and he can work together for similar ends." (Nevertheless, Alfred's focus appeared to have been on converting others to his view.)

June 5 was a perfect day to go walking to Bondville to an auction. It was also, Alfred might say, borrowing a phrase from President Roosevelt, "a date that would live in infamy." Norma finished the Lulu room first, then set out at noon down the Bondville road, which was obstructed with fallen limbs. The first house on the Bondville side had been rebuilt. The sale was beyond the Brownings, the property of a Finn whose wife had died the previous autumn, and whose despair was such that he hanged himself in the spring.

Alfred took no interest in the sale, feeling that Hilltop was nearer to closing down than anything else, not because of the draft, but for internal reasons (itemized in his letter to Philip)—and soon went off with the Nearings to work a bit with Scott. Norma stayed, and about 5 o'clock came along with a look of "very determined naughtiness," announcing that she had bought a horse named Dickie for $60.

They took Dickie to the Fields, where Norma stayed with him, intending to ride him home on Monday, despite the fact that she admitted to being afraid of horses and had never ridden one! Alfred cut through the woods, aiming rather too high and coming out above the farm above the stone bridge. On the way he saw a small animal, black and white, with a very bushy tail which it held high in the air. He wisely left it alone.

The next day Norma, who had not, after all, ridden Dickie home, discovered a flower in her garden, and a pea pod in the bucket that had been planted on March 1. They harvested the first whole lettuce from the garden. Poor Penny bled underneath, and there appeared to be blood and mucus in her droppings. Janet Jackson, Helen Knothe, and Natalie Field drove up with the new horse and a borrowed buggy, a 12-mile trip around through the village. While they were having supper, Dickie decided to go home again. Natalie chased him down the road and out of sight. Harold couldn't bring him back. Norma went down with the gang and they found him on the Pikes Falls road. Norma spent the rest of the night with a neighbor, and rode the horse up the next morning.

On Friday, she rode to the Jacksons' and walked back, unable to mount while holding papers in one hand. Alfred took his first ride. Norma hitched up the buggy and drove to the village, bringing back a sack of goat feed, a dozen tomato plants, and Janet Jackson.

Norma wrote again to Lucia in the Brudercoop. She had asked Lucia if the children, finished with school for the summer, could stay at the Brudercoop for a day or two while she was attending a meeting.

"It's all settled, then. Barring something unpredictable like measles, we'll spend the night of Saturday the 19th with you. I believe the sensible thing would be if Teresa and I stayed over with

you till Monday morning, instead of having to rush out to West Chester and back again next day to see the doctor. Piers, we could perhaps send out to his cousins on Sunday. He would probably enjoy that more than hanging around in the city where it will certainly be very hot.

"Your suggestions [that she take a week to simply lounge around and enjoy hot baths, going to concerts, and being spoiled] sound wonderful, but I simply can't put in the time on this trip. I think one who is shortly to be a C.P.S. widow should stick around as much as possible. Anyway, I can't leave any sooner, as Alfred has to go for his physical examination in the middle of the week and he'll probably have to be away for the better part of three days. But I am definitely toying with the idea of spending a while with you later, say the end of October.

"I'm bursting to tell you the really sensational bit of news. I went to an auction on Saturday and BOUGHT A HORSE. His name is Dick and [although] he's a lovely little horse, I am scared to death of him, especially as I learned, after buying him, that he has a reputation for bucking people off. I never was on a horse before last Saturday, but Dick has such an easy gait that by Sunday morning we set out together actually at a trot. I haven't been able to get him up to Hilltop yet, but I feel the world is positively at my feet if I can only conquer my stupid fear of horses. I'll tell you the whole story all in good time, if I don't break my neck before the 18th.

"Phil Mayer of the Walden Round Robin blew in Monday afternoon, just after I got back from the horse-trading episode (ignominiously afoot). He stayed until Tuesday midday, and that same evening as Alfred was digging the garden and I was writing an article about maple syrup, an incredible, almost forgotten sound was heard: a car coming up the hill! It was the oldest car I've seen, even in Vermont. Two young people bounded out and introduced themselves as Clara and Dick. Luckily I remembered corresponding with them about a goat, so I managed to place them. We spent a gay evening together putting the world to rights, and they left at 1:00 a.m. with two goats, which just about offset my equine indiscretion. Such delightful surprises have been too few in our lives lately, and I hope [their arrival] means the summer is beginning again at last. Alas, they brought nothing up in the car except their own groceries from the A&P, but we had those for supper.

"I just had word from England that my opus on the New England Town Meeting, the fruit of 18 months' work in the intervals of cooking, laundering, caring for children and coaching hopeless freshmen in Spanish at Dartmouth, is to be published shortly by 'The Countryman,' one of the definitely better magazines. That's why I'm writing up the maple syrup now, as they might want some more about Vermont, and even if they don't, someone else quite possibly will. It's a great life."

Letter from 7-year-old Teresa at Manumit dated June 9th, 9143 [*sic*]:

"Dear Norma and Alfred. How are you I am fine. I had so much fun swimming that I could not send you a letter any sooner. I am going to bring you some radishes, lettuce, and spinach. I am hungry."

Subsequent letter: "Dear Norma, How are you? I am fine. Is the snow all gone. Vacation begins June 19. Please send me some shorts."

Norma wrote to Dear Family June 11:

"After a long period of relative peace and quiet, the children being away and the road closed to all but foot traffic, life has suddenly become very exciting again. It all began on Saturday when Alfred and I walked down to an auction at Bondville four or five miles away by the old woods road which once was the main highway. Do you remember Kipling's poem, 'The Road [Way] Through the Woods'?

> *They shut the road through the woods*
> *Seventy years ago.*
> *Weather and rain have undone it again,*
> *And now you would never know*
> *There was once a road through the woods*
> *Before they planted the trees.*
> *It is underneath the coppice and heath,*
> *And the thin anemones.*
> *Only the keeper sees*
> *That, where the ring-dove broods,*
> *And the badgers roll at ease,*
> *There was once a road through the woods.*

"It's not quite that bad but very much like it, especially since the ice storm which brought down so many trees. Since we are probably not staying here more than a few months, I was determined not to buy anything, and I let pass all sorts of things on which ordinarily I would have been bidding, such as a battery radio which went for much less than I would have paid for it (I did bid on this but desisted when reminded that I might not be able to buy batteries for it any more).

"We were just about to leave when they started selling a saddle horse. Bidding was very slow, evidently there were no horse-buyers present, and he was on the point of being sold for a miserable fifty-seven fifty when I heard myself say 'Sixty!' and the next thing I knew, the rope was being thrust into my hand. I had bought a horse! This kind of thing is apt to happen at auctions, but I never before got stuck with anything half as large or alarming. Of course I wanted the horse desperately, and could give all kinds of excellent reasons why Hilltop needs one, but still, I had only five dollars in my pocket and hardly more than sixty in the bank. And I simply couldn't think what Alfred would say.

"Natalie Field, however, was delighted, she wanted the horse too, and believed she could work on Harold to let her buy it from me before the end of the summer, and Harold luckily had his check book in his pocket and was willing to ride the animal home barebacked. Someone found a bridle, the late owner came up and told me the horse's name was Dick, and half a dozen fragile-looking young women clustered round and told me they had ridden him at one time or another and he was a very gentle horse and as clever as a kitten. He really was a beauty, just a nice size, not too wide to ride but big enough to do light farm work too, brown with black trimmings and a white star on his forehead. And he certainly appeared calm and good-natured, though brisk and cheerful. In fact, an admirable horse for a novice.

"Well, we got him back to the Field's without incident, they dug out a handsome saddle and bridle which they were willing to lend me (since horse furnishings these days often cost more than the animal itself), we saddled him and Natalie and I and little Barbara rode him around the pasture in turns. We found he had a beautiful easy gait and a very sensitive mouth. [One wonders how Norma would know this if she'd never ridden a horse before.] In fact, it all seemed to be too good to be true (and to set your mind at rest I will say at once that if there is a flaw, I still haven't discovered it). I didn't feel I could ride eleven miles home on my first attempt, the woods road being too badly blocked to attempt, so I stayed the weekend, meaning to drive him home on Monday harnessed to the Field's buggy. However, on Sunday night he ran away, back to where he came from, and on Monday morning it was raining, and so we declared a temporary moratorium on the whole business and I went home on foot.

1943

"On Wednesday I started down to the village and met the road gang coming up to fix the road, nearly three weeks behind their usual time, owing to the exceptionally bad weather. (Everything in New England is three weeks behind the calendar this year—and in Canada too, from what we hear). Then, passing the dilapidated house bought by our friends the Jacksons for a summer home, I heard myself hailed and there was Janet Jackson doing some spring cleaning. And to top off, I next met Dick drawing the Fields' buggy, with Natalie, Helen and little Barbara. They all stayed to supper, and Harold Field drove up later, bringing some of our bulky packages which had been waiting down in the Post Office since last November. While we were having supper, Dickie ran off, and we finally overtook him well beyond the village, going rapidly in what he thought was the direction of home (poor animal, he didn't realize he was only five miles from home when he started, and was going back the way he came, a whole thirteen miles)!

"Harold rode him back to Jamaica, the butcher found an empty stall in his cow stable, I found a hospitable house to take me in, and I was more than glad to call it a day.

"Next morning, I saddled the beast and set off boldly to ride the four miles up the hill. I don't mind admitting I was in a state of considerable apprehension, but the journey was absolutely uneventful—even negotiating the town truck, which was practically blocking the road on the last stretch which was being fixed up.

"We keep him in the goat stalls at night and tied to a long rope in the pasture by day, just until he stops being so homesick. The goats look very small by comparison. I hope Nancy Montague and her children are going to appreciate him—of course horses are all in the day's work at Manumit and I shall doubtless find my children far more accomplished riders than myself. I'm told Teresa has a good seat; she certainly has the temperament.

"Next week I start out for a hectic round of visits—to someone in New York who is organizing a co-operative farm for the wives of men in C.P.S. somewhere down in Connecticut, to a committee meeting which has been specially fixed so I can attend, to fetch the children at Grand Central on a Saturday evening, thence to Philadelphia to visit our friends there, thence out to West Chester for a brief visit to the family. On the way back I pick up Nancy Montague, her three children and her young sister, and I hope Alfred and Dick and the buggy will be in the village and we shall ride home in style [three adults, a teen, and five children, plus baggage], instead of dragging ourselves up the mountain, always a deplorable ending to a long day's journey.

"By then, too, we should have another man with us—we are expecting him hourly, one Norman Williams, an undergraduate from Oberlin College, son of a missionary in India. So there will be no more peace and quiet from then on. In fact there is none even now, as I am pretty busy having to look after one horse, six ducks, nine hens and 12 rabbits, and the children's bedroom is being plastered and re-decorated." At that time the goats were totally Alfred's responsibility.

Norma wrote to Piers' school friend Craig Work's mother, Minta, on June 14:

"I have had some prints made from your negative and am sending it back with many thanks. Perhaps I ought to explain a little more why I was so pleased with the picture. You see, my husband and I are Quakers and it was a great shock to us when we arrived in this country from Europe to find that, generally speaking, Negro children are not admitted to Quaker schools. For this reason we have refused to send our children to one of these schools, and we try not to miss any opportunity of driving home to our Quaker relatives how strongly we feel about this matter.

"If this picture were to appear in some Quaker publication, or one that Quakers read, it would help bring it home to many among the older Friends who are responsible for this policy, and who are simply refusing to face it (because of course they know better) and also it would be an encouragement to many of the younger Quaker parents who dislike this policy as much as we do but don't see quite what they can do about it.

"I also liked the picture because the German child was in it—we are so very anxious that in times like these our children shouldn't get any pernicious ideas about other races and nations, and if I find Piers getting militaristic later on and saying hard things about the Germans just because he hears others do it, I'll have something to remind him of the time when he had a German friend. Is that your boy in the picture? From what I hear he must be somewhat older than Piers, but if they are friends, I'd love to have you bring him for a visit. It is too bad we are such a terribly long way from anywhere, but if the Montagues get this far, perhaps others will manage it too."

Piers: Indeed, I never had any prejudice against foreigners, being one myself, or folk of other colors, thanks to Craig. So my mother's effort in that respect was successful.

Alfred left for Rutland for the Selective Service physical exam, under some misgiving as whether it was the right thing to do, feeling he was being "led by the nose through easy stages into irremediable complicity."

Norma and Norm plastered the children's room and cleared up a lot of mess. (This is the first reference to Norm Williams actually being at Hilltop: he must have arrived in the past few days. He worked regularly on the ongoing chores thereafter.)

Alfred returned the next day, having been examined from head to toe, and apparently characterized by the psychiatrist as unsuited for any form of military service.[58] (Rough translation: anyone opposed to war has to be crazy.) The nervous wait was over: Alfred was now reclassified as 4-F.

Norma took the morning bus to Brattleboro, on her way to pick up Piers and Teresa in New York. Alfred and Norm accompanied her down the short cut, then returned to the gardening. They had long conversations. They tried plowing with the horse, but he, not having been trained for this type of service, wouldn't give a slow and steady pull: He either refused to move at all, or suddenly lunged forward and broke the traces.

Norma wrote to her Family on June 27:

"The children and I are just back from a visit to the grandparents and other friends and relatives in Pennsylvania. I started out from here on Friday morning, hoping to see Valerie and [baby] David in Brattleboro on their way back to Canada (it proved too complicated for them to come and visit us here), but a card came from Valerie saying they were going back by a different route, so I had a day on my hands. I spent some of it very pleasantly with a young couple to whom we recently sold two goats. Then I took the night bus down to New York, arriving at 5 a.m., and wandered around the city a little, visiting various places such as the Battery and Wall Street, which I had read about and never seen. Wall Street certainly is amazingly unimpressive, little more than an alley, a short, deep, dark chasm between two blocks of enormous buildings. How it ever came to give its name to a whole financial system I can't guess, it is as though there is hardly room for one financier, let alone all those who are supposed to operate there.

"Just opposite Wall Street stands a much more interesting spectacle, a small church (or maybe it only looks small among the skyscrapers) in the purest eighteenth-century style, probably the oldest building I've yet seen in America, with a monument to some British general (not Wolfe) who distinguished himself at the taking of Quebec."[59] She gave further details about her travel. Then:

"No doubt you will have got my letter saying that Alfred was classified in 4-E, which meant a C.P.S. camp within the next few weeks. Just before

---

58. The possibly apocryphal story goes that Alfred picked up a letter opener from the examiner's desk and inquired whether it would be acceptable for him to kill the man, as killing was the purpose for which he was being conscripted. The examiner hastily scrawled across the registration form, "This man is totally unfit for military service."
59. This would probably not be Trinity Church, which at one time was, because of its soaring spire, the tallest building in the country. Perhaps it was the smaller French Gothic Revival Grace Church a few blocks away.

I left, he went to Rutland for his final medical exam. I telephoned the draft board just before leaving Philadelphia (not having dared to do so before, because this particular draft board has about the nastiest reputation of any draft board in the country, and has been in the papers more than once for refusing to accept a recommendation from the President himself.)

"However, they couldn't bite me over the telephone and quite civilly volunteered the information that Alfred was now in 4-F (physically disqualified). This was an unexpected result to say the least of it; the only thing they could have done, actually, to take the Army off his trail. Unless the case comes up for review at some future date—and Larry says his case has never been reviewed—Alfred is as free as the proverbial bird. We shall of course try and find out the ground of the disqualification; a doctor down there who knows Alfred's medical history says it was probably on account of a spot on one of his lungs. We knew about this, and also knew it was inactive, but the Draft Board probably snatched at the opportunity to get this troublesome case pigeonholed for good without seeming to concede anything to the rights of conscience as laid out by law.

"After spending three or four days very pleasantly with Alfred's family, I started back here with the children—another terrible journey. It got hotter and hotter and there were no seats in the air-conditioned carriages, so we traveled in a coach with an open window directly behind the engine and arrived here covered head to toe in soot. Fran Bacon met us, with Dick and the buggy. The Bacons suddenly decided to leave the place where they had seemed pretty well settled (I gather, though they haven't been very explicit, as the result of a row [disagreement] with the owner of the place) and having nowhere else to go, they came back here. They are, I think, a little shaken up by the failure of the other arrangement and are ever so much easier to get along with than they were last summer. Of course, there was always a possibility of their coming back, as they moved out principally because they felt it was too lonely up here in winter for people with a small baby. But Judy is expecting another in January, so I don't imagine they will plan to settle here.

"Later. Norman Williams brought your letter of June 1st back from the village; he went down to meet his girlfriend, who is supposed to be spending a week or so with us, but she didn't arrive. He also brought news that the invasion of Europe has apparently begun, though he hadn't considered it interesting enough to buy a copy of the paper. I do find men very irritating sometimes. It is fearfully hot—only 85°, actually, which is nothing excessive, but very heavy, probably a storm coming. I went out to the kitchen to make a cup of coffee to try and keep awake (Judy has already given up and retired to bed) and found Alfred reading aloud a book on economics to the other two men, who were asleep with their heads on the table.

1943

"Here is a photo showing Piers with two of his school friends, a Negro and a German refugee. I have taken pains to send copies to all my Quaker relatives who always want to know why I don't send my children to a Quaker school, which would be so much cheaper (since there are huge endowments for the children of Friends). It's a matter of principle; it seems particularly shocking to me that Quaker schools should discriminate against Negros and Jews, and I can't feel that the Quakerism taught in such schools will be of very great value. At Manumit our children are really learning that people of different races are as good as themselves, or better. [*Teresa*: Evidently that did not apply to the Japanese, who, at school, were referred to with insulting epithets. We also learned war songs and slogans, which did not seem to trouble Norma. This would never have been tolerated at a Quaker school.]

"The other picture I want to enclose is one of me shearing a sheep [see photo]. We always heard it was so difficult, but though we found it slow and strenuous, it wasn't otherwise hard. Of course electric clippers get more wool off, but we got nine pounds from Heather, who was only a lamb when we bought her a few months ago.

IMAGE 15: *Norma shears a sheep with hand clippers.*

"I am very pleased with the children's progress at school. Everyone comments on how they have grown (especially Teresa, who is now taller than Piers), how well they look, and how much their behavior has improved. The only distressing thing, apart from the accents, which I expect will gradually fade during the summer, is their bad language [which also would not be tolerated in a Quaker school]. I suppose it's inevitable and certainly progressive schools tend to produce that sort of superficial phenomenon more than a school where much stress is laid on turning out little ladies and gentlemen—but Judy and I did look at each other with raised eyebrows when she heard Piers in a dreamy voice saying something about a 'goddamned tree.'

"Eleanor is still in Philadelphia, and I had lunch with her a week ago She has had every kind of misfortune; Gene's application for parole seems definitely refused for the present, she lost the whole final draft of her book in a suitcase which she left on a train, and finally, Herb Willits, who looks after her like a brother, has been ordered to report for military service, which means prison for him too. There are a couple of points I think are worth making about this matter of prison. Almost all our friends who are there deliberately chose prison sentences of indefinite duration (as soon as the first sentence expires, or a few months later, they are sentenced again for essentially the same offense, instead of the very faint likelihood that they would ever be asked to enter the army.)

"It was registration, not mobilization, to which most of them felt driven to object. Some of them were ordained ministers or theological students, and thus were permanently guaranteed against any kind of military service. Others were physically handicapped. Others were married—and remember, the American conscription law works on quite a different principle from the British, [where] married men with children haven't been called even yet. Two and a half years ago, when most of these boys had to make the decision, they chose between a prison sentence which was quite certain, and military service, which was highly improbable. A woman whose husband goes off to the war has, I suppose, at least a three to one chance of getting him back substantially undamaged. Gene Garst's career is permanently blighted; as long as he lives he'll be an ex-convict, he'll probably never have any children (since Eleanor must be my age or older, and there is no end visible to their separation). He has not really chosen so very much the easier part.

"The other consideration is that when deciding whether a particular action is right or wrong one can't let oneself be much swayed by considerations of personal safety, either one way or the other. A number of C.O.'s were condemned to death during the last war,[60] but it is not recorded that this

---

60. When war broke out in Europe in 1914, there were immediately dissenters who would not cooperate with the military. In Great Britain and its empire, men were conscripted by the tens of thousands. Out of these, approximately 16,000 became conscientious objectors to war. They were often greatly mistreated; in many other countries they were imprisoned or even executed. Their stories provided inspiration to American COs when the U.S. entered the war in 1917.

caused any one of them to change his mind and accept the superior chances of survival in battle. A good many died in prison as a direct result of the treatment they received. And at any moment the positions may be reversed and the man who now goes to prison rather than going to the front may find his conscience pushing him into a position where his life is endangered, while the returned soldier sits safely at home.

"Alfred's quite unexpected classification in 2-F has altered all our tentative ideas about the immediate future. I think very possibly he'll stay on here and I'll take three months off in the middle of the winter: a brief holiday for myself, a chance for the children to spend the Christmas vacation somewhere a little more suitable, and time for me to do some work at Pendle Hill on the volume 'Quaker Spanish' on which they are now at work. This seems like a fairly reasonable compromise."

She wrote to Friends of the Brudercoop:

"I am sending Alfred along, and probably he will show up at your Philadelphia branch on Tuesday or Wednesday next week. At the moment we are seven: Norman Williams' girlfriend is expected this afternoon, and four more children and one mother in about three days' time. It's chaotic and happy.

"The garden is sprouting all over the place. We had about a bushel of spinach last night, the first time we've ever been able to grow it in an adequate amount. Strawberries too. There would have been green peas, but the goats finally ate the two little vines we had been nursing in a sugar bucket since the beginning of March. We look at everything with new eyes now [that] we are no longer going to be forcibly separated from it during the next few weeks. Future still pretty uncertain, however.

"The car is about ready to start (yes, we have a car temporarily—the Bacon's—and are taking advantage of it to collect girl[friend], goat & hen food, laundry, groceries and children's luggage. I shall saddle the horse and trot idly about the fields rejoicing in not having to drive the buggy down to the village after all."

July 1943

Norma wrote to Larry Hall on July 2:

"I've been reading [Karl] Menninger under circumstances of considerable difficulty, since not only are two or three others reading it at the same time, but the house is full of people, noise and confusion, and concentration has been almost impossible. It throws a great deal of light on things which have been sources of difficulty here.

IMAGE 16: *Escaping from the turmoil inside the house, Norma finds a way to kill two birds with one stone.*

"What he says about frustrations in babies is very illuminating indeed, and the average male reader probably doesn't realize how revolutionary it is. For several generations now it's been the absolute rule (and I imagine still is)

1943

that babies must be fed by the clock and that their inclinations have nothing to do with it at all. When I was a baby, I got fed every two hours, as that was the fashion then. Then there was a swing of the pendulum and my children got fed every four hours, with no night feed. Now it's swung backward, and they get fed every three hours and do get a night feed—and so on—and the baby was put on the scales before and after feeding to discover to a fraction of an ounce how much it had eaten.

"Now it looks as though we who tried to do the very best for our children only succeeded in doing the very worst. Teresa, when she was first born, cried almost incessantly; I used to lie in bed listening to her crying in the next room and feeling that it was all wrong—but both she and I were in the nurse's hands, and I was just as much a slave as the nurse to the belief that routine was essential to the child's development. If I'd been in charge, probably maternal instinct could have caused me to break the rules occasionally and then be tormented by guilt. Now I wonder if this offers some explanation of the extreme aggressiveness which has always been a feature of Teresa's character (much less so since the school interlude, by the way)."

Teresa: With no direct experience for guidance and according to British custom at the time, my mother was never comfortable around children or babies. We enjoyed no physical or verbal affection, no endearments or pet names, no comforting hug or welcoming lap. My father even liked to mention how selfish and inconvenient what he called my "insistence on being born" had been, as though it were my choice.

Norma continued: "Judy Bacon, who has one baby raised the scientific way and is expecting another, is greatly impressed by this part—I wonder if it will reflect itself in the treatment of the newcomer! I hardly imagine so, as the idea of regularity has been so drilled into us that we can hardly give it up without a struggle. Probably just the same thing applies to goats. We took the unconventional step of allowing our goats to raise their own kids, though some of them who'd never had a kid near them since the instant of birth were rather disconcerted at first."

The same day Alfred wrote to his brother Philip:

"I am glad for your letter, and your view is very sane.

"My reclassification into 4-F after the physical examination has raised problems which the government might have solved by taking me away. Then this place would have closed down for an obvious reason, and though it wouldn't have been the true reason, it would have served a purpose. Now we are driven back to the necessity to make up our own minds. I am beginning to feel that there is nothing useful to be done here in the circumstances except the thing I wanted to come here for: to live as if I were a pacifist, instead of simply holding pacifist views. I was willing, I thought, to apply the touchstone of pacifism to everything I did with my time. Of course I did not realize what opposition would arise here; and I know of no other place where such a life is being attempted.

"Failing that, there is nothing I would place greater confidence in than in your own activities, and my next choice would, I think, be to see whether by taking your chores off your hands I could liberate you next winter for the activities they may have prevented you from undertaking. It does not mean that Norma will live here in the winter in any case, and I do not think I would willingly spend the winter just minding the stock. I think it would be wiser to sell off everything, except perhaps two goats, and arrange to have them dry from November to April while Norma is away, and go away myself too.

"I want a chance to talk with you. Norma has encouraged me to leave next week to talk with people in Philadelphia and with the parents. I had thought of including you in the visit, but I may be wiser to spend only a week away, and go to you somewhat later in the summer. Is there any time you would suggest?"

On July 4, Norm walked down to the village to meet his girlfriend, Winnie. Nancy Montague also arrived, with her 14-year-old sister Caroline, and three young children.

Nancy wrote about her experience at length in an article published in an English paper:

"It must have been late afternoon when we drove into Jamaica. We crossed the bridge and kept a sharp lookout for a lane leading up the hill to the left. Just as we began to jolt uphill, we met the buggy. Norma nervously grasped the reins and called out, 'Can't stop now! Go straight on up, I'll be back later!' The children in the buggy waved to ours and the horse staggered and the wheels jounced on down the lane.

"At the top, on a knoll to our left, appeared the house, standing desolate and drab in its faded red paint amidst a scatter of every sort of litter. A line by the house held a string of snow-white banners [diapers], the signal of a well-cared-for baby.

"On a plaid blanket by the door reclined a handsome young woman, with beside her a red-cheeked infant with brilliant blue eyes. 'I am Judy Bacon and this is Bert,' she greeted us. 'Alfred is somewhere around.' She was under doctor's orders not to move around, having just suffered a miscarriage, and as Bert's father was not there, I took over as his foster mother. This community baby was used to strangers and did not complain as I managed his bath and meal before Fran, his father, came and finished up the bedtime routine.

"Norma returned, Alfred appeared, and so did Norm and his new fiancée, Winnie, and we all had supper. [Later on], after meals we tended to sit at the table with our elbows on each side of the wooden bowls from which we ate, our chins on our hands, discussing life, religion and ethics until it was too dark to see. We always meant to finish the washing-up before it was time to light the lamp, but it never seemed to work out that way."

Nancy gave her impression of her hosts in a letter to her family: "They really are fun: Norma with her brisk ways, erect blond hair and sharp sense of humor; Alfred slow & quiet & rather impish with a blond beard & big eyes and an incredible tan. He lives on salads, bread & queer drinks made with nutmeg & ginger & vinegar and thinks deeply & when roused talks long and forcibly with good logic."

Her report continued: "There was an Elsan, a beautiful sanitary toilet placed discreetly in the porchway to the front door which no one ever used, the key having been lost. Somewhere in the house was the necessary chemical to render human excrement harmless and odorless. But around the corner of the house was the privy with the smooth old wooden seat and the huge bucket and ill-built door with a hole and a string and two nails, inside and out, to keep the door shut. That was Alfred's source of manure; the valuable gathering place of what he fed to his vegetables. Why deprive his garden of what it needed by using an Elsan? [*Teresa*: It would be typical of Alfred's abhorrence of any kind of waste, even of excrement. I do not remember there ever having been a chemical toilet! In the winter the men simply opened the door and relieved themselves in an adjacent snowbank. As a child, I once bravely voiced my objection to this unsightly practice during a group meeting.] Perhaps, said Norma wistfully, when winter comes again we shall start using the Elsan when it's below zero outside. So it sat snugly in the porchway, and it was nice to know it was there, like the never-used cast iron bathtub.

"It would have seemed that to make a subsistence farm support the 14 or so souls who could be accommodated there, some sort of work plan should have been made and put into operation. Norma was excellent on paper and was, I am sure, a good committee woman; Alfred was a really hard worker, and deep in his sober head lurked some thread leading him through the maze of things which 'really must get done,' but none of this came to the surface.

"After a few days I suggested the children might have jobs, and it was arranged that Donald [age 8] and Teresa fed the ducks and hens and collected the eggs. Teresa cuddled the hens a lot, too. Bella [age 6] and Piers were in charge of the [rabbits]. Caroline asked to be allowed to milk the goats, and Alfred allowed her to learn on the quietest nanny. Caroline also set about clearing up the cans and broken crockery the previous occupants had simply tossed from the back door. Shoes were required for the children, and the sordid air of neglect around the house offended our tidy British eyes. A wheelbarrow was found, and Alfred lent her a spade to use when he did not need it himself, to dig burial holes in the swamp. She set herself the task and followed through on it. After two weeks at two barrow loads a day, she had created an area safe for bare feet.

"Judy was the official cook and baked all the bread cheerfully despite the struggle to get manpower to chop wood chunks the right size for the stove. Alfred had a magnificent vegetable garden which did have a master plan of sorts. But the plan should have assigned so many vegetables to so many jars per week. As it went, if anyone wanted to preserve and could find Alfred and get him to allow that there was really a glut of beans and get enough extra wood together and pick the beans and string them and put them in jars, well then something got put into the cellar for next winter.

"A lot of work did get done. Someone would have an idea and might mention it at breakfast, especially if they wanted female help. The women always seemed to find household jobs for the morning anyway, as there were a lot of mouths to fill and beds to make.

"Alfred would go doggedly on and not demean himself by demanding assistance. He scythed day after day in the meadow behind the barn and the sun shone day after day and the hay was dry and raked into rows. One Sunday a great dark cloud was spotted, and everyone, children too, ran outside to save the hay. We tried carrying it to the barn by the armful, then on a sort of stretcher, then on a tarpaulin, everyone running back and forth for hours as the thunder rolled and the cloud moved on and overhead . . . but not a drop of rain fell. Fran was not there. He appeared at supper time and somewhat sheepishly admitted that he had been reading a book in the upper pasture, as Sunday was supposed to be a day of rest.

"The record hay gathering showed that we could get a job done when a crisis arose, but that did not happen often enough. The crises were ahead, next winter, and meanwhile the woodshed lay unmade and the jars languished empty in the cellar. The only critical, not even uncharitable remark I ever heard at the farm was this: 'The summer visitors don't see the thing as a whole and so they don't work consistently toward providing for the winter.'"

July 8: The goats got in the garden and ate two rows of sweet corn and the two best cabbages. In the afternoon Dickie was saddled and the children had rides. Norma tried to ride him back to the barn and was thrown off. Nancy concluded that Dickie and Norma were simply incompatible, as he invariably misbehaved when she tried to direct him.

July 10: Nancy's daughter Bella fell and cut her leg badly when carrying a glass jar, and Piers accidentally got bumped on the head. At the swimming hole [the Salmon Hole in Jamaica] Dickie ran away and a man in a car gave chase and helped Judy to catch him.

July 10: Norma wrote to Mrs. Spruyt, in part:

"Maybe I told you that Alfred was put in 4-E, so we were quickly selling off the animals and finding homes for others which we thought we might possibly want later. Then after his physical exam they put him in 4-F as physically unfit. This seems perfectly extraordinary and I think it's just an example of buck-passing by a draft board who don't want to recognize conscientious objectors if they can possibly get out of it, but still, it makes Alfred greatly sought-after by people with jobs to offer, and would also make it possible for us to stay here. Whether we shall or not isn't clear at the moment.

"The basic trouble is that he wants to live at a standard which I believe is too low to be right, and he feels my insistence on a slightly higher standard makes the whole thing meaningless. It's no good trying to carry on unless we can bring our two divergent points of view together. And so many of the animals have been either sold outright or promised, that there will be hardly any left.

"Did I tell you that we actually have a horse? He is just full of life and spirits, really just the horse for us if he were big enough to pull the mower and not quite so set in his ideas."

Nancy commented: "Norma didn't really like Dick; she freely confessed she was afraid of him and told grisly tales of his wildness and how hard he was to catch and impossible to control. [This comment must have been to add drama to the article she was writing, as it was really not the case.] Caroline and I found that he was quite a sensible, ordinary horse; I was a trifle nervous the first time she decided to go down to get mail and stores, but she and Norm had him captured in no time and saddled up without a whinny. Norma and Dick have no confidence in each other at all. Whenever he was out with her he remembered his former owners, and Jamaica to him meant a chance to run off back to them." Norma's uptight manner tended to foster unease in animals—or children.

Nancy told of an incident in which she rode Dickie down to the village, realizing along the way that the saddle girths had come undone and were dragging on the roadway. "I meditated as to whether I should dismount at once and chance the saddle coming off with me, or Dick bolting as he was rumored to do whenever near the village, leaving me with a saddle and no horse. I decided to sit tight. At the store I took both feet out of the stirrups and vaulted off. The saddle remained as though glued on. Dick looked at me over his shoulder as I buckled the girths, as though to say, 'Why bother? I knew they were undone! We managed all right, didn't we?'"

Norma wrote to her Family:

"I now have two letters of yours to answer—June 13 and June 21. Both came through unopened [by the censors], but it didn't seem to make them much quicker. I have been on the point of writing for days, but what with this heat and seven children underfoot, life has been rather hectic. Nancy Montague, her three children and her fourteen-year-old sister Caroline have been here for about ten days, and the Bacons and their baby are also here—I think I said that in my last letter.

"There is also Norm Williams, the young man from India (who is so delighted to know that there are some English people who are not anti-Gandhi!) and his fiancée Winifred Frost, who was with us for a week. She's gone now, and Norman is returning to his usual hard-working habits. While Winnie was here the two of them went about in a kind of rosy cloud. When they announced their engagement, we felt it was proper to seem surprised, but we simply couldn't be convincing about it!

"On top of everything else Alfred has been away for a week; he thought it was time he went to see his parents, whom he has seen only once, and that very briefly, during the past two years. So I had to do the milking and look after the garden. Fortunately Judy was there, because Nancy never gets up before eleven (having worked very hard at Manumit and being in serious need of a rest) so someone had to see to providing breakfast for her charming but completely undisciplined children.

"Caroline also has been a tower of strength. She washes the dishes, keeps the children in order, does odd jobs around the place like gardening and disposing of tin cans, feeds the rabbits, and this morning she has ridden off on Dickie to fetch the mail. She spent last summer in Arizona riding cow ponies and is much the most accomplished horsewoman on the place. I don't know what we'd do without her.

"The Montague children are Donald, a few months younger than Piers, but much more sophisticated and given to tantrums, which are rather disconcerting; Bella, aged six, beautiful but also cursed with a temperament, and Paddy, aged three, a cherubic child with the most infectious smile. He is very annoying, but you can't stay annoyed with him for long. All three are obviously highly intelligent and quite unused to any kind of discipline.

"I find it hard to know what to do about my children, who do have certain fixed rules which it is desirable for everyone's sake they should observe, such as not leaving food on their plates (the Montagues are terrible about this) and not playing wild games inside the house. I have had to relax the rules a good deal, but they still feel, with some justice, that they are the victims of discrimination. However, they take it very well. No doubt things will shake down in time.

"Meanwhile it's splendid for them to have children their own age to play with and Nancy is most entertaining company. She was born in Oxford and lived there most of her life, though she went to London University. Her father and husband are both Balliol men. [Alfred went to Exeter College.] Her husband (who incidentally is a c.o.) is a son of C. E. Montague[61] and a grandson of C. P. Scott and worked on the *Manchester Guardian* before he became a fireman in 1939. Nancy and the children came in 1940, a couple of months before we did. They have applied for passage to go back, but we are told it will be months or even years before there is room for them on a boat. [All available space was commandeered for the transportation of battle troops.] I do find it wonderful to have someone in the house who speaks the same language as I do and thinks in the same way and has the same general background. I'm afraid, though, the Bacons and Norman must get rather tired of our Oxford reminiscences.

"I have quite a lot more pictures for you now. Here are a couple more from the school, sent to me by Mrs. Work, mother of the Negro child. It turns out that she herself is German, which I hadn't realized. For a white woman to marry a colored man is about the most revolutionary thing that can happen: this case and one other are the only ones I ever heard of. Apparently the boy is only about a quarter Negro, his father was part Red Indian and part white. Strangely enough, Indian blood is considered to confer quite a distinction, whereas Negro blood, however small the percentage, condemns you to the submerged half of the population unless you are a genius (like Paul Robeson) or so light in color that you can pass for a white person in a place where your history isn't known. Little Craig Work, judging by his pictures, will never be able to do that. I have told his mother we'd be glad to have a visit from them, [as] I think Craig sounds a much more suitable friend for Piers than Donald.

"You will be surprised at how Teresa looks in the picture—I would hardly have recognized her if her hair hadn't been just as long when she came from school. It was really quite becoming, though rather a nuisance to comb, but her grandfather volunteered to cut it, and to everyone's dismay gave her what was practically a convict crop—it is just beginning to recover now." (*Teresa*: My father cut my hair once and somehow nicked my earlobe, which still bears a scar. He was not asked to do it again.)

Alfred wrote to Leslie Johnston in part:

"I think that both Norma and I recognize that we do not share a unity of aim, and consequently no program of work can really be evolved. She

---

61. Charles Edward Montague (1867–1928) was a well-known English journalist, critic, and writer of novels and essays. At age 47 he dyed his hair black and enlisted in the Army, where he rose through the ranks and became an armed escort for various celebrities. Nevertheless, by the end of WWI he wrote strongly against it. He was the father of one of the Olympic athletes depicted in the film, *Chariots of Fire*.

feels the most important thing to be done in July is to redecorate the same room that was redecorated last July. I feel that the most important things are the garden weeds, the potato bugs, the hay, and planting of roots for winter stock feeding. Unfortunately [these aims] are largely mutually exclusive, and this means that while I have been away, much of the potato crop has been shorn of its leaves by plump orange insects. I regard this as part of the price of my journey. There is no way to judge the essential rightness or wrongness, since we have no criterion to judge by. The fact is, many criteria are brought into play at different times, and my difference from the community at large is that I think there should be a main one.

"I am trying to get light from other friends on the question of the validity of practical applications of moral principle. It occurred to me that we might have been fundamentally mistaken in taking the view that because we [the original organizers] came to an intellectual conclusion on our responsibility to human society with reference to those elements in it which cause war, we should therefore modify our lives to fit our conclusions.

"We had thought we could devise a life in which Christian behavior was possible in every situation. In thinking so we may have been thinking that water runs uphill. In any case, Christian behavior has not appeared to be more current among us here than it may be in the midst of civilized society. I think we have passed the stage where the problem can be solved by allocating blame. We have labored to hold the place together until a suitable group could be formed; but the original impetus belonged somehow to the original group, and its momentum has been lost. No one visiting here in order to size us up would get any idea of what the original project was.

"I do not myself expect any satisfaction from wage-earning. I depend morally on my sense of the worthwhileness of the work I am doing, and I still feel that nothing is so worthwhile as the original Hilltop purpose as I understood it. If this must be abandoned, for whatever cause, it is difficult to see what can replace it, unless there is a complete moral breakdown and total acceptance of the forms of the war-creating society.

"On the other hand, my relatives insist that in whatever situation in which one may be, enlightened conduct is possible, and small advances made in such an environment are more positive than large advances made in isolation. This may be a matter of personal preference only, in which case I prefer the isolation (from war-economy, not from people) of the original Hilltop aim. However, if they are equally valid, no doubt I should abandon my personal preference and do the job in the other way.

"There is no physical difficulty in the way of continuing to live here, but if it means the children must be maintained away from home and Norma and I must travel a good deal to keep in touch [with them], the financial drain would be tremendous. As you know, I would have wished to apply the community standard even in the sphere of children's education. That is, since $2000 a year [is] available for child education, before sending two children to Manumit with the $2000, I would have made a thorough study of the local situation, in case that same sum might have facilitated a solution for all the local children in some way, including our own. It might be that a $4000 teacher instead of a $2000 one could have been secured; or an extra one to divide up the variegated grades; or a teacher might have been got for the Pikes Falls school only two [actually three] miles away; or in several ways I am not able to see (not being conversant with the situation) a yearly donation of $2000 to the Jamaica schools might have made a great difference to everyone.

"Of course, it may have made a difference to Manumit; but M seemed to be running all right without our help. I know there are reasons why Norma felt it necessary to concentrate more than our full financial resources on our two children's education away from home, and sometimes such steps are inescapable. But it does provide a useful example of how social thinking might have been applied.

"We had expected this summer to plan the work ourselves instead of having any form of group planning. But it is impossible for two reasons. One is that people don't want to have the work planned—each feels he must do the thing that to him seems pressing; and the other is that Norma and I can't evolve a concerted plan, because we do not have a common criterion.

"In the midst of it all I have had to take refuge in a queer kind of device, trying to realize what a remote corner of the physical universe this is and that nothing really matters. Certain things that affect me personally in a very direct and obvious way, I comment on, such as a child dragging an expensive fur coat [Edward's heavy raccoon coat] in the mud. Or leaving my goat-feeding pans lying around in the grass without telling me. But most things I have learned to let be, I hope in good grace.

"If as a group we have no purpose, then there is nothing by which to judge the rightness or wrongness of anything that happens. Although what I describe as no purpose can just as readily be described as a purpose by default: our purpose is to continue living off unearned income [the funds provided by his father] as long as there is any to live off. If this is really the purpose, however, then it is reactionary of us to grow spinach; for we could apply ourselves to our purpose better by buying it and then using some more of our unearned income. I hate to call it unearned, because somebody obviously has earned it, only we haven't.

"Living on so-called earned-increment or wages, would not however, satisfy me very much, since the whole point of modern business seems to be to get as much as you can without earning it. I wouldn't know whether I had in fact produced wealth by the full extent of my wages or whether I had gotten a share in someone else's wealth by some remote trickery.

"My brother Edward distributes among his workers one third of the net profits that presently occur after depreciation has been deducted and a sum for capital reserve laid aside. Are we to assume that he puts twice as much talent into his business as all of his workers together? If not, is he not appropriating to himself, because he is in a position to do so, something which they have earned but cannot claim? [The workers presumably receive wages, so this distribution might be considered a bonus.]

"He may say, 'But other employers do not distribute any of their profits; therefore I am doing more than my share.' The same reasoning came up here this morning: we are probably living at a lower standard of living than anyone in the village. Therefore, we are doing as much as we need.

"You will want to know where you come in. I suppose you should think of possible answers to two questions:

1. Is there any basis on which we could stay here?

2. Is there any basis on which we could leave? At present, both seem equally negative; and while the life of civilized society seems to have nothing to offer in any real way, continuance here is sort of living a lie.

"My own end of the work is getting out of hand: the winter roots are not getting planted; the barn is not being kept clean and fly resistant; the goats are not being fed carefully and dipped, nor restrained within their domain; the hay is not being cut regularly, nor the fencing secured; the roofs are not being leak-proofed nor the barn timbers braced; and so on.

"Again and again, I have to remind myself: none of this really matters. We are not dependent on me, but on that obscure army of unknown workers who provide us with the money we have not earned but which we spend. So if I plant the root crops, it will be only because it interests me to do so. Nothing else seems at all realistic.

"I hope Norma will continue from here. She often feels that I emphasize the wrong things, and it might be that if you know our varying emphases, you could discern some common ground."

Norma added: "Why redecorate the living room when so much needs to be done out of doors? Well, partly because it was done hastily and badly before, and it's part of a scheme for morale-building by making the interior of the house less of an offense to the eye; but chiefly because we have not ever been invited to help with the outside work, and have in fact been suffered with a pained expression, if not actually warned off, when we made fumbling attempts to be helpful and received no direction.

1943

[Alfred's habit was not to instruct, or even warn of danger to, anyone, including children, preferring to let them work out a course of action for themselves on the basis of their interpretation of a situation and then experience any unsatisfactory consequences, for which they alone would be held responsible.]

"No doubt it's time for me to make myself quite clear on the various points Alfred raised, then we may know a little better where we stand.

"I have reached the point where, for me, there is no longer anything to be gained by staying here. What could have been done here, what still could be done if certain attitudes were different, is still to me the most valid and important of all the possible things that could be done, and I realize my attitude is a good deal tempered by a deep-seated disappointment and bitterness.

"Whatever I may say, don't think I am suggesting that I have been blameless in our failure to achieve what we hoped, but it's never so easy to be objective about one's own failings as about other people's. I have certain plans for trying to get competent help in finding out where I failed to hold my own end up in this particular enterprise, and why, so as to avoid repeating the same mistakes in the next thing I undertake. However, stated in the simplest terms, the position seems to be this. We are doing nothing worthwhile because we have no plan. We have no plan because we have no agreement as to either ends, or means.

"Why not? I can't escape the conclusion that it is principally because Alfred has a personal set of ends and means which are not in any way attractive to anybody else, with the possible exception of Herbert Leader. That leaves him free to face the choice, either of living here alone (unless he can persuade Herbert to join him) and doing things his own way, or of living here with others on a basis of mutual agreement, everyone modifying his or her own ideas to some extent in order to arrive at a continuum. If he decides on the latter alternative, he has to make a further step and decide to do it with a good grace. His present emotional attitude, though he naturally doesn't recognize it (others do) is that of the small boy who says, 'If you don't play it my way, I won't play at all.' So we don't play at all, since his way of doing it is unacceptable. In fact, to me it is actually morally repugnant, for reasons of a highly mystical and subjective nature which I have found it is no use trying to explain.

"Now, the world is in too much trouble for us to continue living in relative ease and comfort [?!] on a mountain top, having trouble with our own souls. I have therefore made up my mind (barring some decisive change during the next few weeks) to be away from here for a good part of this winter, exploring other possibilities [for] bearing my share of the world's troubles, and trying to get rid of the hindrances which have made me so ineffective here. I would still rather stay here and do what we originally planned (as I understood it, and believe that others did too) than anything else I can think of, but I am not pursuing a mirage any further over these mountains while there is work waiting to be done elsewhere.

"Still, [you should not] feel our achievements are so entirely negligible as we make out. The garden is doing splendidly, we've made lots of hay, goat sales are booming, we have a large and happy group here, larger and happier (strangely enough) than any previous summer. The Bacons are back, considerably disillusioned, and now thinking seriously of remaining, though of course they can't unless the points mentioned above are straightened out. And two young couples have recently got engaged while visiting here or immediately thereafter, and both (in writing) attribute this happy result to the persuasive example of the Hilltop idea and the harmonious [!] Jacob management. Make what you can of it!"

Further matter by Alfred, who offered the following rationale:

"What I have been trying to stand for is what I thought was implied from the beginning: a balanced budget. In view of settling on cheap land which required a lot of labor and attention before it could be made at all productive, we therefore had to be prepared, while getting our means of production into productive condition, to consume the very minimum of bought goods, and only use freely those which we could produce readily, like corn. Since everyone undergoes some voluntary self-limitation at the beginning of any new enterprise, I never could adjust to the failure of our group to accept any such necessity.

"Secondly, one or two alternatives had to be chosen (if we may assume that we didn't want to live forever on unearned money).

1. The men only should labor, in which case the group would have to live at a very low standard, avoiding almost all cash expenditure. This is a thing that civilized women would not readily accept.

2. Both men and women should labor, in which case the availability of products for both consumption and sale would be considerably higher.

"The usual arrangement in the past was that men worked continually on the major jobs—forestry, dairying, potatoes, sheep, or other cash crop, while the women maintained the continuity of the house and feeding, including the household vegetable garden, milk supply, making butter & cheese, weaving, knitting, making clothing, and so on. But [again], this is something civilized women will not readily accept. [In Alfred's childhood home, those tasks were undertaken by hired women of low status.]

"The present situation appears to be that the men do much of the women's work and some of the men's, while the women devote themselves to taking longer than necessary to provide more elaborate meals than are necessary [no need to waste time making food look or taste attractive; it merely needs to sustain life] mind the children, and do the laundering. This means that men are not free for forestry or any other main cash crop, so that no cash income is possible. Yet the women are not willing to face the consequence of the distribution of labor they have enforced, and feel they have a right to the same abundance of products for consumption and sale as there would be if point 2, above, had been in operation. But that abundance has just not been produced, does not exist, and cannot be enjoyed.

"Unfortunately, the feminine mind does not follow the chain of consequences and can only infer that the men don't want them to have the things that would make them happy. [This bizarre statement, in which Alfred presumes knowledge of "the feminine mind," reveals the root of his resentment about the failure of the intended community: it is clearly the women's fault.] This is an absolute deadlock within a rural situation. It is only capable of solution in an urban situation where the men can earn enough in factory or office to maintain the women at home.

"I have not expected the women to do outdoor work, and so, logically, I had to expect them to accept the limitations imposed by the fact that only the men were available to do all sorts of tasks. This meant a very careful husbanding of resources. In this I have made myself unpopular, as if I had withheld from them a lot of comforts which really existed. On the other hand, when the suggestion was made last summer that the men should work in the forest, leaving the household, stock, and garden to women's care, this was rejected by the women [who recognized that it was unrealistic. The time required for child care is nowhere mentioned].

"In the circumstances, there is no choice but either to live on interest, or reenter industrial society, forget our principles, and live not in terms of production for use, but in terms of wages, rents, and ration books. Scott Nearing may be right after all: that people will not do as we had planned to do here unless driven by very harsh necessity. We had thought we could do it simply out of a sense of its rightness."

Norma wrote to Leslie:

"Your letter as usual was illuminating and tonifying and I feel moved to answer right away, though the answer probably won't get sent off for weeks. Your diagnosis of Hilltop's troubles is profound, and I think perfectly correct. The breakup of the original group of course was something we couldn't do anything about, but the unsatisfactory personal situation at the bottom of our failure to agree is another matter.

"In the past two years I've tried to tackle this first from one angle and then from another, without seeming to get anywhere. Just lately, however, since reading Menninger's *Love Against Hate*[62] (lent and recommended by Larry, who seems to have found it illuminates some of his perplexities) I've felt as though at last I had a line on the real source of the trouble.

"A good part of my reason for wanting to plan to be away this winter is that I feel I can't follow this line up without skilled help. Up here, you see, we have to struggle with things all by ourselves with no wiser person to help us untie small knots before they get to be big ones, and incessant pressure from the material environment makes it all more difficult.

"If I went to Philadelphia for a month or so, maybe Alfred might go and work with Phil at Sebasco. Phil needs help so he can be more free for cooperative work, and his example is always helpful. We are just back from a visit there, using our tenth wedding anniversary (yesterday) as an excuse for walking out on all the people here. We suddenly felt we had to get things straight, and Phil was the person most likely to be able to help. We couldn't stay long, and he was very busy, so we didn't get very far, but I think we did open up some new avenues of thought.

"As regards the possibility of making a completely fresh start with a new group, we do rather unexpectedly have a couple of new possibilities in this direction. One is the Bacons, considerably sobered by their experiences in the past year, and now seriously entertaining the idea of making a home here. For purely personal reasons (some of them connected with them, some with ourselves) I feel rather doubtful whether this would work out, but I feel one can hardly fail to explore the chances of some kind of modus vivendi [manner of living].

"The other is a young couple named Bennett, whom I met at the United Pacifist conference in New York in February and again recently at the School of Living. They think they are looking for a place like Hilltop, but how can one tell? I saw them only so very briefly, and they can't come for even preliminary conversations till September, by which time we ought to know what we are going to do this winter, though we probably can't. It seems to be our destiny to spend every summer waiting for someone else and unable to make binding decisions—the first summer waiting for the Johnstons, the second waiting for the Bacons, and now waiting for the Bennetts. I suppose it just can't be helped.

"The deep-lying difficulty here is, as it seems to me, the fact that a group here can no longer grow organically as the first one pretty well did. I

---

62. *Love Against Hate* (1942), in which the American psychiatrist Karl Menninger "examines the war of instincts within each of us. Recognizing the instinctual forces of love and hate and applying science for the encouragement of love instead of self-destruction will result in the achievement of human happiness" (Wikipedia).

1943

mean, we were originally a group of people who liked being together, and the rest followed from that. Maybe that isn't important, or maybe it's very important indeed. How can we tell if we really want to share our lives with the Bennetts? But what other course is there, as things are now, than to wait and see?

"Alfred's 4-F is a mystery. Two possible explanations are put forward. You remember perhaps when we had the entire family X-rayed at the time Teresa's illness was diagnosed, and a few months later the hospital called for another X-ray on Alfred because one of their specialists taking a second look at the plates had seen something he thought suspicious. They finally decided the small lesion he had was inactive, but Dr. Stokes told me he thought that might be grounds for disqualification (in that case it would disqualify some others we know, including Phil, and Fran Bacon, but I find it hard to believe they would put a man permanently in 4-F without even checking up).

"I rather incline to the belief that the Media [Pa.] draft board didn't want any more C.O.s on its books and leaped at some trivial defect to pigeonhole the case. When I called up and gave Alfred's name the clerk said 'Oh, he's a conscientious objector, isn't he?' There wasn't any connection between that and 4-F (which is for those 'physically, mentally or morally unfit'). They might have snatched at the report of the psychiatrist who, Alfred says, wrote him down as unfit for any military service, though that could surely be said of any man who demonstrated a sincere objection.

"I further wonder if we oughtn't to follow it up just in case the X-ray did show anything serious. That of course would bring all the tentative plans and ideas down in irremediable confusion. It's so odd they didn't tell him the grounds for the disqualification, as I understand they usually do. But Vermont is very rigorous in its checks on suspected TB cases (the district nurse [visited] the other day to inquire about Teresa) and I feel if anything like that had cropped up, we'd have heard about it from some source. Maybe we still shall.

"It's nice to have English people in the house again. The Montague children are simply full of character—by the way, they are grandchildren of C. E. Montague and great-grandchildren of C. P. Scott who made the *Manchester Guardian* what it is. Their father is a C.O. who took training as a fireman when he saw the war was coming. On the other hand, they are very undisciplined and waste food in a way that makes me writhe. We got through fifteen pounds of butter in almost two weeks!

"The Bacons are horrified at what Nancy tells them about progressive education (she teaches at Manumit, as maybe we told you). But personally, I feel it's the one method that may turn out well-balanced citizens at maturity, though the present effects, for instance the dreadful language, are rather alarming in comparison with the young products of a system that exists really to keep children from getting too much on their parents' nerves. I keep reminding myself about the Cadbury children, who were said when younger to be the terror of the Haverford campus![63]

"I do wonder rather what is the wisest thing to do about the blasphemy, which is so painful to Judy (I think it is pretty ugly myself). Just by the way, the effect on Piers of five months of school has been exactly what I hoped; he has acquired poise and lost all his nervous mannerisms. Teresa's defects at the moment are rather accentuated than otherwise by the pose of being a 'tough guy.' But I feel we must be patient. According to Menninger (op. Cit.) she is so aggressive because I didn't feed her when she cried as a baby, which was practically the whole time. [*Teresa*: In later life my mother invariably mentioned how much I cried and how "haggard" the nanny looked in the morning, and as mentioned, my father blamed me for my "insistence on being born."] You should really read what Menninger says before putting your next baby on a schedule! Phil and Teddy are having another (unplanned this time) in January and Teddy hinted she might like it if I came and helped out, which would please me.

"The living room redecoration reached rather a startling consummation. The paint we bought for the floor expecting it to be maroon, turned out bright orange when applied. I don't know just what we can do. At that, it's better than the plain floor.

"We are in funds right now; Alfred's father rashly offered us $2,500 cash down and I accepted it, to make sure next year's school fees are paid and the children can have a few decent clothes to keep their ends up among their fellows. Up to now they've managed on a combination of cast-offs and Sears Roebuck's cheaper efforts. Not conducive to savior-faire." [She did not send this letter immediately, continuing it on September 22, below.]

Alfred wrote to his father, Edward, and Caroline, in part:

"We went to Philip's 8 days ago, conveniently hitch hiking from Bath to Sebasco, and while he was much too busy to spend much time in pure conversation, and had to be away two evenings out of the four, [Teddy's parents] the Lintons were there part of the time, and Sunday we spent at the Baily camp, nonetheless we felt we were adequately celebrating our tenth wedding anniversary—as far as we could remember it was the first time we had been away together since we went to Seville in early 1940 for the AFSC.

"We haven't come to any decision about anything. I felt it would be open to me to winter at Philip's if, in the time I saved him, he could do

---

63. Henry Cadbury was one of the three most well-known, "weighty" (experienced, respected) Quakers of his time.

cooperative organizational work. On the other hand, once we establish the precedent of leaving here during the winters, we shall become summer people, with all that implies. I feel that if we stay here it should be in earnest, with determination to do what we came for. But that cannot even be begun while the children are away, nor carried out without considerably more dedication than we have given it so far.

"Naturally, I might work for a local or a Pennsylvania farmer over the winter; but once again I would not feel a sufficient purpose in that, however much I sympathize with the difficulties of farmers. But rather than help an individual farmer to solve his temporary difficulties, I would feel more useful if I could get at the root of the thing which has caused those problems, which is war. It is too easy to treat symptoms and leave fundamental causes untouched.

"We have purchasers for all the goats except one adult & 2 kids. Even if I stay here over the winter without Norma, I would not want livestock, since they absorb time out of all proportion to the benefit they may give. I'm not keen to live alone, but of course I do not know now who might choose to live here then. Two more visitors came on Friday night, and have been speeding up our work program. One of them installed our new front door today. He is a silversmith. The other has been working in the woods. Norm Williams, who came in June expecting to leave for a Quaker work camp, has stayed instead, and we hope he will end up at Pendle Hill.

"The garden is beginning to feed us with peas, beans, and squashes, and everything is growing pretty normally. We haven't planted as much as I hoped, because of doing other things during planting season. The same is true of hay, which won't be good or abundant. We have yet to learn that a farm requires that things be done at the right time. As Summer People, however, we could please ourselves, and just buy anything which we failed to produce.

"We cleared up the Westtown-Negro business. It is of course true that the Council made no decision to admit them; but there is hope that future students will be admitted on the understanding that the school may be opened to all citizens.[64] "The Bacons are at Pendle Hill just now, and will have to decide what they are going to do in the future. Meanwhile, their goat is our best milker. There is still no news for [his brother] Edward. I hate to turn down such a generous offer; on the other hand, I would not want to accept it unless it was right to do so. When the matter becomes clear I'll

---

64. In later life Alfred recalled with chagrin how, during his youth, the family had a Black maid who was not permitted to use the family toilet but had to go outside to a separate privy. Homes in which servants used to be employed might have a toilet in the basement for their use, and back stairs that gave access to their sleeping quarters.

write him. I sometimes feel in a way which is best expressed in religious terminology: that if God gave me a 4F classification, it must be in order to leave me free to do something for Him. The question now is not What do I want to do? but What does He expect me to do? [Again, Alfred hopes someone else will tell him what he should do.]

"It may be after all that the thing to do is to stick to this. How many years did Father have to stick to his business even though it was failing and running him into debt, before he got it running profitably? [He became one of the most prosperous businessmen in West Chester, Pennsylvania, with a national reputation as The Mushroom King.] I ought to stick here at least that long."

July 28, to August 1, from the journal:

A fly campaign was undertaken in which Alfred agreed to kill all the flies in the house if the others would see that doors and windows were kept protected, and fly-attracting odors not created. Alfred did the deed while all were out berrying in the patch Herbert Leader discovered, toward Rawsonville. Norm worked on the hay, which was finally inundated on Saturday while he was in the village and Winnie and Alfred in the garden. He had gone to fetch Winnie from Manchester on Friday afternoon, arriving back for supper.

Fran Bacon arrived back from Pennsylvania with a job at Westtown School in the orchard; and Saturday morning went off to Bridgewater to fetch their belongings. The road-menders came up Saturday without visible purpose or results, but Mr. Williams paid the money promised for winter roadwork, which consisted of carrying up their own parcels and sacks of feed and fertilizer. They harvested the first potatoes, finding that the chipmunks were digging them up and eating them.

July 31, Norma wrote to Family:

"The joint Jacob-Montague ménage continues to go as well as could be expected. It's amazing how little friction there is, with so many children and all so full of life and determined to get their own way. Nancy is just as easygoing as I am, in fact I think even more so, so we don't wear ourselves to shadows worrying because the children are noisy and untidy but patiently bear with it and tidy up after they have gone to bed. Which saves trouble in the long run. The way they waste food continues now be my chief cross; when we have to bake such huge quantities of bread every two or three days, and it's so hard to get the wholemeal flour which we use, it's maddening to go round the table after a meal when the supervision has been inadequate and find a great heap of crusts and crumbs by every child's place.

"We've managed to bring our butter consumption to something like a normal level, helped by the fact that butter, though rationed, is still often

1943

unobtainable and one can always say, 'Make this last, because there may not be any more.' Meat is unpurchaseable unless we go thirty miles to Brattleboro and hunt through one shop after another for a piece of pork, which is all that can be found usually. So that saves a lot of bother and expense. I think, of all the war shortages the only one that really bothers me is the absence of metal materials for scouring pots. Cooking porridge every morning for ten or twelve means at least two very dirty pots every day, and all the outsides of course are black all the time because of using the wood stove. I couldn't calculate all the hours I've spent clutching a black saucepan to my bosom and trying to get the inside clean with an inadequate little piece of cloth or a sponge.

"Speaking of shortages, the American press is now beginning to be full of alarming stories about the starvation that is ahead of us. What they mean by 'starvation' probably is no beef or mutton, not much pork, less milk than a quart per person per day, potatoes not more than three times a week or so. Still, it does seem to be true that the altogether abnormal weather and spring, and the altogether incomprehensible goings-on in Washington (for instance setting the price of maize [corn] for the market so low that it was cheaper to feed pigs to bursting-point and farmers wouldn't sell the stuff for other farmers to maintain their cows, and so on) are going to make things difficult in spots this coming winter.

"This further complicated my problem as to what to do about staying here. If we stay, we shan't go hungry no matter what happens, as we can raise unlimited quantities of milk, potatoes, green vegetables, and even meat if we go in for sheep on a larger scale. But shall we freeze to death, or become victims of melancholia? I really don't know. My impulse is to make the very most of this summer's harvest, have a cellar bursting with home-grown food of all kinds, as we have in previous years only more so, then take a long mid-winter holiday, say three months, during the coldest part of the winter, and cheer myself up with a little city life, probably in Philadelphia, then returning like a giant refreshed [Psalm 78, verse 66], to grow even more food next year. Our productive season is so very short, hardly more than four months, that we have to raise everything we want to eat for the whole year at one time.

"One thing that really worries me—the Montague children will run about barefooted and there are all kinds of unsuitable things to tread on all around the house. Bella has just come in howling with a rusty nail in her foot. We'll have a case of tetanus on our hands one of these days. It won't be one of my children, because I have thoroughly drilled into them that we never walk about outside without shoes, but it will be unpleasant just the same.

"Speaking of sheep, our two produced eight pounds of knitting wool (extracted by the mill from the incredibly grubby and tangled fleece we sent to them). It's lovely stuff. I plan to make thick warm natural-colored sweaters for the whole family, as well as quantities of caps, gloves, and socks. If two sheep will produce all this, I ask myself, why not have a dozen? We have, in fact, just bought another—a pedigreed Scotch ram lamb to replace Ramsay MacDonald, whose tragic story I told you last year. Today, I realize, is the anniversary of the death of Ramsay the First. This time we were wiser and left him with his dam until he was weaned.

"Dickie the Horse is doing wonderfully and now he has become used to me I find him perfectly easy to handle. His one fault is impetuosity—you can't trust him to stand a single minute, not even to allow a rider to mount, unless someone is holding his head. We took him out last week and dragged several big logs up the hill. Otherwise he has not done much in the way of serious work; he can't be taught to plow because he always starts off with a rush and either uproots the plowshare or digs it into the ground.

"Last week Alfred and I made a lightning dash over to Maine to visit Phil and Teddy. I'd never been there in the summer before, but as the landscape is mostly sea and pine trees it looks very little different, really. We thought we would justify a brief holiday to celebrate our tenth wedding anniversary. Coming home we chose the route through the White Mountains in New Hampshire. They really are mountains, almost as high at the Pyrenees in places, but we didn't see much because it was a cloudy day. This choice of route obliged us to hitch-hike the last thirty miles. I really believe we walked more than half the distance, and it took us all night—from half past eight in the evening till seven in the morning, counting three hours which we spent sleeping in a covered bridge on a pile of hay which providentially had fallen from some farmer's load.

"It's time to start cooking the lunch—past time, in fact. We feed the children and ourselves in separate shifts, which means that each meal takes between three and four hours from start to finish. When I've got rid of one, as likely as not I look at the clock and discover it's time to begin the next."

On Sunday, Nancy, Norma, Judy and all the children went to church down in the village.

Nancy Montague: "The gas in the car was only for essential journeys. The women and children decided that church was an essential journey. The children were dressed in their Sabbath garments, sandwiches were packed, prayer books and swimming suits collected. Baby Bert was a trifle young for church-going but could not be left with the men. With his polished red cheeks he crawled up and down the aisle during the sermon, helping to keep the neighboring pews alert. Sitting in a pew with six children who cannot read is not conducive to meditation, but we stayed for the sermon, as leaving earlier would have shocked the neighborhood.

"After the service our angels made a dive for the back seat and a fight to find bathing suits broke out, with some ungodly expressions picked up in previous contact with civilization. The Salmon Hole was a perfect spot; sand and pebbles for the very young, deeper water downstream, with hot sun and deep shade to rest the eyes. Down the lane was a long hedge with juicy blackberries to go with our sandwiches."

Winnie, Norm, Ted Horvath, and Alfred went swimming at Pikes Falls, with an oat-pudding picnic, not quite finding the diagonal shortcut. Discussion was on pacifist responsibilities, practical pacifism, and CPS.

August 1943

On August 1, stepmother Caroline wrote to Alfred:

"Father is sending a check and possibly a letter, so that I feel lured on by thy two letters to continue the discussions which we carried on—at some length!—when thee was here.

"Regarding thy first letter: I didn't mean to imply when thee was here that thee was going through 'long mental processes with the real purpose of avoiding earning a living!' It just did seem to me that thee was being rather superior in attitude toward those who were doing so, either by necessity or choice, while thee was actually enjoying the privilege of a private income from invested funds. There is nothing wrong in doing that, i.e. using the income for the support of thyself and family, and spending thy time and energy in exploring new patterns of life, but it's hardly fair to criticize the motives of other people who are doing just the ordinary work of the world. But I realize that your [Caroline slips in and out of the Quaker thee/thou "plain language"] situation is an emergency one; you were uprooted from the life you would have followed in England and Spain, and it is far harder for you to find the right path here than for someone who had been living here continually and had no doubts about staying.

"Of course, one might hope that really concerned Christian people would all be interested in exploring the causes of war and trying to do something about them. I think thee and Norma are right in putting that first in planning your lives. But not everyone can agree with you that the roots of war are found in our competitive economic society.

"This does not mean one shouldn't work for changes in the organization of society; but it seems to me it broadens the field in which one can find useful work. While at Pendle Hill, you were contributing to the spirit of the place while you were washing dishes, having tea together, worshiping, studying, even more than the times when you were meeting in committees to work out changes. Using your own terminology: perhaps God gave thee the 4F classification so that thee might do something far more difficult than staying removed from all the complexities of human society, that is, join in with some of the ordinary work of the world with other ordinary people, doing nothing very extraordinary or world shaking but just living out the principles of love and brotherhood and understanding with actual people with whom you are in close contact. It seems to me that there is a more basic principle involved than the one thee is operating on, and being true to that more basic one might lead to the abandonment, or at least a modification, of your present way of life.

"We hear that Francis Bacon and wife are to be at Westtown, living in a neat little white cottage which I used to have my eye on as a place to retire to in my old age. [Caroline had taught at Westtown for 23 years before marrying Grandfather Edward.] If you keep on seeking wisdom in the right spirit, the right course for your particular situation will open up, perhaps unexpectedly." (Quakers believe that "the way will open" if an honest effort is made to resolve an issue.)

On August 3, Alfred wrote to his brother Edward, whose business was making and selling Flavor-Glo seasonings for use by restaurants.

"Within another month you will need to know where you stand with regard to mixing up your brew. I have been reflecting and talking with people about my responsibility in the matter, and so far have not found encouragement to accept your offer, which nonetheless I feel is too generous and with too many redeeming features to be taken lightly.

"One friend said: 'But he wants you to give up your way of life in order to preserve his.' I had been explaining what might happen to your factory if all your reliable manpower were taken from you. I recognize that it isn't just to preserve your business that you want reliable helpers—you have always had a frank interest in my choices and decisions, and you pretty obviously feel I am misusing a large part of my time and would like to see me put it to better use.

"But I feel there is something I have to do here, though the obstacles are greater and more subtle than I had ever realized. Still, if there is the slightest hope I could get something real done here, it would be worth sticking. We can never hope to form a dedicated group here unless we stick to it ourselves. Who is going to stick to a thing we haven't stuck to? There must be a period of failure near the beginning of almost any enterprise, but that may not be sufficient ground to give it up.

"I had thought of asking permission to live in your trailer and arranging my living habits so as to put away a regular $100 a month; or perhaps doing so in the winter as a means of maintaining this place in the summer. But I really don't feel I have any right to engage in business. There is too much in the world that needs to be done. We are responsible to a wider circle than just our family. There is a type of social thought which I very much want to develop, and I do not see how to do so except to stick to this kind of life, either here or elsewhere.

"I have said the same to Philip as I am saying, substantially, to you. I should like to help him for himself alone; but apart from the matter of brotherly affection, I would not feel it was right to help him, or you, just to earn your livings, or to spend much time just earning mine. I would want to feel that through you or him I was giving service to something much greater and more necessary in the world than the living of a small family. If I could release Philip for cooperative organization, or release you for some similar work of importance in the welfare of the population at large, I would feel that I was using my time properly. I don't know that I shall ever make the matter clear. You will just have to assume that my mind works in a special way and leave it at that.

"We are expecting a couple to come in September who might stay the winter, and there is hope that another couple might do the same. As long as anyone is interested, it isn't advisable to think of leaving here. And even if no one were interested, there are reasons why it might be better to stay here than make a change. I am sure Father will be disappointed that I am not of more use to you. But I am driven back always to the view that it is not what is nice, interesting, agreeable, and remunerative that matters. What matters is what is worthwhile; not just worthwhile to me, but worthwhile to the whole human family if possible."

Meanwhile, Norm chopped wood and prepared to paint the south roof of the house. It rained in the afternoon, so nothing much got done outdoors. Next day Norm started painting the roof, interrupted by occasional showers. Alfred tried to work in the garden but was interrupted by the rain and went to sleep with a toothache. The duck pond (a swampy depression between the barn and the house) filled up.

On Friday, Alfred's toothache recurred, and he wasn't good for much work. (He was resistant to all types of medical intervention, even had something been available, believing that the body would heal itself if left alone.) Not noted in the record, Piers had his ninth birthday on August 6. There were Northern Lights in streaks and waves all over the sky.

Norma wrote to Edward Senior and Caroline:

"Perhaps I ought to have made it clear that though I am doubtful whether it is wise for us to spend the winter up here in present conditions, I do not think it would be right for Alfred to accept the job that Eddie offers. I do not think it would work out at all, and the Bailys and others whom we have consulted think the same. It's too bad we missed seeing you all at Sebasco. We left on Thursday morning early and had to hitch-hike the last

30 miles; I calculate we walked more than half the distance. We were pretty tired when we got home, as you can imagine.

"There is a possibility that Winifred Frost, who visited us here a couple or three times and is to marry Norm Williams, the young man who has been with us most of the summer, might get the job of teaching at the little school in Pikes Falls, two or three miles away from us. If she did, that might alter all our plans, as it might be possible to send her and the children down on a sleigh each day, now that we have a horse. [*Teresa*: This did not happen. We walked. The rocky woods trail would not have permitted the passage of other than human feet and certainly not a sleigh.]

"But there are all sorts of doubtful factors still, and until I am clearer about the whole thing, I shall stick to the plan to send the children back to Manumit. I simply can't have the incessant worry as to where they are to go, whether they are being properly taught and properly looked after and so on, and the constant changes are so very bad for them too. I am sure the sensible thing is to make one plan and stick to it unless there is some very good and definite reason for making a change. One complicating factor is that Norman may be sent to a C.P.S. camp at any time, and of course Winnie might want to move nearer to where he was. So I don't put very much reliance on this possibility, though it would be very satisfactory from our point of view."

On Monday, Norm walked to the village and talked to the school superintendent, Mr. Bullis, about the possibility of Winnie's teaching at the Pikes Falls school.

Alfred wrote to stepmother Caroline. Some excerpts:

"Thy letter opens up the possibility of an extensive discussion, and I think I shall number my paragraphs to keep the headings clear.

"1. It's a pity I gave the impression that because I realize I have opportunities which other people lack, I am therefore intrinsically superior to them. I should criticize them for not using constructively the freedom they do have. I feel I have to do first what I wish others would do too, and this amounts to trying to use my abilities in a socially constructive way rather than a selfish one, just as I wish they would.

"2. We set out so to live as to remove the roots of war from our lives. We did not set out to make others live so as to achieve that result. We cannot control society, but we can control ourselves, and have the obligation to work with what we control, and not throw stones at the moon.

"I think it is a mistake to regard us as removed from the complexities of human society. We are just as much identified with the larger problems of the world as anyone; perhaps we see them even more clearly than the avid newspaper reader. Surely one doesn't have to imitate other people's errors to be identified with them.

1943

"If there is a more basic principle than the one we are operating on, we want to know it. We felt that a project of rural community living was more basic in connection with the wellbeing of human society than relief work was, or else we might have gone to Mexico or Santo Domingo.

"We are going to cover the south side of the house, where the siding has shrunk and warped, with asphalt shingles to keep the wind out and give extra insulation (instead of filling the partitions with rock wool). [The (non) progress of this project is illustrated in the kitchen wall mural.] Also there seems to be more sense in putting money into this place, where we always have it, than into Manumit School where it goes to pay for much that we are already providing here."

August 13: Norma wrote to Johanne Madsen, in China. (There is no information enabling the identification of this person.)

"Your questions are searching and not easy to answer. You see, this project arose out of the discussion of a group of students at Pendle Hill, and as usually happens, I imagine, when we had a chance to put our theories into practice, we found we were a long way from being as much in agreement as we thought. Even Alfred and I find that there is far from being an identity of aims and methods between us; we can agree on paper, but we find ourselves in all our daily actions unconsciously working to a pattern and often it isn't the same pattern. These things are hard to get at and put straight since both parties are sincere and feel a strong need to do what they are doing. If we cared less, it would be easier! But I'll try and give you an outline of what we hoped (and still hope) to do.

"The real father of this plan was a young Englishman, a teacher and member of the I.V.S.P. [International Voluntary Service for Peace], who with his wife, whom he married during our year at Pendle Hill, wanted to start a school, which should be really part of community life, where all that the children learned would tie in with their daily lives and form part of a whole to which they would be adding all their lives. Also, he and we felt, when faced by the challenge of conscription in this country, that we must get at the roots of war, and that those roots were primarily in human attitudes and human relations.

"So we wanted to build a small model of a society all of whose relationships—spiritual and material—would be kept on the highest possible level, i.e. one would want those who ministered to one's physical needs, like the milkman and the baker, to have a fair return for their labor because one thought of them as friends, and one would seek to organize a society on a basis of complete fairness in sharing the necessary work and the available rewards, because that is the way friends wish to treat each other. It seemed to us that agricultural life was the only one sufficiently near the source of things to make this possible, so we and this English couple and three others (who later lost interest) looked around for a farm and settled on this one. People often ask us why on earth we picked such a lonely and remote place, such poor land, and so on. [The 600-acre property was purchased sight unseen.]

"I think these things were essential parts of the design. Loneliness, we felt, was good for a social experiment, and as for 'poor' land, we felt that we could demonstrate that such land with proper methods could and would produce a livelihood. I don't think anyone who saw our vegetable garden this year would continue to maintain that this land was correctly classed as 'sub-marginal,' and when you consider the difference between five dollars an acre and a thousand dollars an acre, which 'good' farm land costs in Pennsylvania, you'll see how we feel that we are pointing the way for a great many people with little money to invest to get back to a simple and healthy way of living after the war.

"Also, a simplification of our own material needs was a vital part of our testimony against the things in society which ultimately lead to war. At this point there is one of the basic differences of opinion, not merely here but throughout the peace movement. Some feel that only identification as far as possible with the completely dispossessed will allow us to make a real contribution towards bettering their lives. Others, of whom I'm one, feel that for people of our background to lower the living standard too suddenly, and too far, means wasted energy and lowered efficiency, and also has the effect of making the experiment unattractive to the very people whom it is meant to help.

"Sometimes we feel we are achieving absolutely nothing, since we can't even balance our budget, and then we get a letter, as we did the other day from a young Jew who had been going through, to him, a very exciting experience in the spiritual world, and went so far as to say that it was his short visit to us which gave him the first push in that direction. Such a letter is worth months of loneliness, cold, and hard work, even though we don't feel we deserve it.

"When the school opens, we shall get to see more of our neighbors in the next valley, among whom are some very interesting people including Scott Nearing, the famous economist. There is no Friends Meeting within fifty miles, but there is an F.O.R. group in Brattleboro, 30 miles away, which we can reach by bus for occasional Sunday evening meetings. This winter, with at least a small stable nucleus to the group, perhaps we can have a meeting of our own. With so much ebb and flow [during the summer], it hardly seemed possible.

"Teresa is quite well now. The doctor saw her in June and said she need not come again—and from such a good doctor I feel that really means something. He would not discharge her unless he were absolutely sure. [*Teresa*: For many years I continued to have an annual chest X-ray, until it was felt that the possibly deleterious effects of the radiation outweighed any diagnostic benefit.]

"About the Quaker silence being appropriate, I have doubted that here too, and I am inclining to prefer the kind of meeting which is largely on a basis of silence but given a direction by a selected reading, a piece of music or something of that kind. [Quakers call this worship-sharing; participants speak out of the silence if they wish to. There is no discussion.] Most people need these helps, I think, and even the most experienced Quaker is wrong to despise them. In such a way I think people can gradually come to feel a need for silence, rather than having it forced on them."

Norma wrote to Mrs. Fincke of Manumit School on August 18, explaining why the children would not be returning in the fall.

Norma wrote to her family on August 20.

"You'd hardly believe how difficult it has been to find time to sit down and write this letter. For the past six weeks my letter-writing has been confined to occasional hasty notes scribbled while someone was waiting to go to the village. We've had the house constantly full of people, reaching a climax last weekend when our numbers rose to fourteen. Eight have left in the course of the week, however, and I'm reveling in the brief period of quiet, though it's not complete quiet by any means since we still have two of the Montague children as well as our own. But with Nancy they are much easier to handle.

"Since our cooking methods are relatively slow, and we use the kind of economical foods which need long preparation anyway to make them acceptable, each meal lasted approximately four hours from start to finish. And since I was the only woman on duty all the time (the others came and went, and Nancy never got up till eleven), by far the biggest part of the work fell on me. Sometimes when I saw from the clock that I had worked five hours at a stretch in the kitchen I would go on strike and announce that someone else could get the next meal, and then I would go out for a walk or up to bed. It seemed the only way to get any time to oneself at all. Don't get the idea that I didn't enjoy it, but it was very strenuous, and the brief interlude is more than welcome. Things will be just about as lively again by this time next week.

"It has been weeks and weeks since I heard anything directly from you, though Piers' birthday letter came, not very late, and also his birthday parcel. I thought the choice of books was particularly happy this time, and Piers was very pleased with the letter and said he would write you another one. The English mails have been very irregular lately; Nancy hasn't had a word from her husband since the beginning of June. But papers and magazines have been coming through quicker than usual. I am sure either of us would exchange issues of the *Manchester Guardian Weekly* or the *New Statesman* for one nice fat letter, but that's the way it seems to be arranged. Nancy says her husband has very illegible handwriting so perhaps that accounts for the delay. [Letters were subjected to censoring en route.] Did I tell you he was a fireman in Manchester?

"I expect I have written about Norm Williams, the nice boy from Oberlin who came to spend the month of June with us. His fiancée, Winnie Frost, is planning to teach in the local school nearest to us. The distance is less than two miles [that must be as the crow flies, as on the map it is more like three] and that means that our children will be able to attend. The school was closed before, but now that it is to be re-opened and someone in whom I have confidence is to be in charge, it seems obvious that our children should go. I am sorry to take them away from Manumit, but the burden of the fees was something terrific and they had raised them this year till they were well above our entire yearly income. We can spend the money much better on making the house more comfortable for winter and helping the local school to provide better teaching.

"When I got to this point, I smelled burning, rushed to the kitchen and found the spinach scorched and the bread rising out of the pans. Then the children began clamoring for supper and I had to feed them, so my brief period of concentration is over. You see how difficult it is to do anything connectedly in this house! If I can find the time, I'll copy you some copious extracts from the children's school reports. I think they made considerable progress in all spheres, not least in that of size. I am now ordering their snow suits for the coming winter from the mail order catalogs and I find that whereas Piers can still wear a size 10, Teresa needs a size 12! It might be better to get Piers a 12 to allow for expansion, but the particular suit I want for now, with a sheepskin lining, is not made in the larger size. Teresa has a sheepskin which keeps her warm under anything."

September 1943

Norma wrote again to Family on September 3:
"It has been a very long interval between [your] letters this time; the last was dated June 21st and arrived here the middle of July. Nothing at all since then except Piers' birthday letter and books. Nancy Montague never heard a single word from her husband the whole two months she was here, and we concluded that some mysterious new factor must be at work hindering the transatlantic mails (mysterious, since on the one hand we were told that the submarine menace was on the decline, and on the other hand newspapers continued to arrive regularly and still do). But I don't think I have had a word from anybody in England for nearly two months.

1943

"I am beginning to get seriously worried. It's true that through all these years of war and slow communications I have schooled myself from sending off telegrams when there was a long silence—and seven years [the length of time since she had seen her family] is a long time in which to acquire discipline!—but enough is enough. I'll give it another week anyway before I start burning up the underwater cables.

"I think I told you in my last letter about Norman Williams and Winnie, who are going to join us here. They were to have been married on Wednesday, and were coming straight up here to start getting ready for the opening of the school year next Tuesday. We have been scurrying about getting two rooms ready for them, made as attractive as possible with our very scanty and uninteresting furnishings, and now expect them at any minute; I only hope they come in time for supper, as I have it all planned and don't want to waste an extra-special gala meal on just ourselves. On the other hand, if I fall back on something dull they will probably arrive just as it's being served. That perhaps is the big disadvantage of hitch-hiking as a method of travel (aside from the risk of getting sun-stroke or pneumonia from standing about waiting to be picked up)—one can never form even the vaguest idea of when one may be going to arrive at any particular destination, though people who undertake a long journey by this means, for instance across the continent, can work out an average and tell you proudly they went to San Francisco at the rate of 300 miles a day.

"I hope Winnie won't be too exhausted when she arrives, for there is lots to be done before the schoolhouse, which has been closed for more than a year, can be ready for use again. If it keeps on being as cold as it is today, they'll have wood-cutting for the stove to add to all their other tasks. The School Board was reluctant to re-open the school because of the expense involved, and the parents concerned who were anxious to have it opened undertook to be responsible for all kinds of things such as fuel, maintenance of the building, and hot lunches for the children. I hope we may in time build up quite a flourishing social life around the schoolhouse.

"What is certain is that we shall be able to see much more of our congenial neighbors on the other side of the mountain, who before were practically cut off from us between December and April because of impossible traveling conditions, and [we] can arrange social events like dances, exchanges of books and gramophone records and so on. Maybe we'll even have some amateur dramatics or buy a tenor recorder and give concerts in aid of the Red Cross or other worthy causes, since Helen Knothe is a skillful recorder player. There are all sorts of possibilities, if the weather doesn't frustrate them all. It seems absolutely impossible that this coming winter should in any way equal the severities of the last.

"We've also been working hard on the house, making it winter-proof and more comfortable to live and work in. Asbestos shingles are being tacked over the nice red boards on the south front. It will look very odd—fortunately this is the side away from the road—but the boards were so much weathered that the south wind blew right through and some days one sat in a perpetual draft. The front door, which was an ill-fitting affair of rough boards, has been replaced by a proper door with frame, and we no longer have to scurry in and out of the house in the teeth of a northern blast, in fact the north door will probably be sealed up completely for half of the year.

"Then, cupboards are being built in the kitchen which will give much better storage space as well as looking very smart, the ceiling is being insulated with wall-board so that all the heat of the stove doesn't go to the room above (I hope by this and other means we'll be able to keep the kitchen warm enough this winter so that the dish towel doesn't actually freeze to the fingers any more—maybe even warm enough for us to follow our original plan and take our meals in the kitchen). And redecoration is going on spasmodically, though this is less urgent than many of the outside jobs like building the woodshed, which have been little more than beautiful dreams for three years now.

"The Montagues left—most of them last Saturday. The Manumit term doesn't start just yet, but Nancy was asked to go back early to do an urgent piece of work in the place of a friend who went off to join her husband in Texas. Before that she took a week's holiday, leaving two of the three children with us. It went fairly smoothly, but still I would rather deal with two children than four any day.

"Of course it was different when Nancy was here to take responsibility for hers, but when I alone was responsible, their undiscipline complicated life a great deal. For instance, when Nancy returned she found that Paddy, the youngest, had, despite all my vigilance, gone out bare-footed and got a thorn into the ball of his foot which had become quite badly infected. Nothing was noticeable on the surface and Paddy never said it hurt till his mother came home. I was glad it hadn't been worse, as it easily might have been.

"Still, Nancy in particular was like a fresh breeze blowing through the place and life will be much duller without her. Her young sister and brother [?; a brother had not been mentioned anywhere before] stayed a few days more and then went off to some other destination. A boy from Brattleboro was also here for a few days, and Helen Hanford, who owns the nearest house—nearest but one, rather, two miles away—has been in residence, so we haven't been lonely up till now. But the quiet after two months of constant pandemonium is refreshing.

"I took a lot of pictures this summer and the prints have just come home, but they are extremely disappointing. [*Teresa:* My mother tended to jab the shutter release rather than simply squeezing it, which jiggled the camera and caused photos to be blurred. Film in those days was very slow, and the slightest movement caused a loss of focus.] I'm sending you one very poor specimen showing Nancy giving Teresa a ride on Dick. Just one or two came out decently, and mostly you would not be interested in them, which is a pity. If the letter isn't too bulky, I'll try and enclose a paper mat which Piers made specially for you. If it doesn't arrive you might express interest all the same, he won't know the difference. It is a piece of yellow paper folded and torn so as to make a pattern when spread out, but he will be hurt if he thinks I haven't sent it. He was so pleased to have your birthday letters."

Meanwhile, the farm work continued apace as they got ready for winter.

On September 6, Norm, Winnie, and Norma went to the Pikes Falls school to get it in trim for the grand opening. Next day, the school formally started.

Piers: There is no mention in the Hilltop record, but speaking as one who was there, I can report that on the first day of school the entire Hilltop group made the long walk west along the forest trail about a mile to the corner, then turned south for another mile until it intersected the Pikes Falls road, which we then followed another mile up to the schoolhouse. Next day we took a slightly different route: Norm had explored and discovered where a trail ran diagonally across the square, saving a significant amount of distance, so the three-mile trek became a two-and-a-half-mile trek. The long walk was no problem; everyone walked at Hilltop and we thought nothing of it. We two children generally walked with Winnie, but when she was busy we walked alone. Speaking as a person who at one time was an English teacher before going full time into freelance writing, I can report that Winnie was competent as she handled four grades in one room: 1st, 3rd, 6th, and 8th. Teresa and I were in the third grade. I skipped second grade once I finally learned to read, and later I also skipped 5th grade, catching up with my peers. I believe that was in significant part because Winnie had taught me well. I salute her, in long retrospect.

The Williamses rearranged their room, to everyone's great satisfaction. Alfred took the goats for a run after breakfast and discovered so many large spruces in the southeast corner of the property that he wanted to measure them. In due course the whole Jacob family set out with measuring tools, and spotted a hundred trees of more than 10½-inch diameter outside the bark at a convenient height, with some up to 18 and 22 inches. It seemed likely that there must be many more in the part they didn't measure, perhaps around 25,000 board feet, Vermont scale.

In the afternoon Alfred read several chapters of history to the children. After supper there was a short group discussion in which 30 jobs were listed and labeled, for men or women, to see whether the spruce could be cut without completely disregarding the other jobs waiting to be done. They decided to spend this week working on the barn, next week on the winter wood, and after that the house roof.

Norma wrote to Horace and Mary Jane Reed, of Walhalla, Michigan:

"When you speak of 'a functional school of community living' do you mean the kind of thing Stephen and May Leeman are seeking to establish at Teaberryport? Or do you visualize some operating community group undertaking to train people for that kind of life? Our own idea here originally was more for a school on general lines, where the younger members would get the conventional kind of instruction, though not perhaps in the conventional ways, while the older members were improving their general intellectual equipment through study groups etc. as well as learning about the realities of group living.

"Some months ago I wrote in answer to an inquiry by Don F. Gans, of Walhalla, telling something about the origins of this project and its material assets. At that time we were expecting to have to give it up, as my husband had been classified in 4-E, but at the final medical examination they changed it to 4-F, and now another family has come to join us, so we have taken on a new lease on life. Mrs. Williams, one of the new people, is teaching in a rural school not far away to which our children are able to go, and this is a very interesting opening for us, as it not only makes it possible to do something in the direction of better education, which was our original hope, but it gives us a really functional relationship to local community life. I'll return to that later.

"Your account of the three different types of community life which you considered is of interest to us because we went through a very similar process. We settled as you did, on the third alternative, the self-supporting rural community, though we made the mistake, which you appear to be avoiding, of thinking it was better to start such a community for ourselves rather than look for an existing one where we might fit in. I think this is the chief thing we'd do differently if we were starting again, but at that time there was no one to tell us that other such community groups did exist. However, we were warned against founding our own community by two representatives of the Bruderhof[65] who were in this country getting

---

65. A religious intentional community founded in 1920 in Germany, similar to the Hutterites.

1943

support for their move to Paraguay, and we [have] often wished since that we'd realized how important the warning was.

"There are many people who are still making the same mistake; for instance, a friend recently out of Danbury told us of the group there studying rural cooperative living—but each one wanting to start a community for himself! I'm inclined to think that this centrifugal tendency, arising out of the individualism—which of course makes the C.C. what he is—is one of the biggest dangers to the movement at this time.

"What we didn't realize when we chose the third alternative was the importance of local contacts and the difficulty of making these satisfactory if the relation of the group to the local community has no real functional basis. Why should people accept us just because we come to live in their township? They are much more likely to mistrust us for our queer ideas (we have the additional handicap of being aliens [foreigners, though Alfred was hardly a true foreigner], and thus our experiment threatens to become turned in upon itself, and to get its renewal only from outside contacts with people at a distance, who can very seldom be visited. [Quite possibly no one in the village of 500 had ever known someone who spoke, as Norma did throughout her life, with a British accent.]

"I at any rate am inclining toward the first of your alternatives, that of selecting an existing community and seeking to make oneself a part of its life. At least that is the direction in which we are tending now; the fact that the schoolteacher is a member of our group gives us a direct influence over the principal center of community activity. It's true that our local [Pikes Falls] community is by no means typical. It consists of ten households (11, counting ours, though we live at some distance from the others) strung out along a valley over a distance of three miles, without a post office or store, and with no common activity except the school. The church is a Seventh-Day Adventist church, and though ordinarily we would regard it, too, as a community-building factor, in this case I'm afraid it works if anything the other way, since the different families don't even worship on the same day. (SDA's worship on the '7th Day,' that is, Saturday.)

"Moreover, the ten households are extraordinarily mixed, ranging from a retired professor whose name was not long ago a household word, to a family with lots of children very little above the peasant level. The re-opening of the school has brought all these diverse elements together and there is an excellent spirit of co-operation. Community square dances and canning for the children's hot lunches are included in our plans, and I have the idea that a co-operative buying club might be a possibility, perhaps even leading eventually to a small co-op store, though I doubt if so few families could bear the financial burden.

HILLTOP FARM

IMAGE 17: *The now-overgrown schoolhouse as it was in 2018.*

"There is some hope, though, that if we can help bring life back into this community, several houses which have been closed may be re-opened, and as the valley is fertile and famous for its maple syrup, it can maintain many more people and ought to do so. Co-operative production of maple syrup is already being practiced and we feel the principle could be extended much further. There is a great deal to be said for rural Vermont as the locality for a community experiment, but I won't go into that now. I hope we shall hear further from you about your plans and how they develop; a visit from some member of your group would be more than welcome. May I suggest you add a couple of goats to your ten hives of bees? We can recommend all sorts of literature on the subject!"

On September 22 Norma continued the letter to Leslie Johnston that was started on July 23:

"Much of the foregoing is of course out of date. I send it to show we did react to your letter, only our reaction just got overlaid in the general hurly-burly.

"Things are settling beautifully into a routine. For the first time we have a plan of outdoor work and are following it. Four men (Alfred and Norm, Herbert Leader and Clif Bennett) have worked a couple of days cutting wood and have a pile that looks almost enough for our winter's supply waiting to be sawed up when we get the buzz saw fixed. Inside the house I have actually found it possible of late to get the essential tidying up done by about 10, and then turn my attention to something else.

"I have undertaken to do a good many of the outdoor jobs, like painting the house and digging potatoes, so that the men can get on with the urgent things which only they can do and be through in time to cut some wood before Norm goes off to C.P.S. He received his 4-E [re]classification the other day, and we imagine he will now be called within a few weeks. He hopes to get sent to the Brattleboro unit after the necessary two months in camp. The trouble is, only two camps supply men for Brattleboro, and he can't be sure of getting in to either of them. One is Powellsville, which we believe has no vacancies; it's silly, because they have trouble getting volunteers for Brattleboro because it's so far from any large city, though it's one of the best of the mental hospitals so far as working conditions are concerned.

"I imagine the mechanical saw plan will come to nothing as Norm is against it too; his thinking is strikingly like yours in many ways. Maybe it wasn't such a good idea after all. Alfred will probably write about it if he has time. I think his principal object was to get rid of the weed trees, huge hardwoods (beech & maple up to 24" diameter) which have blocked the growth of the good stuff for years because it seemed too big a job to get them out by hand. There is a definite market for these at present. We also went through one of our spruce groves pretty carefully and calculated that there were at least 25,000 board feet of good lumber there, which would pay for the log saw in a month or less. But it's a complicated question. We are making pretty wide inquiries.

"The school plan continues to work well. Scott Nearing built some beautiful swings, Harold Field supplied the necessary rope, and the children on their own initiative picked ferns [used by florists in the city] to get the money to pay him for it. Now they are building an outdoor fireplace and are inviting the whole community to a corn and apple roast (there being no hamburgers!) next Monday night. It's complicated because most of [the valley people] are 7th-Day Adventists, who keep the Sabbath from sundown on Friday till sundown on Saturday, and then work on Sunday.

"The Adventists had a convention in the church about 10 days ago; we were invited and I went.[66] Did you meet with any Adventists among your fundamentalist colleagues, and if so, what was your opinion of the possibility of working with them to further Christian unity and Christian social ideals in general?

"We are just bursting with money and will certainly renew your subscription. You see, I extracted from Alfred's father two thousand dollars to pay for the children at Manumit this year. We don't want to have it just sitting in the bank and it is already proving to be a bone of contention. Alfred wants to invest it in a co-op, I want to invest part of it, very conservatively, in Hilltop, i.e. in ourselves. The Williamses very properly refuse to make up our minds for us.

"We had a sharp frost the night of the 18th and brought in 65 lbs. of green tomatoes. Strangely enough, some plants which we overlooked in the dark are still flourishing, apparently unharmed. Maybe we should have left them all alone. This has been an exceptionally bad season in every possible way, except for hay—we had a long spell of perfect haying weather in June. But everything else is sadly behind our reasonable expectations. I have only two quarts of blueberries canned, as against 40 last year."

Stepmother Caroline wrote on September 22:

"Your possibilities for the winter sound good, though difficult, and I hope it will be a happy winter for you all. In spite of the advantages of Manumit School for the children I'd somehow rather see you stay together as a family, though that feeling may be based on sentiment rather than reason.

"How many children will be in the school, I wonder, and what ages will they be? My brother, Francis, spent his first eight school years in that sort of ungraded country school and seemed to thrive on it. [Francis became an administrator in a large Philadelphia bank.] My own first year of teaching was in a country High School where one other teacher and I gave all the

---

66. The small Seventh Day Adventist church near the Pikes Falls swimming hole has been converted into a summer retreat. On Memorial Day Winnie took the children down to the old cemetery to place lilacs on the graves of the Pike family, who are interred there.

courses, mostly in one room. I taught a Cicero class of one on a front bench while all the rest pursued their History or English in the rear. I boarded with a farmer whose wife gave us pie and molasses for breakfast! It was really fun, though I don't know how much the 12 pupils learned in the process.

"There is no guarantee that the simple way of life you want to follow will conform more nearly to the Kingdom of God than some other more complex one. In a small community, even in one family there may be tensions and pride and misunderstandings which on a larger scale cause war and are, in my mind, the real seed of war." This paragraph encapsulates the insidious and unanticipated difficulties that eventually undermined the noble experiment.

Animal mischief that day: The Angora goats got into the chicken yard and were diving at the garden fence with such eagerness that it might have been they who committed the ravages of two nights before. Alfred was trying to keep billy goat Patrick from impregnating Ann, and when his back was turned Patrick focused his amours on teenage Lucy instead. Just eight months old, she would freshen February 22. The next day Norm and Herbert brought the horse back from Hanford's, whither he had escaped, having a mind of his own.

Mr. Halsey Hicks came up to advise on the forestry program. They spent the rest of the day going over the conifers in the southeast corner, the same hundred or so that Norm and Alfred had marked earlier. They reviewed another, slightly smaller stand of spruce along the south border and into the Tibbett lot, and discovered the old sugar bush [a stand of maple trees suitable for sugaring] they had heard about. They continued to the west slope, where beech trees predominated. In the afternoon they went along the Bondville road, where there was a beech grove, and there were conifers in the area. All in all, there were fair quantities of spruce, beech, soft maple, hard maple, hemlock, balsam, white and yellow birch, and occasional logs of white pine, basswood, white ash, and cherry.

They went with Mr. Hicks to Petrie's sawmill, who claimed to need all types of logs, the prices ranging from eighteen to twenty dollars at the mill. He needed 3,000 board feet of beech by Wednesday, which Alfred and Norm undertook to supply, and was willing to go in with his tractor to haul them out. They had busy days ahead!

Winnie went to Bellows Falls for a teachers' conference, so the children were home from school. From her report it appeared that the Vermont schools were free to follow an enlightened policy. The matter of saluting the flag was also satisfactorily settled. [*Teresa*: Extending one's arm toward the flag was discontinued as too much resembling a Nazi gesture. The cadence-disrupting words "under God" were not yet mandated.]

September 27, Norma wrote to Family:

"This has indeed been a long interval. The children have been going to school for three weeks now, which should theoretically have meant lots more time for letter-writing, but rashly I disposed of this extra time before enjoying it at all and undertook to do all sorts of outdoor jobs, such as puttying the windows and harvesting the potatoes, so as to set the men free for the larger work like mending the barn roof and cutting the winter wood. At present they are cutting 3,000 board feet of beech to sell to the local sawmill to be made into chair legs.

"They need the horse to help them drag the big logs out of the forest, but unfortunately after one day's work the horse decided he didn't care for it, and ran away. The first time we found him and brought him back, but he hasn't been seen now for three or four days. I spent six solid hours yesterday tramping up and down the mountain following his tracks, some of which looked so fresh that I expected to come upon him around the first corner. [Dickie's escapades could have been prevented by the simple expedient of roping one leg to a cinder block or log that he would have to drag. Hobbling, by strapping the two front legs together, is also efficient. The horse has to hop around and can't move very fast or far, but has a certain amount of freedom.]

"Meanwhile the work is held up, and we can't deliver the wood when we promised unless we can borrow a horse from someone else. To me it all seems to reinforce what a luxury an animal like Dick is, fond as I am of him. A larger horse could be ridden, though not so comfortably, and he could pull a cart up and down the hill, which is Dick's principal function at present, and he could also plow, rake hay, harrow and drag logs out of the woods. You'd think it was pretty obvious, but I have not been able to convince anybody yet; perhaps Dick's spell of French leave [AWOL] will make them feel differently, or it may simply make them feel horses are a nuisance and not worth their keep. [Which was, of course, Alfred's oft-stated opinion.]

"Norman Williams is going through the process Alfred went through early in the summer—first the summons to attend a preliminary medical examination, then the principal examination, which for most men is the immediate prelude to induction into the Army—then, if he passes that (which Alfred didn't) an interval of anything up to two months before he gets sent to camp. He will do his best to get sent to the Brattleboro unit—that is, to work in the mental hospital there, or failing that, perhaps to a similar unit working in Concord, New Hampshire. Either way he will at least be able to get occasional glimpses of his bride, though she will be too busy here to go and visit him very much.

"The school plan seems to me to be working out very well; Winnie gets discouraged at times, but she admits herself that she had all sorts of

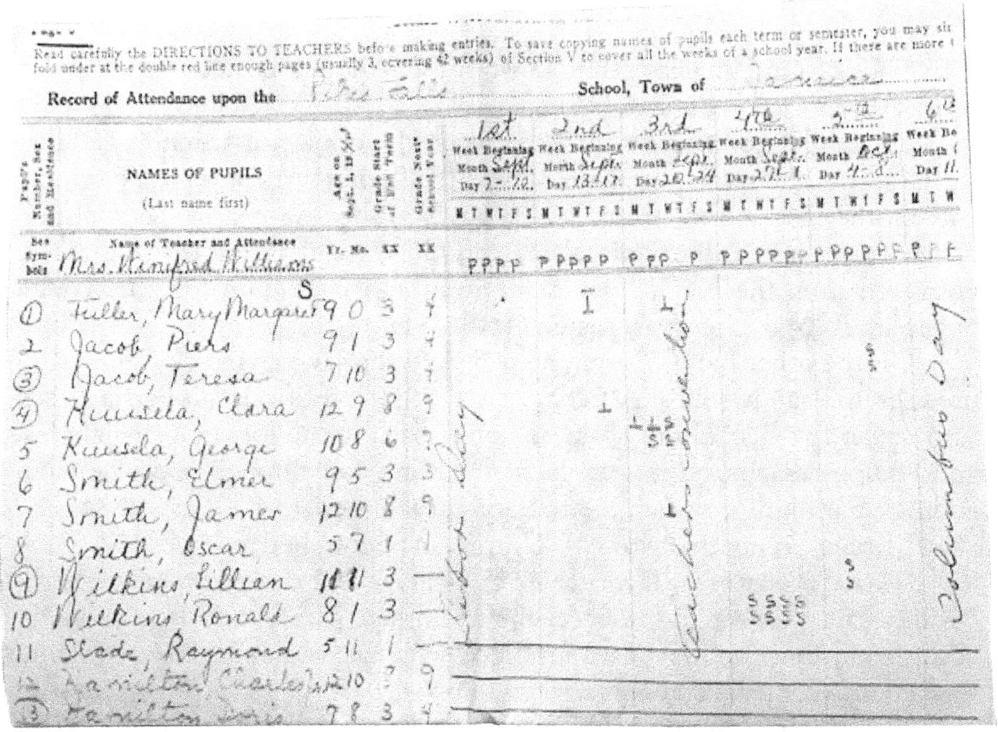
Read carefully the DIRECTIONS TO TEACHERS before making entries. To save copying names of pupils each term or semester, you may six fold under at the double red line enough pages (usually 3, covering 42 weeks) of Section V to cover all the weeks of a school year. If there are more

Record of Attendance upon the .... School, Town of ....

Pupil's Number, Sex and Residence	NAMES OF PUPILS (Last name first)	Age on Sept. 1, 19.. Yr. Mo.	Grade Start of This Term	Grade Next Annual Year	1st Week Beginning Month Sept. Day 7–12	2nd Week Beginning Month Sept. Day 13–17	3rd Week Beginning Month Sept. Day 20–24	4th Week Beginning Month Sept. Day 27–1	5th Week Beginning Month Oct. Day 4–8	6th Week Beginning Month Day 11
	Mrs. Winifred Williams				PPPP	PPPPP	PPP P	PPPPP	PPPPP	PPP
1	Fuller, Mary Margaret	9 0	3	4						
2	Jacob, Piers	9 1	3	4						
3	Jacob, Teresa	7 10	3	4						
4	Huusela, Clara	12 9	8	9						
5	Kuusela, George	10 8	6	7						
6	Smith, Elmer	9 5	3	3						
7	Smith, James	12 10	8	9						
8	Smith, Oscar	5 7	1	1						
9	Wilkins, Lillian	11 11	3	—						
10	Wilkins, Ronald	8 1	3	—						
11	Slade, Raymond	5 11	1	—						
12	Hamilton, Charles	12 10	?	9						
13	Hamilton, Doris	7 8	3	4						

IMAGE 18: *A school attendance record including Piers and Teresa.*

magnificent ideas about all that she was going to accomplish right at the start, and naturally it doesn't work out that way. But it seems clear that she is being successful, though she may not feel so in comparison with her exalted hopes.

"Anyway, the people down in the valley are very glad to have the school opened again and we are already taking steps to have it function as a kind of community center; tomorrow night, for instance, there is to be a picnic to which everyone in the valley is invited, including those who haven't any children to send to the school. About a dozen families live there altogether, but there is nothing in the way of a village—no shop or post office, nothing but the school and the church, and the latter happens to be a Seventh-day Adventist church so it seems to have the effect of keeping people apart rather than drawing them together.

"Not all the families are Adventists and those who are, regard those who aren't as headed for perdition.[67] They don't even all belong in the same town, half of them live in Jamaica town like ourselves, a couple of families in Stratton town, which is merely a geographical expression, and a couple more in Windham town, which is actually in the next county, though they all get

67. Adventist beliefs are similar to those of other churches in many respects, but include a conviction that the "unrighteous" will be annihilated and "cease to exist."

their letters from Jamaica and do most of their shopping there." (This letter continues on October 4, below.)

September 30: Norm and Alfred started work again around 8, felling the largest of the remaining trees. One difficult one turned out to be rotten, and another had a huge trunk, and though cut down to eight feet, neither of the horses [huge draft animals named Comet and Cupid that had been borrowed from the Fields, four miles away] nor even both together could budge it. "A lot of time was wasted on those two [trees]."

On the other hand, Norma helped with the sawing and skidding, and brought up a sandwich for Alfred, to avoid a lunch interval. But Petrie didn't turn up, and at dusk Norm took the horses back to the Fields, losing chains and equipment along the way, having a horse fall through a bridge, and ending up walking between them, leading them both.

Miriam Fredenthal wrote to Norma on September 30:

"I have a very great favor to ask of you. When I decided to come here, Mother said that she did not feel she could take care of both the children and [goats] Junie and Leona. I arranged with David Barrett to keep them for me until I knew what I was going to do.

"By now you have probably heard from Rosina about their plans for the winter. My own are so uncertain that I have been worrying about my goats a lot. I do not know how they will figure into my winter. If I am in Chester, they will probably be with me, but if not, what then. It occurred to me that perhaps I could board them with you at Hilltop Farm for the time being, and then if it should be that I couldn't keep them, you might be in a better position than I to find them new homes.

"You have been so darn generous and good hearted about giving me every kind of advice, that I hate to impose any more of my problems on you. But I feel broken-hearted about Junie and Leona—I really owe them a lot, and love them both very much—this spring they were literally life-savers for me, and now by fall they are accessories in a sense which I do not think you will misunderstand [perhaps referring to marital difficulties]. But I will not cast them off, because they mean too much to me.

"How are you and your family? I hope well and happy. We may get to see you soon."

October 1943

Norma's letter to her family of September 27 was continued on October 4.

"This letter is, as the Americans say, getting nowhere fast. Perhaps I'd better recapitulate briefly what I've been doing since I left it in the typewriter nearly a week ago.

1943

"On Wednesday I rode down to the village with the truck that came to fetch the beech logs, did the shopping and rode back, which took altogether about three hours; then I went off to the picnic at the school. This was a hilarious, and on the whole a very successful, occasion, except for one local family which hung about rather sadly on the edge of the crowd and couldn't be drawn in. Scott Nearing came (he takes a great interest in the school and has built some wonderful swings); he and Helen played an uproarious game of baseball with the children and Helen played her accordion to encourage people to sing. We all got home around 9, somewhat exhausted after the two mile walk through the black forest.

"Thursday, I set off immediately after breakfast and walked six miles or so to fetch Dickie and bring him home—the people who found him had sent a message via the postman. After that I worked the rest of the day until dark with the men in the forest, helping saw down trees and cut them into logs and then drag them out with the larger horses we had borrowed from Harold Field. This operation is called 'snaking', and the name seems very appropriate when you see the huge logs, twelve feet long and anything up to three feet thick, wriggling down the path behind the horse. We had to hitch both horses to some of them, and there was one that couldn't be moved at all, though three of us and two horses worked over it for several hours.

"It's fascinating work and highly skilled, as you have to be constantly in two places at once: at the horse's head urging him on (or restraining him) and behind, with the log, watching for snags and helping it around bends with judicious shoves with a pole. You are lucky if you don't get your feet trodden on by the horse or crushed by a rolling log. I wouldn't want to do a great deal of that kind of work and ordinarily of course it is right outside my province, but this was an emergency, and everyone had to help.

"Friday, I spent the whole day in the kitchen trying to catch up, baking bread and cooking meals for two days. Saturday, I got up at 5 and the children and I left the house at 7 [walking four miles to the village to catch the bus] to go to Brattleboro to see the dentist and buy good strong shoes for the winter. There is an excellent shoe shop in Brattleboro where they take a personal interest in the children's feet, and a good hour (and lots of money) was invested in this serious business, but I felt it was a necessary job well done. Feet are almost the most important part of one's anatomy in winter.

"Piers had his teeth X-rayed to see if the bad fall he had when quite tiny had damaged one of the second teeth, which was very late in appearing. The tooth is there all right, but the two front ones which are already down are very crooked as a result of the same accident and they will have to be straightened sooner or later. Teresa had one small filling in a baby tooth at the back. That was about all we had time for except struggling for some lunch; we unfortunately chose a place which was serving soldiers in relays and it took us an hour and a half to get the slenderest of meals. [The presence of a mother with young children did not seem to influence the behavior of soldiers, on trains or elsewhere.]

"I bought the groceries and we took the bus home, and arrived pretty well exhausted. It is always so hard having to climb a hill three miles long at the end of a hard day. [The bus must have dropped them off at the foot of the road rather than in Jamaica proper, which would have saved a mile.]

"Now [that] I have finished this and written a couple more of the most urgent letters, I must start off and look for Dickie, who has run away again.

"Your letter of Aug. 30th came two days ago and that makes three I haven't answered properly. I think I'll have to deal with them all next time, or this will never get off. Tomorrow I go to Brattleboro again to finish the dozens of small errands I had no time for on Saturday—taking advantage of the fact that Natalie Field is driving down. So everything must somehow get done today, and I haven't written a letter to anybody else in I don't know how long. Patience!"

Norma also wrote to Edward Senior and Caroline on October 4:

"Caroline's long letter of Sept. 22nd has waited for an answer much longer than it deserved, and I have an uneasy feeling that we haven't even answered Father's letter of the 10th. I always think life here can't possibly get any more crowded, and yet it always does!

"These last two weeks, which should have been weeks of peace and quiet and hand work since the children were away at school all day, have, I think, been the worst yet. The horse has run away three times and hours have been spent—mostly by me—looking for him and bringing him back. I have to start out and look for him again in about an hour's time, otherwise I won't be back in time to meet the children coming from school—and so it goes on.

"Last week we took an order for 3,000 feet of beech logs—board feet, that is—and couldn't deliver on time because of the horse running out on us. We had to borrow two horses from a friend, and Alfred and Norm are over there today working out our debt, helping him cut his winter wood. This beech order will be 54 dollars and will give us some idea of our earning capacity. Fifty-four dollars would pay the household expenses for a month, and it could have been earned in four or five days if everything had gone smoothly. But then everything never does.

"Did Alfred mention that he had been thinking hard about buying a mechanical saw? This idea has several advantages; it would enable Alfred to work alone in the forest after Norm has gone to C.P.S., which will probably be in a couple of months at the outside. The saw would almost certainly pay for itself in a few weeks, as both the supply and demand are unlimited in the wood business just now. And it would enable us to practice some forest improvement by taking out the weed trees which have allowed us to grow bigger and bigger [trees] and shade more and more of the valuable young growth.

"On the other hand, it would take three months to get delivery of the saw (though we've heard of a second-hand one which we might be able to move around in the forest); and finally, both Alfred and Norm have a deep-rooted distrust of machinery. I guess they aren't going to want to put their trust in horses either, after this last week's experience. To me, a saw and a strong horse to pull it and the logs would be an admirable investment of the extra money so unexpectedly at our disposal because of the children going to school locally. But I can't sell the idea to anyone else.

"Caroline's letter was most interesting and thought-provoking. I do agree so thoroughly with the suggestion that it is the personal tensions which exist in the family and the small community which are the real seeds of war. But I miscalculated in several respects. For one thing, I failed to realize how tensions would be increased by a life of considerable physical hardship and loneliness, such as ours here has been. Also, I didn't allow enough for the difficulty met with by people like ourselves, aliens and of unpopular views, in attempting to become part of a local community. Physical isolation has a great deal to do with that also. I make a special point of going to meetings of local women's organizations when I can, but it isn't easy, and any community function that takes place in the evening is of course impossible for us.

"Lately we had to court still more estrangement by refusing to help the War Bond drive. In Jamaica they were nice about it, but Scott Nearing, who happens to live in the next town, was threatened with unfavorable publicity in the papers because he refused. Knowing him, I expect he was a little bit truculent about it too! We recently read the record of his trial in 1919, which was in many ways as interesting as the trial of Arle Brooks—in some ways even more so. I wish it could be read by all young men facing trial now for pacifist convictions.

"When do you leave for Florida? Sometime in November I am promising myself a vacation, provided things are going smoothly here and I feel Winnie can manage two jobs for a short time. I told the Brudercoopers in June that though I couldn't possibly stay there I would, without fail, come back and stay for a few days with them later, and I also have plans for doing some research in the various public libraries in Philadelphia to help a friend who is writing a pamphlet on a subject I happen to have studied. My idea of the perfect vacation is to spend it in a library!"

On October 4, Clif Bennett painted a mural of the house as it was at that moment, as seen from the Shack, on the kitchen wall. A caption below it, later painted over, read: "Let not the seeds of war be found on these our

IMAGE 19: *The mural in the kitchen.*

premises." In 2018 the mural, now a historical record and still in excellent condition after 75 years, remained, though the appearance of the house has changed substantially.

October 9, Norma wrote to Nancy Montague:

"Your letter deserved an answer long since, but life has been a kind of kaleidoscopic whirl of chopping down large trees, escaping horses and 'flu. Dickie now runs away every day, that is, provided we manage to catch and

1943

bring him back daily; if not, he runs away as many times as we bring him back. Norm put him to work hauling out logs from the forest and he did quite well, so they made a contract with the local sawmill for a rush order of 3,000 board feet of beech. Dickie apparently got wind of this, because he escaped and almost wrecked the whole plan; not much more than half the order was delivered on time, even with the Field's horses, which we borrowed in desperation at the eleventh hour.

"And no one has been able to put Dickie to work, since he breaks the harness and then while the harness is being fixed, he somehow gets away—a new way every time. I'm on my way down to the village now for mail and hope someone will tell me where he is this time, and hope it won't be too far, so I can get home tonight. I just spent some time in bed struggling with a short, sharp germ which made my sinuses feel as though they were packed tight with heavy clay, so I am hoping Dickie will not make me walk too far.

"I should have started with the most important thing—your ration books. I didn't find them anywhere around (and I've had everything upside down several times lately looking for other missing objects). Moreover, I have a distinct impression that you took them with you. What I recall is that the envelope appeared from somewhere, I said I had thought those were mine, and you pointed out that your name was on the envelope. This is situated in my memory in those last few hectic moments before your departure. Have you looked in the pocket of the car? And have you by any chance a camera which looks just like yours but has 'W. Ward' scratched on the metal part in front? There certainly are gremlins around here.

"Well, here is the sad news, and I wonder if it will distress you as much as it does me—we are buying a cow, and selling all the goats. We need more milk very badly, with our larger family, and at this time of year we couldn't get it from the goats unless we bought another for quite a high price. Then some friends, one of whom expects to go to jail very shortly, as his C.O. status has not been recognized, begged us almost with tears in their eyes to take charge of their Guernsey, Gardenia, and her calf. Gardenia is giving 14 quarts a day and that would solve our nutrition problem for good and all. We would practically live on milk.

"At the very same time two other friends in the same situation begged us to give a home to their Jersey heifer, Juno, to freshen next July. It looks as though we are going to become cow people willy-nilly, since in our exceptionally fortunate position we ought to help where possible. I don't really know if we can manage Juno, all the same, but Gardenia and daughter are coming this next Monday and we are already starting to look for possible purchasers for goats.

"Thanks ever so for the five-dollar check. I'll buy the ice cream this afternoon if I don't have to chase after Dickie to Rawsonville or worse.

[Nancy may have told Norma to 'Treat yourself to some ice cream,' knowing what a rare indulgence this would have been.]

"The school is going splendidly. Winnie has some slight trouble with discipline as the [valley] children expect to be beaten when they misbehave, but I don't think she is much worried about it. They had a roast down at the school; the children built an outdoor fireplace (which threatened to collapse in the middle of the proceedings) and we had a wonderful gathering, most of the families from the valley and members of the school board too, including those who had been snooty about the scheme in the first instance. A Halloween party is now being planned. Sometime all the school mothers plan to get together and can vegetable soup for hot lunches during the winter.

"I am anxiously awaiting the arrival of one Polly Robinson, who is coming to take charge of the domestic end of things, at least while I take a short holiday I feel I have earned. She has been for some time the dietitian at the Catholic Worker C.P.S. camp not far from here, where they managed with practically no money in most uncomfortable surroundings, yet their morale was reported to be far better than in the Quaker camps where they spent twice as much. I feel Polly has the perfect preparation for life at Hilltop!"

Norma, Norm, and Alfred went with Mr. Worden to West Unity, N.H., about 45 miles from Jamaica, where they bought Gardenia Cow and Gladiola Calf, and brought back goats Leona, Junie, and Leonora. Polly Robinson arrived. She was soon busy putting up pear [?], apple, and squash preserves for the winter.

Form dated October 12, 1943:
PERMIT OF LOCAL BOARD FOR REGISTRANT TO DEPART
FROM THE UNITED STATES.

This is to certify that Alfred Bennis Jacob Order No. 748, serial No. 400, Class 4, Division F, a registrant of this local board, has applied for a permit to depart from the United States, and this local board being convinced that the registrant's absence is not likely to interfere with the proper administration of the selective service law, hereby authorizes the said registrant to depart from the United States and to remain absent therefrom from October 12 to October 23, 1943. In his application the registrant gave this information:

1. *Countries to be visited*: Montreal, Canada.
2. *Individuals or organizations represented*: Personal.

Nature of business: Pleasure.

Description of registrant: White, Height approx. 5'10" weight 160 Eyes Blue Hair Brown complexion Dark. Other obvious physical characteristics that will aid in identification Mole on chin.

Date of birth: May 16, 1909.

1943

This trip, the need for which is not explained, was never undertaken, despite the amount of red tape involved.

One day they had a late breakfast and meeting, at which Norm mentioned their insensitivity to the suffering of others, notably people of India in famine conditions. Opinions were expressed that nothing could be done without achieving greater group unity, and also that the lack of group unity might result from too great subjectiveness and too little concern with the welfare of others. There was a pretty clear division, for Norm and Alfred wanted to move in the direction of simpler living with a view to sharing with others less fortunate, or encouraging valuable organizations such as the Fellowship of Reconciliation, while Norma opposed action in this direction. She wished to build up the farm, concentrating on the group's own well-being, and also maintain certain appearances of farming which might be irrelevant in this case—a horse, plowed fields, etc. This terminology, "maintain certain appearances of farming," clearly reflects Alfred's view of the irrelevance of such optics in the face of global disaster.

Work continued. They found it difficult to get any common basis on which to establish a simple life. Piers asked, "What is fascism?" and after various efforts at definition Norma said: "What it boils down to is this…" with a further definition. Piers responded, "Will fascism boil away to nothing?"

Norma wrote to Family on October 20:

"We have bought a cow! And a calf too, to add to our already considerable livestock. We took her over partly because we now have a more or less permanent family of seven [the four Jacobs, Norm and Winnie Williams, and Polly Robinson] and simply have to have more milk, partly to oblige some friends who had to part with her and didn't want to sell her to just anybody because she was a special pet. She is a large light brown Guernsey named Gardenia; the calf is a smaller replica and is named Magnolia and they make a handsome couple. Gardenia was raised by some child in a calf [4-H] club and is extremely gentle, manageable and affectionate. At first I thought a cow [was] just an unresponsive hulk in comparison with goats, but now I am coming to know Gardenia better and am acquiring a real respect for her good nature and patience in putting up with amateur handling. She gives about two gallons of milk a day and it's wonderfully creamy; I certainly appreciate cream with my breakfast porridge, but I still think goats are more intelligent, more fun and more sweet-smelling. However, we have to get rid of the goats now, and I have the sad task this afternoon of drafting an advertisement to put in the local paper.

"We have, at least for the present, what I've wanted more than anything else since we came here; a competent woman to take over the kitchen department. Her name is Polly Robinson and she is accustomed to feeding large numbers of hungry men on a very reduced budget. The difficulty is that she naturally has some professional pride and likes to cook well and interestingly, even if cheaply, and both Alfred and Norm have a perverted idea that there is something sinful about this! Polly says she is used to people complaining about the food, but she never before was in a place where they complained because it was too good!

"With regard to life on a mountain top being good for serenity and detachment, of course that is true to some extent (though not nearly so true as you'd imagine, since the fundamental and most disturbing problems of life are present wherever there is more than one human being). But remember, I too have been where bombs were falling. The presence of actual danger, I've found, conduces to a kind of simplification, often over-simplification in fact, which causes one to become oblivious of the real reasons why things are as wrong as they are. It's only too easy to get into the habit of thinking that once the raid is over, everything will be solved. And that does give 'Serenity of mind,' believe it or not.

"You speak of the hatred induced by people who have witnessed atrocities like the bombing of refugees, but I wonder how many people who talk like that remember that it was [Generalissimo Francisco] Franco who invented this particular form of horror (the most dreadful of all, I think, with the exception of the food blockade—and I speak from knowledge of the effects of both). And I am sure a great many people in England still think Franco is a great Christian gentleman.

"In re your question, 'What would pacifists do with Hitler?' I always feel that's about as logical as the man who is dying of a disease brought on by every kind of wrong living and sends for the doctor and says, 'What are you going to do to cure me?' There isn't any answer. One thing pacifists would not do and that is to execute him and allow him to become a martyr and plague humanity for hundreds of years after he was dead."

On the 22nd, Teresa's 8th birthday, Norma wrote to Rosina Bennett:

"I'm sending out S.O.S's to Clif and Herbert, but the trouble is they are both so mobile I really can't be sure of making contact with either. [The men] are working like demons trying to finish off a logging job that should have been completed two weeks ago.

"Tomorrow I start on my so eagerly-awaited vacation, unless we get a last-minute visit from Paul and his wife. They wrote they'd be up this weekend and I wrote begging them to arrive Friday if they possibly could because I want to be in New Haven Sunday morning for a meeting of the Connecticut Valley Association of Friends. But a friend in the hand is worth twenty in the Connecticut Valley and if they can't come till later, I'll put off my trip till Monday. [She mentioned several books she's taking to read during the trip. Throughout her life she never traveled without books.]

"Gardenia is doing fine; I think she likes us all right, in fact the other day she tried to put her arms around my neck! I was touched by this proof of affection, but I was also knocked flat on my back (for the second time), so I told her we would just be good friends in future, and I keep my distance. Little Gladiola frolics about the barnyard, evidently mistaking herself for a goat.

"Thanks for the stove bolts. We haven't found time to get the stove installed yet, but Helen Knothe wants a stove and offered to trade her good battery radio for the extra one. This would be a bargain almost shamefully to our advantage, so perhaps it's a good thing the men still have their faces set against a radio. I expect we'll end up by just giving Helen the stove; goodness knows we owe them enough, for help, entertainment and maple syrup these last two years."

On Sunday, October 24, Norma's 34th birthday, there was a meeting followed by discussion. Winnie suggested that to please both parties, they should try to earn and save simultaneously, the men earning an amount equivalent to that saved by the household. They spent time working out the possible details of such a plan, almost to the point of beginning again in a new place, because Hilltop had so much expenditure and was so much larger than necessary.

Norma felt she could not go along with such a plan and did not believe that further household economies were possible or desirable, and that too much emphasis was being placed on the economic side of life, while the personal side was in ruins. The group eventually concluded that they should drop all thought of the economic side and try to make the personal side more harmonious. They would try for more group activities, with no immediate purpose beyond that of cooperating together.

Norm and Alfred expressed their concern that they should feel identified with the world's need, as, for instance, with the starving people in Bengal, and make sacrifices for their good. But Polly pointed out that nothing truly constructive could come out of an inwardly destructive interrelationship. The men therefore proposed to continue working on forest improvement to the extent they felt desirable, and any money that might accrue could be used by Norm for any purpose that interested him. The group confirmed that Norm and Alfred might devote such time to reading as seemed proper to them.

It is hard to see how this plan would benefit the "starving people in Bengal."

Both children stayed in bed much of the day, Piers with a cough, and Pearl and Walter (no hint of who these people were or why they were at Hilltop) had to amuse themselves as well as they could. The group read around the fire in the early evening, and discussed war and political action for peace.

Norm went to Rutland for his final physical, and Norma to Philadelphia. Alfred did the chores and read to the children about Vesuvius and Pompeii, and Polly made a Vesuvius pudding for supper dessert.

The next day there was supposed to be a meeting, but only Alfred showed up. He wondered whether other things were getting to be more important than God and group worship. "One would think that if they had any importance at all they would have first importance—certainly more than meals, milking, or sleep. We will sit up and lose sleep to talk with almost anyone who comes; yet when God comes, we are inclined to do the milking during the time appointed to see Him, and probably miss Him altogether." Alfred's persistently Christocentric views were at variance with the more casual beliefs of most of the others, who merely wanted a harmonious work environment.

Alfred went to the school for the Halloween entertainment. The schoolhouse was full, and after the play there were simple games and contests and a variety of cakes and cocoa. Norm arrived just before the show, and reported that he had been rejected by Selective Service, though the classification was not certain.

November 1943

Alfred wrote to Leslie and Valerie Johnston in Canada on November 1:

"Norma has gone off to Pendle Hill and environs & expected I would have answered your letter a week ago. We might have gone up to see you last weekend, but the draft board's permission had expired & we had no [passport] photographs. Whether we do so when she comes back remains to be seen. I have it in mind also to try to see my parents before they go Southwards. [They customarily spent the winters in a waterside house in St. Petersburg, Florida.]

"We can't have kept you well enough posted. There has been a horse all summer, amusing himself grazing & occasionally [continually would be a better word!] running away. Sometimes people have taken him with a borrowed buggy to the village, but on the whole, I don't think anyone believes he justifies his existence. There are no dogs and cats, but plenty of rats and mice and chipmunks. The latter had a lot of our sweet corn, the rabbits have all [gone] to Ruzine [Rosina] Barrett, and we are vaguely hoping the goats will get disposed of somehow. Not because we don't like them, but because Norm and I rather wanted to do a little forest improvement work, and the goats last winter took 4 man-hours daily.

1943

"We have supplied the local mill with 3000 feet of beech at $18 (at the mill) & are cutting 6000 of spruce at $20 or $22; also cordwood at $8 a cord, stacked up here in the woods. So we could get rich quick if we wanted—indeed we even decided one week to try to begin to move toward a sort of equivalence between income and outgo, but abandoned it after a week.

"The Pikes Falls school arrangement works quite nicely. There was even a Halloween party and the local lumbermen from a temporary mill came with wives & children. Winnie is, I expect, rather overworked, trying to pull her weight both here and at the school, but that's what she seems to want to do. Norm was just examined by Selective Service & rejected, so we hope it will mean a 4F like mine. What we should do about that I don't know. He is keen to do something really valid here, not just maintain ourselves and keep ourselves warm for our own good, so he and I have lots in common.

"For myself I have plunged into a reading program, with a view to giving 5 hours a day to it, since that seems more valid to me than many of the ways we tend to spend our time. My main text is [Peter D.] Ouspensky's *Tertium Organum*.[68] We have no end of personal and group problems, even with a nice like-minded group. Of course that is what we came here to have, and to solve. So we have it, but we don't solve it."

On November 8 Norma wrote to Valerie:

"I see in answering your letter Alfred forgot your question about money for winter clothes. Of course the answer is yes—what do you think you'll need, and how? For once in a lifetime, we have money to burn and would much rather do something more constructive with it. Speak up quickly before Alfred's conscience gets to hurt so badly that he gives it all away to the F.O.R.! We've invested some of it in the co-operative movement already. Be sure to indicate quite clearly how it should be sent, as we don't know the regulations.

"I'm just back from a ten-day vacation: would have liked to stay away another week as all sorts of exciting things were happening, including a conference at P. H. [Pendle Hill] with A. J. Muste, and W. H. Auden reading his own poems at the N.Y. public library (what news of Day Lewis, by the way?) But Winnie's parents were coming to visit, and I felt I ought to be on hand. I got a ride with them all the way up from N.Y. and I think probably Alfred will ride down with them tomorrow to see a few people.

"I saw a psychiatrist in Philadelphia who advised me strongly to put myself under treatment, both mental and physical, to get my digestive trouble cleared up before it gets any worse. I've been having difficulties with it almost

---

68. As Alfred regularly alluded to the many tasks that needed to be done, planning to spend five hours a day reading this impenetrable book instead of working was perhaps a sulky act of defiance.

constantly for a year now, am much underweight and consequently overly subject to fatigue and discouragement—both things we can't afford here.

"Winnie seems to be getting on wonderfully with the school. She had some trouble with discipline till one of the children suggested some system of the children disciplining themselves which he had learned at a previous school, and apparently it works like a charm. The public relations angle is also very encouraging. They had a Halloween party at the school, with entertainment by the children, which I understand was a howling success, and a square dance last Saturday night.

"There is a regular lumberman's village of tarpaper shacks springing up at the corner by our mail box. [Had mail been delivered to this box in Pikes Falls rather than being retained in Jamaica, it would have saved countless miles of trekking up and down the mountain—but of course there were social advantages to going to the village. And it would not have been wise to leave packages awaiting pickup in such an isolated location.] It seems the lumbermen are very nice people, and it's interesting bringing such migrants into a local community and making them a part of its social life. To me this is far and away the most hopeful development since Hilltop started. Another piece of good news—Norm was classified 4-F as psychopathic! We think the beard was what turned the trick. His account of the proceedings was very funny.

"Polly is away today with Harold Field in Brattleboro, inquiring about food in bulk for the winter. We are lamentably short, for a variety of reasons. And another member may be joining us, a German refugee whom we knew in Spain and whom I saw in Long Island last week. By the way, Harold Field is also asking to be put in 4-E. I'm afraid his appeal will be turned down and it may mean jail, but it's interesting that he should feel that way. We knew he was sympathetic but never thought of him as a pacifist; it seems Scott Nearing's example (and ours perhaps in part) has been contagious. Norm thought at first that he (Harold) wouldn't go through with it, but he made a special trip over yesterday to talk with him, and thinks he is really in earnest."

Norma wrote to Paul [Rosenthal] and Shirley on November 9:

"I finally arrived back late Saturday night, after spending an extra day in New York, as the people I was ready to ride with weren't ready to go by Friday. I took the time to visit Ejan Adrich and other friends and see Paul Robeson[69] as Othello—a milestone, I think, in the history of race relations in this country.

---

69. Paul Robeson was an immensely popular African American stage and film actor, singer, and political activist who was blacklisted in the 1950s during the McCarthy era despite his international reputation.

"Paul, if there's a vacant place on your mailing list after you get to Danbury (or wherever) we'd appreciate being asked to fill it. We don't have any correspondent in any of the Federal prisons, though we have many friends there. Just these last few days, Harold [Field] has appeared as a C.O. and has applied for Form 47 and will appeal his 1-A classification. It doesn't seem very probable that the appeal will be successful, but Norm thinks he is in earnest about it and will go through with the business to the bitter end. By the way, they decided Norm was psychopathic and put him in 4-F. It's a big thing for Hilltop but I am finding myself a little uneasy at what seems to be a settled policy to deny any C.O.'s recognition by the device of deciding that they aren't entirely sane.

"Work is terribly in arrears and I have now been placed in sole charge of the barn—will take over the cow and calf from Winnie at the end of this week, in addition to the dozen remaining goats and the sheep. I'd rather do that, though, than the cooking any day."

The Frosts [Winnie's parents] left about 7:30 a.m., in the rain. Alfred rode with them as he left for his autumnal visit to friends and relatives. The road was a mass of rushing water, washed out in numerous places, and it was only by good management that the car got down at all.

There is 10-day gap in the Hilltop record while Alfred was away. He had, because it was not his habit ever to take the initiative, not specifically asked that someone else keep it up, no doubt assuming that this would somehow be understood. He returned the evening of Friday the 19th and resumed the record the following day. During his absence, Norm hurt his back and continued suffering from stomach weakness, but managed to plow the rest of the barn field and the lower part of the garden. On his return, Alfred was unable to observe any improvement in working out a mutual plan of life; the complex of resentments, frustrations, and resignations was still there. There was no agreement about what was needful and what was superfluous, or what was to be bought and what produced.

On November 13 Norma wrote to Phil and Teddy:

"Thanks ever so for the check—I had forgotten about it too. I don't believe Bobsie will ever give you any floods of milk now, but she ought to give you some kids with sensational pedigrees, if mated to your five-star buck. If and when we ever get back into the goat business, I hope we'll be able to afford one. At present we are on our way out of the business, having bought a cow—with a more or less permanent family of seven, we simply had to have more milk. But I never will get as fond of that cow as of the goats, though I admit it's grand to have so much cream. She is just an unresponsive hulk in comparison—not that she isn't a very delightful cow as cows go, but you probably know what I mean.

"We are working on a new arrangement now whereby Polly Robinson (who has been dietitian at various C.P.S. camps) looks after the cooking, Winnie takes the children to school every day and brings them back at supper time, Alfred and Norm work hard in the woods (we've sold quite a lot of lumber already) and I take charge of the barn.

"If we didn't write about your being put in 4-F, [actually 4-E, see comment later on] it wasn't that we didn't care. Well, maybe Alfred did write, but I was away visiting the parents and others and hadn't much time, and anyway I was so upset by the news that I didn't really know what to say. Eddie thought Phil ought to appeal and use every possible device to spin the thing out as long as possible. I said, perhaps not very tactfully, that I didn't feel Phil would want to do it that way. Please let us know what it turns out to be!

"Most of our [goats] are dry, but the one that is still milking (Deborah) is still giving double that without any particular pressing. They didn't just go dry (though production dropped shockingly) but I dried them off because I couldn't manage so many animals single-handed. It will be easier to ship them, too, if they get sold.

"The school seems to be working splendidly. Lots more families are moving in, mostly lumbermen living in tarpaper shacks and working on the next piece of woodland to ours. They are really migrant labor and it's interesting to get this contact with them. They seem very decent people. Winnie now has 14 children in the school, and I think is finding it lots easier than she did at first. We've had several parties at the school and feel we are making a beginning on the job of community-building, which is a good deal needed down there. Our next idea (Polly's and mine) is a co-operative buying club.

"I'll be delighted to get the lamp even if it doesn't work perfectly—most of ours at present are working so imperfectly that we seem to spend most of our time plunging around and falling over things in semi-darkness. We bought one at an auction, but it turned out to be a thirty-year old model for which it is difficult to get new parts—we are right out of mantles at present and don't know for sure if we can get more to fit.[70] "Alfred is away this week visiting the parents, Arthur Moore, etc. Norm has been put in 4-F (psychopathic!) and is just waiting for confirmation from the draft board at Oberlin.

"The Garden has been perfectly deplorable, and we have to buy vegetables for winter use. Of course, bad weather had much to do with it, and particularly the fact that we didn't expect to be here this winter when we were making the plans."

---

70. This type of kerosene lamp was pressurized and used a fragile bell-shaped mantle which, when heated by the flame, glowed brightly.

1943

Work continued, and progress was made. The Williams' apartment was warmed for the first time. One day it snowed around six inches in the night, and continued all day. Winnie and the children took two and a half hours to return from school through the snow, which had drifted during the day. Teresa had been week-ending with the nearby [to the school] Fields.

Norma wrote to Family on November 14:

"I don't think I have written since before Teresa's and my birthdays—I didn't even find time to thank you for the books, which arrived actually on Teresa's [8th] birthday. The book about Greece was charming, and I was struck by the resemblance between Greece as described there and Spain, particularly southern Spain. Both countries, too, are capable of exciting the same kind of attachment in people who really get to know them.

"Teresa enjoyed her books a great deal; interestingly enough, Piers enjoyed them even more—he actually started reading them on his own account, the first time I've seen him spontaneously interested in a book. In fact, he read me several of the stories aloud, with obvious pride. They are getting along pretty well now at school, from all that I hear, and Piers is at last beginning to realize that reading can be pleasurable.

"Teresa and I had a joint birthday party because I was planning to leave the next day for a couple of weeks visiting in Pennsylvania. I went down to Philadelphia and spent three or four days with our friends there, just doing nothing but resting. I really was very tired indeed and had been looking forward to this holiday literally for months, ever since our strenuous summer with the Montagues. I didn't feel I could leave before the end of October because of all the harvesting and canning, but as it turned out the garden produced practically nothing for winter storage. The weather was quite exceptionally bad. We've had every imaginable kind of bad weather here during the past year and a half, with the exception of a blizzard—and believe me, there are more kinds of bad weather in New England than can even be conceived of anywhere else, all the way from long droughts to ice storms and torrential rains.

"This past week we had some of the latter, and the road at one place was completely washed out, with gullies in it a foot deep, absolutely impassable by anything less durable than a tractor. In fact I'm not so sure even a tractor could negotiate it. This is a bad business, as there are probably less than two weeks left before the snow falls to stay, and we still have a good part of our winter supplies to get in, including about three tons of hay. I just can't get used to feeling so continually helpless before the forces of nature. In England, nine times out of ten you know pretty much what the weather can do and can be prepared, but here the human race just seems the sport of not very well-intentioned gods. If they decide that your crops are to be a failure this year, or that your road is to be closed to traffic for seven months, there just isn't anything you can do about it."

Norma wrote a mea culpa [my fault] letter to Mr. Davis on November 16 about Dickie's latest escape:

"We are extremely sorry to hear that our horse has been up at your place and that it has done so much damage. We have had considerable trouble with this [for the] last week or two because the pasture up here is used up and [the horse] has got into the habit of breaking loose.

"For a long time we couldn't discover how it [perhaps it was the British custom to refer to animals as "it" rather than by gender] was getting through the fence. I now have it tied in the barn and hope it is secure. We have spent literally hours hunting for it, trudging up and down the mountain, following reports that it has been seen in different places and so on. Twice it was seen at Dr. Ebeling's and we went down and hunted around but could find no sign of it; I suppose it must then have been up at your house. Several days were lost last week because the weather was so appalling that I simply hadn't the moral courage to go out horse-hunting.

"We hope to sell the horse soon, and in the meantime, I can assure you that we are making every effort to keep it at home. Of course we are responsible for the damage, and I hope you will allow us to pay for it as far as is possible; I understand that lawns can't be easily replaced, but please believe that we regret what happened and will not try to avoid responsibility."

Norma wrote to Family in an undated letter, but probably late November:

"I now have four letters to answer, but if you could see me now, you wouldn't wonder at what has happened to all my intellectual pursuits like writing letters! I inherited the job of looking after the cow, calf, and horse as well as all the goats. Winnie had insisted on doing the milking, but she really needed the extra sleep in the mornings and besides there was so much work during the day that she simply couldn't do, like watering the animals and cleaning out the barn. So I became dairymaid-in-chief. I get up at 5:30, light the kitchen fire, cook myself an early breakfast (coffee and eggs), go out to the barn and milk, and do the most urgent jobs like distributing grain and hay to everybody. The sun hasn't even begun to appear by the time I get back to the house—if it has, I know it's late and we shall all be behind.

"By 6:45 everybody is up, and Polly is cooking the breakfast as Winnie and the children are getting ready for school. They leave at 7:30, by which time it is pretty well daylight. Then I sit down, eat my main breakfast, and relax slightly. After breakfast I go out and finish the barn jobs, which usually take me till nearly eleven, now that water has to be carried for all the animals—Gardenia the cow drinks eight to ten gallons all by herself! Then

I clean up the kitchen, and by that time lunch is usually ready. All afternoon I'm busy with various tidying-up jobs or laundry, unless I have to go down to the village—for various causes I had to go down four times within a week just recently.

"Then just before supper I put the goats to bed, distribute more hay and generally make the barn all ship-shape for the night. After supper I milk once more, and then I'm ready for bed. It would be completely impossible if Polly didn't take all the preparation of meals off my hands. If I could teach her to do the washing-up too, everything would be perfect! She came of a rather wealthy Virginia family where they always had droves of faithful, colored servants to clear up after them, and she admits herself that that's one aspect of voluntary poverty she finds it almost impossible to learn. But I don't mind washing a few dishes for the sake of her company, conversation and cooking.

"I really am very fortunate in the women who come here, they all are cooperative and congenial—far more so than the men, as a rule. Polly recently made a trip to Brattleboro (our local metropolis) and ordered in six months' supply of food, and a large part of Saturday and Sunday was spent in getting [the supplies] in. They arrived at the village after the first heavy snowfall, so that the road was closed to wheeled traffic, at least the last stretch. Friends brought them up to the foot of the last hill by car and Dickie, with a light sled, made five journeys and brought in nearly a ton of stuff—all for human consumption! The animal food was in long ago.

"The last two days Polly and I have spent trying to fit the whole lot into our not very large larder while still leaving room to turn around, and having the things needed first on top. It isn't very easy when you consider that a large part of the supplies comes in bulky forms, such as hundred-pound sacks of rolled oats and five-gallon cans of soybean oil for cooking.

"We spent the equivalent of about £40 and we have everything in that we'll need to eat for the rest of the winter. Not bad, I think, for a family of seven people with hearty appetites. No, I'm forgetting, we get our eggs by post every week or so from a friend who has a poultry farm, and of course we get milk fresh each day and there is a seventy-gallon drum of molasses down in the village waiting to get up somehow, and a sixty-pound can of honey on its way to us still. But the statement is substantially correct.

"We had a brief but very satisfactory visit from Phil last week. He has just managed to escape being put into a C.P.S. camp, which would have been absurd as he is certainly as valuable as possible in the place where he is. The stupidities of the system often are exasperating, for instance taking a man like that and putting him in a camp to do forestry work, leaving his wife and three children (the third is due next month) without his support, since C.P.S. men get neither pay nor dependency allowances. [This would have been the 4-E classification.]

"In Phil's case it was possible to side-track the system, since he is favorably known locally and managed to get the draft board to agree that he was a bona fide farmer. Considering he supplies milk, eggs, green vegetables and quite a bit of meat to most of a village of several hundred, I don't think it was an exaggerated claim. There is no other farmer in the village, and they have no other source of fresh foods (except fish), and without Phil would have to rely on tradesmen from the town nine miles away who deliver by truck and of course charge accordingly. Phil also does all the transportation of goods for the village store, as well as being guide, philosopher and friend to half the village. You never saw such a universal man.

"Teresa reads omnivorously. The local doctor who makes regular school inspections says she should be encouraged to read less and play more, but it isn't easy. Poor child, I know just what a struggle is before her, a whole lifetime with hardly ever enough reading matter to meet the demand! [*Teresa*: As there were no children's books, I read such things as Dr. Grantly Dick-Read's *Childbirth without Fear* and *Look to the Mountain* by LeGrand Cannon, Jr.]"

On November 20, Norma wrote to Valerie:

"At the moment you'll be interested to know that Hilltop is actually paying its way. About six weeks ago we decided to see whether we could run the place on what all or any of us were earning, including Winnie's salary, which of course is the lion's share, and whatever came in from chopping wood. I added up the very incomplete figures this morning, and discovered we'd earned about 160 dollars and spent about 150. On the one hand the biggest bill for November hasn't come in yet, on the other, none of the work anyone did in November has been paid for yet, so I personally feel a modest hope that we may come out more or less level by the end of the year.

"The psychiatry question isn't settled yet, but the man I consulted down in Philadelphia said he thought there might be someone suitable in the Brattleboro Retreat, a mental hospital with an excellent reputation. We had already gathered that pretty much from the 25 C.P.S. men who are working there. It compares most favorably with the awful stories one hears from other mental hospitals, Byberry for instance, where John Morgan is. It wouldn't be impossible by any means to go down to Brattleboro once a week. And I think the tonifying effect of seeing people, reading in the library, eating in a restaurant (!!!), would be at least as valuable as the psychiatry.

"Well, we've got a cat. I decided that now I was in charge of the barn there was no reason why I shouldn't have one there to keep me company and incidentally keep down the rats. It's a nice little marmalade-colored kitten. We spent all supper time the night it came trying to give it a suitable name, I had the right one buzzing about in my subconscious but couldn't bring it to light. We finally settled to call it Scherezade, Sherry for short, and it wasn't till next morning that I remembered I'd meant to call the next cat Egypt. After Cleopatra, you know."

On November 20, Norma also wrote to "My very dear Lucia and other friends":

"I write this by lantern light and the lantern doesn't shine directly on the paper, so every so often I pick it up and wave it around to see what I've written. Polly Robinson laughs at me waving the lantern at the typewriter.

"You ought to see me now, the Compleat[71] Dairymaid. I get up each morning at 5:30 and trudge out to the barn through the snow with a lantern and an assortment of pails. Having negotiated the rear end of the horse (though he has never yet kicked) I induce the cow to rise, unless as more often happens she has eluded her stanchion in the night and is in entirely the wrong part of the barn. I then have to dissuade her from lying down again while being milked; she is apt to flop on her knees in a desperate attempt to extract further nourishment from a completely vacated grain pan. Milking takes me around 25 minutes, and I don't think that's bad at all for one as new to it as myself. But I still infinitely prefer the goat. After struggling with the larger brutes, it gives me so much pure happiness to go into the goat barn and see the row of intelligent, sensitive faces looking up at me. I am supposed to be selling them off, because otherwise our winter grain bill will be something appalling, but it tears my heart and I'm afraid the conflict is such that I'm not putting very much energy into the sales talk.

"Looking out the window into the black night and meditating at this point, I suddenly saw reflected a great conflagration, and looking around quickly I saw all my aprons hanging on the back of the kitchen door going up in flames. Polly and I leaped to put them out, and Piers said, 'I was just playing with a piece of string.' I think the child must be a pyromaniac; I have tried not to inhibit him, because I was afraid if he wasn't allowed to play with fire in public, he would do it in private, but I have put my foot down now.

"Alfred saw [the psychiatrist] Dr. Freed, but all I can learn about the interview was that they agreed there was absolutely nothing to be done with me except have me taken to bits and rebuilt.

"Tuesday: Here we are recovering from a blizzard, or something very like it. I've never seen a real New England blizzard, it's the one kind of damnable weather I haven't seen in these past two and a half years. You'd be amazed how many kinds of bad weather we have in these parts, the variety

---

71. Merriam-Webster: "Compleat ... having all necessary or desired elements or skills." An archaic form.

being as astounding as the degree. Sunday night everything was lovely, relatively speaking; Monday morning we found ourselves in a whirling world of white. It snowed all night, all day and all night again. Now it's stopped, and I am going to try and struggle down the hill, that is if I'm not too much out of practice for snowshoeing, or if the snow isn't too sticky, as it certainly is for skiing. Between the house and the barn the drifts are nearly waist deep, no fun at all to struggle through before dawn with a lantern and pails. I never saw so much snow fall all at one time.

"The Brudercoop does seem like home to me, in fact it really feels like all the home I have. This place is just a battlefield. Sometimes I enjoy fighting to keep alive, sometimes I wonder if it's worth so much trouble. Today is one of the latter times. I'll be seeing you again, but not for months and months unless it all gets too much for me. I have a powerful conviction that I am through at Hilltop, and next summer will see my definitive departure. You needn't tell anyone else this. Where I'll go, what I'll do then, I don't know. Yes, Lucia, you guessed right, something did go wrong. I don't want to go into it particularly, but I'm bluer—even purple in spots—than I've been in a long, long while. Nothing to be done but sit tight and wait for spring, and spring is a hell of a long way off. Write to me sometimes, you do cheer me up."[72] On the 26th she wrote to Rosina:

"At last, at long, long last, I'm getting around to some of my arrears of correspondence. There was a long delay in returning the [egg shipping] box for various reasons but I'll try and be more prompt in future. I don't believe we really need three dozen every week; at first I thought perhaps it would be simplest just to take them as they come, and keep sending the box back and forth. From my point of view it would be easier to have the box arrive on Friday or Saturday as I nearly always do go to the village on a Saturday, and if they come other days they may have to wait, but they are so nice and fresh I don't believe it will hurt them to wait. I'd rather do that than be encouraged to use them faster than I really need by getting them every week. Of course we can use them that fast, but it wouldn't be very economical. On the other hand, if for any reason at all any particular arrangement is easier for you (for instance if you have a surplus now and may not have later), arrange it the way that suits you. We'll welcome anything that comes.

---

72. Norma was later diagnosed with what was then called manic depression—bipolar disorder today—and vacillated between energetic optimism and deep depression. The strained relationship with Alfred would have exacerbated any negative feelings she experienced because of this condition. The reference to "blue" and "purple" is troubling, as it could suggest that he had actually struck and bruised her in one of his rages. It had happened before. As Alfred could read the carbons of her letters, it was advisable to be circumspect.

1943

"We are pretty badly behind with our winter arrangements. The barn, for instance, still leaves a great deal to be desired. I have sent for a steel stanchion for Gardenia and hope to goodness they can still supply it [perhaps because of wartime restrictions on the use of steel?]."

Life and work on the farm continued on several fronts. Teresa fainted unexpectedly. Norma's letter to Dr. Joseph Stokes dated November 29 covered it:

"I thought I had better write to you about a trouble of Teresa's which has been causing us some alarm. About five weeks ago, she suddenly fainted in the middle of the afternoon. She was very pale for a long time after coming to, and complained of pain in the lower part of the abdomen. I sent immediately for the local doctor, and he arrived within about an hour, while she was still in a state of partial collapse, and examined her very carefully all over without being able to discover anything at all to account for the fainting. It was the day after her birthday, and though she hadn't eaten much she had nevertheless had rather richer food than usual. We finally put it down to a digestive disturbance of some kind. [This seems to have been the doctor's go-to diagnosis for most ailments.]

"After a few hours she seemed perfectly all right and after keeping her at home quietly for a few days, with the doctor's permission I let her go back to school. Everything seemed to be going perfectly, when one day last week she fainted again, this time at school. The teacher, who is a friend and lives with us, wrote out an exact account of what happened, and this I enclose.

"Apparently the attack wasn't so bad as last time, but they left her at a neighbor's house for the night to avoid the long walk home. When I went to fetch her the next day, she was perfectly all right, and has been ever since. The doctor was not called on this occasion because the telephone wires were down after a storm. [Where was there a telephone? Norma would have had to walk miles to find one.] I went to his house on Saturday hoping to talk the case over with him, but didn't find him at home.

"The neighbor with whom Teresa was left said that in her opinion the trouble might be a tapeworm. She described the symptoms she had observed in her own children which seemed to correspond with some that Teresa had shown—capricious appetite, excessive craving for sweet things, a rather pinched look about the mouth (though she is plump in the body and weighs 65 lbs.) and irritability. These various things I had of course noticed, but I had put them down to psychological strain resulting from some rather unhappy events at home recently.

"Before mailing this I shall try again to see the local doctor and see what he thinks of our friend's suggestion, but I don't want to delay further in writing to you. With your knowledge of Teresa's case, you might be able to suggest some possibility we have overlooked. Until I can find out something definite, I am keeping Teresa home from school (she goes to the local school now, about 2½ miles away, which has been re-opened after being closed last year). We have definite evidence of something wrong and I don't want to take any unnecessary chances. I shall be most grateful if you will let me know what you think."

Piers: I remember that schoolhouse faint. I think Teresa was sitting on the right side of the room, got up, walked a few steps to the left, and fell to the floor. It was certainly a surprise.

Teresa: I continued to faint from time to time as I grew up; years later my daughter did so as well.

Work continued. Alfred, still clinging to the original concept of a religious community, regretted that there was no meeting (for worship), no grace, no reading, and no discussion, because discussion was impossible without bad feeling, with even simple questions difficult.

Tractor advertising arrived, and Alfred was intrigued with the idea of using one to speed up the outdoor work without the daily chores required by a horse. [The hand-labor-only concept apparently was fading.] There seemed to be little remaining Hilltop philosophy.

December 1943

December 3: Alfred and Norma had a discussion in which they sought to find three concrete objectives they could agree on, and three obstacles that could be removed. The objectives were presented to the others in the evening:

1. To do work which has a wider social significance than their own living.
2. To earn their own living.
3. To achieve a group harmony or morale.

A somewhat testy letter from Family in England, probably written by Norma's father, dated December 5, said in part:

"As to your quotation from 'a religious paper,' I'm surprised you do not seem to have noticed something wrong about it. Apparently this paper draws attention to 'the incongruity of publishing in the same paper horror stories about the Japanese treatment of prisoners' and also 'American boys . . . being scientifically taught how to gouge out an opponent's eyes'. I am not advocating brutality anywhere, but can't you see that there is a difference in what is legitimate behavior towards a helpless prisoner and towards an opponent who will certainly take your life if you do not prevent him from doing so? In view of this difference between 'prisoner' and 'opponent' I cannot see the relevance of the newspaper's conclusion that 'It's an atrocity if the other side does it'.

"You say 'Are they the mad dogs that we have to exterminate?' If by that you mean the German nation, we have never undertaken to harm them in any way. It is Hitler and his murderous gang we are out to exterminate. Oddly enough—or perhaps misunderstandings can arise only too easily— you seem to have misunderstood my question 'What would the Pacifists do with Hitler?' I did not mean what would they do with him in the future, but how would they deal with him now? How would they stop him from exterminating the Poles and the Jews, and poisoning the minds of German children so that they may learn to glory in nothing but bloodshed and war? If the Pacifists know of any other means than this terrible sacrifice of our young men, will they not tell us what it is? Many Quakers seem to have faced up to what you call the 'appalling and inescapable dilemma' and are doing most wonderful and useful work to help their fellow men. There is tremendous admiration and appreciation in England of the work being done by the Friends Ambulance unit."

December 7: Alfred prepared a proposal that he thought met everyone's need, as far as it could be met. It consisted in continuing to live at any level that anyone wants; but at the same time fixing a minimum budget of necessity that could be lived on if they were driven to it, and earning enough cash to meet the cash outlay for this lower budget. Norma accepted this, substituting for the minimum budget a three-day works scheme by which to determine how much might be earned.

As for machinery, one approach required hand methods and borrowed equipment throughout; another required the most efficient methods, irrespective of capital cost. There was no personal cleavage on this point, only a consciousness of various approaches. The crux of it appeared to be that if they were going to expend on a level corresponding to machine production, they had to produce by machine; if they were going to expend on a level corresponding to hand production, they might produce by hand. The machinery could be either a horse and separately powered log-and-limb saw, or a tractor with log-and-limb saw. If Harold Field were mobilized [into the Army], his horses might become available.

December 12, they wrapped and addressed Christmas boxes, which Polly was to take and mail in Brattleboro after attending the coop meeting. Next day the pump froze and took some time to thaw. Work on different fronts continued. Winnie dyed Santa Claus' trousers after supper, while discussing the fact that she had not realized that Norm's and Alfred's interest in practicing voluntary poverty was intended to be the first step in the search for a method of attack on poverty in general. Since that was not going to be possible, they needed to search for a different group aim, even if they did not stay at this place or stay together, though many valuable aims were compatible with both.

Winnie felt that a sincere life purpose must coincide with the means whereby one earns a living; that is, take care of the purpose and the living will take care of itself. Norm suggested that for those who are not even earning a living, maybe the first step is to do so, and the later steps will then appear. Alfred thought the matter was complicated by the fact that in some ways it was wasteful to spend time [always his focus] getting a thing that you already have to start with, and the real problem might consist of the right use of your real endowment.

Norma started to windproof the cow barn, but Alfred, who customarily rejected temporary solutions even to immediate problems, felt a couple of structural jobs should have preceded any finishing work. In the evening Teresa was upset, perhaps ill. In the morning Norma took her, on the sled, to the Fields'. The overnight temperature was 18° below. There was discussion of Norma's proposals for next year, with some doubt whether earning capacity would be sufficient to equal the spending capacity without either slavery or mechanization.

Alfred and Norm went to the school Christmas play, then got off in one corner with Scott Nearing and discussed economics and history in all the intervals. Norma went with the Fields as far as Bennington, where they continued to Pennsylvania. (No indication of where they, or she, were going.) Polly and the children stayed with the Nearings, and Alfred walked home alone.

On Christmas Day the Williamses came back to Hilltop for the distribution of presents, then they all went back to the Nearings for dinner. Alfred, Norm, and Winnie explored the far reaches of the property in the vicinity of the stone bridge and made fair progress, but couldn't trace all the markers. The extent of the property seemed much greater than they had realized. The following day Alfred tracked the boundary from the Bondville road until he intersected their footprints in the snow from the prior day.

Norma wrote a letter dated December ? to Friends [Leslie and Valerie Johnston]:

"Here finally is the check, approved by the banking and treasury department after a brief period of panic. We are still solvent! And we have around a ton of food in storage for the winter, as well as a cellar full of wood. It's a very satisfying feeling altogether. It almost seems as though we may be going to be warm this winter—the temperature in this kitchen now is nearly 80! Such a thing has never happened at Hilltop before, not in winter anyway.

1943

"We had a big snowfall—about 2 feet a couple of weeks ago, which closed the road before we had half our winter supplies in, so Dickie and a light sled have been pressed into service, and on Sunday afternoon almost everything was brought up the last stretch. You just stow about 400 lbs. on the sled, make sure it's trimmed and tightly lashed down, then give Dickie the word and he takes it straight to the top. Alfred was impressed, I think, as previously he had regarded Dickie as a lamentable error on my part and looked at him only from a distance. Now he has started to talk about getting [a horse] twice his size to haul a log saw about the woods!

"He is also beginning to talk about a tractor ... Leslie, if you have any thoughts on tractors, now is the psychological moment to produce them. I don't object to the tractor per se, but I did think there were good reasons why Hilltop was to be a tractor-less paradise, and I don't feel those reasons are any less good than they were. However, if Alfred feels he must have a tractor I shan't shed any tears, it will certainly speed things up and remove many of the petty discomforts such as being snowed in all winter and having no ready cash except unearned income (since it will be employed in the production of wood for sale).

"We've been doing some group singing, which has given us a lot of satisfaction. With Norm singing the bass, which he does with excellent effect, and Winnie holding up the alto part and Polly cutting capers all around, it really goes very well. Alfred takes the tenor parts and I make an extra soprano, completely unnecessary but still fun. We do, however, have deplorably little time for any sort of group-building activities. Winnie leaves at 7:30 and doesn't get back much before 6, and after supper she has to prepare for next day's work, and at the weekends she has to catch up on her laundry and letter-writing.

"Supposing we do by some miracle get ourselves on a paying basis, and supposing we don't buy a tractor, and supposing both Alfred and I don't get ourselves let in for several thousand dollars' worth of psychoanalysis, and supposing our German refugee friend doesn't call on us to redeem our promise of help—it ought to be possible for us to help out on your co-operative house if you ever get it going. I feel that's a project that would meet with group approval. You know the Brudercoop in Philadelphia gets along on 27 dollars a month from each of 10 members. Their rent is only 30, their grocery bills run around 130 and they have a surplus."

Alfred added a postscript: "About the tractor, it's just that I have been casting around for some ground for agreement on a work program, and thought for a while I would approach it from a different direction, not 'What tools do we prefer to work with?' but 'What is the most efficient method of forest management?' It occurred to me that a tractor for dragging

& hauling and a tractor-powered tree, log, & circular saw might represent greatest efficiency; particularly since in the case of a horse, time would have to be taken out from the cutting to care for him and get hay for him; while during a large part of the cutting he would just be standing around in the cold fretting, and in any case wouldn't be available [able?] to pull a cord of wood. A caterpillar tractor would reach the most inaccessible spots in all seasons & pull a full cord anywhere with ease, while also providing power for sawing both logs and limbs. This is a long story, and doesn't represent an about-face in my philosophy, but more a determination to try, if not one thing, then another, until there is something we can all work unitedly on."

This thinking had already been done by other farmers for generations, but Alfred had refused to accept their conclusions, as they did not have the same long-range goal—the salvation of humanity—as he did, and therefore their methods were morally circumspect.

While Alfred was away checking on tractors, the pipe froze again, and "the girls" had to carry water from the spring in buckets.

Norma wrote to "My dear Lucia" on December 28:

"I can't think why the typewriter isn't frozen, everything else is, and it always has frozen up in the winter before. Since we only have one warmed room and have to keep from five to seven of ourselves in it, we have to keep almost everything else outside, and only give space to the things which simply mustn't freeze, like oranges. We didn't suffer nearly so much in the twenty-below weather last week as we did the same time last year. I am mildly curious to see how we'll survive forty below, if that happens again, which Heaven in its all-seeing wisdom forbid. If anyone had told me last year I'd be getting up and milking a cow at 6 a.m. in twenty-below weather, I certainly wouldn't have believed it.

"The Brudercoop scored a double bulls-eye, if there is such a thing: they sent both the nicest Christmas card, and the most appreciated present. Piers simply loved the kaleidoscope. We had quite a gay and foolish Christmas, largely thanks to Polly, who made fancy star-shaped cookies to hang on the tree and amusing presents for everyone. Polly is just what Hilltop has needed for three years, and be sure and tell Walter I said so. It's so wonderful for me to have intellectual companionship and someone to take off my hands the job I most hate [the cooking]. I'd far rather struggle with freezing metal objects and frozen fingers in the barn.

"We went over to have Christmas dinner with the Nearings—eight of us, four Jacobs, two Williamses, Winnie's young brother Justin, and Polly. They fed us an all-vegetarian meal, which didn't have the distressing after-effects of too much turkey and plum pudding, and presented each of us with the pair of chopsticks with which we'd eaten the meal. They eat everything

IMAGE 20: *Scott Nearing and Helen Knothe. Photo courtesy of The Scott and Helen Nearing Papers at the Walden Woods Project's Thoreau Institute Library.*

with chopsticks, from wooden bowls. I rashly boasted about my proficiency with chopsticks, but it turned out that these were Chinese ones, heavier and thicker than the Japanese kind, and I didn't do so well. Piers was the best; he evolved some wonderful method that seemed almost mechanically perfect.

"The Nearings—or more accurately, Scott and Helen, since they are not married—are the best possible kind of neighbors for the back woods. They not only know all about living on top of mountains in Vermont, can build a house as easily as cook a dinner or split wood, but they are a constant source of intellectual and artistic stimulation (Scott can talk entertainingly and instructively on any subject yet discovered, and Helen plays the recorder with real mastery) and they have a library that makes the mouth water. I am volunteering to do some work for the Pacifist Research Bureau on the strength of it."

Nancy Montague, in a magazine article she wrote for consumption back in England, had described this household as "an ex-professor and his secretary, a charming young woman of education who was quite unacademically unrepressed." They had visited the Nearings during the summer and Nancy found that "their establishment was a model of modern intelligent building in perfect taste and fitted up superbly." Scott offered the adults cocktails, "but oh, disillusionment! They were vegetable juice cocktails and had a kick of cabbage and leek which to my untutored carnivorous tongue was quite nauseating. He was a man of tact, however, and brought out tomato juice for those whose palate could not appreciate the fine flavor of raw compressed veg." Afterward they had an all-vegetable lunch "finished up with magnificent strawberries and cream."

Nancy went on to remark that, "I understand that since he gave up professing, the old gentleman [Scott was in his mid-50s at that time] had supported himself, apart from his writing, entirely from the sale of his fruit, vegetables and maple sugar. It seemed to me there was a lesson for Hilltop: you couldn't live well or improve your land, firstly, if you choose so out-of-the-way a farm, and secondly, if you only set forth to create a subsistence farm."

Norma continued, "I had a bowl full of narcissi, carefully nurtured, and so hoped for flowers on Christmas Day, [but] on the morning of the 24th I came down to find the kitchen temperature -20 (-22 outside) and the flowers hopelessly wilted. Never mind, they were beautiful while they lasted. "I think we have all had the flu, not the disease itself (we are too hardy

now for germs to thrive on us) but the after-effects. My back aches as though I'd been beaten up by a Fascist prison guard. Anyway, I can't have flu yet because I have made a solemn contract with myself to have an article on maple syrup in the mail for England by the end of this week. I made a similar bargain with myself this time last year and it netted me twenty-four dollars. My only earnings of any kind in several years, and am I proud.

"Talking of earning, Alfred is getting all set to buy a caterpillar tractor and go in for forestry in a big way, and not only maintain Hilltop off the proceeds but offer paying jobs to C.P.S. men on furlough, which seems to me definitely a good idea. I feel quite sure the government will not let him have a tractor, but once the idea has really caught on, he will find some other way around it.

"I am not so depressed as when I last wrote, backache or no backache. We've been through a very bad spell but at the moment I think we have grounds for some modest confidence in the future, and it's the first time I have felt that with any sort of conviction since Leslie and Valerie and Walter left us so long ago. The psychiatric situation continues pretty involved. It seems there is a man in Brattleboro who is just what my digestion [perhaps a euphemism for her mental state] needs, but he is so busy with the hospital patients that he can't spare even an hour a week. So that throws me back on another doctor in Bennington with whom I have already had some conversation. I like him pretty well, but the awful thing is, I can't go to Bennington without being away two whole days, from 7 a.m. one day till 6 p.m. the next, and that's a serious matter for a farmer's wife. For two hours of consultation, I'd have to spend huge sums in fares, not to speak of the night away from home, meals, etc.

"On the other hand, he could arrange it so I could work in the Bennington College library. It might definitely have some points. If only Bennington weren't such a one-horse town [pop. 12,257 in 1940], only one movie and I am sure it never shows anything I could bear to see. Twenty-five hours in that place at frequent intervals is pretty awful to contemplate. I could cut down the time somewhat by hitch-hiking and a long walk at this end, but hitch-hiking is very poor around here now and no fun at all in sub-zero weather [26 miles as the crow flies, 43 miles by car.].

"You may see something of Alfred around the 14th of next month, en route for a conference at P.H. where he has to open a discussion. He'll be staying with his sister, but I expect he will float around your way at least once."

Norma wrote to friends Reg and Rica Brown on December 28:

"I think I have the flu, so probably this letter won't get very far. At any rate there is an epidemic going on all around and I have a backache as though I had been trying to lift Mount Everest—it may just be the effect of the mountain of manure I have carried out from the barn during the last six weeks, since I became a dairymaid and personal attendant on one cow, one calf, one horse, a dozen or so goats, and three sheep. We decided to buy a cow, by name Gardenia, because we had a greatly enlarged family (we are seven now) and the goats just couldn't increase the milk supply fast enough. Alas, we must now sell the goats. I know it has to be, but it breaks my heart.

"I gladly took on the barn work, to set the men free to work in the forest, even though it does mean struggling out to milk before dawn at twenty below zero. We had some vile weather just before Christmas and it looks and feels as though we are in for more—out of the corner of my eye, out of the window, I can see the clothing on the line simply lashing in the north wind. I almost think I'll go out and milk before it gets any colder or my back aches any worse, even though Gardenia will be much upset at such irregularity.

"The summer was successful but very, very strenuous. It wasn't much of a success from the gardening point of view because we had such awful weather. It snowed even in May, then it poured with rain for weeks, and all over the country, and in Canada too, the season was from three to six weeks behind the normal. In these northern latitudes you just can't afford those three weeks. Still, we had enough fresh vegetables to deal with our army of visitors during the summer, but practically nothing for winter storage."

[She explained why they think the draft board reclassified Alfred as 4-F, because "they classify all C.O.'s as psychopathic, especially if they wear beards!" and went on to describe how she happened to purchase Dickie, the horse. "I think Alfred still thinks poor Dickie is a parasite, but he makes a big difference to me."]

"What you say about the general state of things in England fits in pretty well with the indirect impressions we had been forming from our reading and correspondence, except that lately I had been coming to feel that after all we should emerge from the war with the essential social structure still unchanged, so that though on the surface things might seem permanently jolted out of their traditional ways, actually in time 'normality' would gradually be restored. I am almost sure that will be the case in this country.

"I can't help being somewhat amused at Americans taking for granted that theirs will be the moral leadership of the post-war world, when actually they are likely to be the most old-fashioned of the surviving nations, having suffered the least. I'd like to think of Britain assuming this position, but I still wonder a lot about Russia. Isn't she perhaps going to come out of this stronger and with more potentialities than any of the others?

"I do hope I'll manage to write to Molly [her closest friend in and after college] fairly soon; it was good to have news of her. She is so silent, I worry sometimes, because she is still such an important part of my life, even though I never write to her either—but then I hardly write to anyone any more. I can't remember when I last wrote a letter that overflowed on to another page. You deserve extra because I haven't sent you any of the recent news. [She goes on to muse about the possible political future of Spain under Franco.]

"Please send lists of things you might find useful. We are going on a new, very tight, budget because we intend to pay our own way, which we've never been able to do before, but there still will be a little cash knocking about and I think a few creature comforts for friends in England ought to come out of that."

Norma wrote to Eleanor Garst on December 30:

"The only person I feel I can write to in my present depressed condition is you, and I hope you are complimented! We have just had a prolonged spell of subzero weather with frozen pump and all the other oddments and it finally told on us, physically and morally, and then my internal digestion went back on me again—just before Alfred left on a twice-postponed expedition to see a man about a tractor. I thought he'd better go just the same, but here are Polly and I struggling with a barn full of animals and the two children, and the pump has frozen again. We lug the absolute minimum into the kitchen in pails. But you see how it is that I'm not feeling very bright!

"It would be a great deal worse, though, if it weren't for Polly. I don't know where I'd be without her in the present crisis. Alfred will be back tomorrow night, I hope and pray—I didn't tell him what the trouble was, just tried as hard as possible to impress on him how much I wanted him to be back at the scheduled time, but he is liable to go following the bright eyes of some tractor to Springfield or worse. You may be surprised at this development, and I must say I am myself. The fact is we've been giving a whole lot of thought lately to the question of putting the establishment on a really self-supporting basis, providing needs such as books and travel besides mere food, and also providing a small cash-producing industry at which people can work for a guaranteed return.

"A C.P.S. man with a ten-day furlough might find it worthwhile to come and work in our forest if we could guarantee him a fixed return, say four or five dollars a day. I think it can be done with hand methods, Alfred thinks it can't be done without mechanization, and he is willing to sink some of the capital his father gave us in buying the necessary machinery once he's explored all the possibilities. [This is a complete reversal of Alfred's initial views.] Hence the exploration trip. I have a sort of fear he'll come riding home on a tractor—tempered by my conviction that the Government won't let him have one to play with!

"I am now trying to work on an article about maple syrup—I had promised myself to have it in the mail by the end of this week, but I see it won't be possible, there is too much noise and confusion, with the children and the frozen pump and Alfred being away and all, and I am not feeling very bright anyway on a diet of milk. [The present belief is that milk is, in fact, to be avoided as a palliative for ulcers, as it promotes stomach acidity. Fresh fruits and vegetables, not available at Hilltop in the winter, are recommended.] Maybe if I get it off in time, they may still be willing to publish it next March or April.

"School starts again on Monday, and then I hope some peace will return, and I also hope we are through with sub-zero weather for a time! You know how little one can think when one is cold. Even though the kitchen may be fairly warm, the rest of the house is an icebox and tidying up is a penance."

There follows Alfred's summary of the Hilltop experiment so far:

"The years 1941–43 mark the preliminary years of Hilltop's life, with the usual slow orientation and initial setbacks. They will have sufficed to provide some basis in experience for future decisions; and it does appear that 1944 may see the evolution of a more coherent group life and economic plan. There will be a turn away from extreme simplicity of living & simple methods of production, towards a reasonably free type of expenditure and consequent mechanized production methods. But the main thing will be to see if we can stay together and work as a group, finding the proper evolution for ourselves as we are, rather than the ideal evolution for an ideal group.

"The farm is to become a forest farm, with no effort to produce agricultural crops other than hay, and that in a minimum, as well as livestock at a minimum; so that manpower can be devoted fully to the forest, both for its improvement & our own income."

1944

This functional poverty business does lack something on the cultural side, simply because one has not the necessary energy to cope with intellectual and spiritual problems on top of what is required for the day-to-day struggle with an abandoned farm.

January 1944

On New Year's Day, the Nearings, Fields, Costellos, and Julius (?) came over.

Norma wrote to Father and Caroline:

"The children loved your presents, especially the colored pencils and the block [of paper]; those fell to Piers and he's been doing wonderful drawings ever since. He did a colored portrait of Teresa which was really quite a resemblance, and says he thinks maybe he'll be an artist when he grows up. Polly is encouraging him, as she knows quite a lot about art work in general. I had meant to have the children write their own thank-you letters this year, but it just seems like more than I can cope with along with everything else. I remember how my own mother used to toil over my letters of thanks—I am sure now that they cost her far more effort than they did me, although that seemed impossible at the time!

"We have finished the oranges and grapefruit. They arrived in very good condition in spite of the long journey and I don't think more than one was spoiled. It's just the kind of thing to have at Christmas time, too. We had guests to lunch yesterday and it gave us great satisfaction, as they are strong vegetarians, to be able to give them a big raw salad with fresh grapefruit in it. Fresh fruit for the winter (except perhaps apples) is one thing I don't think we can ever hope to produce here.

"Perhaps Alfred wrote you that he is arranging to buy a second-hand tractor from the man who operates the sawmill in the village. It seems a sensible arrangement, as this man doesn't use his tractor except when he needs more logs for the sawmill, and if we supply the logs from our own land we get the money, and the sawmill man doesn't need his tractor. Probably we can pay part of the purchase price in lumber. Alfred thinks he can organize things so that we have a real self-supporting industry in our forest, since lumber prices are now so high, and we may even be able to provide a source of earned income for some of our friends, for instance C.P.S. men on furlough who may feel the need of adding to their $2.50 a month.

"Incidentally I do so hope the A.F.S.C. is really going to take a strong line about this question of dependency allowances for men in C.P.S. It seems a dreadful blot on their good name if they let these people have to go on accepting charity, and suffering hardships, for the sake of their husbands' convictions, which the Friends themselves share. If the Society of Friends as a body isn't going to stand up for these people's human rights, who will? We know all too many cases where a man had finally to accept military service, entirely against his conscience, because his dependents couldn't be cared for. But from the Quaker periodicals that we read, we sometimes wonder if the more comfortably situated Friends are aware of this. They are very generous with money, but maybe that isn't quite all that is needed. (You understand we raise these questions that are on our minds because we feel you are, so to speak, a kind of pipe-line through which what the younger Friends are feeling very strongly may get to circulate among the older Friends too. Sometimes there is rather a frightening feeling that the different generations within the Society are out of touch with one another on essentials).

"Alfred is out hunting boundaries, to establish just what timber we do have available for cutting. He has discovered that our land stretches much farther than we had realized and there is still good lumber to be got out; apparently the lumber company which had the place before, lost its sawmill by fire before the place was worked out. Won't it be gratifying if Alfred turns out to be a businessman after all!"

Norma wrote to Clif and Dolores on January 5:

"You can have Dickie for sixty dollars whenever you say the word, but I'd like the sale to be definite, because I've not been well lately and have been forced to conclude that horse exercise (including bumping along on a sled) is out for the present. Therefore, since we are very short of hay and no one used Dickie much except me, I advertised him for sale. I don't want to turn down a prospective purchaser and then maybe have to advertise him again later on if your plans fall through—do you see what I mean? If it weren't for the hay problem it wouldn't matter so much, but since he won't be working here anymore we can't afford to pass up any opportunity that presents itself of selling him. We may have to board him out at Field's. Poor Dickie, he's a good horse, I really believe, and will work well for you if you employ strictly pacifist techniques, but he doesn't pretend to be anything he isn't, and a heavy farm work-horse is one of the things he isn't. I think myself he's just ideal as light transportation for people in our situation."

Norma wrote to Janet Hall at Pendle Hill:

"I was most touched by your sending the parcel, and contents so well chosen too—you should have heard Polly's shout of joy when I showed her the thyme. Polly is doing our cooking just now and she is particularly strong on herbs and suchlike. Teresa also took eagerly to the first aid book and has started bombarding me with awkward questions like 'Do you know the doctor's telephone number?' From the ruthlessly logical standpoint of the child mind, it matters nothing that a) we have no telephone, b) if we had, all that would be necessary would be to lift the receiver and say 'Give me Dr. Hefflon, please'. [Telephone calls, at least locally, were handled by a central operator at that time.] She rightly dismissed such thoughts as typical grown-up evasions. The book says so, and it must be true. An intellectual in the making, I'm afraid.

"I say 'leisure' but that, as always at Hilltop, is a relative term. At the moment I'm deep in the preparation of a circular letter. We haven't sent one out for more than two years, which is pretty disgraceful, but they have been years of flux and whenever I started to write such a letter (as I did several times) large parts of it became meaningless before the herculean task could be completed. This time we had to start by cooking the gelatin from the hectograph in a bain-marie [a water bath]; I haven't yet dared embark on the next stage, which is looking for the special hectograph typewriter ribbon. As Norm says, the office is so like a jungle that it's useless to start out looking for anything without a machete, and besides I remember that last time I had to send to Sears for a new [ribbon]. So if your copy is too long in the coming, don't be surprised; be surprised, rather, if it does come.

"At last, yesterday, it snowed, after holding off for nearly eight weeks. I never thought I would be glad to see snow, but I was so tired of the remains of what fell on November 20th. We had a few flurries but not enough to keep the surroundings clean even. Yesterday it snowed all day and the children and Winnie didn't come home from school—we had made a provisional arrangement for them to sleep at a neighbor's house not far from the school if the weather seemed too bad to come home.

"One can't help having mental pictures at such times of them wandering in the forest, lost in the blizzard, just a stone's throw from home (one always is) and ourselves sitting toasting our feet by the fire all unaware. Seriously, I wish Winnie had more respect for the New England winter as an adversary. She still had the idea I used to have, that weather is something that can be conquered by a sufficiently resolute soul."

Norma wrote to Family on January 11:

"The kitchen is pandemonium, both children are tired and cross, having been home all day (Piers with pink-eye, which is a mild epidemic in the school just now, and Teresa with a backache which seems suspicious, though she is otherwise perfectly well, as there is so much influenza around). Polly is getting the supper, Winnie is bathing her eyes because she thinks she is getting pink-eye too, and altogether concentration is almost impossible.

"The crowning inconvenience this week has been my fruitless attempt to cash the money order sent by 'The Countryman' (my article did appear; I've forgotten which issue). They made it payable at the Post Office at Townshend. Now it's true Townshend is the next village, but from the transportation point of view it is almost impossible to access anything in less than a full day. I wasted the whole of yesterday afternoon in an abortive attempt to get there by hitch-hiking [which would have required walking down to the main road, waiting in the freezing cold in hopes of being picked up by a passing motorist, who were few and far between because of the wartime ban on pleasure driving, then walking back up the mountain in discouragement, not something that a person in fragile health should attempt]. Now I have put it off till Saturday, when there is a combination of buses which may enable me to make the trip.

"If I seem incoherent it's because Winnie has now seized the axe and is splitting firewood a few feet away. Only the grimmest determination is enabling me to persevere with this!

"The parcel of books also arrived last week and you should have heard the cries of joy with which the children fell on *Mumfie* [a little elephant], so long awaited. Teresa has read both books through already. The one about Stella Benson looks very interesting—I remember how much impressed I was by the novels of hers that I read.

"Alfred is leaving for Pendle Hill tomorrow, where he has been invited to speak about Spain on 'Spiritual Reconstruction in Europe.' This is a great honor, as the other speakers are quite distinguished people. Thanks to the peculiarities of the local bus service, he would in any case have to leave at 7 a.m. in order to catch the only bus of the day, but he also has to drag three miles down the hill a crate containing a goat which we are sending to be a pet for a little girl in Massachusetts. The truck that takes goats and suchlike goes only three times a week and it passes the end of our road about 7.45, so one must start hours before dawn to allow plenty of time for all the difficulties which may arise on the way down. I hoped he would take Dickie, but then someone would have to go down with him and drive Dickie back, and it's no fun on a pitch-dark morning with the temperature at zero or below. We shall all be up about 4 a.m. to make sure he gets off in good time with all his respectable clothes, books, papers etc.

"Piers had a stamp album for his Christmas present from us. I have been collecting stamps for him for years and have an envelope full of choice specimens garnered from our correspondence in Spain. Alas, I omitted to order any stamp hinges with the album, and I find the poor child has innocently been pasting them down to the pages. Not much harm is done as yet, provided I can restrain him till the hinges come. Now Teresa says she wants to start a collection; I know she won't take it seriously, but it does no harm for her to make a beginning on her own. Piers is really interested. I had some difficulty today explaining why a stamp labeled 'Poste Italiane' should go under 'Italy' instead of under 'Italian East Africa' which it obviously so much more resembled. I see now that stamp collecting can be an instrument to grammar as well as to geography." (*Piers:* I remember with fondness both Mumfie the Elephant and stamp collecting. *Teresa:* A modern equivalent might be Babar the Elephant.)

Norma wrote to a Mr. Fretz, from a Philadelphia address:

"It has taken me a very long time to write the letter I promised about the possibility of rural re-settlement in Vermont. I have a job which takes me a great deal of time and energy and am only just now enjoying a short respite which enables me to catch up with other things.

"Briefly, the situation is like this. In the town of Jamaica ('Town' in the New England sense, meaning a hundred or more square miles of largely empty forest land) there are three pacifist units, each owning its own land. Scott Nearing is the one who has been there longest; he has a large sugar bush and gets his living by producing and selling huge quantities of very high quality maple syrup. He also has a garden which provides for almost all his needs, as he is a strict vegetarian.

"I believe he would welcome co-operation from like-minded people and could help them build a suitable small house on or near his property; he is a good builder among other things and built his own house, which is very handsome and all made of stone and wood from his own trees. But I don't think he would have much patience with bunglers or people who didn't really know what they wanted.

"Then there is the Field family, who own land almost next door to his; they are Pennsylvania people who moved up here in the summer of 1942. They have a good deal of equipment for diversified farming—team, wagon, hay rake, mower and so on—which they are hardly able to make full time use of because of labor shortage. Harold Field is a clever mechanic and has a well-fitted shop in which he has no time to work. Their idea is to get several other congenial families to join them, build more houses (at present they have just the one small farm house in rather poor condition) and set up a kind of craft community, perhaps doing ironwork, since Harold has a forge. He wants to use water power, which he has on the property. People interested in all kinds of crafts would fit in there, or even people interested in straight agriculture who could set Harold free for the kind of work in which he is really interested. They are very congenial people.

"Finally, there is our own project. This was established in 1941 by a group from Pendle Hill who wanted to build a fully co-operative community. But it has run into many difficulties, including the loss from various causes of all the members of the original group except Alfred and myself. It has proved very difficult to re-build the original groups and I hardly think we could say we've achieved it yet. We are still a long way from what we originally planned, and may indeed never get back to that idea at all. Also, experience has led us to feel that the collection of semi-independent homesteads (one house, one family) offers a more stable foundation than a group in which everyone has everything in common. We are hampered of course by the difficulty of getting time and materials to build, although materials lie all around and hardly any of them need be bought, as Scott Nearing's example has shown us. At present we have two families on the project. We are anxious to have several more, but our standard of living is exceedingly low, and so far it has not been possible to find any other family willing to share it with us."

At the end of January Norma wrote to Family:

"I put Polly on the early morning bus this morning and have just (3.10 p.m.) come pretty nearly to the end of the task of cleaning up the kitchen. Polly is a good cook and a wonderful companion, but she is far and away the untidiest person I have ever met; in comparison with her I am a model of order, if that tells you anything. All last week she was frenziedly preparing huge stocks of storable food. We have plain bread, fruit bread, big cakes, little cakes, dried onions, dried carrots, a home-made dried soup powder, flavorings for puddings and I don't know what all. Uninterrupted pandemonium reigned in the kitchen throughout the entire week as almost everything we have is too small for even the day-to-day needs of seven people, let alone their needs for a month.

"While Polly cooked, Winnie and I in our spare moments worked on her wardrobe. Winnie made her a beautiful black woolen skirt, I surprised myself by making her a really coquettish red crochet hat and a pair of crochet gloves. She is to be away for four weeks looking after Scott Nearing's son's household while his wife has a baby. We shall eat less well in her absence, but it remains to be seen whether the extra time I spend cooking will more than offset the time I shan't have to spend trying to keep the kitchen livable.

"The week before, I was more or less out of commission, suffering from what I decided was a combination of pink-eye and laryngitis. I think I told you Piers had pink-eye. He didn't have it very badly, in fact no one did except me, and I suffered real misery from the persistent and combined discomforts of eyes and throat. I anxiously took my temperature at intervals to see if I was ill enough to go to bed and leave my work to be done by others, but it obstinately refused to rise above 97. However, I went about in a kind of stupor and did no work beyond what was immediately necessary. So you see this is really my first lucid interval in some considerable time.

1944

"In addition to all the other excitements last week I made three trips to the outer world, two of them to try and get a goat off; the truck driver put every sort of obstacle in the way and this particular goat is a delicate little thing and I am afraid she will come to real harm if she can't get to her new home and settle down soon. I have written to the owner of the express truck, more in sorrow than in anger.[73] I really believe he is helpless; he can't fire his drivers because he might never get any more, and meanwhile they do just what they please amid the mounting irritation of the people in the valley. C'est la guerre. [Rough translation: That's how it is, in wartime.] No, four trips – I hitched-hiked through a snowstorm on Sunday to hear Albert Spalding play the violin, my first concert since we came here, and attend a co-op meeting. Fancy forgetting that! I thought A. S. a virtuoso and very little more. [Norma played the violin in addition to piano and recorder. She once remarked of violin virtuoso David Oistrakh, "Doesn't the man know that what he's doing is impossible?"]

"Finally last week, your long-awaited letter with news of Rowena's wedding. I read the account of the ceremony with great interest and with even more interest the story of Reza's career. He certainly sounds like a notable addition to the family, and I hope he won't have dashed off to his chosen field of enterprise before I have an opportunity to meet him.

"We had a real storm in a teacup over the school last week; at one moment it threatened to become considerably more. Winnie had been having increasing trouble with some of the children who would use bad language and tell unpleasant stories, and she decided the unhealthy atmosphere was largely due to their ignorance and morbid curiosity on the subject of sex. So, acting on an impulse, she gave them a lesson on the subject, and I guess went into it with the utmost thoroughness, diagrams on the board and all. She felt the atmosphere was much better in the school [after that] and the children seemed really interested and glad of the information.

"However, fireworks soon began. Some of the children, it appeared, had actually been very shocked, and they went home and complained to their parents, who in their turn complained to Mr. Bullis, the Superintendent. He, fortunately, is a good friend of Winnie's, and he came out at once to see what was going on and was very nice about it. He encouraged her to talk to the parents herself, which she did, and after some interviews in which poor Winnie really suffered horribly, the matter was more or less patched up, and in fact local relations were somewhat improved.

---

73. From Shakespeare; Horatio is describing Hamlet's ghostly father's "countenance" when the phantom appeared to the guards at the castle gate.

"But of course the children and parents are both left in a bad position; the children will want more information and their parents won't give it to them any more than they would before, and Winnie no longer feels free to do it, so their last state may be worse than their first. All in all, it's a difficult community to teach anything controversial in, especially on the subject of sex. In the past twenty years or so there's been considerable swapping of partners and several of the children (no one knows for sure how many!) are illegitimate.

"Then the other half of the valley population is composed of Seventh-Day Adventists, whose morals are almost intolerably severe. One good lady rose and walked out of the Christmas celebration at the schoolhouse because the children were playing a game with a certain amount of action to it. She said it was dancing and Winnie had promised her there wouldn't be any dancing . . . Natalie Field and I of course backed Winnie, though we felt she'd been a little rash considering the kind of families she had to deal with, and the fact that the children were all ages from five to thirteen or fourteen. One other mother backed her at first, but got a little doubtful when she saw what a storm was raised. If it hadn't been for the good sense of the superintendent the trouble would have been much worse, and there still may be repercussions in the larger community of Jamaica. [*Teresa*: I remember that sex education lecture, with the charts and so on! I've always believed it was precipitated by Winnie's having come upon me about to be taken advantage of by an older boy down in the woods, something Norma may never have known about.]

"I broke my glasses some weeks ago, and on Friday this week I have to go to Bennington and expect to have my eyes tested for new lenses, that being apparently the nearest place where there is a reputable oculist. I broke the frames across the bridge and in the Christmas rush one half completely and mysteriously disappeared, and not a sliver was ever found. This makes it inevitable to have new lenses, but I feel it was probably about time anyway. Not being able to see so well as usual just added to my general misery at the time of the pink-eye. It's very hard to have even slightly defective vision when one lives in a house lit only by oil lamps. However, we have lost the coupons for our new oil ration and shall be in total darkness by the end of this week."

February 1944

Norma wrote to Judy and Fran Bacon on February 4:
"We're very sorry, though not specially surprised, to hear that Fran is headed for Big Flats [a CPS camp] in the near future. It's all the fault of living in Pennsylvania, where conscientious objection is a familiar part of the

1944

landscape; here in Vermont he might have profited by the prevailing belief that all C.O.s are a little touched in the head! By the way our neighbor, Harold Field, decided a few weeks ago that he couldn't accept 1-A and put in an appeal, and his draft board, in Downingtown (Pennsylvania) gave him 4-E without a murmur. Now it remains to be seen whether he will pass his physical here in Rutland, and if so, then what.

"Our first thought was 'How nice if Judy could come back and be with us again!' I don't know if you've considered that at all, but we hope you know you have friends here who will be happy to share their roof (even though it leaks) and such potatoes as they manage to extract from the unwilling soil. Our crop last year, by the way, was about one bushel more than what we planted. Anyway, we think you and Fran will be interested in the new plan on which we're now working, since it owes so much to experiences you shared with us. We decided that we just couldn't bear any longer living on unearned income, and must become self-supporting at the earliest opportunity, now that we were assured of two men at least for a few months (it's always been obvious this place could never be a one-man farm). Also, it was clear that our cash crop must be forestry.

"At present we are budgeting for forty dollars a week, of which about one-third is Winnie's salary and two thirds is the proceeds of the two men working in the woods three days a week. The other three [days] at present they have to devote to the essential jobs around the house which can't be done by the women—some of them will get done once for all, but then there will be others, so we doubt if the men will be able to put in more than half a week's work for cash in the coming year at any rate. However, we must be independent of Winnie's salary by the time school ends in June, and we are planning to ear-mark most of the unearned income for buying equipment which will increase output in the woods (this was a compromise we couldn't see any way to avoid).

"Also of course we hope to get our cash expenses down quite a bit, especially in the sphere of food. After such a bad year as last, we couldn't hope to have enough food in storage for seven people. But we shan't produce anything much edible before July. We also agreed to pool everything we had and divide the proceeds. The way this works at present is that everyone gets five dollars a week (four for each of the children) and out of that, pay back 1.50 for food and .50 for takes [?] and other expenses which come under the general heading of rent. The rest has to stretch for clothing, recreation and about everything else that the individual needs to spend money on. There's a balance of seven dollars a week that goes into a general fund for the things that haven't been budgeted for otherwise, like postage (except on purely personal letters) and books for the library. We've only been on this scheme a little over a month and we don't know just how it will work, but so far it hasn't been bad at all.

"The chief difficulty is that the two men who definitely contracted to buy the wood that was cut haven't been up to fetch it, and so we haven't much real money and have to issue scrip to ourselves to keep the accounts straight. There must be well over a hundred dollars' worth of wood stacked up by the roadside for which we hope to collect pretty soon. Meanwhile we are managing on the money we got from selling stock. Dickie has gone, and Gladiola the calf, and several goats—all are to go in the end.

"Since the men are kept pretty busy, the barn work and the gardening come on the women's shoulders. I do those while Polly looks after the house, which is an arrangement I greatly prefer. Still, we all work a sixty-hour week, and Winnie in addition puts in an extra twelve hours a week walking to and from school with the children. I don't know just how long we can keep this up, as we are all pretty tired and certainly we could use another woman, especially when the gardening season comes along.

"I hated to see the goats go, but we had to have more milk quickly, so we had to buy the cow, and now we need to cut down on labor in every possible way and the men won't have much time to spare for farming, so it looks as though it's cow milk for us from now on. I enjoy having cream on my cereal, but looking after a cow is just a chore, while looking after goats is enjoyable in itself. The men clean the barn out for me and do various other heavy jobs."

Piers: Polly was fun. When she was away she would send me cards addressed to "Dear [Capital P followed by three little drawn ears]" put together. P-ears, or Piers, with other word symbols in the text. She may also have shown the "dear" as a little deer figure; I don't remember. She was heavyset, and diabetic, but generally cheerful and humorous. She suffered fits of sneezing in the mornings. *Teresa*: I remember knitting Polly a "nose warmer," a little square secured by strings around her head.

Letter from Dr. Joseph Stokes dated February 9, 1944:
"In going carefully over your account of Teresa's spells, I am a little disturbed to think that they might be petit mal. The other possibility is that they are mild attacks of hypoglycemia. Both of these possibilities should be investigated carefully by your local physician. If they continue, I believe it would be quite important to have her studied here at the Children's Hospital or at some other hospital where facilities are adequate. Indigestion might account for both of the affairs, particularly if she has been under any great strain due to the household difficulties. I hope those latter have not been at all serious."

1944

Norma wrote to Polly:

"Your letter just came tonight, and if it's this coming weekend you are going to spend in N.Y. I'm terribly afraid your jumper [sweater] will not be there to share it with you. I'm very penitent, but the truth is with Norm's parents and subzero weather and whatnot, the workbasket just got pushed out of sight and out of mind. I am working on your gloves and hope I may get them finished tomorrow, though I fear not in time to join the other parcel which I'll try and get made up tonight. I leave first thing in the morning for another little jaunt to Bennington [where she was seeing the doctor] and am all excited about getting out into the wide, wide world—even though to my disappointment the new dress hasn't arrived.

"Alfred is running around looking for his dictionary, and Norm says, 'Ask Polly.' Have you any suggestions as to where it may be? I don't even remember what it looks like, that's how innocent I am. From your boyfriend's letter I don't really think you are in as deep as I thought you were, though I still think you need to watch your step, as one who, out of sheer kindness and inertia and not wanting to lose an entertaining correspondent, very nearly married the wrong man and caused a lot of unhappiness in the process. It's fatally easy to get into this kind of thing and impossible to get out without causing horrible pain—and I don't mean 'worse than death' [seduction or rape], either.

"Nothing else much has happened, it's been too cold. Winnie is having more trouble arising out of her sex talk. Teresa finally saw the doctor because she complained so much about her back, but he couldn't find anything wrong. [Not even a "digestive upset"!] Now, I am arranging for her to spend 2 nights a week at Kuusela's, at any rate while the snow is deep. Mrs. Smith says I'll regret it. . . .

"Valentine party Monday. The cookies didn't come yet, but the cake came, and went, all in a flash, even though I told the men about the egg-whites. You got a hymn of praise for that but loud jeers for the dried soup (in the glass jar) which turned out so salty that even Alfred couldn't eat it. Norm did, and Winnie said he woke up several times in the night with his mouth all swollen up calling out for water. . . . I don't know what went wrong. The salt box was empty, which seems suspicious, except that I distinctly remembered emptying it into the cereal the night before. My belief is I never even touched the soup. We'll conduct a controlled experiment on the remainder of the mixture when we get our courage back.

"If you think your return is going to be delayed, be sure & let me know in good time because I'll probably want to fit in another doctor appointment in early March."

Norma wrote to Roger Robison:

"Your letter and Bob Mueller's made a great impression; you mustn't judge the depth of the impression by the time it takes to get an answer, because everybody is working a ten-hour day and our hours are staggered in such a way that we never really get together except at supper time and on Sunday mornings.

"Polly Robinson, to put first things first, is a girl who has been dietitian for several C.P.S. camps in New England (we met her first at Royalston) and now out of the goodness of her heart is doing some reconstruction in our kitchen department. It's a thankless job and I dread the inevitable day when she will decide we are no longer worth bothering over, because not only shall I be thrown back upon a job I loathe and do excruciatingly, but I shall lose a companion who's been nearer to me in many essential respects than anyone who's stayed any time here yet.

"Status with the natives? Well, yes and no. From one point of view it's improving, from another the increased contacts via the school have inevitably brought our peculiarities into sharper focus. Winnie will write you no doubt about her special problems: I gather a major one is achieving pacifist discipline among children who expect and actually demand to be beaten. She gets despondent, but I think that's largely the time of year. Each time I go down to the schoolhouse I am struck by the happy atmosphere there, and people in the village are still saying what a good teacher they've got out at Pikes Falls. I think there's no doubt at all that Winnie does have the toughest assignment (which is something she won't tell you—nor will she tell you what courage and resourcefulness she is developing to meet it).

"As for the religious community idea, people disappoint and irritate one and finally something really disillusioning happens and there is a bad collapse. I have been so much exasperated by people lately, so much disappointed by them (beginning, always beginning with myself!) that insensibly it has been chipping away such genuine belief in God as I had managed to achieve—till I got a pretty bad shock [perhaps referring to marital problems?] and discovered that I had left myself practically nothing to go on with if fellow humans failed me. The psychiatrist has been patiently trying to build up in me a belief in people, their essential goodness, to counterbalance the general fear of life I somehow acquired before I'd had much of a chance to know it. From his point of view, lose your belief in people and what have you got left? Well, I found I did have something left—essentially, the knowledge of the nature and depth of real goodness in the world which I somehow got from Pendle Hill. There is a balance that sometimes has to be achieved between trying too hard, and not trying at all. So many religious writers have struggled with this from one point of view or another. I feel a lot of spiritual dryness comes from too much consciously directed effort—since after all 'the spirit bloweth where it listeth.'[74]

"Have you read Silone's 'The Seed Beneath the Snow'?[75] I rather hope not, it's a major experience and I would treasure the privilege of being the one to bring it to your notice!"

Norma wrote to Dear Friends:

"We love to be visited, but I don't feel we ought to encourage anyone from as far away as New York to try and come up here at this time of year! It can just be done at a weekend if you can get away on Friday night and don't mind spending two nights out of three in the train. You would get up here by noon on Saturday (the last three miles is a steep hill which has to be climbed on foot, part of the way through deep snow). Then you'd have to leave immediately after lunch on Sunday to get back to New York by Monday morning. Anyway, this is the worst time of year here, cold and miserable (the house has no furnace), with nothing stirring on the farm except a couple of baby goats. They are a joy, to be sure, but I wouldn't claim they were worth coming all that way for! In any case you would be shocked at our interpretation of Mildred Young's 'Functional Poverty,' which is seen at its very worst during a New England winter.

"I do wish there were some chance you might be able to come a little later, say in May, which I think is the most beautiful time of the whole year. I can't imagine what there might be that you could learn from us; we are very amateur farmers and pretty poor communiteers. The profit would be all on our side, since we get so few visitors except during the summer (when we get them by dozens) but I honestly don't believe so long, tiring and expensive a trip would be worthwhile from your point of view. If you were only going to be in the East a little longer, we'd urge you to try and come up to Putney the last weekend in April, when we are having a small local conference and a few very worthwhile people will be around, and then you could come on and see us after that. But I suppose it's no good.

"I feel this functional poverty business does lack something on the cultural side, simply because one has not the necessary energy to cope with intellectual and spiritual problems on top of what is required for the day-to-day struggle with an abandoned farm. There are interesting possibilities, but so often one hasn't time to stop and take that up. It's all rather complicated, trying to lead two kinds of life at once. At present the men are working at

---

74. John 3:8, "The wind bloweth where it listeth, and thou hearest the sound thereof, but canst not tell whence it cometh, and whither it goeth."
75. Ignazio Silone, *The Seed Beneath the Snow* (1942), portrays socialist heroes who try to help the peasants by sharing their sufferings in a Christian spirit.

forest improvement, which seems to offer a chance to combine a public service with earning the necessary minimum of cash. This summer we plan to start a crop-rotation, soil-building scheme. That will exhaust our energies for the coming year, I should think.

"We have thought several times of the possibility of having a Japanese American family here. The big difficulty, I feel, is that since we are already foreigners and considered rather strange, we should not be good sponsors for them, and they would start out inevitably in an atmosphere of suspicion, which is probably what they most need to avoid. I suppose most pacifist farmers are in a similar position, though most don't have the added handicap of being foreigners to contend with. Still, if you discover any possibilities in your new work, we'll be interested to hear of them. Please write sometimes, and come and see us in the spring or summer if you possibly can."

That day Norma also wrote to Polly:

"We made a solemn resolve that before sugaring started, we'd finish four outstanding jobs. The women would finish the shingling on the south side and the inside plastering, and the men would put insulation around the cellar stairway (underneath) to keep cold breezes from freezing up all our potatoes for a fourth year, and would cut three cords of wood as a beginning towards the ten cords we ought to have in stock for next winter. I've just come in from hammering on several acres of shingles. It's about done now except for a strip about four shingles deep across the top of the library windows, but the higher it gets the harder it is to manage, with the step ladder continually sinking in the snow and jerking one to and fro.

"I put on lots of plaster in the kitchen too, behind the stove, but to my mortification it has been falling off into the food ever since. I don't know if I used the wrong kind of lime, or spread it too thin, or whether it dried out too fast, or what, anyway I'll have to start again. But I have done a really nice job upstairs, using a different batch of lime, and I hope I get my assignment finished after all if the warm weather only holds up. I would make a great effort to get the kitchen kalsomined [whitewashed] before you return, but I don't know what your preferences are in the matter of color. We have white, dirty yellow, and deep rose, and in the library I used equal parts of all three, but the combinations are multiple.

"You must hurry home, Polly, if only to meet [goat kids] Fancy and Mercy before they lose that first fine, careless rapture.[76] They are Lucy's babies, born quite unexpectedly last Sunday evening. You may remember I was very worried about Lucy, but she fooled me and produced them when I

---

76. Robert Browning, "Home Thoughts from Abroad": "That's the wise thrush; he sings each song twice over / Lest you should think he never could recapture / The first fine careless rapture!"

was suspecting nothing. I never expected two girls and while I am delighted from one point of view, for the moment it's a strain on the fresh milk supply which is Lucy's contribution of a little under two quarts a day.

"The hay situation became so horrifying that we had to pack Gardenia off to Kuusela's in a hurry. Mrs. K needs the milk as her cow is going dry, and she will send us up a quart or two each day after school if production keeps up. It's all rather discouraging, but we have lots of home-canned milk and shall probably hold out all right till the next goat freshens and I can get Fancy and Mercy on to skim milk, which Dolores is sending me from Putney. Don't you think 'Green Mountain Fancy' is a lovely name? Fancy has most of the beauty, Mercy most of the brains.

"Wonderful cakes arrived yesterday—we're saving the best till Norm's & Winnie's best man comes to visit Sunday."

Norma wrote to Dr. Hefflon:

"Thank you for your letter about Teresa. I will do my best to follow your suggestions, but this will mean keeping her home from school. They have to leave the house at 7:30 a.m. which means of course no time to rest after breakfast; and they don't get back till 6 p.m. or later. This gives me no time at all for making sure about bowel movements and things like that. Also, since she necessarily has a light lunch at school, I have to give her the chief meal of the day just before going to bed. I have felt for some time that this was not at all a good way to arrange things, but it seems the only way we can arrange for her to go to school. She is well up with her work and for the present she will have to study at home.

"I hope you are right in thinking it's just digestive trouble, but I'd like to be able to settle the question of petit mal once and for all. I understand it can be diagnosed definitely by the use of an electroencephalograph and that there is one at Brandon. Do you think we could arrange for a test to be made?" (*Teresa*: I think I remember this test, but I never knew I was suspected of having epilepsy!)

On Leap Day, February 29, Norma wrote to "Lucia and Walter, to each of whom I owe letters":

"Well, time marches on and one moment I feel everything is really turning out wonderfully and infinitely better than we had any right to expect, and the future unrolls like a brightly-colored carpet full of beautiful designs, and the next minute I am about ready for them to bring on the straitjacket. [This fluctuation would be typical for someone with bipolar disorder.]

"The only thing is, [our] new world is getting fashioned closer to Alfred's and Norm's heart's desire, and it proves to be a world in which I feel lonely and lost. What with extra work and the feeling of being one against the world, I am feeling a little low right now. It just shows how careful one should be not to have one's prayers answered. I know I am ungrateful and foolish, but my ideal world was so different from this! I'll feel fine again soon; when Polly comes back and I have someone's eye to catch again and haven't to struggle with the nightmare of preparing meals for people who like to suffer. She is planning to do a few days' typing for the Catholic Worker and be back the end of the week.

"I have been very uneasy about Teresa, who has been having fainting spells, rather alarming. In between she seems absolutely all right and the local doctor thinks it is just nervous, perhaps connected with the fact that she doesn't get on at all well with the other children at school. I think the fact that the walk to school and back is so long, and she never gets any time to sit down quietly and relax after her meals, has a good deal to do with it. She too has the ulcer temperament, poor little thing, and I expect this is just the first step in that direction. There are, of course, more alarming possibilities; I am trying to persuade the local man to make the necessary tests [for petit mal] and get them eliminated. He insists she is in perfect physical condition. I hope he is right. My own digestion died on me just before the New Year and I'm still living on slops because I haven't the enterprise to think up anything else. That too will be remedied when Polly comes back.

"We too have twins—Fancy and Mercy—born a week ago last Sunday. That evening, after a brief absence I went out to the barn and heard two faint squeals and there were Fancy and Mercy running around. They are the first kids of the season and as always, a source of intense joy to me. When things seem at their blackest, the goats never fail to revive my morale. They always think I'm wonderful, no matter what I do. Gardenia the Cow has left us temporarily for greener pastures. We hopelessly under-estimated the amount of hay she would consume in a winter, and it being too snowy to get more in, we boarded her out with a neighbor who had extra hay and whose cow was going dry. It's an excellent arrangement; the only snag is that Lucy was intended to be the milk supply. We expected one kid, which might very likely be a buck and not be kept, and Lucy's two quarts a day would supply the family table. But I'd rather have Fancy and Mercy any day."

Alfred wrote to Clif [Bennett, who painted the mural on the kitchen wall] a completely dateless letter, so it might even date from before Clif came to Hilltop, but the context seems to be later. It chiefly consists of philosophical musing about magic, what it is, who might benefit, how it relates to religion. In closing he opined that: "Much nonsense has been written about magic, as about alchemy; and the same was true about evolution in its day & psychology in our day. I no longer doubt that there is movement in that sphere.

"We look forward to seeing you whenever you can come. The snow is not deep yet, but drifted in places; we don't go much above our knees in the woods. H. Leader is expected sometime this month too."

March 1944

On March 1 Norma wrote to her sister Rowena:

"It seems only about a week ago I got the news about your wedding, and now I hear about the expected happy event. It all moves too fast for me. I would have written a lot sooner, though, if I hadn't been delayed by one thing after another. First I was ill, then I was much too busy, what with looking after a cow and a dozen goats and acting midwife to the goats, as well as substituting in the kitchen while the girl who usually does the cooking took a month off; and then I thought I'd wait till I was less completely penniless and could send off your wedding present. It's on its way now, I hope—three or four small woodcuts of Vermont scenes by rather good local artists. Framing, I decided, was out of the question because of the risk of breakage, though I don't know how easy it may be for you to get things framed at present. [Paragraph about the discomfort of morning sickness, baby clothing one should have, and wardrobe matters.]

"My letter-writing time is more than up; the men are out in the woods dragging logs to the roadside with borrowed horses, and as the temperature is nearly zero and the wind is howling down from the snowy wastes of Canada, I promised to bring them some hot soup at midday. Just as a matter of curiosity, does the institution you are attached to have an outdoor thermometer? People so often ask me 'How cold does it get in England?' and I find I haven't the slightest idea. I feel quite certain, though, that even in Edinburgh it never gets to 42 below zero."

Norma wrote to Family ten days later:

"My latest responsibility is two kids, first of the new season's crop, one of which has been out of sorts for about a week so that I am keeping it in the kitchen and trying to restore it with frequent feedings, vitamin capsules, and general attention. The big difficulty is that we have no box with high enough sides to keep a kid in, and I can't keep her in a warm, dry place away from drafts, so half my time I spend nursing her on my lap. I really have no idea what is wrong with her but expect she will either recover or die within the next few days.

"The weather continues horrible, sub-zero temperatures and deep snow, though it is time for the sugaring season to start. On the whole, though, we've had a very mild winter and we mustn't complain. There haven't been more than a couple of days when I felt it necessary to keep the children at home simply on account of the weather. They have had about two colds each, which is somewhat below average, and escaped the influenza entirely. Probably during the next week the weather will suddenly get very warm and the snow will begin visibly to disappear, but somehow it's when you know winter is at its very last gasp that it suddenly becomes almost impossible to bear. It will be six weeks before we have any leaves on the trees, and in between there's a long wretched period of brown trees and fields and mud which is almost as trying as winter itself.

"This year's Town Meeting was last Tuesday. I didn't manage to go, but the two men went and reported that the proceedings were somewhat tame. Winnie sent her three oldest children from the school with special instructions to watch and see how the democratic process was working, whether people were really interested in keeping it alive and so on. She was considerably annoyed when the children came back and reported that her own husband had read the newspaper all through the proceedings, especially as she had taken pains to warn him he'd be under observation!

"Winnie, I'm glad to say, is not producing a baby just yet. I fervently hope we'll be able to get things into better shape here before she does. She is still having various kinds of trouble with the parents, though one of the more difficult families moved out—the husband demanded more money and got fired instead. What will happen next year we don't yet know, there will not be nearly so many children and I think quite possibly Winnie will prefer to stay here and teach our children and perhaps a couple of others without benefit of the School Board. She complains of being so much handicapped by her lack of experience and special vocational training, but from what I've observed [our] children are making excellent progress, which is probably not due entirely to Winnie but also to the really excellent textbooks, infinitely better than any that ever came my way. One of them wrote you a letter which I must be sure and remember to enclose.

"The spring cleaning is about to start (even in the absence of any signs of spring) and I am making all sort of wonderful plans for re-decoration. We couldn't decide what color to make the kitchen walls and at last had the brilliant idea of painting them white and embellishing them with designs in bright colors. Then I plan to remove a whole series of ugly shelves from the north wall of the large living-room, as well as the old sink which is now nothing but an eyesore, and put bookshelves the whole way along the wall about three feet high. And finally, I mean to move Alfred's and my bed into the large sunny room the children had before they insisted on rooms of their own, put new curtains and wax the floor, as well as plastering and painting where necessary. It won't be a big or an expensive job since all the materials are already to hand, but it is going to make a big difference to the general appearance of the house.

"The one remaining eyesore will be the kitchen floor. It is in too bad a condition to paint, and good quality linoleum for it would cost about thirty dollars, which is out of the question. The best solution all around is to give it a new hardwood floor from our own forest, but the trouble is this means waiting nearly a year for the flooring to season after it is cut and sawn into boards. For the present it looks as though we'll have to bear it the way it is. I scrubbed part of it this morning, but with people's snowy boots continually tramping in and out the effect doesn't last more than a couple of hours."

Norma wrote to Craig Work's mother, Minta:

"I was so glad to have a letter from you. The children are on the whole very well and happy, though I've had them both home with coughs this week. I wouldn't want anyone to think I took them away from Manumit on account of a difference of ideas or because I wasn't fully satisfied; on the contrary I thought it a very good place for them to be and would have wished to keep them there. But it happened that a friend of ours, a girl from Oberlin, was coming to live here and teach at the little one-roomed schoolhouse not far away (which was closed last year). We felt we had to support her and the cause of better education for the public schools in general, so we thought it was up to us to send our children. Of course the question of fees did bulk rather large too, as one reason for sending them to Manumit in the first instance was that there was absolutely no school of any kind near enough for them to attend, and so we had no choice but to pay boarding-school fees.

"I feel sure Piers would like to see Craig again and I still hope perhaps you could come up and visit some time and bring him. Or if you can't get away, could you perhaps send him for part of the summer vacation? I might be down that way myself, though I don't know yet, and in that case I could bring him back with me. It's really beautiful up here in summer and it is nice for our children to have others to play with.

"I'll get them to write you a letter if I can, but you know how it is! They still often talk about Manumit, but I think they like being at home in spite of the long cold walk through the forest between here and the schoolhouse. Luckily we have had a mild winter, otherwise it would hardly have been possible."

Norma wrote to Dr. Stokes on March 13:

"I am sorry for the delay in answering your letter about Teresa. I was just about to write and tell you that there had been no further trouble, when she fainted again. This time no one was near to catch her and she fell rather heavily, struck her head and bit her lip quite hard. After this I determined to get to the bottom of the thing. I showed your letter to Dr. Hefflon (the local man) but he said he still thought it was a form of nervous indigestion. However, another doctor whom I've been consulting about my digestion (which has been giving trouble again) told me some of the symptoms of both petit mal and hypoglycemia—it doesn't seem as though Teresa has any symptoms of the latter—and also said that a definite diagnosis of petit mal could probably be made by an electroencephalograph, and suggested that I write to the Superintendent of the State School at Brandon, Vt., where they have one of these machines.

"So I wrote to him and arranged to take Teresa there as soon as possible, which will probably be early next week. I will of course let you know what happens. I kept her home for a couple of weeks after the last incident, and for several days she did seem to have an upset stomach; I just hope that Dr. Hefflon will prove to be right."

On March 14 Norma wrote to Valerie Johnston:

"We have mapped out a campaign for bringing several acres of Hilltop back into productivity the biodynamic way, which as you know takes time, patience, labor and lots of organic materials. We'll have to gather up manure, forest hummus, sawdust and so on from all over the place and get them composted or laid out on the fields at the very earliest opportunity, and we've figured we can just get it done before the middle of May (along with all the other things that have to be done) if we stick pretty strictly to business. I think Norm feels this more strongly than anybody, and his sense of responsibility is so new and refreshing for a Hilltopper that I hate to do anything to weaken it. So I don't feel I ought to press any more for Alfred to take time off, though from my personal point of view that time would be better used going to Montreal to see you, than putting compost on the fields. Also, he thinks his passport has expired, and he prefers not to renew it just at this juncture. [Alfred, having become a British subject, would have had a British passport.] Mine was renewed three months ago.

"Here's one of the things I was going to write about most urgently. My young sister was married last year (she married a Persian, did I tell you?) and now she is going to have a baby. She is a medical student in Edinburgh (so is her husband, who is planning to be a medical missionary) and I imagine she will have all kinds of trouble getting together suitable garments, so I am going to make some. I have a woolly coat about half finished already. What I am wondering is whether you, when you are in Montreal, could look around and tell me what it would cost to buy a nice woollen baby blanket, the dark kind preferably for putting on the outside of the pram [perambulator, baby carriage], and send it directly to England, thus avoiding the U.S. customs. It would almost certainly cost me less that way even than buying wool here and knitting it. I understand one is allowed a certain amount of stuff [to bring] in tax free after a personal visit to Canada so I might be able to get some knitting wool that way if I came up to see you. The baby isn't actually due till September, so it isn't really so urgent as all that, I suppose.

"From one point of view the new scheme is working very nicely indeed (except for the technical snag that owing to weather conditions the wood hasn't yet been hauled away and hence the money hasn't come in; so we are living on Winnie's salary). But there's a malaise somewhere. As far as I can trace it, it's due to the men's feeling that forty dollars a week is too high a budget for seven people wedded to the simple life. I rather think so too, but no amount of thought has yet shown me where it can be cut down, at any rate before we start to produce our own food in July. I'm rather afraid that we have here a fundamental difference in philosophy and as time goes on I get less and less hopeful of reconciling it. But in outward matters things are really running very nicely indeed, infinitely better than they have at any time hitherto."

Norma also wrote to Rosina, about other matters, but the letter included this paragraph: "I write under difficulties, as I have a kid on my lap and she won't sit still. This little one made a good start but has been ailing almost ever since. I have tried all sorts of things but the thing she seems to thrive on is nursing—being held hour after hour, coaxed to drink hot milk with vitamin capsules and so on. Every time I think she's better and send her back to the barn, she has a relapse. She might have held up this time, though, if sub-zero weather hadn't happened to coincide with her having to be turned out of the kidding-pen to make room for another newcomer."

At the end of March Norma wrote to Dr. Chatterjee of Antioch College with this thoughtful proposal:

"During a recent visit to Philadelphia I happened to read in the *Friends Intelligencer* your very interesting article suggesting that preparations be made now for eventually resettling C.O.s on the land. I would like to urge that you add another point to your suggested program; that is, the making of a careful survey of existing farms owned or worked by pacifists, with a view to finding out how many extra families could be settled on them and whether some of them could make preparations for larger numbers if they had a little help of the right kind now.

"Quite a number of pacifist families besides ourselves have bought farms very much more extensive than would be needed for their own support, because they believed in the thesis of your article, that some such opportunity of earning a living would be needed by large numbers of men immediately after the war. I know that a few attempts have been made to canvass such people, but nothing systematic has been done. What is needed is information as to the acreage on each farm, the character of the land, the possibilities of various cash crops, school facilities and so on, and an estimate of the number and kind of families whom the existing farmers think they could make room for if a certain amount of help were available. It is infinitely cheaper to expand the productive capacity of an already existing farm than to buy and equip a new one almost from scratch.

"Several of the existing farms may have to be abandoned during the next few months unless some organized help can be given. We ourselves are in a specially fortunate position, because we not only have a small financial endowment which has enabled us to survive several bad years and an infinity of mistakes, but we have at present two men classified in 4-F working on the farm. We constantly hear, however, that people who started out with similar ideas to ours have had to give up, chiefly because they had not sufficient manpower or because they could not meet mortgage payments.

"Some of these farms could be kept in being by a policy of encouraging the few men still available to work on them for the sake of the movement as a whole, rather than buying still more farms and abandoning them in a few years. Others could be helped over the present difficulties with a loan of some kind, perhaps to help them buy equipment to put themselves on a cash basis right away. If they are abandoned, not only is everyone discouraged, but a great deal of money is wasted, since the farm and the stock have usually to be sold at a loss. Moreover, the soil improvements which have been started represent wasted labor if they cannot be continued.

"Isn't there someone who will make a survey of this kind? It would mean some hard work, but it would undoubtedly save a great deal of money which might be used to help pacifists in other ways."

Norma also answered Ralph Templin of the School of Living, who had queried them in a letter dated March 23 about the availability of Norman and Winnie Williams to join them.

Norma replied, "I've been away during the past week and have only just read your letter to us. I think Norm has explained more or less what our position has been. Of course we should miss them a great deal if they went, but we have not tried to make this weigh with them, since the decision was an important one which they had to make entirely for themselves. And there isn't any kind of 'contract' from which they could be released by us—simply the understanding, which we all share, that we can't make any sort of plans for the future without some idea of what we have to plan for in the way of members to feed, and available man-power. I do not think considerations of that kind would hold them back, though, if they felt a strong call to go and work with you.

"We do greatly hope you will find a suitable couple, and please be assured that if Norm and Winnie change their minds we won't stand in the way."

April 1944

Norma wrote to Family on April 1:

"I'm just back from one of my brief trips to Philadelphia, which help me to bear the monotony and isolation of life on top of a mountain. This time I went down to attend part of the Yearly Meeting. I am oppressed by the feeling that the Society of Friends, which should be a live element in society (as it is in England) is becoming almost entirely fossilized over here by the influences of money and responsibility. It just isn't possible for Quakers to have money and social position without losing their distinctive and valuable features as the leaven working in the lump.[77] I confess I was much discouraged by what I saw of the Yearly Meeting. They all seem complacent, and the younger Friends in whom we might have some hope are simply doing their best to become Weighty Friends [experienced, respected] as quickly as possible.

"However, I enjoyed the opportunity of talking with Caroline, who in spite of her impressive official position (she is Recording Clerk of the Yearly Meeting, which means she writes all the minutes) is nevertheless still very far from being fossilized. [Norma and Caroline maintained a warm relationship for almost fifty years. Both died in 1991: Norma in May at age 81, Caroline six weeks later, age 99½.] And of course I enjoyed the brief time with my energetic young friends of the Brudercoop, many of whom are actually trying to do in their small way the things I'd like to see being done by the Friends as a body.

"Well, it's April but the prospect is still covered with snow and the laundry still freezes on the line. The sugaring season should have been in full swing for the last three weeks, but it has hardly begun; our two men are working with Scott Nearing and I don't think they have been over there more than five days altogether. I don't know just what Scott will do if the season goes on as it's begun. It can't go much after mid-April anyway because then the buds begin to open and the character of the sap changes. So many farmers around here depend on the maple syrup harvest for most of their year's cash. I thought we had seen every kind of exceptional weather, but evidently Nature still has something up her sleeve. It's at this time of year that the weight of the winter suddenly seems intolerable. I find it harder to get up in daylight with the thermometer at twenty above than I did in midwinter in darkness with the thermometer at twenty below. Then one expected it, now one feels it ought to be spring. The spring will suddenly arrive, but the interval just before it does is an agonizing one.

"Anyway, Winnie and I have started on the spring cleaning. We began with the attic in the traditional manner and then revised all the bedrooms. Alfred and I have moved out from our little cubbyhole under the eaves into the larger room the children used to have (the children now have demanded cubbyholes of their own). And I filched the prettiest curtains from other parts of the house and cut them to the right shapes and sizes so that I now have the beginnings of quite a nice bedroom in a severely simple style. I plan

---

77. Galatians 5:9, "A little leaven leaveneth the whole lump."

to re-finish a couple of chests of drawers to get a weathered oak effect and perhaps weave another rag rug for the floor. Then we'll have a guest room into which we can put important visitors, ourselves retiring to the attic.

"Now we are starting the big north room downstairs and spent some happy hours yesterday with a crowbar ripping out the ugly old sink which has been an eyesore ever since we came. It's a well-proportioned room when all the excesses are removed, and I hope with a little redecorating we can make it really pleasant. The trouble is that so far we've found it impossible to heat a north room in winter. Our stoves just aren't good enough.

"Wonderful plans are being made for the garden, which I have rashly undertaken to manage this year. It is necessary that the women should do this work in order to leave the men free for something on a larger scale, but I never grew a vegetable before, and I'm committed to growing enough for ten people on our fenced-in quarter acre. Fortunately the soil is in good condition, and thanks to our distance from all other cultivation we suffer from very few insect pests. Birds aren't a problem either, as they are in England. I don't know if it is because there are fewer birds or because with so much forest all around they don't need to get their nourishment from the small pieces of land tilled by men.

"The kidding season has begun. A couple of weeks ago we had an obstructed kidding where, following the textbook, I had to put my hand in and straighten the kid out. The textbooks warn you it may someday be necessary, and I felt sure we should lose the kid at last after so many struggles (we misinterpreted the situation at first and gave entirely the wrong treatment). But she turned out to be the biggest and most beautiful kid ever born here and both mother and child are flourishing."

Norma wrote to Mr. Wend, the author of a book just read (probably Milton Wend, *How to Live in the Country Without Farming*):

"Your book arrived last week and has been read with interest by everyone. I'm not quite through with it yet myself because I have found so much to absorb, but I feel it is time to let you know we received it and how grateful we are. It is really astonishingly full of practical information on every imaginable subject. I really never expected to learn such useful but remote things as what to do in an earthquake! And what you say about such topics as the best way to split wood finds several echoes here.

"As for the goat versus cow controversy, I feel you left out one or two things to the goat's advantage (such as her resistance to disease) but I have to admit you also glossed over other things which are definitely to her disadvantage. I would have credited the cow with one very solid asset—the fact that in sub-zero weather she gives off such a lot of heat at milking-time! Re horses, I wish I knew how to buy a horse, buggy and harness for seventy-five dollars; but no doubt that is just my inexperience. I thought I had done pretty well to buy a horse, who proved to be perfectly sound, for sixty dollars without fixings.

"Several of us hope to be over at the conference at Putney at the end of this month and we look forward to seeing you there. Meanwhile you may be sure this particular copy of your book is going to be very thoroughly read and is going to improve the quality of our living and that of our friends in a great many respects. We shall feel it a privilege to lend it about as much as possible."

Norma wrote to Family:

"Spring is in full blast, and so is spring cleaning, so that between the two of them I am kept in a constant rush except for intervals when I sink down to rest my legs or arms before starting again. Today, however, is too wet to do anything outdoors and too cold to do anything in the house. We started with the attic about two weeks ago and have been bringing order and cleanliness slowly down. I shifted our bedroom into a larger room, arranged new curtains (or rather old ones in a new arrangement), scrubbed and waxed the floor, altered the arrangements for storing clothes, then cleaned out the children's rooms and am now hard [at] work trying to catch up with the arrears of laundry which the spring cleaning revealed.

"Meanwhile Winnie has been at work on the cellar and the big north living room which has been completely stripped with a view to altering its whole interior arrangement and making it a much larger and more useful room for summer parties, dances etc. and finally yesterday I finished going through the office, sorting through three years' accumulation of papers (and you know how we accumulate papers!) and relentlessly throwing away anything that couldn't justify the place it occupied. This took the better part of four days. I am moving the office up to my new bedroom, where I expect to do most of my reading and writing this summer, and the former office is being made into a sewing-room, with the sewing machine, the work basket and other untidy but necessary furnishings, while the top shelves are being used for magazines.

"Very possibly we'll alter the whole arrangement of our library, too, since it now occupies a set of temporary shelves in the Williamses' bedroom. I have visions of built-in shelves all along the north living room wall, below the level of the windows. We still have some redecoration to do, but our great effort has been to make tidiness and cleanliness substitute for new paint. I got a complete new bedroom for no more expenditure than about one shilling for floor wax.

"Books here have now begun to show signs of the economy you mention, though not yet to the extent that the English ones show it. Personally, I like the smaller and more manageable ones, though the much smaller type is a little trying to the eyes. I'm glad, though, that the bindings are still good, and I hope there may be permanent change in the too-lavish and excessive make-ups of so many books before the war. One doesn't need to pay for all that extra paper. The one I sent you had of course been out a considerable time.

"It looks as though we are to have some interesting visitors. First, little Craig Work, Piers' Negro friend from Manumit, who by all accounts is in every way an unusual child. He is 12, and quite phenomenally intelligent [Craig was reputed to have an IQ of 180], which makes me glad that he feels it worthwhile to bother with Piers. His presence may let us in for some difficulties; you wouldn't believe the things a Negro can't do, even in this part of the world. But I feel very strongly on this point and mean to fight for every one of his social rights that can be secured without making the child himself suffer.

"Then, Norm's younger brother Jerry and a girl who was their bridesmaid and is said to be very interesting; and just possibly Nancy Montague and her children again. No doubt there will be others whom we don't yet know of. Polly has a friend, a young man recovering from a nervous breakdown, who might welcome the chance to spend a quiet summer here, and another friend who has been having bad trouble with his digestion is toying with the idea of building a cabin, or setting up a tent, in some remote part of our property beside a spring and spending a few months on a diet of goat milk and berries. The result, as usual, is bound to be quite different from all our expectations.

"Yesterday I walked over to Nearing's to talk to a man who works for them about bees, and to pay one of my infrequent visits to other friends down in the valley. Scott couldn't drive us more than a mile on our homeward way because the road was in such an appalling condition. I asked him why Vermonters didn't realize that in the long run they would save money by fixing their roads.

"'Well, you know,' he said, 'they take a kind of pride in a bad road.' Certainly the badness of these roads has an epic quality. Even the main mail route between here and Rutland is a mass of potholes, with streams running across it at intervals, and occasional huge holes due to a subsidence. When this happens, probably a car or truck falls in; a team of horses is sent for to pull it out, and a piece of wood is left sticking up in the hole to warn other drivers. This goes on till about the middle of May, when most roads are dry enough for the road repair gangs to fix them for the summer. Ours may not really dry before the end of June. It's the melting snow, of course, that causes all the damage, as practically no drainage was provided when the roads were built. Some of them in fact can't be said even to have been built at all. For a progressive nation, it is an amazing phenomenon. However, one can understand how an impecunious [having no money] township, with perhaps 500 inhabitants and 100 miles of country roads, might find it hard to raise the money to do an efficient job.

"The size of this country still is a source of amazement to me—and this is one of the smaller, tighter corners! I can't help hoping I may yet find some absolutely foolproof excuse to make a journey to the West coast before I return to Europe. [Once again alluding to her expectation of returning after the war to assist in recovery efforts.] I believe I would hitch-hike if I could find anyone to go with me. It would probably take a couple of weeks each way."

Norma wrote to Dr. Stokes again:

"Last week I finally managed to make the trip to Brandon with Teresa, and had her brain waves recorded on the electroencephalograph. Unfortunately, we seem to be pretty much as we were; I had hoped the machine would show definitely that there was no irregularity, but apparently there was something out of the ordinary, only the Superintendent did not feel able to say what caused it. He did say he thought it not likely that Teresa would prove to have epileptic tendencies, but he was unable to be certain either way. He asked a great many questions and had a talk with Teresa herself and seemed very well satisfied with her general mental and nervous condition, though he thought she had some emotional instability. He took down your name and I had the impression he intended to write you about it.

"Dr. Thorne's advice was that for the present we should not give Teresa any treatment for these attacks. He seemed to feel there was nothing we could do unless they became much worse, in which case we should have to use some kind of drug. I feel it is all very unsatisfactory, but there seems really nothing we can do."

There are a fair number of letters dated in April or May, no year given, and some completely undated ones. Others are from other people and addressed to Hilltop, whose relevance to the operation of the farm are peripheral. So while activity continued unimpeded, this record skips a month.

May 1944

On May 12 Norma wrote to Family:

"No letter at all came from you for a very long while, then finally one dated some time in March. I know it has been longer than usual since I've written, and I'll try and make this one double length to make up, but it is pretty late, and I am tired. Gardenia the Cow came home yesterday (I think I wrote you that we had to board her out as we ran out of hay). This means five animals to milk, feed and clean up after as well as all the housework and cooking, Polly having gone off to visit her family in Virginia.

"In addition, I have all the spring work in the garden, which amounts to several hours every day, and every day for the past two weeks has been fine. I never thought I would find myself longing for a wet day! I have burnt my back to a crisp weeding, preparing the soil and planting rows and rows of peas, carrots, onions, spinach and so on, and the end is not in sight. We had no idea how many vegetables we wanted to produce for the coming year, so we took an estimate of what was required for a family of five and doubled it. The result is rather staggering, but at least we are reasonably sure of not going hungry, if we harvest even two-thirds of what we hope.

"Add the laundry (I make it a principle never to let a fine day go without washing something, and [am] now washing all the winter clothes preparatory to storing them away—and winter clothes on a farm in Vermont can accumulate almost unbelievable quantities of dirt!); also add baking bread about every other day and a little flower gardening now and then, and you will have a picture of a pretty busy life.

"One transitory headache just now is finding ways to get six people, three of whom are away all day, to consume almost four gallons of milk a day. We shan't be troubled with this very long, however, if we sell three or four goats as planned.

"I read your letter about [Rowena's Persian husband] Reza losing his job, aloud at the supper table. It evoked appreciative snorts from Norm, whose parents are missionaries and who disapprove heartily of the whole clan. He on his side was reading with scorn a report on some Methodist conference to which his father had been a delegate—full of flowery observations about the work in the mission fields. However, I don't think all missionaries are quite so bad. I think Reza ought to go and see someone at Friends House to see if they want extra people for their hospital in India. They have two, I believe, and might jump at the chance to get someone with an oriental background and medical training.

"Yesterday it was such a wonderful day I decided to play truant and walk over to talk to Scott Nearing about some research work I am doing (with the aid of his large library and encyclopedic knowledge). However, I met the Fields going to Manchester (another lovely place, as different as you could possibly imagine from the English one) and went with them on a joy-ride instead. Manchester is an artist's resort, you might perhaps compare it to [the picturesque village of] Broadway in the Cotswolds, except that the architecture is more modest and the scenery grander. It's really summer over there, here it is still spring but very beautiful. I put the tomato plants out in the sun each day and bring them in at night in case of frost, though I don't think it is at all likely as the weather is so very warm. What I am really more afraid of is the sheep; they percolate through fences in the most mysterious way and are apt to appear browsing around the house in the early morning after being firmly shut in the pasture the night before. Our pasture at least is fenced all the way around and the goats didn't get out once today, except when I inadvertently left a gate open. Only one of them noticed it, but he walked into the cow barn (which I had also left open) and gorged himself on our expensive cow feed, scattering it all over the floor.

"You may just possibly be getting a visit from Nancy Montague, who spent last summer here with us. I say 'possibly' but I really think it's very unlikely; her home is in Manchester and as she has three small children, her mobility is just about nil. She had been expecting to spend this summer here too, but last week we had a hasty letter from her saying she was to sail almost at once. She had had her name down on the waiting list for about two years. She was born and brought up at Oxford, and altogether she and I had much in common and I shall miss her this summer, though her children were holy terrors and made hash of our budget by refusing to drink goats' milk or eat half the things we could provide for them. I have sometimes complained that the children of American intellectuals were undisciplined, but nothing to compare with the Montagues! No doubt they will all grow up to be intellectual leaders.

"If I had known when Nancy was leaving, I might have been able to send something for Rowena by her, but all she could say was that she couldn't say when it would be, but it was very soon. Her younger sister Caroline left her bicycle here, and as there isn't time to send it, I suppose we are the richer by one bicycle. Not an English one, unfortunately. The English bicycle is much esteemed over here, the American ones for some reason being built like dreadnoughts [a battleship with large-caliber guns] and so heavy that only the strongest can push them up a hill.

"Teresa just came running in, all out of breath, to announce that one of the kids was in trouble. I hastened out to the barn in bare feet but found only little Linda, my newest pet, calling for her breakfast. Linda is a couple of weeks old, very tiny but simply full of life and spirits. She is as good as a pet dog, in fact prettier and livelier, the only disadvantage is that she is now learning to nibble green things so I am nervous about taking her to keep me company when I weed the garden, in case she should eat the precious asparagus. But she is a wonderful companion. She bounds about as though she had springs in all four feet and a sort of double joint in the middle of her spine, enabling her to do the most bewildering leaps and twists in mid-air. And she has such an intelligent little face. No one could want a more lovable pet than a baby goat! Just now she made a flying leap onto the table, landed on something which slid away from under her, and fell on the floor on her back, which disconnected her [rest of line absent because of bottom of carbon paper.]

"The children have recently discovered the delights of fishing, which is now in vogue among the people around here (mountain trout, you know ...). This morning they spent a long time digging for worms and getting ready to fish in the small brook in the pasture where the cow is watered; it is hardly more than a trickle, and of course they found very soon that there were no fish. So off they went to join the neighboring children fishing in another brook about two miles away—very businesslike, with their own lunch box. Piers abandoned his worms to Alfred, who is encouraging them to multiply in the garden (the very latest in scientific agriculture); he wrote out a notice which read 'Worms! Worms! Worms! For SAIL!'

"I took my pressure cooker down to a 'clinic' last Saturday to have its various mechanisms tested by the nice young girl who comes around to teach Vermont farmers' wives how to run their homes. I am astonished at the tact with which she manages these meetings, always getting the information across without seeming to be dictating to her elders. My pressure cooker was the newest and most streamlined but also the dirtiest—years of use over a wood fire have taken the bloom off it forever, and though I had spent about an hour trying to make it presentable I was quite ashamed of it. However, it proved that the gadgets are working all right, which was a relief. The pressure cooker is such a formidable and incomprehensible piece of equipment that I am still quite scared of it. We had some speculation at the meeting as to what would happen if a pressure cooker ever blew up. Nobody knows, of course, as they are fitted with all sorts of elaborate safety devices. It makes an enormous difference in the winter's food. This morning it is in use to preserve some of our surplus milk, then I shall do some chicken, and I even hope we may put up at least one jar of asparagus. If I do, I shall save it for Christmas Day, like the solitary jar of wild strawberries we had last year.

"The big disadvantage is that canning necessarily has to be done in the summer, when the extra heat in the kitchen is so unwelcome and everyone else is too busy to help. Six or seven quart jars of snap beans, for instance, can mean an entire afternoon's work. On the other hand, a jar of absolutely fresh, straight-from-the garden beans in midwinter is something worth working for. This year we are going to try putting some of the beans down in brine, which will be less trouble though they may not taste so good.

"Winnie is still suffering agonies of mind trying to decide whether or not to teach again next year. The School Board has offered to renew her contract, but she feels it is only because they can't get anyone else, some of the children are very troublesome and some of the parents still think she is a Wicked Woman because of the talk she gave the children on sex. I don't know just what the outcome will be but I imagine, barring some unexpected development, she will teach our children in any case."

1944

More correspondence on different subjects, such as dealing with stultified local draft boards, finishing May.

June 1944

June 2 Norma wrote to Family:

"The fine weather has been unbroken for about five weeks now (it has rained, by some convenient arrangement, only on Sundays) and to my surprise and gratification I am pretty well up with my outdoor jobs, including planting and cultivating a garden more than twice the one that took all Alfred's time last summer, all the milking and barn work, and shearing the sheep. I finished the last sheep about an hour ago, and am in a state bordering on exhaustion. [She would of course have had to use hand clippers; see image 15.]

"It's a pity to write letters when one is tired, but after one of these long, sunny days I am always exhausted by supper time. I come in from the garden at six or later, the family expects to be fed by 6.30, and after that I have all the milking to do, and then it's letter-writing time, but as you can imagine I feel more like bed. Meanwhile the other indoor jobs are completely neglected. I have had the living-room ceiling half papered for six or eight weeks. It's a nasty job, but with one good wet weekday I might finish it. As for the mending, the less said about that the better.

"It seems probable that we'll have another mother and children staying with us this summer. This year it's a young woman named Miriam Fredenthal, wife of quite a well-known artist. We got to know her when we sold her a couple of goats last summer. Now she writes that she's getting a divorce and this costs a lot of money, and could she and her two young children spend the summer here and work for their board? She is very accomplished at several things that would be useful here, for instance weaving and gardening, and knows how to manage goats, and I think she and I would get on well together. Nothing is decided yet, however.

"Our other summer guest was to have been Piers' little Negro friend from Manumit, but his mother writes she's sending him to a camp instead. I am disappointed about this as I was anxious to meet this child. Perhaps I told you about him, he is the one who is supposed to have an I.Q. of 180, which I presume will mean something to Daddy anyway. By the way, some weeks ago Winnie conducted a rough I.Q. test on the school children, and as I recall Teresa scored about 130 and Piers about 125. That didn't seem very high to me, but it wasn't any kind of official test. [Norma herself later became a member of Mensa, for those with IQs over 150, which put her in

0.1% of the population. The children's scores were actually very superior, but might not have seemed so to her!]

"Saturday Morning

"When Winnie is through with her teaching for this year—in a couple of weeks' time—she will take over the housekeeping and I shall, I hope, be a little less burdened. At the present time I am doing three full time jobs—the cooking and housework, the sole care of the garden, and the work in the barn.

"Have you read 'Conditions of Peace' by E. H. Carr?[78] It's a wonderful book, what Americans call a 'must'."

Norma wrote an undated letter about this time to Rosina, which said in part:

"Saturday, with an awful wrench, I parted with my adorable Linda, the one whose birth kept Alfred from the conference. She was the sweetest of all the kids I've raised and that now is saying a good deal! She played around by herself like a happy child and kept me company in all sorts of dull jobs. But some people came Saturday to fetch another kid they'd bought, and Linda was playing in the roadway and they couldn't pass her.... I know she had to go, and I'm glad she went to someone I knew slightly. I wish I had a picture of Linda, but both our cameras are out of action. I won't ever quite forget her."

Norma wrote to Miriam Fredenthal:

"You must have wondered whatever happened to us. To begin with, your letter didn't reach here till late Thursday, on account of Memorial Day coming on one of our two weekly mail days. And then, though everyone was pleased at the idea of your coming, we felt we ought to explain the changes that have happened here since I last wrote, as we were in the midst of a discussion which went on for two days. I'll describe the present state of things pretty fully—in case you want to back out!

"You see, the others here have some pretty definite ideas on the subject of simplicity, home produced food and the like. There are various complicated reasons for this which I'll try and explain fully when I have a better opportunity; anyway, one of them is precisely that we want to be free to keep open house at all times and not have a big cash budget for food, so our guests can always feel they are not being an extra burden on the economy. We've cherished the Open House principle through all sorts of vicissitudes, and we still do. But this last revision brings the diet

---

78. "In his 1942 book *Conditions of Peace*, Edward Hallett Carr argued that it was a flawed economic system which had caused World War II, and that the only way of preventing another world war was for the Western powers to fundamentally change the economic basis of their societies by adopting socialism" (Wikipedia).

down to something you may feel is inadequate, that's why I am going to describe it in a good deal of detail. Mostly it rests on lots and lots of green vegetables, potatoes (soon), native fruits and berries, and at present plenty of milk. And the cereals we are planning to use are mostly wheat—whole grain for cereal, home ground flour for bread. No corn flakes, etc., no butter, no meat, fish or eggs (except very occasionally), no oranges. I have explained that I feel the children may need extras, and if so it's up to me to provide them.

"Now how do you feel about it? Do you think you could regard a diet of mostly milk and green vegetables as a sort of 'nature cure' for a couple of months? Because if so, we'll be delighted to share our rabbit-food with you and your children. There will, I hope, be almost unlimited quantities of rabbit-food, at any rate there should be, judging by the size of the garden I'm cultivating, and it tastes pretty good too. We had some early spinach last night that was superlative. I never knew before I came here how utterly different vegetables tasted when they were straight out of the garden.

"All the things you suggest you could do are things I'm needing help with this summer. How are you on plastering? Because one of the two rooms we could give you needs plastering terribly badly and I am very doubtful if I can find time for it on my own. It's quite easy, just needs strong arm muscles. And how I would love to have someone to work with me in the garden! I spend hours a day there now entirely alone, as Winnie is off at school all day and the men mostly are working in the woods. Sometimes I let the goats in, at imminent danger to my precious green peas, just to have company.

"I felt in fairness to you I had to give you the chance to back out, but I hope you won't! I haven't said anything about your troubles, but that doesn't mean I don't sympathize."

Norma wrote to Family:

"By a happy chance your letter of May 14th arrived on the second solidly wet weekday we've had since the end of April, the first one being yesterday. (It rained all day a week [ago] last Saturday but I was out on the road, hitch-hiking north to visit a friend whose husband is in prison; I got myself as wet as if I'd swum the Channel and of course no letters got written). The drought has driven farmers in New England—and elsewhere, for all I know—to despair and gnashing of teeth. Many gardens have dried up completely and had to be re-planted, and as if that weren't enough, a sudden sharp frost the first week in June killed nearly everyone's tomato plants. The New England growing season is so short anyway that something like this means a real food shortage, and this is the second year running—last year the same calamitous effects were produced by too much rain. A great many good dairy cows will be slaughtered this coming winter for lack of food. I hope ours won't be one of them, but it is very unlikely we'll be able to buy hay.

"In other respects we have suffered less; our land is naturally damp, being in a kind of bowl on top of the hill with a clay subsoil, and the frost when it comes out of season never strikes up here as it does below. One night we spent about an hour desperately working in the garden, putting wooden sugar buckets over every hill of sweet corn and laying flannel sheets over the long rows of beans. (Without flannel sheets in winter, one would scarcely have the courage to get into bed.) All the time the thermometer was dropping, but stopped at 32 and nothing was harmed. Now we are in the proud and happy position of having the second-best garden in the neighborhood, the best being Scott Nearing's, as it always is. One can never hope to compete with him! I get plenty of satisfaction out of being able to supply fresh green vegetables to neighbors who've been living on the land ten times as long as I have.

"I feel that between Scott and ourselves we are giving a pretty good demonstration that agriculture can be learned, at least partly, out of textbooks. [Although] people who've been here all their lives know that it's absurd to plant a garden before May 15th, ours went in, at least part of it, in the week beginning April 15th, and now we have fresh spring greens every day, while they have none but what they buy. Probably about one year in ten the frost will catch us and we'll lose all our early planting, but even then, we can always begin again. And we are experimenting with greens that can be wintered over, either in the garden under a protective covering, or in the cellar, or even in window boxes inside the kitchen. We now have fresh vegetables straight from the garden for seven months out of the twelve, which would enormously surprise the people who built this house.

"The children got the cards and were very pleased; they get so little mail. Polly has been very good in this respect and has sent them picture post cards about once a week, usually ones they can learn something from, for instance two pictures from which I myself learned for the first time the difference between a stalagmite and a stalactite. No one ever thought to tell me (as Polly thought to tell Teresa) that you can tell the upside-down one is a stalactite because it has to hold tight to the ceiling!

"Churchill's latest speech created consternation over here even in the most unlikely places. It is being said now, by all sorts of people, that we'll have to get rid of Churchill after we've got rid of Hitler. Hitch-hiking the other day, I was picked up by a Navy chaplain who talked to me about it for nearly twenty miles (just as I reached my destination, we discovered we had several friends in common). How a man with American ancestry [Churchill] can so regularly do these catastrophic things has long been a puzzle, but this time has certainly been the worst yet.

"For the first time in nine months, in fact nearly the first time in a year, we are temporarily reduced to just ourselves. The Williamses are taking a well-earned holiday, their first since their marriage—they never had a honeymoon. Possibly Alfred and I will take a similar trip sometime after they get back. Now [that] the goats are nearly all sold, there is less to keep me here. When there were five animals to milk, either Alfred or I had to be here morning and evening as no one else had time for the extra work. The cow gives about ten quarts a day. I still greatly prefer goats, but it can't be denied that when you need milk for a large party you can get it with less labor from one animal than from six.

"Alas, if only the rainy days had come before school ended last week! Now of course the children are on the rampage and peace and quiet are unknown. They wake as early as I do in the mornings, and I am too tired to sit up and enjoy the blessed peace after they are in bed at night. On fine days they can be kept happy for hours picking wild strawberries, but on a day like this there seems nothing for them to do but to run about the house and scream. Every now and then someone gets hurt and then there are tears and recriminations. They have read nearly all the available books, and games of the sedentary variety don't amuse for more than half an hour or so. Polly has just sent a basketful of books, which were extremely welcome. Piers gets a good deal of pleasure out of drawing and some of his productions are quite good, but Teresa has to be bounding about all the time and won't leave him in peace for long. His reading difficulty has quite vanished. Last week another boy from the school—aged ten—came to stay overnight and I was impressed to find Piers reading 'Pinocchio' aloud to him.

"Much to everyone's disappointment, Craig Work, who should have been here today, isn't coming until August. His mother misunderstood the invitation and thought I didn't want him for the whole time of the holidays. Negroes are so terribly sensitive, and you may make a mistake without meaning it at all. She herself isn't a Negro but a German, but she has learned, poor woman, that her son has an almost fatal handicap and she is hyper-sensitive on his behalf. I think I told you he was reputed to be a child of altogether abnormal intelligence and now I learn that a New York newspaper published a column about this not long since. They are strong on inter-racial understanding, and I imagine they took him to demonstrate that the children of mixed marriages are not inevitably morons or criminals, as some people appear to believe. Miscegenation is regarded by some with a superstitious horror that would be funny if it weren't so tragic.

"I mentioned my trip North last weekend. In Tunbridge, not very far from Hanover, where Dartmouth College is, there live two young people whom we met when Alfred was teaching at Dartmouth. They were formerly Civil Servants but decided to go back to the land and did it with real thoroughness, on a capital of $200, or about £40. Half of this capital went to buy 50 acres of land, the other half to provide a minimum of equipment and some food for the first winter. Now they grow everything they eat, except for spices and salt and a little sugar. Elizabeth told me their total cash expenditure for last year was $185.

"Now Henry is in prison; Elizabeth doesn't know what for. Henry wrote and told the military authorities he wasn't going to open any more letters from them, and one day they came and took him away, and after a while Elizabeth received a postcard saying that his sentence was three years. Their place is just a little less remote than this one, [as] there are several inhabited farm houses almost within sight, but the house is in far worse condition, in fact half of it has already fallen down. They have a horse and a cow which they maintain on grass or hay all the year round, and apart from milk all they eat is wheat and vegetables (yes, it's true, they do have to buy the wheat, though they hope to grow it soon). They certainly look like a good advertisement for the diet, and when Henry is home they are perfectly contented; I don't know another family so happy.

"But of course they can't go on like that. I feel myself they are evading their responsibilities to society, as educated and able people, but it is impossible to argue with them. Elizabeth won't even consider living anywhere else; she will stay on there, all alone with the child all through the long winter, with four feet of snow all around and not a single convenience of any kind and only half a house, just keeping things going as [best] she can until Henry comes back as mysteriously as he went away. It's futile, I think, but not without its epic qualities.

"It seems such a pity that people must run a good idea into the ground. It's a wonderful thing to be able to provide yourself with a perfectly satisfying life on the land when you have nothing in the world but £40 in cash, an old car (they traded that for the cow) and boundless determination. But I feel that they have carried the demonstration beyond the point where it can be useful to others who want to get back to the land and be healthy and happy as they never can in a city. Only very unusual people would be able, much less willing, to live as they do. I want to demonstrate a way of life which can be some use to L'homme moyen sensual.[79] "Of late I have learned to make both butter and cheese. At least I hope I have learned to make cheese; I have a shelf of cheeses in varying stages of ripeness, but not one has yet been broached. They smell very cheesy anyway. We are keeping them for the time when the cow is dry, if they keep that long. They are made by different processes and some are Cheddar style while others look more like Brie. If

---

79. The concept of *l'homme moyen sensuel* refers to the response of a reasonable person when presented with some form of information either by image or sound, or upon reading a book or magazine.

1944

the first one turns out I'll be tempted to try and send you one; but I fancy there are restrictions on all kinds of perishable foods."

June 11, Miriam Fredenthal wrote to Norma: "You have no idea how happy I was to have your sweet letter of the 5th. I appreciated your writing to me the way you did, although it was not necessary in one sense, Norma. I have a bit of an idea what you folks are working for and trying to achieve at Hilltop, and if I hadn't wanted to be with you, and work with you, and live the way you are living for a while I wouldn't have suggested it in the first place. I am speaking for myself in that statement—I had considered even before I first wrote to you that because of your circumstances (and I do not mean in a monetary sense, either) I might want to supplement my children's diet with a few simple things (a supply of which I could bring with me) such as fruit or tomato juice, canned fish, cod liver oil, chocolate for their milk, butter when I could get it from Jamaica. Would such a thing be acceptable?

"Both the children [ages 4 and 6] had a very bad winter—with one sickness after another for almost six months. Tomorrow morning they were to have had their highly infected tonsils and adenoids removed, but due to a very bad and persistent cough of Sparrow's (which I am afraid may be whooping cough) the operation had to be postponed perhaps a week, perhaps the whole summer. While the children seem well and strong, I feel that they do need a bit richer diet than that which you outlined to me. I would not want you to go to any trouble to prepare for us—Sparrow and I are used to sleeping together—if that would simplify anything for you, and I have a small folding bed which I could bring if it could be gotten conveniently to the farm. Also, I would bring my own sheets and bedding.

"I had hoped to be able to come to Hilltop about the first of July unless of course Sparrow is sick, in which case it might be nearer the middle or end of the month. On Friday we are leaving Claremont to spend a couple of weeks with my mother at a cottage on Lake Sunapee. Sparrow and Robin are both elated over the prospect of a possible visit to Hilltop, and both being real lovers of the country, and used to it—I think that it would be a wonderful thing for them if all of this is agreeable to you.

"I shall be very eager to hear from you again, I read your letter many times before I wrote because I would not feel that I could come if I would cause a breach in your communal etiquette.

"P.S. I have done only minor plastering, but am certain that I could muster up plenty of muscle for that or any other job that you would need help with." (*Piers:* I remember their visit. Miriam wore her hair in two long braids, and her children were good-natured and fun. Sparrow was the elder, I think younger than we were, who was just beginning to assert herself by asking that she be called her given name, Ruthie, instead of Sparrow. The story was that she was so small when she was born that she was nicknamed after that small bird, and it stuck, but I can hardly blame her for preferring a more formal name. Robin was younger, but a big boy. He was invariably cheerful. I remember them both with pleasure.)

Many letters traveled to and from Hilltop in June and July that relate mostly to personal connections, the placing of goats, and other matters not directly related to the operation of Hilltop Farm.

July 1944

Norma wrote an undated (the dateline was off the carbon paper) but probably July 1944 letter to Family: "Your letter of June 4th arrived yesterday—it seems as though a terrible lot has happened since then, in fact it seems like almost another world in some ways, but in the circumstances, I suppose it's surprising the letter wasn't even more delayed. My silence has also been somewhat prolonged. All through May and June I worked desperately in the garden, digging up, weeding, planting, watering and weeding again. For several weeks we've been having fresh vegetables, but today we had a grand celebration with new potatoes, green peas and young carrots.

"As soon as school was over Winnie went away for a couple of weeks, which left me single-handed to deal with everything, including the livestock. On July 1st she came back, and on the next day there arrived the first of our regular summer visitors, a young woman named Miriam Fredenthal with her two children. She is the wife of a rather famous artist, David Fredenthal, who has been doing some official war paintings, and who, I gather, is now shortly setting out for England, or Europe anyway. Oh, dear, I suppose the censor [all mail was censored, and references that might be helpful to the enemy were blacked out] won't like that, though heaven knows what difference it can make to anyone. Her two children, attractively named Sparrow and Robin, are a few years younger than ours but very bright and quick, and as ours are still very lacking in sophistication, the quartet gets along famously.

"This means that we now have three women where we had one before (Miriam, fortunately, is a formidable gardener, specializing in weeding). The goats too, have almost all gone and the last two are going at the earliest opportunity. So Alfred and I feel we can now contemplate taking a short vacation, the more so as the big saw they've been using in the woods is broken and a week or more may pass before the spare part arrives. We are planning to leave Tuesday afternoon and be away perhaps for a week, perhaps a little longer.

"Here's an item of news I think will interest you. A man who happened to visit us last week (about buying a goat) called our attention to a newspaper paragraph saying that the UNRRA [United Nations Relief and Rehabilitation Administration, founded 1943, closed 1947] is now recruiting people for reconstruction work in Europe. They want people for agricultural rehabilitation, among other things. Now, as you probably know, a large part of the purpose of this experiment has been to prepare us for just such work. So we think we'll go to Boston on Wednesday and inquire at the office where the people are being recruited, so that at least we'll have some idea of what the possibilities are. We would, of course, very much prefer to work for the Friends Service Council, or failing that, the American Friends (and probably in Philadelphia, we'll have a talk with the A.F.S.C. office too).

"But there might be definite advantages in being with an official organization. It might be very difficult for unofficial people to get passage back to Europe immediately after the war. Of course it is all very vague and up in the air, but it does represent a definite step in the general direction of home [England remained Norma's "home"]. I don't want to consider taking the children across the Atlantic in wartime, and there are many other considerations. For instance, Alfred is very suspicious of American economic imperialism; he doesn't want to feel he is working for an organization which is just going to result in fastening upon European peasants the yoke of General Motors or Imperial Chemicals, or any of the huge concerns that [in his opinion] exist largely by creating a demand for things people don't really want.

"There is, unfortunately, evidence that the power given by relief funds to the people who administered them in Europe was very unscrupulously used after the last war. In the *New Statesman* not long ago I read an article by Brailsford on some doings of the Hoover organization which at first seemed incredible, but I found later that these things are well-known over here. This makes me feel, however, that there's all the more need for disinterested people on the field of action. We are going to Pendle Hill this coming week for the special purpose of talking over all these things with Redolfo Olgiati, a Swiss with whom we worked in close collaboration for a long time in Spain. He is the head of a large relief organization and is over here to confer with the American Friends.

"Another small but interesting development occurred this last week in our special fields. A call has been sent out for gifts of goats to be sent to Malta. Nothing is said about the European mainland as yet, and the kind of goats they want for Malta are not the kind we have been raising, but it shows things are stirring. Although we are getting rid of our goats, we still have the experience and I would like to be associated with some kind of goat-recolonization scheme more than almost anything I can think of. Not only do I like goats and get along splendidly with them (often better than with humans!) but goat milk is a life-saver in so many situations where nothing else will do. There will be thousands of babies in Europe who will owe their lives to goat milk if someone comes along with the goats at the right moment.

"You may well ask, where do the children fit in in all this? My idea is that by the time we do actually get back to Europe [Norma resolutely clings to this dream] it will be perfectly in order to send them to boarding school, most likely one of the Quaker schools or St. Christopher's at Letchworth (where Molly could keep an eye on them). But we mustn't let our minds jump ahead too far. After all, the Atlantic supposedly still has submarines in it and I still don't like the idea of them very much. If we go on living so economically we'll be able to pay all our passages by Clipper—if there's room!

"The heat today is appalling. It's not that the temperature is so very high, I don't think it has been much above 80, but the humidity must be very high. We seem certain to get a thunderstorm and probably it will then begin to rain and all the rain which has been failing to fall for the past two and a half months (except for a catastrophic downpour in mid-June which ruined half the crops which had managed to survive the drought) will start to fall on Tuesday, just when Alfred and I start on our journey. What a climate!"

Polly Robinson, to Norma's regret, never returned from visiting her family, and by October had moved to Greenwich Village in New York City, to learn singing.

August 1944

On August 1 Norma wrote to Merle [no last name]:

"The place is such a hive of activity at present that you'd barely recognize it. Just outside the back door Alfred and Norm Williams are hard at work sawing up about five cords of wood for our winter fuel supply. We've never had so much before, or so early. They are using the Ottawa log saw, which we got to speed up work in the woods, since we've decided that the forest is to be our cash crop. We've sold almost two hundred dollars' worth of cordwood and a good many logs. The cordwood, we know, goes to keep people in Jamaica warm, and the logs are made into chair-legs at the sawmill in the village, so we feel reasonably sure we aren't helping along the war very much, and also we think we can earn enough to be sure of paying our cash expenses and have time left over for necessary repairs and improvements about the place.

"Meanwhile, the women look after the garden and the animals. We have a big garden, more than twice as big as in previous years, and expect it to produce maybe three quarters of all we eat for the coming year, maybe more. If we can get used to doing without extras, we can get through the winter buying hardly anything except whole wheat to grind up for bread. We got started early with the garden—too soon, everyone said, and we did have a bad scare when there were two sharp frosts in the first week in June and many people lost their tomato plants and other things. We rushed out and covered up the tender plants and lost nothing except one grape vine and a bean or two. Now our garden is way ahead of everyone else's, except Scott Nearing's of course (he always has the best garden anywhere around), and we have been able to give away big heads of lettuce, beans, Swiss chard and beets to all our neighbors who said we shouldn't plant so early. I'm afraid this gives us some satisfaction—it may do some good if it persuades them that you can plant the garden before May 15th!

"The weeding of the garden takes us more time than anything else. It got terribly overgrown with witch grass during June, when Winnie was away and I was single-handed. I don't think any of the vegetables have suffered much, but we spend hours and hours every day pulling up witch grass and digging out those terrible long roots. I hope we'll get the benefit of all this work next year too.

"As well as the garden, there are the animals. We have regretfully decided to get rid of the goats, because for such a large family we really had to have a cow, and to keep cow and goats means too much work. Only one is left and she is to go on Thursday. She is going to the Catholic Worker farm at Easton, Pa., where they had all their goats killed by dogs a while back. The sheep are going too, for the same reason. We even think that this winter we'll board out Gardenia, the cow, because it has been such a poor year for hay and we have practically none of our own. We have quite a lot of milk canned.

"There are nine of us at present and another friend is expected today or someday soon, and also Norm's younger brother and his friend from the University of Pennsylvania and a little Negro boy, a friend of Piers', and maybe a couple more—all due to come sometime this month. If they all turn up at once I don't know just where we shall put them, but we'll manage somehow—we always do. Oh, yes, I forgot a Nisei [second-generation Japanese American] friend from Philadelphia who also may be coming to see us, so we shall be really interracial as well as full up.

"Next time you write, tell us a bit about what you're doing out there. Did you put out the big fire?[80] One of our friends, Keith Hillman, has just transferred to Glendora [CPS camp], but I understand California is a big

---

80. Presumably the Tillamook Burn, "a series of forest fires in the Northern Oregon Coast Range that destroyed a total area of 350,000 acres of old growth timber in what is now known as the Tillamook State Forest" (Wikipedia). Evidence of the Burn could still be found along roadsides as late as 1970

state and it may be hundreds of miles from where you are. We did know someone at Coleville [CPS], but I don't think we do any more. Tell us about California, too. Is it really as wonderful as they say? I'd like to go out and take a look at it someday, but at present I don't quite see how."

August 5, Norma wrote to Dear Friends:

"If we haven't sent a shoulder of fatted calf[81] along yet it's just because we are so darn busy—not that we didn't appreciate with loud hosannas the news that you had decided that this was, after all, a place to settle. In fact I've been going round looking speculatively at likely spots with Bennetts in mind. Norm and Winnie have also been prospecting with thoughts of building in mind. We haven't yet made any inquiry into sordid matters like cash, but if and when we do, we'll share our discoveries.

"There's a nice little field, maybe two acres, just to the left of the short cut, on the road that starts at the four cross roads as you come up. Has a nice view and though heavily screened by forest, isn't more than a quarter mile from Route 30. You could live there in almost absolute privacy unless you yielded to the urge to carve out a driveway and set up a mail box, which I suppose you'd have to do if you were going to make your living by a mail order business.

"There are lots of other possibilities, of course. The Rome house, the nice little white one at the foot of our short cut, is reported for sale on account of the parties broke up. We peered inside; the ground floor is one large, irregular room, all paneled, with a cocktail bar and three built-in beds with handsome springs. Nice kitchen and all fancy plumbing. Would run into thousands, I imagine. Finally, Charles Jackson was just here, and he thinks there's just a possibility Janet might consider selling their place. I imagine they would want to get back what they've put in it, which must be in the neighborhood of $1,000 [for the] house and twenty acres (more or less).

"I got hold of the *Letters of Lincoln Steffens*[82] and after that his autobiography, which has given me lovely masses of verbal ammunition to sling around in arguments here. I'm afraid, though, I overdid it in the end. They visibly balked when I read them the bit about the man whom Steffens advised to continue drawing money from houses of prostitution so as to have a salutary sense of how much he was a part of this sinful world. Now

---

81. Fatted calf is a metaphor or symbol of festive celebration and rejoicing for someone's long-awaited return. It derives from the parable of the Prodigal Son in the New Testament (Wikipedia).
82. Lincoln Steffens (1866–1936) was the most famous of the American muckraker journalists of the period 1903–1910. His exposés of corruption in government and business helped build support for reform (Encyclopedia.com).

I'm afraid they will write Steffens off as something like Bernard Shaw (not serious, you know) and fail to read him, which will mean a big bit missing from their education.

"Helen has been off to a musical camp of some kind while Scott is lecturing to people in a Gunnery School (yes, honestly, I don't believe they are Gunners though). Mrs. Smith caught a neighbor picking raspberries she considered hers: she remonstrated, he kicked her, she says she'll have him arrested. . . . The Lightfoots have had a whole catalog of misfortunes and their son has been seriously wounded in Italy. The school is to be open again, though with fewer children, and Mr. Bullis has found Winnie an organ."

Piers had his tenth birthday on August 6, when he almost managed to eat ten pan-sized pancakes to celebrate the occasion. Norma's August 10 letter to Family noted: "Last Sunday was Piers' birthday and we had a picnic planned, but most unfortunately it rained just at the time we should have been starting out. It was a swimming picnic, and the walk to the swimming hole is at least two miles, so we gave it up and had the party indoors—after which of course the sun came out again. Piers got a tool chest, a large very businesslike affair in which he takes great pride."

Norma's August 7 letter to "Jim" said in part:

"We received [your letter] just as we were starting off on a short vacation, and part of our plan was to go to Boston to see the UNRRA office there, but we changed our minds and went straight to Philadelphia instead, otherwise we'd have looked you up the very next day.

"We spent a week at Pendle Hill working on a Spanish manuscript which they are getting ready to publish, and on the way home my typewriter got a bang and has been out of action ever since, so I quietly gave up letter-writing till the pile of unanswered correspondence grew so alarming that I was reduced to borrowing a friend's machine.

"We still don't have a team. Not long ago there was a rumor—in fact it was told to us as definitely true—that a local farmer had a horse he wanted to give away because it was too old for the heavy work he needed from it! We duly investigated this, but it turned out to be (so to speak) a mare's nest [an illusory discovery]. So since Dickie left us in mid-winter we are horseless, and as far as I can see likely to remain so, though to me it's the biggest single gap in our economy.

"We do have a soil-improvement program, having come to feel that understanding the conservation of natural resources is one of the biggest contributions we ourselves can make; but it's badly held up for lack of the necessary motive power to carry it through. Alfred has become intensely interested in earthworms, which at least don't need the assistance of a disc harrow to perform their useful function in renewing the topsoil. And we've started to exploit the forest for cash, though I note 'exploit' is the wrong word, as the definite purpose has been to improve the forest while removing the weed trees which are hampering the growth of the better stuff.

"You'd hardly recognize the road; quite a long distance has been opened up to the sun and air by the wholesale cutting of the trees which were crowding in on it. These and others have been sold locally for cordwood and this has brought in some honest hard-earned cash, potentially enough to balance our budget with a maximum of production of food. One difficulty is that the road is still so bad that the wood cut during the winter can't be got out before June at the earliest and after it's been removed we still have to collect payment, and the present imbalance of the budget is directly due to the fact that we haven't yet been paid for wood cut last year. Still we feel more self-respecting than we did.

"Quite a number of things have got done around the house. Most of the upstairs is plastered, though some of it was done with more zeal than skill and will eventually have to be done again. The kitchen is quite transformed, with large cupboards all along one side, nice white paint and even a mural painted by one of last summer's guests! Outside we've improved the fencing and shifted the position of the outhouse, but that's about all. Oh yes, we've put asbestos shingles on the south side of the house and plan to extend them eventually to the other three sides: they don't look so nice as the red boards, but the condition of the woodwork on the south side was so bad that the winter winds blew straight through and something had to be done soon.

"The Williams family are still with us and Winnie is to teach again this year in the local school, which is a valuable contact with the outer world. During the past year we've learned to know a lot more about our neighbors and their special problems, though we do sometimes wish they wouldn't try to drag us into their internecine feuds.

"We tried square dancing at the school house, but many of the valley inhabitants are Seventh-day Adventists to whom anything resembling dancing is sinful, and to make things worse some of the local lumberjacks turned up in a partially intoxicated condition, so we didn't persist too long in this attempt at community organization. Maybe this coming year we'll try again. The local religion is anything but helpful because of all the prohibitions involved, and also because they can't attend any kind of jollifications on a Saturday, which is when the others are free.

"We've another family, a mother with two small children, spending the summer with us, and a number of people are promising to come and visit during August—including Roger Robison, the Williams' best man, John Farger, a medical student from the University of Pennsylvania, Norm

Williams's younger brother, and a colored child whom Piers made a friend of during his brief excursion to boarding school. Also a lady journalist from New Bedford, member of the nearest Friends Meeting which we are thinking of joining, is due to arrive almost any moment."

(There are a number of undated letters in and out, around early August, some carbons too faint to be legible.)

A letter to Family dated August 10:

"In despair of getting this letter written any other way I resolved to get up extra early this morning and write it before breakfast, but as luck would have it, I overslept instead. I get up at six and on Tuesdays and Thursdays I leave the house soon after eight to walk the two miles down through the forest to the mailbox. [This must have been the box in Pikes Falls; Jamaica would be four miles.]

"Sometimes even then I haven't time to put the cow in the field after milking, and have to ask Winnie to do it. Gardenia can be extremely difficult when she chooses and one day last week it took all morning to get her safely tied (she can't be left loose in one field because she climbs out over the [dry-laid stone] wall. Alfred says undoubtedly she was a goat in a previous incarnation.)

"During the day there is so much noise and confusion, with four children constantly running in and out, that I have almost given up trying to write letters even in the few minutes I can snatch from weeding the garden. The days are so full and yet nothing seems to happen that is worthy of record. Day after day I get up and milk goat and cow, tie them out, eat breakfast, go for the mail if it's a mail day, do the laundry, tidy up the kitchen and occasionally a bedroom or two, eat lunch, weed the garden, pick beans or Swiss chard for brining or canning, help prepare the supper, milk again and go to bed. Very rarely I have a breathless excursion somewhere, such as a walk over the hill to see the neighbors or even a trip on the bus down to Brattleboro to see the dentist. But there really isn't any material for letters.

"I wonder if you ever got my postcard saying not to worry any more about the hernia; I found I'd forgotten to mention it in the letter I sent in answer to yours, so I sent a postcard after it which very possibly arrived first. That's ancient history—the doctor in Media told me he couldn't find a trace of it, and either it got better of its own accord or the Spanish doctor made a mistake in diagnosis. I think that's perfectly possible in view of the fact that he failed to diagnose a case of jaundice—of all things!—in one of our friends.

"Last Sunday was Piers' birthday and we had a picnic planned, but most unfortunately it rained just at the time we should have been starting out. It was a swimming picnic and the walk to the swimming hole is at least two miles, so we gave it up and had the party indoors—after which of course the sun came out again. Piers got a tool chest, a large very businesslike affair in which he takes great pride. Piers is still very unsophisticated and doesn't mind at all playing with small fry like Robin and Sparrow. He is very friendly with the local children and often goes off to visit them, which is an excellent thing. It's much harder for Teresa, [as] there are no girls anywhere near except one very much older than herself. She would love to play with the boys, but they don't see it that way.

"Our friends the Fields, as well as a baby girl, have a baby horse, the most delightful creature. I saw it when it was three days old and it looked just like a beautifully-made toy; it tossed its little head and tail and came trotting to the fence for me to rub its nose. Harold has offered us the next one if we'll pay the breeding fee. It certainly would be a joy to have, but it would be years before it would do any work. This one indirectly has set some of our plans back a year, because we had been counting on borrowing Harold's team for some necessary work which has to be done now or not till next summer. I do wish we had a horse, one larger than Dickie, who could really be a help. But it seems pretty hopeless still."

Norma wrote to Araminta, Craig Work's mother, probably in August.

"Your letter came just before my husband and I went away for a short vacation, and as I'd forgotten to take it with me, I couldn't answer it because I hadn't the address. It sounded rather as if you were not sure if Craig would have time to come up here at all—I do hope that isn't so because we are still counting on him and the children are beginning to get thoroughly annoyed with me because he doesn't show up. I have tried to explain, but they seem to feel it is some kind of conspiracy! Also Sally Cleghorn has written twice (you know she lives near here) saying how anxious she is to have him for a few days' visit when he comes. So do please let us know soon.

"About the other child you mentioned, I'm in a difficulty. The truth is I haven't been extra well lately, and I rather quail at the idea of another completely strange child (we have four here at the moment), especially a sophisticated one from the city. The latest development is that the doctor has advised me to go away from here for a while and take intensive treatment for a demoralized digestion. This won't be till September anyway.

"I don't want to put you in any embarrassing dilemma if you've already spoken to the other child's parents, and if you have mentioned it to them, please do send him along, I expect we'll manage all right. But if nothing has been said yet, I'd rather leave it till next year. Now I have your friend's name and address, I could write to her some time during the winter and see if we can't arrange for one of her children to come up for a good long visit. I feel mean about this, but it seems really the sensible thing to do as I really have been pretty much overwhelmed lately with so much work and so much to worry about.

"All the above, though, doesn't apply at all to Craig. He isn't at all an unknown quantity and I am sure he will fit in beautifully. Please don't disappoint us again, we really do want him!" (*Piers:* Craig's visit was a high point of the summer for me.)

On August 23 Norma wrote to Family:

"I'll be single-handed again all too soon, when school begins again in a couple of weeks' time. There has been some doubt as to whether the school would be opened this year, as two of the older children have gone on to High School and a couple of other families have moved away from this locality. If they decide the survivors are too few, Winnie will teach our children at home instead.

"It's impossible from over here to form any real idea of what is going on [with the war], which makes it all much worse, as no doubt you realized at the time of the bombing of Barcelona. I can only tell myself that worrying doesn't do any good, and hope that they will get the business finished one way or another before too long.

"Just after I'd written my last letter to you, an event occurred here which caused a good deal of upset. I was just leading the cow home one evening when a car appeared suddenly up the hill—this is an unusual sight at any time and this particular car, I saw to my amazement, was a taxi. There are no taxis in Jamaica and I realized it must have come from Brattleboro, thirty miles away. It proved to contain Miriam's artist husband who, as I told you, she is in the process of divorcing, accompanied by his lawyer. No one knew just what they'd come for. We were entirely unprepared for any such visit, and for a few minutes we just didn't know what to do. However, we pulled ourselves together and gave them a polite greeting and as good a supper as we could produce on the spur of the moment. The children were delighted to see their father and dragged him all over the place showing him the sights, while Miriam talked to the lawyer, and after about an hour they left, in a general atmosphere of cordiality.

"Miriam, however, was very much upset and has been very depressed ever since. She says he's been living with a girl in Australia for the past year. He is now off to some other battlefront. This week one of the best illustrated magazines ("Life") published six or eight pages of his drawings and paintings made in the South Seas. Quite possibly you might be able to get hold of a copy. Soon after that Miriam had to go off to her old home in New Hampshire to sign legal papers, arrange about packing up furniture and so on, so Winnie and I coped with the children. They are really no trouble at all, and Sparrow, the older one, does the most remarkable imaginative drawings with a distinctly Chinese appearance.

"That's about all the local news, except that I spent the night over at the Field's on Saturday helping with the new baby, Gretchen, who has just been brought home. It's a very tiny baby, weighed 5½ lbs. at birth. I never handled one so small, but it's very vigorous and one soon learns that it is not by any means as frail as it looks.

"Simply as an experiment, I am going to enclose a check for ten dollars. I have no idea what are the rules about sending money, and it would take a long time to find out. I imagine that you will be asked to cash it within a limited time and through some official agency. Possibly you won't be able to cash it at all, in which case no harm will be done. We've been so economical that I could send a little more if this gets through all right, and you could put it down as a gift to the new baby, to buy anything it specially needs. American dollars are still legal tender almost anywhere (or if they aren't legal one can get fantastic sums for them on the black market!) but if I send actual cash and it goes to the bottom of the sea that's too bad, while a check that disappears means nothing. Let me know what happens.

"Our last (and first) goat, Junie, left on Saturday and is now safely at her new home in Pennsylvania. We sent her and a couple of others to some friends who had theirs killed by dogs. I hope the same fate won't overtake Junie. She was quite a member of the family, having come to us quite soon after we came here ourselves. No doubt I'll see her again from time to time.

"Soon we must start going through the catalogs to choose the children's snow suits. It's difficult to know what to buy; even at twenty below zero, they get warm in just a few minutes walking through the woods and I've found that if I buy the very warmest woolen coat with a sheepskin lining (which is impervious to anything), as like as not the child will begin to perspire and throw open the coat. I begin to understand why windproof cotton clothing is so popular in Canada. Feet are the real problem; no method has been discovered of keeping them dry and warm in any condition, though sheepskin-lined boots are perfect as long as everything is frozen hard and there's no moisture to seep in through the seams." (*Teresa*: Our wool snowsuits were closed with buttons; when there was a crust of ice on the last downslope above the house, we liked to slide down on our stomachs, which tended to rip the buttons off).

Norma wrote to Family, undated—off the carbon—probably late August or early September:

"The mail on Thursday brought two letters dated August 14th. I was so much relieved to know that the green dress arrived; I had been beginning to wonder whether, if it didn't arrive till late September, Rowena could still wear it in the post-natal period. The battle to keep up with the correspondence seems to be increasingly a losing one. This year we are growing almost all our own food and almost the entire responsibility falls on me, except for the two months when Winnie doesn't have to be away teaching all day. In September everything ripens at once and a sharp frost must be looked for not later than the last week in the month, so it's a race against time to get all the perishable stuff in. Bushels of tomatoes go into glass jars (Vitamin C for the winter) [the high heat of the canning process would destroy much of the vitamin or cause it to leach into the water], bushels of snap beans go into the brine, bushels of sweet corn into the drier, not to speak of oddments like hot red peppers which Alfred is growing in his little garden [which was always identified as the Pepper Garden] (we've never yet, to my deep regret, had any success with the delicious aubergine [eggplant]).

"I work away at all this in the midst of cooking the meals, trying to keep the visible parts of the house at least superficially clean, looking after the cow and in odd moments struggling with my own literary work. I don't want it to sound like unremitting drudgery; as a matter of fact I've managed several small excursions lately. First I went over to spend the night at the Field's when Natalie brought the new baby home; I calculated, quite correctly, that the baby would howl all night [as had infant Teresa], but Harold, to my surprise, proved perfectly competent to deal with it, so I went home the next day.

"After that, Alfred and I arranged to visit our friends the Baumgardts, who spend their summers at Dorothy Canfield's home on the other side of the mountains—twenty miles to hitch-hike, there being no bus. I wasn't feeling extra well but I went anyway, as there wouldn't be another opportunity. Dorothy Canfield invited us to spend the night in her very comfortable house. By this time my temperature was rising fast and I tossed about all night wondering how in the world I should ever get home. One can't, I felt, be ill in the house of a famous novelist whom one hardly knows, and who besides is in delicate health herself.

"Next day, feeling worse and worse, I consulted a doctor. He took my temperature and pulse, gave me a startled look and advised immediate bed. So there seemed nothing for it but to go all the way home in a taxi, which caused a major sensation at home. I spent several days in bed in considerable discomfort, but was back at work at the end of the week, very much rested and feeling altogether better than before. I forgot to say that the doctor's verdict was influenza. In three and a half years that we've spent here, it's only the second time that I've been obliged to spend even a day in bed. There's no doubt this way of life is healthy.

"My next excursion was again to Manchester; I started out, once more, to hitch-hike but on my way fell in with Helen Knothe who said she was driving over next day, so why didn't I stay the night. (I'm not sure if I've explained Helen; she used to teach music at Manumit while Scott Nearing was lecturing there and his wife was the director. Exactly what happened is not clear, but according to Helen, Scott's wife misinterpreted their friendship and threw Helen out, whereupon Scott felt he must be responsible for her, so they've been living together ever since. It sounds fishy, but if one knows Helen one can't help liking her, and I don't much care what really happened. Anyway she had no reason to tell me anything but the truth, as I know perfectly well what the present state of things is). [Scott and Helen did eventually marry, after his long-estranged wife died.]

"They had a houseful of interesting guests, so I had a wonderful time, with more intellectual conversation than has come my way in many months. Next morning we drove to Manchester where I was to pick up our long-awaited guest, Craig Work, from Manumit. On arriving I found they were already in Jamaica—he and his mother had arrived at Hilltop soon after I left the previous day! So back I went over the hill, apologetic but having thoroughly enjoyed playing truant, and there was my guest in the kitchen, baking bread.

"She's a large, blond woman of German extraction, an extraordinary contrast to her small, dark child. He is very far from black, one would say Italian or southern Spanish. He is an exceptionally intelligent and very attractive child, fortunately not at all sophisticated and quite willing to play games with Piers and Teresa. While they are at school he helps me in the kitchen and keeps me constantly entertained with anecdotes, snippets of the latest scientific knowledge, thoughts on life and so on. He is only just 13 but the other day he beat me at one of those word games at which you know I usually excel. Quite an acquisition in fact. He is to be with us another ten days. I hope knowing him will provide our children with the best kind of protection against the vicious race discrimination which it's so hard to avoid over here.

"I needn't say how relieved I was to learn that the robot bombs had finally stopped coming. How I pored over the newspapers, on the rare occasions when I saw them, trying to make out what was happening through the fog of censorship! I imagine the effect must have been similar to that of the shelling we experienced in Barcelona which was so extremely disagreeable. No one over here has any conception of what these things are like.

"Poor Winnie is washing the dishes all alone; we are about to start for our weekly trip to the village, so no more for now. I'm sorry about the bad typing—my machine is still out of order and Miriam has reclaimed hers now. Teresa came home bursting with pride to say that she could pick out 2 tunes on the harmonica at school! I think I shall ask Helen to give them music lessons."

September 1944

Norma wrote to Minta, Craig Work's mother, September 14:

"We broke the news to Craig that he was to stay till the 25th and he didn't raise any objections, while our children uttered howls of joy. It has been rather dull for him since you left, as it has rained a lot, but today he went off with the school party. Monday morning he got lost in the woods but resourcefully found himself again by climbing a tree to spy out the land. I sent you a telegram yesterday morning and hope the address was sufficient. Yesterday was my letter-writing day but I had to make an unexpected trip to the village, so I'm behind on my schedule. It was nice to have your card and know you enjoyed your brief visit. We so much enjoy having guests, but often I feel they probably have a terrible time getting used to everything and the satisfaction is all on our side! Just now the Williams' friend, John Ferger, is here for his third visit. We always feel flattered when people turn up again.

"I went to Brattleboro Monday to hear Scott Nearing give a very interesting talk on the future of civilization (he thinks it is headed for the scrap heap and a good thing, too). In the library I read an extract from what I understand is the forthcoming autobiography of Richard Wright ('Native Son'), describing some of his experiences in the CP [Communist Party] and how he left it. It's beautiful writing as well as very interesting. If you haven't seen it yet I recommend you get yourself the last two issues of the *Atlantic Monthly*.

"Arrears of correspondence are mountainous so I mustn't stop and gossip. But I hope from now on we shall count you among one of our regular correspondents (with visitors too of course). It does us lots of good to meet people who don't fully share our ideas but nevertheless think much as we do so that a real exchange is possible."

Norma wrote to Elizabeth [Thorsen?] on September 16:

"We hoped we could send someone up to join Herbert in cutting wood this week, but a chapter of accidents got in the way. We have a contract to cut 10 cords of wood for a man in the village (we are about the only source of supply, as everyone else is busy with war work) and last week Alfred hurt his foot in the woods, and then it rained for four days, so the product of the week's work was only 1 cord. The men feel they must have this out of the way before they take on anything else. But we have good hopes of sending someone up a little later. Would any special time be better than another for you? It's a matter of planning—if we plan ahead of time we can usually take a particular day or even a week off, but it's difficult to fit into a schedule that is already pretty full.

"We had a very brief visit yesterday from Dick Gore, and hope we may see more of him later. Herbert passed through Jamaica but hadn't time to climb the hill—I hope he isn't taking our name from his visiting list! Everything is a scramble here, the men trying to get their 10 cords out as well as 3 or 4 for a friend who spent the summer here and now, to our great satisfaction, has rented a house in the village; Winnie is back at school and I am trying to get everything perishable in from the garden before the frost. I think we shall pretty well meet our estimates for winter food.

"Alfred is contemplating going to the F.O.R. conference shortly, but it all depends on those wretched 10 cords and he won't make it unless the weather improves. The big wind the other night was a hurricane, did you know? We never would have except for the radio sets of our friends in the valley, which convey news to us via the school. Apparently it did a lot of damage in some places." (*Piers:* I remember three days of dark clouds scudding rapidly across the sky; I wondered where they were going in such a hurry. But we did not suffer wind damage at Hilltop; we were evidently beyond the danger zone.)

October 1944

On October 3, Norma wrote to Lucia:
"Here I am just sitting down to make plans, the month of October having begun, when comes your letter. The plans range from correspondence with doctors, to ordering silk underwear from the Sears catalog (not very much, I mean to splurge and have something really exciting from Wanamaker's [an upscale department store in Philadelphia], symbol of the New Life, if you see what I mean). I can hardly imagine anyone on whom fancy underwear is more wasted than a grass widow [a woman whose husband is away for prolonged periods], but perhaps you got the idea. Farewell to the hair shirt [a shirt made of rough uncomfortable cloth or animal hair that some religious people used to wear to punish themselves], as it were.

"Things on the agricultural front are coming along nicely. I just came in from harvesting six bushels of carrots, one of onions and one of beets. There will probably be eight or nine more bushels of carrots, so you see I am not leaving my family to starve. The men are fetching in field corn, apples and potatoes, and the shelves in the cellar are groaning with canned stuff. Altogether it's been a good year.

"[My] morale on the whole is good, I suspect because this is the month I've fixed to see the end of this rather unsatisfactory epoch in my own life.

Not that I don't expect to return, but unless it's on an entirely different basis, my trip to Philadelphia will have been in vain.

"The children just rushed in like the Assyrian coming down[83] and concentration is at an end. I've been greatly reassured to see how much more smoothly the school machinery is working this year. The early morning rush is not nearly so hectic, the children remember to brush their teeth and put on their rubbers [galoshes], and there's no more fuss about coming home alone through the woods. This eases my mind a good deal as I didn't see who, in my absence, was going to get them into all the innumerable garments required and out of the house by 7.30—not to speak of hunting out dry things every other day. It looks as though they will be able to manage a good deal for themselves.

"This Peace Chest business interests me. As I don't know where Martha is at the moment, do you think you could pick up your telephone and ask her to write and tell me whatever she knows about it, including (especially) her personal not-for-publication opinion? Two things I need to know without fail—first, is it full-time, because I don't think I can give much more than half time to anything for a start; second, is the Peace Chest in the fight against peacetime conscription, because that's where I somehow or other intend to be this winter. Working out publicity is a thing I am pretty good at, but talks I feel would not do so well, on account of my being an alien and this strictly a domestic matter. Or don't you think?

"Time to start the supper cooking. I hope there are steaks in Philadelphia, I am all set to go carnivorous after a summer living entirely off the produce of the garden. You'll be hearing from me."

Mrs. John H. Arnett, secretary of the United Peace Chest, wrote to Norma at length on October 20, describing the work the organization was engaged in and inviting her to join them as the "field director, as they felt she was well qualified for the position."

Piers: Norma worked there for years, and it was my impression that it was ideal for her. As for me, one afternoon I waited in the Peace Chest office while she wrapped up her day's work. There was an old magazine lying around which I started reading. It was *ASTOUNDING SCIENCE FICTION*, a magazine of stories. It changed my life, literally. It introduced me to the science fiction genre, part of what is now known as Speculative Fiction, embracing science fiction, fantasy, and horror. In due course I

---

83. "The Destruction of Sennacherib," by Lord Byron: "The Assyrian came down like the wolf on the fold / And his cohorts were gleaming in purple and gold / And the sheen of their spears was like stars on the sea / When the blue wave rolls nightly on deep Galilee."

became a highly successful science fiction and fantasy writer, using the name Piers Anthony. The Peace Chest was peripheral, but that may have been how my literary career started.

Norma wrote to Family on October 24:

"You'll be pleased to know that the birthday books [for Teresa's 9th] arrived in the nick of time, on the evening of the 21st. [They] were received on Sunday morning with loud acclimations. The party was to be held on the 23rd—a joint celebration of all the birthdays this month, including Norm's twenty-first, which was on the 11th. I baked two cakes and Norm's mother also sent one, so we had a real feast.

"Your letter describing the new baby arrived in record time—about two weeks. I see Rowena has achieved what always used to be my ambition, to have a dark-haired child. I now wait eagerly to hear its name [Susanna] and other particulars. I finally finished knitting another coat and pair of socks, but they got so dirty being worked on in the intervals of weeding the garden that I had to give them a very vigorous washing and their pristine beauty is a good deal impaired. Keep letting me know if anything special is needed which you can't get. A friend's son recently wrote from England saying he couldn't buy any laundry soap, but I suppose babies have priority on this kind of thing. I'm so glad to hear the blanket arrived and was satisfactory, and must let Valerie know.

"Wednesday. I didn't get very far after all. The children came in from school and I had to go out and pick spinach for supper before it was too dark to distinguish it from grass. The final burst of harvesting is now in progress; I have promised myself to have everything in by the end of the month, and it looks as though we shall manage it except for a few turnips, which are really Alfred's responsibility. We harvested altogether over a ton of potatoes and the garden did exceptionally well, which gratified me considerably, as it was my first serious attempt at vegetable gardening. I didn't do all the work, of course, but I planned and planted the garden and took my share of the weeding, and most of the harvesting has fallen to me. Our cellar is full of food of all kinds, all home produced—hundreds of jars of tomatoes, greens and fruit, bins full of carrots and potatoes, dried beans, cheeses and so on. All very gratifying and reassuring, particularly when we remember that we had almost nothing ready this time last year.

"For the past two days everyone has been saying it was going to snow. We scoff at the idea, but some nasty-looking clouds have suddenly rolled up. I think I'd better go and get my cabbages in before it is too late; if they get thoroughly wet with snow they will be difficult to dry out for storage. I also have sunflowers to get in. They are eight feet tall and proportionally tough, and cutting off the heads is a major problem.

1944

"I finally managed to secure just one film for our smaller camera, and have been using it with extra care. It will be just my luck if the carefully selected pictures are all failures. One exposure is saved in case something comes along that I don't want to miss, but we'll use that up soon anyway and have the roll developed. You may hope for pictures in a week or two, anyway, with reasonable luck.

"The children are hard at work preparing a play to be given at the school for Halloween, which is quite a celebration in these parts. There are only five children in the school this year [three valley boys and Piers and Teresa] so their choice is somewhat limited, but they are putting enough energy into it for a dozen. The subject-matter and everything about the play is strictly secret, but the title is 'The Haunted House'. The Arthur Ransome[84] book, by the way, is wonderful—I am reading it myself with keen enjoyment. I see there's a whole series, and this should solve the birthday-present problem for some time to come."

On October 25, Norma wrote to the Rev. H. T. Sutton:

"We have no printed matter describing our project; we do put out a hectographed or mimeographed news-letter from time to time, and I will put your name on the mailing list. But this project is far too small for any large-scale publicity. We are still feeling our way and have changed our plans too many times already to want the embarrassment of being tied down to a definite program which might need revision in the light of experience. At present we are two families, six people in all, living co-operatively and trying to get our whole livelihood from the land. Our immediate objectives, which take up most of our energy, are to try and produce almost all our own food and to sell enough forest byproducts (cordwood and lumber) to meet our very small needs for cash. We are anxious to have others join us, but many have felt that what we were trying to do was too extreme and that living conditions were too hard, so we urge no one to even think of coming to join us without making an exploratory visit first. We need more living accommodation, and in order to find time for building we should need to be able to count on more man-power than is available at present, so that it's really a question of asking people to come and build their own houses. Guests, however, we always manage to squeeze in somewhere, provided they don't mind the discomforts of over-crowding.

"We have several hundred acres of land, most of it wooded, and the forest provides us with a guaranteed source of income, as the demand for

---

84. Arthur Michell Ransome was an English author and journalist. He is best known for writing the Swallows and Amazons series of children's books about the school-holiday adventures of children, mostly in the Lake District and the Norfolk Broads (Wikipedia).

wood locally is always ahead of the supply. This means that we can offer any single man a chance to earn a living at a modest rate provided he can learn to use an axe and a cross-cut saw. As for agriculture, we have done nothing as yet beyond producing our own food; we are much interested in soil conservation and building up fertility, but have not been able to do very much in that direction as yet. Apart from pasture and hayland we have only a little less than an acre under cultivation. We are not contemplating growing anything for the market, as we are very isolated and transportation is already a serious problem.

"Will you let us know what your special interests are, if you feel you would like any more information? It is always hard to know just what people need to know.

"PS—I will see that you also get a copy of the New England Newsletter. We hold informal conferences from time to time and if you could come to one of these you would meet a number of people in the community movement and perhaps learn of some project which would meet your requirements. Theoretically we are confined to New England, but I have always felt that northern New York might be included."

November 1944

There are no records from Hilltop in November, as Norma had left by then and no daily journal was kept.

December 1944

Norma wrote to an unnamed person, evidently a longtime friend [Molly?] in England, December 12, from Philadelphia:

"This letter has waited six months to be finished. Things boiled up and first I couldn't write because I was in such a state of mental distress that I couldn't do anything but purely mechanical jobs, and hardly even them; and then when it got settled I didn't want to write to you because I couldn't do it without telling you what happened, and I have been at considerable trouble not to let my parents know (not wanting to distress them unnecessarily), and if you should meet them you would be in such a difficult position. But I thought of you very often."

She went on at length about her new job in Philadelphia and the race issues she encountered and a new friend, Lee, a psychologist, with whom she felt a close connection.

1944

"I went up to Hilltop last month and found everything going splendidly. Alfred is making an excellent job of looking after the children, and I think it is good for both him and them (I never would have left them if the doctor hadn't said he thought it would turn out to be a good thing all around, and he was right). We have a friend in the village, a very sensible person, who watches to see how things go, and next week they're all coming down for the Christmas holidays. We're going to have a wonderful time—new clothes for the children, free movies (educational!), family parties, friend— we had so few friends at Hilltop, but the wonderful thing about Lee is that she is going to be just as good for Alfred as she has been for me. She has a way of handling an unhappy or mixed-up person which works miracles.

"And they will enjoy the Brudercoop (that's the name of the house) and learn, I hope, of simple, co-operative, cheap living that still has graciousness and a minimum of concern for the needs of the body. We have been flagellating ourselves up there. It's got to stop, and I think I am getting ready to be able to stop it." (*Piers:* The Brudercoop, which I take to mean Brother Co-op, was another fun place, useful to stay at temporarily. I remember our trip to Philadelphia with pleasure. Part of the trip I rode with Natalie Field, and remember she hit 80 miles an hour at some point: she was an urgent driver. That Christmas was fabulous, a dream come true. A few years later I stayed briefly at the Brudercoop myself.)

Alfred wrote to Edward Rapp on December 25 from the Brudercoop, marking the return address "as from Hilltop Farm":

"It's always nice to hear again from old friends and know they are still, so to speak, cultivating the same garden. What can I have said to imply we weren't expanding the community idea just then? What I did no doubt say was that our physical expansion was somewhat constrained by an extreme shortage of housing room. We do however very much welcome [you] even if it isn't exactly the line you were trained for. We none of us are in the work we are trained for anyway.

"We are not farming so much as we are seeking the proper means of self-maintenance. This seems to mean retaining a large proportion of what we produce, rather than attempting to sell it. No one ought to belittle the need for hard cash no matter how you live in modern civilization; but we have found people who are willing to come in on a potentially permanent basis, think in terms of building themselves a house, and don't mind the inconveniences of sharing what accommodation there is in the meantime. Right now we still have the one farmhouse which holds two families; there are plans for building this coming year; that is, one of our families is longing to build for itself on nearby land, meanwhile continuing to share the communal garden, fields, animals & equipment.

"We rather hope to find what degree of independence & what degree of communality is most appropriate to the needs of those involved; obviously complete identity in all spheres of living is not the thing, nor is the other extreme, complete individuality. But it is true that the more you share—one woodpile, one barn, one main garden, one tax bill—the more efficient is your living at the material level.

"As we have gone on, we found that this need can be reduced in many interesting ways, one of which is by adapting ourselves to other modes of doing some things so that no exchange of cash is necessary. Self-adaptation is important. It is in many ways a new way of life, and so of course you have to surrender some parts of the old. Some of what is surrendered is amenable, and we would prefer to conserve it; but we remind ourselves of the many compensations and advantages we enjoy in other directions, not the least of which is the conviction of living according to some social principles, rather than entirely on a basis of individual self-interest.

"In a way we have plenty of room—we do not use nearly all the house; though to you (who knows) it might seem cramped. The only way is to experience what is here. We would welcome a visit long enough to test us out & hash over our experiences to date. Many people I think have been made extremely critical of our way of living by brief impressions they have had of it; but some return to visit again and again, and this makes us think we are not wholly mistaken. Each person, each family, has to try out its own ideas, and the question is whether you might try out yours in basic cooperation with us. That would be welcome.

"We want to encourage you, and everyone interested, to try to find out & indulge to the full in the advantages of rural living and working; and in principle the Hilltop property & equipment is at the disposal of the pacifist movement for all appropriate uses along these lines. It is not private property, but available property. You might have quite different needs and ideas from ours, but you would still be welcome to make any use of the property which suited your needs and fell within the general sphere of pacifist land settlement. There can be no one mode of life which is right for everyone on the land; but if there were, it would only be discovered by experimenting in hundreds of ways at the start; and we feel that such experimentation is to be encouraged.

"We think ours is a good area. Consciously and unconsciously, families seem to have gathered within walking distance [in Vermont, walking distance meant several miles] who, as they come to know each other, may develop very interesting capabilities for common action. The teacher of the local one room school, who is one of our colleagues, will not continue to teach next year. Are you interested? It's no easy task, yet in some ways it is a worthwhile one.

1944

"So please let me know, here at 'The Brudercoop,' what you think the next step to be, & I shall try to follow it out."

1945

*Even if we should establish what looks like a secure and happy
family life in this house, it would have a canker at the heart.
People who talk as we talked in 1941 are either pioneers
or escapists; only time could show which,
and I'm afraid time has shown.*

January 1945

NORMA WROTE TO FAMILY ON JANUARY 9, from Philadelphia, describing in detail the Christmas holiday the family had enjoyed there:

"The children have had a wonderful time, eating all the exciting and frivolous foods not available on the farm. Teresa, for instance, had a secret dream that she wanted to eat six ice cream [sundaes], so Alfred bought her three for a start and lined them up in front of her on the counter, but she gave up in the middle of the second!

"At the Brudercoop the amounts of dry cereals, like corn flakes and shredded wheat, that they have consumed have brought horror to me and some amusement to the others. I'm afraid we have made serious inroads upon their sugar ration, but we fortunately had a couple of extra sugar coupons to contribute."

She went on to mention their visits to the natural history museum, the Planetarium, and the zoo, and described the residents and way of life at the Brudercoop, where there were individuals from other backgrounds and races.

She continued: "The holiday was partly damped down by the fact that Piers spent four days in the hospital. We determined to get to the bottom of the bed-wetting trouble if we possibly could and they kept him under observation and took several X-ray pictures to see if any abnormal condition could be causing it. They concluded that the child's trouble was psychological in origin, which of course we had expected all along. As you know, he is extremely highly strung and sensitive and easily upset by things other children would take in their stride, and he is apt to get nightmares and be afraid of things under the bed and so on. It's the penalty, I think (for the parents) of having an exceptional child. Piers has a well-balanced personality [and] I think will be a real contribution to society."

1945

On the 13th Norma wrote to Dear Friends:

"To return to Dick [Mitchell, Polly's boyfriend], I like him, but I'm sorry to hear, through indirect channels, that he is engaged to a girl who lives in Philadelphia. This isn't Polly, because he told me himself that Polly was in Virginia. We haven't heard from her in some time but now [that] we know where she is, we're planning to send her the money for the bicycle. We did think of taking her on as extra office help, but it was decided that we must have a man.

"Alfred is reading the Bible aloud at mealtimes [Alfred always enjoyed reading aloud material that he believed would educate or enlighten the listeners] and of course came the day when the children wanted to know what adultery was. He told them that, roughly speaking, it was living with people you weren't married to, or words to that effect. Piers at once said 'Scott and Helen.' Teresa said, 'Norm and Winnie, before they were married.' We aren't altogether sure we made the distinction clear!"

On January 15 Teresa [age 9] wrote to Norma:

"We are back at school again! We had to tramp down the path a lot with snowshoes for 2 days, but now I am going to tell you our trip! First when you saw us off, we sat on the bus for a long time, and pretty soon we came to the end of the city and I said Norma is somewhere out there. (I felt sort of sad.) And then pretty soon about 15 or 20 miles on, the bus broke down and the driver told funny stories while we were waiting for another bus to come and take us there. Once he took a packet of cigarettes out of his pocket and went ½ way up the aisle saying cigarettes, candy! Although he only had cigarettes! And the bus came and the driver on that bus found out what was wrong and we fixed it. Then we were on our way again. Then we came to New York. We went to the Grey Hound bus house, and we found out that the next bus that was going where we wanted left at 5:30! so we went to Grand Central and had some breakfast. Alfred bought some comics to read on the train. Piers and I had a rest before the train came. When it came we found out it had rather hard seats so we couldn't go to sleep very well but in the end we went to sleep. Then we had to change in Springfield to the Brattleboro train. We got there at 11:00 A.M. but we had to wait till 3:00 for the bus. We got nearly to Jamaica and we had to turn back to get some school kids. Well we finally got to Jamaica and I went in to get the mail, then we went up to miss Miriam's and we found out that Grandfather's oranges had come. We are eating them now. Well good-bye sweet mimi! I have to get donte [?] KISS KISS KISS KISS KISS KISS KISS KISS KISS Hug Hug Hug Hug Hug Hug Hug Hug Hug Hug HUG KISS With all that I am Your daughter.

"P.S. I have not wright very well."

Letter from Piers to Norma dated January 27:

"I am sorry I haven't wrote to you sooner, but I just couldn't find time.

"On the other paper is a dream I wrote at school. I hope you like it. I forgot to put in all of it, but I hope you will see what it is about.

"Winnie is making cookies out of some left over bread batter. Alfred has just finished pouring some black strap [molasses] into some jars. Teresa is eating a grape fruit she should have eaten last Friday. Now I must sharpen my pensul so good by for the moment. There, I have sharpened my pensul, wich is a red one and can write much better.

"This is the week after the middle of the school year. I wish school was over, because both I an Teresa just hate going past the lumber camp. There is a dog there called Sandy, and he most always barks at us and acks as though he is going to bite us. Last Friday he did make Teresa's leg bleed a little, but it had stopped bleeding when she looked at it. We are very glad when he stays in his house.

"Alfred has written to a lady in New York about my wet beds, and is wating for an ansur. I hope she can do something about it.

"Pleas tell every body at the Bruder coop that I liked it there very much."

Piers: my spelling and syntax were evidently works in progress at that time. The lumber camp was not the original Lumbercamp Corner referred to in these records; it was a temporary camp set up on our route to school, and the folk there were okay, apart from the obnoxious dog who did nip us on occasion. Barking dogs *do* bite.

In due course Alfred did take me to see the lady, Mrs. West, who explained to me how some things like electricity you can't see but they do have power. I never believed in God or the supernatural, but I appreciated the way she clarified her belief. She also bought me a child's book with puzzle pages that was about the best such book I remember from my childhood: I spent many delightful hours on them. So while I was a skeptic on their belief in God, I did appreciate my father's effort to help me: it showed that he cared, and that knowledge contributed to my slow recovery from, yes, the bed wetting and other personal complications. I loved every part of the trip.

February 1945

Mother-in-law Caroline, in her characteristically kind and thoughtful way, wrote to Norma from their winter home in St. Petersburg, Florida, revealing how deeply they were concerned about Alfred, and his family:

1945

"I had thee on my mind for a letter; the very intriguing books on 'Herbs' had arrived and never been acknowledged, nor thanks expressed which I really felt strongly; then just now came thy long letter.

"From thy letter I gather that thee and Alfred may even now be together in New York, and perhaps some uncertainties may be cleared up by now, though it's equally possible that more may have appeared. Certainly the draft situation has not cleared up, nor do I see any light on it. We have thought about it a good deal and wondered how it would affect Alfred and Philip, as well as Eddie's business. It seems to me probable that they will let well enough alone, knowing that there is no possibility of using Alfred in any way for the benefit of the war, and realizing he might as well be allowed to produce a little food and cord wood as be sent to prison or into C.P.S. of some sort.

"I wish I had some light on the kind of work which would appeal to Alfred and which would take him away from the present type of life on Hill Top. The only pattern I can see is for thee to have some kind of a job where thee could make some kind of a 'home' for thyself and children (apartment or preferably cottage with land attached), in which there would also be a possible chance for work for Alfred, and would hence serve as a lure to remove him from Hill Top.

"I'm just thinking on paper without having come to any conclusions: thee might find a small farm or suburban place near Philadelphia, keep on thy present job for another year, put Piers under treatment from thy doctor or someone else, and send them both back to Media school, have for Alfred some 'bio-dynamic farming' on a small scale and some translating and tutoring perhaps in connection with A.F.S.C. workers. Or he might have some work with this 'School for Living' group which would take him out a good deal, but he would have a home base. Some arrangement might be made by which Hill Top turned temporarily into a summer proposition.

"The same sort of pattern might be set up with some other job at some other place, such as a school like Manumit, or a farm like the Fellowship Farm or any kind of place where you would be furthering a cause you believe in, but where you could have some kind of a home where thee had some kind of a job and where there would be a pull for Alfred to join you and a place into which he could fit. If there is no home center, it seems to me it will be more and more easy for Alfred to drift more and more into solitude.

"I've tried to think how it would work to have the children in another home, but it seems to me that would tend to increase Piers' insecurity and anxiety. In many ways I would really love having them, but we are too old, and don't have a settled all year round home ourselves. Francis and Evelyn [Nicholson—Caroline's younger brother and his wife] might take them, with thee nearby in Philadelphia to keep in close touch, and with us to visit frequently, and Westtown School nearby. Evelyn is anxious to have companionship for her little Joan and I think Piers especially might have things in common with Joan, but it would be another home to adjust to, and Francis and Evelyn as two very practical 'extroverts' would be so different from thee and Alfred that all sorts of differences might arise."

Piers: I find this reference startling. Joan was my age, and we were in schools together for six years, but we had little in common. She was a militant girl who became the outstanding female athlete of our class at Westtown School and went on to pursue her objectives so vigorously as an adult that she spent time in prison. I believe her group raided an FBI office and distributed formerly secret papers from it to the newspapers. I was essentially nothing in those years, and retain a certain admiration for her spunk.

Caroline continued: "I think that Eddie and Dorothy would be glad to have Piers but wouldn't be able to take two children, and then what would happen to Teresa? Also the possibilities of 'differences' in education and attitudes and everything else would be even greater, I fear. [*Piers:* That's another surprising but significant connection. Their son, Teddy, was my closest cousin, a year my junior, attending the same school, but he got leukemia and died at age 15. I became quite close to their family and to his little sister, Dotsy, in a manner filling in for her lost brother. But I felt survivor's guilt: It seemed to me that if fate found it necessary to take one of us out, I should have been the one, not Teddy.]

"Altogether my thinking on paper doesn't seem to be getting me anywhere, and I wish it would! Somehow in the last six years my affections seem to have got very much tied up with Jacobs of all ages, sizes, shapes and colors! I'd like to see Alfred in the place where his best gifts could flourish; I'd like to see Piers freed from his anxieties; and thee being able to have a family and still expanding in the kind of work and community that thee loves . . . nor is your family the only one with needs and problems that I'd like to help solve!

"It does seem to me that Piers ought to have some special attention, and somehow I imagine he may suffer most from thy being away. It seems to me that a boy especially needs a 'mother' in his early life, while a girl is more affected by the absence or the ill-adjustments of a father. Thee might arrange for him to come down a while this spring. We would be at home then, and could have him mostly with us, in fact we could have you both with us so that he could see more of thee, even though thee was commuting to thy job on the trolley every day.

"Teresa might be all right for a few weeks up there without Piers. Of course this might affect schooling too much, and perhaps would have to be postponed until after school, and by that time perhaps thee would be returning anyhow. But two or three weeks at the time of spring vacation might do no harm. However, we won't be back until toward the end of April."

Piers: Norma was not very motherly in person—reviewing her letters three quarters of a century later made me surprised to see how much she had been trying to do for me: I simply hadn't known. I still longed to wake up and discover that the entire Spanish and American experience was all a bad dream, and that I was safely back with the English nanny, who was closer (in her manner) to being a real mother figure.

March 1945

Norma wrote to an unnamed person on March 2:
"It's less than a week since your letter came. It reached me during a brief visit to Hilltop in which I was plunged into the depths of despair because everything seemed so hopeless and I felt like a stranger in my own home, in fact I didn't feel as though I had a home at all. I've been away four months and shall probably be away a couple of months more before I get wound up with this job (this is my office address by the way). I simply must be back at Hilltop by early May in time to take charge of the cow and the garden.

"As I say, I was suffering from horrible despair and came back here on Monday in a fit of blackness such as even I have seldom equaled. Tuesday night (I was still feeling pretty bad), I was just walking through the hall at the Brudercoop when the front door opened and there was Alfred! I don't see quite how I can convey the effect of his having suddenly decided to follow me more than three hundred miles, only a day after I'd left, and after he himself had been away from home over two weeks. It was quite a startling step for him to take, and symbolical of a complete change of mind on his part.

"I really think we'll be able to pull together from now on. He only stayed 3½ hours but we made all sorts of new plans and feel like a honeymoon couple. The only sad part is that now I've acquired a real taste for city life and several new friends I hate to lose, and I'm going to find it harder than ever to bear being buried in the country! I think I was designed by nature to work in an office and live in a flat. I like hot water to come out of taps instead of kettles, I like radio and a good road with a bus passing the door and a grocer on the corner and a public library and the letters delivered three times a day [as they were in England!]. No, probably I would forgo all those things to live in the English countryside, Somerset for instance, but here the country is too vast and terrifying.

"I wonder if you've read a fascinating book called *The Peckham Experiment*.[85] We ordered a copy from England, and it's now going the rounds. I think that helped a great deal to produce Alfred's change of heart, and I know it had lots to do with the other thing that has lifted the burden off me—the fact that the Williamses have decided they want an independent home right away. [The book] lays great stress on a) the family as the natural unit in society, [and] b) the necessity of allowing the family to function as much [as possible] in a suitable social environment.

"I don't believe you are getting colorless—you don't sound like it. I think you are going to find when the children are bigger that you still have all your old interests and capacities. That's what I found to an astonishing extent when I came here. I thought I'd become the complete drudge, and instead I am able to keep my end up in any conversation, and choose clothes that suit me, cook reasonably good meals, read intelligent books and thoroughly enjoy classical concerts and Shakespeare."

Piers wrote again to Norma on March 17:

"I liked all your letters very much. They are very cheering up.

"Spring is coming here too. All reddy there is grass growing. But still you can go up to your wast in snow. That sounds rather funny, doesn't it? But its trou.

"All I could read from your last letter was 'I hope you can read my writing'. That's what I want to say about my writing.

"Love to all the Brudercoop."

On March 28, Norma wrote to Judy Bacon, Bert's mother:

"Don't take any notice of Alfred—he always says the wrong thing, especially to ladies! And then he wonders why they get upset. I guess he just wrote a postcard because he knew I would write a letter. He certainly thinks it's a fine idea for you to come, anyway for the summer (we aren't making positive plans beyond that, even for ourselves—so many things may happen, this Work-or-Fight Bill [the question of whether the Selective Service draft could be used for nonmilitary workforce purposes], for instance, may change the whole picture at any moment.)

---

85. Innes H. Pearse and Lucy H. Crocker, *The Peckham Experiment: A Study of the Living Structure of Society* (1943). The experiment was designed to determine whether people as a whole would, given the opportunity, take a vested interest in their own health and fitness and expend effort to maintain it (Wikipedia).

1945

Piers: In my biography of Alfred (Xlibris Corporation, 2007) I conjectured that he suffered from undiagnosed Asperger's syndrome, a mild form of autism that became more evident as he grew older. It is characterized in part by low empathy. He thought that empathy was a fantasy others had; he did not acknowledge its existence, and was upset when I or others argued the case. This seeming insensitivity to the concerns of women or, indeed, of children or strangers or animals, may be evidence of that, part of the larger syndrome. He simply was unable to put himself in their emotional place, and so was prone to misstepping, no malice intended.

Norma continued: "I don't know about this Selective Service business, but I do know that about 2 weeks ago we heard all transfers were suspended and since then two of our friends have got transfers to the East from California. One of them has actually arrived, the other is expected next week. So if that is what you have been hearing about, I don't think it is very likely to interfere with Fran's transfer. But it isn't quite clear just how you feel that might affect your personal plans.

"Your ideas on food, I think, are running pretty well parallel to ours. We did relatively less canning last year and concentrated more on root vegetables for cellar storage and string beans, which were brined. We also dried quite a bit of corn in the fine new drier Norm built, but unfortunately it was built to fit on the stove we had while you were with us, and we sold that to Miriam Fredenthal and put in another which is more efficient but a different shape, so the drier no longer fitted. It works nicely in the sun provided the stuff ripens early enough, but towards the end of the summer, sun heat wasn't sufficient.

"I do think we can have a pretty good and varied diet based pretty largely on things that can be stored without canning, which after all is a fairly modern invention. Alfred is considering ways to hitch the grinder to the 5 HP motor from the log saw; as you know, I've always thought it was a fine idea to grind our own flour but I didn't feel hand grinding was satisfactory. Maybe now we can have it all fine and beautiful as Mildred Loomis has it, with satisfaction and better health to all.

"I do feel strongly that the basis of the diet should be lots of MILK and we should either make or buy sufficient hay to keep the cow over the winter and not have to board her out, even though she is a tie and it's been very helpful that everybody was able to be away, for instance over Christmas.

"The local community is becoming a lot more interesting—new people moving into the village and others who've been there before and whom we are just beginning to get to know. We're thinking hard about how we can improve our local communications; I'm bound to say almost the only practical means seems to be a horse. Did you get any echo of the more or less nation-wide excitement about the Pikes Falls mail route? The Govt. decided to do away with it on the grounds there weren't enough people and it didn't pay, apparently thinking that if they got away with it they would quietly drop other mail routes all over Vermont—but unfortunately for them they didn't pick on a community of semi-literate farmers, but one which contained Scott and Helen, the Fields, the McGurdys and several other people willing and able to get up and speak for themselves.

"It was reported in the *N.Y. Times*, and Plumley made a speech in Congress, and finally they agreed to restore the mail route, but now Scott is practically demanding a Congressional investigation and insisting that at the very least they should pay the mailman for the weeks he was wrongfully laid off! I guess they are wishing they hadn't thought of it, and it's been a wonderful thing for healing local feuds and bringing everyone together in protest. Mass meetings and all kinds of things.

"Did I tell you we had a prospect of about 9 children this summer? That will include three or possibly four colored children from New York, two daughters of a friend of mine here in Philadelphia, and a boy from Jamaica whose father wants him to stay with us instead of going to summer camp. It will be pretty lively, I think. A couple of other people connected with the office I work in are also thinking of spending part of the summer in or near Jamaica, so that ought to brighten life up quite a lot."

April 1945

Alfred wrote to Lowell Naeve, he of the sod house, answering Lowell's letter of the 6th:

"I'm very glad to hear from you and be able to write. Many people who come here ask about you, and your house is one of our show places, tending to lean now, though. [*Piers:* Yes, it slowly leaned, and a tree grew out of its roof, but it lasted for years, demonstrating that stone, brick, or wood were not essential to building a house, though I think there were some supportive planks. *Teresa*: In 2018 Lowell's house had crumbled into a low, grass-covered mound in a swampy field.]

"We are not at all sure about returning to England. But one of our main purposes in getting so much land was to protect it from the slaughtering of the lumber companies. If we should leave, it would probably be placed under the administration of a trust, or of the rural cooperative Communities Council, or some such body. In any case, if you wished, we would always be glad to mark out your corner and deed it to you—always with the proviso that it should not afterwards be sold into the commercial market. This land is intended for use as homesteading and rural settlement only, as long as we have jurisdiction over it.

"We are entering our 5th year, after a good winter of abundant home grown produce, plenty of heat and a good deal of regular activity. Last winter was the second one we worked regularly chopping through the winter; and now that we have disposed of all the stock except a cow in the summer & a goat all year, we have more time to devote to the main tasks. Norm and Winnie Williams have been with us since June 1943, and this year expect to start homesteading for themselves nearby.

"Scott has published two books recently, and two more are promised, after 12 years without a publisher. He also lectures more, but without neglecting his means of support. Herbert has been around, sugaring with the Fields, after wintering in an orchard in New Jersey. With his help, and Norm's, Harold built his sugar house over the winter in time to use it this spring; but there was a very poor season—it got warm much too early. We are about a month ahead in our apple blossom.

"Arthur Moore has asked about you. He is still teaching at Adelphi College, but I understand they have not renewed his contract for next year and he is looking for a new opportunity. With stimulation from him, I have come into a school of religious thought which has met my need during the past year, and which it would be good to discuss with you—though it seems that the more we talk about some things the less we live them. I have been devoting the early mornings to study—from 4 to 8—which is uninterrupted and very satisfactory. I do it in a little building in the woods behind the shack, where we also keep the tools.

"The blueberries have never been so abundant as the year you were here; but our apples have done us very well—not your tree, however.

"I'll get the Johnsons' address and send it to you. They have a kiln of their own. Perhaps if you let us know the name of one of your regular correspondents, we could give him any news that would interest you. Naturally we hope you will come here again when you get out, for as long as you like." (*Piers:* I believe Lowell had written from prison as a conscientious objector, a common fate for folk of conscience.)

Norma, back at Hilltop, wrote to Friends [at the Peace Chest office], April 25:

"I have just finished milking and tidied the kitchen, and now I notice it is just past nine. I mustn't think about [our office routines] too much or I shall burst into tears! It's raining today, the country looks its very worst, and the prospect of Chestnut Street is terribly attractive in retrospect. Only a few trees have leaves on them yet, and the apple blossom isn't out, though we have one cherry tree in flower. But there are asparagus and rhubarb ready to eat in a day or two.

"Everybody is well and active. The children get themselves ready and go off to school without a murmur—their clothes are literally in rags, but that's the usual thing in the village school and I think it makes them less conspicuous! I hope we can soon put the winter clothes away for good. Alfred and I finished papering the kitchen yesterday and it really looks beautiful, all white and red. Arthur [Zeben, who was mentally unstable] is painting some of the furniture—he seems in very good form too.

"The Williamses have almost finished making over a chicken house to live in, with an outdoor fireplace—it really looks nice, and much cozier than I supposed possible! We think we'll fix up the other chicken house to make a guest house, and any of you of course will be welcome. Please, someone write and tell me all the news—you know I'll want to know when you get to $16,000 and all sorts of things like that —especially gossip! One of these fine days I'll get so homesick I shall leap on a bus and appear suddenly one morning. Meanwhile I miss you all very much; I can't possibly tell you how much the goodwill and understanding of all of you helped at a very difficult time, but I hope the recording angel has it credited to you at its full value."

Then to the Brudercoop:

"I'd like to write you a long, chatty letter, but it is sheer torture using Alfred's machine. Mine is down at Miriam's in the village, and though I am planning to go down this afternoon there are several more urgent things that will have to be carried up first. Also it is raining, and I don't feel particularly gay. Everyone about here (even the children) is so sensible and works so hard all the time!

"I have not had an opportunity yet to see Scott about the cabin, but maybe I'll walk over there this next weekend. I ought not to be writing letters just now, I remember I should be getting bread to rise, but I want at least a brief note to go off to you this afternoon. The spring is really hardly beginning here, though it's an extra early year. About half the trees are in leaf but there's a long way to go yet. The asparagus can be cut in a few days and I'm planning on fresh rhubarb for supper tonight. You don't know what that means to us—in April!

"Piers planted an early garden in which a number of things are coming up, but every so often the cow gets in and walks on it, which has a rather negative effect. However, she is providing about fourteen quarts of milk a day, so I suppose we ought not to grudge her a few baby radishes, provided she leaves some for us. Two quarts per person per day is quite an allocation and theoretically we ought not to need very much else, but in practice the men still seem to consume potatoes in the accustomed quantities. It will take me some time to re-adjust to their appetites! Last night I made some vegetable soup which was really pretty good, but it went practically nowhere towards filling them up. Fortunately the men aren't chopping in the woods at present so they don't have their maximum capacity right now. Norm is hard at work building a fireplace outside the chicken house which they are making into a summer home. The rest of us are getting the garden ready and also doing some work on the house. You ought to see our kitchen now, all papered and painted in red and white. Everything all modern except the floor and a few places around the sink, which are scheduled to be fixed as soon as the materials arrive.

"A. [as they customarily referred to Arthur Zeben] is painting a small cupboard which has been an eyesore ever since Valerie bought it at an auction in June 1941. When it's all done, no one will believe how it looked before. I wish I could make a water-tight excuse to come down at the time of the Bach festival at the end of May, but it's much too soon.

"Alfred wants the machine now, and I don't know that I can bear it anymore anyway. Please, somebody write to me soon!"

Then Alfred wrote again to Lowell Naeve:

"Norm Williams is expecting to build a stone house not far away this summer too—beginning this summer—so you will be able to profit by any mistakes he makes. We very much like the idea of gathering more people into this hill and valley, and in your case we just assume anyway that you belong to the particular area you chose, which is always referred to as Lowell's Field. [*Piers:* It was a very nice section, with fields and trees and stone walls. I was fascinated by Lowell's project and went over there so often that I was told to stay away, which was hard for me to do. In long retrospect I regret being a pest.]

"That whole field, in between all the walls, is, I think, supposed to be eight acres, and includes a good proportion of woods. According to your description, you would want a deed for only about half of it. Actually, if you took the whole field, its boundaries on two sides would be outside boundaries, so to speak—former lines of former properties. The boundaries you want would have to be marked in some way in order to be described, and the wording of the deed would then be:...."

There followed a legalistic statement formally deeding that section to Lowell Naeve "for the sum of one dollar and other valuable considerations."

On April 26, Norma wrote to Family:

"I have to plead guilty to having been a bad correspondent of late. I certainly am not becoming an American, in fact I get more and more homesick with every month that passes; but this has been a time of unsettlement, not propitious for letter-writing.

"I don't want to burden you with my relatively minor troubles when you have so many major ones of your own. Several changes have happened recently, though. For one thing, the Williamses have decided to set up separate housekeeping, and yesterday they moved into one of our former chicken-houses which they have been making over into quite a pleasant little cottage. They were fine fellow-workers but we never were really congenial, and I think we shall get on much better at a slight distance. The principal difficulty from my point of view was that they reinforced just those tendencies of Alfred's which I found it hardest to deal with, especially his extreme asceticism. On points connected with the amenities—even the necessities of daily living, I was constantly in a minority of one.

"Another very helpful development is that I think Alfred is now [not?] set on remaining here. I could see this place as valuable interim experience, but it becomes less and less satisfying as possibilities open up again for the kind of work in which I am really interested. Ultimately, I want to get back into the field of European reconstruction, where the experience we've been acquiring here should be very valuable. But it can't be right away, since I think the children [ages 9 and 10] have the right to be with their parents for a year or two more at any rate. What I want is to feel that we are moving in that direction and preparing ourselves as adequately as possible, which might mean moving on from here, and I now think Alfred is more open to the idea, though I don't expect anything will happen at all soon.

"Meanwhile I feel the need for more outward activity; I have traveled around a good deal more this past winter, made new friends, and so on. And I intend seriously to do some writing—starting perhaps with a pamphlet on race relations which someone in Philadelphia wants to publish.

"As for the place here, we are already hard at work fixing it up for the summer. The kitchen is all papered and painted and Alfred is installing laundry tubs and a hot water system. Then we have plans for upstairs too—the bedrooms were redecorated, very hastily, two years ago, and it all needs doing again. This should make it easier either to stay or to find someone else who would want the place as a home. It's the ideal setting for a young family with the right tastes and talents, but I am not the person who belongs here as a permanent thing. For the summer it is fine, and allows us the chance to offer hospitality to our city friends who need a holiday in the country, and several such are in prospect for this year. But I wish some people would come along who would want to take over the whole thing and build on the foundation we have laid. It might happen—but most such people are in jail or in work camps, and likely to remain there for the duration. At present another man [Arthur Zeben] is here, discharged from the Army for bad eyesight. He is a scholar and good company.

"No, we've seen nothing of Polly for a year now. She planned to spend the winter here and sent a huge trunk, which was a nuisance to get up the hill and a worse nuisance to store. Then she wrote she'd decided instead to settle in New York and study singing. No more news came, and when I was

1945

in New York I looked for her in vain. Her friends didn't know where she had gone. I am rather uneasy about her.

"Spring is early this year, but still that isn't saying much. A good many of the trees have small leaves, but we are still waiting for the apple blossom. I was just going out to see whether we can pick a few stalks of asparagus for supper—asparagus in April will be really unprecedented! The cow and goats seem to be finding enough pickings to give quite a lot of milk, and seven of us are making away with fourteen quarts or so a day. And all the vegetables have kept well in winter storage—we've never had such an abundance of food at this time of year before. Scarcely anything needs to be bought, except wheat to grind into flour. I buy a few luxuries such as coffee, now that things are no longer so tight on the idealistic front. Our living expenses are really about down to rock bottom, and everybody's health is fine.

"I notice the contrast between my children and the children of friends in the city. They are becoming very resourceful, get themselves off to school with no pushing or supervision, cook Sunday's breakfast, keep their room tidy, and so on. I am sorry they haven't more friends of their own age and interests, but I think we can make up that deficiency for them during the summer to some extent.

"My machine is down at Miriam's in the village, and writing on Alfred's is exasperatingly slow. I think I'll finish this when I go down on Saturday, as it can't be posted before then anyway.

"Monday. An active weekend as usual. On Saturday we carried up huge quantities of food etc. from Miriam's; also materials for redecorating the house. At this time of year everything has to be carried up on people's backs, and we are almost out of permanent supplies, so many journeys will be necessary. By the middle of May, we hope, if this wet weather doesn't go on too long, a truck can come up with the bulk of the supplies.

"Yesterday we started out with axes to open a trail over the mountain to Scott Nearing's. I think we now have it fairly clear at least halfway, but it is difficult going, part of it through thick underbrush along a steep hillside—the trees blot out the landmarks and one has to steer by the compass all the time. When we have our trail blazed and cleared, anyone will be able to walk over it without hesitation. This will make communications with the outer world much quicker and easier.

"I think I told you about the Great Mail Route Controversy, which actually got into the columns of the *New York Times*. The fuss raised by our tiny community was so effective that the Postmaster General climbed down and restored the mail route. This coming Saturday there is to be a grand celebration in the Town Hall in Jamaica and no less a person than the Governor of Vermont is coming to speak on Rural Improvement.

"Helen Knothe wanted me to play a recorder duet with her, but we couldn't agree on any music we could play even tolerably well together, and I must say I am just as glad not to have to make a public exhibition of myself! I'll tell you all about it when next I write. Look out for pictures, too, I finally got some film for Valerie's camera."

On April 29 Norma wrote to Marian, in Philadelphia:

"Your letter came at just the right time; it found me in a depression and helped to drag me out of it, along with a rather touching note from Marjorie Woznicki (it seems they do actually miss me a little in the UPC office!) and a typical brevity from Lucia at the Brudercoop. These small outward signs of the existence of other people are pretty important to me. So please, keep on writing, and I expect I shall answer, too.

"I am trying to make a cast-iron rule that I have each morning from 9 to 12, at any rate on the days the children are at school, for occupations completely distinct from life on the farm. As my day runs from 6 a.m. to 8 p.m. I feel it ought to be perfectly possible. And letter-writing is and always has been my favorite extra-curricular activity. Getting a letter sets me up for about forty-eight hours, and then I can spin out the pleasure of answering for anything up to a week. A little bit each day is the secret; I am just putting in this couple of paragraphs before I start out to the Nearings' to practice the recorder. We are going to take compass and axe and blaze a trail over the top of the mountain which so unkindly keeps neighbors apart. Probably the day's program will include felling trees and building a bridge over a stream too deep for wading at this time of year. You see we are real pioneers! I am torn between the desire to wear my smart new slacks and my knowledge that they will be ruined before I get there.

"I'm terribly afraid that the country for me is just a romantic dream, something attractive if served on a silver platter, but in the raw, something to be avoided. I seem to be allergic to the extremer forms of Nature; when the sun shines I can bear it and even feel a faint pleasure in it, [but] when it's gray, and I wake up to a vision of bare boughs before the window, I am depressed actually to tears. The summer must be coming, I know that intellectually, but for a would-be intellectual I am shockingly bad at making my feeling follow my beliefs!

"Tuesday. It's still raining, with an appalling persistence, and Scott (usually no mean weather prophet) says it won't change for another week. This kind of thing really gets me down—universal grayness, and everyone underfoot, the kitchen full of muddy rubbers and wet clothes hanging up to dry, dirty laundry mounting up, and the monotonous sound of rain on the roof morning and night. And the house full of men all day! However this has certain advantages, because there is a huge amount of indoor work to be done. Almost the whole of the upstairs is scheduled to be done over, some of it quite ambitious structural repairs and alterations like building a new partition where none was before, and on rainy afternoons I get the manpower to work executing the ideas as they come to me—'Let's have this here, and that there'—and so on.

"A. [Arthur Zeben] is quite a help in many ways, but the last two or three days he has seemed much disturbed in mind. He rushes about the house in a distressful manner apparently trying to be invisible, which is pretty well impossible here. Just as a meal is announced he flies out of the back door as though pursued by furies, reappearing a couple of hours later with a hungry look just when I have given up and put everything away. I'm sure it is useless to inquire and one can only take no notice and wait and see what develops.

"Tuesday. I didn't get this into the mail this morning because I forgot to ask Alfred for the check overnight. Our mail service takes a bit of explaining. The mail man brings it round to the school (nearly 3 miles away) on Tuesday and Thursday mornings and the children bring it back when they come home about 5. Saturdays I usually walk to the village and pick up letters at the post office after the evening delivery. So a letter that's mailed, say, Saturday, is likely to reach here by Tuesday evening. If it's mailed Sunday it may not reach here in time to go out with the mailman first thing Tuesday morning, in which case I wouldn't get it till Thursday night.

"On the other hand, your letter sent off Friday morning reached me (at the post office) Saturday afternoon. This now probably won't get to you before Friday night, unless I make an extra trip to the village tomorrow, which I contemplate doing, as we are out of almost all groceries. But an eight-mile hike, in the rain, 1100 feet down and ditto back, is not undertaken lightly! [That is, 1,100 feet in elevation, as well as the distance.]

"It's still raining, as it has been for a week almost without intermission (except when it snowed). Strangely enough, however, my morale is creeping up. I expect I am just getting acclimated, or re-acclimated, if there is such a word. I expect, though, it's partly due to the fact that I am in progress of figuring out a way that it might just be possible for me to have the UPC job another year without badly disrupting the rest of the family. At present this is just in the general category of castles-in-Spain, something to keep up the spirits on a wet morning—I am not taking it seriously at all, but it's nice to play with.

"I think we'd like to redeem your pledge to the choir. I know just how much you and Suzie put into the interracial aspect of it, and I have confidence in you to keep plugging away. I wonder how my interracial experiment this summer is going to turn out? I was talking the other day to the couple in the village who think of sending their boy to spend some weeks with us, and let fall that I expected we'd have some colored children about then, but [there was] no reaction one way or another that I could see. The man is a retired Professor of economics and maybe has some openings on the subject. Native Vermonters on the whole are very indifferent to the race question. I only recall seeing three Negroes in nearly five years I've spent in Vermont, and one was our guest, Craig, last summer. The other, I'm ashamed to say, was the chauffeur of a distant Quaker relative who drove up to visit us in her limousine. There is a rumor that there are a couple of Negro families in Brattleboro, our local metropolis, but no one's even seen them that I know of.

"On the other hand, you may have read about the experiment last summer when several farm families in one of the northern towns invited a group of Harlem children for the summer. By all accounts it worked out extremely well. The local minister I think was responsible for that. I wish I dared suggest it to the man here—but he is very deaf, which makes communication difficult (I am almost unable to make myself heard by the deaf, for some reason) and also any suggestion emanating from here is apt to be regarded with some suspicion. They tolerate us, so long as we stay within bounds, and are even cordial, but there is a strong undercurrent of distrust.

"Oh, how I wish I could make myself a good enough excuse to dash down for the Bach festival, but it's better husbandry to save my one promised trip for later."

May 1945

Norma wrote to Judy Bacon:
"Your letter of April 15th got here just a few days before I did, but somehow it got buried under piles of papers, so I've only come across it in the process of tidying up.

"I'm so glad to hear you really are planning on coming in early June. I don't know just where we'll put you, but perhaps anyway the best thing is to let you choose. I've had a big cleanup upstairs and lots more is in prospect—redecorating and all, though nothing really ambitious. I just want the house to look decent.

"Ossining isn't very far from New York, I guess you would have to go down there and start again from Grand Central as I always had to do when I wanted to visit any place in or near the Hudson Valley. Cross-country communications are terrible. But still New York is only five hours from Brattleboro by train and you can go off any time you are prepared to trust us with your children for a day or two. In return I'll probably load my responsibilities on to you at least once or maybe twice.

"About the children, the only ones I'm certain of (as far as one is certain of anything) are two little girls belonging to a Jewish friend of mine in

Philadelphia. One is eight, the other six. Then in mid-June Craig Work (from Manumit) may be here, and two or three friends of his from New York. Craig is 13 but the others are rather younger. I really know awfully little about them as yet, and it is quite time I wrote to find out.

"And finally there will probably be Billy Knight, whose parents live in Jamaica—they think he needs a change of surroundings or something, and want him to spend part of June at least up here. The whole thing is a bit vague but I am certainly happy at the prospect of having someone around who handles children more easily than I do!

"Keep us posted, if we possibly can we'll arrange with Scott to meet you in Manchester. But the more warning we have, the better the chances will be."

Norma wrote again to Marian:

"We took our little hatchets and chopped ourselves a way through the jungle to Scott's on Sunday, and I remembered to ask him about lending the stone cabin for a honeymoon. He said yes, certainly, you could have either the little one up in the woods or the bigger one opposite the schoolhouse. The small cabin has two rooms, the big one three, and moreover the big one has a bath and a flush toilet, though I don't guarantee the plumbing works. It was put in to satisfy a city purchaser. We don't bother with such refinements in this neck of the woods, but you might feel it lent class to your honeymoon.

"Both cabins have the necessary minimum of furniture. The bigger one belongs to a man named Hank Meyer, an engineer from somewhere in the Middle West, who's only been there once since he bought it (he can't persuade his wife to abandon the city). He is a friend of Scott's and told them their friends could use it any time. Moreover Helen, quite of her own accord, said, 'They wouldn't have to bother with food, we'd let them have what they needed.'

"Although from what you say Jim's tastes in many matters have a lot in common with Scott's, still I think you at any rate might feel a bit starved on only what they live on, which is mostly vegetables, and you could bring in a few sophisticated foodstuffs in a suitcase, but anyway it's a good offer and I'm sure you needn't have any hesitation about accepting it. They are very successful gardeners and grow and store masses of everything and always have plenty, even in June which is the leanest month of all, hereabouts.

"We have spent the morning in a perfect orgy of house-fixing and have put wallboard on two pieces of ceiling that had been dropping dirt and spiders in our hair for five years. My hair is full of dirt and spiders right now, but I can bear it if I think it's the last time. The house is getting painted and papered in all directions and as soon as the road is open for traffic (which won't be for at least a month if it keeps on raining the way it's done ever since I got back here) we'll have a hot water system before midsummer. [*Teresa*: I don't recall any hot water system: Water for dishes or bathing was heated in a tank attached to the side of the stove.] No nonsense with flush toilets, though, thank you."

The next day Norma wrote to an unidentified person, perhaps her psychologist friend Lee, probably never sent, as it is not a carbon copy.

"There is a certain difficulty here with the question of open correspondence (where letters are read, and sometimes postscripted, by others in the house before being sent). I feel it is most desirable that the correspondence should be open; it doesn't have to be, but the fact that it was not, would naturally be rather a dampening one. So I think I may on occasion have to resort to the same type of deceit which I have had, unhappily, to practice on my mother—the type which consists simply in suppressio veri, not saying everything, thereby of course as a by-product creating a false impression without actual falsehood.

"So these extra sheets will just go in with another, more general letter. Be assured I won't do this any more often than seems necessary. You, if need should arise, might do the same—stick in an extra sheet. See what I mean? [*Piers:* One of the problems she had with my father was that there were topics that triggered his massive denial and possible rage, and had to be avoided if association with him was to be maintained.]

"The situation here is in many respects just what it was. Alfred still gets up at 3 a.m. to read and he goes to bed even earlier—7.30 usually. I am seldom through with the chores before 8. I do usually go to bed then—however being quite unaccustomed now to these hours, I lie awake for a long time, which is not the happiest thing. I thought at first, let it go for the present, I am grateful for a breathing-space anyway and when I get ready I will try to change it.

"But in this particular respect, and it's a very important one, I am feeling some discouragement. Alfred's astrological interest has hold of him to an extent far beyond the normal. It blots out everything else. He doesn't want to do any kind of work; I have to coax constantly to get him to keep a semblance of regular work hours and put up an appearance of activity so that A. doesn't get left completely high and dry (not being able to think things up for himself or work without direction) and at least the most obvious things get done.

"On my suggestion, Alfred now comes and cleans out the barn while I am milking in the morning, and the thought was that this would allow at least a little time for discussing our personal adjustments, plans and so on. But we don't talk of anything but astrology; he has nothing else in his mind. I have challenged him a couple of times on this, have said how important I feel it to be (as I wrote him more than once before coming back here) that everything should be subordinated to the building up of better understanding between us, and a more regular family life.

"When directly challenged in this way he will say, yes, maybe it's a good thing . . . but nothing further happens. This morning while milking I said I had a passage from William James I'd like to share with him some time. His perfectly casual reply was, 'That will be nice, but I don't know when you are to get access to me, unless you can let me have at least five more hours a day to get on with my studies.' Just let that sentence sink in, particularly the middle part, and you'll see what dismays me about our immediate future."

Piers: Astrology is integral to my novel *Macroscope*. I studied it enough to understand it, impressing Alfred with my knowledge of its details. Its fundamental principle is that just as the stars and planets as seen from Earth seem to travel in their courses, and these courses can be determined, and their future courses predicted, so also do human events travel in their rather more obscure courses, but can't be predicted.

Norma continued: "I am inclined to think—though maybe this is just the outcome of ten days of incessant rain, with no relief in sight!—that we ought to face a fact which is implicit here. Looking back over our mutual lives, I feel I have abundant evidence that Alfred really does not want any closer life. It frightens him [this would be consistent with autism] and he will retreat instantly from any approach. You think otherwise, I believe, but it does seem to me that one can tell what really interests a person by his conduct in regard to that, contrasted with his conduct in regard to other spheres of life—and I have never known him to show a fraction of the interest in our mutual affairs that he has shown in a whole succession of largely academic subjects, culminating in this.

"I happen to think this a less desirable subject than some of the others, but that really is beside the point. At first I thought, if I showed interest, maybe it would give us a meeting point and he could be gradually drawn into more real channels. But I am beginning to think that may have been entirely the wrong decision. I may be just helping him to get further from life.[86]

---

86. *Piers*: In my experience, Alfred was as open to family values as was Norma, but neither of them had the interest or ability here that they did for intellectual pursuits. My opinion and that of my sister Teresa tend to fall into Alfred and Norma camps, echoing the differences of our parents. *Teresa*: I disagree, having seen no evidence, ever, of Alfred placing family values above his own tightly focused interests. He himself had stated that he "never gave it a thought." Some might say that he was "too much in his own head."

"I think the retreat from actual life is the salient factor in his make-up and I think it can only be changed by some intervention from outside. Psychiatry, I feel, has shown itself to be inappropriate in his case—he is one of those people whose minds move very slowly at the deeper levels and if we had five years and ten thousand dollars perhaps it could be worked, but none of the measures now available to us is likely to be any real good. Some terrific shock might do it, but that one can hardly engineer. What W. James describes as 'conversion' is what is needed, but that requires certain preconditions, and perhaps the chief of these is an intolerable dissatisfaction with one's present state of things, which is totally absent in Alfred's case. Possibly a subconscious process such as W. J. describes is going on in him, one can never tell, but I see no evidence.

"Now there are other kinds of outside influences which can work miracles—falling in love is said to be about the most effective of all!—but we here are almost entirely protected from the impact of the outside world. I feel very strongly that the only hope of getting Alfred out of his present mental furrow (much deeper than a rut or a groove) is to get him away from here and into an environment where, willy-nilly, he is blown upon by events, other people's emotions, and intellectual stimuli of a varied kind.

"That I will stand by him I think is now as certain as it is ever likely to be, but a tree can't hold up another tree unless its own roots are in the ground, and there is no soil for my roots here."

Norma had been trying for years to resolve her own confusion and depression by going to doctors in Brattleboro and Philadelphia, visiting Phil and Teddy, writing to Bob at Gould Farm and sympathetic friends, and pondering how she could better fit in with the overall goals, understanding that "it takes two to tango." In spite of everything, she was willing to "stand by" Alfred if he would make an effort to resolve troublesome issues, the way she herself was doing, rather than abandoning him altogether, despite the occasional physical abuse. Others in his own family—his stepmother, and years earlier his sister—had expressed concern about his mental state.

She continued: "It seems inevitable that there should be one wage-earner in the family, and pretty clear that Alfred's preoccupations do not allow him to be that person. There has never been a time throughout our whole marriage when we were financially self-supporting. There have been reasons for this, some of them good reasons, for instance the four years he spent as a volunteer working for the Friends. But still, over twelve years, the general picture acquires some significance. He will work to support the family, but only at the minimum sacrifice of his other interests, which means at the minimum level on which he finds it possible to live, and that in actuality is below the minimum level on which I find it possible to live. In practice, that means dependence on the in-laws.

"He just hasn't the motivation to give up more of his time to providing what I consider a minimum standard. I am quite prepared to accept that, and become the wage-earner for such part of the family income as corresponds with the things I need and he doesn't—I really have no adverse feelings about this, it seems plain common sense. But I'll work at what is congenial to me, not at chopping down trees.

"As I look back, it seems to me that I checked the vital development in myself a number of times by running away from life just as Alfred does; my case is similar to his, only not so bad, because I have more objectivity and can select and set in motion the process which is capable of making me over. I, in other words, can decide to let the world get in its stab at me, whereas he never can.

"Coming here originally was, from that standpoint, one of my worst acts of self-protection. Despite any evidence you may think you have to the contrary, I am genuinely lacking in initiative in any matter of personal relations, and could only become permanently different as the result of some very profound change. It would be easier for me to go on in the condition of anhedonia [the inability to feel pleasure, a common symptom of depression as well as in other mental health disorders] which has been my refuge until now.

"There was perhaps a point—I'll never know for sure—at which the whole direction of things could have been reversed, at which Alfred could have come fully out into mutual life and I could have followed him instead of having to drag [him]. That would have been when he made his unexpected trip down to Philadelphia at the end of February. But it is vain to speculate, because in practice it was impossible for me to go along just at that point. I was going through a process of deep transformation which couldn't have been speeded up any more than I have speeded it up already. If I'd come back here even a week sooner, I might have gone under right away. The events of my last week in Philadelphia, anyway the last two weeks (I mean interior events) were the decisive ones in providing me with the strength I now find I have.

"Because we do have one really new and hopeful element here, and that is that now apparently I am better able to take it. I became aware of the change rather suddenly on Monday, when Alfred came down from the corn crib where he studies, sat down at the table, buried his head in his hands and moaned something about having to find a way to get through a bad week— he meant the malevolent influence of Mercury!

"The important thing is to keep struggling to reduce the gap, to unmake the dualism, rather than let it harden into a permanent state, like those who despaired of this life all the more because they hoped for so much from Heaven. For me it should be easier than for most, because I have so many other genuine interests which can fill my life without my feeling cheated at all."

This concludes her private letter.

Norma wrote to Sheema Buehne, the mother of Sylvia and Judy [Jutta] and a close friend of Lee's:

"I've been thinking about you a lot, especially these last few days, and as a matter of fact I had a letter all ready to mail to you when yours came. But it was a cross letter (not at you, at things in general!) and I decided to scrap it. Things have been kind of demoralized around here the last couple of days, both indoors and out. Inside, we had the kitchen almost completely torn to pieces because a new floor was being put down, and the kitchen is the nerve center of this house. Outside, of all things, we had a blizzard. I had to laugh at the picture of myself this morning, Friday, May 11th, plunging to the barn to milk through at least eighteen inches of wet fluffy snow! Winnie and the children set out for school on snowshoes but had to turn back before they'd gone half a mile, so we had them on top of us to add to the confusion. [*Teresa*: I remember that. I had always thought it was April 15.] Altogether my temper was a little strained.

"I will get Alfred to add a footnote if that makes you any happier, but there certainly isn't any objection forthcoming from his side. The question is, just when are they coming, and that's what I was writing about. I have two suggestions to make, either of which would save you some travel and train fare. One is that Alfred and I, on our way back from the Y[early] M[eeting], meet you and the children in Springfield on the night of the 15th and bring them back with us. The other is that I make my projected trip to Philadelphia right after the 25th and bring them back with me. It isn't entirely important to me just when I go, except that I want the plans made well ahead of time so I can be sure and see the people I want to see in Philadelphia—some of them may be out of town later in the summer.

"I'd really like very much to have you come up here, and you might feel you wanted to see for yourself just what your children were getting into. I am pretty sure I can arrange for our friends the Fields to meet you either in Brattleboro or Manchester and bring you all the way up, which would simplify the journey a great deal.

"Well, that's the set-up from our point of view; let us know how it fits in with your plans. Everything is flexible except the Yearly Meeting date. You say you have no utterance from Alfred, but you know how he is much like Lee in that respect—he never utters unless absolutely bullied into it!

"Saturday. There is still six inches of snow all over everything and the poor cow is standing bellowing with rage because she can't find anything to eat. I sympathize with her, but how can I explain that the hay is all gone, but since the sun is now shining, the grass will probably reappear within a few hours? The dumb thing just stands and bellows, she doesn't hunt about for the places where a little grass is already showing through. Just like the human race. A friend was planning to drive up tomorrow and bring us our laundry tubs and hot water boiler; luckily he did manage to get up on Wednesday, just before the snow, and brought us the kitchen floor covering.

"The kitchen is now transformed—it needs another coat of paint on the new floor, and the hot water and laundry fixings, and then it will be really pretty good. Upstairs we are constructing another bedroom out of a tiresome space that used to accumulate junk. The problem now is what to do with the junk! There are moments when I feel we'll have to burn the house down finally to get rid of that, and the floods of papers of all kinds that accumulate all around us whenever we go. I have got in some work on the diet, it is still mainly milk and vegetables, but I think it is more interesting and it seems adequately nutritional. That is except for me, as I can't eat much of it except the milk.

"Here I am forgetting altogether to give you any news of A. [Sheema's brother.] He is very helpful around the place, cheerfully does the tiresome little jobs that everybody shies away from, like scrubbing vegetables or getting doors ready for painting, and I find studying languages with him very agreeable, though the pity is that we have so little time or energy for intellectual pursuits. I was supposed to get each morning free for study, but it hasn't worked out one single morning this week—maybe that accounts in part for my bad temper: mental malnutrition!

"A couple of days ago A. talked of moving on somewhere else—he has been interested of late in post-graduate study at Madison, Wisconsin, but this seems hardly the time of year for a beginning there. I think perhaps he was a little piqued at something and now feels better and in a mood to stick around a bit longer. We are trying to work out a schedule which will give him the opportunity to earn a little cash, the difficulty [being] that men more or less have to work in twos in the woods and both Alfred and Norm are pretty busy at present with house-building, and anyway have enough cash in reserve for their simple needs so they had planned to postpone woods work till June. But I expect we'll work it out somehow.

"I don't feel I am doing right by A., but I hope to be given time to learn better. My own affairs have been absorbing perhaps too much of my attention."

Norma wrote to Martha [Wakefield] on May 13.

"Reports on your condition reach me from here and there and seem to be reassuring. Only the person who has it knows the real misery of a sore throat. I had one in Spain which put me in the hospital for 10 days while Alfred was in jail in Madrid. I couldn't swallow anything except liquid in small gulps and they gave me some pills which were too big to go down and too hard to dissolve in water. The best I could do with them was, by long pounding, to reduce them to three or four jagged pieces—the torture of trying to wash those pieces down I'll never forget. [Such a sore throat might well have been a symptom of mononucleosis, which also would have caused persistent fatigue.] I have a sore throat right now—everyone has a cold—but it's a puny thing in comparison.

"I met our minister on the street yesterday and he told me he was just back from Philadelphia. I restrained the imbecile impulse to ask if he'd seen any friends of mine there, and asked instead what the weather was like. Pretty bad, he admitted. Today he's conducting Thanksgiving services [V-E Day, the unconditional surrender of Nazi Germany to Allied forces, was observed on May 8, 1945, in much of Europe and the U.S.] and I thought it would be a nice gesture if we attended, but with everybody having such a bad cold and the road three inches deep in slippery wetness, I didn't really feel it was possible. Not that I wish to stand aside from the Thanksgiving—I do think the end of actual fighting is a solid good in itself, however many fears one may have about what is to come after. No doubt it will be even worse than we imagine, but I was reassured to see that Truman finally came out and told the Japanese it was not planned to exterminate or enslave them. Maybe he has the makings of a statesman—neither Roosevelt nor Churchill ever showed that much imagination.

"As regards the question of environment, I was much impressed, the same evening I got your letter, by reading a letter from a man I knew who is now in the jaundice unit in Philadelphia. He said, 'In spite of the unpleasant aspect of our guinea-pig existence, the morale of the whole group is high. Frustration, a most depressing aspect of the base camps, is completely absent. . . . The regimentation and bickering, so evident in other places, does not exist here.' The men he is writing about are the same men who were so unsatisfactory in C.P.S. Only the environment is different; and the real difference is not a greater or lesser degree of comfort, but the fact that they now have an environment to which they can establish a creative and functional relationship. The roots of this kind of thing go very deep, and it's those roots I have been pursuing in my mind this past week.

"That same night, at supper, Norm Williams was talking about a letter he'd just received from his father, to whom he is immensely devoted. The letter was a little sharp and critical of his way of life; Norm was very upset indeed and had sat down right away to dash off a justification. Specifically, he was counter-attacking on the ground that his father, a very liberal minded person, had come around to accepting atrocity stories and talking to his students about them. Norm's argument was: If a man like my father can be affected by the current propaganda, then no one's integrity is safe, and the only thing one can do is isolate oneself altogether from these influences.

1945

"I responded a little tartly that I'd been exposed to them pretty steadily all winter [in Philadelphia] and I didn't feel my soul was in any more danger than before; and I maintained that unless one could be exposed to the full blast of propaganda, yet keep one's intellectual integrity to some extent, and find the way to stand out against it, one wasn't much use to one's fellow-men.

"He reiterated that, on the contrary, absolute isolation was the only way of salvation. That discussion pretty well focused my four or five days' thinking on the perennial question: What goes on here? When I came back [to Hilltop] I was brought face to face again with the same thing that haunted me all last summer; the persistent feeling of something wrong, like a bad smell because a rat had died under the floor. I tried to discount it last summer by telling myself that it could easily be all a product of my own disordered state of mind, but it returned in such force that it has convinced be it has objective validity. My approach is genuinely different, but the phenomenon is the same. As the man said in 'World's Beginning,' it's time at last to go down to the cellar and find out who it is that's dead.

"I think when we came here in 1941 our thinking was: We will save ourselves, and thus point a way for others to do the same. That was an attitude which could be justified—in 1941. But now, I feel, our thinking is: We will save ourselves, and as for those who are too feeble to follow us, well, it's just too bad for them.

"So I have come to believe that even if we should, at least, establish what looks like a secure and happy family life in this house, it would have a canker at the heart. People who talk as we talked in 1941 are either pioneers or escapists; only time could show which, and I'm afraid time has shown.

"I am going to be very disappointed if you don't get to see us, but I shall understand how it is. Just possibly I'll be down in Philadelphia the end of June."

Norma wrote to Marian on May 15, saying in part:

"The Pikes Falls Citizens Association holds a meeting this evening in the schoolhouse. We go, bearing cookies. I am not a good cookie maker and compounding these absorbed most of yesterday afternoon as well as precious materials, but it's expected, and we want to show goodwill.

"This association arose out of the spontaneous get-together which allowed us to save the mail route last winter. Rural Improvement is now the subject and I am rather fascinated to know what form it will take. At the governor's meeting a letter was read from Frederick Van de Water saying he was sure we'd soon have a trolley car. I asked Scott if he'd been intending to work to get Pikes Falls a trolley car, and he gave an exaggerated shudder—I don't imagine he even wants us corrupted by electric light. As for us, we need something more drastic.

"Piers composed a poem:
> *Funiculi, funicula,*
> *We're going to have a cable car.*

"This morning it isn't just raining, it is pouring, with thunder and lightning thrown in. I'm sorry to keep harping on this theme, but it's hard to think of much else. Along about midsummer I'll be writing to complain of the awful drought—that's the way farmers are, never satisfied. As a matter of fact, we never have a drought up here. In our four summers of residence, three have been abnormally dry, but our spring has never failed nor our garden wilted.

"We continue pretty much unaware of what goes on in the world below. One October day when rain was coming down so hard you could hardly force your way through it, I was obliged to make a trip to the village (I rode down in someone's car but got drenched to the skin between the car and the Post Office). I made some annoyed remark and the postmaster snapped back: 'I don't know about you people, but down here we've been carrying water since the middle of August.' In the village the wells seem to dry up regularly every summer. That's a disconcerting feature of life here, people seem friendly and suddenly hostility flashes out. This same postmaster, we've been told by half a dozen people, was the one who wrote to Washington suggesting our mail route be dropped, an unfriendly gesture if ever there was one—maybe it's just gossip but it seems common knowledge. Gives one a sinking feeling to be told things like that.

"Then Miriam Fredenthal discovered that some of the foulest rumors were circulating about her in the village, and she traced them to the store where we all prefer to trade because the people seem so friendly. [In] the other store [that] I seldom patronize the man never says more than 'Yes' or 'No,' but maybe what I took for personal animosity is just discretion and unwillingness to be a rumor-factory. One doesn't know who are one's friends, or if one has any at all. With eccentrics like ourselves, it's safest to assume we have none, be courteous all the time but never give anything away. Miriam, for instance, still trades in the same store, but she just passes the time of day and no longer sits down for a friendly chat.

"One person who was a very outspoken and bitter enemy is now very friendly, and yesterday sent us a gift of dandelion greens and—butter! We had seven asparagus tips for supper in honor of Alfred's birthday, and as I gathered them I thought, 'Oh, if we only had some butter!'—it seemed, as they say, like an answer to prayer. This woman in winter used to stand on her front porch and yell abuse at Winnie and the children as they went by to school, till Alfred finally forbade the children to go near her house at all and hacked them out a back way through the woods. I wonder if she is at all aware that her spasm of hate was not reciprocated, and if so, what is the impression. Winnie said [that] as she handed over the dandelion greens she said, 'Give them to Norma—if she'll take them!' I must make a point of thanking her for them tonight. I'm afraid my attitude has not always been completely non-violent but one does the best one can."

Piers: That was Mrs. Kuusela, mother of one of the boys in school. One day when the snow was fresh Teresa and I enjoyed making tracks in it, holding on to small trees so we could run around them making circles. They were along the road in sight of Mrs. K.'s house, and when we passed the house she screamed at us that those were her trees we were despoiling. Then she sent a message to the school and we were required to return about a mile to her house, where she bawled us out for some time with her baseless charges, accusing me of cutting up one of her tires, I think. But further thought over the years may have yielded the true reason. I had written a creative story about wild events at Pikes Falls, naming particular residents, all in a spirit of fun, and she was one of them. Winnie thought it was hilarious—it seemed I had some talent for humorous fiction—and shared it with those residents. But I suspect that Mrs. K. was not really amused, and had it in for me thereafter. So when she had a pretext, the damage our circling around her trees supposedly did to them, she struck back. I think that later she discovered that one of her own children had cut up that tire, but could not bring herself to apologize for her error, so simply became friendly without explanation. She caused us an immense amount of distress, for nothing.

Teresa: She threatened to "send us to reform school" if we even stepped off the road onto what she called her property. I was terrified for a long time and finally confessed my fear to my mother one night when she came to tuck me in during our stay at the Brudercoop. But Mrs. K. also several times welcomed me to stay in her home on snowy nights, or when I was sick. I have no memory at all of these visits.

Norma continued: "Here I go after all, wandering on. By all means share with L. if you think fit, the poem especially. [Perhaps referring to the sonnet that appears at the front of this book.] Oh, I did mean to make an observation about your triangle figure. I find it rather unsatisfying, both too much and too little. Piers came home from school last week with a figure something like this: [*Piers:* There is no figure on the carbon, but I remember such figures, triangles overlapping triangles so there are more than can readily be counted. Such things fascinated me.] You have to guess how many triangles there are altogether, and you never guess right, there are so many. Now imagine such a figure in three dimensions and you would have a better picture, I think, of human relationships in geometrical terms."

May 17 Norma wrote to Anna Brinton, co-director of Pendle Hill:

"Alfred and I have been giving some thought to plans for next winter, and we have wondered whether, if we decided to give ourselves a leave of absence from here, there might be some corner we could fit the family into at or around Pendle Hill. Would there be, for instance, a couple of rooms anywhere that could be a sort of housekeeping apartment for a few months? Or could you make any other comparable suggestion? There are a number of factors—for instance the local school here is closing and I have several times thought how much I would like the children to go back to the Media Friends School for a while (it's the only school they ever liked).

"I am offered the same job again next year with the Peace Chest, and feel I could do better at it now I have more experience, whereas a newcomer each year just flounders around wasting the movement's time and money as I did at first. Also, Piers needs some treatment for some of his mannerisms—and a number of other things which I won't enumerate at length. But the financial end of it would be pretty complicated if we had to set up housekeeping somewhere on the ordinary basis. We are planning a trip to Philadelphia at the end of next week, and we thought we might come out to Pendle Hill perhaps on the Sunday (27th) and talk things over with you and Howard Brinton if you are going to be there. I suppose we ought to fit in a trip to West Chester too, and there are a number of other people we should see.

"I expect to be arriving in Philadelphia some time Friday morning. Could you send me a message either here before Thursday, or by Friday in care of the Peace Chest office (1924 Chestnut) saying if you're home that weekend and when might be the best time to talk to you?"

Piers: This seemingly incidental letter set in motion events that were to transform my life. We did return to Pendle Hill for several months, when I was eleven. I attended The School in Rose Valley for two years, which I regard as my second-best school of ten attended, Goddard College being the first, and discovered speculative fiction as mentioned before.

May 19 Norma wrote to Family:

"I wrote to you not long ago that we had been turning over in our minds plans for next winter. I am feeling more and more that the children are now reaching an age where they need a wider environment and more friends. There have only been three other children in the school this past year and next year the school itself I imagine will be closed, since Winnie has definitely said she doesn't want to teach again. Natalie Field is qualified to teach, but she can't go away from her house because of the baby, and they live five miles from here, so I hardly see how a school over there would be much use to us.

"Until now, I think, the quiet life has been good for the children, after so many vicissitudes, but they are both getting to need more varied intellectual feeding now that they are past the stages of learning the three R's. Piers is showing a good deal of skill with his hands—for Alfred's birthday the other day he made a small box with a fitted round lid which was really quite impressive. Teresa is quicker than he is at most of the regular school subjects (except arithmetic), but she doesn't seem to show any special aptitudes. Altogether I am coming to feel that we should give ourselves a six months' leave of absence during the coming winter, and perhaps go back to Pendle Hill, near which there is an excellent school run by the Friends (I don't want to put our poor children into one of the big public schools).

"We expect to make a trip down to Philadelphia this next weekend to discuss possibilities. Money would be something of a problem, as it's always so expensive to live for a short time anywhere, but we have a good deal saved just at present, as opportunities for spending are so few, and there is a temporary job I have been offered which would probably pay enough to make up the difference. Anyway, no sort of move is contemplated for several months. We have invited a number of our friends to bring their children here for the summer, and this is certainly the healthiest place for the children to be.

"I have some film now and hope to be taking some pictures to send you, but for the past four weeks it hasn't done anything but rain. Except twice when it snowed—ten days ago we had a blizzard. Winnie and the children weren't able to get to the school even on snowshoes. In the whole four weeks there's only been one fine day when I could wash any sheets and the laundry problem is becoming really serious. Our laundry arrangements are terrible anyway. Alfred ordered two special laundry tubs and a hot water boiler, but they are sitting down in the village waiting—no one can drive up. We have spent hours working on the road, but no sooner do we get it into shape than a deluge comes and washes it all out again. People say they've never seen anything like it—I'm getting so tired of hearing that! Sometimes the exceptional weather is good, for instance a long fine spell in early April, but that brought all the trees on too early and many of them have lost their leaves again. The outdoor prospect is a very dreary one just now.

"Things inside look a lot brighter. The kitchen is all modernized now, except for the laundry tubs. We did manage to get some linoleum up the hill, and now we have a nice smooth floor which can be kept fairly clean, or would if it would stop raining, so that the house wasn't full of muddy boots all the time. Upstairs, we are evolving a new small bedroom into which we hope to put one of our summer guests—a new partition had to be built. And

I have started painting the bedroom floors in bright colors. Probably I shall paper some of the walls too, as the plaster is pretty rough; the ceilings also need plastering, but that we hope to get done very soon.

"I feel it is none too soon to have a decent house even if we aren't going to live in it all the year round. Now that the Williamses have their separate establishment, I'm able for the very first time to organize things and take pride in feeling that it's my house and if it looks all right, people are not going to come and upset it by trying out their own ideas.

"I think I told you that little Gretchen is now standing by herself; I fancy she is about a month older than Susanna—I don't remember exactly when she was born—but it seems to me she is a very precocious child. When I say she stands by herself I mean she stands holding on to something in her play pen. She certainly is a fine argument for the healthiness of country living—you never saw a finer-looking baby.

"It's a week since we heard any news from the outer world. The news of victory in Europe did reach us, because we happened to make an extra trip to the village and heard about it on Miriam Fredenthal's radio; otherwise it would have happened as I always expected; the war would come to an end and we'd remain completely oblivious for days or weeks. No signs of rejoicing were noticeable around here, and a friend wrote to me from Philadelphia that the celebrations there seemed very lacking in spontaneity. I've heard the same thing about other large cities too. I think people over here, thankful as they are that their sons are now less likely to get killed or captured, nevertheless are sobered by a feeling that whatever the war was fought for is pretty well lost already. It seems a pretty general feeling here that World War III is only a matter of time. The discouraging thing about that is that no one seems seriously concerned to do anything about it. They are content to sit back and let matters take their course.

"It's true that [but] for the casualty lists nothing ever happened to make the average American aware there was a war on at all, and they don't have a real emotional incentive to work hard to prevent another war later on. I'll be interested to see whether the English turn out to be different. I am pessimistic, but not disillusioned, because in this matter I never had any illusions anyway. Perhaps it will prove that those of us who never hoped the war would bring them anything good will suffer less from emotional shock and be able to get to work sooner.

"What our personal sphere of usefulness is likely to be I don't know, though I do very much want to get back some time into the reconstruction field. But that doesn't look like an immediate possibility since we should have to make some stable arrangements for the children, and they are not at the right age now to be farmed out anywhere while we went off into danger-zones. Perhaps something will turn up which can employ us usefully while giving an opportunity for the children to stay with us. Being on the wrong side of the Atlantic certainly complicates matters from this standpoint.

"I enclose a brief cutting [clipping] which Daddy may find interesting, about the mental hospitals in Ohio." [Norma's father was head of a mental facility.]

Also on May 19, Norma wrote to Dear Friends:

"We were delighted with the book which arrived yesterday—it's wonderfully generous of you to make us such a present, and I imagine we'll be having exciting new dishes for quite a while now. I've heard a lot about your visit and am sorry I wasn't here to meet you. Winnie says you thought of coming over again, and we wanted to suggest the Sunday following the school picnic on June 3rd. I think that will be June 10th—I don't have a calendar handy.

"On that day the Fields are planning to come up and see us, and we gather you didn't manage to see them last time you were over. By then I think we can reasonably hope the road will be passable, if only it stops raining! Ten days ago a small truck did manage to get up the hill and bring us the linoleum for the kitchen floor, but immediately after that it snowed, and now I guess the road is worse than before. However, we have worked hard on the drainage ditches, and since I really don't see how it can possibly go on raining much longer, I think we can reasonably hope the road will be dry three weeks from now.

"We don't want to impose our date on you if another suits you better, but Alfred and I will be away at the end of the next week, the Sunday after that is the school picnic, and so the tenth is about the earliest we can be here to receive you as we like. I did think of making a trip over to Bennington some time during the summer, but I've no idea when it will be, if at all. Without a car it is pretty hard to reach the other side of the mountain from here. So I hope very much you'll be able to come over again before too long."

Norma wrote to "Martha Dear" on Sunday, which would be May 20:

"This is just a hasty note—I have a chance to send it tomorrow by someone who will be at the school picnic. This is the high point of the scholastic year, but I'm afraid in practice it just means a ten-mile hike through the rain. Of course it's raining—what did you expect? (Alfred says that according to the *Farmers' Almanac* we shall have fine weather the last week in September.) Piers has a sore throat and obviously ought to stay home, but I haven't the heart to make him—the picnic is the only thing about school that gives them pleasure in the whole year! And he is depressed already, I have not succeeded in finding out why. [*Piers:* I don't remember specifically, but it was a depressive time for me. I really did not enjoy my life, overall, and concluded that, were I magically able to relive it exactly as before, or to vacate my existence entirely, I would prefer the latter. But I never believed in magic, however tempting illusion might be. I was locked into reality.]

"My trip to Washington was perfectly awful. I am writing to Sheema about it [see letter in June 1945] as she asked for particulars—you can ask her if you're interested. They gave me a regular third degree, and my friends will certainly not get their visa."

Norma wrote to a person whose name is not on the carbon: probably Lee Brodersen:

"Here I am in wicked luxury in the middle of the morning sitting down in the midst of everything waiting to be done to drink cocoa and write a letter. It's a soft day, the sun not shining but present behind light clouds, the air full of birdsong and little green leaves. Spring here is more behind than I had expected, but it promises well. Some sort of tree is in blossom near the house. On the whole, the prospect is one of desolation but not devoid of hope.

"Inside the house, things are rather the same. Some of the very worst eyesores in the kitchen have been dealt with, but my, what a lot remains. In the bedroom Alfred has rearranged the furniture, swept the floor and put flowers in a vase. I must say I like my bedroom, it is monastic but not an affront to the eye like the rest of the house. Up there this summer I intend to do some writing—and not only pamphlets! As I rode up in the train there suddenly came to me a short story, growing from the germ of something I'd attempted before but entirely new. The idea of the whole thing was there and the latter half almost word for word.

"I wish I knew what was incapacitating me with the Williamses, or at any rate with Norm (Winnie alone I could manage, could even become fond of, probably). But he sits there as immovable as the Rock of Gibraltar, at least to my eyes, and giving out something I simply don't know how to deal with. I have to recognize that it's perfectly possible he is simply giving back what I am transmitting to him. Anyway, it must be worked on. Their house is not yet ready, so they haven't moved.

"I'll be all right as the conviction gains ground in me that this really is my house now (I don't mean in any exclusive sense). Except for sudden moments of despair and incredulity, I am more or less the captain of my soul.[87] And I am not forgetting it will hurt less and less, though that in itself is a painful thing, as others have found out.

---

87. A reference to "Invictus" by the Victorian poet William Ernest Henley: "It matters not how strait the gate, / How charged with punishments the scroll, / I am the master of my fate; / I am the captain of my soul."

"When I came in last night, I found A. playing the Op. 132 quartet. I had just stacked the milk things (this would be about 9:05) when he started to play the 'Heilige Dankgesang'—the one we listened to in Presser's [a music store]. It was too much, song of thanks or no song of thanks, I went upstairs, flung myself on the bed and howled. Maybe he heard me, since I left the doors open to hear better and the walls are thin. Anyway he broke off after the first record and played 'Sheep May Safely Graze,' and after that, part of Beethoven's 7th. I'll never know if it was accident or design—no doubt you would say it could be both. But it helped a lot and I will be grateful to A.

"Thursday morning. The Williamses completed their transit last night in a storm of rain, and oh, the difference to me![88] I hope cordial relations will now have a chance to grow between the two households instead of the non-belligerence which was too much the former state of things. They stole away like the Arabs,[89] without announcement or farewell—after all these years! I honestly don't think that indicated hostility so much as a total absorption in their own affairs. It is still an enigma to me how two groups could live side by side—practically superimposed—without any kind of interchange in so many months. I feel closer to A. even after so short a time. We had a pleasantly goofy conversation as we walked down to Miriam's yesterday.

"Rural elegance notes. An elderly farmer limping down the main street of Brattleboro, wearing one of those gray cloth caps suitable for milking and such pursuits—with a pink Bambi pin stuck in it! We finally got the presents home last night. Teresa fell on 'Bambi' with joy. This morning while I was getting the breakfast she rushed in exclaiming 'Look, there's Bambi!' I looked out, and sure enough there was a deer, a big one, though, strolling past the house.

"Wrote-in-the-stars-above Department. Alfred is up to the eyes in his astrological studies; I've seen him in the grip of a whole series of obsessions, but this is the biggest yet, I think. He evidently was much afraid I would disapprove or hinder, and can't quite make out the change.

"Alfred has worked out that for him there are several bad periods (especially matrimonial) during the coming year. The discouraging thing about this is that he may produce the effect by subconscious expectation. However, the first of these bad periods is to coincide with an extra good one for me, so there's hope! Tell us your birth time as exactly as you can. I

---

88. William Wordsworth, "She Dwelt among the Untrodden Ways": "She lived unknown, and few could know / When Lucy ceased to be; / But she is in her grave, and, oh, / The difference to me!"
89. A quote from Henry Wadsworth Longfellow, "The Day is Done": "The cares that infest the day shall fold their tents like the Arabs, and silently steal away."

altered mine to make it more exact, from 12.05 to 12.03, and Alfred had to re-draw all the charts and shift me from the influence of Capricorn to that of Sagittarius.

"Even my outward appearance has changed—you'll be interested to know that I am not tall and red-haired with a tendency to stamp with the feet! Some other discoveries about me are that the period right after my last birthday (October 24) was an excellent one for travel, making especially congenial friends, and spending money. . . . And right now the stars indicate I have a secret sorrow which is likely to stick with me for several months. Well, well. Dr. Freed, it seems, makes no recognizable appearance anywhere in the charts. No dark man in my life as yet. . . . I'm sorry, it's all kind of humorous to me." (*Piers:* Here I agree with Norma, as I am as much a skeptic as she. Even were astrology valid, that kind of detail would be illusory. Alfred evidently needed something to help him make sense of the confusing world, and this seemed to be a way. For others it can be politics, religion, a sage friend—Norma's case—or magic.)

Norma continued: "Obiter dicta [incidental remarks]. The children have been avidly reading—guess what?—*Black Boy* [Richard Wright's autobiography]. . . . I have made a start on *Varieties of Religious Experience*. Robin Fredenthal (age 4) calls his sister, 'You naughty, naughty, goddam son of a bitch.'. . . People in the village tell me I look much fatter. . . . Asparagus for supper tonight I hope. . . . Greetings to the Literature Department, I forgot this was a Letter of Welcome too. . . .

"Friday. I had sworn this shouldn't run on to another page, but evidently it is going to do so. I am exercising my privilege of writing when I feel bad. It's a lousy day, raining again, I feel a terrible desire to GET AWAY FROM IT ALL, and of course just because it's raining the house is full of men and noise. Alfred and A. get their periods of recollection in the early morning, while I am doing the chores and getting the children off to school. Come nine o'clock, I want to relax and have my bit of privacy, but by then of course the day is in full swing.

"At this moment I am experiencing the extreme frustration of not being able to let myself think freely aloud (this being the equivalent of aloud) for fear of someone reading over the shoulder at any moment. I am mad at the interruption of the schedule I was trying to build for myself. Why can't they go and hoe the potato field, for heaven's sake? It isn't raining as hard as all that. It's 10.30 and half my precious three morning hours are gone, not to return, so is my philosophic calm, what there even was of it. Oh, how I loathe rain in the country.

"This morning in a caprine [goatly] transport Hyacinth leaped off the milking stand somehow carrying away the whole of the length of heavy chain by which she was supposedly fastened. She wouldn't let me get near her to unfasten it, but now goes bounding around with it clanking over the stones. I hope she won't have a nervous breakdown; she is already pretty neurotic.

"A. is plugging away at Op. 132 till I could almost scream. I am tempted to ask him not to, but somehow I feel one doesn't do that with A. Perhaps it is exerting some healing influence on him. Unfortunately, the emotions it produces in me are so strong and so impossible to coalesce with the daily routine that I find it becoming very painful. If it's good for him, I suppose I should be glad. He seems cheerful on the whole, and I think the atmosphere here is now fairly suitable for him. I fancy what he needs is people who will take him for granted, let him come and go, talk or be silent, as the mood takes him, and never be surprised or demanding. He still doesn't look anyone in the face, but he goes industriously about the small jobs, doing them better than before, sings in a formless way as he works, is occasionally loquacious and from time to time throws off a remark that gives me real pleasure of a quiet kind.

"Saturday. Yesterday was a pretty difficult day. Alfred too, was in one of his horrible sarcastic moods, and around noon he came down and announced with somber satisfaction that the matter with both of us was that Mercury was in the wrong place and would remain that way for more than a week. I told him tartly that Mercury or no Mercury, I expected to be much better in a few hours. After that it began to snow. After that, with typical feminine inconsistency, I became very cheerful and energetic, organized the men, got lots of useful indoor work done, and went to bed in a glow of achievement. [Textbook bipolar disorder!] Today there's snow on the ground and a bitter north wind, and all the asparagus I was so tenderly watching is frozen."

Piers: This is a rare insight into Norma's secret heart, the thoughts she can't afford to express elsewhere. They simply did not understand each other, and their marriage was foundering. I, from my cynical agnostic perspective, see astrology as no more misguided than the average religion. Who in his or her right mind can believe the supernatural precepts of either? But some mythology is more fashionable than others.

June 1945

Norma wrote to "Dear Sheema (and Lee if she is interested), Here are the gruesome details of the interview in Washington.

"First of all, it was disconcerting to find myself confronted by a tribunal of five men, two of them soldiers, perched up on a kind of dais while I sat meekly below with a typist, I mean a stenographer, who chewed gum and took down every word I said, frequently asking me to talk slower because she couldn't keep up. I swear I don't talk at 120 words a minute even at my most hectic!

"The man in the middle was elderly, with gray hair with a most beautiful wave; every so often it would flop forward and then I would find myself visited by a strange impulse to fix it for him with a couple of bobby pins. . . .

"I no sooner came in the room than they started gabbling an oath at me—I thought I had better make my position clear from the start so I said, as a Quaker could I be allowed to affirm instead (not that I really care a hoot, but solidarity, you know, and all that. Well, now I suppose I must give up drinking and smoking too!) [Obviously a joke, as Norma did neither.] The man with the wave said, 'Off the record—do you know why you do that?' [To affirm rather than swear.]

"He clearly thought I didn't, so I gave him a resume of the historic Quaker testimony on the subject of oaths. He said he'd once had a rabbi before him who refused to swear on the grounds that he couldn't possibly undertake to tell the truth which was known only to God. I said I hadn't thought of it that way before, but I would certainly subscribe to that position.

"Then they asked for my passport, etc., and took down all the names and numbers. I think it was then that one of them said, why had I not taken out first citizenship papers? I had expected that question, so I gave him the only possible answer which was that it was on account of my religious beliefs; I couldn't take an oath to defend the country of my adoption by force of arms and therefore I had dismissed the idea of ever becoming a citizen. In an ill-judged burst of frankness I went on to say that since I took the responsibilities of a citizen of a democracy very seriously, I now thought it probable that I should ultimately go back to England, where I could enjoy my full civil status.

[Norma did eventually take the oath of citizenship, and she reported with satisfaction that a special exception had been made for her, that she would not have to swear to take up arms in the country's defense!]

"They asked if Alfred had ever considered trying to regain his American citizenship and I said no, which of course made a very bad impression, and the interview got stickier and stickier from that point on. Then they asked what I knew about the Maison family, a German Jewish couple we had known in Spain and for whom we'd been trying to get visas ever since we came here, which really is practically nothing—I made the most of the little I did know. They said that in the papers, his wife was described as of Protestant birth, did that mean she wasn't a Jew?

"I said I had no idea, I supposed so.

"They said, how do you know he is a Jew? I couldn't think of a thing to say except, 'Why should he say he was if he wasn't?' It turned out that what was worrying them was the idea that he might be an enemy agent masquerading as a victim of persecution. They wanted to know how long he'd been in the concentration camp in Spain and I couldn't tell them. I said rather heatedly that it hadn't been my business to inquire into his politics, I was a relief worker and as such forbidden to take such things into account.

"'Ok,' said one, 'so you would help an enemy agent to get into this country?' That stung me and I told them how a Franco officer threatened to hang Alfred in the Plaza de Catalunya for feeding Red children, and Alfred had said it was all the same to him what color they were. I don't think they got the point, and the atmosphere dropped another several degrees. They seemed to think it highly suspicious that I didn't know whether the Maisons had any brothers or sisters, though I pointed out that they were elderly people and perhaps had no more living relatives. I can't say why that was so important, can you?

"Then they got back to me again. They wanted to know what we were doing now, and I said farming, except that I'd had a temporary job last winter. They wanted to know how many acres under cultivation, and as it obviously wouldn't have done to say, 'About two,' I evaded it somehow and said all we produced for the market was cordwood. They then wanted to know what was our income last year. I told them as near as I could tell, around 1800 dollars. One of the soldiers gave me a look that obviously meant, 'You're a liar!'—It was Elizabeth Smith's hat, I suppose. I'd have dressed the part of the subsistence farmer's wife if I'd been able to anticipate what was going to happen!

"Then he asked, did we file an income tax return last year, and how much tax did we pay—I said Alfred did all that while I was in Philadelphia, very lame but strictly true. I don't believe we paid any tax, actually, because there were so many deductions for doctors' bills, but I couldn't see how that was their business. I realized again, though, how utterly crazy our way of life appears to any normal person.

"Then they asked Alfred's draft status, and I actually had to think a minute before I could remember it was 4F. They asked why, and I said I didn't know, they never told him, but I had observed that conscientious objectors in Vermont were usually put in 4F, as obviously of unsound mind. Even though that was true, it was certainly not judicious—the two soldiers looked at each other, stupefied. One said, hadn't Alfred asked the draft board why they deferred him, and again I had to say no, he had never taken the trouble. [Typical of Alfred, who never asked questions.]

"About then one soldier fixed me with a glare and said, 'Are either you or your husband buyers of War Bonds or donors of blood?' I said no, no War Bonds, for the religious reason cited above; as for the other matter, I would have wished to be one myself (I thanked heaven just then that Alfred wasn't there) but that on medical grounds it was not possible for me. I was thinking just as fast as I could and checked in the middle of a sentence, thinking if I said I was subject to hemorrhages they would think I had T.B. and was a bad risk as a sponsor.

"Not till about an hour later did it strike me that the effect I'd probably left on their minds was that I had syphilis—which would consort rather oddly with the high moral tone on which I'd been conducting my case up till then! I'm inclined to think that was about the worst mistake I made all the way through, though Heaven knows among so many it's hard to choose. The other soldier then said he didn't see what my religious principles had to do with not buying War Bonds, so I patiently explained that I thought it was just about as bad to pay someone to do my killing for me as to do it myself.

"The insignificant civilian at the far end then piped up and said, 'Doesn't that apply to paying taxes too?' so I smiled sweetly at him and said that was why we lived on as little as we could. I felt I had scored, but I don't suppose it did anyone any good by that time. Along about then both the gray-haired man and the solider on his right pointed at me with their pencils and said more or less in unison, 'In other words, you are accepting the protection of this country, letting all those American boys die to keep you and your children safe, and you won't do anything to help'! (I forgot to say that earlier they asked why we didn't go back to England when we left Spain, and I told them I had seen what war did to children and I thought one of the most important things I had to do was to see that my children grew up with healthy minds and bodies).

"I said no, that wasn't a fair way of putting it. They insisted that really was the position, but I insisted that I couldn't accept that as a true statement of the case. Right there I missed my big chance to explain why I felt that their American boys were not making the world safer for my or anybody else's children, but rather the reverse, but I couldn't get my ideas in coherent order before they had passed on to the next thing.

"We argued back and forth a little more, and I asked them to believe that I didn't take my responsibilities in this matter lightly. They said very heavily, 'Well, that is a matter between you and your conscience; we can't see it the way you do. If that is all you have to say, you may go'.

"So I went. I was just about all in by that time and was thankful to get out before I lost my temper, which miraculously I'd managed not to do up to that point. I hardly see how it could have gone worse, unless I actually had lost my temper. Of course the Maisons won't get their visa, though I don't let that worry me too dreadfully, because it seems obvious that they had no chance anyway, with such paucity of definite information about the applicants. Just possibly it might have gone through if I'd turned out to be a D.A.R. [Daughter of the American Revolution] with three sons in the Pacific and ten thousand in War Bonds and giving a pint of blood every Friday.

"So now about the journey. A. will definitely not be here the 24th; he is planning to leave for Wisconsin in about a week and is all signed up for summer courses at the University and very pleased about everything.

"As regards transportation from Brattleboro, Kent said he would be very glad to bring you up on a Sunday morning—you would just have to phone him when you arrived. I will send you his phone number when I can get it. Supposing you waited till the next weekend, you could leave Philadelphia, say, Friday night, arrive in Brattleboro Saturday morning and take the 10 a.m. bus to Jamaica. Saturday is the only day the morning bus runs. Or you could leave Saturday morning about 6 and catch the 3.30 bus from Brattleboro (9.20 train from Grand Central). Or you could leave Saturday night and ride up with Kent Sunday morning.

"I'll be writing a letter about getting the cow tested in the morning. I've been working in the woods a good part of the day, rolling huge logs around, and my muscular fatigue is just about the equal of my spiritual depression. If it's still raining when I wake up I rather think I shall jump out of the window. . . .

"Tuesday. As soon as I came to think it over, I realized what should have been obvious all along, that I couldn't go to this meeting anyway—far too many things I can't leave here. I was counting, when I made the plan, on having Judy Bacon here to look after the children, and now she isn't here, so about the only solution would be to take the children along—which I refuse to contemplate. Now I must cope with some of the myriad other matters, before the children get up and there is no more peace. I hope both I and the weather will be more cheerful before you come!"

On June 11, Norma wrote to Family:

"One more letter has arrived, dated May 2nd. Actually, it came about ten days ago and though I expected to answer it almost at once, something intervened. Alfred and I had arranged to make a trip to Philadelphia to attend the Bach Festival (a friend of ours was singing in the choir, and we had supported her efforts to get Negro singers included, which represented a remarkable victory over prejudice). We also planned to talk to several people about possible arrangements for next winter, and I hoped to be able to report something definite, but nothing is decided as yet. I do feel that we ought to be away at least part of the winter, if only to give the children a rather wider social life, but these things are very complicated to arrange.

"The day we arrived there, I received word that I was to go to Washington at the end of the following week to testify on behalf of a German Jewish couple we had known in Spain, and for whom we'd been trying to get visas ever since we came here. So I stayed away a whole week longer than I had expected, and had a good time going around visiting friends.

"Finally I went down to Washington, but the hearing went very badly, partly because I really know almost nothing about the people concerned; it was impossible for me to convince a hostile tribunal that they weren't enemy agents. I am sure they are not, but the onus of proving they weren't turned out to be on me, and there was nothing conclusive I could offer. Even the fact that the man was a Jew they wouldn't take on trust, and wanted me to prove it. How could I? He had been a year or more in a concentration camp, but they didn't think that was evidence either.

"I came home very upset and discouraged about the whole thing, thinking about that poor old couple hoping for five more years to get to America, the land of promise, and now having to be told that their hopes will be in vain. They are living in Barcelona supported by some Jewish organization, but how long that can go on I don't know. The man is an architect and a good one, but it is almost impossible for foreigners to get permission to work in Spain. The whole business cast a deep gloom over me, and the continued bad weather here hasn't helped me to throw it off. Hence my silence, since I didn't feel I had anything of any interest to say to anybody.

"I finally got one roll of film exposed (I am using them with extreme caution as they are so hard to get) and sent it away to be developed about a week ago. I don't know whether or not to wait till the prints come back before sending this, but on the whole I think they had better wait till next time. They may be disappointing anyway, as there is something wrong with the camera.

"Yesterday we had a big party here—nineteen people including eight children. It rained, so the house was pretty crowded, and the noise was appalling. I rather unwisely volunteered to take charge of a neighbor's son for the summer, as his parents said they wanted him to have more congenial company than is provided by the village boys. I had undertaken to look after a number of other people's children this summer, partly in the belief that Judy Bacon would be here to help—she was supposed to be coming with her two in early June, and she is much better with children than I am. But she made other arrangements, and now I not only have this child but his younger brother, who insisted on coming too.

"Moreover the older boy, aged thirteen, was represented to me as quiet and studious and only wanting to be left alone with a book—now I find he fights with Piers continually, and has about the most painfully harsh voice I've ever had to listen to. He arrived yesterday and my nerves were all on edge before he had been in the house an hour. [*Piers:* An older boy I fought with? I have no memory of that. I wish she had named him. *Teresa*: It was Billy Knight. I don't remember him either. Perhaps he didn't stay very long. Norma was not very good with children, and deserves appreciation for taking on these responsibilities, especially without the expected help.]

"Tuesday. The situation is a little better, both as to the weather and the noisy children, so I don't feel quite so depressed. The worst of it is that our own children so seldom have guests that they forget all the rules of the house—carefully built up so as to make living in such a ramshackle place as comfortable as possible for a large number of people—and I have to be continually saying, 'Don't,' which is very discouraging for everybody. However I think things are settling down a little.

"I presently bought a new game called 'Monopoly,' said to have been invented by a Professor of Economics to teach the iniquities of the present financial system. Perhaps it does have that effect for grown-ups, but for children it's wonderful fun—each trying to outdo the other in every possible way and make more money. A game started yesterday afternoon and went on for three solid hours, and now I hear them beginning again. At any rate it keeps them quiet—except for the interludes when they come to blows—and it's simply wonderful for their mental arithmetic, dealing with large and complicated sums in their heads. Everyone has to think for himself and see that the others don't take advantage of him, which teaches them to calculate quickly. I suppose it's a degree better than the war games that seem to be the only pastime of city children. [*Piers:* I certainly remember Monopoly! I loved it and played it so much I soon had the board memorized. If it was supposed to turn us off the capitalist system, it failed phenomenally. *Teresa*: Piers later invented a board game called Modern War. In the absence of other children, he undertook to play all the positions himself.]

"Thursday. I am stiff all over today; yesterday I walked to the village and back, and on my return found that Gardenia had wandered off in search of a bull. We had to pursue her to the nearest inhabited farm, about three miles away, and she was very reluctant to come back. Altogether my total walk for the day must have been sixteen miles. Alfred was watching the road to forestall any attempt at escape on Gardenia's part, but she set off innocently in the opposite direction and then made a detour through the woods. No one knew she'd gone till I came back from the village and reported fresh cow tracks on the road. It's about the only time she has ever manifested anything resembling intelligence. Poor creature, all it means is that she is confined to the barn instead of being allowed to roam about under observation. [The ankle tether mentioned earlier for Dickie would have worked here.]

"I hope the photographs have come, and just possibly the mail man will bring them this morning, but I won't wait any longer to send them off. And I'll try to make my next letter a bit quicker."

To the president of the Media Friends School, June 13:

"Our two children, Piers and Teresa, were pupils in the Media Friends School four years ago—Piers for the whole year and Teresa only for a few months. Lately they have been attending the rural school here, but that is now to be closed, and for other reasons I think it is time for them to have a slightly different type of education. I'd like to be able to send them back to the Media school, which they liked better than any other.

"The difficulty is that we do not want to give up farming operations here entirely, nor do we want to break up the family. We could all be away from here during the winter for a maximum of about six months—probably mid-October to mid-April. Would it be possible for you to take the children for this limited period? And what arrangement could be made about fees? I feel that if you could let me have a list of the books to be studied in the fifth grade next year, I could see that they were not too much behind the other children when they came to start. I realize such an arrangement as I propose has many drawbacks, but I feel that from the children's point of view it would be greatly preferable to having to remain here throughout the winter."

To Dr. Freed, June 17:

"I am sorry to trouble you with a problem like this, but it's a little difficult for me to know whom to consult. Alfred is now trying to diagnose Piers' trouble by astrology, and his present theory is that the child may have one or more vertebrae out of place and should be taken to a chiropractor. I am willing to put up with a good deal of this kind of thing if in exchange I may be free later on to get the treatment which I feel he needs; but I do feel that it could be very dangerous to have some possibly incompetent person manipulating a child's spinal column. Can you tell me whether you feel that real harm might be done, or whether the experiment could be tried without too much risk? And is there any way in which I can inquire into the qualifications of any chiropractor Alfred may propose?

"In the normal way I would have taken this up with Dr. Stokes, since he made a thorough physical examination in January, but Alfred has asked me not to tell other people about his interest in Astrology, and I too, for obvious reasons, would rather it didn't get around unless it seems inevitable."

A dateless missive to no address, evidently another to Lee, circa June 1945:

"Alfred had one of his worser moments and I came back to find both children suffering from what looks like pink-eye (conjunctivitis to you) and if you ever had that you'll know its unhappy effect on the temper. The only cheerful member of the party is A., who for some reason is at his gayest.

He plans to leave very soon for Wisconsin. Alfred told him according to his horoscope he was due to emerge about now from the troubles that have been besetting him these last few months, and that seems to have pleased him a lot.

"The longing to get back to [relief work in Europe] becomes stronger and stronger. So many wonderful countries still to see, so many exciting people to meet and love.

"We had the school picnic on Sunday. One of the valley boys was there in uniform, just invalided out of the Army. On the way home Teresa said to me that she was so glad he had been there; she said, 'I thought he must be thinking about the battlefields and I was glad he was there having fun among friendly people.' She went on to confide to me that the only man she'd ever wanted to marry was a chopper who worked in our woods the winter before last.

"Part of what's getting me down is uncertainty—no decision yet on next winter. I don't know what it's waiting for, but I do wish I knew definitely what to expect. Discussion however seems impossible.

"A. left us this morning on the first lap of his journey to Wisconsin, having carefully inquired from Alfred as to a propitious day and hour to make a start. He seemed in the best of spirits. If only things turn out well for him there, I shall feel we did perhaps achieve something by giving him a space for re-orientation. I shall miss having him around, popping up now and then in the conversation with some philological brain-twister, or singing 'Heiden-roslein' to himself in a bumbling kind of way as he scrubbed the kitchen floor. The children I am sure will miss him; he read 'Don Quixote' to them and taught them military drill, which they loved. You should have seen them all going around in single file—first A., then the children, then the goats, who never want to be left out of anything, and as like as not the cow bringing up the rear. Wouldn't this make a wonderful illustration!

"Our next regular guests aren't due till Sunday, and I calculated that we were going to have two whole days of plain family life, the Williamses also being away—the first since November 1942, believe it or not. But sure enough, someone else turned up at lunch time. The tourist season is beginning in Vermont.

"I am fighting a pitched battle with this house. My ambition is to have it running by the end of the summer like a piece of well-oiled clockwork, but it just isn't that kind of house—even if I were that kind of person. However, little by little the frontiers of chaos get pushed back. The trouble is that if I turn my back, the bit I tidied yesterday gets as bad again. I have to keep after it continually, there is such a strong will to disorder in the place. And heaven knows, though I keep cheerful by comparing it in my mind how it looked a year or two years or three years ago, anyone coming from outside would think it looked perfectly frightful even at its best. But it gives me an activity.

"It isn't so much that this life is distasteful, rather it's the wrong life. So much effort, to absolutely no purpose. Imagine Sisyphus pushing his stone up the hill if ever it occurred to him that there wasn't any real reason why the stone should even reach the top; how do you think he would feel about it after that? No, I want a fresh start, a new direction, some road to travel that I can feel is going somewhere. This has lasted altogether too long. There are moments when my rebellion becomes so extreme that I don't know how I'll even see the summer through. I know I must and shall, but I remember my mother who lived fifteen years in a place she loathed, and always said the last two weeks were the worst.

"Vermont farmers are being encouraged to take Negro children again this summer, the experiment having proved successful last year. Our children are eager to have us apply for one. I think it's a good idea, but I shall see if we can get some other families to do likewise—seems to me one solitary little Harlemite might feel rather lost in so completely alien an environment."

June 14, Norma wrote to Lee:

"This one is off the record—no carbon copy! You know my habit of keeping copies of even the most trivial note. But this is just a small conversational interlude chiefly to tell you that I am better; the lump of dry ice in place of the heart has vanished away, as all such things do in the fullness of time.

"We had a sort of tragi-comedy climax last night, precipitated by the cow. She's in heat again, that makes it three weeks since I was getting ready to start for Philadelphia. Alfred was watching to see she didn't go off down the road, but she fooled him by starting in the opposite direction and sneaking around through the woods, which tells you something about the power of Sex, though whether good or bad I don't quite know. Anyway, returning from the village, with about ten miles already hiked, I found her fresh tracks on the hill, though Alfred swore she hadn't left the premises.

"I didn't feel much like a further six miles, pursuing her and bringing her back from the farm where the silly creature thinks there is a bull, though by this time she ought to know there isn't. But I thought, it's a beautiful evening, nice and romantic for a stroll through the woods in the twilight, and if I can't get Alfred to come strolling for my sake, maybe he'll be tricked in to doing it for Gardenia. But it didn't work out a bit; on the way down we exchanged perhaps two casual remarks, and on the way back Alfred made some disagreeable remark (I expect I provoked it, though I don't know just how) and we walked the rest of the way home in total silence, one leading the recalcitrant cow and the other urging her along by periodical swipes at the rear end.

"After breakfast I sat down and took stock. I said to myself, you have fallen back into expecting Alfred to be all sorts of things you know he can't,

1945

and holding it against him. You think because he's all the man you have, therefore he has to be Apollo and Casanova and Romeo all rolled into one. And why should you feel entitled to what most women don't get? I still think monogamous marriage is the ideal, but I am pretty tired of my own line of thinking which never could let me admit that half a loaf was better than no bread. I gave up writing poetry, though it gave me real pleasure, just because I knew I'd never be as good as Keats.

"This is being written June 14th, but it won't be mailed for days and days, or maybe even weeks and weeks. I feel you have fully earned a rest from me and my private thunderstorm (sometimes I feel a lot like the hired man in the Thurber story!)

"I'd volunteered to take one of the village boys for a while, counting on Judy Bacon to help out if the child population got out of hand, but Judy isn't here, and this boy not only came, but brought his little brother too. And whereas he'd been represented to me as a quiet, studious boy, wanting nothing so much as to crawl off somewhere with a book, he turned out to have a high, shrill, nasal voice which set my every nerve straight up on edge, and most of his time the first two days he seemed to spend fighting with Piers. I went about desperately trying to get some semblance of quiet, at least inside the house, which is bad enough, Heaven knows, without children fighting continually in it, and feeling I could shoot everyone in sight, beginning with myself.

"It quieted down after a few days, he really is quite a nice boy and anxious to do what people want once he grasps what it is, and I've become more or less used to the voice. I think maybe he's tone deaf or something. Anyway, something more like order has been restored. I guess, though, I came as near cracking up on Sunday and Monday as I'm ever likely to do."

On June 26 Norma wrote to Family from Philadelphia.

"I told you when I wrote some weeks ago that some changes were possible, and now things are moving faster; I'm down in Philadelphia on a lightning visit looking at the possibilities of moving our whole family here for perhaps six months during the winter. I've nothing definite to report as yet, except that it seems likely we'll be away from the farm during the winter months, and that I'll work here in the office of one of the peace organizations for which I have already done some voluntary work; they need a secretary for just the months I happen to want to be away from Vermont, and this is the kind of work I know something about and would probably do all right.

"Alfred may also find something of the kind, or he might decide to do postgraduate work at the University, or follow some special course in preparation for going back to active relief work—there are a number of possibilities.

"Around Philadelphia there are a number of good private schools run by the Quakers. The chief difficulty is that for two children the fees would probably turn out to be beyond our means, which will be pretty limited, especially if Alfred decides to study instead of getting a regular job of some kind. So I am now inquiring pretty actively into the various elementary schools in the Philadelphia suburbs. The city schools are huge and terrifying, at least to me. I visited one this morning, and though it was highly recommended I couldn't help thinking our children would be lost among perhaps forty-five others in the same class.

"Tomorrow I'm going out to visit Pendle Hill and see what the possibilities are around there—that would be a very pleasant place to live—and then on to West Chester to see Alfred's parents before they leave for their summer holiday in Maine. On Thursday I'm going to see schools in two of the northern suburbs. By Friday I ought to have some ideas, but I am going to be kept so busy that I thought I'd better write this letter while I had a few minutes to spare. The idea would probably be that we would leave Hilltop about mid-October, when all the harvesting was done, and stay away till towards the end of April, when it would be time to start next summer's gardening. It is rather a complicated scheme, but it represents a compromise, since Alfred doesn't really want to leave the farm at all. He is perfectly happy there, and there's no doubt it is a very healthy life for the children.

"But for me it is terribly lonely and confining, and now that Winnie is no longer planning to teach, the small local school will be closed and it's hard to know just how we should get the children down to Jamaica. I don't much care for the school there anyway. And though we did once before meet the difficulty by sending the children away to boarding school, they don't want to do that again.

"It might be simplest for all concerned if we just moved out during the inactive winter months. We'd have to bring with us a truckload of the most essential furniture and probably vegetables too. The cow can be boarded out as she has been before, and the Williamses very probably would occupy the house, since the one they have started to build for themselves won't be ready to live in for many months yet."

July 1945

Norma continued her Family letter:

"July 2nd. Quite a long hiatus occurred here because I was kept so busy seeing schools and so on. On Saturday morning I started back from Philadelphia, bringing with me a friend's two children who are to spend the summer holidays here. It's the American equivalent of a Bank Holiday weekend, as I should have realized, and the traveling conditions were simply appalling. We couldn't find a porter to help with the suitcases, so I had to carry everything myself except the small parcels, which the children managed. Also we had to stand up for about half the journey.

"The heat was high up in the 80's and the trains had no air conditioning; all the windows were open, the result being that we reached Brattleboro looking like chimney-sweeps. Nor could we buy anything to eat on the journey except some perfectly nauseating sandwiches which not one of us was hungry enough to eat—and they cost the equivalent of a shilling apiece! I have traveled in such conditions in wartime Spain, but even there I don't believe I was ever quite so hot or so dirty. No doubt it's been like that in England for a long time now, but in England you don't have to cover some three hundred miles in a day's journey, nor is it so hot.

"We arrived back in Jamaica on Saturday evening, and according to plan slept at Miriam Fredenthal's, and a friend drove us up the hill the next day.

"Almost immediately after we'd got here Teresa hurt her thumb turning cartwheels, and this morning I took her to the doctor to see whether it was broken. The doctor said he thought not, but it was too swollen to tell. In a few days, if it doesn't regain its normal shape I'll have to take Teresa to Brattleboro for a X-ray. I hardly think it can be broken since it doesn't hurt her at all now and she can move it just a little, but it seemed wise to inquire further so that we shouldn't run any risk of having her go through life with a deformed thumb."

Norma wrote to Mrs. Nowell on July 6:

"After discussing the question between ourselves and with the children, we feel that on the whole the plan I tentatively outlined to you would suit us best. That is, as far as we can see now, we'd like to send Piers to [The School in] Rose Valley (beginning around mid-October) and Teresa to the elementary school in Wallingford.

"We feel that on the whole the most important consideration is that Piers needs the assurance that would come from starting out in a new society on his own, without his bright little sister constantly around. As I said, he has a good mind and has got on with the children in the small school here, but I think he has sometimes been made nervous and anxious by having his sister always there and inclined to put herself forward, sometimes at his expense.

"As regards helping at the school, my husband thinks he probably isn't going to have time; he has a program of study he wants to follow and wants to feel that his time will be free. In any case that would depend on whether or not we were able to find a place to live near at hand; so I expect you had better discount it altogether."

Norma wrote to Lee on July 7 (though name and year are not on the letter).

"Everything is exquisitely peaceful. Piers and Sylvia are playing Monopoly in one room, Teresa and Jutta are playing school in another.

Although it seems much too good to be true and I can't help wondering how long it will last. We had a slight scene yesterday, when Jutta decided to be tiresome and Sylvia wound up by hitting her in the face (bringing up once again the problem of how to explain to children the doctrine of turning the other cheek).

"But apart from that, everything has gone so smoothly and pleasantly it just seems like a miracle. Fine weather has helped a lot, but really Sylvia and Jutta are astonishingly well-behaved and biddable. They even like the food—we've always had trouble over that before with visiting children. It's true I've been carrying on a determined campaign ever since the end of April for palatability to be regarded as just as important as nutrition. That's heresy by Hilltop standards!

"(Speaking of violent situations, at this moment we had an interruption—the bees swarmed. While I was rushing to get out the new hive they disappeared, and with them I suppose most of our honey crop for this year.)

"The pacifist tendency to assume that there's good in every man which only needs to be appealed to in the right way is probably sound, but it is apt to be rather dangerous if used to pretend that phenomena either can't be explained or didn't happen. The fact is many of them at present just can't be explained in terms of any hypothesis brought forward either by the Vansittartites[90] or by the Man of Good Will. So the more of this kind of reporting, the better.

"Sunday. Alas, the heavenly calm was too good to be true. The cow ran away during the night; Alfred knew she was in heat and looking for any chance to escape, and he knew there was a hole in the pasture fence, but nevertheless he put her in the pasture instead of leaving her tied in the barn. I said nothing, his mood being such that any remark of mine would have provoked an explosion. Today he has sat all day studying his astrology, and when I asked whether he planned to go after the cow he answered no, he had assumed that I was going. The farm she goes to at these times is three miles away through the woods, and she won't be led or otherwise conducted by me when she is in heat, in fact it takes a strong man to hold her. The walk there and back, even if she came quietly, would take me away from here for more than two hours.

"I'll have to go, of course, and do the best I can—maybe she will be quiet by evening, and if I put the children to bed early maybe they won't

---

90. Followers of Baron Vansittart, British diplomat and extreme Germanophobe, who warned the British government of the growing military power of Germany and insisted that Great Britain should rearm.

kill themselves before I get back. (Alfred has already voiced a grievance at being asked to look out for them while I was away on Monday taking Teresa to the doctor because she fell on her thumb and it looked as though it might be broken.) I have to be away all day tomorrow too, taking Teresa to Brattleboro to have her thumb X-rayed and possibly re-set at the hospital.

"The reason I'm writing about all this is that if Alfred keeps on this way I don't see how I can continue taking responsibility for Sheema's children. I don't want to worry Sheema unnecessarily, but I do want someone to understand the difficulties in case I have to write and say, 'I can't manage.' Life here is impossible without a man to do the heavy jobs, and I can't count on the Williamses, who are away working on their new house all day. [It's] impossible to tell what makes Alfred this way, or for how long. But unless he recovers, [gets] some kind of treatment, and some responsible person vouches for his improvement, I can't face another summer up here without another man. It looks to me as though we shall have to hire somebody.

"The depth of bitterness inside me I am frightened to contemplate; I am trying to be aware of it and not let it go to bed on me, but I feel cheated of the absolutely elementary support I must have from him if we are to carry on mutual life. What am I going to do, if next winter doesn't bring some kind of improvement? Such complete insecurity it just isn't possible to bear.

"Miriam has a letter from A. which she thinks hints strongly at some kind of amatory experience, though I think she is reading more into it than is actually there. It does seem clear, though, that he's sitting on top of the world out there in Wisconsin. He sent us a whole lot of books, carefully chosen to be of interest to different members of the family, by which we were really touched. The one he ear-marked for me has some pretty queer philosophy in it (for instance the author stresses that Buddha, Socrates and Jesus all consorted with courtesans to elevate them morally).

"Tuesday. Well, my pilgrimage in search of the cow was just about as painful as I expected. She tried to knock me down twice before we were out of sight of the farm where she'd been visiting: I armed myself with a big stick and set out to teach her which was the Master Race. Before giving in she tried every other trick she could think of, including leading me a long way through thick woods and across a brook which was just too wide for me to jump, so that I fell in. By the time we got home I was simply incandescent with rage, and realized I was beating her just for the pleasure of beating, although she was by then completely submissive.

"After this incident Alfred seemed just a little better (I think subconsciously he must have felt rather guilty) and I was able to leave the other three children with him yesterday while I took Teresa to Brattleboro. It turns out that her thumb is broken and will have to go in a splint for a couple of weeks. [*Teresa*: The splint was created out of a broken-off section of a folding wooden ruler. I think it was yellow.]

"Don't say anything to Sheema about all these troubles, because I think probably I can make out all right. We've had a run of bad luck, with Teresa's thumb getting broken and all, and the cow running away just when Alfred was at his worst, but I hope there won't be any more bad luck for a bit, and his mood now shows signs of letting up a little. He's had it since the beginning of June, after all. I am tormented (when I let myself think about it, which is as little as possible) with thinking how different everything would be if we could only establish some kind of contact with one another. But every attempt I make seems to be interpreted by him as some kind of indirect aggression, an attack on his precious solitude, and he lashes out in order to keep me away from it. Sometimes I tell myself, 'Let's try again'—it would make such a difference if I could only reach him—he wouldn't do what he does if he knew how it makes me feel.

"But however carefully I prepare the approach, however hard I hold on to my temper, he is so afraid of me that it only ends in another brawl. I don't honestly believe I am as terrifying as all that. He is more afraid of me than anybody simply because I am nearest to him and therefore constitute the worst threat. If I were completely above the battle, it might come out all right, but in the nature of things it is my life too, that is being wasted in this way, my deepest desires that are being frustrated, and I can't keep my own disappointment completely out of the picture. Every time I make an attempt at an understanding, it makes things worse and I vow I won't again, but I never can forget that we used to be happy together and could still be as happy as we were then, and more so, now some of the obstacles on my side are removed.

"I suppose absolute passivity and making as few demands on him as possible is the only safe course. But when I think that he is making arrangements to have the whole of next winter for his astrology, and I have made it clear that when I can get help from other sources I won't ask him for anything at all so that he can be entirely free—and he can't spare time even to help me with the little things here and now that make such a big difference in the country—oh well, what's the use?

"I didn't mean this to be such a Jeremiad. I am writing under difficulties; I've had no time to myself the last ten days in which I could write letters, except after the children are in bed and then I can't type in case I wake them. The lack of privacy is another thing that tells. Even at night I can't call my soul my own; one night I got woken up four times.

"You can tell me to mind my own business if you like, but it still seems to me in a way you are playing the trick that Alfred plays on me, passivity as a form of indirect aggression. You make the other party make all the suggestions, and then if things don't turn out as you want, you have a grievance. [Textbook passive aggression!] Are you quite sure you won't say to yourself, some day, 'Well, I might have done much more in this sphere of going out and establishing myself in the inter-racial world, but [her friend] Jeannette always wanted to go to a movie instead'?

"A battle is going on downstairs. I'm afraid they'll just have to fight it out while I go for the mail. Things still go much better than I dared to hope, though Jutta has now begun to display some of her tricks. Since I genuinely am not impressed when she cries, I think she will soon decide not to bother. She came up just now whining 'Sylvia put a crumb in my cereal!' I firmly said, 'That won't do any harm,' turned her around and conducted her gently out of the door. No more sounds from her. The spider menace has completely ceased to be, though at first I just didn't know what we could do about it."

Piers: This letter offers another remarkable insight into Norma's situation and frame of mind, and I think she has a case. The cow showed the limits of pacifism, and Alfred clearly was a trial at times.

Norma wrote to Arthur [Zeben] on July 10:
"It really was nice of you to send us all those books, and specially chosen for our special interests, too. It is now pretty well settled that we shall be away from here during the winter, and I have written to say that I want Piers entered at the Rose Valley school (near Pendle Hill). A couple of weeks ago I made another hasty trip down to Philadelphia to see about schools and houses, and as a result we decided that the Rose Valley school was the one that would suit Piers best. It's a small school, but very progressive; they seem to have a number of interesting new teaching methods. I don't suppose we can possibly afford to send both children there, but I think Teresa will do all right in the near-by elementary school, which is also small and pleasant-looking. I want to have the children in separate schools, as I think they may both be happier that way for a while.

"The girls seem to be settling in quite all right, much to my relief. We had some trouble at first because they are both so much afraid of spiders, (and you know how many we have here!) but to my surprise it took only a few days before Jutta was saying she had found the way to get rid of them with a piece of paper."

Norma wrote to an unnamed person—surely Lee—"July 15 or thereabouts."
"My reflective mood was set off by a conversation at breakfast. Sylvia talking about a Negro girl who came to their house and stole a number of

her toys. Piers interjected something in defense of the Negro race which I didn't quite catch (I was in the kitchen) and Jutta piped up that she had two colored friends and they didn't steal anything, and moreover her best friend was a Chinese girl. Sylvia went on to say: 'So I told the other girls who used to beat her up on the way home from school, and they beat her up even worse!'

"She glowed with satisfaction over this manifestation of justice, so I told her I supposed she didn't know that children who stole always did it because people were unkind to them, hence this particular girl would be likely to steal even worse in the future. Of course, it made no impression.

"I fell to musing, as I washed the dishes, on the brutalizing effect of mass education as demonstrated in these two children. How can we give the next generation a chance to grow up into a better generation than ours? Because if we don't, we are wasting all our propaganda for peace, freedom and all the rest. Sylvia and Jutta will lose the trick of saying 'Them there' and 'I don't want none,' but what will rid them of the belief that Might is Right and getting the better of an opponent by cunning is best of all?

"Every child has a right not only to food, clothing and shelter, but to affection and a stable family life, and to education suited to its special needs, and to a social life which produces a genuine indigenous culture instead of a state of things which is just the law of the jungle under a polite disguise. But where can we possibly start to give our children these things?

"The system, bad as it is, does sometimes throw up (or fail to suppress) an individual who is really creative, who conceives the kind of idea that can transform society and is able to give it currency. I suppose for the sake of those few individuals it's worthwhile stumbling on, doing the best we can in full awareness of its imperfections.

"Bambi and his mother met me in the woods the other day; I didn't get much of a look at them because they vanished in their usual uncanny way. Last night an extra beautiful bright red little deer was licking at our salt block. I always feel that deer are creatures of another world—if you could get near enough to touch one, your hand might go right through it. Partly it's because they are so silent and graceful; to see one run, you'd think its feet didn't touch the earth at all. And their faces have a kind of other-ness. Their incorporeal presences are all around us here, though we don't see them very much except in spring. A tub of clear water stood outside and half of it was gone by morning; it reminds you of the stories about the brownies who used to come in the night and drink saucers of milk which the housewife left for them, or was that leprechauns?

"Thursday—date unknown. The structure of life is crumbling, the cow has gone dry! I suppose she has eaten something poisonous, but while she seems well enough, just a little dejected perhaps, we are thrown into confusion and deprived of the staple of our diet. Four gallons of milk a day laid a pretty comprehensive foundation for anything, and when they are suddenly withdrawn, no one quite knows what to do.

"Last night I was meditating sadly on the fact that I am no longer able to write anything—not even letters most of the time—it isn't the pressure of occupation, at least not always, I told myself, but something more subtle. And I vowed to take my two or three hours out of this morning at whatever cost. My morning's program, however, included walking four miles for mail (nothing worth walking for, either), a fruitless struggle to administer a whole pound of Epsom salts to a cow who wasn't interested, and arbitrating in a fight over the kitten (a new member of the household).

"What disconcerts me constantly is that I am accustomed to dealing with children who are trustworthy, that is, by and large capable of understanding what is wanted and doing it without constant supervision. But my experience with Sylvia is that she will do the exact opposite of what she's been asked as soon as the adult's back is turned. I hate having to bend myself into a dictatorial pattern, but our children are the victims if I don't enforce the rules made for everybody's better enjoyment. I can't blame Sylvia, in fact I am very sorry that she feels justice is so lacking in the world that she must use fair means or foul to gain her ends, but it does complicate and sadden life at times, and I am often at a loss for the right thing to do in a particular situation. What would you do with a child you knew was lying when you couldn't prove it? I suppose I'll develop a technique.

"At this point I rushed down to yank Sylvia, by the hair if necessary, out of my Bach records—but was completely melted when she said, 'But I like Beethoven!' So I dug her out the Eroica and let her loose on that. After all, the effect of great music should be to elevate the mind. Don't get the idea I don't like the child, I do, but she presents me with a new set of problems and often my irritation is at my own inadequacy to meet them.

"Friday. What a day yesterday was! The cow is better anyway, though everything else including (again) the domestic situation is pretty much of a mess.

"Sylvia's latest gambit is to hint to our children at nameless horrors in the ordinary facts of sex ('Do you know what they were doing?—Something bad!') I realize she gets it from her associates, but I find myself wondering whether we have been successful in giving our children the kind of sex education that will protect them when they get into the hurly-burly again.

"Saturday. I learn from Lucia that you and Sheema came to play recorders with Roger—I hope you appreciated the beautiful myrtlewood boxes. That must have been quite an evening: I hope I was with you in spirit.

How would you like to be all alone except for children day after day? I think I never spent such a lonely summer since my unhappy teens.

"Despite everything, I feel the desire to build myself a career in the peace movement. I must have a definitive peg on which to hang my life, and this looks like the thing that is most my size. The only immediate step that can be taken is by preparing the mind; I intend to be a lot more studious the rest of this summer, and make up on the subjects I always regretted not having studied at Oxford; P.P.E., or Philosophy, Politics and Economics. I sent to the U. of Chicago Press for *Philosophers Speak for Themselves*.

"Sunday. I just had another shock; Jutta was telling me solemnly how Philadelphia is full of Bad Men who will kill you if they get a chance; they come out of dark alleys, and Sylvia was nearly killed once, but fortunately her grandmother heard her calling and she was saved. And, 'When we are sitting on the porch, if we see a bad man coming, we run inside and lock the door—that's what Mother told us to do.'

"Does it really have to be that way? I do so believe that children should feel their world is friendly for as many years as possible. Sooner or later they will learn different, but the longer the discovery is put off, the more secure they will be, since that kind of security surely is built up chiefly in one's earliest years. Alfred [who tended to see bogeymen behind every bush] thinks I am mistaken about this.

"I rode part way home with Scott last night. He is just back from Haverford, where he said he met 'Several of your Peace Chest people.' I asked if he would do some speaking for us on conscription in the fall, and he said yes. I know there were doubts about using him last year, but this year I mean to try and get over that. He draws a crowd and puts things across so clearly that you can't see any other way out—not till afterwards anyway!

"The children at supper were discussing the transmigration of souls; I was interested to observe that they all took it for granted, including ours. I wonder what Dr. F. would make of Piers' admission that he is afraid of being reincarnated as a wolf? [*Piers:* This is curious, as I regard reincarnation as supernatural, and I never believed in the supernatural. Maybe I was merely playing with the concept.]

"Tuesday. I got bitten by a mouse the other day; I caught it with my bare hand, meaning to put it Buddhistically out in the garden. Our kitten, by the way, after a week of furry angelhood, suddenly threw off the mask and caught three mice this morning before breakfast. Oh, dear—but what is one to do? They make life almost intolerable and Alfred's method is strychnine, which seems to me the ultimate low of cruelty, as well as being no use at all. A few mice die in agony, the rest flourish.

"The cow was in heat again and she and Alfred set off to find the bull. They've been gone seven hours, and privately I'm worried he doesn't realize what a fury she can be when she conceives herself scorned, or perhaps frustrated is the better word.

"Alfred's astrology has scored a distinct success. He wrote to his sister saying she must be wrong about her birth time, she had obviously been born in the middle of the night instead of the middle of the day. This crossed with a card from her saying that from an old family record of some kind she had discovered that she was born at 11.10 p.m.! For the moment the wind is completely out of my sails. Yes, I told him so too. [*Piers:* She told us, too, later, saying that caused her to investigate astrology more thoroughly, but she concluded that it had no validity. Coincidences happen.]

"Saturday. I dreamed that Alfred and I were singing alto in some mammoth choral work. We were the only two altos and they put us at opposite ends of the hall, with hundreds of sopranos in between. The entire composition concluded with a solo bar for altos, but as I couldn't hear Alfred so far away, and couldn't pitch the notes by myself, the rest was silence. . . .

"You should have heard Alfred trying to explain the fourth dimension to the children. He got nowhere at all, and neither did I. Piers insisted that the round cap on the ink bottle which we were using for a demonstration represented a fourth dimension.'" [*Piers:* I don't remember that, but later was satisfied that Time is the fourth dimension.]

Norma wrote to Sheema on July 17:

"I hope to get the children to write to you today, too. Tomorrow isn't a mail day, but I am planning a trip to the village for supplies. I don't usually go down in mid-week, but just now when most of last year's stores are used up and the garden has hardly started to produce, we rely more than usual on stuff from outside.

"This morning they all went for a swim—the swimming place being only just beyond the mailbox (some two miles from here). We were to have gone on Sunday, but it rained. After the heavy rain the river was very full, and the Falls (where we swim) quite spectacular. However, there's one pool which is shallow and safe at all times, so long as they stay in it and don't venture out to where the water is deep and runs swiftly.

"Piers patched up an old inner tube, and although it still leaked it gave everybody a great deal of entertainment. Coming home, we brought back a kitten which was offered as a contribution to our mouse problem. The house is overrun with them and they even keep me awake conducting a kind of Walpurgisnacht[91] in the middle of my bedroom floor in the small hours of the morning. After being wakened twice in one night by Sylvia who was frightened at the noise

---

91. The night of April 30/May 1 was said to be a time when witches and warlocks (male witches) would gather around a bonfire for "wild and orgiastic convocations" at the beginning of the new season.

they made, I resolved that this couldn't go on any longer, traps and poison having proved quite ineffective, and that a cat must be sought. We haven't had good luck with our cats hitherto, largely because I am the only one who likes them, and they seem to kind of wither in the face of so much hostility from other members of the household. [Norma could relate to this herself.] But now that I am 50% of the adult household, maybe it will be better. Alfred is as tired of the mice as I am, and probably ready to admit defeat, after three months of effort on his part have left things just about where they were. As for the children, they are of course overjoyed, and I shall have to exercise some supervision if the kitten isn't to be loved to death in the first few days of its stay. It's an extremely ordinary kitten, but strikes me as having a personality of a sturdy Cockney kind.

"There's a funny scene downstairs now, Piers is playing the accordion and the other three are sitting around and counting, 'one, two, three, four. . . .' On the whole they all get on very well together. Teresa and Sylvia are becoming bosom friends, which I hope is a good thing for both [they have remained so until the present day]—Teresa becoming more feminine and Sylvia less so. Jutta has been as sweet as anything since she realized that tantrums were wasted on me, which she did surprisingly soon. The only person she tries them on now is Sylvia, who has an unfortunate habit of saying 'no,' sometimes to quite a reasonable request, and then giving in after twenty minutes of pandemonium. As she gives in she usually gives me a dirty look, as if to say 'How can you be so cruel to the poor little thing?'

"On the whole, we have surprisingly few scenes of any kind. The most difficult are those which arise over personal possessions, where I can't arbitrate—I have no idea which is whose handkerchief, for instance. This morning a storm blew up over toothbrushes—I hope they haven't both been using the same one all this time, but each is perfectly convinced that the green one is hers. More slight difficulties over conflict of authorities; for instance Sylvia once maintained that thunder was caused by clouds banging together, and Piers exclaimed, 'Listen to the superstition!' Whereat Sylvia said, 'They do so!—Mother told me so!' and began to cry.

"This evening there was a slight dispute because Sylvia said Lee said rice was a vegetable (she began to explain to me who Lee was, but broke off, to my disappointment, and said, 'Oh, you know who Lee is!'). Teresa claimed it was a cereal, and I was obliged to side with her. But these little things are of no consequence and I cite them to show how small our troubles are.

"A regular routine is gradually getting established, for instance we have instituted a rest after lunch as this seems to help prevent short tempers in the evening. And on wet days we pair them off to prevent a brawl from developing. Piers gets on best with Jutta and Sylvia with Teresa, though we sometimes have to break up this particular combination as it gets too excited.

"Once, Sylvia demanded to be paired off with Piers. I could have told her what would happen, but she was thoroughly disgruntled when she found he just wasn't interested in her a bit. With so many girls in the house, most of the time he just keeps to himself and plays solitary games of his own devising. Jutta has pleased Alfred by showing an intelligent interest in goats and earth worms; she has a bucket in the cellar full of earth and worms, and goes to visit them at least once a day. She also enjoys waiting on the kitten, which proved to be house-trained to everybody's surprise and pleasure (especially mine!)."

Norma wrote to Nancy [Montague] on July 20:

"Life continues to be pretty energetic here. Last summer we had a friend and her two small children to stay, and in the autumn she bought a house in the village and settled there, which has made a great difference to us. She finds it too lonely, though, and the people too uncongenial (I think she has outraged some of their rather rigid standards of propriety) and she plans to be away for this winter.

"We've more or less given up wintering here ourselves, at least for the present. I was away last winter, on the doctor's advice, because I simply couldn't get my digestion into sufficiently good order to cope with the diet and the cold and everything else. Alfred took care of the children, with Norm and Winnie's help, and it seemed to be an educational experience for everybody.

"This winter we all plan to be away, probably somewhere near Philadelphia, for about six months. I had a job last year with one of the peace organizations, which I enjoyed a great deal, and since it's a seasonal job I can arrange to go back to it again in October. It's mostly organizing the collection of money, which is a thing I didn't expect to find myself doing, but it involves quite interesting sidelines like talking to small groups of women and getting them enthused about various good causes (just now it's the fight against permanent peace-time conscription), or organizing meetings with a good speaker on the particular subject we're working on at the time.

"I've made the interesting discovery that the majority of the American middle class apparently can't read; if you want them to understand something you have either to call them up on the telephone or go and see them in person. After some experience of trying to unwind the tangles that apparently intelligent people would get into after reading instructions which were as clear as we could make them, I'm just about ready to give up on the written word altogether as a means of communication.

"Norm and Winnie are still here; they bought a piece of land on Briggs Hill (just where we wandered about that day we tried to take the short cut and got lost) and are clearing the ground and getting ready to build over an old cellar hole. Meanwhile they are living in one of the chicken houses which they have made into a desirable summer residence by adding a front porch and a stone chimney and open hearth. Separate living-places for the two families is a great advantage for both, but we co-operate on care of the cow, work in the woods and so on.

"I hope they'll condescend to use this house during the winter, because it is in much better shape now. All the inside is plastered and most of it is painted, and the kitchen has a linoleum floor and washable paper (red and white) on the walls and even a couple of laundry tubs (you can imagine the difference that makes). There is a hot water tank too, waiting to go in.

"Our chief job this summer has been the famous Sanitary Privy, which finally is just about finished; about two weeks ago we solemnly towed away the awful old outhouse and began to use the new one, though it still had no roof, which was disconcerting in wet weather. Fortunately we had a dry spell which lasted pretty well until the roof was on. It's an enormous improvement. We also seem to have reduced the fly population a good deal, though I don't know just how this has been achieved, and they will probably come in their millions in August and September.

Piers: I remember the whole group organizing every week or so, holding dishtowels and waving them in unison to drive the flies forward and out of the house, with the door slammed behind them. But mainly we used fly paper hanging down in spirals from the ceiling: the flies would sit on it and be unable to depart. When one was thoroughly coated with dead and dying flies, it was thrown away and replaced with a new one. As for the privy, it was indeed an improvement. Alfred or Norm opened the back panel and emptied out the accumulated refuse once a week and took it to the compost heap for processing into next year's soil. It was efficient organic recycling.

"Gardenia is still with us, and a couple of goats, but that's all the livestock except for a kitten we got this week to try and keep down the mice. It saddened me greatly to see the other animals go, and I think my hope of ever making a farm out of this finally died when Dickie and the sheep were condemned. I just can't visualize farm life without animals, it doesn't seem to make any sense. But I was the only one who felt that way, so no doubt the change was right.

"This summer we again have children visiting, but without their parents this time. A friend I made in Philadelphia, who has a job that keeps her fully occupied six days a week, didn't know what to do with her two little girls during the summer holidays, so I volunteered to take them. They are nice children, though some of the habits produced in them apparently by the American public school system (such as lying their way out of a situation wherever possible) make new problems for me. Their mother lost her husband in the war in very tragic circumstances and she hasn't been able to have them with her much, and it certainly shows in their behavior. I am learning more about child management, which I suppose is all to the good, and they've been here nearly three weeks without any catastrophe.

"A few others have been here for shorter or longer periods, but no one steadily. Next week some people connected with some labor organization are coming—I expect they will be rather interesting. On the whole, though, it's a quiet summer where visitors are concerned.

"We'd like to hear how things are going in the Montague family, even though our silence hasn't seemed much like it perhaps. I find it terribly difficult to detach my mind enough from the daily worries to write any kind of letter. But if we hear from you, I hope you won't have to wait so long for an answer this time. I am still hoping to get back to England before too long, but don't want to take the children over till I feel more sure of what awaits them on the other side. Their health is fine, and I want it to remain so."

On July 22 Norma wrote to Lucia, saying in part:

"Running ragged is about the word; it isn't only the children, but the cow has been sick this past week and other complications have arisen, such as Teresa breaking her thumb. I had supposed it would be easy to turn the children loose and have peace, since there seemed nothing around here that could hurt them, such as traffic or rattlesnakes, but I hadn't reckoned with man's inhumanity to man. Either through inhumanity or mere thoughtlessness, they seem unable to play for more than an hour at anything not entirely sedentary without one or another coming back to the house damaged and yelling. The damage is always slight, the yell always tremendous. Sylvia in particular seems to be accident-prone; even in a friendly game she is bound to fall and chip pieces off herself.

"In this respect, having them here is much more strenuous than I had expected, though in other respects, such as food, it has proved easier. They are very adaptable and don't complain about this so very different kind of life. Another thing I had omitted to realize in advance is that since they are unable to walk the distance to the village and back [and Alfred refused to 'babysit'], they are entirely cooped up here, and so am I—the little excursions that used to diversify the summer, such as a trip to Arlington to spend the day with the Baumgardts, are out this year.

"And since the Williamses are busy house-building all day, every day, I find it very quiet and dull around here, and long desperately for some adult to talk to.

"Emily Cooper, pillar of the Peace Chest as well as innumerable other good causes, is expected to arrive tomorrow to spend part of her vacation in Jamaica; I had been looking forward greatly to this, but I don't know how much I am going to see of her. Those four miles and 1,100 feet of altitude are an almost insuperable barrier, cutting us off from all but the most active among our acquaintances."

To Sheema, July 26:

"I meant to send you a letter with the mail man each Thursday, but we've had a perfectly distracting week and I am completely off schedule. First, the cow was sick and for about a week we've had practically no milk except about a pint a day from the goats, and a few cans I managed to get in. Now we've sent for the veterinarian to find out what is the matter with her, but meanwhile the feeding problem is acute, since milk is the basis of practically everything we eat.

"Then a whole lot of other things came along, such as a picnic and an auction—all classified as entertainment but much more resembling hard work, especially when small children are involved! And as a further complication, Jutta got her finger mangled sliding in a gravel-pit and I've been working over it two or three times a day. I think it's definitely on the mend now, but I did think I might have to take her down to the doctor, which would consume the greater part of the day as she couldn't walk the full distance, and we'd have to try to take advantage of part-way transportation.

"I shan't get this mailed before Saturday, so you'll get a further report then. What between first rain, and then sultry heat, and bad tempers all around due to the weather, and guests who had to have special treatment—I am in rather a jangled state of nerves!

"We have a young couple here for a few days, Morris and Grace Milgram from New York. He is the Executive Secretary of the Workers' Defense League and very strong against conscription, and when we can get some peace, which is practically never, we amuse ourselves laying plans to defeat conscription decisively in the fall. His wife is very sweet but she thinks she is pregnant, and having recently had a miscarriage she is taking special care of herself, and that also complicates life a bit.

"Then just to add the crowning touch of lunacy, our cow made herself scarce this morning and a friend's cow also chose this day to run away, and the forest is full of tracks and no one knows who is pursuing whose cow. At least no one did know. Alfred set off early this morning following a trail which we supposed was Gardenia's, then about 2 p.m. Gardenia strolled into the barnyard from the opposite direction as though she'd never been away at all, and heaven only knows where Alfred and the other cow are now, especially as they don't know they are looking for each other. We are helpless and can do nothing till he gives up and comes home, by which time he will be in a perfectly terrible temper, and I shan't blame him one bit. Meanwhile I should have spent the day doing the laundry and baking bread, but I wasn't able to do either, and I am wandering about in a demoralized condition wishing it would be over so I could make a fresh start tomorrow morning.

[In retrospect, a cowbell would greatly have simplified these excursions! The Swiss knew what they were doing.]

"Friday. I finally did get the jobs done today, and feel much better. The vet came to see Gardenia, shot her full of sulfa drugs, said the milk from two of her quarters was all right to use (but I'll boil it for a few days for safety) and left, promising to look in again on Monday.

"The children are sitting outside, stark naked, gazing at a big deer which is licking the salt block quite close to the house. They were all out pouring pans of cold water over each other when the deer appeared. That's the second they have seen this week—I got them out of bed in the misty early morning to see the other, for they don't come so near very often at this time of year.

"Jutta's finger is coming along fine. It was a gory mess after the gravel pit incident, and before that she had got it shut in a door, but the incident taught her once and for all not to take bandages off, and now everything is going well and it is practically healed. I impressed on her that she was lucky, she might very well have got blood poisoning.

"I am undertaking three small campaigns, in such spare time as I have. The first is to get your children to realize that when I say, 'No,' I mean just plain No, not Maybe or Ask me again. I'm having some success, though not as much as I should like. The second is against what I believe in the Army is known as gold-bricking—pleading illness in order to get out of something or get some kind of preferential treatment. I fancy this must have worked on Mrs. Willis, but it doesn't work on me. Actually, apart from innumerable cuts and abrasions, neither one has had anything at all the matter with her for the entire four weeks. Even Sylvia's cold, which she wrote about, was a product of her imagination. (We treat diplomatic indispositions with a strict application of rest in bed and perfect quiet—the patient always recovers very fast!)

"The third campaign is to improve their grammar, and I have their hearty co-operation because they know how much it will please you if they lose the idioms you don't like. We have our chaotic moments, but on the whole I am very well satisfied with how we are getting along."

On July 29, Norma wrote to Family:

"My resolution to write more often didn't turn out very well after all. I have had 4 extremely strenuous weeks since I brought my friend's two little girls back from Philadelphia at the end of last month. They are quite nice children, but their life has been a difficult one and they've been badly trained. Their father is dead, and their mother works in an office to support the family, so that she can't look after them at all during the day, and when the school term is over, she doesn't know what to do with them. For a while she had them in a foster home in the country, and though it seems they were not badly treated there, still they were badly mismanaged and have all sorts of bad habits, such as whining for attention and lying, which I am having a good deal of a struggle to correct. In fact, I don't suppose I shall correct them, I am just kept busy trying not to let things get too involved or allow our children to be the victims.

"On the whole we get along all right, but since these children need constant supervision, my time is fully occupied. When they first came, they used to call me in the night, sometimes three or four times, so inadequate sleep was added to my troubles, but they seem to have got over that now. I suppose it was the effect of being in a strange place. They also were terrified of spiders, which of course abound here. To my surprise they got over this fear in a few days, and it hasn't given us any trouble since.

"Their mother has only had them at home for a short while, and of course sees very little of them as she is away from home from 8.30 till 5.30, and though I know she has done her best with them, she hasn't had much of a chance yet. In particular their grammar must be a horror to her—she is a very intelligent woman, a graduate of one of America's best colleges, a Greek and Latin scholar, and would never dream of saying the kind of thing her children picked up in the foster home. I think I can give her some help here, especially as the children know it distresses her to hear them say, 'Them there,' or, 'I don't want none,' and I fancy there is a steady improvement. Luckily our own children's grammar is sufficiently established for them to be out of danger of being corrupted by the example.

"The younger child, age 5, is a flaxen-haired angel in appearance and trades on it; evidently people have always given way to her and favored her at the expense of her older sister. She feels that she has only to screw up her face and begin to cry for everything to be arranged just the way she wants it. I have made some slight headway in getting her to realize that the technique doesn't work on me, but today after four weeks of abstention I finally spanked her. I hope I shan't have to do it again.

"All this is not, of course, as bad as it sounds—we don't have trouble all the time by any means, but I am on duty day and night with little or no relaxation, and can't even write a letter without being called on three or four times. Frankly, I shall be glad when they go back to school at the beginning of September, though I'm glad I was able to take some of the worry from their mother, who has a very difficult time altogether.

"On top of all this our cow is seriously indisposed, and we've had no milk for more than a week. The trouble seems worse than ever today, and I am beginning to wonder if we aren't going to have to destroy our beautiful cow. The vet came two days ago and gave her all sorts of remedies which he evidently hoped would have the desired effect, but she is noticeably worse today. He is coming again tomorrow, luckily. She is supposed to be milked every two or three hours, on top of all my other tasks.

[Some material missing here.]

"Most of the people we know regard Churchill as a great military leader, but they were worried about what was going to happen after the war, when his special talents in that line were no longer required. People, too, are very pleasantly surprised by the way Truman is turning out—he was generally thought to be a complete figure-head, and every time he acts in what seems like an independent way you can almost hear the sigh of relief. A good many people, though, are bitterly regretting the loss of Henry Wallace as vice-president,[92] since he has a very large following among progressively-minded people. Some thought he was too idealistic and regarded this as dangerous, but almost everyone agreed that he was honest—a tribute that, as far as I can tell, is practically never paid to an American politician.

"Our plans for the autumn are not any more settled. As the matter stands now, we leave here in the middle of October and hope it will be possible for us to live at Pendle Hill for six months. The children then will probably go to different schools—Piers to a private and experimental school, Teresa to the local elementary school which is small and well-spoken of. It's possible that Pendle Hill will not have room for us, and then house-hunting will begin, though I think in any case we shall try and stay in the same general neighborhood. I specially want to get the children into different schools, because I think Piers is very much oppressed by having Teresa around all the time. Even since the two other girls have been here, occupying Teresa's attention, he has seemed in much better spirits and his bed-wetting has practically stopped.

"My photography has been very unsuccessful this summer; I have a film now waiting to be developed, but I can't hope for much from it judging by the disappointing results from the two previous ones. I am particularly sorry that I don't seem able to get a good snapshot of Teresa, for she is really blossoming out in the last few months; she is becoming very tall and graceful and looks splendid in more grown-up clothes. But somehow, when I do get a picture she is always either screwing up her face or moving so fast that her limbs are nothing but a blur.

"This next winter I'll try and get a family portrait; I hoped to last Christmas, but was frustrated by Piers' stay in the hospital. Teresa of course

---

92. Roosevelt designated Wallace as his running mate over the considerable objection of many convention delegates. Four years later, in 1944, Roosevelt jettisoned him in favor of Harry S. Truman. Although widely judged a failure as vice president, Wallace was in many ways a forerunner of modern vice presidents.

isn't the only one who is growing up. Piers is now shorter than she is—I think he will be relatively short and broad, like the other Jacob boys—but he is very strong and getting to be quite ingenious. This afternoon, for instance, entirely of his own accord he made a replacement part for the back door latch, which has been a source of irritation for months. Our latches are of wood, and in theory anybody could have fixed it up, but somehow nobody ever did. Piers worked out in his head what was needed and then went and whittled it out with Alfred's tools. He is also learning to play the accordion.

"Teresa too, was learning, but her lessons were held up because of the accident to her thumb. I think I told you that she hurt it and we were afraid it might be broken. An X-ray shows that it was, but not seriously—the bone wasn't out of place—and she has now had it out of the splint for a week and it is almost back to normal again. I don't think any mark will be left."

Norma wrote to Minta [Work] on July 30:

"Your two letters should have been answered last week, but as you know I have two extra children here, and there isn't much in the way of deviltry that these two innocent babes won't think up—and what they don't think of, mine do. Also, poor Gardenia is very sick, and I not only have to nurse her but to contrive feeding the household with such canned milk as I can carry up from the village with all the other groceries. It has been a strenuous time. Tomorrow I'm taking twenty-four hours off and leaving Winnie in charge; Alfred and I are off to meet a very old friend from England who is staying near Rutland. Communications being so bad, we'll be spending the night in Manchester, which will make a little outing for us.

"First of all, I'm sending back your check—I can't imagine how you figured you owed me anything like that. At the outside it would be about $3.24 or whatever, if you absolutely feel you must, but that's all. I would subtract it from the fifteen and return the balance, but we're all out of check forms. We have a sweatshirt of Craig's and I think a couple of other things—I'm afraid it may be a long time before I get around to making them into a tidy parcel, that being a thing I always put off if there's anything else I can do first, and so unless you send an S.O.S. I'll return them to you when you get back to New York.

"These two children who are here now would make an interesting study for you. They are the daughters of a German father and an American Jewish mother; their father most probably was killed in the war, as nothing has been heard from him for three years. Their mother has a fearfully hard time of it, and had them in a foster home for quite a while. This proved so unsatisfactory that she brought them to her apartment in Philadelphia, but as she works long hours in an office their home life even so is reduced to a minimum. The poor little things show the results of being fatherless and batted around from one person to another. I know I have not been the best possible influence for them, but we get on increasingly well and at least they are out of the city and not at large in the streets. It means a few difficulties for my children, who in matters such as honesty are accustomed to a much higher standard than theirs, but there have been corresponding advantages. Teresa has met her match for bossiness, and I think is getting a very salutary lesson. As for Piers, he has Teresa off his neck for the first time in his life, and the improvement has been most noticeable; he has given up bed-wetting, for one thing. This makes me feel sure I am right in planning to send them to separate schools this next year.

"About schools, I considered the Philadelphia public schools but only very briefly. I went to visit one which was specially recommended and was appalled by its size and impersonality. It would be like throwing one's children into the jaws of a sausage machine, except one wouldn't have much idea of what would emerge at the other end.

"Did you hear of The School in Rose Valley? It's a relatively small private day school in a small town not far from Media—about fourteen miles from Philadelphia. I've heard of it often, and on this trip I visited it and was very much impressed. It seemed to me to have most of the good features of Manumit, and as it's a day school, the things our children disliked there would be obviated. The present plan is to send Piers there and to let Teresa go to the local elementary school, which is small and also well-spoken of. I was a little afraid that Teresa might feel this was discrimination, but she doesn't seem to. I think she would prefer to be on her own and in a public school.

"I am hoping we can live at Pendle Hill; if not, we'll have the home-finding problem all over again, but it would be quite possible to live in West Philadelphia, where we have an apartment more or less offered, and send the children out to school by train each day. This would actually fit in better with my office hours, though in other ways it wouldn't be so good."

Piers: Norma really worked at seeing to the children's education, and though we did not like Manumit, she also found The School in Rose Valley, and later Goddard College in Vermont, the one that truly changed my life. That was where I became a vegetarian, decided to become a professional writer, and met the girl I married.

Norma continued: "[It's] time I went and put my little charges to bed. I had the bright idea this evening of improvising a seesaw, which has kept them amused for about two hours, but it is now starting to pass and I think it's time to bind up the day's crop of cuts and bruises and get them tucked away. How thoroughly and thankfully I relax when silence settles down upstairs!"

August 1945

On August 2, Norma wrote to Edith Wood:

"I'm happy to report that I arrived home quite safely with all the groceries and found everything well with the children; the poor cow, though, is very sick and the vet thinks she will die, though she herself seems to be making a determined effort to live. I do hope she will survive at least until Alfred gets home.

"On my way up through the woods I saw my first skunk, which I recognized at once from your description. It was going quietly in the opposite direction, so I didn't stop to speak to it.

"We so much enjoyed our visit to you, and it was very kind indeed of you to think of it. I hope perhaps by next summer, if the gasoline situation is better you may be able to come and see us, though I'm afraid we have nothing to offer to compare with the Rogers farm! I hope we may see something of you this coming winter."

Piers: It is not mentioned in the correspondence, but on August 6 I had my 11th birthday, and on that day the United States dropped the atomic bomb on Hiroshima, effectively ending that war and inaugurating the era of nuclear weapons. The date of it bothers me, as well as the ethics; I suspect they could have made a demonstration on an uninhabited island to persuade Japan to surrender.[93]

On August 8, Norma wrote to Dick and Cynthia:

"Hilltop news is of a mixed order. Congenial people are moving gradually into the area and the rudiments of co-operation are beginning to be visible. But it's very slow, and Hilltop's remoteness means that we are almost entirely left out. One can't co-operate very effectively even with one's nearest neighbor if one has no transportation, since 'near' means as much as five miles away.

"I keep hoping things will loosen up, but there are a variety of other things which make me feel that for at least this coming winter we ought to be somewhere else. So we are planning to be away from here from mid-October to mid-April. We have no livestock to keep us here, except a cow

---

[93]. While there were those who advocated for a demonstration bomb in an unoccupied area, more of President Truman's advisors felt that the true destruction and resulting terror would not be achieved if only a relatively few people were affected. Seventy thousand were killed in the initial blast, another 70,000 died of radiation exposure, and 80,000 died in Nagasaki three days later. Japan surrendered on August 14, 1945.

who has been boarded out the last two winters anyway, and she at the moment has a perfectly terrible case of mastitis and has been condemned to death by the vet. She herself seems to think she will live, but it's extremely doubtful if she'll come back into milk, and I'm afraid she has a good chance of being beef before October.

"I don't see what can be done in the co-operative field before next Spring except wood chopping, and this leaves the women entirely out, and the loneliness is more than I can stand. The Williamses, who have been with us more than two years, are building their own house about a mile away. They hope for a baby in April.

"Please let us know how things go with you. It was grand to see Leslie and Valerie—and how much I'd like to see you too! I simply have never been within possible distance to visit you, and all my absences from home are as short as I can make them. But this time maybe we can really bring it off."

Norma's letter to Polly Robinson of August 15 said in part:

"Well, there's quite a lot of news with us, as you might imagine after so long a time. [She went on to mention the cow, the visiting children, and the Williamses. In addition, there is some missing material here.]

"So as soon as the weather permitted, [Norm and Winnie] moved out into the chicken house, which by now they have made into a really comfortable residence. I came back about that time, and we did a good deal of fixing up in the house, principally in the kitchen, which is really quite something now. Feeling that it was my own house at last made things a lot easier in many ways. However, many of the old difficulties remained, as you can imagine, and I think you'll see why I grew to feel that we should all move out this coming winter and get our batteries re-charged by a closer contact with the outer world. All the Jacobs, that is. Hilltop simply won't meet the essential needs of any of us all the year round, at least the way things are at present.

"So, after some thought on all sides, this is what has been settled. I go back to my winter job with the Peace Chest, which luckily runs just during the months that no agriculture is possible here. Alfred spends the winter in study (he might take a post-graduate course at the U. of P.) and perhaps in giving some voluntary help to the F.O.R., which is expanding its Philadelphia office and needs help very badly. The children go to school, probably near Pendle Hill, where I hope it will be possible for us to live. When spring comes and my job peters out, we return here for the next agricultural year. After that, no one knows.

"Meanwhile, the house here will be in the Williamses' hands. They still want separate family life, but they expect to keep a guest room available for the casual visitors who drop in and out at any season of the year. They have bought a piece of land in the field that you go through on the short cut down to the school, and are starting to clear it and believe they will be building soon. But they obviously can't build anything weathertight before winter, so it's lucky this place will be available. Especially as Winnie is now pretty sure she is pregnant—poor girl, she has all the signs, such as nausea and depression—and the baby should be along some time in April, just about when we are due to come back.

"It all fits in rather neatly, I think. Hilltop gets continuity, the Williamses get a home, and the Jacobs get a sabbatical leave, and how they do need it by this time! I still hope fervently that the right people to be bosses here will come along, if C.P.S. demobilization gets going. We would stand down if a couple came who obviously had what it took to make the place a success on good decentralist lines. I long more and more to get back to Europe and back into the relief and reconstruction field. If you know of any possible people, send them along.

"Things are getting quite changed in the valley, by the way. All the old timers are moving out except perhaps the Smiths, and even they may do so when the son comes back from the wars. And more of our kind of people are moving in. Some people called Hazard from Connecticut, strong School of Living enthusiasts, are negotiating to buy the Twing place, and expect to be in before winter. The Fields and Scott are still going strong. I think we really have the makings here for a loosely-knit co-operative group of families in the valley.

"For me, though, I'm afraid it is too late. The point came, and passed, where I could no longer hold on to my hopes and shifted them elsewhere. My real center of gravity now is somewhere out in the wide world, and willy-nilly I expect I shall find myself driven out to look for it. These movements of the human mind are rather mysterious things but very inexorable in their effects.

"One other piece of news, and this is a sad one—poor Gardenia will probably be beef before very long. She was going along in fine style, giving four gallons a day, when suddenly she developed acute mastitis. That's a month ago. The vet thought she would die when the infection was at its height; he dosed her with sulfanilamide and she now seems to be recovering, but it's doubtful whether she'll ever be worth her keep as a milker again. And can we expect anyone else to board her if we can't do it ourselves? Little Gladiola (remember her?) is now giving huge quantities of milk over at Field's. There's just a chance someone might take Gardenia to get another calf from her, as she showed up so well."

September 1945

Norma wrote to Family on September 5:

"Your letter saying that Dorothy Emmet's book had been sent off 'some weeks ago,' or words to that effect, arrived by the same mail as the book itself. I'm very happy to have it, and plan to settle down to some serious reading in a couple of days' time, when our young guests will have gone. They are to leave early tomorrow morning, and I can assure you I shall heave a sigh of relief!

"They have not been altogether easy children to look after, and of course the responsibility is very heavy—I shall be so happy if I can get them safely shipped back to their mother, after nearly ten weeks without any major calamity. In fact, nothing has been wrong the whole time except for the inevitable cuts and scratches.

"But they have made pretty heavy demands on my patience and time; in particular their habit of waking up and calling out in the night was a trial, since after a day of heavy manual work, I felt a real need for my eight hours of undisturbed sleep. Yesterday I went to bed dog tired after an afternoon spent working in the woods, and was called three times! I plan to spend tomorrow clearing up and putting away, washing sheets and so on, then spend the whole of Friday in bed, just luxuriating in my own laziness and being waited on.

"I'm not sure whether I told you that Piers' birthday book came in plenty of time. Books, I should say. The one about woodworking had lots of ideas in it and he has been trying some of them out. He is really very clever with his hands. Speaking of birthdays, I can't really believe I shall be thirty-six next month.

"This is the time of year for casual visitors, and people drop in almost every day, especially now that they can buy gasoline freely for the first time in about three years. Three arrived yesterday. It's pretty difficult to feed them, since we still have no milk except the little the goats give. The cow is condemned to become beef as soon as we get in touch with the butcher—a terrible tragedy for one so young and beautiful, but it is hopeless to think of keeping her through the long winter with hay so expensive.

"By the way, another very pleasant young couple is thinking of spending the winter up here. We like to have our house used as fully as possible, and if it stands empty any time the chipmunks (attractive little animals like tiny red squirrels) find their way in through cracks and make nests in the bedding. Also, hunters may break in during the deer season. So, the more people around, the better.

"We expect to move about the second week in October, or possibly a little before; I had been sticking to my provisional date, but now I have a communication from the new School Superintendent (evidently wanting to impress the local people with his zeal) telling me I must make sure the children get the full school year; if they are going to be late in starting in the new school, they must attend the local school here during the interval. This will be very difficult to arrange, and I think not very good for our children. As the man is within his legal rights, though previous Superintendents have been willing to trust us to see that our children were sufficiently educated, it may mean moving a little sooner, as the school I want Piers to go to opens on September 29th. The one we planned for Teresa I'm afraid opens some weeks earlier. It is all rather complicated. Bother the officious man.

"I see your letter which reached here on the 4th was postmarked August 12th—this is really encouraging. Two postcards from you have also come for each child. The pictures of Sussex cottages excited them very much, and Teresa was especially thrilled to be told that she was born in a thatched cottage something like that. Now they want to know if we'll live in a thatched cottage when we go back to England!

"We are beginning to think seriously about Europe now that travel restrictions seem to be slackening up much earlier than we had expected. I even entertain the idea of coming over for a visit next summer, that is unless something unexpected makes it seem advisable for us all to move back [to England] about that time. I had previously been thinking of about this time next year as a possible time for a move. One has to see what possibilities exist in any field we might want to go into, and at present there is the difficulty that I am very anxious to get back into relief work, and Alfred is somewhat against it, so it's really impossible to look ahead. But I do entertain the hope that within the next year you may see something of us, though I don't know in what circumstances.

"Teresa wrote another letter and I hope I haven't lost it—it has been lying about on my desk for about a week. I simply couldn't write letters while those children were getting ready for departure. The last ten days were terrible; their uncle [Arthur Zeben] was here, and his presence encouraged them to behave worse than they'd thought of doing all the rest of their stay. Poor man, it wasn't his fault. He seemed very distressed to find them so difficult, but I couldn't exactly say, 'Don't worry, it's only because you are here!' He finally took them off on Thursday morning. The original plan had been for their mother to come and fetch them this weekend."

September 9, Norma wrote to Father and Caroline:

"I somehow felt as though school and all that sort of thing was a long way off, and suddenly I find myself confronted with the fact that school has already begun in Jamaica, and the local superintendent (a new man, full of zeal) wants to know why our children aren't attending. I wrote him that we expected to be sending our children to school down in Pennsylvania this winter, but he seems inclined to insist that they must attend for the full school year even if they have to put in two or three weeks here. That seems to me perfectly silly; it will be extremely hard to send the children to Jamaica, and I do not at all like the kind of children that go to the Jamaica school. Piers and Teresa, after their one brief experience there, are very anxious not to be sent there again. [*Teresa*: All I remember about the Jamaica school was that they provided grapefruit juice and graham crackers at snack time, both of which were unfamiliar treats for us.]

"All this is making me wonder whether we oughtn't to change our original plan, which called for moving in the middle of October, after all the harvesting was done here.

"Here's what I have just been suggesting to Alfred, and I'll be glad to know how it sounds to you. We might move—that is, the children and I might come down by train—about the last week in this month—and perhaps stay a little while with you. If the children are to go to school, one in Wallingford, the other in Rose Valley, which is the present idea, we could easily send them from West Chester on the train for a while. [*Teresa*: Which is what happened; I recall making that long walk through town to reach the train station. It may have been during that time that I got chickenpox and the house was quarantined. I spent time in the guest bedroom with its embroidered linen sheets, being waited on by the black maid—quite a change from Hilltop.]

"I could stay about a week, see them safely started, and meanwhile look round for a place for us to move into. I had hoped to have this all settled by now, and in fact made two trips down to Philadelphia in the summer, each time hoping to get it all fixed up, but we still are pretty much where we were, and I am afraid some further exploration is inevitable before we can know just where we are to live and what to bring. (I'm afraid it will have to be not further out than Wallingford, because I should lose so much time commuting to and from Philadelphia—I have to arrange to be home as soon as possible after the children get back from school, and I feel Wallingford is about the outside limit of the journey I could find time for each day).

"However, before I start work West Chester would be all right, if you were willing to have us for a short while. Then I thought perhaps when I'd found where we were to live, I could come back up here—leaving the children with [Alfred's brothers] John or Eddie if it seemed better—and help Alfred with the final packing-up, and we could come down with the truck about the time we originally planned—some time in the second week in October. Alfred thinks it might be better for us all to plan to move out—truck, goat, furniture and all at the end of this month, and for him to make a trip back later, if necessary, for the final clearing-up. I see difficulties about that, but it isn't a very important point.

"This afternoon I am hoping to see the superintendent and may be able to make some other arrangement with him, so we could stick to our original plan. But there is much to be said for letting the children start in the new school, or schools, as early as possible, if it doesn't mean too much sacrifice at this end. We have a good deal of clearing up to do, as others will probably be occupying this house during the winter.

"Will you send us a card to say how it all strikes you?"

Norma wrote to Miriam Fredenthal on September 14:

"Sylvia and Judy [Jutta] finally left a week ago, and I've been recovering more or less ever since. [For] the last ten days Arthur was here, and they behaved like little fiends. I think they had a subconscious feeling that he was one of them and would protect them against any discipline that was irksome, also they took a wicked delight in embarrassing him, and you know he embarrasses so easily. The last week was perfectly hellish, and when he finally took them off I retired to bed for 36 hours just to get up my energy again.

"Almost immediately after that we decided to accelerate our move, and as it stands now, we'll be out of here by Sunday week (the 23rd). So now I am going through all you went through in the way of sorting out and packing up, except that I have three extra handicaps—I have the accumulation of four and a half years of junk, I don't know where we are going so don't know what to pack with us, and finally I don't know who, if anybody, will be living in this house during the winter or what we'll want to have left or how.

"At first, you know, Norm and Winnie thought they would move in here. Then a proposal was brought forward that the Ladds should occupy the house, and the Williamses the corn crib. I think that's a fine idea, but I have heard not a word of it from the Ladds—only indirectly through Winnie. No one seems to think this at all strange! So now I have to leave things so that the Ladds will find them as they want, without any sort of direct communication with the Ladds whatever.

"I know Paul has been out in the Middle West looking at homesteading projects, and I understand they won't make any decision till he returns. But I hope very much that I'll see Eva at least, next Monday when a gang of us is going over with Helen (I hope) to a meeting in Manchester. If I don't get a chance to talk with Eva then about linen, china, etc. [of course generic terms, as Hilltop had nothing remotely like that!] I shall be in a still worse complication, time being so short. Alfred will probably be here for part of

October, finishing up the harvesting and odd jobs, and may take a truckload of stuff down, but what am I to pack? I don't even know whether we'll be living in a furnished or an unfurnished place!

"However, my spirits are rising. I've written my office and told them I'll be in to see how they are getting along, probably on the 24th. And the tidying-up is so thorough that I'm finding things that had been missing for years, and have a real sense of achievement.

"For the first week or so, we'll go to Alfred's parents in West Chester. After that, we hope to get a small (very small!) apartment at Pendle Hill where we can do our own cooking and have our own family life, but be within the general sphere of activity of a lot of congenial people. It's an excellent arrangement for us, and I hope it works out. I can't give you an address, but I shall give people here my office address (1924 Chestnut, Philadelphia 5, Room 301) which will always find me. We'll probably have most of our mail sent there, as Pendle Hill's mail service is a little erratic.

"We certainly miss you in the village. There isn't any gossip, as far as I know, but that doesn't prove anything. I didn't even know, till Natalie told me the other day, that the F.B.I. was reported to have found a short-wave transmitter in our barn! The source for this lovely story was apparently someone who spends her summers in Wardsboro, but I have no doubt it's widely believed."

The last Hilltop letter of 1945 is Norma's to Valerie Johnston, dated September 20.

"Many congratulations both on [new baby] Erica and on Leslie's job. A frivolous friend of ours wants to know whether you named her after Eric Johnston of the U.S. Chamber of Commerce?

"I'll have to stay [here] till some time next week, as the Williamses are away just now picking apples in Bennington. We are leaving the house for the winter to Paul and Eva Ladd (with whom Norm and Winnie are staying this week) and I am very busy clearing away junk and getting things ready for them to move in, probably some time next month. They will take over the goats, which will mean we won't have to board them out or take them with us as we expected. All in all, it's a very satisfactory arrangement. They are very community-minded and I hope will stay a full year and make Hilltop more of a community center than it's ever been yet, though they are adamant against staying here permanently; they say it's too remote for the kind of community life they want to see established.

"Anyway, we get more time and the ideal solution [to the original community concept] may still come along, especially if they start releasing men from C.P.S., which I gather depends on whether Congress gets around to passing some bill within the next ten days. Apparently it's a bill to delay releasing any C.P.S. men until all men in the armed forces are released, so I certainly hope that their calendar is so full they'll forget about it. If they pass it, it seems as though Friends' European relief is impossible, as they won't be able to draw on their manpower reserve. But I know there are plenty of men in Congress dumb enough to dig out this bill and insist on trying to force it through, if they happen to remember it.

"We had a horde of guests yesterday—a boy from the Retreat unit who's been here before (his wife was one of the original Fellowship Farm committee) and his neighbor, a farmer with an idea for reforming the entire social system. I can't pretend I fully understand it, but he was very enthusiastic about it. After dark there came a couple we met only last Monday over in Manchester—they live near the Fishers & Baumgardts in Arlington. They seem to have taken to us at sight, and after our brief meeting Monday made this long trip over after dark just for an hour's visit. Encouraging, but too rare. Their name is Edson, and both worked in the Boston Public Library before coming to Vermont. I hope we see more of them in the spring."

Thus did the Hilltop experiment end,
"not with a bang, but a whimper."
—T. S. Eliot

1945

IMAGE 22: *This unusual artifact—an engraved tree ear fungus—was donated to the historical museum in Jamaica by Piers, who supervised the signing. It is displayed in a glass case.*

The community picnic at which this memento was created was extensively photographed and the local circumstances (and inhabitants) described in Rebecca Lepkoff and Greg Joly, *Almost Utopia: The Residents and Radicals of Pikes Falls, Vermont* (Vermont Historical Society, 2008). At that time Piers had just turned 16 and Teresa was 14.

Epilogue

For several years after the war the family lived in a tiny two up, two down "gardener's cottage" in Wallingford, Pennsylvania. Alfred soon left to move into the city, and Miriam Fredenthal and her children shared the house briefly. Piers and Teresa went to Westtown School. Alfred and Piers sometimes spent summers at Hilltop, but Norma did not, and it was no longer a subsistence farm. It was doomed from the start, because Alfred and Norma were incompatible in many essential ways and could not make a life together, though they shared many views about the futility of war.

After a long separation they divorced in 1952, and Alfred remarried. Both went on to obtain PhD degrees at the University of Pennsylvania. Norma spoke and wrote extensively about mental health issues, obtained a Master of Social Work degree, and in 1980 was a delegate to the Democratic Convention, where she shook hands with President Jimmy Carter. Alfred taught Spanish at Franklin and Marshall College for a few years, but preferred to spend his time on arcane scholarly projects that did not involve any social interaction. He and his second wife, who did not drive, returned to Hilltop in the summers. She became concerned that an accident might occur for which she would be unable to summon help, and they sold the property to Stuart Dauchy in 1960, to be maintained as a forest farm.

Herbert Leader married, worked at several blue-collar jobs, survived surgery for a benign brain tumor, and remained a free spirit until his death in 1988.

Nancy Montague returned to England in 1944 and was reunited with her husband after five years. She had three more children, suffered declining health in the postwar conditions, and eventually had a mental collapse from a sort of Post-Traumatic Stress Disorder. "She was a wonderful mother to us," her son Donald recalled in 1994. "She gave us a sense of adventure and a love of words." Nancy died in 1992.

Norm and Winnie Williams built their house in the old cellar hole, calling the homestead Welkincroft, "small farm under the sky." After some years, with a growing family, they sold the property back to Alfred in 1955. Eventually economics drove them away too, to settle finally near Washington, DC, where Norm became involved in top-level government issues.

Scott Nearing and Helen Knothe married and moved to Maine in 1952, where they established another subsistence farm that became a mecca for back-to-the-land enthusiasts. Scott died in 1983 at age 100, having decided that he had lived long enough, and it was time to go.

Miriam Fredenthal's children, Robinson and Ruthann, became recognized artists in their own right, Robin as a sculptor, Ruthie, as an abstract painter. Robin developed multiple sclerosis at age 24 and spent many years confined to a wheelchair before his death in 2008. Miriam purchased a house adjacent to Pendle Hill and established a community art center there, later moving to Bennington, Vermont.

Teresa and Piers grew up to make their own lives with their own complications. Piers is a popular author of many science fiction/fantasy novels, using the pen name Piers Anthony. He lives in Florida with his wife and daughter. Teresa obtained a master's degree from Pennsylvania State University, worked as an editor at the corporate headquarters of the Quakers in Philadelphia, and traveled widely, indulging the sense of adventure noted by her Manumit teacher.

A number of the participants in the Hilltop endeavor stayed in the vicinity, and their descendants remain in the Pikes Falls area.

Following its sale, many upgrades were made to the house, inside and out (but not including plumbing or electricity). Following Stuart Dauchy's death, it remained unfinished and unoccupied except for vacation use or storage. His son Jim, who lives at Lumbercamp Corner with his family, is now the owner. A tree-filled cellar hole marks where the barn once stood. Mice and spiders have reclaimed their territory.

Could it have worked, had our parents been more compatible? Perhaps, but the burden of the children, the rigors of the remote location, and most importantly the unanticipated social conflicts, made it unlikely. Norma's physical and mental health challenges, Alfred's difficult personality and tunnel vision, and from beginning to end the naivete of all those involved, made success virtually unachievable.

It is ironic that we, as the only survivors, have compiled this history, learning for the first time as we did so of the ultimately insurmountable personal trials that led to the collapse of the dream.

Piers Anthony Jacob
Teresa Jacob Engeman

Appendix I

My Experience in Civilian Public Service Camps

Jan Long, one of a number of essays contributed by former COs to the book *Men of Peace: World War II Conscientious Objectors*, Mary R. Hopkins, editor (2010)

I DECIDED I WOULD BECOME A CONSCIENTIOUS OBJECTOR while I was a student in college, and registered that intent with my draft board in New York City. I was sent in 1943 to Gorham, New Hampshire, to a camp that was engaged in timber-stand improvement in the national forest, run by the National Forest Service. There were two people who were Jehovah's Witnesses, one who called himself Walking Jerusalem and the other, Peaceful Brother. In the dormitory, some were conscientious objectors for purely political reasons, draft dodgers for all I know. They were unhappy and were causes of worry to the director of the camp. They were notable for not doing any assigned work, or as little as possible. The group I was in was nice, quiet Quaker types who did as they were told and enjoyed the experience, or at least didn't resent it.

During the day we were loaded into trucks and taken into the forest, where we were trimming the timber stand, thinning them out to get better tree growth. At lunch time we would leave our section of the woods and come to a central area where the foreman had lunch ready for us. After half an hour we'd go off again in pairs to the area where we were cutting. The wood was cut into cord lengths and stacked. I don't know what it was for; it may have gone to pulp mills for all I know.

Two things I learned there; one was a lifelong appreciation of peanut butter and jelly sandwiches, and the other was that I decided to read the Bible, cover to cover. I did get through a good deal of the first book, Genesis, but not a great deal further. I came up against Leviticus, and that is what stopped me.

In March that camp closed, and we were given a choice of going to California, Nevada, or Oregon. My friends and I chose Oregon, going out by the Union Pacific railroad to Portland, and then by bus down to Elkton.

There, the project was under the direction of the Oregon and California Revested Lands Administration, a division of the Department of [the] Interior. We were to work on both sides of a right-of-way for the railroad, being available to fight fires during the dry summer. I don't know whether they were concerned about the possibility of the Japanese setting incendiary fires as a form of attack on the United States. In any case they needed men to fight fires, and young men weren't readily available, because they'd been drafted.

Our group was given a choice of going to the Big Creek camp where they were building a logging road, or another camp, McKinley, where they had a tree nursery. The logging road seemed like more direct helping in the war effort than we were interested in, so, nursing our tender consciences, we decided to go to McKinley. The work there was to develop trees that could then be used in re-planting.

It turned out that the cook needed a helper, and when no one else volunteered for such an unpopular job, I decided to try it. After I helped with lunch the next day, the cook walked out, saying, "All right, here's the menu, the food is around. Get supper." That was the beginning of a challenge that went on for quite a while. Supplies arrived once a week, with a menu. The problem was to make the supplies last until the next truck came! Because there was meat rationing, meat was highly desirable, and when there was a deer kill out on the road one day, I went out and got it. I forget whether I was going to bring it back to camp, or butcher it out in the bush. In any case I brought the liver in, and we had deer liver for dinner one night. But before I got any further, someone from the county appeared and took it off for the county home, so that was the end of that.

Some months later I was shifted to the main camp at Elkton, where I became the property clerk, keeping track of where the beds were and the mattresses, and how many blankets there were *here*, and how many *there*.

After that I was sent out to two tree-planting camps. One of them was in Veneta, Oregon, not far from Elkton, where we were re-planting an area that had been burned over. You started off with a bundle of a thousand trees and started up a hillside, walking a fixed number of paces. There was a long line of men working together. Everybody stopped, made a hole in the dirt with a mattock, stuck a tree in it, kicked dirt over it, and then the whole line moved up again. The result was that the whole hillside got planted in a reasonably effective manner.

The other tree-planting was at McMinville, part of what was known as the Tillamook Burn. The Burn was a catastrophic series of forest fires that lasted at intervals from 1933 to 1951, destroying 355,000 acres, or 554 square miles, of old-growth timber. Traces of the Burn could still be seen along the roadsides well into the 1970s.

APPENDIX I

In March of 1945 a friend and I were sent back east, to New Haven, to a "guinea pig" unit there. Research was being done about the cause or transmission of infectious hepatitis, which had become a considerable problem, particularly in the campaigns in Italy, and they needed some guinea pigs to try out different methods of spreading the disease. We were given capsules, we didn't know where they had come from or what they had in them. If there was a baptismal font with water, could it be a source for transmission of hepatitis, or could it come from the drinking water? For whatever reason, I came down with it. It wasn't much fun, but at least I was in a medical school with a good hospital (with pretty nurses who gave fabulous back rubs!). During my long convalescence I managed to get through both volumes of *An American Dilemma* by Gunnar Myrdahl [Myrdal].

The other work I did there was on polio research. There was an epidemic in Paterson, New Jersey. Another man and I were sent down there in a pickup truck to set out traps to catch flies. We went around once a day and collected the traps and froze the flies in a refrigerator in which there was dry ice, so it was a quick freeze. Back in New Haven we sorted them by species, the idea being that perhaps some species of flies were involved in polio transmission, and not other species.

I also at some point worked in the Yale "mouse house," filled floor to ceiling with cages of mice, like stacks in a library. My job was to start in the morning and work my way down, cleaning the cages, restocking the food holders and making sure the water bottles were filled. The odor from the mouse house would cling to your clothes, so I had one set of clothes to work in and a fresh outfit to wear back at the dormitory.

Finally, I was sent to Big Flats, New York, a forestry camp where they raised seedlings. I remember hardly anything about it, as I was discharged fairly soon afterward, in April of 1946.

The stated purpose of the CPS camps was to accomplish "work of national importance, under civilian direction." Little attempt was made to interpret the work or relate its significance to the national need. The result was a good deal of poor morale. The people doing it had no background in whatever their assignment was. Often they were from urban or suburban areas, and working out in the countryside or the woods was not a satisfactory way to be protesting the war.

We had little contact with the surrounding community. The camps had been used under the Roosevelt administration for the Civilian Conservation Corps, "a public work relief program that operated from 1933 to 1942 for unemployed, unmarried men." The CCC was disbanded and the camps, mostly in isolated regions, were repurposed for the CPS workers.

I'm not sure of any real impact the experience had on me, except that as a result of my service there I got a job at a Quaker school [Westtown] whose headmaster was specifically looking for CPS "graduates." For the most part I have no continuing relationships with people I worked with in the camps.

JL, 1987

Appendix II

LIBERATION magazine was published from 1956 to 1977 and was run by David Dellinger, Bayard Rustin, Sidney Lens, Roy Finch, and A. J. Muste. It was a bimonthly printed by Dellinger from his shop in a small anarchist community in Glen Gardner, New Jersey. It supported unilateral nuclear disarmament and opposition to Jim Crow and the Vietnam War thru nonviolent resistance, and was the first to publish Martin Luther King Jr.'s "Letter from a Birmingham Jail." Norma's article appeared in 1962.

Community Examined. . . .
Community—But Not Utopia

Norma Jacobs [*sic*]

I BELIEVE THAT THERE ARE WAYS OF LIVING in which human beings, through a high degree of mutuality, can develop capacities which ordinary competitive life thwarts or twists out of shape. On the other hand, I recall some rather disillusioning experiences with attempts to bring this ideal to practical fulfillment. I am left with a number of firm convictions about the things which work against the realization of the community ideal.

First is the tendency to overestimate the amount of self-sacrifice of which human beings are capable over a long period. In a brief emergency, almost anyone can perform feats normally beyond him, but for this effort to continue there has to be continued pressure from outside. Just the task of keeping alive day after day, even in an ideal society, doesn't make us able to work at an abnormal level. Inevitably a slowing-down occurs, work schedules can't be met, disillusionment creeps in, harsh words are exchanged, and the community begins to crumble at its edges as people move away.

So the first essential, from my point of view, is a realistic assessment of what we can expect of ourselves, not just when enthusiasm is high, but later, when routine has become established. That means much better planning than is usual with groups full of desire to abandon the world of shifts and compromises and build a new heaven on earth. We are people, not angels, and should face that fact at the start of our experiment, rather than have it thrust crudely upon us at its end.

Non-material Needs

Second is the disregard for non-material needs. Plain living and high thinking sound good, but they do not make up a balanced diet. We need art, music (better music than we can make for ourselves), learning new things from new minds, recreation; many things that seem to unbalance the Spartan budget in the direction of needless luxury. After a long period of deprivation, the experience of hearing a symphony can be as painful as that of feeling blood return to a frost-bitten finger. I am thinking now of a group [at Hilltop] which refused the offered loan of a piano on the ground that "too much time was being wasted already." This same group sternly rebuked one of its members who liked to cook and had expended love and skill in making an attractive dish out of the available materials; they said she had been wasting time, which was the property of the community.

This is simply a slow form of death, comparable to the quicker death which comes if we deprive ourselves of the immediate material needs like food, clothing or sleep. We cannot provide ourselves with a sufficient cultural universe out of our own resources.

Third obstacle—the insistence on too much communal living. I believe myself that one communal meal a day is about as much as flesh and blood will stand. Every family must have its own separate living space, preferably its own separate house. Children are not community property: they belong to themselves, and our task is to see that they enjoy their birthright, which is family life. I learned from Stephen Spender's book, *Learning Laughter*, that this realization is beginning to creep into the most communally minded of the settlements in Israel.

Obstacle number four is the attempt to get along at too low a standard of physical subsistence. This is insidious and does not show itself in most ways until the damage has gone quite far. Unnecessary fatigue cuts into working efficiency. Hunger dulls the edge of creative thought. Even a succession of adequately balanced but unappetizing meals (worse yet when they are eaten off bare boards with a wooden spoon) can fail to give us what we need to live at our fullest capacity. We do the world no service when we reduce our bodies to nothing better than ill-fueled, ill-lubricated machines. This is another area where we need to keep well in sight the difference between saints, who are rare beings in more ways than one, and plain people like ourselves, trying to find a way which other plain people may want to follow.

Community Isolationism

Finally, and most strongly, I protest the tendency to strive for the impossible goal of economic self-sufficiency. If we called it "autarkie" [*sic*] [economic independence or self-sufficiency] we would see it more in its true colors. Not only does commerce with the world outside provide us with better balanced living on the physical plane; it also gives that indispensable exchange on higher human levels without which we become monsters of self-satisfaction. There are many people not living in communities who are far more satisfactory human beings than those who do live in communities, and we forget this at our peril.

I would be so unorthodox as to suggest that the plan for the first year or so should be based on the earning of wages by several members of the group working on the outside. Even at its highest development, a community should have certain of its members who regularly exchange skills with the larger society, just to keep gangrene from developing when the circulation of the common life is stopped. We can all quote, "No man is an island." Why, then, do we fail to allow for the fact that all humanity is the continent to which we belong?

What I am asking for is a deeper realization of the true nature of sharing at the very highest level, not just of maintaining a common purse. We would do better to love each other and have separate bank balances than to have everything so much in common that indifference or even hatred become the emotional climate of our days. Let our mutuality begin where it counts most, and work its way gradually down till it fills all the crevices of daily life. To work from the bottom up has meant for too many community-minded groups that they never reach the high places at all.

NPJ

Index of Happenings, 1941–45

1941

Introduction
- Spanish civil war
- Generalissimo Francisco Franco
- Oxford University
- Somerville College
- Exeter College
- Charlbury village
- Barcelona
- Madrid, Alfred's jail sentence
- HMS *Excalibur*
- Duke/Duchess of Windsor, Salvador Dali
- New stepmother Caroline Nicholson
- Westtown School
- Pendle Hill
- Original rationale for Hilltop
- Dodge telephone truck
- Purchase of King Farm
- Jamaica village, Vermont
- Hurricane of 1938

May 1941
- Alfred arrives at Hilltop, alone
- Description of Farm as first seen
- Fellowship Farm
- Alfred records his daily diet as guide to anticipated subsequent experimenters
- Asperger's Syndrome, what it is
- Alfred's 32nd birthday
- Maple sugaring
- Alfred as British subject
- Ambitious plans envisioned for future improvements to the farmstead

June 1941
- The family leaves Pendle Hill, heads north
- Arrival on the farm
- Perceived importance of potatoes to general well-being
- Albert and Helen Baily
- Vernon's girlfriend Abbie
- (Brother) Ed Jacob, wife Dorothy and son Teddy (Edward III)
- Leslie's deed of partnership
- Leslie and Valerie make business trip to Canada, anticipating prompt return

July 1941
- Why Walter and Ed abruptly abandoned the project
- Ernst Sollwitz also leaves
- Arrival of Junie Goat
- Hilltop Ghost, "Ann Boleyn"
- Pat, Sheila, and (baby) Barbara Beatts
- Alfred complains to Leslie Johnston about loss of original focus
- In Alfred's view, the importance of God to the project
- Alfred outlines two alternatives to enable project to continue
- Abstractions and autism
- Alfred's rock-bottom subsistence plan, shared by few
- Brother Edward, stepmother Caroline, sister Elinor, aunt Louisa
- Mr. Buchanan, county agent, Brattleboro
- Mr. Turner, forester
- Letter to Dick and Cynthia (3rd founding couple?)

443

Pikes Falls vs. Salmon Hole for swimming
Description of Native American archaeological site on West River
Leslie and Valerie anticipate their return
Author Dorothy Canfield Fisher
Discontent already bubbling up; Alfred ominously alludes to his violent temper
Mrs. Smith, mother of Oscar and Elmer
Local residents come to pick blueberries, an annual custom
First mention of Herbert Leader
Norma's ill health is exacerbated by circumstances
Christian Science (and Alfred's) view of illness
Alfred's frustration continues to surface
Meeting with Johnstons at Canadian immigration office, Derby Line
Devastating result of Derby Line meeting

August 1941

Piers' 7th birthday
First mention of Scott Nearing
Helen Knothe
Excavation of cellar and the unanticipated consequences
Norma's determined support of plan
Dorothy Canfield Fisher's letter explaining situation
Alfred rethinks importance of hand labor, and orders tools
Decision to buy Hope House for the winter, for $800
The garden begins to produce
Anna Brinton's letter offering encouragement
Brother Phil and wife Elizabeth "Teddy" Linton arrive
A descendant of the Kings, former owners
The Pinnacle, its significance in local lore
Norma describes her life to her family, glossing over difficulties
Seventh Day Adventists
American Friends Service Committee

Alfred muses about the human cost of war

September 1941

Mr. Crowninshield, often mentioned
The Jacksons find a house
Juliet (puppy) and what subsequently happened to her
Anna Brinton and other Pendle Hillers visit
Scott Nearing stops by
Purchase of Singer sewing machine in cabinet for $5
Alfred attempts to make sileage in a barrel
Letter to Domingo Ricart, Spanish colleague
There is a possibility of a job at Dartmouth College
Johnstons' belongings are packed up

October 1941

Summary of expenditures January–September 1941
First daytime fire for warmth
Excavation made for cistern and concrete poured
Sara Cleghorn's famous verse about laboring children
Norma and Teresa leave for Philadelphia
Alfred sends barely 7-year-old Piers to walk alone on forest road
Herbert Leader
Rationale for eating unappetizing food
Alfred explains why Hilltop was (in his opinion) the perfect choice for the project
The first potatoes are dug and stored
With little supervision or guidance, Piers falls asleep in odd places
Scott Nearing drops off some seasoned wood for the stove
Piers steps on a nail, isn't taken to the doctor
Teresa's 6th birthday, Norma's 32nd
Making copies with a hectograph
Letter to Jorge Guillen, a Spanish friend, describing their escape from Spain
Puigcerdà, Spanish resort village on the French border

1941–1942

Scott Nearing, sighting of three bear cubs
Herbert Leader with two sisters

November 1941
Teresa's thousand "birthday trees"
Myron Stark, a former resident on the farm, reminisces
King farm's two-family occupation, explanation of mysterious door in outside wall

What Piers and Teresa had as playthings
Herbert Leader
Phil and Teddy's lifestyle
How Alfred learned that WWII had been declared
Fremont Johnson, a draft resister
Helen Knothe and Scott Nearing
Alfred gets the job at Dartmouth College

1942

January, February, March and April are spent at Dartmouth

May 1942
Five of Mrs. Spruyt's goats arrive
Herbert Leader gets six hens in the village
Richard Gregg's walking plow
Herbert Stark, with plow and harrow, prepares garden
Alfred's 33rd birthday
Will Connolly offers to buy Hope House
Scott Nearing's stone house, built into the landscape
Scott Nearing and Helen Knothe
Herbert Leader

June 1942
Herbert Leader
Ginger (goat): her shocking death
Dr. Ebeling's corncrib is available for repurposing
Fran and Judy Bacon
Lowell Naeve
Ramsay MacDonald (lamb)
Norma's reaction to USO request to support "our boys"
Fran Hall, draft refuser
Discussion of ends and means

July 1942
New England Pacifist Farmers' Conference notes
Leslie and Valerie Johnston letter
Albert Lloyd Bacon (baby)

Pendle Hill asked not to bring Negroes to local restaurant again
Scott Nearing and Helen
Harold and Natalie Field
Alfred's letter to Domingo Ricart detailing his ongoing frustration, and Norma's postscript
Fran Bacon
(Brother) Phil Jacob

August 1942
Norma describes Farmers' Conference attenders, discussion, notes
Fran, Judy, and baby Bert Bacon
Scott Nearing and Helen
Norma describes conference in a letter
Herbert Leader
Piers' 8th birthday
Discussion of ethics and morality at Baumgardts'
Scott Nearing
Norma formulates a plan similar to Paul's
How baths were managed in the absence of a bathroom
Goat herd gets lost in the woods for several days
Broody Hen and Half Chick
Lowell Naeve
FBI agents show up as anticipated to arrest Francis Hall
Fran Bacon
Junie goat is finally found, at Charlie White's

Alfred goes to Ohio conference
Norma describes nightmare train trip in letter and laments lack of cohesion in group

September 1942
Letter from Herbert Leader (in San Diego)
Norma writes to Mildred Young, another subsistence farmer, about problems
Fran and Judy Bacon
Beech tree with cryptic 1902 carving
Norma writes to Leslie and Valerie proposing "a different arrangement" for the project
Lowell Naeve
Letter from Arle Brooks

October 1942
Norma writes to Leslie and Valerie lamenting the substitution of endless talk for meaningful action
Paul Rosenthal
Lowell Naeve
Mrs. Spruyt takes (some of) her goats back
Norma writes to Mrs. Fincke at Manumit School asking about policy regarding Negroes
Hay is purchased from Mr. Crowninshield @ $15/ton
Alfred works on air intake for fireplace
Letter from Mildred Fincke at Manumit re: fees, and acceptance of Negro children
Norma writes to Eleanor Garst, offering land @ $5/acre
Teresa's 7th birthday, Norma's 33rd
Alfred excavates for new privy
Scott Nearing and Helen
Norma writes to her family, enthusing about Manumit
Nancy Montague
Communities Conference at Gould Farm

November 1942
Norma writes to Judy Bacon, expressing discouragement
Herbert Leader arrives, leaves, returns CPS camp Patapsco
Norma writes end-of-her-rope letter to Phil and Teddy
Paul Rosenthal and Zionists
Letter from another "Phil," not brother, questioning validity of Hilltop concept
Alfred offers lengthy justification for the initial plan
The Bacons and Thanksgiving
Norma and children leave for Sebasco
Lowell Naeve
Alfred and Norma, who describes another "awful journey," exchange carefully worded letters that fail to address the core of the problem
Alfred laments the ill-advised decisions of others

December 1942
Herbert Leader
Bill Clark, a mental health professional at Gould Farm, writes to Norma in Sebasco
Norma writes to Janet Hall, giving reasons for her trip to Sebasco
In a long letter Alfred mentions "skimping to the utmost" as a desirable subsistence practice
Mildred Fincke provides Manumit enrollment details
Alfred itemizes several ways in which he believes the children's school needs are undermining the Hilltop plan
Herbert leaves for Bennington, not wishing to be present when Norma returns
Wallace Crowninshield
Stepmother Caroline writes to Norma approving Manumit decision and outlining financial help
Norma and children return from Sebasco at dusk and walk four miles

home in the snow, with temperature 15° below zero
Temperature reaches 31° below zero overnight, +24° inside house
Reg and Rica Brown come for the holiday
Yet another discussion of the future of Hilltop

1943

January 1943
The children leave for Manumit
Janet Hall writes from Pendle Hill
Brudercoop history
The Bacons' plans
Alfred and Norma develop a new plan
Eleanor Garst and Herb Willits arrive
Road commissioner offers 40¢/hr for baggage hauling
The diarist complains of noncooperation
Wallace Crowninshield
Mildred Fincke reports on Piers' progress at Manumit
Brother Phil questions the Hilltop plan
Alfred writes long letters to Leslie, and Phil, expressing his frustration in general, and repeats his views about spending money "needlessly" on children
Norma has difficulties trying to ship goats
Scott Nearing
Letter from Manumit about Piers

February 1943
Herbert Leader walks up from Bondville
A frightening fire in the office
Morning temperature 38° below zero
Alfred takes advantage of Norma's absence to fill the library with seedlings in flats
Carl Covey, "a student of religio-communism," writes to ask about the Hilltop "colony"

March 1943
Norma hitchhikes to visit children at school, stays at an ashram in Harlem, NY

Alfred responds to an inquiry with description of hardscrabble life, asserting that "physical discomfort is a minor evil"
The children return from school for spring vacation
Detailed plan is worked out for placement of 98 vegetable varieties in the proposed garden
Maple sugaring begins
Alfred makes a cart for billy goat Patrick to pull, with negligible success
Herbert Leader turns up, leaves again the next day
Scott Nearing's maple sugaring cooperative
Hilltop's sugaring process
An FBI agent drops in unexpectedly

April 1943
Herbert Leader's wealthy, yet tolerant, family
Class system in Britain vs the U.S.
Norma is shocked at the treatment of Negroes in the U.S.
Artist David Fredenthal's biography
Alfred is classified 4-E, his future uncertain

May 1943
Two dozen Angora rabbits arrive for boarding
Alfred responds to letter from "Ed," repeating at length his view of rightly ordered consumption
What is birthright membership for Quakers?
Impassible road results in famine for stock

INDEX OF HAPPENINGS

Alfred's 34th birthday
First reference to Norm Williams
Alfred complains to Leslie about wrong-headed choices of others in society
Scott Nearing's prediction about the war
Norma writes to Norm Williams to welcome him to the project
Reference to super-intelligent Negro boy at Manumit (Craig Work)

June 1943
Alfred laments sadly to Phil (not his brother) that "everything is gone."
In another letter Alfred muses about "the whole question of the nature and purpose of life."
Dickie horse joins the family—and runs away, the first of many times
A photo of Craig Work with a German boy interests Norma as possibly useful propaganda for hidebound Quakers
Alfred fails the physical exam and is reclassified 4-F
Fran and Judy Bacon return to Hilltop unexpectedly
Norm brings news of the invasion of Europe
Making the choice between registration and prison

July 1943
The generationally strict rules of infant care and consequences thereof
Progressive education: good or bad
Alfred ponders going to brother Phil's for the winter
Winnie Frost (Williams) arrives
Nancy Montague arrives with her family and meets Judy and baby Bert Bacon
Nancy's amusing description of Hilltop life, for publication in England
Alfred again laments failure of original project and money "wasted" sending his children to a private school when others are in want
Nancy assigns tasks to the children, and teenage Caroline cleans up decades of accumulated trash outside back door
Dickie horse's demeanor and behavior
Alfred writes to Leslie about "the validity of practical applications of moral principle" and complains about money spent on children's schooling
Perceived difficulty of women wanting to assist men with their work
Norma expresses her "deep seated disappointment and bitterness"
Alfred's opinion of how "the feminine mind" is sabotaging the original plan
To his parents, Alfred muses about "the relation of principle to practice"
Nancy describes a Sunday church/swimming excursion to the village

August 1943
Stepmother Caroline alludes to Alfred's "superior attitude"
Piers' 9th birthday
Possibility of Winnie becoming the local schoolteacher
Alfred responds to stepmother's comments, tries to explain his motivation
Children will not return to Manumit
Scott Nearing and Harold Field prepare schoolhouse for use

September 1943
Norm and Winnie get married
The Montague family returns to Manumit
Opening day for Pikes Falls school
A grove of 100 spruce trees is discovered, the right size for cutting
Norma advises another couple about the pitfalls of establishing a community
Stepmother Caroline recalls her early days as a teacher in a one-room school
Sawmill owner Petrie orders 3,000 board feet of lumber for prompt delivery
Dickie horse's peripatetic habit creates

1943–1944

ongoing problems
The Seventh Day Adventists in Pikes Falls and elsewhere
Miriam Fredenthal gets in touch re: goats

October 1943
Norma helps with the logging tasks with borrowed horses
Pros and cons of a mechanical saw
Clif Bennett paints the iconic kitchen mural, on October 4
A report on the status of Francis Hall in jail
Gardenia cow and Gladiola calf join the family
Official permit is granted for Alfred to leave the country
Alfred and Norm complain that Polly Robinson's meals are unnecessarily ("wastefully") elaborate
Description of poor treatment of prisoners and refugees in wartime
School reports for Piers and Teresa
Teresa's 8th birthday, Norma's 34th
Norma's view of essential underlying principles "on which the whole of life is based"
Norma rejects a proposed plan, annoying Norm and Alfred
Alfred fears that the original importance of "God and group worship" has become lost in the demands of daily life
Norm is classified 4-F by the draft board

November 1943
Norma's physical and mental health are suffering
The Zionist movement is reflected upon
Norma takes over management of the cows, goats, and sheep
No progress is made in working out an overall plan
14 children attend the Pikes Falls school
Prolonged bad weather sabotages food production
Dickie tramples neighbor's lawn and garden, Norma writes to apologize
The daily work routine is described
A psychiatrist in Brattleboro might be helpful for Norma but scheduling (and cost) is a challenge
Norma makes ominous statement in a letter to friends: "I have a powerful conviction that I am through at Hilltop. Yes, something did go wrong." *See footnote.*
Dr. Stokes is advised of Teresa's fainting spells

December 1943
Yet another operating plan is formulated
Norma's father questions her viewpoint about warfare
Winnie finds herself at odds with Norm's view of poverty
Christmas dinner is enjoyed at the Nearings'
The acquisition of a tractor is considered; Alfred is beguiled by the possibility
Scott Nearing and Helen's enviable homemaking skills
Which country will assume moral leadership of the postwar world: unscathed U.S. or bomb-ridden U.K?

1944

January 1944
Unrepentant Dickie goes to a new home, at last
The challenges of producing a newsletter
Norma's unending daily duties described
Scott Nearing, Harold Field, Hilltop project as mentors for would-be homesteaders

INDEX OF HAPPENINGS

Winnie teaches schoolchildren about the birds and the bees, horrifying their families

February 1944

Norma invites Judy Bacon to come while her husband is in Big Flats Civilian Public Service (CPS) camp, describes budget plan

The importance of focusing on the essential goodness of people, to counteract disillusion

Dr. Stokes thinks Teresa may have petit mal epilepsy, but local doctor says it is merely a digestive upset

The challenge of possibly hosting a Japanese-American family: why it wouldn't work

Four "outstanding jobs" are agreed upon, and commenced

Hay supply runs out, Gardenia must be boarded at the Kuuselas' place

Norm shares Alfred's ascetic views, leaving Norma feeling "lonely and lost"

Problems of producing the New England Newsletter

In a letter, Alfred philosophizes about Christian teaching

March 1944

Teresa has another fainting spell; local doctor says indigestion, his go-to diagnosis

Norma considers going to Montreal to visit Valerie

The men think seven people don't need a $40/week budget

The back-to-the-land movement may be fizzling out

School of Living tries to lure Norm Williams as staff

April 1944

Are Quakers developing social strata?

Scott Nearing's sugaring operation threatened by bad weather

An obstructed kidding requires veterinary skills; Norma copes

The house is cleaned and reorganized, again

Hilltop's possible summer visitors are reviewed

Scott maintains that Vermont takes pride in its epically bad roads

Teresa is tested, probably does not have epilepsy, but there is "something"

May 1944

Norma must take over all animal care, gardening, and household duties in Polly's absence

Manchester, Vermont, compares favorably with Manchester, U.K.

Treatment of "foreigners" in wartime

June 1944

Miriam Fredenthal mentioned as summer guest

IQs of Craig Work, Piers, Teresa, and Norma

Norma accumulates war-scarce items to send to sister Rowena

Hilltop diet described for Miriam F. as a warning; she is undeterred

Winston Churchill's policies as a political threat

July 1944

Winnie returns from a post-school vacation

Miriam Fredenthal arrives, with children

Norma writes an update to Family, and outlines plans to return to war-ravaged Europe to aid in reconstruction

Polly Robinson does not return, will remain in New York City

August 1944

Norma reviews housing options for the Bennetts

Piers' 10th birthday

Alfred develops an interest in earthworms as soil cultivators

Upgrades to house described
Square dancing is considered sinful by local Adventists
Norma references her ongoing poor health to Craig Work's mother, Minta
Miriam Fredenthal's estranged husband arrives in a taxi, with his lawyer
The problems of trying to send money abroad
How Scott Nearing met Helen Knothe, at Manumit

September 1944
Norma becomes ill during visit to friends, is sent home in a taxi
Craig Work arrives, with his mother
Harvest bounty described
Scott Nearing gives lecture on "The Future of Civilization"
Men work to cut more than 10 cords of wood despite Alfred's foot injury and steady rain
A hurricane misses Hilltop

October 1944
The harvest has been bountiful
Norma makes trip to Philadelphia to find a psychiatrist, hoping "to see the end of this unsatisfactory epoch in my life"
Norma is offered a salaried position with a peace group in Philadelphia
The Hilltop project is described to yet another inquirer
A three-way birthday—Teresa, Norma, and Norm—is celebrated, with three cakes

November 1944
There are no records from November, as Norma had left, and no one else was making notes.

December 1944 (in Philadelphia)
Norma writes to a close friend in England, alluding to an "intolerable" life and her "state of mental distress" after "things boiled up" at home. She stresses that her parents do not, and *must* not, know either of Teresa's recent TB illness or of her own difficult circumstances
Brudercoop housemates described
How persons of color are treated in the U.S.
In a letter, Alfred explains and justifies the overall Hilltop approach from his point of view: "Many have been extremely critical of our way of living."

1945

January 1945
A detailed account of the family's much-enjoyed Christmas at the Brudercoop

February 1945
Stepmother Caroline expresses concern about Alfred and tries to think of "work that he could do" and ways Piers and Teresa could be taken care of, perhaps by other family members

March 1945
After a quick trip back to the farm, Norma laments that "Everything seemed so hopeless and I felt like a stranger in my own home."
Norma's mood of despair lifts when Alfred unexpectedly travels 300 miles to visit her at the Brudercoop for a few hours
In a letter Norma writes, "I would forgo hot water, good roads, and frequent mail delivery to live in

INDEX OF HAPPENINGS

the English countryside.... [T]he call of Europe is more and more imminent."

April 1945

Alfred writes to Lowell Naeve to bring him up to date, mentions that he studies religion four hours a day

Back at Hilltop, Norma greatly misses Philadelphia and her new Peace Chest friends

Lowell is deeded eight acres of meadow and woodland "for the sum of one dollar and other valuable considerations"

The Great Mail Route Controversy was resolved, to the satisfaction of Pikes Falls residents

Norma makes a determined plan to reserve three hours for herself every morning for nonfarm activities, like letter writing

Scott Nearing predicts unending rain

The local mail delivery system is explained

May 1945

Norma writes to Judy Bacon, looking forward to her arrival in June to help with the anticipated influx of children

In a private letter to her friend Lee Brodersen, possibly never mailed, Norma writes about Alfred's increasing obsession with astrology to the exclusion of all else

Plans are made with their mother, Sheema, for the arrival of Sylvia, age 8, and Judy (Jutta), age 6, in July

A late spring blizzard makes the walk to school, even on snowshoes, impossible for the first time

V-E Day, Germany's surrender, occurs on May 8; this is learned accidentally during a trip to the village

The Pikes Falls Citizens Association holds a meeting

Animosity to the Hilltop group is sensed among Jamaica villagers, who circulate negative rumors

Norma writes to Anna Brinton, asking if the family can stay at Pendle Hill temporarily next winter

Americans had no personal experience of the just-ended war, unlike the Europeans, who endured it

June 1945

A detailed account of Norma's meeting with unsympathetic government officials in support of a refugee couple

Arrangements are worked out for bringing Sylvia and Judy from the city

Judy Bacon "made other arrangements," and won't be coming to help Norma after all

Gardenia cow wanders away for three miles in search of romance and is retrieved

The Springfield Plan for Japanese Americans explained

Alfred attempts to diagnose Piers' nighttime problem by means of astrology

Comparison between the British in colonial India, and the Southern U.S. slaveholders

"It isn't so much that this life is distasteful, rather it's the wrong life. So much effort, to absolutely no purpose"

Norma reports to Family on plans for the winter and the possibility of Alfred getting "a regular job"

Norma's depression increases: "The depth of bitterness inside me I am frightened to contemplate"

Judy and Sylvia arrive to spend the summer

Piers' and Teresa's school plans are settled; Norma is relieved that Piers will be able to avoid Teresa's "negative influence"

1945

- Alfred is not interested in a paying job or in volunteering, claiming he needs time for his astrological studies
- Why is violence so prevalent in society?
- Alfred focuses on astrology, does not assist with animals or household
- "The brutalizing effect of mass education" is contemplated
- Norma sadly comments that "I never spent such a lonely summer since my unhappy teens"
- Norma feels drawn to a career in the peace movement
- The problems of managing other people's children
- Scott Nearing agrees to talk about conscription to Peace Chest constituents
- A report to their mother on Judy and Sylvia's behavior
- After four years of making do, the new privy is finally ready

July 1945

- Norma brings Sylvia and Judy to the farm on July 4th weekend on crowded, hot, sooty train
- Teresa breaks her thumb turning cartwheels
- Schooling for Piers and Teresa is settled
- Cow runs away, and Alfred, absorbed in astrology, refuses to look for her
- "The depth of bitterness inside me I am frightened to contemplate"
- Norma struggles to accommodate to Alfred's stubborn astrological fixation
- Gardenia Cow develops mastitis
- Daily life with the visiting girls is described
- Plans for the winter—schooling, housing—are explained to Norma's family and other friends

August 1945

- Piers observes his 11th birthday on August 6, the day the atomic bomb is dropped on Hiroshima, incinerating tens of thousands of "the enemy"
- "I long more and more to get back to Europe and back into the relief and reconstruction field"
- In a letter to Polly, Norma laments that although Norm and Winnie moving to their own "house" has made things much easier, "many of the old difficulties remain." She explains that, "The point came, and passed, where I could no longer hold on to my hopes and shifted them elsewhere"

September 1945

- Sickly Gardenia cow is condemned by the local vet
- Local school superintendent Bullis insists the children must attend school while they remain at Hilltop, an impossible requirement
- Judy and Sylvia go home, after ten weeks
- Norma asks parents-in-law whether she and the children might stay with them briefly
- Paul and Eva Ladd will move into the Hilltop house
- An amusing rumor is heard that a shortwave transmitter had supposedly been discovered by the FBI in Hilltop's barn
- A final four visitors, two of them after dark, drop in unexpectedly the day before the family's scheduled departure.

There are no further entries.

IMAGE 23: *Piers and Teresa.*

www.ingramcontent.com/pod-product-compliance
Lightning Source LLC
Chambersburg PA
CBHW051156290426
44109CB00022B/2483